WELCOME TO ARGENTINA

Argentina's magnificent landscapes create memorable backdrops for amazing experiences. Wine lovers can sample world-class Malbecs at Mendoza's high-altitude vineyards with Andes Mountain views; adventure seekers revel in the colorful canyons of the Northwest; and nature lovers marvel at the thundering torrents of Iguazú Falls. In Patagonia, top-notch outdoor activities beckon, from scaling translucent glaciers to spotting penguins and whales. Urban adventures also await in Buenos Aires, with its thriving foodie scene, chic shopping districts, and vibrant nightlife.

TOP REASONS TO GO

★ **Stunning Landscapes:** From Iguazú Falls to the Perito Moreno glacier, beauty reigns.

★ **Buenos Aires:** The capital city combines European glamour with Latin American verve.

★ **Food:** Modern Andean cuisine, Patagonian seafood, and some of the world's best beef.

★ **Tango:** On packed dance floors or at ritzy shows, people move to the 2/4 beat.

★ **Mendoza Wineries:** Flavorful vintages flourish in vineyards along the Andean foothills.

★ **Outdoor Adventures:** Riding in the pampas and fly-fishing are just a few top options.

Fodor's ARGENTINA

Publisher: Amanda D'Acierno, *Senior Vice President*

Editorial: Arabella Bowen, *Editor in Chief*; Linda Cabasin, *Editorial Director*

Design: Fabrizio La Rocca, *Vice President, Creative Director*; Tina Malaney, *Associate Art Director*; Chie Ushio, *Senior Designer*; Ann McBride, *Production Designer*

Photography: Melanie Marin, *Associate Director of Photography*; Jessica Parkhill and Jennifer Romains, *Researchers*

Maps: Rebecca Baer, *Senior Map Editor*; David Lindroth, Mark Stroud (Moon Street Cartography), *Cartographers*

Production: Linda Schmidt, *Managing Editor*; Evangelos Vasilakis, *Associate Managing Editor*; Angela L. McLean, *Senior Production Manager*

Sales: Jacqueline Lebow, *Sales Director*

Marketing & Publicity: Heather Dalton, *Marketing Director*; Katherine Punia, *Senior Publicist*

Business & Operations: Susan Livingston, *Vice President, Strategic Business Planning*; Sue Daulton, *Vice President, Operations*

Fodors.com: Megan Bell, *Executive Director, Revenue & Business Development*; Yasmin Marinaro, *Senior Director, Marketing & Partnerships*

Copyright © 2015 by Fodor's Travel, a division of Random House LLC

Writers: Amanda Barnes, Allan Kelin, Karina Martinez-Carter, Melissa Kitson, Sorrel Moseley-Williams, Victoria Patience, Dan Perlman

Editor: Luke Epplin (*lead project editor*), Mark Sullivan (*Buenos Aires editor*)

Editorial Contributors: Denise M. Leto, Sue MacCallum-Whitcomb

Production Editor: Jennifer DePrima

8th Edition

ISBN 978-0-8041-4285-4

ISSN 1526–1360

SPECIAL SALES

This book is available at special discounts for bulk purchases for sales promotions or premiums. For more information, e-mail specialmarkets@penguinrandomhouse.com

PRINTED IN THE UNITED STATES OF AMERICA

10 9 8 7 6 5 4 3 2 1

CONTENTS

Fodor's Features

CONTENTS

MAPS

ABOUT THIS GUIDE

Fodor's Recommendations

Everything in this guide is worth doing—we don't cover what isn't—but exceptional sights, hotels, and restaurants are recognized with additional accolades. **Fodor's Choice★** indicates our top recommendations; and **Best Bets** call attention to notable hotels and restaurants in various categories. Care to nominate a new place? Visit Fodors.com/contact-us.

Trip Costs

We list prices wherever possible to help you budget well. Hotel and restaurant price categories from $ to $$$$ are noted alongside each recommendation. For hotels, we include the lowest cost of a standard double room in high season. For restaurants, we cite the average price of a main course at dinner or, if dinner isn't served, at lunch. For attractions, we always list adult admission fees; discounts are usually available for children, students, and senior citizens.

Hotels

Our local writers vet every hotel to recommend the best overnights in each price category, from budget to expensive. Unless otherwise specified, you can expect private bath, phone, and TV in your room. For expanded hotel reviews, facilities, and deals visit Fodors.com.

Top Picks	Hotels &
★ Fodor'sChoice	Restaurants

Listings

⌂	Hotel
⌧ Address	⇲ Number of
⌧ Branch address	rooms
☎ Telephone	⦿ Meal plans
🖷 Fax	✗ Restaurant
⊕ Website	⌂ Reservations
✉ E-mail	🏛 Dress code
🎟 Admission fee	▭ No credit cards
⊙ Open/closed	Ⓢ Price
times	
Ⓜ Subway	**Other**
⊹ Directions or	⇨ See also
Map coordinates	☞ Take note
	🏌 Golf facilities

Restaurants

Unless we state otherwise, restaurants are open for lunch and dinner daily. We mention dress code only when there's a specific requirement and reservations only when they're essential or not accepted. To make restaurant reservations, visit Fodors.com.

Credit Cards

The hotels and restaurants in this guide typically accept credit cards. If not, we'll say so.

EUGENE FODOR

Hungarian-born Eugene Fodor (1905–91) began his travel career as an interpreter on a French cruise ship. The experience inspired him to write *On the Continent* (1936), the first guidebook to receive annual updates and discuss a country's way of life as well as its sights. Fodor later joined the U.S. Army and worked for the OSS in World War II. After the war, he kept up his intelligence work while expanding his guidebook series. During the Cold War, many guides were written by fellow agents who understood the value of insider information. Today's guides continue Fodor's legacy by providing travelers with timely coverage, insider tips, and cultural context.

1

EXPERIENCE ARGENTINA

WHAT'S WHERE

Numbers refer to chapters in this book.

2 Buenos Aires. Elegant boulevards and cobbled streets give the capital a European air, but the chaotic traffic and frequent protest marches are distinctly Latin American. The home of tango is *the* place to take in a show. Also visit Argentina's biggest selection of boutiques, restaurants, and museums.

3 Side Trips from Buenos Aires. Varied scenery lies an hour's bus, ferry, or plane ride from Buenos Aires. Traditional *estancias* (ranches), waterways, windswept dunes, and mind-blowing Iguazú Falls are only some of the attractions.

4 Side Trips to Uruguay. Cobbled lanes and colonial buildings define Colonia del Sacramento. East along the Río de la Plata lies Montevideo, known for its eclectic architecture and down-home dining. Beautiful beaches and beautiful people are what the glamorous resort town of Punta del Este is all about.

5 The Northwest. Rock-strewn mountain passes, deep red gorges, verdant valleys, humid forests, Inca ruins, and the arid landscape of the Puna: the backdrop in the Northwest changes constantly. Rich Andean traditions live on in the region's food and

folk music, beautiful Salta city has a colonial feel, and wines from nearby high-altitude vineyards are the latest thing.

6 Mendoza and the Wine Regions. Argentina's vintners use desert sun, mountain snow, and extreme altitudes to craft distinctive wines—especially Malbec. Mendoza's wineries enjoy the greatest reputation. The Pan-American Highway passes through hot springs, Inca ruins, and incomparable views of Mount Aconcagua.

7 The Lake District. Alpine scenery on a gigantic scale is one way to describe this region's pine forests and snowcapped peaks. Posh resort towns like San Martín de los Andes and Bariloche are Argentina's best ski spots. In summer, you can climb, hike, and bike in the region.

8 Patagonia. Patagonia really is the end of the world. The monumental natural beauty of the Perito Moreno glacier alone is worth the trip south, but on the Chilean side of the Andes, Parque Nacional Torres del Paine competes in grandeur. Penguins, whales, and sea lions are the natural attractions on the windswept, wave-battered Atlantic coast.

ARGENTINA PLANNER

Visitor Info

The umbrella organization for all regional tourist offices is the **Secretaría de Turismo** (Secretariat of Tourism ⊕ *www. turismo.gov.ar*). The website includes basic information on the country.

Travel Agents

Argentina-based travel agents can help you pack a lot into a short trip. The 24-hour support many offer is particularly good when internal flights are delayed, a common occurrence. Argentina Escapes and Buenos Aires Tours are reliable local agencies that can arrange trips all over the country. Limitless Argentina is a U.S.-based company with offices in Argentina.

Argentina Travel Agents
Argentina Escapes
☎ 11/4322–4141 ⊕ *www. argentinaescapes.com.*
Buenos Aires Tours
☎ 11/4785–2573 ⊕ *www. buenosaires-tours.com. ar.* **Limitless Argentina** ☎ 202/536–5812 *in U.S., 11/4772–8700 in Buenos Aires* ⊕ *www. limitlessargentina.com.*

Driving

Argentina is a fantastic place for a road trip: the vast distances and unique windswept scenery are some of the most driveworthy on the planet. If you're heading to the Lake District or Mendoza or Córdoba province, for example, try to spend at least a little time driving around.

If you don't fancy dealing with driving yourself, you can also hire a *remis con chofer* (car and driver) in most cities. You can arrange this through hotels or local taxi companies. For trips to and from a specific destination, you pay a pre-agreed-upon flat fare. Otherwise most companies charge an hourly rate of around 150–300 pesos (usually with a two- or three-hour minimum) to have a driver at your disposal all day. Rental companies also offer this service, but are more expensive.

Some major highways are maintained by private companies, others by provincial governments; surface conditions vary greatly. Many *rutas* (national highways) have only one lane in each direction; you get two or three lanes on an *autopista* (freeway), but these only connect some major cities. Local driving styles range from erratic to downright dangerous, and the road mortality rate is shockingly high. Heavy truck traffic can also make some routes slow, frustrating, and tricky for passing. Don't count on good signage leading to estancias or wineries. Do as the locals do: pull over and ask directions. In towns, intersections without traffic lights or signs function like two-way stops: a car approaching from your right has right of way.

Your rental-car agency should have an emergency help line; the best is usually through the Automóvil Club Argentina (ACA), which can dispatch help to nearly anywhere in the country within a reasonable amount of time. In the event of an accident, stay by your car until the police arrive. To report a stolen car, head to the nearest police station.

Contacts American Automobile Association (*AAA*). ☎ 800/564–6222 ⊕ *www.aaa.com.* **Automóvil Club Argentino** (*ACA*). ☎ 11/4808–4000, 800/777–2894 *emergencies* ⊕ *www.aca.org.ar.* **Police** ☎ 101.

Dining: The Basics

The size of a restaurant's *milanesa* used to be the yardstick establishments were measured against. Quality has finally elbowed quantity aside. Argentina's more discerning urban food scene includes molecular morsels, high-end interpretations of comforting classics, and unusual fusion (Korean-Argentine BBQ, for instance).

Of course, the first thing most visitors want to try is the beef, and a traditional *parrilla* (grill or BBQ restaurant) is the place to do it. Locals handpick the cuts they want, but ordering a *parrillada* (mixed grill) is a good way of sampling more parts of the cow than you knew existed.

In the central Pampas region, including Buenos Aires, the focus is on simple flavors done well—spice and sauce don't get much look-in. The heat gets turned up for the spicy dishes of the Andean northwest, often featuring traditional pre-Columbian ingredients. River fish and yucca root are staples on the border with Brazil, while in Patagonia lamb often upstages beef.

Wherever and whatever you eat, expect to do so later than at home: lunch doesn't start until 1 pm and dinner until 9 pm (or later). Thankfully there's the *merienda* (afternoon tea or snack) to keep you going between the two.

Argentine Wine

From *asados* with friends to nights on the town to family dinners, the glass most often raised at special occasions in Argentina contains a locally produced wine. Although simple table wines were traditionally the local go-to drink, the market is now awash with varietals and high-end blends.

Many of the country's grapes grow in the foothills of the Andes. Mendoza produces more than half of Argentina's wine. Regions like Lujan de Cuyo and the Valle de Uco are renowned for their Malbec, often said to be the world's best expression of the grape, and Cabernet Sauvignon. Growing conditions are similar in neighboring San Juan, known for its Shiraz (usually referred to as Syrah in Argentina). The high-altitude vineyards of Cafayate, in Salta, turn out unusual Malbecs and the country's best Torrontés, a flowery white.

Wine lists at bars and restaurants are still hit and miss: for sensational wines you need to go to a specialty wine bar or wine shop, called a *vinoteca*. For everyday tipples, most supermarkets have a reasonable selection.

When to Go

Remember: when it's summer in the Northern Hemisphere, it's winter in Argentina.

Buenos Aires is least crowded in January and February, when locals beat the heat at resorts along the Atlantic and in Córdoba Province. City sightseeing is most pleasant during the temperate spring and fall. Try to visit Iguazú Falls August through October, when temperatures are lower, the falls are fuller, and the spring coloring is at its brightest.

If you're heading to the Lake District or Patagonia, visit during the shoulder-season months of December and March. Southern seas batter the Patagonian coast year-round, and winds there often reach gale force. In Tierra del Fuego, fragments of glaciers cave into lakes throughout the thaw from October to the end of April.

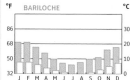

ARGENTINA TODAY

The only thing certain in life is change, and no one knows it like Argentineans. Recession and growth, busts and booms, they've seen it all. Though their country's economic star rises, falls, and occasionally sputters out with alarming regularity, the things that really matter in Argentina don't seem to change. The beef and wine-laden table of a family asado; a penalty kick at a fútbol match; the rhythms of tango, cumbia, and chacarera—these are what make locals' hearts beat faster. They might just win yours over, too.

Political Divisions

Since the country hit rock-bottom in 2001–02, Argentines have taken increasingly vehement positions on the actions of the three Kirchner administrations (one led by Néstor Kirchner and two by his wife Cristina Fernández). Critics accuse them of corruption, populism, and cutting Argentina off from the global market. But the renationalization of the country's pension scheme, airline, and petrol giant YPF have earned them many supporters. So has their social spending, including a new universal childcare allowance and low-interest credit for first-time homeowners.

For many, soaring inflation and a plummeting peso are causes for concern, as are clamp-downs on foreign currency purchases to prevent capital flight. Argentines feel strongly about this, and they show it, often by taking to the streets. City avenues and highways are regularly blocked by drum- and banner-toting crowds, and large-scale strikes are becoming common. Sometimes demonstrators are protesting a law; at others they're celebrating political or sporting victories, or marking an event.

Going Global

Locals can't get over the number of out-of-towners flooding the country. And more and more of the 2.6 million annual foreign visitors are staying on. Tango enthusiasts are snapping up old apartments in Buenos Aires, wine aficionados are investing in vineyards, outdoors enthusiasts are buying chunks of Patagonia. The number of exchange students at universities in Buenos Aires has soared, and there's a thriving expat scene complete with how-to blogs and magazines.

Comparatively low property prices and a favorable exchange rate mean that some of these European and North American newcomers can afford not to work: would-be novelists, painters, musicians—and former investment bankers—abound. Popular tourist sites are getting the

WHAT'S HOT IN ARGENTINA NOW

Being out. In 2010 Argentina became the first country in Latin America—and only the ninth in the world—to fully legalize same-sex marriage, sealing Argentina's claim to the title of Latin America's gay capital. It's not just bars and clubs, either, but also tango schools, *milongas* (tango dance halls), hotels, travel agencies, and wedding planners. The annual Marcha del Orgullo Gay (Gay Pride March) attracts tens of thousands of revelers in Buenos Aires each November.

Made in Argentina. One of the upsides of the sinking peso is the prominence of local over imported brands, which are restrictively expensive for Argentineans. The country's food is produced almost entirely within its borders, most clothing and housewares bear the label "Industria Argentina," and half of Argentina's

spit-and-polish treatment, and tourist-friendly attitudes are being promoted.

Grappling with the Past

The military juntas behind Argentina's 1976–83 dictatorship called their reign the National Reorganization Process, a grim euphemism for six years of state-run terror during which 30,000 people "disappeared" and countless more were brutally tortured. Justice has been slow in coming: although some military officials were brought to trial in the 1980s, President Carlos Menem later pardoned them all. But after years of tireless campaigning by victims and human rights groups such as the Madres de Plaza de Mayo (Mothers of Plaza de Mayo), the Kirchner administration has revoked these pardons, and military officers responsible for torture and disappearances are being sentenced for crimes against humanity. Former clandestine detention centers have been transformed into cultural centers, and the anniversary of the start of the dictatorship, March 24, has been made a public day of remembrance.

Abuelas de Plaza de Mayo (Grandmothers of Plaza de Mayo) continues to search for missing grandchildren, stolen at birth from kidnapped mothers and often raised by the very people who killed the children's parents. The creation of a genetic information bank has meant that 113 such cases have been solved, leading to many children—now in their thirties—being "found."

Foodie Culture

Foodie culture has hit Argentina in a big way. Celebrity chefs are enthralling TV audiences, and former table-wine drinkers now debate varietals and name-drop boutique vineyards. Their beer-drinking peers are turning from the ubiquitous bottles of Quilmes lager to local craft beers. A growing number of food blogs and food tours alert locals and visitors to the dishes of the day, often found behind the unmarked doors of clandestine restaurants. The food scene is rife with contradiction, however. Argentina is one of the world's largest producers of organic fruits and vegetables, but nearly all of it gets exported. A small slow-food and farm-to-table movement is fighting back at farmers' markets in big cities. Saddest of all, the growth of GM soy farming is pushing Argentina's famed grass-fed cattle from the Pampas and into feedlots—these days only very high-end restaurants can guarantee you a grass-fed and -finished steak.

electronics and nearly all its TVs are now made at a specialist industrial park in Tierra del Fuego.

Geek Is Good. After decades of *fuga de cerébros* (brain drain), 850 top Argentine scientists have been tempted back from abroad by government investment programs. The country is betting on future techies, too: free netbooks have been given to 4 million public high school students. Local techie achievements past, present, and future are on display at Tecnópolis, a temporary technology exhibition in Buenos Aires that attracted so many visitors it's been made permanent. The sky's the limit—literally: in 2011 Argentina's space agency launched its first satellite, SAC-D Aquarius, in collaboration with NASA.

ARGENTINA TOP ATTRACTIONS

Iguazú Falls

(A) On the Argentine–Brazilian border some 1.7 million gallons of the Iguazú River plummet over a precipice each second, forming a 275-meter-wide (900-foot-wide) wall of water. Trails, metal catwalks, and Zodiacs all allow for spray-soaked close-ups.

La Quebrada de Humahuaca

(B) Dramatically colored, craggy rock faces overlook the traditional villages that nestle in this gorge. The most stunning section is the Camino de los Siete Colores (Seven Colors Trail) in Purmamarca, with its red, ocher, and mossy-green rock layers. Music pouring from area *peñas* (folk bars) is the perfect soundtrack.

Laguna de los Pozuelos

Thousands of Andean flamingos form a salmon-pink swath across this remote lake near Argentina's border with Bolivia. The harsh beauty of the Puna region's gritty slopes and scrubby high-altitude plains offsets the birds' extravagant plumage perfectly.

Mendoza Wineries

(C) Malbec is the grape that has made Argentina's name in the wine world, and Mendoza is where they do it best. But getting you tipsy isn't all the 20 or so area wineries do: informative tours, atmospheric accommodations, and top-notch dining are also on offer, all within spitting distance of the Andes.

Plaza de Mayo and San Telmo, Buenos Aires

(D) Revolution, mass protests, Evita's inflammatory speeches: never a dull moment for the square that is the historic heart of Buenos Aires. The past also lives on in the cobbled streets of the San Telmo neighborhood. Its elegant 19th-century mansions once housed brothels, tenements, and tango dens. The tango remains, but these days it's antiques and hip designers that draw crowds.

Perito Moreno Glacier

(E) A translucent blue-green cliff of frosty majesty forms where this glacier reaches Lago Argentino in southern Patagonia. Blocks splinter off the ice face all the time, but they're ice cubes compared to the tons that come crashing down roughly every four years as a result of pressure building from behind.

Camino de los Siete Lagos (Seven Lakes Route)

(F) Between San Martín de los Andes and Villa La Angostura, the partly paved Ruta Nacional 234 winds alongside seven beautiful bodies of water fringed by pine forests and overlooked by the Andes. You can do the trip in a day, or stay on at inns or campsites for the gorgeous sunsets and sunrises.

Península Valdés

(G) Graceful *ballenas francas* (southern right whales) are literally the largest attraction at this Atlantic coast nature reserve. They come for mating season, June through November. Orcas, sea lions, elephant seals, and vast penguin colonies keep the beach busy the rest of the year.

Salta

(H) Stately colonial buildings, hopping nightlife, and fabulous local food and wine make the city of Salta more than just a gateway to the Northwest. When you do decide to get out of town, hiking, rafting, and tours to wineries and salt lakes are all options.

Punta del Este

This exclusive Uruguayan resort town may be small but it's as perfectly formed as the celebs that adorn its sands. Choose from calm waters at La Mansa or rougher ones at La Brava, Punta's most famous beaches, or make your own waves on the dance floors of La Barra.

QUINTESSENTIAL ARGENTINA

Beef

Argentina is cow country. The beef is so good that some Argentineans see little reason to eat anything else, though chicken and Patagonian lamb are tasty alternatives, as is *chivito* (kid) in some parts of the country. *Carne asada* (roasted cuts of beef) might be done on a grill over hot coals (*a la parrilla*), roasted in an oven (*al horno*), or slowly roasted on a metal spit stuck in the ground aslant on a bed of hot coals (*al asador*). A family *asado* (barbecue), where men show off their barbecuing skills, is the classic way to spend a Sunday afternoon. The nearest restaurant experience is to order a *parrillada mixta* (mixed grill). Expect different cuts of beef—both on and off the bone and usually roasted in huge pieces—as well as chorizo sausage, roasted sweetbreads, and less bloodthirsty optional accompaniments like provolone cheese and bell peppers.

Vino

Given their high consumption of beef, Argentines understandably drink a lot of *vino tinto* (red wine). Although much of the wine consumed here is nondescript table wine, the wine industry has boomed, and Argentine vineyards (especially so-called boutique vineyards) are firmly on the map. The most popular grapes are Cabernet Sauvignon, Malbec, and Shiraz (known locally as Syrah), but Tempranillo, Tannat, and Merlot are also popular. If you prefer *vino blanco* (white wine), try a Sauvignon Blanc or Chardonnay from Mendoza, or from lesser-known wineries in Salta, where Torrontés, another local specialty, thrives. This varietal exhibits a dry white with a lovely floral bouquet.

It's easy to enjoy Argentina's daily rituals. Among other things, you can enjoy some fancy footwork—on the playing field or in the ballroom—or savor the rich flavors (and conversation) of a leisurely meal.

Fútbol

In a country where Diego Maradona is revered as a god, nothing unites and divides Argentineans as much as their passion for soccer. Local teams are the subject of fiery dispute and serious rivalry; the national team brings the country together for displays of unparalleled passion and suicidal despair, especially during the World Cup. Nothing, it seems, can lift—or crush—the spirits of the nation like the result of a soccer match. Every weekend, stadiums fill to bursting with screaming fans toting drums and banners and filling the air with confetti and flares in their team's colors, which—together with the play on the field—makes for a sporting spectacle second to none.

Tango

There's no question as to what the soundtrack of Buenos Aires is: the city and the tango are inseparable. From its beginnings in portside brothels at the turn of the 19th century, tango has marked and reflected the character of Buenos Aires and its inhabitants. Although visitors associate tango with dance, for locals it's more about the music and the lyrics, and you can't help but cross paths with both forms. You may hear strains of tango on the radio while sipping coffee in a boulevard café, see high-kicking sequined dancers in a glitzy dinner show, or listen to musicians in a cabaret. Regardless, you'll experience the best of this broody, melancholic, impassioned, art form.

IF YOU LIKE

Wild, Gorgeous Nature

Argentina's climates range from tropical to subantarctic, and altitudes descend from 22,000 feet to below sea level, so natural environments here vary hugely. Plants, birds, and animals thrive undisturbed in their habitats. Along the south Atlantic coast, sea mammals mate and give birth on empty beaches and in protected bays. To the north, guanaco, rhea, and native deer travel miles over Andean trails and across windswept plains, while birds pass above in clouds of thousands or descend on lagoons like blankets of feathers.

Glaciar Perito Moreno, Patagonia. Tons of ice regularly peel off the 60-meter-tall (197-foot-tall), 4-km-long (2½-mile-long) front of this advancing glacier and crash into Lago Argentino.

Cataratas de Iguazú, Northeast. Iguazú Falls National Park protects 275 waterfalls and countless species of animals. Trails disappear into a greenhouse of creepers, epiphytes, orchids, and bromeliads.

Península Valdés, Patagonia. Small boats bring you alongside southern right whales as they feed, mate, give birth, and nurse their offspring.

Parque Nacional Nahuel Huapi, Bariloche. Rich forest surrounds the sapphire-blue waters of Lago Nahuel Huapi. Smaller bodies of water nearby make this Argentina's lake district.

Quebrada de Humahuaca. Vibrant pinks, yellows, and greens color the walls of this northwestern canyon like giant swaths of paint.

Reserva Faunística Punta Tombo, Patagonia. This Atlantic peninsula is home to the world's largest colony of Magellanic penguins.

Adrenaline Rushes

If an eyeful of natural beauty doesn't make your heart race in the way you'd like, why not try an adventure sport? Argentina is great for winter rushes—skiing, snowboarding, and dogsledding among them. When temperatures soar, you can cool down by white-water rafting or leaping (with a parachute) into the breeze.

Ice Trekking on the Glaciar Perito Moreno. You can trek over the glacier's 1,000-year-old ice, then celebrate your ascent with cocktails served over cubes of it.

White-water rafting in the Río Mendoza. This river's medium-to-difficult rapids course through Andean foothills. You can combine one- or two-day descents with horseback riding in the mountains.

Skiing and snowboarding at Las Leñas, Catedral, and Chapelco ski areas. Las Leñas near Mendoza, Catedral near Bariloche, and Chapelco near San Martín de los Andes offer groomed runs, open bowls, and trails that follow the fall line to cozy inns or luxurious hotels.

Tierra Mayor, Patagonia. This family-run Nordic center near Ushuaia has such novelties as dogsled rides, snowcat trips, and wind skiing.

Mountain climbing at Aconcagua, Mendoza Province. Close to the Chilean border, this 6,959-meter (22,831-foot) peak is the highest in the Western and Southern hemispheres and is surrounded by a host of other climbable mountains.

Culture and History

Buenos Aires is a city of European-inspired boulevards and historic neighborhoods. Beyond the urban sprawl, gauchos work ranches that reach the horizons. The Andes tower above the age-old vineyards of Mendoza and San Juan, while Salta and Jujuy retain traditions that stretch back to before the arrival of Europeans. Some of the world's largest dinosaurs once roamed the windswept reaches of Patagonia.

Museo de Arte Latinoamericana de Buenos Aires (MALBA). One of the world's few museums specializing in Latin American art is in a stunningly simple building.

Festival de Tango, Buenos Aires. The world's most important tango festival is a two-week extravaganza culminating in a huge milonga along Avenida Corrientes.

Festival de la Vendimia, Mendoza. At the grape-harvest festival, during the first week of March, parades, folk dancing, and fireworks take place. The crowning of a queen marks the grand finale.

Museo de Arqueología de la Alta Montaña, Salta. The rich pre-Columbian heritage of Argentina's Northwest is explored here.

Carnaval. Brazilian-style feathers and sequins characterize February parades in Entre Ríos and Corrientes provinces, but pre-Columbian rituals mark celebrations in Salta and Jujuy provinces. In Buenos Aires, neighborhood troupes take to the streets to sing and dance murga.

Museo Paleontológico, Trelew. You can marvel at dinosaur bones and watch archaeologists at work at this impressive paleontology museum.

Shopping

On weekends town squares become *ferias* (open-air markets); street performers wind their way between stalls of handmade offerings. Big shopping malls stock local and international brands. Wine, chocolate, cookies, and preserves are some of the consumables for sale.

Handmade jewelry and housewares, Buenos Aires. Artisans sell wares for you and your home in alpaca, wood, and leather.

Silver and leather, San Antonio de Areco. Modern-day gauchos can stock up on saddles, bridles, asado knives, belts, and even handbags and jewelry in this town of leatherworkers and silversmiths.

Ceramics and weavings, Salta and Jujuy. Salta is famed for its rich red and black ponchos. Woven wall hangings and alpaca knitwear are ubiquitous in Jujuy. Red-clay figures and cookware abound.

Wine, Mendoza and Salta. Tour the vineyards, sampling malbec, cabernet, and torrontés at leisure, before stocking up on those you liked most.

Cutting-edge designer clothing, Buenos Aires. In trendy Palermo Viejo and San Telmo, cobbled streets are lined with the boutiques of up-and-coming designers.

Chocolate and beer, Bariloche. Many of Bariloche's founders were German, hence the thriving trade in craft beer and chocolate in flaky sticks (*en rama*) or bars filled with locally grown berries.

FLAVORS OF ARGENTINA

Argentina's food traditions combine wild foods native to the region with crops cultivated from pre-Columbian times. Add in techniques brought by the European colonizers: first the wheat and cattle that built the country's reputation as the granary—and slaughterhouse—of the world; then the wines, pastas, and ice creams brought by 20th-century immigrants from Spain and Italy.

Compared with other Latin American fare, Argentine cuisine is found bland by some. And while there are parts of the country that love their spices, the local food philosophy is more about letting top-notch ingredients speak for themselves. Here are some of the flavors that might cross your plate.

Beef

Admit it: a juicy steak comes to mind when you think of Argentina. Locals proudly boast that the grass-fed cattle of the pampas produce the world's tastiest beef. Although the exponential growth of soy farming is elbowing the cows off the pampas and increasing local beef prices, Argentina's inhabitants still manage to consume 122 pounds of carne per capita per year, second only to neighboring Uruguay and well ahead of the U.S.'s 58 pounds. Sunday *asados* (barbecues) are a sacred national ritual. Whether they're grilling in the garden or ordering a *parrillada* (mixed grill) at a restaurant, Argentines typically go for at least two cuts of beef, one on the bone and one off. *Tira de asado* (prime ribs) and *vacío* (flank steak) are the standard selections, and are usually slow-roasted in huge pieces weighing 5 to 10 pounds. Choicer cuts like *bife de chorizo* (porterhouse) or *lomo* (tenderloin) are more likely to be cooked and ordered as individual steaks.

The preludes to the meat include chorizo, *morcilla* (blood sausage), and grilled offal: crispy curls of *chinchulines* (chitterlings) and rich *mollejas* (sweetbreads) are especially popular.

Cow culture doesn't end at the barbecue. Mildly spiced ground or sliced beef is the most traditional filling for *empanadas* (a pastry turnover), the country's star snack. Another local favorite is the *milanesa,* a plate-sized breaded beef cutlet served with fries or a salad, in a sandwich, or topped with tomato sauce and melted cheese (*a la napolitana*). Other beef-centered classics include *bifes a la criolla,* thin slices of steak cooked with onions and red peppers; and *carbonada,* a rich beef stew containing corn and dried peaches.

Andean Ingredients

Maize is the backbone of Andean fare and comes in an impressive range of sizes and colors. The most ubiquitous corn-based dishes are *humitas* and *tamales,* fist-sized balls of maize meal stuffed with cheese or ground beef, respectively, and steamed in corn husks. Sweet corn spiced and mixed with goat's cheese is also a popular filling for the area's tiny but incredibly addictive empanadas. Large, nutty-tasting ears of rehydrated dried white maize are popular additions to salads and stews. You can even drink maize: it's fermented into a dangerously powerful alcoholic beverage called *chicha.* Bucketfuls of the soupy-looking concoction fuel the action during the long nights of Carnaval, Pachamama, and other traditional festivals.

The Andes are the spiritual home of the potato. Forget big fluffy brown spuds: Andean potato varieties (of which there are scores) are tiny and dense, and might be purple, crimson, green, or rich yellow. Fresh, they're a common side dish, and

form part of spicy stews. They're also preserved by being left to freeze outside and then dehydrated. The resulting starchy balls (or a flour ground from them) are known as *chuño* and are a common addition to soups and stews.

Once a staple of the Incas, quinoa continues to grow in these parts. This nutty, protein-rich grain was traditionally incorporated into stews, but these days it's just as common to find it served as a risotto. Llama steak is more fibrous than beef and has a sweet, gamey edge to it. *Charqui* (the local word for jerky or dried salted meat) is also commonplace in stews. At dessert, don't pass up a plate of *quesillo* (raw goat cheese or stringy fresh white cheese) with *dulce de cayote* (a sweet cactus preserve). It's usually served with a handful of nuts and dribbled with *arrope* (a thick, dark fruit syrup).

Patagonian Wild Foods

In the southern half of Argentina the cow plays second fiddle to wilder fare. The star catch along the Atlantic coast is *centolla* or king crab, but mussels, clams, octopus, and shrimp are also regional specialties, as are freshly caught sole, salmon, hake, cod, or silverside. Fish is on the menu in Andean Patagonia, too, which is famous for its wild river trout. Avoid the cheesy sauces local chefs favor and go for something simple that lets you appreciate the star ingredient—*manteca negra* (browned butter) is a fail-safe choice.

If you're feeling game, *jabalí* (wild boar), *ciervo colorado* (red deer), and *liebre* (hare) are the land-lubbing southern specialties. They're usually served roasted or in stews, often accompanied by sauces made from berries or craft beer (or even berry-flavored beer), some of the other products Patagonia is famous for.

Best of all, you can take it all away with you. Boar, venison, hare, trout, and seafood are sold pickled and canned (a product known as *escabeche*), and there's a roaring trade in homemade jams and jellies concocted from *rosa mosqueta* (rosehip), *guindas* (morello cherries), and all manner of berries.

Dulce de leche

Milk, sugar, and not a whole lot else go into this rich brown milk caramel, which is practically a food group in Argentina. Get your first hit each day by spreading some on your toast at breakfast, where you may also find dulce de leche oozing out of cylindrical millefeuille pastries known as *cañoncitos* (little cannons) or long, ridged donuts called *churros*. Midmorning you might encounter it sandwiched between two cookies to form an *alfajor*, the nation's favorite sweet snack.

Dulce de leche is a standard flavor for ice cream; you'll also find chocolate-chip dulce de leche, or dulce de leche with swirls of—you guessed it—extra dulce de leche. Diners think nothing of asking for a dollop of dulce de leche on the side of already sugar-laden desserts like *flan* (crème caramel) or flambéed pancakes. Super-sweet chocolate cakes filled with dulce de leche are a common fixture in bakery windows. Bananas and dulce de leche are a killer combination: imitate local kids and mash the two together for an instant sugar fix.

All the same, connoisseurs insist that the best way to appreciate it is on a spoon straight from the pot. Why not line up some jars of brands like La Salamandra, Chimbote, and Havanna, and do a dulce de leche tasting of your own?

GREAT ITINERARIES

THE BIG CITY, WATERFALLS, AND WINE

Day 1: Arrival

Arrive in Buenos Aires and pick up a city map from the tourist office right before you enter the main airport terminal. Ignore the drivers asking if you need a cab; head straight for the taxi booth, pay up front for your ticket (about 250 pesos), and let staffers assign you a driver. Spend your first afternoon in La Recoleta, whose famous cemetery contains Eva Perón's tomb. Make your first meal a memorable one at a grill with a bife de chorizo.

Day 2: Plaza de Mayo, San Telmo, and La Boca

Have your morning coffee and croissants at ultratraditional Gran Café Tortoni. Stroll down Avenida de Mayo to take in Plaza de Mayo, including a quick look round the Museo del Bicentenario. Hop a taxi to La Boca, the port neighborhood where tango was born. The main strip is Caminito, which though colorful and iconic, is too touristy to merit more than an hour. Lunch at El Obrero is a classic.

Another characteristic old neighborhood, San Telmo, is a short taxi ride away. Set aside an hour to get up close to its history with a visit to El Zanjón de Granados, a fascinating house loaded with history. After coffee (or a beer) at one of San Telmo's many traditional cafés, spend the rest of the afternoon wandering through the antiques and clothes shops.

Day 3: Palermo

After a leisurely breakfast, head for a stroll, skate, or cycle through the Parque 3 de Febrero, and linger at the Jardín Japonés or the Rosedal. Walk or take a short taxi ride to MALBA, which opens at noon, and work up an appetite viewing Latin American art.

Hop a cab to the cutting-edge Palermo Viejo neighborhood, where you can lunch on sushi, Vietnamese, or far-out fusion. Afterward, browse the city's coolest clothing, shoe, and homeware stores. When night falls, have coffee or a cocktail near Plaza Serrano, and finish with dinner at a modern restaurant. If you're up for a nightcap, you're already where all the action is.

Day 4: Buenos Aires to Puerto Iguazú

Catch an early morning flight up to Puerto Iguazú. After a quick stop at your hotel, head straight for the Argentine side of Parque Nacional Iguazú. Spend the rest of the day wandering the trails and catwalks and getting soaked on a Zodiac ride through some of the spectacular waterfalls.

TIPS

1. The Big City, Waterfalls, and Wine itinerary works best if Day 1 (arrival) falls on a Thursday or Friday.

2. A 10-day apartment rental in Buenos Aires could save you money, even if you aren't spending all your time there.

3. Most flights to and from Puerto Iguazú and Mendoza use the Aeroparque in Palermo, although some also operate from Ezeiza, the airport for all international flights, which is about 40 minutes from downtown. If you can't avoid same-day arrival and departure, allow at least four hours between landing at one airport and leaving from the other.

Day 5: Iguazú Falls: the Brazilian Side

Spend your second morning at the falls at the Parque Nacional Foz do Iguaçu, Brazil's national park, for amazing views of the Garganta del Diablo (Devil's Throat). (Note that to enter Brazil, U.S. citizens need to have obtained a tourist visa in advance, which costs US$160. In Buenos Aires the Brazilian consulate has a three-day visa service and is open weekdays 9–3.)

Days 6-8: Mendoza

Catch an early flight to Mendoza via Buenos Aires. Spend your afternoon on the first day wandering through the stately city streets of Mendoza and people-watching in its main square, Plaza Independencia.

Divide your next two days between Mendoza's main wine-producing valleys: Uco and Luján de Cuyo. The wisest way to go is with a wine tour, which will help you make the most of your time, not to mention avoid drinking and driving. Let the wining and dining spill over into the evening with dinner at some of Mendoza City's excellent restaurants. And if raising your glass isn't your idea of exercise, spend the day rafting, hiking, horseback-riding, biking, or kayaking in fabulous natural settings only an hour or two from the city.

Days 9 and 10: To Buenos Aires and Home

Catch a morning flight to Buenos Aires and head to your favorite neighborhood for a late lunch.

You could spend the rest of your last day catching up on culture at the Museo Nacional de Bellas Artes, history at the Museo Evita, or street art on a tour with Graffittimundo. Later, try out your footwork with a tango class and a visit to a milonga, or see the pros in action at an evening show.

If you need to do some last-minute shopping, divide your time between the chain stores on Avenida Santa Fe, high-end mall Paseo Alcorta, and the boutiques in Palermo. On your last day, allow at least an hour to get to Ezeiza for your flight home. If you kept your rental car so that you can drive yourself to the airport, make sure your hotel has a garage, and allow an extra half hour before your flight to return the car.

ALTERNATIVES

You could combine this 10-day itinerary with a day or two in gaucho country. The town of San Antonio de Areco, in the heart of the pampas, is home to

several estancias, country houses turned hotels where gauchos tend to the horses. Most estancias include four meals per day in the room price, along with horseback riding or buggy rides. You can also visit just for the day, including a huge midday meat fest, often accompanied by a musical performance with whooping gauchos— cheesy, but fun. Set aside a couple of hours to browse the silversmiths' and artisans' stores that San Antonio is famous for, check out the gaucho museum, and wander the sleepy streets.

Another add-on or replacement side trip is to Uruguay. The port town of Colonia del Sacramento is easily accessible by Colonia Express, a fast ferry, which also has connecting buses to Montevideo. In summer the exclusive beach resort of Punta del Este is another option. Spending two or three days in Uruguay isn't just a fun way to get an extra passport stamp—it's a window into a country whose cultural differences from Argentina (their heightened obsession with maté, for instance) are readily apparent.

BARILOCHE TO PATAGONIA

Day 1: Arrival and on to Bariloche
It's a long trip to Patagonia. After you arrive at Buenos Aires's Ezeiza International you need to transfer to the downtown Aeroparque for your flight to Bariloche. Rent a car at the airport, and drive to your hotel (consider a place on the Circuito Chico outside town). If you could use a beer after all that, choose a laid-back downtown pub to enjoy a local craft brew.

Day 2: Bariloche and Circuito Chico
Spend the day exploring the Circuito Chico and Peninsula Llao Llao. Start early so you have time for a boat excursion from the dock at Puerto Pañuelo on the peninsula's edge as well as for some late-afternoon shopping back in Bariloche. Spend the evening devouring Patagonian lamb *a la cruz* (spit-roasted over an open fire).

Day 3: Circuito Grande to Villa La Angostura
Villa La Angostura is a tranquil lakeside retreat that marks the beginning of the legendary Circuito Grande. Driving there is a gorgeous experience, as you hug the shores of Lago Nahuel Huapi on Ruta 237 and Ruta 231. Relax to the full by checking into a hotel in quiet Puerto Manzano, about 10 minutes outside Villa La Angostura.

Day 4: Villa La Angostura
Spend your second day in Villa La Angostura skiing at Cerro Bayo if it's winter and that's your thing. In warmer weather, explore the Parque Nacional Los Arrayanes, the only forest of these myrtle trees in the world, or simply relax by the lake— if you're staying at Puerto Sur, this might be the most appealing option.

Day 5: Ruta de los Siete Lagos to San Martín de los Andes
Head out of Villa La Angostura onto the unbelievable Seven Lakes Route (Ruta 234), which branches right and along the way passes seven beautiful lakes: Correntoso, Espejo, Pichi Traful, Villarino, Falkner, Hermoso, and Machónico. If you leave early, add the hour-long detour to Lago Traful, where you can stop for lunch. The route brings you to smart San Martín, where you can spend the late afternoon shopping, trying rainbow trout

and other delicacies at the smoke shops, then enjoying them all over again for dinner. Note that the Seven Lakes Route is closed during particularly heavy winter snowfall, when you have to go through Junín de los Andes to get to San Martín.

Day 6: San Martín de los Andes

In winter, skiers should plan on at least one full day at Cerro Chapelco, near San Martín. Otherwise, spend the day relaxing on the beach, fishing, horseback riding, rafting, or just strolling the town.

Day 7: Flight to El Calafate

Get an early start from San Martín de los Andes for the four-hour drive back to Bariloche and then the two-hour flight to El Calafate, the base for exploring Parque Nacional Los Glaciares. From San Martín, be sure to take the longer but faster route through Junín to Bariloche (Ruta 234 and Ruta 237). If you follow the Ruta de los Siete Lagos, you'll have little chance of making an early afternoon flight.

In El Calafate, grab a taxi to your hotel, have dinner, and get some sleep in preparation for glacier-viewing tomorrow. If money is no object, stay at Hostería Los Notros, the only hotel within the park and in view of the glacier. The sky-high rates include all meals and excursions. Otherwise, stay at a hotel in El Calafate and book your Day 8 glacier visits through El Calafate tour operators (preferably before 7 pm).

Day 8: El Calafate and Perito Moreno Glacier

Spend two days taking in Perito Moreno from different angles. Devote today either to the Upsala Glacier tour, which traverses the lakes in view of an impressive series of glaciers, or the hour-long Safari Nautico on a boat that sails as close as possible to the front of the glacier. Enjoy a well-deserved dinner back in El Calafate. Make arrangements for a Day 9 ice trek by 7 pm.

Day 9: El Calafate and Perito Moreno Glacier

Don crampons and trek across Perito Moreno's icy surface. The trip is expensive, but worth every penny. You crawl through ice tunnels and hike across ice ridges that seem to glow bright blue. After all this, dinner—and everything else—will seem insignificant.

Day 10: Departure

Board a bus or taxi for El Calafate's renovated airport, and take a flight back through Buenos Aires and home. Note that if you are not connecting to another

Aerolíneas flight home, you may have to spend an additional night in Buenos Aires on the way back.

ALTERNATIVES

Sports and outdoors enthusiasts can really customize this itinerary. Skiers, for example, can skip southern Patagonia, spending a day or two in Cerro Catedral, near Bariloche, and a day at Cerro Chapelco. Rafters can work with Bariloche operators to create trips that range from floats down the Río Manso—an 8-hour outing with easy rapids through a unique ecosystem—to 13-hour excursions to the Chilean border. And serious hikers can boat across Lago Mascardi to Pampa Linda, then hike to the black glaciers of Tronador, continuing up above the timberline to Refugio Otto Meiling, spending the night, walking along the crest of the Andes with glacier views, then returning to Pampa Linda. Day hikes to the foot of Tronador leave more time for a mountain-bike or horseback ride in the same area.

The most adventurous travelers drive from Bariloche to El Calafate instead of flying. It adds about a week to the itinerary, but it involves an unforgettable trip down the largely unpaved Ruta Nacional 40. Don't attempt this route without a four-wheel-drive vehicle equipped with two spare tires. And pack plenty of extra food and water as well as camping gear. Getting stuck in a place where cars and trucks pass only once every day or two is dangerous.

TIPS

1. In the dead of winter limit yourself to the ski resorts in the Lake District. That said, Bariloche is teeming with kids on high-school vacation trips July through September.

2. Book your flight to Argentina and your round-trip ticket to Bariloche at the same time. Booking a separate flight with another carrier will mean you won't be able to check your luggage through, and you'll have to time things very carefully to avoid missing your connection.

3. It's difficult to tour the Lake District without a rental car. If you don't want to drive, confine your visit to southern Patagonia, spending more time in El Calafate or extending into Tierra del Fuego.

A PASSIONATE HISTORY

by Victoria Patience

If there's one thing Argentinians have learned from their history, it's that there's not a lot you can count on. Fierce—often violent—political, economic, and social instability have been the only constants in the story of a people who seem never to be able to escape that famous Chinese curse, "May you live in interesting times."

Although most accounts of Argentine history begin 500 years ago with the arrival of the conquistadors, humans have been living in what is now Argentina for around 13,000 years. They created the oldest recorded art in South America—a cave of handprints in Santa Cruz, Patagonia (c. 7500 BC)—and eventually became part of the Inca Empire.

Spanish and Portuguese sailors came in the early 16th century, including Ferdinand Magellan. The Spanish were forced out 300 years later by locals hungry for independence. Though autonomous on paper, in practice the early republic depended heavily on trade with Europe. Conflict and civil war wracked the United Provinces of the South as the region struggled to define its political identity and the economic model it would follow.

Spanish and Italian immigrants arrived in the 20th century, changing Argentina's population profile forever. Unstable politics characterized the rest of the century, which saw the rise and fall of Juan Perón and a series of increasingly bloody military dictatorships. More than 30 years of uninterrupted democracy have passed since the last junta fell, an achievement Argentines value hugely.

(left) Ferdinand Magellan (c. 1480–1521)
(right) Stamp featuring Eva Duarte
de Perón (1919–1952)

TIMELINE

Magellan sails down
Argentinian coast

Juan de Garay
founds Buenos Aires

PRE-1500s   INCA INVASION   1500   1600

(top left) Cave paintings, Cueva de las Manos, Santa Cruz; (top right) Indigenous inhabitants of Río de la Plata area pictured by Hendrick Ottsen; (bottom) Relief detail, San Ignacio Miní Mission, Misiones Province.

PRE-CONQUEST/INCA

PRE-1500

Argentina's original inhabitants were a diverse group of indigenous peoples. Their surroundings defined their lifestyles: nomadic hunter-gatherers lived in Patagonia and the Pampas, while the inhabitants of the northeast and northwest were largely farming communities. The first foreign power to invade the region was the Inca Empire, in the 15th century. Its roads and tribute systems extended over the entire northwest, reaching as far south as some parts of modern-day Mendoza.

BIRTH OF THE COLONY

1500—1809

European explorers first began to arrive at the River Plate area in the early 1500s, and in 1520 Ferdinand Magellan sailed right down the coast of what is now Argentina and on into the Pacific. Buenos Aires was founded twice: Pedro de Mendoza's 1536 attempt led to starving colonists turning to cannibalism before running for Asunción; Juan de Garay's attempt in 1580 was successful. Conquistadors of Spanish origin came from what are now Peru, Chile, and Paraguay and founded other cities. The whole area was part of the Viceroyalty of Peru until

1776, when the Spanish king Carlos III decreed present-day Argentina, Uruguay, Paraguay, and most of Bolivia to be the Viceroyalty of the Río de la Plata. Buenos Aires became the main port and the only legal exit point for silver from Potosí. Smuggling grew as fast as the city itself. In 1806–07 English forces tried twice to invade Argentina. Militia from Buenos Aires fought them off with no help from Spain, inciting ideas of independence among *criollos* (Argentinian-born Spaniards, who had fewer rights than those born in Europe).

IN FOCUS A PASSIONATE HISTORY

(left) Julio Roca
(right) Monument to
General San Martín;

BIRTH OF THE NATION: INDEPENDENCE AND THE CONSTITUTION

1810—1860s

Early-19th-century proto-Argentinians were getting itchy for independence after the American Revolution. On May 25, 1810, Buenos Aires' leading citizens ousted the last Spanish viceroy. A series of elected juntas and triumvirates followed while military heroes José de San Martín and Manuel Belgrano won battles that allowed the Provincias Unidas de América del Sur to declare independence in Tucumán on July 9, 1816. San Martín went on to liberate Chile and Peru.

Political infighting marked the republic's first 40 years. The conflict centered on control of the port. Inhabitants of Buenos Aires wanted a centralist state run from the city, a position known as *unitario*, but landowners and leaders in the provinces wanted a federal state with greater Latin American integration. The federal side won when Juan Manuel de Rosas came to power: he made peace with indigenous leaders and gave rights to marginal social sectors like gauchos, although his increasingly iron-fisted rule later killed or outlawed the opposition. The centralist constitution established on his downfall returned power to the land-owning elite.

RISE OF THE MODERN STATE

1860—1942

Argentina staggered back and forth between political extremes on its rocky road to modern statehood. Relatively liberal leaders alternated with corrupt warlord types. The most infamous of these was Julio Roca, whose military campaigns massacred most of Argentina's remaining indigenous populations in order to seize the land needed to expand the cattle ranching and wheat farming. Roca also sold off services and resources to the English and started the immigration drive that brought millions of Europeans to Argentina between 1870 and 1930.

(top left) Juan Perón and his wife Eva Duarte attend a party in 1951; (top right) Juan Perón addressing the congress, Buenos Aires, May 6, 1949; (bottom) Perón in discussion c. 1950

THE RISE AND FALL OF PERONISM

1942–1973

A 1943 coup ended a decade of privatization that had caused the gap between rich and poor to grow exponentially. One of the soldiers involved was a little-known general named Juan Domingo Perón. He rose through the ranks of the government as quickly as he had through those of the army. Uneasy about Perón's growing popularity, other members of the military government imprisoned him, provoking a wave of uprisings that led to his release and swept him to the presidency as head of the newly formed labor party in 1946.

Mid-campaign, he quietly married the young B-movie actress he'd been living with, Eva Duarte, soon to be known universally as "Evita." Their idiosyncratic, his'n'hers politics hinged on a massive personality cult. Together, they rallied the masses with their cries for social justice, political sovereignty, economic independence, and Latin American unity. Then, while he was busy improving worker's rights and trying to industrialize Argentina, she set about press-ganging Argentina's landed elite into funding her social aid program. Their tireless efforts to close the gap between rich

and poor earned them the slavish devotion of Argentina's working classes and the passionate hatred of the rich. But everything began to go wrong when Evita died of uterine cancer in 1952. By 1955, the Marshall Plan in Europe reduced Argentina's export advantage, and the dwindling economy was grounds for Perón being ousted by another military coup. For the next 18 years, both he and his party were illegal in Argentina—mentioning his name or even whistling the Peronist anthem could land you in prison.

(top left) Leopoldo Galtieri led the last military dictatorship in Argentina. (top right) Argentina military junta during the Falkland's War; (bottom right) Argentine prisoners of war—Port Stanley;

DICTATORSHIP, STATE TERRORISM & THE FALKLANDS

1973–1983

The two civilian presidencies that followed both ended in fresh military coups until Perón was allowed to return in 1973. Despite falling out with left-wing student and guerrilla groups who had campaigned for him in his absence, he still won another election by a landslide. However, one problematic year later, he died in office. His farcical successor was the vice-president, an ex-cabaret dancer known as Isabelita, who was also Perón's third wife. Her chaotic leadership was brought to an end in 1976 by yet another military

coup widely supported by civil society. The succession of juntas that ruled the country called their bloody dictatorship a "process of national reorganization"; these days it's referred to as state-led terrorism.

Much of the world seemingly ignored the actions of Argentina's government during its six-year reign of terror. Throughout the country, students, activists, and any other undesirable element were kidnapped and tortured in clandestine detention centers. Many victims' children were stolen and given up for adoption by pro-military families after their parents' bodies had

been dumped in the Rio de la Plata. More than 30,000 people "disappeared" and thousands more went into exile. Government ministries were handed over to private businessmen. Massive corruption took external debt from $7 million to $66 million. In 1982, desperate for something to distract people with, the junta started war with Britain over the Islas Malvinas, or Falkland Islands. The disastrous campaign lasted just four months and, together with increasing pressure from local and international human rights activists, led to the downfall of the dictatorship.

(top) President Carlos Menem mobbed by the public; (top right) a revitalized economy brings new construction. (bottom) Argentine riot police drag away a demonstrator near the Casa Rosada in Buenos Aires.

1982–1999 RETURN OF DEMOCRACY

Celebrations marked the return to democracy. The main players in the dictatorship went on trial, but received relatively small sentences and were eventually pardoned. Inflation reached a terrifying 3,000% in 1988 and only stabilized when Carlos Menem became president the following year. Menem pegged the peso to the dollar, privatized services and resources, and even changed the constitution to extend his mandate. But despite an initial illusion of economic well-being, by the time Menem left office in 1999 poverty had skyrocketed, and the economy was in tatters.

2000–PRESENT CRISIS & THE K YEARS

The longer-term results of Menem's policies came in December 2001, when the government tried to prevent a rush on funds by freezing all private savings accounts. Thousands of people took to the streets in protest; on December 20, the violent police response transformed the demonstrations into riots. President Fernando de la Rúa declared a state of emergency, then resigned, and was followed by four temporary presidents in almost as many days. When things finally settled, the peso had devaluated drastically, many people had lost their savings, and the future looked dark.

However, under the center-leftist government of Argentina's following president, Néstor Kirchner, the economy slowly reactivated. Kirchner reopened trials of high-ranking military officials and championed local industry. In a rather bizarre turn of political events, he was succeeded by his wife, Cristina Fernández. Her fiery speeches have inspired both devotion and derision, but her social and economic policies ensured her landslide re-election. Times may be better than a few years ago, but Argentines have lived through so many political ups and downs that they never take anything for granted.

MADE IN ARGENTINA

There's no doubt that Argentinians are an inventive lot. And we're not talking about their skill in arguing their way out of parking tickets: several things you might not be able to imagine life without started out in Argentina.

Una *birome* (ballpoint pen)

BALLPOINT PEN
Although László Jósef Bíró was born in Hungary and first patented the ballpoint pen in Paris, it wasn't until he launched his company in Argentina in 1943 that his invention began to attract attention. As such, Argentines claim the world's most useful writing instrument as their own.

BLOOD TRANSFUSION
Before ER there was Luis Agote, an Argentine doctor who, in 1914, was one of the first to perform a blood transfusion using stored blood (rather than doing a patient-to-patient transfusion). The innovation that made the process possible was adding sodium citrate, an anticoagulant, to the blood.

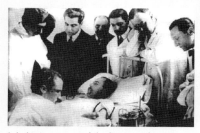

Luis Agote was one of the first to perform a nondirect blood transfusion, in Buenos Aires on November 9, 1914.

FINGERPRINTING
In 1891, Juan Vucetich, a Croatian-born officer of the Buenos Aires police force, came up with a system of classifying fingerprints. He went on to make the first-ever criminal arrest based on fingerprint evidence. Although his method has since been refined, it is still used throughout Latin America.

Huellas digitales (fingerprints)

■ Other useful Argentine claims to fame include the first working helicopter (1916); the first one-piece floor mop (1953); and the first one-use-only hypodermic syringe (1989).

ARGENTINA LODGING PRIMER

Booming visitor numbers have sparked dozens of new accommodation options. There's plenty of variety, whether you're looking for a tried-and-tested international chain, a boutique property, the Old World charm of an estancia, local hospitality at a family-run B&B, or a cheap hostel that's not only clean but stylish, too. All hotels include breakfast in the room price.

Estancias

For a taste of how Argentina's landed elite live, book a few nights on an *estancia* (ranch). Most estancia accommodation is in grandiose, European-inspired, century-old country mansions. Rates include activities such as horseback riding and four generous daily meals, usually shared with your hosts and other guests.

Estancias vary greatly: some are still working cattle or sheep farms, but many have switched entirely to tourism. At traditional establishments you'll be hosted by the owners and stay in rooms that once belonged to family members. Accommodations are usually old-fashioned and tastefully furnished, but rarely luxurious: you might have to share a bathroom, and some rural locations don't have round-the-clock electricity.

Other estancias still belong to their original owners, but a private company runs the accommodation side of things. These properties are hit-and-miss: some are more luxurious and professional than traditional establishments, while others have become bland and generic. Many properties that advertise themselves as estancias are actually redevelopments of old rural houses, which may not have been estancias originally. These emulate traditional estancia style but are generally more luxurious and have modern amenities.

Apartments and Cabins

Self-catering options are plentiful in Argentina and increasingly popular with visitors. The savings are especially significant if you're traveling as a family or group. In Buenos Aires and other big cities you can rent furnished apartments (and sometimes houses) daily, although weekly and monthly rates are usually cheaper. Some properties are in new buildings with pools, gyms, and 24-hour concierges; others are in atmospheric, but less luxurious older buildings.

Cabañas (cabins) often outnumber hotels in destinations popular with Argentinean holiday-makers, such as the Atlantic coast or Bariloche. Some are independent holiday houses, most form part of vacation complexes and include maid service and breakfast. Being outside busy town centers in natural surroundings is a boon, but you usually need your own vehicle to reach properties comfortably.

Bed-and-Breakfasts

In many smaller destinations large midrange hotels tend to be impersonal, institutional set-ups aimed at passing business travelers. If you're looking for local flavor, consider a smaller hotel or bed-and-breakfast. Some are simple family-run affairs, others are boutique properties; many are housed in recycled old buildings that pack plenty of charm. Friendly, personalized service is another major appeal. Although many now use the term "B&B," you may also find them labeled *posada* or *petit hotel*. Hotels with fewer than 10 rooms are very common outside of Buenos Aires—as hotels in Argentina always include breakfast, these properties could be considered B&Bs, even if they don't actively advertise themselves as such.

BUENOS AIRES

WELCOME TO BUENOS AIRES

TOP REASONS TO GO

★ **Dance the Night Away:** This is the capital of tango, that most passionate of dances. But porteños also dance to samba, salsa, and DJ mixes until the wee hours.

★ **Shop 'Til You Drop:** High-quality silver and leather goods as well as fashionable clothing and accessories are available at world-class boutiques and malls. Open-air markets carry regional and European antiques and provincial handicrafts.

★ **Get Your Culture On:** The architecture, wining-and-dining, and arts activities rival similar offerings in any major capital. But the lifestyle, lower prices, and warm locals are more typical of Latin America.

★ **Meat Your Destiny:** The capital of cow country has more parrillas than you'll be able to sample.

★ **The Beautiful Game:** Top matches play out in Buenos Aires's colorful stadiums, stuffed to bursting with screaming fútbol addicts.

GETTING ORIENTED

Most visitors see only a tiny part of Buenos Aires. It's actually a mammoth megalopolis that stretches more than 200 square km (75 square miles) into the surrounding pampas, Argentina's fertile plains. Around one-third of the country's 40 million inhabitants live in or around the city, making it the center of social as well as economic, political, and cultural life. Venturing out into the city's affluent northern suburbs or grittier west and south give you a very different perspective on Buenos Aires.

1 Centro. The heart of the city is filled with bars, cafés, and bookstores—not to mention crowds. The Plaza de Mayo is the hub of political life and home to some of the city's oldest buildings.

2 Puerto Madero. An elegant boardwalk and the Museo Fortabat are among the draws in Puerto Madero. Its high-rise towers—many designed by big-name architects—are flanked by a sprawling nature reserve.

3 San Telmo. Antiques shops and hip clothing stores compete for store space along San Telmo's dreamy cobbled streets—ideal for lazy wandering and relaxing at cafés.

4 La Boca. Gritty La Boca was the city's first port, which explains a name that means "The Mouth." Visitors come for a snapshot of the colorful Caminito area, and soccer fans fill the Boca Juniors stadium.

5 Recoleta. The elite live, dine, and shop along Recoleta's gorgeous Paris-inspired streets. They're also often buried in the sumptuous mausoleums of its cemetery. Art galleries and museums—including the Museo Nacional de Bellas Artes—are also draws.

6 Almagro. Peruvian restaurants, fringe theater, and a lively tango scene distinguish Almagro. The area is home to the sprawling Abasto shopping mall.

7 Palermo. If it's cool, chances are it's in Palermo Viejo: bars, restaurants, boutiques, galleries, and hotels line the streets surrounding Plaza Serrano. The hipster action spills over into Palermo Hollywood. There are excellent museums in Palermo Chico.

Darsena A

Antepuerto

PUERTO MADERO

2

Reserva Ecológica

Dique 4
Dique 3
Dique 2
Dique 1

LA BOCA

4

Darsena Sur
Av. Pedro Mendoza

Brandsen

Viala

0   1/2 mile
0   1/2 kilometer

Updated
by Karina
Martinez-
Carter, Sorrel
Moseley-Wil-
liams, Victoria
Patience, and
Dan Perlman

For 500 years, Buenos Aires has been in the throes of a powerful identity crisis. The unlikely lovechild of a troubled marriage between Europe and Latin America, Argentina's capital has never wholly aligned itself with either of the cultures that spawned it. Each wave of immigration has brought new flavors to the mix, and the resulting fusion—or creative confusion—is attracting more visitors to this city than any other in South America.

There's no denying Buenos Aires' architectural appeal: the graceful stone facades of its 19th-century townhouses and civic constructions speak of Paris or Madrid, so just wandering the streets is a memorable experience. The shopping is world-class, too, whether you covet contemporary couture or quality handcrafts; and the electric nightlife further heightens B.A.'s cosmopolitan ambience. Many of the city's classic cultural institutions have been renovated, and bleeding-edge spaces are keeping hipsters happy. Traditional dance floors, moreover, have come back to life thanks to a booming tango—and tango tourism—revival. Meanwhile, marriage and equal rights for same-sex partnerships plus a thriving scene have made the city a prime gay destination.

But grit offsets the glamour. Crumbling balconies, uneven sidewalks, and fresh layers of photo-worthy graffiti are reminders of your real coordinates. The devalued peso means that Buenos Aires keeps getting cheaper for anyone with hard currency, despite rising prices—though growing numbers of homeless people and ever-expanding shanty towns within the city limits speak of tough times to come for on-the-edge residents. In the face of so much change, however, some things do remain the same. Food, family, and fútbol are still the holy trinity for most *porteños* (as the locals are called), and they still approach life with as much dramatic intensity as ever.

PLANNING

WHEN TO GO

Remember that when it's summer in the United States, it's winter in Argentina, and vice versa. Winters (July to September) are chilly. Summer's muggy heat (December to March) can be taxing at midday but makes for warm nights. During these months Argentineans crowd resorts along the Atlantic and in Uruguay.

Spring (September to December) and autumn (April to June), with their mild temperatures—and blossoms or changing leaves—are ideal for urban trekking. It's usually warm enough for just a light jacket, and it's right before or after the peak (and expensive) seasons.

The best time for trips to Iguazú Falls is August through October, when temperatures are lower, the falls are fuller, and the spring coloring is at its brightest.

GETTING HERE AND AROUND

Intriguing architecture, an easy-to-navigate grid layout (a few diagonal transverses aside), and ample window-shopping make Buenos Aires a wonderful place to explore on foot. SUBE, a rechargeable swipe card, can be used on the subway, most city bus lines, and commuter trains.

PUBLIC TRANSIT

Service on the *subte* (subway) is quick, but trains are often packed and strikes are common. Four of the six underground lines (A, B, D, and E) fan out west from downtown; north–south lines C and H connect them. Single-ride tickets cost 5 pesos. Monday through Saturday, the subte opens at 5 am and shuts down between 10:30 and 11 pm, depending on the line. On Sunday, trains run between 8 am and 10–10:30 pm.

Colectivos (city buses) connect the city center with its barrios and the greater Buenos Aires area. If you pay by SUBE card, fares within the city cost 2.50 to 2.70 pesos, but are double that if you pay cash (on-board ticket machines accept coins only). Bus stops are roughly every other block, but you may have to hunt for the small, metal route-number signs: they could be stuck on a shelter, lamppost, or even a tree. Stop at a news kiosk and buy the *Guía T,* a route guide.

TAXIS

Black-and-yellow taxis fill the streets and take you anywhere in town and short distances into greater Buenos Aires. Fares start at 11.80 pesos, with 1.10 pesos for each click of the meter. You can hail taxis on the street or ask hotel and restaurant staffers to call for them.

SAFETY

Although Buenos Aires is safer than most Latin American capitals, petty crime is a concern. Pickpocketing and mugging are common, so avoid wearing flashy jewelry, be discreet with money and cameras, and be mindful of bags and wallets. Phone for taxis after dark. Police patrol most areas where you're likely to go, but they do have a reputation for corruption.

Protest marches are a part of life in Buenos Aires: most are peaceful, but some end in confrontations with the police. They often take place in the Plaza de Mayo, in the square outside the Congreso, or along Avenida de Mayo.

TOURS

Known for superlative customer service, Buenos Aires Tours arranges everything from city walking tours to multiweek Argentine vacations aimed at different budgets. Informed young historians from the University of Buenos Aires lead private tours that highlight the city's art and architecture as well as its intriguing past at Eternautas. Academics also serve as guides at Cultour: the highbrow history- and culture-oriented excursions are complemented by general city tours and boat trips.

For a different take on local life, contact the Cicerones de Buenos Aires. Its resident volunteers take groups of up to six visitors on informal outings, providing a true porteño perspective along the way. The experience is free, but donations are welcome. For serious insight into the city's Jewish community, sign on for one of the full- or half-day outings organized by Deb Miller's company, Travel Jewish.

B.A.'s new and growing network of bicycle lanes has led to a sudden surge in two-wheel travel. La Bicicleta Naranja has scheduled tours led by bilingual guides; it will also supply do-it-yourselfers with excellent route maps and deliver rental equipment to your hotel. Graffiti and street art are the focus of one unusual tour run by Biking Buenos Aires; another includes live performances by actors recreating key moments in civic history.

Large onboard screens make the posh minibuses used by Opción Sur part transport and part cinema. Each stop on the city itinerary is introduced by relevant historical footage (picture Evita rallying the masses at Plaza de Mayo); trips to outlying areas are available, too. If you would rather rely on public transit and foot power, try Buenos Aires Local Tours, a popular pay-what-you-like service (advance online registration is required).

Tour Companies Biking Buenos Aires ☏ *11/4040–8989* ⊕ *www.bikingbuenosaires.com.* **Buenos Aires Local Tours** ☏ *11/5984–2681* ⊕ *www.buenosaireslocaltours.com.* **Buenos Aires Tours** ☏ *11/4785–2753* ⊕ *www.buenosaires-tours.com.ar.* **Cicerones de Buenos Aires** ☏ *11/4431–9892* ⊕ *www.cicerones.org.ar.* **Cultour** ☏ *11/5624–7368* ⊕ *www.cultour.com.ar.* **Eternautas** ☏ *11/5031–9916* ⊕ *www.eternautas.com.* **La Bicicleta Naranja** ☏ *11/4362–1104* ⊕ *www.labicicletanaranja.com.ar.* **Opción Sur** ☏ *11/4777–9029* ⊕ *www.opcionsur.com.ar.* **Travel Jewish** ☏ *877/826–4674 in the U.S. only* ⊕ *www.traveljewish.com.*

VISITOR INFORMATION

The civic tourism board—Turismo Buenos Aires—operates information outlets with English-speaking staff at both airports and seven other locations around the city, including Centro, Recoleta, and Puerto Madero. Hours can be erratic, but the booth at the intersection of Florida and Marcelo T. de Alvear (near Plaza San Martín) is usually open weekdays from 10 to 5 and weekends from 9 to 6.

Visitor Information Turismo Buenos Aires. ⊕ *www.turismo.buenosaires.gob.ar.*

2

Buenos Aires
Metro Network

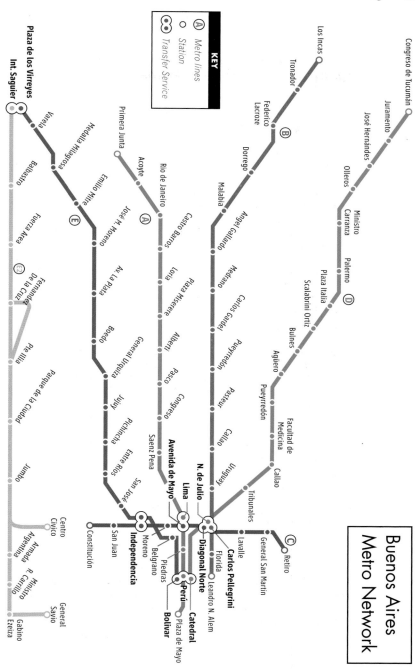

KEY

Ⓐ *Metro lines*

○ *Station*

⊗ *Transfer Service*

EXPLORING BUENOS AIRES

Unlike most other Latin American cities, where the architecture reveals a strong Spanish influence, little remains of Buenos Aires's colonial days. This is due in part to the short lifespan of the *adobe* (mud and straw) used to build the city's first houses, and also to the fact that Buenos Aires' elite have always followed Europe's architectural trends closely. The result is an arresting hodgepodge of building styles that hints at many far-off cities—Rome, Madrid, Paris, Budapest. With their boulevards lined with palatial mansions and spacious parks, Palermo, La Recoleta, and some parts of the downtown area are testament to days of urban planning on a grandiose scale (and budget), whereas San Telmo and La Boca have a more working-class Italian feel.

CENTRO AND NEARBY

Porteños love to brag that Buenos Aires has the world's widest avenue (Avenida 9 de Julio), its best steak, and its most beautiful women. The place to decide whether they're right is the city's heart; known simply as "El Centro," it contains the oldest and newest districts as well as many other superlatives. Cross Santiago the sleek and curvaceous Puente de la Mujer (Bridge of the Woman) and you're in the upscale waterfront neighborhood of Puerto Madero.

CENTRO

The historic heart of Buenos Aires, El Centro is still the focus of contemporary civic and commercial life. Plaza de Mayo is the original main square, and civic buildings both past and present are clustered between it and Plaza Congreso. Many of Argentina's most historic events—including revolutions, demonstrations, and terrorist attacks—took place on this square. Bullet-marked facades, sidewalks embedded with plaques, and memorials where buildings once stood are reminders of all this history, and the protesters who fill the streets regularly are history in the making. The city's most highbrow cultural events are hosted a few blocks away in the spectacular Teatro Colón, and the highest-grossing theatrical productions line Avenida Corrientes.

PLANNING YOUR TIME

Crowds and traffic can make touring draining: try to do a few short visits rather than one long marathon. Half a day in the Centro is enough to take in the sights, though you could spend a lot more time caught up in the shops and boutiques. Office workers on lunch breaks make the Centro even more hectic than usual between noon and 2. If you're planning on hard-core shopping, come on a weekend. The area is quiet at night, and a little dangerous in its desolation.

TOP ATTRACTIONS

Casa Rosada. The eclectic Casa de Gobierno, better known as the "Casa Rosada" or "Pink House," is at Plaza de Mayo's eastern end, with its back to the river. The building houses the government's executive branch—the president works here but lives elsewhere—and was built in the late 19th century over the foundations of an earlier customhouse and fortress. Swedish, Italian, and French architects have since modified

Arenales
TO PALERMO
Plaza Vte. Lopez
Museo de Arte Hispanoamericano Isaac Fernández Blanco
Arenales
Edificio Kavanagh
Maipú
Av. Santa Fe
SAN MARTÍN
Plaza San Martín
RECOLETA
RETIRO
Galería Ruth Benzacar
M.T. de Alvear
Plaza R. Peña
Plaza Libertad
Carlos Pellegrini
Esmeralda
Maipú
Av. Córdoba
Galerías Pacífico/ Centro Cultural Borges
Paraguay
Av. Córdoba
Plaza Lavalle
Teatro Colón
CENTRO
M CALLAO
Viamonte
TRIBUNALES M
Calle Florida
← TO ALMAGRO
Tucumán
LAVALLE
San Martín
LEANDRO N. ALEM
Av. Leandro N. Alem
Bouchard
Lavalle
La Giralda
Av. Corrientes
C PELLEGRINI
FLORIDA M
25 de Mayo
Junín
Ayacucho
Riobamba
Av. Callao
Rodríguez Peña
Obelisco M 9 DE JULIO
Palacio Elortondo-Alvear
Reconquista
Av. Leandro N. Alem
Av. Rosales
Sarmiento
DIAG NORTE M
Maipú
Av. Roque Sáenz Peña
Galería Güemes
Tte. General Juan Domingo Perón
Paraná
Montevideo
Uruguay
Talcahuano
Libertad
Cerrito
Av. 9 de Julio
Carlos Pellegrini
Esmeralda
Suipacha
Bank Boston
Catedral Metropolitana
Museo del Bicentenario
Bartolome Mitre
CATEDRAL
PERÚ M
Plaza de Mayo
Av. de
CONGRESO M
SAENZ PEÑA M
Rivadavia LIMA M
Rivadavia
Museo Histórico Nacional del Cabildo
Parque Colón
Casa Rosada
Rivadavia
Palacio del Congreso
Plaza del Congreso
Av. de Mayo M
Hipólito Yrigoyen
AV DE MAYO M
La Morada
BOLIVAR M
La Manzana de las Luces
PLAZA DE MAYO
Chan Chan
Adolfo Alsina
Salta
Lima
Av. de Irigoyen
Tacuarí
Defensa
Bolívar
Museo de la Ciudad
Plaza A.P. Justo
Combate de Los Pozos
Av. Entre Ríos
Solís
Virrey Cevallos
Luis Sáenz Peña
San José
Santiago del Estero
TO SAN TELMO & LA BOCA
Moreno
Piedras
Bernardo de Irigoyen
Av. J. A. Chacabuco
Roca
Perú
Bolívar
Balcarce
Museo Etnográfico Juan B. Ambrosetti
Av. Paseo Colón
Sarandí
Av. Belgrano

TOP EXPERIENCES

Reflecting: on Argentina's indigenous history at the Museo Etnográfico Juan B. Ambrosetti.

Witnessing: demonstrations in Plaza de Mayo, where Evita waved to crowds.

Listening: to opera singers in the glittering Teatro Colón or to the equally talented songbirds in the Reserva Ecológica.

Wandering: along Juana Manuela Gorriti and Pierina Dealessi to see Puerto Madero's "recycled" warehouses; Avenida de Mayo for 19th-century style; or Calle Florida for hustle, bustle, and souvenirs.

THE TERRITORY

The Microcentro runs between avenidas L. N. Alem and 9 de Julio and north of Avenida de Mayo. There are two axes: Avenida Corrientes (east–west) and pedestrian-only shopping street Florida (north–south). Florida's northern end leads into Plaza San Martín in Retiro. South of the Microcentro lies Plaza de Mayo. From here Avenida de Mayo runs 12 blocks west to Plaza del Congreso. Puerto Madero borders the Centro to the east. The main thoroughfares, avenidas Alicia M. de Justo and Olga Cossentini, run parallel to the river.

SAFETY AND PRECAUTIONS

Be especially alert for "stain scammers" downtown: they squirt foul-smelling liquid on you surreptitiously, then "helpfully" offer to clean it off (as they pick your pocket). Use ATMs only during bank hours (weekdays 10–3); thieves target them after hours.

Centro and Nearby

KEY

✕ Quick bites

Ⓜ Subte stops

QUICK BITES

Chan Chan. Peruvian dishes at bargain prices have made a name for Chan Chan. The the deep-fried corn kernels are almost a meal in themselves. ⊠ *Hipólito Yrigoyen 1390, Congreso* ☎ *11/4382–8492* ⊙ *Tues.–Sun. noon–4 and 8–12:30 am* Ⓜ *A to Sáenz Peña.*

La Morada. Local office workers know where to find the best empanadas. Vintage adverts, 1960s LPs, and photos of late, great Argentine celebrities are hung so close you can barely see the walls. ⊠ *Hipólito Yrigoyen 778, Plaza de Mayo* ☎ *11/4343–3003* ⊕ *www.la morada.com.ar* ⊙ *Mon.–Thurs. 10–4, Fri. 10–4 and 6–midnight* Ⓜ *A to Plaza de Mayo; D to Catedral; E to Bolívar.*

La Giralda. Don't let the small tables or surly waiters put you off—La Giralda's signature *chocolate con churros* (hot chocolate with crisp cigar-shape donuts) are to die for. ⊠ *Av. Corrientes 1453, Centro* ☎ *11/4371–3846* ⊙ *Mon.–Thurs. 8 am–midnight, Fri. and Sat. 7 am–2 am, Sun. 4 pm–midnight* Ⓜ *B to Uruguay.*

GETTING AROUND

The quickest way into Centro is by subte. For Microcentro, get off at Florida (Línea B) or Lavalle (C). Retiro and Plaza San Martín have eponymous stations on Línea C. Stations Avenida de Mayo (A), Catedral (D), and Bolívar (E) all serve Plaza de Mayo. Línea A has stops along de Mayo, including at Congreso. Líneas B, C, and D intersect at Carlos Pellegrini/Diagonal Norte/9 de Julio. Only change lines here if you're going more than one stop. Otherwise, walking is quicker. Puerto Madero is close to L. N. Alem on Línea A, and is connected by the Tren del Este, a light-rail service running parallel to Avenida Alicia Moreau de Justo.

You can take a taxi or bus to the Microcentro, but walking is the best way to move within it. Bus No. 17 connects Centro and Recoleta; so do Bus nos. 59 and 93. No. 130 connects these areas with Puerto Madero. Bus nos. 22 and 24 run between San Telmo and Microcentro.

the structure, which accounts for the odd mix of styles. Its curious hue dates from the presidency of Domingo Sarmiento, who ordered it painted pink as a symbol of unification between two warring political factions, the *federales* (whose color was red) and the *unitarios* (represented by white). Local legend has it that the original paint was made by mixing whitewash with bull's blood.

The balcony facing Plaza de Mayo is a presidential podium. From this lofty stage Evita rallied the *descamisados* (the shirtless—meaning the working class), Maradona sang along with soccer fans after winning one World Cup and coming second in another, and Madonna belted out her film rendition of "Don't Cry for Me Argentina." Check for a small banner hoisted alongside the nation's flag, indicating "the president is in."

On weekends, hour-long guided tours leave every ten minutes, taking in some of the presidential offices and the newly opened Galería de los Patriotas Argentinos del Bicentenario (Bicentennial Gallery of Patriots), a pictorial who's who of Argentina's national heroes. The country's heroines have a room of their own here, the Salón Mujeres Argentinas, which is often used for presidential press conferences. An impassioned Evita presides over black-and-white photographs of Argentina's other great dames. ⊠ *Balcarce 50, Plaza de Mayo* ☎ *11/4344–3714* ⊕ *www. presidencia.gov.ar/visitas-guiadas* ⌨ *Free* ☉ *Weekends 10–6* Ⓜ *A to Plaza de Mayo; D to Catedral; E to Bolívar.*

La Manzana de Las Luces (*The Block of Illumination*). More history is packed into this single block of buildings southwest of Plaza de Mayo than in scores of other city blocks put together. Its name, which literally means "the Block of Lights," is a metaphorical nod to the "illuminated" scholars who once worked within. Most of the site can be visited only on guided tours led by excellent professional historians. Regular departures are in Spanish, but they provide brochures with English summaries of each stage.

The earliest occupant of the site was the controversial Jesuit order, which began construction here in 1661. The only survivor from this first stage is the galleried **Procuraduría**, the colonial administrative headquarters for the Jesuits' vast land holdings in northeastern Argentina and Paraguay (think: *The Mission*). Secret tunnels, still undergoing archaeological excavation, linked it to area churches, the Cabildo, and the port. Guided visits include a glimpse of a specially reinforced section. After the Jesuits' expulsion from Argentina in 1767 (the Spanish crown saw them as a threat), the simple brick-and-mud structure housed the city's first school of medicine and then the University of Buenos Aires. Fully restored, it's now home to a school for stringed instrument makers and a rather tacky crafts market.

The Jesuits honored their patron saint at the **Iglesia de San Ignacio de Loyola** (Church of Saint Ignatius of Loyola), at the intersection of Alsina and Bolívar. It's the only building in the block you can visit without going on a tour. The original sanctuary here was built of adobe in 1675; within a few decades it was rebuilt in stone.

Argentina's first congress convened within another building on the site, the **Casas Virreinales** (Viceroyal Residences)—ironic, given that it was built to house colonial civil servants. The remaining historic building is the neoclassical **Colegio Nacional**, a top-notch public school and a hotbed of political activism that replaced a Jesuit-built structure. The president often attends graduation ceremonies, and Einstein gave a lecture here in 1925. ⊠ *Entrance at Perú 272, Plaza de Mayo* ☎ *11/4342–6973* ⊕ *www.manzanadelasluces.gov.ar* ☜ *20 pesos* ⊙ *Visits by guided tour only: tours in Spanish weekdays at 3, weekends at 4:30 and 6; call 2 wks ahead to arrange tours in English* Ⓜ *A to Plaza de Mayo; D to Catedral; E to Bolívar.*

Museo del Bicentenario. Today, the Río de la Plata is nowhere in sight, but the humming traffic circle that overlooks this underground museum behind the Casa Rosada was once on the waterfront. The brick vaults, pillars, and wooden pulley mechanisms are the remains of the 1845 Taylor Customs House and jetty, discovered after being buried for almost a century. In honor of Argentina's 2010 bicentenary celebrations the structure was restored and capped with a glass roof.

Each vault covers a portion of Argentina's political history, recalling it through artifacts (often personal possessions of those who governed from the house overhead), paintings, photographs, film reels, and interactive screens. Temporary art exhibitions run on the other side of the museum courtyard.

The large glass structure in the center contains the star attraction: a 360-degree masterpiece by Mexican muralist David Alfaro Siqueiros, which originally covered the walls, floor, and ceiling of a basement room in a client's home. When the house was demolished in the early 1990s, the mural was carefully removed in pieces, only to languish in a shipping container for 17 years. Thankfully, Siqueiros's innovative use of industrial paint meant that damage was minimal. Prompted by the campaigns of committed art activists, President Cristina Fernández intervened and the mural has now been fully restored and reassembled here. After donning protective shoes, you cross a small passageway into the work, which represents an underwater scene, against which the feet and faces of swimmers seem to press. The only male figure (swimming upwards on the wall opposite the entrance) is said to represent the artist. A café at the back of the museum offers coffee, sandwiches, salads, and a set lunch menu. ⊠ *Paseo Colón 100, at Hipólito Yrigoyen, Plaza de Mayo* ☎ *11/4344–3802* ⊕ *www.museobicentenario.gob.ar* ☜ *Free* ⊙ *Apr.–Nov., Wed.–Sun. 10–6; Dec.–Mar., Wed.–Sun. 11–7* Ⓜ *A to Plaza de Mayo; D to Catedral; E to Bolívar.*

Museo Etnográfico Juan B. Ambrosetti (*Ethnographic Museum*). Until 2012, the 100-peso bill still honored General Roca—the man responsible for the massacre of most of Patagonia's indigenous population—so it's not surprising that information on Argentina's original inhabitants is sparse. This fascinating but little-visited museum is a welcome remedy.

Begun by local scientist Juan Bautista Ambrosetti in 1904, the collection originally focused on so-called exotic art and artifacts, such as the Australasian sculptures and Japanese temple altar showcased in the rust-color introductory room. The real highlights, however, are the Argentine collections: if you're planning to visit Argentina's far north or south, they'll provide an eye-opening introduction.

The ground-floor galleries trace the history of human activity in Patagonia, underscoring the tragic results of the European arrival. Dugout canoes, exquisite Mapuche silver jewelry, and scores of archival photos and illustrations are the main exhibits.

In the upstairs northwestern Argentina gallery the emphasis is mainly archaeological. Displays briefly chronicle the evolution of Andean civilization, the heyday of the Inca empire, and postcolonial life. Artifacts include ceramics, textiles, jewelry, farming tools, and even food: anyone for some 4,000-year-old corn?

The collection is run by the University of Buenos Aires' Faculty of Philosophy and Letters. Although their insightful labels and explanations are all in Spanish, you can ask for a photocopied sheet with English versions of the texts. It's a pleasure just to wander the quiet, light-filled 19th-century town house that contains both the collection and an anthropological library. The peaceful inner garden is the perfect place for some post-museum reflection. ⊠ *Moreno 350, Plaza de Mayo* ☎ *11/4345–8197* ⊕ *www.museoetnografico.filo.uba.ar* ⊠ *20 pesos* ⊙ *Tues.–Fri. 1–7, weekends 3–7* Ⓜ *A to Plaza de Mayo; D to Catedral; E to Bolívar.*

Museo Histórico Nacional del Cabildo y de la Revolución de Mayo (*Cabildo*). Plaza de Mayo's only remaining colonial edifice was built in 1765 as the meeting place for the city council, now based in the ornate wedge-shaped building on the southwest corner of the square. The epicenter of the May Revolution of 1810, where patriotic citizens gathered to vote against Napoleonic rule, the hall is one of Argentina's national shrines. However, this hasn't stopped successive renovations to its detriment, including the demolition of the whole right end of the structure to make way for the new Avenida de Mayo in 1894 and of the left end for Diagonal Julio Roca in 1931. The small museum of artifacts and documents pertaining to the events of the May Revolution is less of an attraction than the building itself. Thursday and Friday from 11 to 6, a tiny craft market takes place on the patio behind the building. ⊠ *Bolívar 65, Plaza de Mayo* ☎ *11/4334–1782* ⊕ *www.cabildonacional.gob.ar* ⊠ *4 pesos* ⊙ *Wed.–Fri. 10:30–5, weekends 11:30–6* Ⓜ *A to Plaza de Mayo; D to Catedral; E to Bolívar.*

Fodor's Choice ★ **Plaza de Mayo.** Since its construction in 1580, this has been the setting for Argentina's most politically turbulent moments, including the uprising against Spanish colonial rule on May 25, 1810—hence its name. The square was once divided in two by a *recova* (gallery), but this reminder of colonial times was demolished in 1883, and the square's central monument, the Pirámide de Mayo, was later moved to its place. The pyramid you see is actually a 1911 extension of the original, erected in 1811 on the anniversary of the Revolution of May, which is hidden inside. The bronze equestrian statue of General Manuel Belgrano, the designer of Argentina's flag, dates from 1873, and stands at the east end of the plaza.

The plaza remains the traditional site for ceremonies, rallies, and protests. Thousands cheered for Perón and Evita here; anti-Peronist planes bombed the gathered crowds in 1955; there were bloody clashes in December 2001 (hence the heavy police presence and crowd-control barriers); but the mood was jubilant when revelers thronged in to celebrate the nation's bicentenary in 2010. The white head scarves painted around the Pirámide de Mayo represent the Madres de la Plaza de Mayo (Mothers of May Square) who have marched here every Thursday at 3:30 for nearly four decades. Housewives and mothers-turned-militant-activists, they demand justice for *los desaparecidos*—the people who were "disappeared" during the rise to power and reign of Argentina's dictatorial military government (1976–1983). Ⓜ *A to Plaza de Mayo; D to Catedral; E to Bolívar.*

Fodor's Choice ★ **Teatro Colón.** Its magnitude, magnificent acoustics, and opulence earn the Teatro Colón (Colón Theater) a place among the world's top five opera theaters. An ever-changing stream of imported talent bolsters the well-regarded local lyric and ballet companies.

After an eventful 18-year building process involving the death of one architect and the murder of another, the sublime Italianate structure was finally inaugurated in 1908 with Verdi's *Aïda*. It has hosted the likes of Maria Callas, Richard Strauss, Arturo Toscanini, Igor Stravinsky, Enrico Caruso, and Luciano Pavarotti, who said that the Colón has only one flaw: the acoustics are so good that every mistake can be heard. The theater was closed in 2008 for controversial renovations which ran way over schedule and budget, but reopened on May 24, 2010, to coincide with Argentina's bicentenary celebrations. Much of the work done was structural, but its stone facade and interior trimmings are now scrubbed and gleaming.

The theater's sumptuous building materials—three kinds of Italian marble, French stained glass, and Venetian mosaics—were imported from Europe to create large-scale lavishness. The seven-tier main theater is breathtaking in size, and has a grand central chandelier with 700 lights to illuminate the 3,000 mere mortals in its red-velvet seats.

Nothing can prepare you for the thrill of seeing an opera or ballet here. The seasons run April through December, but many seats are reserved for season-ticket holders. Shorter options in the main theater include symphonic cycles by the stable orchestra as well as international orchestral visits. Chamber music concerts are held in the U-shape Salón Dorado (Golden Room), so named for the 24-karat gold leaf that covers its stucco molding. Underneath the main building is the ultra-minimal Centro Experimental, a tiny theater showcasing avant-garde music, opera, and dramatic performances.

You can see the splendor up close and get in on all the behind-the-scenes action with the theater's extremely popular guided tours. The whirlwind visits take you up and down innumerable staircases to rehearsal rooms and to the costume, shoe, and scenery workshops, before letting you gaze at the stage from a sought-after box. (Arrive at least a half hour before the tour you want to take starts, as they fill up very quickly.)

Buy tickets from the box office on Pasaje Toscanini. If seats are sold out—or beyond your pocket—you can buy 10-peso standing-room tickets on the day of the performance. These are for the lofty upper-tier *paraíso*, from which you can both see and hear perfectly, although three-hour-long operas are hard on the feet. ⊠ *Main*

entrance on Libertad between Tucumán and Viamonte. Box office: Pasaje Toscanini 1180, Centro ☎ 11/4378-7100 for tickets, 11/4378-7127 for tours ⊕ www.teatrocolon.org.ar ☒ Guided tours 130 pesos ⊙ Daily 9–5, tours every hr on the hr Ⓜ *D to Tribunales.*

WORTH NOTING

Calle Florida. Nothing sums up the chaotic Microcentro better than this pedestrian axis, which has fallen from grace and risen from the ashes at least as many times as Argentina's economy. It's a riotous spot on weekdays, when throngs of office workers eager for a fast-food or high-street retail fix intermingle with buskers and street vendors who busily hawk souvenirs and haggle over leather goods. You can wander it in less than an hour: start at the intersection with Av. de Mayo and a bench or patch of grass in shady **Plaza San Martín** will be your reward at the other end.

En route, lift your gaze from the brash shop fronts to take in the often noteworthy buildings that house them. At the ornate **Edificio Bank Boston** (No. 99) attention tends to focus on the battered, paint-splattered 4-ton bronze doors—unhappy customers have been taking out their anger at *corralitos* (banks retaining their savings) since the economic crisis of 2001–02.

The restoration process at **Galería Güemes** has left the soaring marble columns and stained-glass cupola gleaming. The tacky shops that fill this historic arcade do nothing to lessen the wow factor. Witness Buenos Aires' often cavalier attitude to its architectural heritage at Florida's intersection with Avenida Corrientes, where the neo-Gothic **Palacio Elortondo-Alvear** is now home to a Burger King. Buy a soda and drink it upstairs to check out the plaster molding and stained glass.

Milan's Galleria Vittorio Emanuele served as the model for **Galerías Pacífico**, designed during Buenos Aires' turn-of-the-20th-century golden age. Once the headquarters of the Buenos Aires–Pacific Railway, it's now a posh shopping mall and cultural center. Head to the central stairwell to see the allegorical murals painted by local greats Juan Carlos Castagnino, Antonio Berni, Cirilo Colmenio, Lino Spilimbergo, and Demetrio Urruchúa. The **Centro Cultural Borges**, which hosts small international exhibitions and musical events, is on the mezzanine level.

Past the slew of leather shops in the blocks north of Av. Córdoba is **Plaza San Martín**, where you'll see a bronze statue of the namesake saint atop a rearing horse. It's overlooked by several opulent Italianate buildings and South America's tallest art deco structure, the **Edificio**

Kavanagh. ✉ *Microcentro* Ⓜ *A to Plaza de Mayo; D to Catedral; B to Florida (southern end); C to Plaza San Martín (northern end).*

Catedral Metropolitana. The columned neoclassical facade of the Metropolitan Cathedral makes it seem more like a temple than a church, and its history follows the pattern of many structures in the Plaza de Mayo area. The first of six buildings on this site was a 16th-century adobe ranch house; the current structure dates from 1822, but has been added to several times.

There's been a surge of interest in it since February 2013, when Cardinal Jorge Bergoglio, then archbishop of Buenos Aires, was elected Pope Francis. The sanctuary now includes a small commemorative display of the pope's personal objects, watched over by a grinning life-size fiberglass statue of the pontiff in full regalia.

The embalmed remains of another local hero, General José de San Martín—known as the Liberator of Argentina for his role in the War of Independence—rest here in a marble mausoleum lighted by an eternal flame. Soldiers of the Grenadier Regiment, an elite troop created and trained by San Martín in 1811, permanently guard the tomb. Guided tours (in Spanish) of the mausoleum and crypt leave Monday to Saturday at 11:45 am. ✉ *San Martín 27, at Rivadavia, Plaza de Mayo* ☎ *11/4331–2845* ⊕ *www.catedralbuenosaires.org.ar* 💲 *Free* ☉ *Weekdays 7–7, weekends 9–7:30* Ⓜ *A to Plaza de Mayo; D to Catedral; E to Bolívar.*

Centro Cultural Borges. There's something very low-key about this cultural center, despite its considerable size and prime location above the posh Galerías Pacífico mall. With a minimum of pomp and circumstance it has hosted exhibitions of Warhol, Kahlo and Rivera, Man Ray, Miró, Picasso, Chagall, and Dalí, as well as local greats Seguí, Berni, and Noé. Occasional mass shows focus on new local artists and art students. Small, independent theater and dance performances are also staged here. ✉ *Viamonte 525, at San Martín, Centro* ☎ *11/5555–5359* ⊕ *www.ccborges.org.ar* 💲 *30 pesos* ☉ *Mon.–Sat. 10–9, Sun. noon–9* Ⓜ *B to Florida.*

Museo de Arte Hispanoamericano Isaac Fernández Blanco (*Isaac Fernández Blanco Hispanic-American Art Museum*). The distinctive Peruvian neocolonial-style Palacio Noel serves as the perfect backdrop for this colonial art and craft museum, which was built in 1920 as the residence of architect Martín Noel. He and museum founder Fernández Blanco donated most of the exquisite silver items, religious wood carvings, inlaid furnishings, and paintings from the Spanish colonial period that are on display. Guided tours in English can be arranged by calling ahead. Shaded benches in the lush walled gardens provide welcome respite for your feet, and the rustling leaves and birdcalls almost filter out the busy Retiro traffic noises. The museum is an easy five-block walk from Estación San Martín on Línea C: from there go west along Avenida Santa Fe and then turn right into Suipacha and continue four blocks. ✉ *Suipacha 1422, at Av. Libertador, Retiro* ☎ *11/4327–0228* ⊕ *www.museofernandezblanco.buenosaires.gob.ar* 💲 *5 pesos (free Tues. and Thurs.)* ☉ *Tues.–Fri. 2–7, weekends 1–7* Ⓜ *C to San Martín.*

PUERTO MADERO

A forest of skyscrapers designed by big-name architects like Sir Norman Foster and César Pelli is sprouting up in Puerto Madero, a onetime port area that's now notable for its chic hotels, restaurants, and boutiques. Original dockland structures have been repurposed: former grain silos now house luxury lodgings, and high-end cafés line the waterside walkways where cargo was once offloaded.

The neighborhood's upswing has even extended to the 865-acre Reserva Ecológica, a nature preserve built on land reclaimed from the river using rubble from major construction projects in the 1970s and '80s.

PLANNING YOUR TIME

Puerto Madero has a few sights, but the best reason to come here is a leisurely stroll along the waterfront. You might want to enjoy a morning excursion to Puerto Madero, then cross the Puente de la Mujer to spend your afternoon in El Centro.

TOP ATTRACTIONS

Colección de Arte Amalia Lacroze de Fortabat. The late Amalia Fortabat was a cement heiress, so it's not surprising that the building containing her private art collection is made mostly of concrete. It was completed in 2003, but after-effects from Argentina's 2001–02 financial crisis delayed its opening until 2008. Amalita (as she was known locally) was closely involved in the design, and the personal touch continues into the collection, which includes several portraits of her—a prized Warhol among them—and many works by her granddaughter, Amalia Amoedo. In general, more money than taste seems to have gone into the project. The highlights are lesser works by big names both local (Berni, Xul Solar, Pettoruti) and international (Brueghel, Dalí, Picasso), hung with little aplomb or explanation in a huge basement gallery that echoes like a high-school gym. The side gallery given over to Carlos Alonso's and Juan Carlos Castagnino's figurative work is a step in the right direction, however. So are the luminous paintings by Soldi in the glass-walled upper gallery. They're rivaled by the view over the docks below—time your visit to end at sunset when pinks and oranges light the redbrick buildings opposite. Views from the dockside café come a close second. ⌂ *Olga Cossettini 141, Puerto Madero* ☎ *11/4310–6600* ⊕ *www.coleccionfortabat.org.ar* ⌨ *45 pesos* ☉ *Tues.–Sun. noon–8* Ⓜ *B to L. N. Alem (13 blocks away).*

WORTH NOTING

Buque Museo Fragata A.R.A. Presidente Sarmiento (*President Sarmiento Frigate Museum*). The navy commissioned this frigate from England in 1898 to be used as an open-sea training vessel. The 280-foot boat used up to 33 sails and carried more than 300 crew members. The beautifully restored cabins include surprisingly luxurious officers' quarters that feature parquet floors, wood paneling, and leather armchairs; cadets had to make do with hammocks. ⌂ *Dique 3, Alicia M. de Justo 980, Puerto Madero* ☎ *11/4334–9386* ⊕ *www.ara.mil.ar/pag.asp?idItem=112* ⌨ *2 pesos* ☉ *Daily 10–7* Ⓜ *B to L. N. Alem (9 blocks away).*

Puente de la Mujer. Tango dancers inspired the sweeping asymmetrical lines of Valencian architect Santiago Calatrava's design for the pedestrian-only Bridge of the Woman. Puerto Madero's street names pay homage to famous Argentinean women, hence the bridge's name. (Ironically its most visible part—a soaring 128-foot arm—represents the man of a couple in mid-tango.) The $6-million structure was made in Spain and paid for by local businessmen Alberto L. González, one of the brains behind Puerto Madero's redevelopment; he also built the Hilton Hotel here. Twenty engines rotate the bridge to allow ships to pass through. ⊠ *Dique 3, between Pierina Dealessi and Manuela Gorriti, Puerto Madero* Ⓜ *A to Plaza de Mayo, B to L. N. Alem; D to Catedral; E to Bolívar (all about 10 blocks away).*

Reserva Ecológica. Built over a landfill, the 865-acre Ecological Reserve is home to more than 500 species of birds and a variety of flora and fauna. On weekends thousands of porteños vie for a spot on the grass, so come midweek if you want to bird-watch and sunbathe in peace or use the jogging and cycling tracks. A monthly guided "Walking under the Full Moon" tour in Spanish begins at 7:30 pm April through October and at 8:30 pm November through March. Even if you don't speak Spanish it's still a great way to get back to nature at night; otherwise avoid the area after sunset. The main entrance and visitor center is across from the traffic circle where Avenida Tristán Achával Rodríguez intersects with Avenida Elvira Rawson de Dellepiane, a short walk from the south end of Puerto Madero; you can also enter and leave the reserve at its northern end, across from the intersection of Mariquita Sánchez de Thompson and Avenida Hernán M. Giralt. ⊠ *Av. Tristán Achával Rodríguez 1550, Puerto Madero* ☎ *11/4315–4129, 11/4893–1853 for tours* ⊕ *www.buenosaires.gov.ar/areas/med_ambiente/reserva* ⊠ *Free* ☉ *Apr.–Oct., Tues.–Sun. 8–6; Nov.–Mar., Tues.–Sun. 8–7; guided visits in Spanish weekends at 10:30 and 3:30.*

SAN TELMO AND LA BOCA

"The south also exists," quip residents of bohemian neighborhoods like San Telmo and La Boca, which historically played second fiddle to posher northern barrios. No more. The hottest designers have boutiques here, new restaurants are booked out, an art district is burgeoning, and property prices are soaring. The south is also a hotbed for the city's tango revival, appropriate given that the dance was born in these quarters.

SAN TELMO

San Telmo, Buenos Aires' first suburb, was originally inhabited by sailors, and takes its name from their wandering patron saint. All the same, the mariners' main preoccupations were clearly less than spiritual, and San Telmo became famous for its brothels.

That didn't stop the area's first experience of gentrification: wealthy local families built ornate homes here in the early 19th century, but ran for Recoleta when a yellow-fever epidemic struck in 1871. Newly arrived immigrants crammed into their abandoned mansions, known as *conventillos* (tenement houses). Today these same houses are fought over by foreign buyers dying to ride the wave of urban renewal—the

GETTING ORIENTED

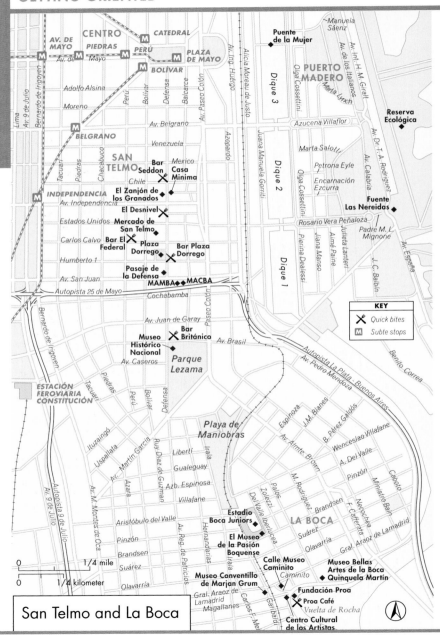

CENTRO
AV. DE MAYO
PIEDRAS
PERÚ
CATEDRAL
BOLÍVAR
PLAZA DE MAYO

Av. de Mayo
Adolfo Alsina
Moreno
Av. Belgrano
BELGRANO
Venezuela
Lima
Av. 9 de Julio
Bernardo de Irigoyen
Tacuarí
Piedras
Chacabuco
Perú
Bolívar
Defensa
Balcarce
Av. Ing. Huergo
Alicia Moreau de Justo
Av. Paseo Colón
Azopardo

SAN TELMO
Bar Seddon
Chile
El Zanjón de los Granados
El Desnivel
Mercado de San Telmo
Bar El Federal
Plaza Dorrego
Pasaje de la Defensa
Mexico
Casa Mínima
Estados Unidos
Carlos Calvo
Humberto 1
Av. San Juan
Bar Plaza Dorrego
MAMBA ◆ MACBA
INDEPENDENCIA
Av. Independencia
Autopista 25 de Mayo
Cochabamba

Puente de la Mujer
Manuela Sáenz
PUERTO MADERO
Azucena Villaflor
Marta Salotti
Petrona Eyle
Encarnación Ezcurra
Rosario Vera Peñaloza
Pierina Dealessi

Dique 3
Dique 2
Dique 1

Juana Manuela Gorriti
Olga Cossettini
Marta Lynch
Av. de los Italianos
Av. Int. H. M. Giralt

Reserva Ecológica
Av. Dr. T. A. Rodríguez
Av. Calabria
Fuente Las Nereidas
Padre M. L. Mignone
Julieta Lanteri
Aimé Painé
Juana Manso
J. C. Balbín
Av. España

Bernardo de Irigoyen
Av. Juan de Garay
Bar Británico
Museo Histórico Nacional
Av. Caseros
Parque Lezama
Av. Brasil
Paseo Colón
Autopista La Plata - Buenos Aires
Av. Pedro Mendoza
Benito Correa

ESTACIÓN FEROVIARIA CONSTITUCIÓN
Av. 9 de Julio
Autopista 9 de Julio
Av. M. Montes de Oca
Tacuarí
Piedras
Perú
Bolívar
Defensa
Ituzaingó
Uspallata
Azara
Av. Martín García
Aristóbulo del Valle
Ruy Díaz de Guzmán
Pinzón
Brandsen
Suárez
Olavarría
Libertí
Gualeguay
Azb. Espinosa
Villafane
Av. Reg. de Patricios
Hernandarias
Carlos F. Melo
Gral. Araoz de Lamadrid
Magallanes

Playa de Maniobras
Espinoza
J.M. Blanes
B. Pérez Galdós
Av. Almte. Brown
Wenceslao Villafane
A. Del Valle
Pinzón
M. Rodríguez
Palos
Brandsen
Del Valle Iberlucea
Zolezzi
Irala

Estadio Boca Juniors
El Museo de la Pasión Boquense
Calle Museo Caminito
Caminito
Museo Conventillo de Marjan Grum
Suárez
Olavarría
LA BOCA
Museo Bellas Artes de la Boca
◆ Quinquela Martín
Fundación Proa
✕ Proa Café
Vuelta de Rocha
Centro Cultural de los Artistas
Necochea
F. Cafferata
Ministro Brin
Caboto
Gral. Araoz de Lamadrid

0 _____ 1/4 mile
0 _____ 1/4 kilometer

KEY
✕ Quick bites
Ⓜ Subte stops

San Telmo and La Boca

THE TERRITORY

San Telmo, south of the Centro, is bordered by Avenida Madero to the east, avenidas Brasil and Caseros to the south, Piedras to the west, and—depending on whom you ask—Chile or Belgrano to the north. The main drag is the north–south Defensa, part of which is pedestrian-only. It forms one side of Plaza Dorrego, the area's tourist hub.

South of Avenida Brasil lies La Boca, whose westernmost edge is Avenida Patricios. The Riachuelo River forms a curving border; Avenida Don Pedro de Mendoza runs beside it.

GETTING AROUND

The subte takes you within about half a mile of San Telmo. The closest stations to the southern end are Independencia (Línea C or E) and San Juan (Línea C). Be prepared to walk nine blocks east along Avenidas Independencia, Estados Unidos, or San Juan to get to Defensa, the main street. To approach San Telmo from the north, get off at Bolívar (Línea E) or Catedral (Línea D) and walk eight blocks south along Bolívar. Bus nos. 22, 24, 26, and 28 connect San Telmo to Centro. The same route by taxi costs 10–12 pesos.

There's no subte to La Boca, so taxi travel is a good bet, especially after dark: expect to pay 18–20 pesos to or from the Centro. Bus No. 29 runs between La Boca and the Centro; so do nos. 64 and 152, which continue to Palermo. Bus No. 53 connects La Boca and San Telmo.

SAFETY AND PRECAUTIONS

San Telmo's popularity with visitors has led to increased police presence in the busiest areas (especially near Defensa). Still, instances of petty crime are common. After dark, stick to busy, well-lighted streets close to Defensa.

La Boca is far sketchier, and you'd do best not to stray from the Caminito area. Avoid the neighborhood after dark; take radio taxis if you must visit then.

TOP EXPERIENCES

Descending: into El Zanjón de Granados's restored tunnels for a different perspective.

Drinking: in the atmosphere—and a cortado—at at time-honored café like Bar El Federal or La Perla.

Watching: the sun set from Fundación Proa's roof café.

Wandering: Caminito (and adjacent Garibaldi and Magallanes), to tick the sightseeing boxes, or Defensa to cruise antiques stalls (on Sunday) and boutiques.

QUICK BITES

El Desnivel. At this classic parrilla the trimmings don't go beyond a mixed salad and fries, and surly waiters virtually fling food at you—but it's all part of the experience. ⊠ *Defensa 855, San Telmo* ☎ *11/4300–9081* ⊕ *www.parrillaeldesnivel.com. ar* ⊘ *Mon. 7 pm–1 am, Tues.–Sun. noon–1 am* Ⓜ *C or E to Independencia.*

La Perla. Right opposite Caminito, this colorful old-time café is *the* place for a *licuado* (milk shake) or *tostado mixto* (a local take on the croque-monsieur). ⊠ *Av. Pedro de Mendoza 1899, La Boca* ☎ *11/4301–2985* ⊘ *Daily 7 am–8 pm.*

reciclaje (recycling), as porteños call it—that's sweeping the area and transforming San Telmo into Buenos Aires' hippest 'hood.

Although San Telmo does have its share of sites, the barrio itself is the big attraction. Simply watching the world go by as you linger over coffee is one quintessential experience. Soaking up some history by wandering down cobbled streets edged with Italianate townhouses is another. You can get closer to the past at two small museums, or even take a piece of it home from the shops and stands selling antiques and curios. However, there's plenty of contemporary culture on offer in the neighborhood's art museums, cutting-edge galleries, and bars.

PLANNING YOUR TIME

San Telmo thrives on Sunday, thanks to the art and antiques market in Plaza Dorrego. During the week a leisurely afternoon's visit is ideal. Start with lunch in a café at the northern or southern end of San Telmo, then spend an hour or two wandering the cobbled streets. You still have time for some shopping before winding up with a coffee or a drink.

TOP ATTRACTIONS

Fodor'sChoice **El Zanjón de Granados.** All of Buenos Aires' history is packed into this
★ unusual house. The street it's on was once a small river—the *zanjón,* or gorge, of the property's name—where the first, unsuccessful attempt to found Buenos Aires took place in 1536. When the property's current owner decided to develop what was then a run-down conventillo, he began to discover all sorts of things beneath it: pottery and cutlery, the foundations of past constructions, and a 500-foot network of tunnels that has taken over 20 years to excavate. These were once used to channel water, but like the street itself, they were sealed after San Telmo's yellow-fever outbreaks. With the help of historians and architects, they've now been painstakingly restored, and the entire site has been transformed into a private museum, where the only exhibit is the redbrick building itself. Excellent hour-long guided tours in English and Spanish take you through low-lighted sections of the tunnels. The history lesson then continues aboveground, where you can see the surviving wall of a construction from 1740, the 19th-century mansion built around it, and traces of the conventillo it became. Expect few visitors and plenty of atmosphere on weekdays; cheaper, shorter tours on Sunday draw far more people. If you want to spend even more time here, you can rent the whole place (including an adjacent building reached via the tunnels) for functions. ✉ *Defensa 755, San Telmo* ☎ *11/4361–3002* ⊕ *www.elzanjon.com.ar* ✉ *Guided tours weekdays 120 pesos (1 hr), Sun. 75 pesos (30 mins)* ☉ *Tours in English weekdays at noon, 2 and 3, Sun. 1–6 (every 30 min). Closed Sat.* Ⓜ *C or E to Independencia.*

Museo de Arte Moderno de Buenos Aires (MAMBA) (*Museum of Modern Art of Buenos Aires*). Some 7,000 contemporary artworks make up the permanent collection at this newly renovated, block-long museum. Formerly the site of a tobacco company, the MAMBA retains its original exposed-brick facade and fabulous wooden doors with wrought-iron fixtures. Inside, galleries showcasing a carefully curated selection of paintings, sculptures, and new media are complemented by large temporary exhibitions of local or Latin American works as well as smaller installations. Recent highlights include the unusual portraits of superstar collective Grupo Mondongo, who eschew paint in favor of materials like crackers, sliced ham, and chewing gum. ⊠ *Av. San Juan 350, San Telmo* ☎ *11/4341–3001* ⊕ *www.museos.buenosaires.gob.ar/ mam.htm* ⌨ *10 pesos (free Tues. and Thurs.)* ⊙ *Tues.–Fri. 11–7, weekends 11–8* Ⓜ *C to San Juan.*

Pasaje de la Defensa. Wandering through this well-preserved house affords a glimpse of life in San Telmo's golden era. Behind an elegant but narrow stone facade, the building extends deep into the block around a series of internal courtyards. This type of elongated construction—known as a *casa chorizo* or "sausage house"—is typical of San Telmo. Once the private residence of the well-to-do Ezeiza family, it became a conventillo, but is now a picturesque spot for antiques and curio shopping. The stores here are open from 10 to 6 daily. ⊠ *Defensa 1179, San Telmo* Ⓜ *C to San Juan.*

Plaza Dorrego. During the week a handful of craftspeople and a few scruffy pigeons are the only ones enjoying the shade from the stately trees in the city's second-oldest square. Sunday couldn't be more different: scores of stalls selling antiques, collectibles, and just plain old stuff move in to form the Feria de San Pedro Telmo (San Pedro Telmo Fair). Tango dancers take to the cobbles, as do hundreds of shoppers (mostly tourists) browsing the tango memorabilia, antique silver, brass, crystal, and Argentine curios. Note that prices are high at stalls on the square and astronomical in the shops surrounding it, and vendors are immune to bargaining. ⚠ Pickpockets work as hard as stall owners on Sundays, so keep a firm hold on bags and purses or—wiser still—leave them at home. More affordable offerings—mostly handicrafts and local artists' work—are on the ever-growing web of stalls along nearby streets like Defensa. ■TIP→ Be on the lookout for antique glass soda siphons that once adorned every bar top in Buenos Aires. Classic colors are green and turquoise. Be sure to look up as you wander Plaza Dorrego, as the surrounding architecture provides an overview of the influences—Spanish colonial, French classical, and ornate Italian masonry—that shaped the city in the 19th and 20th centuries. ⊠ *Defensa and Humberto I, San Telmo* Ⓜ *C to San Juan.*

WORTH NOTING

Museo de Arte Contemporáneo de Buenos Aires. Geometric abstraction is the guiding principle for both the collection and the construction of Buenos Aires' newest museum. Sharply sloped walkways connect four floors of concrete-walled galleries, creating an austere backdrop for the bright lines and shapes of local financier Aldo Rubin's private collection. Regularly changing exhibitions may include pieces by contemporary local stars like Pablo Siquier and Guillermo Kuitca. ⊠ *Av. San Juan 328, San Telmo* ☎ *11/5299–2010* ⊕ *www.macba.com.ar* ⌨ *25 pesos, Wed. 15 pesos* ⊙ *Mon. and Wed.–Fri. noon–7, weekends 11–7:30* Ⓜ *C to San Juan.*

Museo Histórico Nacional. What better place for the National History Museum than overlooking the spot where the city was supposedly founded? Once owned by entrepreneur and horticulturalist Gregorio

CALLE MUSEO CAMINITO

✉ *Caminito between Av. Pedro de Mendoza (La Vuelta de Rocha promenade) and Gregorio Aráoz de Lamadrid, La Boca* 🕮 *Free* ⊘ *Daily 10–6.*

TIPS AND TRIVIA

■ "Caminito" comes from a 1926 tango by Juan de Dios Filiberto, who is said to have composed it while thinking of a girl leaning from the balcony of a ramshackle house like those here. It was chosen by local artist Benito Quinquela Martín, who helped establish the street as an open-air museum.

■ Expect to be canvassed aggressively by rival restaurant owners touting overpriced, touristy menus near the start of Caminito and along every other side street. Each restaurant has its own outdoor stage—competing troupes of stamping gauchos make meals a noisy affair. The best tactic to get by them is to accept their leaflets with a serene smile and "gracias."

■ The Caminito concept spills over into nearby streets Garibaldi and Magallanes, which form a triangle with it. The strange, foot-high sidewalks along streets like Magallanes, designed to prevent flooding, show how the river's proximity has shaped the barrio.

Cobblestones, tango dancers, and haphazardly constructed, colorful conventillos have made Calle Museo Caminito the darling of Buenos Aires' postcard manufacturers since this pedestrian street was created in 1959. Artists fill the block-long street with works depicting port life and the tango, which is said to have been born in La Boca. These days it's painfully commercial, and seems more a parody of porteño culture than anything else, but if you're willing to embrace the out-and-out tackiness it can make a fun outing.

Highlights

Local Art. Painters, photographers, and sculptors peddle their creations from stalls along Caminito. Quality varies considerably; if nothing tempts you, focus on the small mosaics set into the walls, such as Luis Perlotti's *Santos Vega*. Another local art form, the brightly colored scrollwork known as *fileteado*, adorns many shop and restaurant fronts near Caminito.

Tangueros. Competition is fierce between the pairs of sultry dancers dressed to the nines in split skirts and fishnets. True, they spend more time trying to entice you into photo ops than actually dancing, but linger long enough (and throw a big enough contribution in the fedora) and you'll see some fancy footwork.

Lezama, the beautiful chestnut-and-white Italianate mansion that houses it later did duty as a quarantine station during the San Telmo cholera and yellow-fever epidemics before morphing into a museum in 1897. Due to ongoing renovation work, much of the building remains closed at the time of writing; three rooms, however, reopened to the public in 2013. Personal possessions and thoughtful explanations (in Spanish) chronicle the rise and fall of Argentina's liberator José de San Martín. Other galleries celebrate the heroes of independence and foreign forces' unsuccessful attempts to invade Argentina. ⊠ *Calle Defensa 1600, San Telmo* ☎ *11/4307–1182* ⊕ *www.cultura.gob.ar/museos/ museo-historico-nacional* ⊠ *10 pesos* ☉ *Wed.–Sun. 11–6.*

LA BOCA

Although La Boca is more touristy, it shares much of San Telmo's gritty history. La Boca sits on the fiercely polluted—and thus fiercely smelly—Riachuelo River, where rusting ships and warehouses remind you that this was once the city's main port. The immigrants who first settled here built their houses from corrugated metal and brightly colored paint left over from the shipyards. Today you'll see imitations of these vibrant buildings forming one of Buenos Aires' most emblematic sights, the Caminito.

The waterfront near the iconic Caminito area may be the most unashamedly touristy part of town, but the neighborhood surrounding it is the most fiercely traditional. Cafés, pubs, and general stores that once catered to passing sailors (and now reel in vacationers) dot the partially renovated area. For high-brow hipsters, the gallery of the Fundación Proa is the main draw.

Two quite different colors have made La Boca famous internationally: the blue and gold of the Boca Juniors soccer team, whose massive home stadium is the barrio's unofficial hub. For many local soccer devotees, the towering Boca Juniors stadium makes La Boca the center of the known world.

PLANNING YOUR TIME

In La Boca, allow two or three hours to explore Caminito and do a museum or two. It's busy all week, but expect extra crowds on weekends.

TOP ATTRACTIONS

Calle Museo Caminito.

See the highlighted listing in this chapter.

Fundación Proa. For more than a decade, this thoroughly modern art museum has been nudging traditional La Boca into the present. After major renovation work, its facade alone reads like a manifesto of local urban renewal: part of the original 19th-century Italianate housefront has been cut away, and huge plate-glass windows accented by unfinished steel stand alongside it. The space behind them now includes three adjacent properties. The luminous main gallery retains the building's original Corinthian-style steel columns, artfully rusted, but has sparkling white walls and polished concrete floors. With every flight of stairs you climb, views out over the harbor and cast-iron bridges get better. On the first floor, you can browse through one of Buenos Aires' best art bookshops (it has a particularly strong collection of local artists' books and photography tomes displayed on trestle tables). On the roof, an airy café serves salads, sandwiches, and cocktails. Bag one of the outdoor sofas around sunset and your photos will rival the work below. English versions of all exhibition information are available. The museum also runs guided tours in English, with two days' notice. ⊠ *Av. Pedro de Mendoza 1929, La Boca* 🕾 *11/4104–1000* ⊕ *www.proa.org* 🖃 *20 pesos (free Tues.)* ☉ *Tues.–Sun. 11–7.*

Museo de la Pasión Boquense. Inside Estadio Boca Juniors (aka La Bombonera), this modern, two-floor museum is heaven for fútbol fans. It chronicles Boca's rise from a neighborhood club in 1905 to its current position as one of the best teams in the world. Among the innovative exhibits is a giant soccer ball that plays 360-degree footage of an adrenaline-fueled match, recreating all the excitement (and the screaming) for those too faint-hearted to attend the real thing. Jerseys, trophies, and more are also on display. A huge mural of Maradona (the team's most revered player) and a hall of fame complete the rest of the circuit. Everything you need to Boca up your life—from official team tees to bed linens, school folders to G-strings—is available in the on-site gift store (shops and stalls outside La Bombonera sell cheaper copies). For the full-blown experience, buy a combo ticket that includes museum entry plus an extensive tour of the beloved "Candy Box" stadium. ⊠ *Brandsen 805, La Boca* 🕾 *11/4362–1100* ⊕ *www.museoboquense. com* 🖃 *65 pesos, 80 pesos with stadium tour* ☉ *Daily 10–6.*

WORTH NOTING

Estadio Boca Juniors. Walls exploding with huge, vibrant murals of insurgent workers, famous inhabitants of La Boca, and fútbol greats splashed in blue and gold let you know that the Estadio Boca Juniors is at hand. The stadium that's also known as La Bombonera (meaning candy box, supposedly because the fans' singing reverberates as it would inside a candy tin) is the home of Argentina's most popular club. The extensive stadium tour is worth the extra money. Lighthearted guides take you all over the stands as well as to press boxes, locker rooms, underground tunnels, and the emerald grass of the field itself. ⊠ *Brandsen 805, at del Valle Iberlucea, La Boca* 🕾 *11/4309–4700 stadium* ⊕ *www. museoboquense.com* 🖃 *80 pesos* ☉ *Daily 11–5.*

RECOLETA AND ALMAGRO

For Buenos Aires' most illustrious families, Recoleta's boundaries are the boundaries of the civilized world. The local equivalents of the Vanderbilts are baptized and married in the Basílica del Pilar, throw parties in the Alvear Palace Hotel, live in spacious 19th-century apartments nearby, and wouldn't dream of shopping anywhere but avenidas Quintana and Alvear. Ornate mausoleums in the Cementerio de la Recoleta promise an equally stylish afterlife.

RECOLETA

Recoleta wasn't always synonymous with elegance. Colonists, including city founder Juan de Garay, farmed here. So did the Franciscan Recoleto friars, whose 1700s settlement here inspired the district's name. Their

GETTING ORIENTED

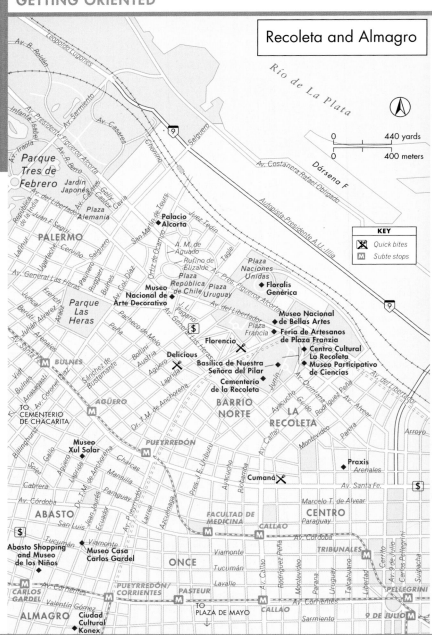

Recoleta and Almagro

Río de La Plata

0 ——— 440 yards
0 ——— 400 meters

KEY

✘ Quick bites
Ⓜ Subte stops

Parque Tres de Febrero

Jardín Japonés

Plaza Alemania

◆ Palacio Alcorta

PALERMO

A. M. de Aguado

Rufino de Elizalde

Plaza República de Chile

Museo Nacional de Arte Decorativo ◆

Parque Las Heras

Plaza Naciones Unidas

◆ Floralis Genérica

Plaza Uruguay

Plaza Francia

Museo Nacional de Bellas Artes ◆

Feria de Artesanos de Plaza Franzia ◆

Florencio ✘

◆ Centro Cultural La Recoleta

◆ Museo Participativo de Ciencias

Delicious ✘

Basílica de Nuestra Señora del Pilar

Cementerio de la Recoleta

BARRIO NORTE

LA RECOLETA

Arroyo

BULNES Ⓜ

TO CEMENTERIO DE CHACARITA

AGÜERO Ⓜ

PUEYRREDÓN Ⓜ

Museo Xul Solar ◆

Praxis ◆ Arenales

Cumaná ✘

Av. Santa Fe.

Marcelo T. de Alvear

CENTRO

Paraguay

ABASTO

FACULTAD DE MEDICINA

CALLAO Ⓜ

CALLAO Ⓜ

TRIBUNALES

Ⓜ

Abasto Shopping and Museo de los Niños ◆

Museo Casa Carlos Gardel

ONCE

Av. Córdoba

CARLOS GARDEL Ⓜ

PUEYRREDÓN/ CORRIENTES Ⓜ

PASTEUR Ⓜ

TO PLAZA DE MAYO ↓

CALLAO Ⓜ

9 DE JULIO Ⓜ

PELLEGRINI Ⓜ

ALMAGRO

Ciudad Cultural Konex ◆

THE TERRITORY

The Río de la Plata borders Recoleta to the north. Uruguay and Montevideo join to form the eastern border; the jagged western edge is made up of Mario Bravo, Coronel Díaz, and Tagle. The area between Juncal and Córdoba—Recoleta's southern boundary—is known as Barrio Norte, whose main thoroughfare is Santa Fe. In Recoleta proper, avenidas Alvear and Quintana are the key streets.

Almagro is officially bordered by avenidas Córdoba and Estado de Israel to the north, Río de Janeiro to the west, Independencia to the south, and Sánchez de Bustamente and Gallo to the east. The Abasto subdistrict, which centers on Gallo and Corrientes, stretches a few blocks farther east into neighboring Balvanera.

GETTING AROUND

True to its elite roots, Recoleta has no subway, so taxis are your best option. Expect to pay around 30 pesos from downtown or 40 from Palermo. Bus nos. 17 and 59 run to Recoleta from Palermo, San Telmo, and Centro; No. 92 connects Retiro and Recoleta, then continues to central Palermo and Almagro.

Heavy traffic means Almagro is best reached by subte. Línea B runs along Avenida Corrientes through Almagro; Carlos Gardel station leads right into the Abasto mall. Bus No. 24 connects Almagro with Centro and San Telmo; No. 168 goes west to Palermo Viejo.

SAFETY AND PRECAUTIONS

Recoleta and Barrio Norte are relatively safe in the daytime, but stick to well-lighted streets at night. Bag snatching is opportunist rather than systematic here: keep a firm grip on your purse in the crowded weekend market and in busy restaurants. Although Almagro is on the upswing, many streets near the Abasto mall are still run-down. Wander with caution.

TOP EXPERIENCES

Seeking: unusual statues in Cementerio de la Recoleta.

Window-shopping: on Avenida Quintana for Argentine designs but buying more affordable ones on Avenida Santa Fe or in the Abasto mall.

Comparing: 19th-century Argentine and European art on the first floor of the Museo Nacional de Bellas Artes.

Wandering: Avenida Alvear for the gorgeous late-19th- and early-20th-century mansions.

QUICK BITES

Cumaná. The hearty stews, steaks, and empanadas at chaotic Cumaná are a far cry from Recoleta's European pretensions. Skip dessert, though (nearby ice-creameries are better). ⊠ *Rodríguez Peña 1149, Barrio Norte* ☎ *11/4813–9207* ⊙ *Daily noon–12:30 am* Ⓜ *D to Callao.*

Delicious. It's a hard name to live up to, but there's no doubt this casual café pulls it off. Delicious does superfresh sandwiches, salads, and smoothies, which you can eat in or pack into your picnic basket. A shot of espresso and a slice of cheesecake provide the perfect dose of caffeine and sugar to get you back in the sightseeing saddle. ⊠ *Laprida 2015, Recoleta* ☎ *11/4803–1151* ⊕ *www.deliciouscafe.com.ar* ⊙ *Tues.– Fri. 9–8, weekends 10–8* Ⓜ *D to Agüero.*

CEMENTERIO DE LA RECOLETA

✉ *Junín 1760, Recoleta*
☎ *11/4803–1594* 🎫 *Free*
🕐 *Daily 7–6.*

■ The city government runs free guided visits to the cemetery in English on Tuesday and Thursday at 11; visits in Spanish operate Tuesday through Sunday at 9:30, 11, 2, and 4. Groups gather at the entrance.

■ If you prefer an independent tour, the administrative offices at the entrance can usually provide a free photocopied map, and caretakers throughout the grounds can help you locate the more intriguing tombs. These are also labeled on a large map at the entrance.

■ It's easy to get lost in the cemetery, so start your independent tour well before closing time.

■ Look out for such intriguing statues such as the life-size likeness of boxer Luis Angel Firpo, who lost the world heavyweight title to Jack Dempsey in 1923. It stands on guard outside his tomb at the back of the cemetery, wearing a robe and boxing boots.

■ The cemetery had its blessing withdrawn by the Catholic Church in 1863, when President Bartolomé Mitre ordered that a suicide be buried there.

The ominous gates, Doric-columned portico, and labyrinthine paths of the city's oldest cemetery may leave you with a sense of foreboding. Founded in 1822, it's the final resting place for the nation's most illustrious figures, and covers 13.5 acres that are rumored to be the most expensive real estate in town. The cemetery has more than 6,400 elaborate vaulted tombs and majestic mausoleums, 70 of which have been declared historic monuments. The mausoleums resemble chapels, Greek temples, pyramids, and miniature mansions.

Highlights

Evita. The embalmed remains of Eva Duarte de Perón, who made it (almost intact) here after 17 years of posthumous wandering, are in the Duarte family vault. Around July 26, the anniversary of her death, flowers pile up here.

Late Greats. If the tomb of brutal *caudillo* (dictator) Facundo Quiroga looks small, it's because he's buried standing—a sign of valor—at his request. Prominent landowner Dorrego Ortíz Basualdo resides in Recoleta's most monumental sepulcher, complete with chandelier. The names of many key players in Argentina's history are chiseled over other sumptuous mausoleums: Alvear, Quintana, Sáenz Peña, Lavalle, Sarmiento.

Spooky Stories. Rufina Cambaceres is known as the girl who died twice. She was thought dead after suffering a cataleptic attack, and was entombed on her 19th birthday in 1902. Rufina awoke inside her casket and clawed the top open but died of a heart attack before she could be rescued. When Alfredo Gath heard of Rufina's story he was appalled and commissioned a special mechanical coffin with an opening device and alarm bell. Gath successfully tested the coffin in situ 12 times, but on the 13th the mechanism failed and he died inside.

church, the Basílica del Pilar, was almost on the riverbank then: tanneries grew up around it, and Recoleta became famous for its *pulperías* (taverns) and brothels. Everything changed, though, with the 1871 outbreak of yellow fever in the south of the city.

The elite swarmed to Recoleta, building the *palacios* and stately Parisian-style apartment buildings that are now the neighborhood's trademark. They also laid the foundations for Recoleta's concentration of intellectual and cultural activity: the Biblioteca Nacional (National Library), a plethora of top-notch galleries, and three publicly run art museums are based here. Combine all of that with Recoleta's exclusive boutiques and its beautiful parks and squares—many filled with posh pooches and their walkers—and sightseeing becomes a visual feast. An unofficial subdistrict, Barrio Norte, is one step south of Recoleta proper and one small step down the social ladder. Shopping is the draw: local chains, sportswear flagships, and minimalls of vintage clothing and clubwear line Avenida Santa Fe between 9 de Julio and Puerreydón.

PLANNING YOUR TIME

Despite the luxury around you, many of Recoleta's sights are free. Blitz through the main ones in half a day, or spend a full morning or afternoon in the cemetery or museums alone. Come at midweek for quiet exploring, or on the weekend to do the cemetery and crafts market on Plaza Francia in one fell swoop.

TOP ATTRACTIONS

FodorśChoice
★

Cementerio de la Recoleta.

See the highlighted listing in this chapter.

Feria de Artesanos de Plaza Francia (*Feria de Plaza Francia*). On weekends artisans' stalls line the small park outside Recoleta Cemetery, forming the open-air market known as La Feria de Artesanos de Plaza Francia. It's usually teeming with shoppers eager to stock up on quality crafts—including leather goods, pottery, table linens, and other textiles, plus lovely pieces of handmade jewelry. Although the market officially opens at 11, many stalls aren't properly set up until after 1. ⊠ *Pl. Francia, avs. Libertador and Pueyrredón, Recoleta* ⊕ *www.feriaplazafrancia. com* ⊗ *Weekends 11–8.*

Floralis Genérica. The gleaming steel and aluminum petals of this giant flower look very space age, perhaps because they were commissioned from the Lockheed airplane factory by architect Eduardo Catalano, who designed and paid for the monument. The 66-foot-high structure is supposed to open at dawn and close at dusk, when the setting sun turns its mirrored surfaces a glowing pink. It's been stuck in open mode for several years due to a faulty petal that no one can afford to fix, but even static it seems stylish. The flower stands in the Plaza Naciones Unidas (behind El Museo Nacional de Bellas Artes over Avenida Figueroa Alcorta), which was remodeled to accommodate it. ⊠ *Pl. Naciones Unidas at Av. Figueroa Alcorta and J. A. Biblioni, Recoleta* ⊗ *Dawn–dusk.*

Museo Nacional de Arte Decorativo. The harmonious, French neoclassical mansion that houses the National Museum of Decorative Art is as much a reason to visit as the period furnishings, porcelain, and silver within it. Ornate wooden paneling in the Regency ballroom, the imposing Louis

MUSEO NACIONAL DE BELLAS ARTES

✉ *Av. del Libertador 1473,*
Recoleta ☎ *11/5288-9900*
⊕ *www.mnba.gob.ar* ✉ *Free*
⊙ *Tues.–Fri. 12:30–8:30,*
weekends 9:30–8:30.

■ Information about most works is in Spanish only; however, free one-hour guided visits in English are offered on Tuesday, Thursday, and Friday at 12:30, and Saturday at 2. Alternately, you can rent an MP3 audio guide (50 pesos) or purchase a printed guide (30 pesos); collection maps may be downloaded for free on the museum website.

■ You wouldn't know it by looking at the museum's elegant, columned front, but the building was once the city's waterworks. Famed local architect Alejandro Bustillo oversaw its conversion into a museum in the early 1930s.

■ The museum owns more than 11,000 works, but restricted space means only 10% of them are ever on display.

■ The large modern pavilion behind the museum hosts excellent temporary exhibitions, often showcasing top local artists little-known outside Argentina.

The world's largest collection of Argentine art is contained in this neoclassical wine-color building. It also houses many lesser works by big-name European artists from the 12th through 20th centuries and hosts several high-profile temporary exhibitions per year.

Since 2010, alternating parts of the museum have been shut for renovation. At this writing, the European collection and 19th-century Argentine works are on display in the 24 ground-floor galleries; the upper floor, currently closed, will eventually hold the 20th-century collection.

Highlights

War and peace. Cándido López painted the panoramic battle scenes with his left hand after losing his right arm in the 1870s during the War of the Triple Alliance. His work spearheaded contemporary primitive painting and is showcased in Gallery 23. Local master Eduardo Sívori's tranquil landscapes (in Gallery 24) portray less turbulent times.

European masters. A whole room (Gallery 8) is given over to Goya's dark, disturbing works. Nearby are minor works by El Greco, Rubens, Tiepolo, Titian, and Zurbarán. The room behind the entrance hall (Gallery 10) contains Rodin sculptures. The right wing includes paintings by Manet, Degas, Monet, Pissarro, Gaugin, and Toulouse-Lautrec.

XIV red-and-black-marble dining room, and a lofty Renaissance-style great hall are some of the highlights in the only home of its kind open to the public here. There are excellent English descriptions of each room, and they include gossipy details about the original inhabitants, the well-to-do Errázuriz-Alvear family. The museum also contains some Chinese art. Guided tours include the Zubov Collection of miniatures from Imperial Russia. ✉ *Av. del Libertador 1902, Recoleta* ☏ *11/4801–8248* ⊕ *www.mnad.org* 🖅 *15 pesos (free Tues.), guided tours in English 15 pesos* ⊙ *Jan., Tues.–Sat. 2–7; Feb.–Dec., Tues.–Sun. 2–7.*

Fodor's Choice
★ **Museo Nacional de Bellas Artes.**
See the highlighted listing in this chapter.

WORTH NOTING

Basílica de Nuestra Señora del Pilar. This basilica beside the famous Cementerio de la Recoleta is where Buenos Aires' elite families hold weddings and other ceremonies. Built by the Recoleto friars in 1732, it is considered a national treasure for its six German baroque–style altars. The central one is overlaid with Peruvian engraved silver; another, sent by Spain's King Carlos III, contains relics. The basilica's cloisters house the **Museo de los Claustros del Pilar**, a small museum that displays religious artifacts as well as pictures and photographs documenting Recoleta's evolution. There are excellent views of the cemetery from upstairs windows. ✉ *Junín 1904, Recoleta* ☏ *11/4806–2209* ⊕ *www.basilicadelpilar.org.ar* 🖅 *Basílica free, museum 8 pesos* ⊙ *Basílica daily 9–9:30; museum Mon.–Sat. 10:30–6:30, Sun. 2:30–6:10.*

Centro Cultural La Recoleta. Art exhibitions, concerts, fringe theater performances, and workshops are some of the offerings at this cultural center. The rambling building it occupies was converted from the cloister patios of the Franciscan monks. ✉ *Junín 1930, Recoleta* ☏ *11/4803–1040* ⊕ *www.centroculturalrecoleta.org* ⊙ *Tues.–Fri. 1–8, weekends 11–8.*

FAMILY **Museo Participativo de Ciencias.** The motto of this mini science museum inside the Centro Cultural La Recoleta is *"Prohibido No Tocar"* ("Not Touching Is Forbidden"), which says it all. Ten hands-on rooms aim to teach kids how things like electricity, music, light, and computers work through thoughtful interactive displays that include giant musical instruments and DIY whirlpools. Explanations are entirely in Spanish, so your little ones may not get the full educational experience, but there's so much to touch and try that they probably won't mind. ✉ *Centro Cultural La Recoleta, Junín 1930, Recoleta* ☏ *11/4807–3260* ⊕ *www.mpc.org.ar* 🖅 *50 pesos* ⊙ *Jan. and Feb., daily 3:30–7:30; Mar.–Dec., Tues.–Fri. 10–5, weekends 3:30–7:30; school holidays (last 2 wks of July), Tues.–Fri. 12:30–7:30, weekends 3:30–7:30.*

ALMAGRO

Almagro lies southwest of Recoleta but feels like a different world. Traditionally a gritty, working-class neighborhood, it spawned many tango greats, including the legendary Carlos Gardel. The Abasto subdistrict has long been the heart of the barrio: it centers on the massive art deco building (at Corrientes and Agüero) that was once the city's central market. The abandoned structure was completely overhauled and reopened in 1998 as a major mall, spearheading the redevelopment of the area, which now has several top hotels and an increasing number of restaurants and tango venues. More urban renewal is taking place a few blocks away at Sarmiento and Jean Jaurés, where the Konex Foundation has transformed an old factory into a cutting-edge cultural venue.

PLANNING YOUR TIME

In Almagro a couple of hours will suffice if you want to pay homage to Carlos Gardel—tango's greatest hero—and get a feel for the district.

TOP ATTRACTIONS

Museo Casa Carlos Gardel. Hard-core tango fans shouldn't pass up a quick visit to the home of tango's greatest hero, Carlos Gardel. The front rooms of this once-crumbling casa chorizo contain extensive displays of Gardel paraphernalia—LPs, photos, and old posters. The maestro's greatest hits play in the background. The back of the house has been restored with the aim of recreating as closely as possible the way the house would have looked when Gardel and his mother lived here, right down to the placement of birdcages on the patio. Concise but informative texts in Spanish and English talk you through the rooms and the history of tango in general. Short guided visits in English are usually available on request on weekdays. ⊠ *Jean Jaurés 735, Almagro* ☎ *11/4964–2015* ⊕ *www.museocasacarlosgardel.buenosaires.gob.ar* 🎫 *5 pesos (free Wed.)* ☉ *Mon. and Wed.–Fri. 11–6, weekends 10–7* Ⓜ *B to Carlos Gardel.*

WORTH NOTING

Cementerio de Chacarita. This cemetery is home to Carlos Gardel's tomb, which features a dapper, Brylcreemed statue and dozens of tribute plaques. It's treated like a shrine by hordes of faithful followers who honor their idol by inserting lighted cigarettes in the statue's hand. On June 24, the anniversary of his death, aging *tangueros* in suits and fedoras gather here to weep and sing. Fellow tango legends Aníbal Troilo and Osvaldo Pugliese are also buried in this cemetery, which is about equidistant from Palermo and Almagro. If you're heading from Almagro, hop subte Línea B at Estación Carlos Gardel for a 10- to 15-minute ride west to the Federico Lacroze stop. Depending on where you are in Palermo, a cab here will cost 40 to 50 pesos. ⊠ *Guzmán 680, at Corrientes, Chacarita* ☎ *11/4553–9338* 🎫 *Free* ☉ *Daily 7–5* Ⓜ *B to Federico Lacroze.*

FAMILY **Museo de los Niños.** The real world is scaled down to kiddie size at this museum in Abasto Shopping. Children can play at sending letters, going to a bank, acting in a mini-TV studio, or making a radio program. You need to speak Spanish to participate in most activities, but the play areas and giant pipes that replicate the city's water system are internationally comprehensible. ⊠ *Abasto Shopping, Level 2, Av. Corrientes 3247, Almagro* ☎ *11/4861–2325* ⊕ *www.museoabasto.org.ar* 🎫 *Tues.–Fri. 30 pesos, weekends 35 pesos* ☉ *Tues.–Sun. 1–8* Ⓜ *B to Carlos Gardel.*

PALERMO

Trendy shops, bold restaurants, elegant embassies, acres of parks—Palermo really does have it all. Whether your idea of sightseeing is ticking off museums, flicking through clothing racks, licking your fingers after yet another long lunch, or kicking up a storm on the dance floor, Palermo can oblige. The city's largest barrio is subdivided into various unofficial districts, each with its own distinct flavor.

Some say Palermo takes its name from a 16th-century Italian immigrant who bought land here, others from the abbey honoring Saint Benedict of Palermo. Either way, the area was largely rural until the 1830s, when national governor Juan Manuel de Rosas built an estate in Palermo. After the dictatorial Rosas was overthrown, his property north of Avenida del Libertador was turned into a huge patchwork of parks. Known as Los Bosques de Palermo (the Palermo Woods), the green space provides a peaceful escape from the rush of downtown. The zoo and botanical gardens are at its southern end. High-brow culture is provided by the gleaming MALBA (Museo de Arte Latinoamericano de Buenos Aires, or the Museum of Latin American Art of Buenos Aires), whose clean stone lines stand out on Avenida Figueroa Alcorta. The streets around the intersection of avenidas Santa Fe and Coronel Díaz are home to mainstream clothing stores and the Alto Palermo mall. More upscale alternatives, meanwhile, abound in Palermo Viejo. Top boutiques—along with minimalist lofts, endless bars, and the most daring restaurants in town—have made Palermo Viejo (and its unofficial subdistrict, Palermo Soho) the epicenter of Buenos Aires' design revolution.

PLANNING YOUR TIME

Palermo is so big that it's best to tackle it in sections. An even-paced ramble through Parque Tres de Febrero should take no more than two hours, though you could easily spend an entire afternoon at the zoo, Japanese Garden, and Botanical Garden. In architectural and geographic terms, Palermo Chico and the MALBA tie in nicely with a visit to Recoleta: allow at least a couple of hours for such an experience.

TOP ATTRACTIONS

FAMILY   **Jardín Japonés** (*Japanese Garden*). Like the bonsais in the nursery within it, this park is small but perfectly formed. A slow wander along its arched wooden bridges and walkways is guaranteed to calm frazzled sightseeing nerves during the week; crowds on the weekend make for a less-than-soothing experience. A variety of shrubs and flowers frame ornamental ponds that are filled with friendly koi carp—you can actually pet them if you feel so inclined (kids often do). The traditional teahouse, where you can enjoy sushi, adzuki-bean sweets, and tea, overlooks a zen garden. ⊠ *Av. Casares at Av. Figueroa Alcorta, Palermo* ☎ *11/4804–4922* ⊕ *www.jardinjapones.org.ar* 🎫 *32 pesos* 🕙 *Daily 10–6.*

Fodor's Choice   **Museo de Arte de Latinoamericano de Buenos Aires** (*MALBA, Museum of*
★   *Latin American Art of Buenos Aires*).
See the highlighted listing in this chapter.

2

Museo Evita.
See the highlighted listing in this chapter.

FAMILY **Parque Tres de Febrero.** Known locally as Los Bosques de Palermo (Palermo Woods), this 400-acre green space is really a crazy quilt of smaller parks. Lush grass and shady trees make it an urban oasis, although the busy roads and horn-honking drivers that crisscross the park never let you forget what city you're in. Near the lakes in the northwestern part, some 12,000 rosebushes (more than 1,000 different species) bloom seasonally in the **Paseo del Rosedal.** A stroll along the paths takes you through the Jardín de los Poetas (Poets' Garden), dotted with statues of literary figures, and to the enchanting **Patio Andaluz** (Andalusian Patio), where majolica tiles and Spanish mosaics sit under a vine-covered pergola.

South of Avenida Figueroa Alcorta, you can take part in organized tai chi and exercise classes as well as impromptu soccer matches. You can also jog or rent bikes, in-line skates, and pedal boats. The park gets crowded on sunny weekends, as this is where families come to play and have picnics. If you like the idea of the latter, take advantage of the street vendors who sell refreshments and *choripan* (chorizo sausage in a bread roll) within the park. There are also several posh cafés lining the Paseo de la Infanta (running from Libertador toward Sarmiento in the park). ⊠ *Bounded by avs. del Libertador, Sarmiento, Leopoldo Lugones, and Dorrego, Palermo* Ⓜ *D to Plaza Italia.*

WORTH NOTING

FAMILY **Jardín Botánico Carlos Thays.** Wedged between three busy Palermo streets, this unexpected haven has 18 acres of gardens filled with 5,500 varieties of exotic and indigenous flora. Different sections recreate the environments of Asia, Africa, Oceania, Europe, and the Americas. An organic vegetable garden aims to teach children healthy eating habits. Winding paths lead to hidden statues and a brook that's watched over by an ever-growing population of cats (the gardens are the traditional dumping ground for unwanted porteño pets). The central area contains an exposed-brick botanical school and library, plus a beautiful greenhouse brought from France in 1900 but sadly not open to the public. ⊠ *Av. Santa Fe 3951, Palermo* ☎ *11/4832–1552* ⊕ *www.buenosaires.gob.ar/ jardin-botanico-carlos-thays* 🖰 *Free* ⊙ *Sept.–Mar., weekdays 8–6:45, weekends 9:30–6:45; Apr.–Aug., weekdays 8–5:45, weekends 9:30– 5:45.* Ⓜ *D to Plaza Italia.*

Museo de Artes Plásticas Eduardo Sívori (*Eduardo Sívori Art Museum*). If you're looking for respite from the sun or sports in Parque Tres de Febrero, try this sedate museum. Focused on 19th- and 20th-century Argentine art, its collection includes paintings by local masters like Emilio Petorutti, Lino Eneo Spilimbergo, Antonio Berni, and the museum's namesake Sívori. The shaded sculpture garden is the perfect combination of art and park. ⊠ *Av. Infanta Isabel 555, Palermo* ☎ *11/4774–9452* ⊕ *museos.buenosaires.gob.ar/sivori.htm* 🖰 *5 pesos (free Wed.)* ⊙ *Tues.–Fri. noon–8, weekends 10–8* Ⓜ *D to Plaza Italia.*

Museo Xul Solar. Avant-garde artist, linguist, esoteric philosopher, and close friend of Borges, Xul Solar is best known for his luminous,

GETTING ORIENTED

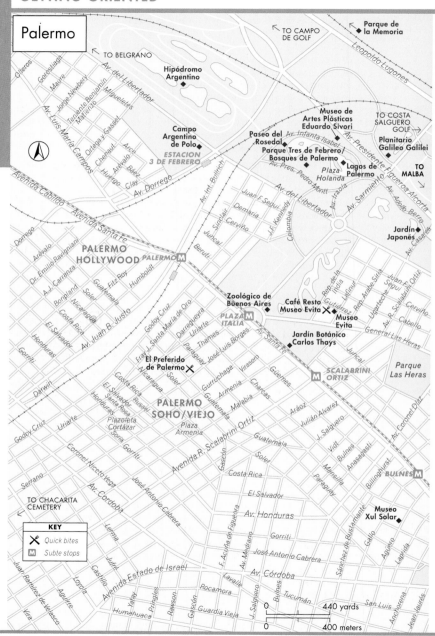

Palermo

TO CAMPO DE GOLF

Parque de la Memoria

TO BELGRANO

Hipódromo Argentino

Campo Argentino de Polo
ESTACION 3 DE FEBRERO

Museo de Artes Plásticas Eduardo Sívori

Paseo del Rosedal
Parque Tres de Febrero/ Bosques de Palermo

Plaza Holanda

Lagos de Palermo

TO COSTA SALGUERO GOLF

Planitario Galileo Galilei

TO MALBA

Jardín Japonés

PALERMO HOLLYWOOD

PALERMO

Zoológico de Buenos Aires

PLAZA ITALIA

Café Resto Museo Evita

Museo Evita

Jardín Botánico Carlos Thays

Parque Las Heras

El Preferido de Palermo

PALERMO SOHO/VIEJO

Plaza Armenia

Plazoleta Cortázar

SCALABRINI ORTIZ

BULNES

TO CHACARITA CEMETERY

Museo Xul Solar

KEY
✕ Quick bites
Ⓜ Subte stops

| 0 | | 440 yards |
| 0 | | 400 meters |

THE TERRITORY

The city's biggest barrio stretches from Avenida Costanera R. Obligado, along the river, to Avenida Córdoba in the south. Its other boundaries are jagged, but include Avenida Coronel Díaz to the east and La Pampa and Dorrego to the west. Avenida Santa Fe cuts the neighborhood roughly in half. Palermo's green spaces and Palermo Chico lie north of it. To the south are Palermo Viejo and Palermo Hollywood, east and west of Avenida Juan B. Justo, respectively.

GETTING AROUND

Subte Línea D runs along Avenida Santa Fe, but doesn't always bring you to the doorstep of Palermo's attractions, so you may need to combine it with a taxi or some walking. Indeed, weekday traffic makes this combination a better idea than coming all the way from Centro by cab (which costs 40–50 pesos). Get off the subte at Bulnes or Scalabrini Ortíz for Palermo Chico; Plaza Italia for Palermo Viejo and the parks; and Ministro Carranza for Palermo Hollywood.

A more scenic route to Palermo Viejo and Hollywood from Centro is Bus No. 39 (Route 3, usually with a windshield sign "Palermo Viejo"). It takes 30 to 60 minutes, running along Honduras on the way to Palermo and along Gorriti on the way back. Bus No. 59 serves Palermo via Centro, San Telmo, and Recoleta. Nos. 29 and 64 link La Boca, San Telmo, and Centro with the northern end of Palermo; No. 152 connects La Boca and Palermo more directly.

SAFETY AND PRECAUTIONS

Pickpocketing is the biggest threat, especially on crowded streets on weekends. Palermo Viejo's cobbled streets aren't well lighted at night, so avoid walking along any that look lonely. Although locals usually hail cabs on the street, it's safer to ask a restaurant or bar to call one for you. The usual caveats about parks apply to the Palermo woods.

TOP EXPERIENCES

Appreciating: the early works in the permanent collection of the MALBA, featuring painters like Diego Rivera, Xul Solar, and Joaquín Torres García.

Exercising: your arms in Palermo Viejo carrying bags on a boutique crawl.

Visiting: with Evita; understand the phenomenon that she was by taking in the Museo Evita.

Wandering: on the winding paths of Parque Tres de Febrero, to smell the roses, or along Honduras—east of Juan B. Justo for boutiques, west of it for bars and restaurants.

QUICK BITES

El Preferido de Palermo. Trends come and go, but nothing changes these tall Formica tables. A plate of cold cuts and pickles or basic (but delicious) sandwiches are the way to go. ✉ *Jorge L. Borges 2108, Palermo Viejo* ☎ *11/4774–6585* ☉ *Mon.–Sat. noon–12:30 am* Ⓜ *D to Plaza Italia.*

Café Resto Museo Evita. The checkered floors and glossy black tables are as stylish as the great lady herself. The sticky, flaky *medialunas* here are some of the best in town. ✉ *J. M. Gutiérrez 3926, Palermo Botánico* ☎ *11/4800–1599* ⊕ *www.museoevitaresto.com.ar* ☉ *Mon.–Sat. 9 am–midnight, Sun. 9–7* Ⓜ *D to Plaza Italia.*

MALBA

✉ Av. Presidente Figueroa Alcorta 3415, Palermo ☎ 11/4808–6500 ⊕ www.malba.org.ar 🎫 50 pesos (25 pesos Wed.) ⊗ Thurs.–Mon. noon–8, Wed. noon–9 Ⓜ D to Bulnes.

The fabulous Museum of Latin American Art of Buenos Aires (MALBA) is one of the cornerstones of the city's cultural life. Its centerpiece is businessman and founder Eduardo Constantini's collection of more than 220 works of 19th- and 20th-century Latin American art in the main first-floor gallery.

Highlights

Europe vs. Latin America. Early works in the permanent collection reflect the European avant-garde experiences of artists such as Diego Rivera, Xul Solar, Roberto Matta, and Joaquín Torres García. These, in turn, gave rise to paintings like *Abaporu* (1928) by Tarsila do Amaral, a Brazilian involved in the "cannibalistic" Movimento Antropofágico (rather than actually eating white Europeans, proponents of the movement proposed devouring European culture and digesting it into something new). Geometric paintings and sculptures from the 1940s represent movements such as Arte Concreto, Constructivism, and Arte Madí.

Argentine Art. Argentina's undisputed modern master is Antonio Berni, represented by a poptastic collage called *The Great Temptation* (1962) and the bizarre sculpture *Voracity, or Ramona's Nightmare* (1964): both feature the eccentric prostitute Ramona, a character Berni created in this series of works criticizing consumer society. Pieces by local greats Liliana Porter, Marta Minujín, Guillermo Kuitca, and Alejandro Kuropatwa form the end of the permanent collection.

Temporary Exhibitions. World-class temporary exhibitions are held on the second floor two or three times a year, and two small basement galleries show art by cutting-edge Argentineans.

TIPS AND TRIVIA

■ MALBA also has a great art cinema showing restored copies of classics, never-released features, and silent films with live music, as well as local films of note.

■ Kids love hands-on kinetic works like Julio Le Parc's Seven Unexpected Movements, a sculpture with gleaming parts that move at the press of a button.

■ Leave time to browse the art books and funky design objects in the museum's excellent gift shop.

■ Young, enthusiastic guides give great tours of the permanent collection in Spanish on Wednesday and Sunday at 4 pm.

■ Give your feet—and eyes—a rest on the first-floor sculpture deck, with views over Belgrano and Barrio Norte.

■ Córdoba-based studio AFT Arquitectos' triangular construction in creamy stone and steel is one of the museum's draws. The main galleries run along a four-story atrium, flooded in natural light from a wall of windows.

MUSEO EVITA

✉ *Lafinur 2988, 1 block north of Av. Las Heras, Palermo* ☎ *11/4807–0306* ⊕ *www. museoevita.org* ✉ *60 pesos* ⊘ *Tues.–Sun. 11–7* Ⓜ *D to Plaza Italia.*

2

TIPS AND TRIVIA

■ Laminated cards with just-understandable English translations of the exhibits are available in each room and at the ticket booth.

■ Take a postmuseum coffee or lunch break at the onsite café (its outside tables are shaded by classy black umbrellas). There's also a small museum gift shop.

■ The gray-stone mansion dates from 1909. It was purchased in 1948 by the Fundación de Ayuda Social Eva Perón (Eva Perón Social Aid Foundation) and converted into a home for single mothers, to the horror of the rich, conservative families living nearby.

■ The Evita myth can be baffling to the uninitiated. The museum's excellent guided visits shed light on the phenomenon and are available in English for groups of six or more, but must be arranged by phone in advance.

Eva Duarte de Perón, known universally as Evita, was the wife of populist president Juan Domingo Perón. She was both revered by her working-class followers and despised by the Anglophile oligarchy of the time. The Museo Evita shies from pop culture clichés and conveys facts about Evita's life and works, particularly the social aid programs she instituted and her role in getting women the vote. Knowledgeable staffers answer questions enthusiastically.

Highlights

Photographic evidence. The route through the collection begins in a darkened room, where 1952 footage showing hundreds of thousands of mourners lined up to view their idol's body is screened. Family photos and magazine covers document her humble origins and time as a B-list actress. Upstairs there are English-subtitled film clips of Evita making incendiary speeches to screaming crowds: her impassioned delivery beats Madonna's hands down.

Death becomes her. The final rooms follow the First Lady's withdrawal from political life and her death from cancer at age 33. A video chronicles the fate of Evita's cadaver: embalmed by Perón, stolen by political opponents, and moved and hidden for 17 years before being returned to Argentina, where it now rests in the Recoleta Cemetery.

Fabulous clothes. Evita's reputation as fashion plate is reflected in the many designer outfits on display, including her trademark working suits and some gorgeous ball gowns.

DID YOU KNOW?

Parque Tres de Febrero, in Palermo, is an oasis of calm. Leave the collectivo exhaust behind and come take a paddleboat ride, stroll through the woods, or just laze in the grass to people-watch with your maté in hand.

2

semi-abstract watercolors. They glow against the low-lighted concrete walls of this hushed museum. Solar's wacky but endearing beliefs in universalism led him to design a pan-language, pan-chess (a set is displayed here), and the Pan Klub, where these ideas were debated. One of its former members, architect Pablo Beitia, masterminded the transformation of the town house where Solar lived and worked. Open stairways crisscross the space, an homage to one of Solar's favorite motifs. ☒ *Laprida 1212, Palermo* ☎ *11/4824–3302* ⊕ *www.xulsolar.org.ar* ☜ *20 pesos* ⊙ *Tues.–Fri. noon–7:30, Sat. noon–6:30* Ⓜ *D to Agüero.*

Planetario Galileo Galilei (*Galileo Galilei Planetarium*). One of the city's most iconic buildings, the Planetario Galileo Galilei is a great orb positioned on a massive concrete tripod in the middle of Palermo's Parque Tres de Febrero. Built in the early 1960s, it looks like something out of *Close Encounters of the Third Kind*—especially at night, when the dome glows with eerie blue lighting. It reopened after major renovation in 2012 with a state-of-the-art projector, new sound system, and vibrating seats for the twice-daily sky shows, narrated in Spanish. Tickets go on sale at 9:30 Tuesday through Friday and at 11:30 on weekends; note that they usually sell out fast. Three meteorites that landed in northern Argentina 4,000 years ago guard the entrance. The nearby pond with swans, geese, and ducks is always a hit with kids. ☒ *Avs. Sarmiento and Figueroa Alcorta, Palermo* ☎ *11/4771–9393* ⊕ *www.planetario.gov.ar* ☜ *30 pesos* Ⓜ *D to Plaza Italia.*

FAMILY **Zoológico de Buenos Aires.** The grandiose stone pens and mews—many dating from the zoo's opening in 1874—are as much an attraction at the 45-acre city zoo as their inhabitants. Jorge Luis Borges said the recurring presence of tigers in his work was inspired by time spent here. Today, the six rare white Bengal tigers (four of which were born at the zoo in 2013) may inspire you to pen a few lines of your own. South American animals you might not have seen before include the *aguará guazú* (a sort of fox), the *coatí* (a local raccoon), anteaters, and the black howler monkey. Some smaller animals roam freely, and there are play areas for children, a petting farm, and a seal show. *Mateos* (traditional, decorated horse-drawn carriages) stand poised at the entrance to whisk you around the nearby parks. ☒ *Avs. General Las Heras and Sarmiento, Palermo* ☎ *11/4011–9900* ⊕ *www.zoobuenosaires.com.ar* ☜ *90 pesos* ⊙ *Tues.–Sun. 10–6 (last entry at 5)* Ⓜ *D to Plaza Italia.*

WHERE TO EAT

Visitors may flock to Buenos Aires for the steak and malbec, but the food scene goes far beyond those two attractions. Over the last dozen or so years, the city has burst onto the international food scene with gusto.

There's a demand for more and more creative food. Here three things have come together to create a truly modern cuisine: diverse cultural influences, high culinary aspirations, and a relentless devotion to aesthetics, from plate garnishes to room décor. Tradition dictates late dining, and the majority of restaurants don't open until 8 or 9 pm for dinner and don't get busy until after 10. Dinner is a leisurely affair, and the *sobremesa*, or after-dinner chat over coffee or digestifs, is nearly obligatory. Rushing from the table is frowned on—anyway, where would you go? Bars and clubs often don't open until after midnight.

The core of the population is of Italian and Spanish heritage, and pizza, pasta, paella, and *puchero* (beef boil) are as common as the *parrilla* (steakhouse). Argentines have taken the classics and made them their own with different techniques and ingredients, but they're still recognizable to the international traveler. Pizzas and empanadas are the favored local snack food, the former piled high with cheese, the latter typically filled with steak or chicken. And while steak is indisputably king in this town, it's got fierce competition in tender Patagonian lamb, game meats, fish, and shellfish. In contrast to that of much of Latin America, Argentine cuisine is not known for its spice, and *picante* dishes are not common.

Cafés, too, are an important part of the culture, and locals will stop in at their favorite for a *cafecito* at least once a day, not only to knock back a little caffeine, but also to see friends and catch up on the latest news and gossip.

Use the coordinate (✛ 2:C5) at the end of each listing to locate a site on the corresponding Where to Eat and Stay map.

WHAT IT COSTS (IN ARGENTINE PESOS)				
	$	$$	$$$	$$$$
Restaurants	Under 66 pesos	66 pesos–100 pesos	101 pesos–160 pesos	over 160 pesos

Restaurant prices are the average cost of a main course at dinner or, if dinner is not served, at lunch.

CENTRO

Centro and the surrounding neighborhoods have something for everyone, from traditional to trendy. At lunchtime, the city's bustling downtown is the place where business deals are negotiated over leisurely lunches of steak, potatoes, salad, and wine. In the evening the area can get deserted, except for the pedestrian strip along Avenida Reconquista, which is jammed with bars and restaurants.

$$ ✕ **Café Tortoni.** Filled with Tiffany lamps, towering columns, and marble-
CAFÉ topped tables. this art nouveau hangout has charm to spare. While you may have to wait in a line outside, depending on the time of day, it'll be worth it to knock back an espresso or sip a *submarino*, the local version of hot chocolate. Nibble on one of the dozens of different sandwiches or fork in one of the exquisite pastries and contemplate that you may well be sitting in the same seat that a former president, a renowned tango singer, or a world-famous artist or writer occupied many a time before. It's a place and time out of the past, and thankfully well preserved. Reservations are a must during the dinner-hour tango show. $ *Average main: 95 pesos* ⊠ *Av. de Mayo 825, at Piedras, Centro* ☎ *11/4342–4328* ⊕ *www.cafetortoni.com.ar* Ⓜ *A to Perú* ✛ *1:D4.*

$ CAFÉ 🍴 **Confitería Ideal.** This century-old café is one of the best spots for newcomers to learn some basic tango steps and enjoy a casual bite to eat. Downstairs, a cavernous space with beautiful marble columns is dotted with tables where you can relax with a coffee and pastry (the glazed tea cookies are famed citywide). If you're feeling a little hungrier, dig in to simple local fare like a *milanesa* (breaded veal cutlet), a pizza, or one of a selection of salads and sandwiches. The kitchen closes at 8 pm. Upstairs is the tango hall, where inexpensive lessons can be had two or three times a day. Outside of class hours there's often a tango show, and in the evenings there's always a milonga, open to anyone who just wants to show up and dance tango. [$] *Average main: 40 pesos* ✉ *Suipacha 380, at Av. Corrientes, Centro* ☎ *11/4328–7750* 🌐 *www.confiteriaideal.com* 💳 *No credit cards* [M] *C to C. Pellegrini; D to 9 de Julio* ✣ *1:D4.*

$$$ ECLECTIC 🍴 **Dadá.** Pop-art posters add some flair to this foodie favorite. With a short but creative menu, this spot serves some of the most interesting food to be found in the district. Don't miss out on the house specialties: phyllo-wrapped Morbier cheese salad as a starter and the perfectly cooked *ojo de bife* (ribeye steak). The kitchen also deftly turns out perfectly cooked pastas, particularly those incorporating fresh seafood. Relax, enjoy a glass of wine, read the paper, sit at the bar and chat, and eat well. Hours can be as eclectic as their food, and they may or may not open at posted times, though likely they won't be too far off. [$] *Average main: 120 pesos* ✉ *San Martín 941, Retiro* ☎ *11/4314–4787* ⏲ *Closed Sun.* [M] *C to San Martín* ✣ *1:D3.*

$$$ PIZZA 🍴 **El Cuartito.** Founded in 1934, this icon of porteño pizza tugs at the heartstrings of locals, who get misty-eyed when they think about the fresh tomato sauce and the mile-high pile of oozing mozzarella on these classics. You'll spot the occasional tourist, but the vast majority of seats will be filled by locals who've been coming here for decades. Every square inch of wall space is dedicated to posters, photos, and memorabilia of sports legends, musicians, tango dancers, and actors, and every local has his or her cherished spot in the dining room. The best pizza? A classic *mitad-mitad,* or half-and-half—one side a straightforward tomato sauce and cheese, the other swimming with anchovies. Dessert here is a winner, with the classic flan leading the pack. [$] *Average main: 110 pesos* ✉ *Talcahuano 937, Centro* ☎ *11/4816–1758* 💳 *No credit cards* [M] *D to Tribunales* ✣ *1:C3.*

$$ ITALIAN 🍴 **Filo.** Crowded and lively, particularly at lunch, Filo is the place for pizza and pasta in the downtown area. True Neapolitan-style pies with smoky, charred crusts direct from the wood-fired oven are among the best in the city. For a real treat, order the Filo, a wheel of a pizza with each slice a different topping according to the pizzero's whims. Pastas are served perfectly al dente—a rarity in town—and come with both classic and creative sauces. If you're dining solo, the bar is a great spot to grab a stool and strike up a conversation. No photos allowed: the management cheekily say some guests "may be dining with someone that they'd prefer their spouse doesn't see." Check out the ever-changing art gallery in the basement. [$] *Average main: 100 pesos* ✉ *San Martín 975, between Alvear and Paraguay, Retiro* ☎ *11/4311–1871* 🌐 *www.filo-ristorante.com* [M] *C to San Martín* ✣ *1:D3.*

CAFÉ LINGO 101

Coffee is taken seriously in Argentina. A morning and evening caffeine jolt is what gets many porteños through their long days and nights. Here's how to order it:

Café: Same as an American espresso

Café con leche: Half coffee and half milk, served in a larger cup

Cortado: A café topped or "cut" with hot foamy milk

Filtro: Brewed coffee

Lágrima: Hot foamy milk with a "drop" of coffee

Ristretto: A small, very strong shot of espresso

Submarino: A tall glass of hot milk served with a chocolate bar submerged into the milk (aka hot chocolate)

Unless you specify otherwise, your café will be served in a short espresso glass. If you want a larger coffee, order a *jarrito,* or medium. If you want an American-size coffee, order a *doble,* or double espresso.

$$$ WINE BAR

🍴 **Gran Bar Danzón.** It's a two-story climb up some steep stairs to the city's best wine bar. Arrive too early in the evening and this might be your worst nightmare: a dimly lit lounge with hard-drinking business executives. Wait until dinner hour—after 8, at the earliest—and the crowd changes to the local wine-geek set wolfing down some of the best lounge food in town, including great sushi (don't miss the crispy prawn rolls), eclectic appetizers and main courses, and a selection of wines by the glass that can't be beat. The place is not too bad on the wallet, particularly in this neighborhood. Wednesday nights there's live jazz early. [$] *Average main: 135 pesos* ✉ *Libertad 1161, 2nd fl., Retiro* ☎ *11/4811–1108* 🌐 *www.granbardanzon.com.ar* ✍ *Reservations essential* 🕒 *No lunch* [M] *C to San Martín* ✥ *1:C2.*

$$$ MODERN ARGENTINE Fodor's Choice ★

🍴 **Restó.** This place became famous when it was run by founder Maria Barrutia, and on and off it was a popular destination for local foodies over the years. Many people held their breath when she sold the place to Guido Tassi, but we can all breathe a sigh of relief because the cooking is better than ever. The menu is more creative, with bolder flavors and more beautiful presentations. Likewise, the service has been stepped up a notch, as has the wine list. There's now nowhere better in the neighborhood for lunch, nor for dinner on the two nights a week it's open late. The star of the lineup is the roasted, stuffed whole quail, but there's not a misstep on the menu. [$] *Average main: 110 pesos* ✉ *Sociedad Central de Arquitectos, Montevideo 938, between M. T. Alvear and Paraguay, Recoleta* ☎ *11/4816–6711* ✍ *Reservations essential* 💳 *No credit cards* 🕒 *Closed weekends. No dinner Mon.–Wed.* [M] *D to Callao* ✥ *1:B3.*

$$$$ ARGENTINE

🍴 **Sabot.** You're likely to be the only newcomer amid scores of older business executives who've been making this landmark a classic for more than 40 years. Day in and day out, this is the spot where behind-the-scenes negotiations take place over French-influenced local fare. The *centolla* (king crab) or *langostino* (prawn) salad is a throwback to another age, but it's perfectly prepared. Tuck into properly prepared pastas and a house specialty, semolina gnocchi, or slice into a delicious steak—the entrecote is king here. Add to the food some of the friendliest and most efficient service you'll find in town, and it's a don't-miss downtown lunch. [$] *Average main: 160 pesos* ✉ *25 de Mayo 756, between Córdoba and Viamonte, Centro* ☎ *11/4313–6587* 🕐 *Closed weekends. No dinner* [M] *B to L. N. Alem* ✥ *1:E3.*

$$$$ ARGENTINE
🍴 **Tomo I.** Despite being one of the more sophisticated dining rooms in the city, being a hotel restaurant means that Tomo I will have a mix of couples dressed to the nines and groups of backpackers in T-shirts. Don't let that put you off, as the fare at this bastion of modern French-Argentine cooking is some of the best in the city. The room was renovated a couple of years ago, and now features a full wall of windows looking out over the city's widest avenue. The food tends toward the lighter side, even when considering meat dishes, and truly shines with its updated versions of classic French dishes. [$] *Average main: 275 pesos* ✉ *Hotel Panamericano, Carlos Pellegrini 521, Centro* ☎ *11/4326–6695* 🌐 *www.tomo1.com.ar* ✍ *Reservations essential* 🕐 *Closed Sun. No lunch Sat.* [M] *B to Carlos Pellegrini; D to 9 de Julio* ✥ *1:C3.*

$$$ SUSHI
🍴 **Yuki.** Getting in requires a reservation, but once you're through the unmarked facade you'll find yourself in the closest thing the city has to a sushi temple. Japanese business executives are quietly making deals in semi-hidden salons lined with tatami mats, while local aficionados are deftly wielding chopsticks around the small tables, or, if they're lucky, seated at the sushi bar in front of sushi-master Kazu-O, whose father opened Yuki some 60 years ago. The fish is pristine and changes daily based on availability, but always goes far beyond the local standard of salmon and cream cheese (the latter thankfully not offered). For a special experience, order either the *omakase* (sushi chef's choice) or *teishoku* (prix-fixe from the kitchen, with or without sushi) menu and let the chef do his thing while you knock back a sake or two from the impressive selection. [$] *Average main: 125 pesos* ✉ *Pasco 740, between Independencia and Chile, Congreso* ☎ *11/4942–7510* ✍ *Reservations essential* 🕐 *Closed Sun. No lunch* [M] *E to Pichincha* ✥ *1:A5.*

PUERTO MADERO

A magnet for tourists, Puerto Madero's restaurants charge amounts that would make restaurant owners in other parts of the city blush with shame. Unless you're on an expense account, the food is generally far better and far less expensive elsewhere.

$$$$ STEAKHOUSE
🍴 **Cabaña Las Lilas.** Probably the best-known steakhouse in all of Argentina, Cabaña Las Lilas draws most of its clientele from the international travelers that crowd into Puerto Madero. It's not just a tourist trap, as it also draws wealthy porteños intent on showing their disregard for the high prices. The service is impeccable, as is the cooking of various cuts of beef from the owner's own ranch. Particularly noteworthy are the *ojo de bife* and *bife de lomo,* better known to Americans as ribeye and sirloin, respectively. It's by no means the best steakhouse in town, but it is the most expensive, by a significant amount. But if you just

want to sit and look out over the water and dig into a steak, this is your place. $ *Average main: 275 pesos* ⊠ *A. M. de Justo 516, at Corrientes, Puerto Madero* ☎ *11/4313–1336* ⊕ *www.laslilas.com* ⚓ *Reservations essential* ✛ *1:E4.*

$$$$ ✕ **La Rosa Náutica.** Aficionados of Nikkei cuisine know the Nautical
PERUVIAN Compass, a chain that started on the beach in Lima, Peru, and now has outposts as far away as Abruzzo, Italy. Located in Puerto Madero, the elegant, white tablecloth dining room has a beautiful view over the water; better yet, sit outside on the covered patio. La Rosa Náutica serves some of the best Peruvian-Japanese fusion food in the city. The stars on the menu are the ceviches, tiraditos and carpaccios, all raw seafood dishes that are impeccable. Service can be a bit slow, but it's worth the wait. $ *Average main: 170 pesos* ⊠ *Alicia Moreau de Justo 264, at Lavalle, Puerto Madero* ☎ *11/4311–5560* ⊕ *www.larosa nautica.com* ✛ *1:E3.*

SAN TELMO

These days San Telmo has an artsy, bohemian vibe. Although most dining spots are inexpensive, there are some true gems.

$$$$ ✕ **Aramburu.** Hidden away on a gritty, graffiti-covered street is one of
ECLECTIC the most beautiful, intimate, and romantic restaurants in the city. Night
Fodor'sChoice after night Gonzalo Aramburu turns out his exquisite 12-course tasting
★ menu of seasonal dishes, each reinterpreted through the lens of what here is called *cocina vanguardia,* or cutting-edge cooking. Aramburu is the undisputed star of the nascent local molecular gastronomy scene. If you're going to splurge, go all the way and add in the 320-peso wine pairing put together by star sommelier Agustina de Alba, one of the best in Buenos Aires. For those who want a more wallet-friendly option, Aramburu Bis opened in early 2014 just down the street at Humberto Primo 1207, offering bistro-style dining with those same cutting-edge influences. $ *Average main: 450 pesos* ⊠ *Salta 1050, between Carlos Calvo and Humberto Primo, San Telmo* ☎ *11/4305–0439* ⊕ *www. aram002uresto.com.ar* ⚓ *Reservations essential* ☺ *Closed Sun and Mon. No lunch* ✛ *1:C6.*

$ ✕ **Bar Plaza Dorrego.** This atmospheric corner building with greenery
CAFÉ tumbling over wrought-iron balconies has what is unquestionably the best view of Plaza Dorrego. It shouldn't be your first choice for a full meal, as there are far better options pretty much anywhere, but do stop in for coffee and a pastry or a beer and a dish of peanuts. Then sit back and people-watch. Given the century-old décor and grime, the nose-in-the-air attitude of the waiters is far misplaced. $ *Average main: 60 pesos* ⊠ *Defensa 1098, at Humberto I, on Plaza Dorrego, San Telmo* ☎ *11/4361–0141* ⚓ *Reservations not accepted* ▭ *No credit cards* Ⓜ *C or E to Independencia* ✛ *1:E6.*

$$$ ✕ **Brasserie Petanque.** One of the few—if not the only—classic French
BRASSERIE brasseries in Buenos Aires, Petanque is a place to drop in, enjoy hearty French fare, and wash it all down with local wines. The ambience is lively, with marble-top tables so close to each other that you may well find yourself participating in neighboring conversations (and vice versa).

The best dishes are the most traditional, often the day's special, which repeat in rotation each day of the week. The sublime *confit de pato,* or duck confit, is not to be missed. The owners have just opened a branch in Santiago, Chile, and have another one coming to Lima, Peru. [$] *Average main: 120 pesos* ✉ *Defensa 596, at Mexico, San Telmo* ☎ *11/4342–7930* 🌐 *www.brasseriepetanque.com* ⏲ *Closed Mon.* ✣ *1:D5.*

$$ STEAKHOUSE FAMILY 🍴 **DesNivel.** Though the name may translate as "uneven," there's nothing remotely so about this classic steakhouse. Don't expect any frills, just great steaks and side dishes (for a real treat order the *papas fritas provençal,* golden french fries tossed in fresh parsley and garlic). Take a table in the cavernous dining room, or grab something to go—steak sandwiches and empanadas fly out the door as fast as they can make them. The portions are huge and the prices are eminently reasonable. Late night the crowd gets particularly interesting. [$] *Average main: 80 pesos* ✉ *Defensa 855, at Giuffra, San Telmo* ☎ *11/4300–9081* 💳 *No credit cards* ⏲ *No lunch Mon.* ✣ *1:D6.*

LA BOCA

La Boca was the dock and warehouse district, and much of that is still in evidence and much of the area is a bit dicey.

$$$ STEAKHOUSE 🍴 **El Obrero.** You'll half expect sawdust on the floor and a saloon fight to break out when you walk into this old-time steakhouse just off the docks of La Boca. While the place is usually filled with locals, it's also a regular stop for touring rock stars who seem to have chosen it as *the* spot to go when in town for a performance. Big, juicy steaks that are perfectly cooked, massive helpings of side dishes, and more ambience than you can shake a stick at make El Obrero a movie director's dream of an Argentine steakhouse. The neighborhood is a little iffy, particularly at night, and it's down a little side street—take a taxi to and from (they'll call one for you). [$] *Average main: 120 pesos* ✉ *Augustín R. Caffarena 64, at Don Pedro Mendoza, La Boca* ☎ *11/4362–9912* 💳 *No credit cards* ⏲ *Closed Sun.* ✣ *1:F6.*

RECOLETA

Arguably Buenos Aires' poshest neighborhood, Recoleta is the epicenter for high-end shopping, museum-going, and white-tablecloth dining. It's home to most of the swankier hotels, and many of them house excellent restaurants, but it's also home to a good number of classic spots that have been serving up high-quality fare for decades.

$$$ AMERICAN 🍴 **Buller Brewing Company.** Smack in the middle of the touristy Village Recoleta strip, Buller is the city's first microbrewery. Turning out an impressive seven different styles (don't miss the Oktoberfest or the Porter), the friendly place also offers a sampler of the whole range that's worth a try. Great sandwiches and one of the better burgers in the neighborhood are more reasons to drop in. The service can seem a bit slow, at least until you get your first beer in hand, but it's worth the wait. [$] *Average main: 140 pesos* ✉ *R. M. Ortíz 1827, Recoleta* ☎ *11/4808–9061* ⏲ *Closed Sun.* ✣ *1:B1.*

$$$$
MODERN
ARGENTINE

✕ **Duhau Restaurante & Vinoteca.** An oasis of elegance and grace in the heart of Recoleta, the Duhau Restaurante definitely shouldn't be overlooked because it's inside a chain hotel. While French techniques may dominate in the kitchen, the ingredients are pure South America. Particularly favored by the chef are seafood and meats flown in from Patagonia. Standout dishes include butter-soft Angus tenderloin, crispy sweetbreads, and a decadent molten chocolate cake. If the weather is nice, grab a table on the terrace overlooking the courtyard gardens. Don't miss a pre- or postdinner visit to the wine-and-cheese bar with a fantastic array of each, and then take an after-meal stroll through the hotel's underground art gallery. ⓢ *Average main: 270 pesos* ✉ *Park Hyatt Palacio Duhau, Av. Alvear 1661, at Montevideo, Recoleta* ☎ *11/5171–1340* ⊕ *www.buenosaires.park.hyatt.com* ⚑ *Reservations essential* ☾ *No lunch weekends* ✛ *1:C1.*

$$
ARGENTINE
Fodor's Choice
★

✕ **El Sanjuanino.** Tourists from the nearby hotels flock to this Northern Argentine regional spot, but you'll definitely also see lots of locals, particularly at lunchtime. It's cramped, crowded, and kitschy, and in hot weather the roaring wood-fired ovens can make the main floor a bit too toasty (head downstairs, where it's cooler), but it's worth it for great empanadas, the city's best *locro* (corn, squash, and meat stew), and, if you're feeling adventurous, one of the iconic game dishes. Don't bother with the wine list, because the house wine served in pitchers is just as good at half the price. The waiters have fun with the crowd, and speak at least basic conversational phrases in a half dozen or more languages. ⓢ *Average main: 90 pesos* ✉ *Posadas 1515, at Callao, Recoleta* ☎ *11/4804–2909* ⊕ *www.elsanjuanino.co/esp/sucursales.html* ☾ *Closed Mon.* ✛ *1:C1.*

$$$
STEAKHOUSE

✕ **Juana M.** It's the salad bar that brings in the crowds—nowhere else in town will you find one this extensive, or one that offers unlimited trips. But that isn't the be-all and end-all of Juana M, where you'll find perfectly cooked prime cuts of steak, along with pork, chicken, and fish. There's also a great selection of pasta dishes and local classics. Oh, and back to that salad bar—it's included in the price of your main course and is packed with everything from fresh vegetables to bean salads, piping-hot chard croquettes, and cheeses. The place is a cavernous basement with few windows, so your view tends to be your dining companions and a selection of ever-changing and sometimes questionable artwork. Our only quibble: the wine list isn't nearly as good as everything else in the place. ⓢ *Average main: 130 pesos* ✉ *Carlos Pellegrini 1535, basement level, Retiro* ☎ *11/4326–0462* ⊕ *www.juanam.com* Ⓜ *C to San Martín* ✛ *1:C2.*

$$$
ARGENTINE

✕ **La Biela.** When the weather cooperates, locals and tourists mix and mingle at La Biela's outdoor tables—this despite the fact that there's a higher charge for the privilege. That leaves the dining room dominated by a local crowd. A blast from the past, this traditional café is one of the best spots in Recoleta for people-watching and celebrity-spotting. For the most part, it's place to linger over coffee and a pastry, or perhaps a savory sandwich at midday, but there's also a full menu of local specialties, and they're not half bad. ⓢ *Average main: 125 pesos* ✉ *Quintana 596, at Junín, Recoleta* ☎ *11/4804–0449* ⊕ *www.labiela.com* ✛ *1:B1.*

2

$$$$
FRENCH
Fodor'sChoice
★

✕ **La Bourgogne.** You'll be welcomed with a complimentary flute of sparkling wine and a selection of hors d'oeuvres when you take your table in this elegant dining room on the side of the famed Alvear Palace Hotel. Chef Jean-Paul Bondeaux (you may meet him as he strolls around the dining room) turns out brilliant French classics updated for modern sensibilities. While not on the menu, the kitchen will happily prepare a completely vegetarian menu. The service is impeccable, and you'll feel exquisitely cared for even as you take your leave, when the staff presents you with a breakfast treat for the next morning. The best value is the seven-course tasting menu that includes six wines—it will run you less than a three-course dinner with a bottle of wine. The wine list is extensive, focusing on the finest from France and Argentina. Jackets are recommended, though not required, for men. $ *Average main: 370 pesos* ✉ *Alvear Palace Hotel, Ayacucho 2027, at Alvear, Recoleta* ☎ *11/4805–3857, 11/4808–2100* ⚬ *Reservations essential* ◷ *Closed Sun. No lunch.* ✛ *1:B1.*

$$$
ITALIAN
FAMILY

✕ **La Parolaccia Trattoria.** Close to the neighborhood's most popular shopping strip, La Parolaccia Trattoria feels like the kind of family-run and family-friendly Italian eateries you could find in any big city. It serves surprisingly excellent pastas made on the premises that are topped with a wide variety of sauces—particularly good are the hand-rolled fusilli. Don't overlook the three-course lunch specials, which can be a great deal. The staff are happy to prepare half portions of pasta dishes for your kids. You'll be greeted at your table with a complimentary cocktail and sent off with a digestif of limoncello at the end of your meal. $ *Average main: 150 pesos* ✉ *Riobamba 1046, Recoleta* ☎ *11/4812–1053* ⊕ *www.laparolaccia.com* Ⓜ *C to Congreso; B to Callao* ✛ *1:B4.*

$$$
ARGENTINE

✕ **Munich Recoleta.** This convivial place looks like a relic of another era—located along a strip filled with casual eateries, it has white tablecloths draping the tables, waiters clad in black vests, and managers in tuxes. The décor is old-school, with coats of arms and mounted animal heads hanging over the dining room. The food is classic porteño, prepared with a flair. The sizzling steaks are delicious, though they tend to be close to "well done" regardless of how they're ordered. At lunch the not-to-be-missed dish is the *revuelto gramajo,* a local classic with ham, eggs, onions, and fried potatoes elegantly plated like a French omelet. For dessert, don't miss the *panqueque de manzana,* a thin crêpe with caramelized apples and flamed in rum. $ *Average main: 135 pesos* ✉ *R. M. Ortíz 1871, at Av. Quintana, Recoleta* ☎ *11/4804–3981* ⊕ *www. munich-recoleta.com.ar* ◷ *Closed Tues.* ✛ *1:B1.*

$$$$
ARGENTINE
Fodor'sChoice
★

✕ **Oviedo.** A tranquil ambience, soft lighting, and sea-theme artwork adorning the walls greet you in this elegant Spanish-style establishment in the heart of Recoleta. In a meat-centric city like Buenos Aires, beautifully cooked seafood is a welcome change, and Oviedo is the best in the city. From classic dishes to modern creations, the kitchen turns out beautifully plated fillets of fish—don't miss the daily catch with pickled baby vegetables. You can't go wrong with any of the pristine shellfish dishes. Top it all off with one of the better wine lists in the area and you're in for a memorable lunch or dinner. $ *Average main: 175* *pesos* ✉ *Beruti 2602, at Ecuador, Recoleta* ☎ *11/4821–3741* ⊕ *www. oviedoresto.com.ar* ⊗ *Closed Sun.* Ⓜ *D to Pueyrredón* ✛ *1:A2.*

$$$$ ✕ **Tarquino.** The city's rock star of molecular gastronomy, Dante Lipor-
MODERN ace, has reappeared in this sophisticated hotel garden setting, where he's
ARGENTINE adding touches of those cutting-edge techniques to a menu dedicated to
Fodor's Choice meat in all its forms. This is world-class cooking with flavors guaranteed
★ to please any carnivore. From the moment you sit down and receive your own baguette with a bowl of beef broth to dip it in until the last shred of beef, veal, or pork (or the occasional fish or fowl) enters your mouth, everything is sensational. It comes at a price, as do the six- and 11- course tasting menus (850 and 1,000 pesos, respectively, not counting wine), but every moment is worth it. $ *Average main: 200 pesos* ✉ *Hub Porteño Hotel, Rodriguez Peña 1967, at Posadas, Recoleta* ☎ *11/6091–2160* ⊕ *www.tarquinorestaurante.com.ar* ⌕ *Reservations essential* ⊗ *Closed Sun. No lunch Sat.* ✛ *1:C1.*

PALERMO

The city's largest neighborhood, Palermo offers something for every taste, style, and budget. It's the city's undisputed culinary hot spot, with enclaves that have their own distinct styles and vibes. If you want the tastiest, most cutting-edge, most traditional, most ethnic, most daring, and most fashionable food in Buenos Aires, then you head to Palermo. It's that simple.

$$$ ✕ **Bardot.** Peruvian fusion cuisine is all the rage these days, but not
PERUVIAN everyone is looking to blend Japanese and Peruvian fare. In Bardot's
Fodor's Choice sizzling lounge atmosphere, chef Germán Cardenas and his staff are
★ bringing flavors of the Amazon basin to the table with exotic fruits like *camu-camu* and the fiery *charapita* chilies. Start off with a cocktail made with one of the dozens of pisco infusions lining the bar, then settle in for some of the best modern Peruvian food in town. Lemony ceviche topped with red onions and cilantro and a truly mouthwatering *paella amazonica* featuring smoked pork and sausage share the list of favorites. $ *Average main: 140 pesos* ✉ *Honduras 5237, at Uriarte, Palermo Soho* ☎ *11/4831–1112* ⊕ *www.restobardot.net* ⌕ *Reservations essential* ⊗ *Closed Mon. No lunch weekdays* Ⓜ *D to Palermo* ✛ *2:B4.*

$$$ ✕ **Chira.** While Nikkei cuisine is taking Argentina by storm, some chefs
PERUVIAN have realized that Japanese isn't the only cuisine that pairs with the
Fodor's Choice explosive flavors of Peru. In this understated dining room, chef Renato
★ Ortigas is turning out fascinating modern Andean dishes that combine elements from the Mediterranean and the Caribbean, to resounding accolades. The name comes from the Quechua word for a chili seed, and there's no question that Ortigas is trying to plant something new. Not to be missed are his *anticuchos de chipirones,* tender baby squid bathed in a smoking red pepper sauce. The service is friendly and faultless, though perhaps over-informative, as the staff seem to have been trained to let you in on every element of the dishes. $ *Average main: 140 pesos* ✉ *Humboldt 1864, between El Salvador and Costa Rica, Palermo Soho* ☎ *11/4777–0724* ⊕ *www.chiracocinafusion.com.ar* ⊗ *Closed Sun.* ✛ *2:B4.*

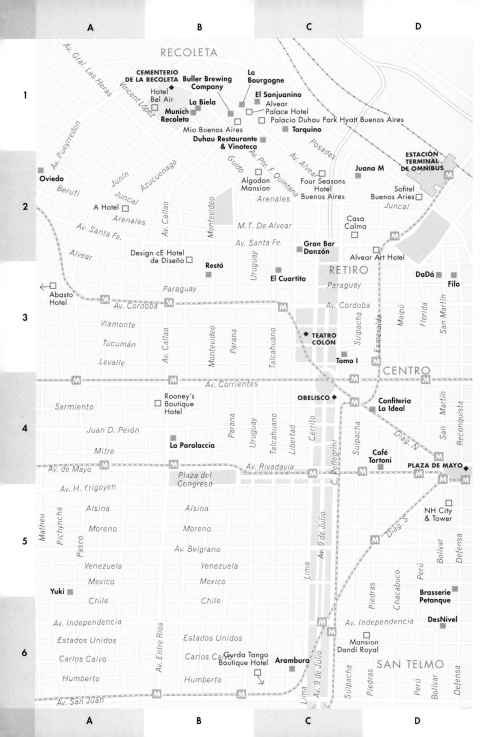

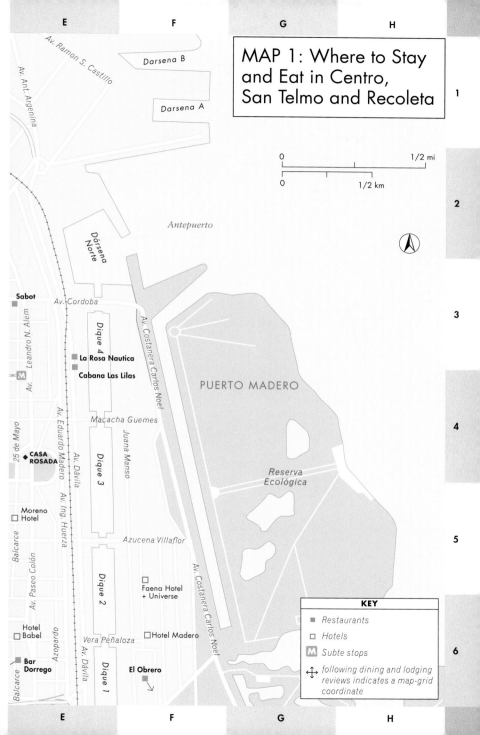

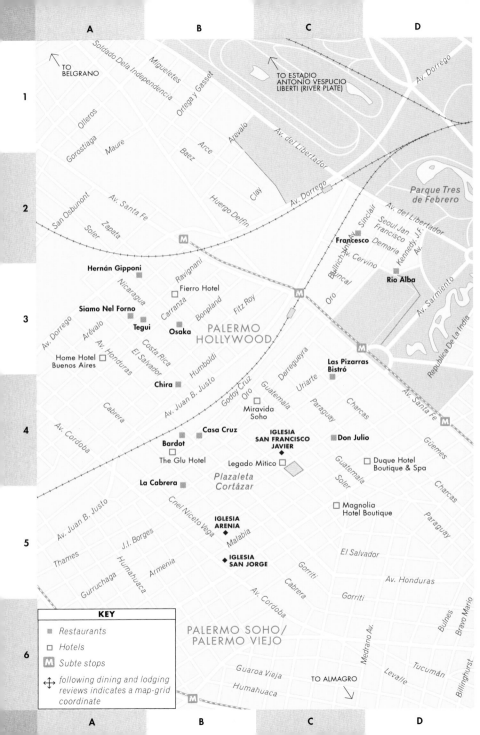

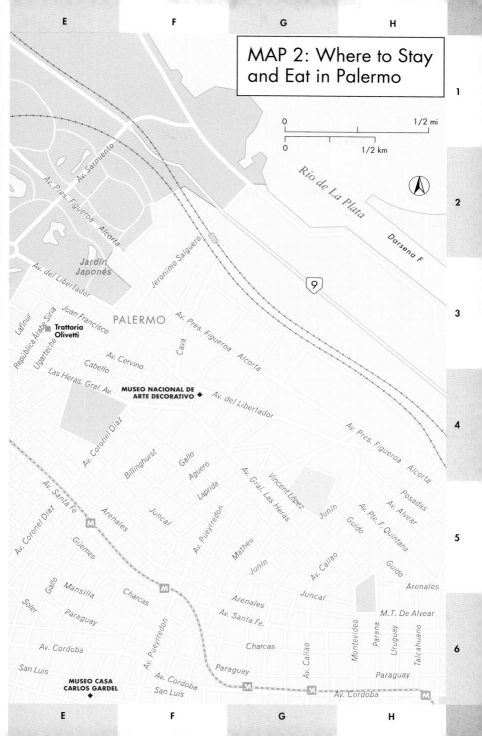

MAP 2: Where to Stay and Eat in Palermo

E   F   G   H

0   1/2 mi

0   1/2 km

Río de La Plata

Darsena F

9

Av. Sarmiento

Av. Pres. Figueroa Alcorta

Jardín
Japonés

Av. del Libertador

Jeronimo Salguero

PALERMO

Lafinur

República Árabe Siria

Juan Francisco

Ugarteche

■ Trattoria
Olivetti

Av. Cervino

Cava

Av. Pres. Figueroa Alcorta

Cabello

Las Heras. Gral. Av.

MUSEO NACIONAL DE
ARTE DECORATIVO ◆

Av. del Libertador

Av. Pres. Figueroa Alcorta

Av. Coronel Diaz

Billinghurst

Gallo

Aguero

Laprida

Av. Gral. Las Heras

Vincent López

Junín

Av. Pte. F. Quintana

Posadas

Av. Alvear

Av. Santa Fe

Av. Coronel Diaz

Arenales

Juncal

Av. Puerredon

Matheu

Junín

Av. Callao

Guido

Guido

Arenales

Güemes

M

Gallo

Mansilla

Charcas

Arenales

Av. Santa Fe.

Juncal

M.T. De Alvear

Soler

Paraguay

M

Charcas

Montevideo

Parana

Uruguay

Talcahuano

Av. Cordoba

San Luis

MUSEO CASA
CARLOS GARDEL ◆

Av. Puerredon

Av. Cordoba

San Luis

Paraguay

Av. Callao

M

M

Paraguay

M

Av. Cordoba

M

1

2

3

4

5

6

E   F   G   H

Restaurant parrillas like this one offer everything from classic bife de lomo to all manner of offal.

$$$ STEAKHOUSE Fodor's Choice ★ 🍴 **Don Julio.** Behind an unassuming facade, one of Palermo's best steak houses features cowhide tablecloths, wagon-wheel lighting fixtures, and rows and rows of empty wine bottles signed by satisfied customers. The place features one of the city's better-curated wine lists—ask for owner Pablo Rivero, who knows the ins and outs of every vintage. Packing the place at lunch and dinner is a mix of locals and expats dining on the fantastic ojo de bife and *cuadril* (rump steak). The chorizo sausages are also great, as is pretty much anything else off a grill. [$] *Average main: 120 pesos* ✉ *Guatemala 4691, at Gurruchaga, Palermo Soho* ☎ *11/4831–9564* ⊕ *2:C4.*

$$$$ PERUVIAN 🍴 **Francesco.** With a privileged view of a quiet residential street in Palermo, Francesco was one of the first high-end Peruvian restaurants in Buenos Aires. While it's still as good as it ever was, these days it faces some stiff competition where the food is just as good or, in a couple of cases, even better. But the ceviches continue to be wonderful, and the chef shows a deft hand with fresh fish. The dining room is elegant, and the service is efficient (if rather formal). The place lacks the bells and whistles of the newer spots, but it's perfect if you want to avoid a "scene." [$] *Average main: 175 pesos* ✉ *Soler 5598, at Fitz Roy, Palermo Soho* ☎ *11/4774–4011* 🌐 *www.francescorestaurant.com.ar* ⊙ *Closed Sun. No lunch Sat.* ⊕ *2:C2.*

$$$ ECLECTIC 🍴 **Hernán Gipponi.** This long, narrow room leading to Fierro Hotel's garden patio may not seem like a hot spot for creative cooking, but don't let appearances fool you. Using skills he honed while working for years in the top kitchens of Spain, chef Hernán Gipponi turns out some of the most creative food in Palermo, particularly fish dishes. While you can order from the à la carte menu, local foodies gravitate toward the

changing seven-course tasting menu for 350 pesos. For lunch there's a three-course prix fixe for 170 pesos. Backing up the kitchen is one of the better wine lists in the city, managed by a team of top sommeliers, as well as an excellent cocktail selection from the bar. Weekends are known for one of the city's most fabulous brunches. [$] *Average main: 120 pesos* ✉ *Fierro Hotel, Soler 5862, at Ravignani, Palermo Hollywood* ☎ *11/3220–6820* 🌐 *www.fierrohotel.com/restaurant/hernangipponi* ✍ *Reservations essential* ⏲ *No dinner Sun. and Mon.* [M] *D to Ministro Carranza* ✣ *2:A3.*

$$$$ STEAKHOUSE 🍴 **La Cabrera.** Spanish may actually be the least common language spoken at this touristy place, but that doesn't mean it's not a great steakhouse. Generally big enough to share, huge slabs of meat are seasoned, seared, and cooked to perfection and accompanied by a variety of condiments. There's also an array of "side dishes," a touch gimmicky, but tasty, ranging from different vegetable purees and pickles. The service is impeccable—it has to be with the international crowd it attracts. *Provoletas* (gooey, slightly crispy, grilled cheese slabs) are a must to start, either the standard cow or the much touted goat versions. The exact same menu is served down the block at La Cabrera Norte, at Cabrera 5127, a location opened just to handle the overflow. While reservations are accepted, they're rarely honored, so expect to stand in line during prime dinner hours. [$] *Average main: 200 pesos* ✉ *Cabrera 5099, at Thames, Palermo Soho* ☎ *11/4832–5754* 🌐 *www.parrillalacabrera.com.ar* ✍ *Reservations essential* ⏲ *No lunch Tues.–Thurs.* ✣ *2:B5.*

$$$ ECLECTIC Fodor's Choice ★ 🍴 **Las Pizarras Bistró.** Quirky and kitschy, this 40-seat hole-in-the-wall looks like any of hundreds of other neighborhood hangouts throughout the city. But take a look at the chalkboard-covered walls (*las pizarras*) and you'll know instantly this isn't your typical spot for cheap steaks and *milanesas*. Chef Rodrigo Castilla is one of the most unsung chefs in the city. He turns out a constantly changing, market-driven menu of a dozen plates of some of the most interesting, eclectic food you'll find in the area, making the local food cognoscenti very happy. There's an equally creative wine list. Pricing is civil, portions are huge, and the service can be a trifle slow, but it's worth the wait. [$] *Average main: 110 pesos* ✉ *Thames 2296, at Charcas, Palermo* ☎ *11/4775–0625* ✍ *Reservations essential* ⏲ *Closed Mon. No lunch.* [M] *D to Plaza Italia* ✣ *2:C4.*

$$$$ JAPANESE FUSION 🍴 **Osaka.** Behind a bamboo facade is the first modern Japanese fusion spot in Buenos Aires, this Lima-based chain combines flavors from across Asia with plenty of touches of Peru. The sushi and other small plates are excellent, though bordering on outrageously pricey, and the service is spot-on, particularly at the gleaming sushi bar. In the evening the crowd can be a bit loud and pretentious as the bar scene heats up and spills over into the dining area. There's also a location in Puerto Madero in the Faena Arts Center. [$] *Average main: 185 pesos* ✉ *Soler 5608, at Fitz Roy, Palermo* ☎ *11/4775–6964* 🌐 *www.osaka.com.pe* ✍ *Reservations essential* ⏲ *Closed Sun.* ✣ *2:B3.*

$$$$ STEAKHOUSE 🍴 **Río Alba.** When you want to go old school, you won't find anywhere in Palermo better than this venerable steakhouse. This longtime favorite has waiters in bowties and vests who maneuver around the green metal columns that define the farmhouse-style dining room. Among

the flavorful, tender cuts of meat, don't pass up the *entraña* (hanger steak) or the *matambrito* (pork flank)—the latter is one of the best in Buenos Aires. Although the menu appears fairly pricey, the portions are massive, and they know it: the steaks are set atop small hibachis to keep them hot. Your best bet is to order one steak for two to share and a platter of the *papas rejillas*, thick waffle-cut chips, and dig in to a classic Argentine meal. $ *Average main: 200 pesos* ✉ *Cerviño 4499, at Fray J. S. de Oro, Palermo* ☎ *11/4773–5748* ✛ *2:D3.*

$$ **✕ Siamo nel Forno.** Every country has its own style of pizza, and in
PIZZA Argentina it's piled high with cheese. After spending a year studying traditional techniques in Naples, *pizzero* Nestor Gattorna took another route. He even imported a wood-burning oven, and brings in specially milled flour and extra-virgin olive oil, all to reproduce the best Neapolitan-style pizza in the heart of Palermo. Italophiles jam into the place for a bite of one of his smoky, perfectly charred pies and equally good calzones. Try a delicious specialty like the potato pizza, and end your meal with a "white pie" filled with Nutella. $ *Average main: 100 pesos* ✉ *Costa Rica 5886, Palermo Hollywood* ☎ *11/5290–9529* ◷ *Closed Mon. No lunch* Ⓜ *D to Ministro Carranza* ✛ *2:A3.*

$$$$ **✕ Tegui.** Germán Martitegui was among the city's first leaders of the
ECLECTIC *cocina de vanguardia* movement, or what people tend to think of as *gastronomía molecular.* After taking the helm at Casa Cruz and then Olsen, he hit his stride with the open-kitchen at Tegui, which still has both local and international foodies lining up at the door. Whether you order from the regularly changing à la carte menu (with one-, two-, or three-plate options), or go for the full experience with an eight-course tasting menu (which, with all the extras, is more like a 12-course food orgy). Martitegui has a deft hand with fish in particular and is fond of using fruit in his savory dishes. Add an option of paired wines under the direction of sommelier Martín Bruno and you'll have an experience like no other in the city. $ *Average main: 220 pesos* ✉ *Costa Rica 5852, between Carranza and Ravignani, Palermo Hollywood* ☎ *11/5291–3333* ⊕ *www.tegui.com.ar* ⤷ *Reservations essential* ◷ *Closed Sun. and Mon. No lunch* ✛ *2:A3.*

$$ **✕ Trattoria Olivetti.** In a city so packed with Italian restaurants that you
ITALIAN could spend years visiting all of them, to claim that one or another is
FAMILY the best is presumptuous. But Trattoria Olivetti's casual style, fantastic
Fodor's Choice service and atmosphere, and prime location in Palermo Chico's Little
★ Italy bodes well for the claim that this is the city's top trattoria. For the more adventurous, don't miss Chef Luca Lepri Berluti's "surf and turf" of *gamberi e animelle* (perfectly grilled prawns and sweetbreads), or his *guanciola* (beautifully braised pork cheeks). For those less inclined to stray into that territory, the multilayer house lasagna may just be the finest in Argentina. There's a great wine list, too. $ *Average main: 95 pesos* ✉ *República Arabe Siria 3200, at Cerviño, Palermo Botánico* ☎ *11/4802–7321* ⊕ *www.trattoriaolivetti.com* ◷ *Closed Mon.* ✛ *2:E3*

WHERE TO STAY

In Buenos Aires, neighborhoods each have their own energy and spirit, and hotels tend to both mimic the identity of their neighborhood and help to shape it. The lodging options here are some of the most impressive of any international, cosmopolitan locale. From luxurious, majestic hotels (many with recognizable chain names) to boutique hotels operating a handful of rooms and injected with local flair, one thing is certain: you're bound to encounter plenty of attractive lodging options.

Though prices have climbed in Argentina in recent years, the city is still highly affordable for international visitors on the dollar, euro, and real. Many visitors, having discovered the intoxicating energy of the city, return again and again. Hotel owners and staff are some of the key players in helping people to fall in love with the city or lure them back.

Downtown—in Centro and Puerto Madero—you'll find sleek, soaring hotel properties; inch toward Recoleta and you can choose from some of the ritziest hotels in town, especially around Avenida Alvear and the Recoleta Cemetery. Boutique hotels are where Buenos Aires' options really shine, and while intimate, stylish spots dot most of the city's neighborhoods, they are found in greatest concentration in the vast, hip barrio of Palermo. Each neighborhood offers visitors the chance to experience one facet of the buzzing, intriguing city of Buenos Aires.

WHAT IT COSTS IN U.S. DOLLARS			
$	$$	$$$	$$$$
Hotels	under $115	$115–$175	$176–$250	over $250

Hotel prices are for two people in a standard double room in high season.

Use the coordinate (✛2:C5) at the end of each listing to locate a site on the corresponding Where to Eat and Stay map.

For expanded hotel reviews, visit Fodors.com.

CENTRO

$$$$
HOTEL

Alvear Art Hotel. The newest property from the country's most respected lodging chain, the sleek Alvear Art Hotel is set back behind some trees on a pedestrian-only street in the heart of the city's business district. **Pros:** gorgeous views from the sky-high pool; well-appointed gym; quiet location. **Cons:** pool and gym areas open only until 9 pm. $ *Rooms from: US$295* ⊠ *Suipacha 1086, Centro* ☎ *11/4114–3400* ⊕ *www.alvearart.com* ⌔ *139 rooms, 2 suites* ❑ *No meals* ✛ *1:D2.*

$$$
HOTEL
Fodor's Choice
★

Casa Calma. This "wellness hotel" in the heart of downtown Buenos Aires has taken the concept of in-house spa to a new level, equipping each of its 17 rooms with jetted tubs—six deluxe rooms also have saunas where you can relax after a day of exploring the city. **Pros:** gorgeous design; serene atmosphere. **Cons:** on a chaotic city street. $ *Rooms from: US$235* ⊠ *Suipacha 1015, Centro* ☎ *11/4312–5000* ⊕ *www.casacalmahotel.com* ⌔ *17 rooms* ❑ *No meals* ✛ *1:C2.*

WHERE SHOULD I STAY?

NEIGHBORHOOD	VIBE	PROS	CONS
Centro and Puerto Madero	The center of it all; you have a little bit of everything here, from history (Retiro and Congreso) to modernity (Puerto Madero). It buzzes by day, but is quiet at night.	Close to all major city sights; good transportation options to other parts of the city. If you're only in town briefly, this is your place.	Certain areas are loud, chaotic, dirty, and deserted at night, which can make them dangerous. Don't walk around alone.
La Boca and San Telmo	The oldest barrios in the city; you can get a real feel for how Buenos Aires has operated for the past 100-plus years.	Old-world charm: cobblestone streets, corner cafés, tango music. You're sure to meet some interesting characters in this area.	Streets are dark and not well policed. Limited public transportation options. Locals have been known to target tourists.
Recoleta and Almagro	The most upscale area of the city, home to Argentina's high society. Certain enclaves will convince you you're in Paris.	Proximity to sights in Centro. It's safe, friendly, and chic. Great eating options; high-end stores and art galleries abound.	Prices are sometimes inflated for foreigners. Streets and sights are often crowded with tourists.
Palermo	The biggest neighborhood in the city; it's a mix of old family homes, soaring new towers, and renovated warehouses.	It's the undisputed hot spot of Buenos Aires' gastronomic scene. The city's biggest park, polo field, horse track, and casino are also here.	The übercool attitude of some locals is a turn-off. Some quality-of-life issues like clean sidewalks have been ignored in recent property developments.

$$ HOTEL 🏨 **Design cE.** With spacious rooms like TriBeCa lofts, the Design cE has rotating flat-screen TVs that let you watch from bed or from one of the leather recliners. **Pros:** supermodern suites; great location; breakfast is served 24 hours a day. **Cons:** common areas are on the small side. [$] *Rooms from: US$140* ✉ *Marcelo T. Alvear 1695, Centro* ☎ *11/5237–3100* 🌐 *www.designce.com* 🛏 *20 rooms, 8 suites* 🍴 *Breakfast* [M] *D to Callao* ⊕ *1:B2.*

$$ HOTEL 🏨 **Hotel NH City & Tower.** Topped with an eye-catching rooftop pool and patio, this enormous art deco showplace is a reminder of an earlier era. **Pros:** central location; amazing views from the roof; transports you back to another era. **Cons:** feels isolated from other attractions; area can be sketchy at night. [$] *Rooms from: US$170* ✉ *Bolívar 160, Centro* ☎ *11/4121–6464* 🌐 *www.nh-hotels.com/nh/en/hotels/argentina/buenos-aires.html* 🛏 *327 rooms, 42 suites* 🍴 *Breakfast* [M] *A to Perú; E to Bolívar* ⊕ *1:D5.*

$$ B&B/INN 🏨 **Rooney's Boutique Hotel.** On the third floor of a century-old building, this hotel exudes such French elegance that you might expect to find Marie Antoinette herself lolling about in one of the guest rooms filled with lovingly restored antiques. **Pros:** complimentary tango lessons three nights per week; lovely rooms and common areas. **Cons:** location in the Centro is far from relaxed. [$] *Rooms from: US$115* ✉ *Sarmiento*

1775, 3rd fl., Centro ☎ *11/5252–5060* 🌐 *www.rooneysboutiquehotel.com* 🛏 *14 rooms* 🍴 *Breakfast* [M] *B to Callao* ✥ *1:B4.*

$$$$ HOTEL **Sofitel Buenos Aires.** Built in 1929 by a Yugoslavian shipping magnate, this was the city's tallest building for many years; it might have lost its lofty title, but it's still considered one of the classiest hotels in Buenos Aires, known for its understated elegance. **Pros:** on a swanky street lined with art galleries; long list of amenities. **Cons:** the lobby can get crowded and noisy. [$] *Rooms from: US$345* ✉ *Arroyo 841, Centro* ☎ *11/4131–0000* 🌐 *www.sofitel.com/gb/hotel-3253-sofitel-buenos-aires/index.shtml* 🛏 *115 rooms, 29 suites* 🍴 *No meals* [M] *C to San Martín* ✥ *1:D2.*

PUERTO MADERO

$$$$ HOTEL Fodor's Choice ★ **Faena Hotel.** Argentinean fashion impresario Alan Faena and famed French architect Philippe Starck set out to create a "universe" unto itself with this hotel, and they succeeded: rooms are feng-shui perfect, with rich reds and crisp whites, sporting velvet curtains and blinds opening electronically to river and city views. **Pros:** quite simply, one of the most dramatic hotels on the planet; luxury abounds; celebrity magnet. **Cons:** an "are you cool enough?" vibe is ever-present. [$] *Rooms from: US$550* ✉ *Martha Salotti 445, Puerto Madero* ☎ *11/4010–9000* 🌐 *www.faena.com* 🛏 *110 rooms, 16 suites* 🍴 *Breakfast* ✥ *1:F5.*

$$$ HOTEL **Hotel Madero.** A favorite for visiting British rock stars, television personalities, and fashion photographers, this slick hotel is within walking distance of downtown as well as the riverside ecological reserve. **Pros:** the lobby bar attracts a cool after-office crowd; see-and-be-seen clientele; central location. **Cons:** the gym and pool are in cramped quarters; no subway service nearby. [$] *Rooms from: US$190* ✉ *Rosario Vera Peñaloza 360, Puerto Madero* ☎ *11/5776–7777* 🌐 *www.hotelmadero.com* 🛏 *169 rooms, 28 suites* 🍴 *Breakfast* ✥ *1:F6.*

SAN TELMO

$ B&B/INN **Hotel Babel.** A 15-minute walk from the Casa Rosada, this 200-year-old former home of late Argentinean president Juan Manuel de Rosas sits on one of the city's most historic streets in the heart of San Telmo. **Pros:** beautiful and welcoming lobby; guests are greeted with a complimentary glass of Argentine wine upon arrival; local artists display their works throughout the hotel and hold monthly openings. **Cons:** it's an old house: rooms are close together and the open-air patio can mean noise—and sometimes rainwater—outside your door. [$] *Rooms from: US$100* ✉ *Balcarce 946, San Telmo* ☎ *11/4300–8300* 🌐 *www.hotelbabel.com.ar* 🛏 *9 rooms* 🍴 *Breakfast* ✥ *1:E6.*

$ B&B/INN **Mansión Dandi Royal.** For a glimpse of early-20th-century high society, look no further than this hotel, where exquisite rooms are decorated with classic wood furnishings and period murals. **Pros:** a tango junkie's heaven; stunning interiors. **Cons:** the surrounding streets are often populated with unsavory characters. [$] *Rooms from: US$90* ✉ *Piedras 922, San Telmo* ☎ *11/4361–3537* 🌐 *www.mansiondandiroyal.com* 🛏 *26 rooms, 4 suites* 🍴 *Breakfast* [M] *C to San Juan* ✥ *1:D6.*

$ ⚎ **Moreno Hotel.** When they were reviving this art deco masterpiece, the
HOTEL   architects ably met the challenge of restoring the 1929 building without
disturbing its original elements, like mosaic tiling and stained-glassed
windows. **Pros:** designed to the max; plenty of charm; great views.
Cons: some rooms are just steps away from the main lobby and elevator.
Ⓢ *Rooms from: US$90* ✉ *Moreno 376, San Telmo* ☎ *11/6091–2000*
⊕ *www.morenobuenosaires.com* ⤳ *39 rooms* ⦿ *Breakfast* Ⓜ *A to
Plaza de Mayo* ✛ *1:E5.*

RECOLETA

$ ⚎ **A Hotel.** This lodging has an impressive ground-floor gallery where
B&B/INN   exhibits of paintings, photographs, and sculptures by acclaimed Argentinean artists change monthly—you might even run into some fabulous
art aficionados sipping wine and admiring the creations. **Pros:** its bohemian vibe will make you feel like you've joined an artists' colony. **Cons:**
rooms are somewhat antiquated. Ⓢ *Rooms from: US$109* ✉ *Azcuénaga
1268, Recoleta* ☎ *11/4821–4744* ⊕ *www.ahotel.com.ar* ⤳ *34 rooms*
⦿ *Breakfast* Ⓜ *D to Pueyrredón* ✛ *1:A2.*

$$$$ ⚎ **Algodon Mansion.** Every detail of this hotel, one of the ritziest proper-
HOTEL   ties in the city, makes it clear that your comfort is of the utmost importance. **Pros:** unparalleled service; luxe location; each room comes with
a complimentary bottle of wine. **Cons:** the hotel's bars, restaurant, and
rooftop draw a crowd. Ⓢ *Rooms from: US$480* ✉ *Montevideo 1647,
Recoleta* ☎ *11/3530–7777* ⊕ *www.algodonmansion.com* ⤳ *10 suites*
⦿ *Breakfast* Ⓜ *D to Callao* ✛ *1:C2.*

$$$$ ⚎ **Alvear Palace Hotel.** The standard-bearer for upscale sophistication
HOTEL   since 1932, the Alvear Palace is undoubtedly the shining star of the
Fodor's Choice   city's hotel scene: scores of dignitaries, celebrities, and VIPs have passed
★   through its doors over the years, and they keep coming back for the
world-class service and refined atmosphere. **Pros:** gorgeously appointed
rooms; top-notch service; beautiful spa features a sauna and steam
rooms. **Cons:** bathrooms are on the small side; one of the country's
most expensive hotels. Ⓢ *Rooms from: US$510* ✉ *Av. Alvear 1891,
Recoleta* ☎ *11/4808–2100, 800/448–8355 in U.S.* ⊕ *www.alvearpalace.
com* ⤳ *91 rooms, 100 suites* ⦿ *No meals* ✛ *1:C1.*

$$$$ ⚎ **Four Seasons Hotel Buenos Aires.** A $49 million renovation in 2013
HOTEL   rendered this hotel even grander than before—quite a feat for what
was already one of the city's swankiest lodgings. **Pros:** all the class
you'd expect; wonderful eateries; swanky bar. **Cons:** the pool is outdoors, making it ideal for sunny spring and summer days but unus-
able in winter. Ⓢ *Rooms from: US$565* ✉ *Posadas 1086, Recoleta*
☎ *11/4321–1200* ⊕ *www.fourseasons.com/buenosaires* ⤳ *116 rooms,
49 suites* ⦿ *No meals* ✛ *1:C2.*

$$$ ⚎ **Hotel Bel Air.** Given the frilly French-style facade, you could mis-
HOTEL   take the Bel Air for a neighborhood hotel somewhere in Paris. **Pros:**
great location on one of the city's poshest streets. **Cons:** the staff are
easily distracted; hallways and common areas are cramped. Ⓢ *Rooms
from: US$180* ✉ *Arenales 1462, Recoleta* ☎ *11/4021–4000* ⊕ *www.
hotelbelair.com.ar* ⤳ *77 rooms* ⦿ *Breakfast* Ⓜ *D to Tribunales* ✛ *1:B1.*

$$$$ HOTEL

🏨 **Mio Buenos Aires.** The Catena family owns this luxurious boutique hotel, so all the rooms come stocked with wines straight from their own Mendoza vineyards. **Pros:** on one of the most picturesque streets in Recoleta; mixes rustic and modern elements; open and airy feel. **Cons:** the ground-floor common areas feel elegant but somewhat somber. [$] *Rooms from: US$320* ✉ *Avenida Pres. Manuel Quintana 465, Recoleta* ☎ *11/5295–8500* 🌐 *www.miobuenosaires.com/en/hotel* 🛏 *30 rooms* 🍴 *Breakfast* [M] *Linea D to Callao* ✥ *1:B1.*

$$$$ HOTEL Fodor's Choice ★

🏨 **Palacio Duhau Park Hyatt Buenos Aires.** This landmark hotel ups the ante for elegance in Buenos Aires—its two buildings, a restored 1930s-era mansion and a 17-story tower, are connected by an underground art gallery and an expansive, leafy garden that's among the city's most attractive outdoor areas. **Pros:** understated splendor; great restaurant; has the city's largest indoor pool. **Cons:** a long walk from one side of the hotel to the other. [$] *Rooms from: US$510* ✉ *Av. Alvear 1661, Recoleta* ☎ *11/5171–1234* 🌐 *www.buenosaires.park.hyatt.com* 🛏 *126 rooms, 39 suites* 🍴 *No meals* ✥ *1:C1.*

PALERMO

$$ B&B/INN

🏨 **Duque Hotel Boutique & Spa.** As the name suggests, this 1920s French-style hotel is fit for a duke—or even a president, as the mansion once served as an Argentinean president's private residence. **Pros:** gorgeous entrance; spacious and inviting common areas; an enclosed patio means many guests use rooms only for sleeping. **Cons:** some rooms are on the small side. [$] *Rooms from: US$160* ✉ *Guatemala 4364, Palermo Soho* ☎ *11/4832–0312* 🌐 *www.duquehotel.com* 🛏 *14 rooms* 🍴 *Breakfast* ✥ *2:D4.*

$$ HOTEL Fodor's Choice ★

🏨 **Fierro Hotel.** Often called "the hotel for the gourmand"—the restaurant's chef Hernan Gipponi is a driving force behind the Buenos Aires foodie scene—the Fierro is a choice lodging for travelers looking for a five-star stay in a boutique package. **Pros:** among the city's best dining and drinking; rooftop pool with skyline views; sleek décor. **Cons:** common areas are small. [$] *Rooms from: US$160* ✉ *Soler 5862* ☎ *11/3220–6800* 🌐 *www.fierrohotel.com* 🛏 *22 rooms, 5 suites* 🍴 *Breakfast* ✥ *2:B3.*

$$$ HOTEL Fodor's Choice ★

🏨 **The Glu Hotel.** Run with great attention to detail by the Glusman Family, this boutique hotel has 11 spacious rooms, all stylishly modern and minimalist and equipped with low-slung furnishings, bright wooden floors, and small bar areas. **Pros:** sought-after location; sleek interior décor; tip-top concierges provide highly personalized and attentive service. **Cons:** its location on a happening street means constant traffic, though rooms are soundproofed. [$] *Rooms from: US$210* ✉ *Godoy Cruz 1733, Palermo* ☎ *11/4831–4646* 🌐 *www.thegluhotel.com* 🛏 *11 rooms* ✥ *2:B4.*

$$ B&B/INN

🏨 **Home Hotel Buenos Aires.** Run by Argentinean Patricia O'Shea and her British husband Tom Rixton, Home Hotel oozes coolness and class. **Pros:** impossibly hip and fun; always interesting people staying here; great pool area. **Cons:** lots of nonguests come here to hang out. [$] *Rooms from: US$165* ✉ *Honduras 5860, Palermo Hollywood*

☎ *11/4778–1008* 🌐 *www.homebuenosaires.com* 🛏 *14 rooms, 4 suites, 2 apartments* 🍴 *Breakfast* [M] *D to Ministro Carranza* ✥ *2:A3.*

$$$ B&B/INN 🏨 **Legado Mítico.** Blessed with city's most gorgeous sitting room, the Legado Mítico also has an enormous library with plush leather couches, antique furnishings, a fireplace, and bookshelves stocked with English- and Spanish-language classics. **Pros:** exquisitely decorated rooms; welcoming vibe; an authentic and unique Argentine experience. **Cons:** common areas and hallways are very dark; the upstairs terrace disappoints for a property of this quality. [$] *Rooms from: US$250* ✉ *Gurruchaga 1848, Palermo* ☎ *11/4833–1300* 🌐 *www.legadomitico.com* 🛏 *11 rooms* 🍴 *Breakfast* ✥ *2:C4.*

$$$ B&B/INN Fodor's Choice ★ 🏨 **Magnolia Hotel Boutique.** This boutique lodging feels like home—if home were a high-ceiling, lavishly decorated Palermo townhouse dating from the 1890s. **Pros:** top-floor terrace is the perfect urban escape; lots of cozy common areas; homemade baked goods at breakfast. **Cons:** some rooms require walking outdoors. [$] *Rooms from: US$210* ✉ *Julián Alvarez 1746, Palermo Soho* ☎ *11/4867–4900* 🌐 *www.magnoliahotelboutique.com* 🛏 *8 rooms* 🍴 *Breakfast* ✥ *2:C5.*

$$ B&B/INN Fodor's Choice ★ 🏨 **Miravida Soho Hotel & Wine Bar.** This enchanting boutique hotel is owned and operated by two German expats who personally see to it that you receive the most thoughtful and personalized service starting the minute you walk in the door. **Pros:** charm to spare; breakfast options like homemade granola will have you eager to start the day; end the day with a delicious tipple by the ground-floor bar. **Cons:** if street noise is a concern, request a room in the back. [$] *Rooms from: US$160* ✉ *Darregueyra 2050, Palermo* ☎ *11/4774–6433* 🌐 *www.miravidasoho.com* 🛏 *6 rooms* 🍴 *Breakfast* [M] *D to Palermo* ✥ *2:C4.*

NIGHTLIFE AND PERFORMING ARTS

Preparing for a night out in Buenos Aires has an element of marathon training to it. Rest up with a siesta, fortify yourself with some protein, and drink plenty of fluids before, during, and after. That's right, the key to porteño nightlife is longevity—after all, an early night means hailing a cab at 6 am.

The scene here rivals that of any capital city, so you'll find something to suit every taste. Trendy cocktail bars, secret speakeasies, classic tango haunts, artsy watering holes, and packed dance floors await. To make the most of them, try following the locals' lead.

Painting Buenos Aires red means looking sharp, going with the flow as you bar-hop, and not challenging your new B.A. buddies to raucous drinking games. Porteños adore going out with their friends, but it's not uncommon to see a large group sharing a liter bottle of beer and swigging from the same glass. Latino lightweights? Not at all. This is just how Argentineans roll—and once a night gets really rocking, they'll move onto their favorite tipple, Fernet y Cola.

Hours are relaxed, but there are general guidelines. The smartest bars kick off an evening with happy hours that begin around 8 pm and often stretch way beyond 60 minutes; downtown drinking establishments

Don't forget your best dancing shoes: nightclubs, like this one in Palermo, are a stylish affair.

start even earlier to lure workers to part with hard-earned pesos, spawning the "after-office" across the city, which is now a nightlife fixture almost any day of the week.

CENTRO

BARS

Dadá. Cozy and colorful, Dadá has a short but sweet list of classic cocktails and an ideal bar to perch at while sipping one. With its owners doubling as bar staff, Dadá sees an eclectic mix of locals and visitors popping in for dinner, a drink, or both. Grab a booth at the back for extra privacy. ✉ *San Martín 941, Centro* ☎ *11/4314–4787* Ⓜ *C to San Martín.*

The Kilkenny. A popular Irish pub that spawned a whole street of imitators, the Kilkenny serves surprisingly good food and has a well-stocked bar. Celtic or rock bands play nightly, entertaining an after-work crowd from nearby offices that comes for the extended happy hour and stays on into the wee hours. ✉ *Marcelo T. de Alvear 399, Centro* ☎ *11/4312–7291* ⊕ *www.thekilkenny.com.ar* Ⓜ *C to San Martín.*

La Cigale. After moving two blocks down the road, La Cigale has undergone a serious upgrade, proving that size does matter. Take advantage of happy hour until 10 pm at its curvaceously seductive first-floor bar, which leads to the streetside balcony and smokers' corner. Another flight of stairs winds up to the stage, ready and waiting for local indie, jazz, and acoustic bands any night of the week. ✉ *Av. 25 de Mayo*

TIPS FOR A GOOD NIGHT OUT

Don't be afraid to stand in line outside. Lines are generally quick and painless—and if there isn't one, the place might not be worth visiting.

Buy a ticket or make a reservation. For concerts, shows, and club events, people often buy tickets in advance, as many do fill up or sell out, especially international offerings.

Go late—really. Otherwise you'll miss out on the atmosphere and find it a bit boring. If necessary, help smooth the adjustment with a *merienda* (a snack of coffee and croissants at around 6 pm) and a "disco siesta."

Find out what's on and where. Scour flyers, websites, ticket agencies, and magazine listings for up-to-date information. There's a lot more going on than you can find out from any single source.

Dress to impress. Porteños like fine clothes, though their style tends to be on the conservative side. So skip the shorts and flip-flops (both social no-nos) in favor of something fashionable. With the exception of one or two scruffy bars in San Telmo, you'll never feel overdressed.

Never imagine you've seen it all. Private parties and last-minute underground events are where it's at. Finding out about them isn't easy, but keep an ear out and tell people you're looking, and you might luck out.

597, Centro 🕾 *11/4893–2332* ⊕ *www.lacigalebar.blogspot.com* Ⓜ *B to L. N. Alem.*

DANCE CLUBS

Fodor's Choice
★

Bahrein. Sheik—er, *chic* and super-stylish, this party palace is located in a former bank. The Funky Room is where beautiful, tightly clothed youth groove to pop, rock, and funk, while the basement Excess Room has electronic beats and dizzying wall visuals. For a more sophisticated dinner-before-dancing vibe, head upstairs to the Yellow Room. This is a great spot to catch local DJs in action. ✉ *Lavalle 345, Centro* 🕾 *11/4314–8886* ⊕ *www.bahreinba.com* Ⓜ *B to L. N. Alem.*

Cocoliche. Cocoliche enjoys cult status in both the straight and gay communities. Upstairs is a diverse art gallery big on young locals; downstairs, underground house and techno drives one of the city's darkest dance floors, while DJs with huge followings line up to take on the decks. ✉ *Rivadavia 878, Centro* 🕾 *11/4342–9485* ⊕ *www.cocoliche. net* Ⓜ *A to Piedras.*

GAY AND LESBIAN

Contramano. This was a pioneering gay disco when it opened in 1984, but—like its clientele—Contramano has grown up. Today it operates more as a small, laid-back bar with an older, male-only clientele. Occasionally there's live music and male strippers. ✉ *Rodríguez Peña 1082, Centro* ⊕ *www.contramano.com* Ⓜ *D to Callao.*

Flux. It took a couple of expats to realize the gap in the market for early-evening gay bars. Their creation, Flux, is a smart, friendly, and sociable basement club that gets going for happy hour and keeps on until after midnight with decent pop music and an ample cocktail menu. ✉ *Marcelo T. de Alvear 980, Centro* ☏ *11/5252–0258* ⊕ *www.fluxbar. com.ar* Ⓜ *C to San Martín.*

LIVE MUSIC

ND/Ateneo. This spacious theater and cultural space mainly showcases midlevel local bands, showmen, and comedians, with a few big Argentinean names thrown in for good measure. Get tickets at the box office (open Monday–Saturday from noon to 8) or through Ticketek (⊕ *www. ticketek.com.ar*). ✉ *Paraguay 918, Centro* ☏ *11/4328–2888* ⊕ *www. ndateneo.com.ar* Ⓜ *C to San Martín.*

Ultra. The owners of this dynamic space for art and live music have run an independent record label for more than a decade. On weekends they throw big parties until daybreak, and on most weeknights there's a strong line-up of local bands. ✉ *San Martin 678, Centro* ☏ *11/4312– 5605* ⊕ *www.ultrapop-ar.blogspot.com* Ⓜ *C to Lavalle.*

TANGO

El Beso. The standard of dancing is usually high at this club, which belongs to La Academia del Tango Milonguero, one of the city's best tango schools. Intermediate dancers can get their footwork up to speed at daily classes before putting themselves to the test at the milongas, run by different organizers Tuesday through Sunday. ✉ *Riobamba 416, Congreso* ☏ *11/3166–4800* ⊕ *www.laacademiatango.com* Ⓜ *B to Callao.*

PUERTO MADERO

BARS

Asia de Cuba. Once *the* spot to be seen sipping Champagne and eating sushi, Asia de Cuba still draws a smattering of Argentinean celebrities, though it's now lost some of its white-hot luster. Candlelight and a red-and-black Asian décor set the mood for an exotic evening—by local standards. Grab a booth to watch and be watched. ✉ *Pierina Dealessi 750, Puerto Madero* ☏ *11/4894–1329* ⊕ *www.asiadecuba.com.ar* Ⓜ *A or D to Catedral.*

TANGO

Fodor'sChoice
★

Rojo Tango. Five-star food, musicians, choreography, and glamour: you wouldn't expect anything less from the Faena Hotel + Universe. Crimson velvet and gold trim line everything from the walls to the menu at El Cabaret, and tables often hold celebs both local and global. The implausibly good-looking troupe puts on a tango-through-the-ages show, which includes jazz-tango, semi-naked numbers, and even the tango version of Roxanne from *Moulin Rouge*. It's worth raiding the piggy bank for. ✉ *Martha Salotti 445, Puerto Madero* ☏ *11/4952–4111* ⊕ *www.rojotango.com* Ⓜ *D to Catedral.*

SAN TELMO

BARS

Bar Británico. Opened in 1928, this traditional corner bar opposite Parque Lezama is an iconic spot. Day and night it's full of characters who engage in passionate discussions or simply watch the world unfold through the oversized windows. Imbued with nostalgia, Bar Británico has a cinematic appeal—which may explain why it has appeared in movies like *The Motorcycle Diaries* and Francis Ford Coppola's *Tetro*. ⊠ *Brasil 399, at Defensa, Barracas* ☎ *11/4300–6894* ☉ *Mon. 8 am–midnight, Tues.–Sun. 24 hrs* Ⓜ *C to San Juan.*

Doppelgänger. With a list of 100 cocktails and an excellent menu to match, this corner bar on the edge of San Telmo is a hidden gem. The fancy glassware and quotations in the menu show that the "double" concept has been thought through down to the finest details. But your focus should be on having a good time as you sip carefully made libations. Happy hour runs from 7 to 9, Tuesday through Friday. ⊠ *Av. Juan de Garay 500, San Telmo* ☎ *11/4300–0201* ⊕ *www.doppelganger. com.ar* Ⓜ *C to San Juan.*

La Puerta Roja. Pass through the titular scarlet entrance and clamber up the stairs to this trendy yet friendly bar. There's a wide selection of spirits and beers on tap, as well as a pool table, and a sociable mix of local and expat regulars. If you need to nibble, bar snacks here are above average. ⊠ *Chacabuco 733, San Telmo* ☎ *11/4362–5649* ⊕ *www. lapuertaroja.com.ar* Ⓜ *C to Independencia.*

DANCE CLUBS

Rey Castro. Just because this Cuban restaurant-bar gets a little wild on weekends doesn't mean things get out of hand: the bouncers look like NFL players. It's a popular spot for birthday parties and great mojitos. After the nightly live dance show, DJs crank up the Cuban rhythms; you're likely to learn some sexy new moves. ⊠ *Perú 342, San Telmo* ☎ *11/4342–9998* ⊕ *www.reycastro.com* Ⓜ *A to Perú.*

GAY AND LESBIAN

M.O.D. Variete Club. Mainly attracting men keen for a pick-up, Friday cabaret nights at M.O.D. are buzzing—expect glamour and fun, with plenty of dancing to indie, rock, and '80s music. Slip into the VIP area to get close to the stars of the show. ⊠ *Balcarce 563, San Telmo* ⊕ *www. modclub.com.ar* Ⓜ *D to Catedral.*

LIVE MUSIC

Centro Cultural Torquato Tasso. Here classic trios and quartets share the stage with young musicians performing hip tango and folk sets. There are also milongas on weekends. ⊠ *Defensa 1575, San Telmo* ☎ *11/4307–6506* ⊕ *www.torquatotasso.com.ar* Ⓜ *C to San Juan.*

La Trastienda. A San Telmo institution, this cabaret-style club is one of Buenos Aires' most popular venues, so grab a table and enjoy an intimate performance for 900. La Trastienda is the place to catch electro-tango or new tango groups, although it takes pains to promote other genres as well. Check out national pop and rock legends, as well as local rock, reggae, and funk. ⊠ *Balcarce 460, San Telmo* ☎ *11/4342–7650* ⊕ *www.latrastienda.com* Ⓜ *A to Bolivar.*

TANGO

Buenos Ayres Club. Rousing live orchestras keep even nondancers entertained at the nontraditional milongas that are this club's hallmark. La Orquesta Típica el Afronte provides the music for La Maldita (☎ *11/4560–1514*) on Sunday, Monday, and Wednesday, while El Toque Cimarrón Salsa (☎ *11–15/3827–7786*) takes charge on Thursday. Tuesday's Tango Queer (☎ *11–15/3252–6894* ⊕ *www.tangoqueer.com*) draws both gay and straight dancers looking to escape the confines of more conservative dance floors; Friday takes a different turn once again with Latin American music. ⊠ *Perú 571, San Telmo* ☎ *11/4331–1518* ⊕ *www.buenosayresclub.com* Ⓜ *D to Catedral.*

El Viejo Almacén. This place was founded by legendary tango singer Edmundo Rivero, but he wouldn't recognize the slick outfit his bar has become. Inside the colonial building lurks a tireless troupe of dancers and musicians who perform showy tango and folk numbers. ⊠ *Balcarce 793–799, at Independencia, San Telmo* ☎ *11/4307–6689* ⊕ *www.viejo-almacen.com.ar* Ⓜ *C to Independencia.*

RECOLETA

BARS

El Alamo Bar. From the outside, it's only the signs asking patrons to leave quietly that suggest this isn't the demure bar it appears to be. The generous drinks promotions (ladies drink free until midnight on Friday) add substantial rowdiness, and it turns into a raucous party zone on weekends. A sports bar at heart, El Alamo also hosts bikini competitions—just so you know. You can also check out its sister branch in Palermo at Córdoba 5267. ⊠ *Uruguay 1177, Recoleta* ☎ *11/4813–7324* ☼ *24 hrs* Ⓜ *D to Tribunales.*

Milión. One of the city's most stunning bars is spread across three floors of a perfectly restored French-style mansion. A cool vibe and cooler drinks (try the basil frozen daiquiri) keep this place packed on weekends. When the back garden fills on balmy summer nights, squeeze onto the marble steps with the beautiful people. ⊠ *Paraná 1048, Recoleta* ☎ *11/4815–9925* ⊕ *www.milion.com.ar* Ⓜ *D to Callao.*

Pony Line. No expense has been spared at the polo-theme Pony Line, a cool watering hole in the Four Seasons hotel. Creative cocktails, its own line of craft beer, luxury bar snacks, and great tunes have made this a go-to spot for sassy ladies and suave gentlemen. ⊠ *Posadas 1086/88, Recoleta* ☎ *11/4321–1728* ⊕ *www.elenaponyline.com* Ⓜ *C to San Martín.*

DANCE CLUBS

The Basement. Owned by an Irish father-and-son duo, this vibrant downstairs nightspot is popular with expats and young upwardly mobile porteño party people. Stop first for a pint at the ground floor Shamrock pub, where you can yap away in English and easily forget you're in South America; then, following the techno beats, descend to the dance

Continued on page 116

The Dance of Buenos Aires

by Victoria Patience

"THE TANGO IS MACHO, THE TANGO IS STRONG. IT SMELLS OF WINE AND TASTES LIKE DEATH."

So goes the famous tango "Why I Sing Like This," whose mix of nostalgia, violence, and sensuality sum up what is truly the dance of Buenos Aires. From its beginnings, tango and its two-four beat marked and reflected the character of Buenos Aires. You may hear strains of tango on the radio while sipping coffee in a café, see high-kicking sequined dancers in a glitzy dinner show, or listen to musicians in a darkened cabaret. But one of the most memorable ways to experience the best of this broody, melancholic, impassioned art form is through dancing it yourself.

DANCING THE TANGO

Many milongas now kick off with group dance classes which usually last an hour or two and cost 15–20 pesos; some lessons are free, though chaotic. These classes are great for getting over nerves and getting you in the mood. However, most *milongueros* (people who dance at *milongas*, or tango dance halls) take tango very seriously and don't look kindly on left-footed beginners crowding the floor. We recommend you take a few private classes first—they can make a huge difference to your technique.

less common to see them on milonga floors. (Confusingly, "milonga" refers both to traditional tango dance halls and to a style of music and dance that predates the tango; though similar to tango, it has a more syncopated beat and faster, simpler steps.)

English-speaking private teachers abound in Buenos Aires; classes generally last 1½ hours and prices can range from $20 to $80 a class. Complete beginners should plan on at least three or four classes before hitting a milonga. Many private instructors organize milonga outings with groups of their students (usually for a separate fee). Others even offer a so-called "taxi dance service": you pay for them to dance with you all night. See the end of this feature for a rundown of some of the best options for lessons and milongas.

DANCE STYLES

Tango milonguero, the style danced at milongas and taught in most classes in Buenos Aires, is quite different from the so-called salon or ballroom tango danced in Hollywood movies and in competitions outside Argentina. Ballroom tango is all fixed steps and staccato movements, and dancers' backs arch away from each other in a stiff embrace. Tango milonguero is a highly improvised style built around a variety of typical movements, not fixed steps. Dancers embrace closely, their chests touching. There are other, historical tango styles, but it's

AT THE MILONGA

Dancers of all ages sit at tables that edge the floor, and men invite women to dance through *cabeceo* (subtle eye contact and head-nodding), a hard art to master. Note that women sitting with male partners won't be asked to the floor by other men.

Dances come in sets of three, four, or five, broken by a *cortina* (obvious divider of non-tango music), and it's common to stay with the same partner for a set. Being discarded in the middle is a sign that your dancing's not up to scratch, but staying for more than two sets with the same partner could be interpreted as a come-on.

To fit in seamlessly, move around the floor counterclockwise without zigzagging, sticking to the inside layers of dancers if you're a beginner. Respect other dancers' space by avoiding collisions and keeping your movements small on crowded floors. Don't spend a long time doing showy moves on the spot: it holds up traffic. Finally, take time to sit some out, catch your breath, and watch the experts.

TANGO TALK

Abrazo: the embrace or stance dancers use; in tango, this varies from hip-touching and loose shoulders to close chests and more fluid hips, depending on style.

Abrazo

Barrida

Barrida: literally, "a sweep"; one partner sweeps the other's foot into a position.

Caminada: a walking step that is the basis of the tango.

Canyengue: style of tango dancing with short and restricted steps; from the 1910s and '20s when tight hobble skirts were popular.

Ocho: eight; a criss-crossing walk.

Parada: literally a "stop"; the lead dancer stops the other's foot with his own.

Petitero: measured style of tango developed after the 1955 military coup, when large tango gatherings were banned and the dance relegated to small cafés.

Caminada

MILONGA STYLE

Wearing a fedora hat or fishnet stockings is as good as a neon sign reading "beginner." Forget what on-stage tango dancers wear and follow a few basic rules.

Go for comfortable clothes that allow you to move freely; a sure bet are breathable, natural fabrics with a bit of stretch. Be sure it's something that makes you feel sexy. If in doubt, wear black. Avoid showy outfits: it's your footwork that should stand out. It's also smart to steer clear of big buckles, studs, stones,

or anything that might catch on your partner. Try not to wear skirts that are too long or too tight. Also a bad idea are jeans or gymwear.

A good example of what to wear for men would be black dress pants and a black shirt; for women, two of many options are a simple halter-neck dress with a loose, calf-length skirt or palazzo pants with a fitted top.

As for your feet: look for dance shoes with flexible leather or suede soles that allow you to glide and pivot. The fit

Parada

should be snug but comfortable. Note that rubber-soled street shoes or sneakers mark the dance floor and are often forbidden. High heels are a must for women; the most popular style is an open-toed sandal with an ankle strap (which stops them coming off). Black lace-ups are the favorite among men, so leave your two-tone spats at home.

TANGO THROUGH TIME

The tango and modern Buenos Aires were born in the same place: the *conventillos* (tenement houses) of the port neighborhood of La Boca in the late 19th century, where River Plate culture collided with that of European immigrants. The dance eventually swept from the immigrant-quarter brothels and cabarets to the rest of the city; rich playboys took the tango to Paris on their grand tours, and by the 1920s the dance had become respectable enough to fill the salons and drawing rooms of the upper class in Argentina and abroad. In the 1930s, with the advent of singers like Carlos Gardel, tango music became popular in its own right. Accordingly, musical accompaniment started to come from larger bands known as *orquestas típicas*.

Carlos Gardel

By the '40s and '50s, *porteños* (people from Buenos Aires) celebrated tango as the national music of the people, and tango artists lent Evita and Perón their support. The military coup that ousted Perón in 1955 forbade large tango dances, which it saw as potential political gatherings, and (bizarrely)

encouraged rock 'n' roll instead. Young people listened, and tango fell out of popular favor.

The '90s saw a huge revival in both traditional *milongas* (dance halls) and a more improvised dance style. Musical offerings now include modern takes on classic tangos and electrotango or *tangofusión*. Even local rock stars are starting to include a tango or two in their repertory. And since 1998, thousands of people from around the world have attended the annual fortnight-long Festival de Tango in Buenos Aires (⊕ *www.tangobuenosaires.gob.ar*), held late winter or spring.

Whether you decide to take in a show or take up dancing yourself, sit down for a classic concert or groove at an electrotango night, there are more ways to experience tango in Buenos Aires than anywhere else on earth.

DID YOU KNOW?

■ Tango so horrified Kaiser Wilhelm and Pope Pius X that they banned the dance.

■ In 1915, before he was famous, Carlos Gardel was injured in a barroom brawl with Ernesto Guevara Lynch, Che's father.

■ One of Gardel's most famous numbers, "Por Una Cabeza," is the tango featured in *Schindler's List*, *Scent of a Woman*, and *True Lies*.

■ The coup of 1930 prompted composers like Enrique Santos Discépolo to write protest tangos.

■ Finnish tango has been a distinct musical genre since at least mid-century and is still one of the most popular in Finland; there's even an annual *Tangomarkkinat* (tango festival) in Seinäjoki, complete with the crowning of a Tango King and Queen.

club. Argentina's finest DJs burn up the decks. ✉ *Rodríguez Peña 1220, Recoleta* ☎ *11/4812–3584* Ⓜ *D to Callao.*

GAY AND LESBIAN

Zoom. Half a block from the very cruisey section of Santa Fe, between Avenidas Callao and Coronel Díaz, Zoom offers a lounge bar, a maze, video cabins, and plenty of dark corners. It can get pretty intense, but there's good security. ✉ *Uriburu 1018, Recoleta* ☎ *11/4827–4828* ⊕ *www.zoombuenosaires.com* ☽ *24 hrs* Ⓜ *D to Pueyrredón.*

LIVE MUSIC

Clásica y Moderna. An older, artsy crowd gathers here for live jazz complemented by dinner, drinks, and a dash of philosophy. Musicians make good use of the vintage venue's grand piano, while singers offer their take on the bossa nova, tango, and bolero. Bibliophiles will also appreciate the on-site bookshop. ✉ *Av. Callao 892, Recoleta* ☎ *11/4812–8707* ⊕ *www.clasicaymoderna.com* Ⓜ *D to Callao.*

Notorious. A jazz bar, restaurant, and record shop rolled into one, Notorious often hosts some of the area's best musicians. Certain nights have a fixed calendar, others are one-off gigs. You can also listen to the club's extensive music collection on the CD players at each table. ✉ *Av. Callao 966, Recoleta* ☎ *11/4813–6888* ⊕ *www.notorious.com.ar* Ⓜ *D to Callao.*

ALMAGRO

LIVE MUSIC

Ciudad Cultural Konex. A mixed bag of live music, film screenings, wild parties, and interactive theater make for an interesting line-up at this huge converted factory. The outdoor space morphs into an inner-city beach complete with hammocks in summer; the winter months see DJs and bands hash it out indoors. ✉ *Sarmiento 3131, Abasto* ☎ *11/4864–3200* ⊕ *www.ciudadculturalkonex.org* Ⓜ *B to Carlos Gardel.*

TANGO

MILONGAS

La Catedral. This former grain factory has been converted into a hip club where the tango is somehow very rock. There are classes and milongas every evening, although Tuesday is the most popular. It's a cool night out even if you're not planning to dance, as you can watch the pros in action later on. ✉ *Sarmiento 4006, Almagro* ☎ *11–15/5325–1630* ⊕ *www.lacatedralclub.com* Ⓜ *B to Carlos Gardel.*

PALERMO

BARS

878. B.A.'s original speakeasy has spawned a spate of followers over the past few years, but it remains a classic for cocktail lovers: 878 has an extensive drinks list, armchairs to sink into, plus a super-cool clientele. Be sure to stick your head around the more private back bar. ✉ *Thames 878, Palermo Viejo* ☎ *11/4773–1098* ⊕ *www.878bar.com. ar* Ⓜ *B to Malabia.*

Acabar. This offbeat bar in the heart of Palermo Hollywood has become a big hit, and the lines to get in are only exacerbated by the abundance of board games inside, including giant Jenga. Those who manage to snag a table are quickly charmed by the easy-going atmosphere. The barstaff whip up some great fresh juices, too. ✉ *Honduras 5733, Palermo Hollywood* ☎ *11/4772–0845* ⊕ *www.acabarnet.com.ar* Ⓜ *D to Palermo.*

Antares. Originating in Mar del Plata in 1999, Antares is now a successful national brewer making seven of its own ales, which you can taste in shot-size glasses. The spacious bar attracts a cosmopolitan group of drinkers who keep it packed from after-office until the small hours. Service is friendly and efficient, the music is feel-good, and the bar snacks are tasty. Also check out the newer outposts in Las Cañitas at Arévalo 2876 and San Telmo at Bolivar 491. ✉ *Armenia 1447, Palermo Soho* ☎ *11/4833–9611* ⊕ *www.cervezaantares.com* Ⓜ *B to Malabia.*

Bangalore. A pub and curry house in Buenos Aires? Well-located, the Bangalore has it all—right down to a blazing log fire in winter. There's limited seating both at the bar and in the tiny restaurant upstairs, and the place is often packed from early evening on. Service is friendly, and there's a wide range of draft beers. Revelers spill out onto the street with their pints in the warmer months. ✉ *Humboldt 1416, Palermo Hollywood* ☎ *11/4779–2621* Ⓜ *B to Dorrego.*

Congo. Beautiful people—in faded fitted jeans, hipster sneakers, and leather jackets—frequent this hangout post-dinner and pre-club. Browse the great cocktail list at Congo's lengthy bar, or head for the large back patio: either way, you'll easily be able to convince new friends to stick around for another drink or three. ✉ *Honduras 5329, Palermo Soho* ☎ *11/4833–5857* ⊕ *www.barcongo.com.ar* Ⓜ *D to Plaza Italia.*

The Harrison Speakeasy. Modern-day guys and dolls embrace the *Boardwalk Empire* vibe at Harrison's, one of the finest speakeasies around. Its time-warp cocktails have earned a cluster of awards, so you're in expert hands. Membership is required; alternatively, you can dine at the shop-front sushi restaurant, and then ask "to see the bodega." ✉ *Malabia 1764 and Costa Rica, Palermo* ⊕ *www.nicky-harrison.com* Ⓜ *D to Scalabrini Ortiz.*

Isabel. Glamour is the name of the game at Isabel, one of Palermo's posher watering holes. You can feel like a star sipping a cocktail under the twinkling ceiling lights, while actually star spotting if you're up to date with your Argentinean models and polo players. Hip DJs spin tunes for a bling-y crowd, so booking is essential—as is a bottomless wallet. ✉ *Uriarte 1664, Palermo Soho* ☎ *11/4834–6969* ⊕ *www.isabelbar.com* Ⓜ *D to Plaza Italia.*

Mundo Bizarro. Longevity is a mark of Mundo Bizarro's success—after all, this place has been perfecting cocktails and building a faithful late-night following since 1997. Red lights, kitsch artwork, rock and roll, and even a pole for dancing provide the backdrop; the rest gets improvised afresh every evening. ✉ *Serrano 1222, Palermo Soho* ☎ *11/4773–1967* ⊕ *www.mundobizarrobar.com* Ⓜ *B to Malabia.*

Sugar Bar. If cumbia and salsa are becoming a bitter pill to swallow, a trip to Sugar will sweeten up your evening. With an extensive happy hour or three until midnight, this Palermo fixture is run by expats and attracts a fun-loving crowd of Argentineans and foreigners looking for good times and big-game matches under the flattering red lighting. ⊠ *Costa Rica 4619, Palermo Viejo* ☏ *11/4831–3276* ⊕ *www. sugarbuenosaires.com* Ⓜ *D to Scalabrini Ortiz.*

Verne Club. Themed around Jules Verne's *Twenty Thousand Leagues Under the Sea,* Verne Club runs a tight ship thanks to Fede Cuco—one of Argentina's best-known mixologists. This old-school cocktail bar serves innovative offerings that are often inspired by the eponymous author's characters, including a Phileas Fogg Martini. ⊠ *Medrano 1475, Palermo* ☏ *11/4822–0980* ⊕ *www.vernecocktailclub.com* Ⓜ *D to Scalabrini Ortiz.*

DANCE CLUBS

Club Aráoz. A serious party crowd is found at Club Aráoz. Bump and grind it at Thursday's block-rocking hip-hop night; Friday and Saturday see DJs spinning rock and electronic dance music for a relatively laid-back bunch of Buenos Aires youth. ⊠ *Aráoz 2424, Palermo* ☏ *11/4833–7775* ⊕ *www.lostshake.com.ar* Ⓜ *D to Bulnes.*

Kika. Right in the heart of Palermo and next door to Congo, Kika is much bigger than you'd guess from the outside. Thanks to its funky musical orientation, its two dance floors fill up quickly. The back room sometimes hosts live bands while Tuesday is all about Hype, an all-in-one electro, hip-hop, indie, and dubstep night that gets students moving till dawn. ⊠ *Honduras 5339, Palermo Soho* ☏ *11/4833–9171* ⊕ *www. kikaclub.com.ar* Ⓜ *D to Palermo.*

Fodor'sChoice
★

Niceto. One of the city's best venues features everything from demure indie rock to the outrageous and legendary Club 69 on Thursday (think under-dressed cross-dressers). Check out live bands and dancing on the A Side, while something contrasting and chill simultaneously takes place in the back room, B Side. ⊠ *Cnel. Niceto Vega 5510, Palermo Hollywood* ☏ *11/4779–9396* ⊕ *www.nicetoclub.com* Ⓜ *B to Dorrego.*

GAY AND LESBIAN

Amerika. This immense gay disco has three floors of high-energy action and shows. Friday and Saturday are fun and frivolous verging on hectic thanks to its one-fee, all-you-can-drink entry. Thursday and Sunday are quieter, with greater emphasis on the music. Amerika remains the city's gay club to check out—and be checked out in. ⊠ *Gascon 1040, Palermo* ☏ *11/4865–4416* ⊕ *www.ameri-k.com.ar* Ⓜ *B to Medrano.*

LIVE MUSIC

Thelonious Club. The best porteño jazz bands (and occasional foreign imports) play at this intimate, upscale spot. Arrive early for a good seat, as it's a long, narrow bar and not all tables have good views; on weekends there are usually two shows per night. ⊠ *Salguero 1884, Palermo* ☏ *11/4829–1562* ⊕ *www.theloniousclub.com.ar* Ⓜ *D to Bulnes.*

Virasoro Bar. This is an intimate art deco venue for local jazz maestros and appreciative audiences. It's a great space and you can get up close and personal with musicians, who draw from a deep well of talent and cover a lot of ground, from improv to standards and experimental. ✉ *Guatemala 4328, Palermo* ☎ *11/4831–8918* ⊕ *www.virasorobar. com.ar* Ⓜ *D to Scalabrini Ortiz.*

TANGO

Fodor'sChoice **Salón Canning.** Several milongas call this large dance hall home. The
★ coolest is Parakultural (☎ *11–15/5738–3850* ⊕ *www.parakultural.com. ar*), which takes place late on Monday, Tuesday, and Friday. Reservations are essential for the last of these—the dance floor is totally packed by midnight, so get here early. Originally an alternative, "underground" milonga, it now attracts large numbers of locals, including longtime expats. ✉ *Av. Scalabrini Ortíz 1331, Palermo* ☎ *11/4832–6753* ⊕ *www. parakultural.com.ar* Ⓜ *B to Malabia.*

SHOPPING

Whether you're looking for a unique handicraft, a cowhide chair, the latest boutique-vineyard Malbec, a one-off pair of rhodochrosite earrings set in silver, or jeans no one's got back home, you're sure to leave Buenos Aires with your bags full. Ever since Argentina's economic collapse in 2001, designers have had to inject a new level of creativity into their wares in order to survive. Innovation is key, and it can be found on every corner and at every street fair and upmarket boutique.

If you love the hustle and bustle, elbow your way to the stalls at the city's outdoor markets. Many artisans set up around squares such as Plazas Francia, Armenia, and Serrano. On weekends in Palermo Soho, some artisans simply lay out handcrafted leather mate gourds or colorful aguayo hair clips symmetrically on the sidewalk, while Sundays at San Telmo's Plaza Dorrego turn into an outdoor theater show, with living statues and tango dancers jostling for space among the antiques.

CENTRO

CLOTHING

La Martina. Feel part of the jet set when you browse the clothing line of Argentine polo team La Martina. It's not just about boots and jodhpurs; there are also corduroy pants and cashmere sweaters perfect for lounging around your country house. Screen-printed tees—including the country's national polo-team shirt—are a must-have. ✉ *Paraguay 661, Microcentro* ☎ *11/4311–5963* ⊕ *www.lamartina.com* Ⓜ *C to San Martín* ✉ *Arribeños 2632, Belgrano* ☎ *11/4576–0010.*

Ona Saez. The ultrafitted jeans at Ona Saez are designed to be worn with sky-high heels and slinky tops for a sexy night out. The menswear is equally slick, mixing dressed-down denim with cool cotton shirts and tees. ✉ *Florida 789, #203, Centro* ☎ *11/5555–5203* ⊕ *www. onasaez.com* Ⓜ *C to San Martín* ✉ *Santa Fe 1609, Barrio Norte* ☎ *11/4815–0029.*

JEWELRY AND ACCESSORIES

Autoría Bs As. Fashion meets art at Autoría Bs As. After browsing the ready-to-wear women's collections by Mariana Dappiano, Min Agostini, and Vero Ivaldi, head to jewelry and accessories. Necklaces may be made of coiled silver by María Medici or crochet by Tatiana Pini. Some handbags have been fashioned from car tires, others from top-quality leather or organic wool. This is one of the few places to pick up a daring one-of-a-kind Manto Abrigo coat, handwoven in luminous colors in northern Argentina. ✉ *Suipacha 1025, Microcentro* ☎ *11/5252–2474* ⊕ *www.autoriabsas.com.ar* Ⓜ *C to San Martín.*

Plata Nativa. Tucked into an arcade, this tiny shop is filled with delights for both boho chicks and collectors of singular ethnic jewelry. Complex, chunky necklaces with turquoise, amber, and malachite—all based on original Araucanian (ethnic Argentine) pieces—and Mapuche-style silver earrings and brooches are some of the offerings. Happy customers include Sharon Stone, Pedro Almodóvar, and the Textile Museum in Washington, D.C. ✉ *Galería del Sol, Shop 41, Florida 860* ☎ *11/4312–1398* ⊕ *www.platanativa.com* Ⓜ *C to San Martín.*

SHOES, HANDBAGS, AND LEATHER GOODS

Carpincho. As its name suggests, this spot specializes in supersoft, stippled *carpincho* leather from the capybara—the world's largest rodent, native to Argentina. Gloves (which also come in more conventional kidskin) are the main attraction, and there's a wide variety of lengths and colors to choose from. ✉ *Esmeralda 775, Centro* ☎ *11/4322–9919* ⊕ *www.carpinchonet.com.ar* Ⓜ *C to Lavalle.*

Casa López. Don't let the drab storefront put you off: you're as likely to find a trouser suit in floral-print suede as a staid handbag for grandma at this two-part place. The right-hand shop (No. 658) has totes in chestnut- and chocolate-color leather that look good enough to eat; there are also classic jackets. More unusual fare—including fur sacks with wool fringes, black cowhide baguettes, and tangerine purses—are sold next door at No. 640. ✉ *Marcelo T. de Alvear 640 and 658, Centro* ☎ *11/4311–3044* ⊕ *www.casalopez.com.ar* Ⓜ *C to San Martín.*

SAN TELMO

ANTIQUES AND COLLECTIBLES

Gabriel del Campo. Gabriel's good taste means 50-year-old Louis Vuitton trunks don't look out of place beside wooden church statues or scale-model ships with canvas sails. Ceramic rubber-glove molds, one of his specialties, are some of the more accessible conversation pieces. The flagship store takes up a sizable patch of Plaza Dorrego storefront. ✉ *Bethlem 427, on Plaza Dorrego, San Telmo* ☎ *11/4307–6589* Ⓜ *C to San Juan (walk 6 blocks along Humberto I).*

Gil Antigüedades. Sequined flapper dresses, dashing white-linen suits, and creamy lace wedding veils are some of the items you might stumble across in this casa chorizo. Period accessories include Castilian hair combs and lacy fans that beg you to bat your lashes from behind them. ✉ *Humberto*

Soda syphons for sale in the San Telmo flea market in Plaza Dorrego

I 412, San Telmo ☎ *11/4361–5019* ⊕ *www.gilantiguedades.com.ar* Ⓜ *C to San Juan (walk 6 blocks along Av. San Juan).*

CLOTHING

Fodor'sChoice
★

Pablo Ramírez. His tiny shop front is unadorned except for "Ramírez" printed on the glass over the door—when you're this big, why say more? Voted Argentina's best designer by the fashion blogger Scott Schuman, Ramírez's couture doesn't come cheap, but these perfectly tailored numbers are worth every centavo. He favors black or white for both waspishly waisted women's wear and slick gent's suits, though a few other shades are creeping in. ⊠ *Perú 587, San Telmo* ☎ *11/4342–7154* ⊕ *www.pabloramirez.com.ar* Ⓜ *E to Belgrano.*

GIFTS AND SOUVENIRS

Artepampa. An artist-and-architect duo is behind these singular works, which are inspired by native Argentine art. They use an unusual papier-mâché technique to create boxes, frames, tapestries, and freestanding sculptures. The primitive-looking pieces, a vision of rich rusts and earthy browns, make highly original gifts. ⊠ *Defensa 917, on Plaza Dorrego, San Telmo* ☎ *11/4362–6406* ⊕ *www.artepampa.com* Ⓜ *C to San Juan.*

Juan Carlos Pallarols Orfebre. Argentina's legendary silversmith has made pieces for a mile-long list of celebrities that includes Frank Sinatra, Sharon Stone, Antonio Banderas, Bill Clinton, Nelson Mandela, the king and queen of Spain, and Queen Máxima Zorrequieta—a local export now integrated into the Dutch royal family. A set of ornate silver-handled steak knives is the perfect memento of cow country, although it will set you back a few grand. ⊠ *Defensa 1039, San Telmo* ☎ *11/4361–7360*

⊕ *www.pallarols.com.ar* Ⓜ *C or E to Independencia (walk 6 blocks along Estados Unidos).*

Marcelo Toledo. Sunlight and the smell of solder fill the rooms of this old San Telmo house, which doubles as a store and open workshop for celebrity silversmith Marcelo Toledo. A huge silver mosaic of Evita gives away who Toledo's main muse is: he has created replicas of her own jewelry (and is the only silversmith authorized by her estate to do so) as well as pieces inspired by her. Eva Duarte Perón isn't the only crowd-pleasing politician Toledo's been associated with: a local magnate commissioned cuff links as an inauguration gift for President Obama. He also designed a maté gourd especially for Prince William and his bride, the Duchess of Cambridge. ⊠ *Humberto I 458, San Telmo* ☎ *11/4362–0841* ⊕ *www.marcelotoledo.net* Ⓜ *C to San Juan (6 blocks away).*

JEWELRY AND ACCESSORIES

Abraxas. "Yes" is pretty much guaranteed if you propose with one of the period engagement rings that dazzle in the window of this antique jeweler. If you're not planning on popping the question any time soon, surely you can find a home for a pair of art deco earrings with the tiniest of diamonds or a gossamer-fine bracelet? ⊠ *Defensa 1092, San Telmo* ☎ *11/4361–7512* ⊕ *www.abraxasantiques.com* Ⓜ *C to San Juan (walk 6 blocks along Humberto I).*

MARKETS

Feria de San Pedro Telmo. Plaza Dorrego is the heart of the Feria de San Pedro Telmo—an open-air market that stretches for more than a kilometer (½ mile) along Calle Defensa each Sunday. Thrust your way through the crowds to pick through antiques and curios of varying vintages as well as tango memorabilia, or watch dolled-up professional tango dancers perform on the surrounding cobbled streets. The unofficial "stalls" (often just a cloth on the ground) of young craftspeople stretch several blocks up Defensa, away from the market proper. As it gets dark, the square turns into a milonga, where quick-stepping locals show you how it's done. ⊠ *Plaza Dorrego, Humberto I and Defensa, San Telmo* ⊕ *www.feriadesantelmo.com* ☉ *Sun. 10–dusk* Ⓜ *C to San Juan.*

RECOLETA

CLOTHING

Giesso. A classic gents' tailor for more than 130 years, Giesso has pulled a Thomas Pink by adding jewel-color ties and shirts to its range of timeless suits and corduroy jackets. A women's line includes gorgeous linen suits and cashmere overcoats. ⊠ *Av. Alvear 1882, Recoleta* ☎ *11/4804–8288* ⊕ *www.giesso.com.ar* Ⓜ *D to Tribunales (12 blocks away)* ⊠ *Florida 997, Centro* ☎ *11/4312–7606.*

CLOTHING: MEN

La Dolfina. Being a no. 1 polo player wasn't enough for Adolfo Cambiaso—he founded his own team in 1995, then started a clothing line which he also models for. If you think polo is all about knee-high boots and preppy chinos, think again: Cambiaso sells some of the best

2

urban menswear in town. The Italian-cotton shirts, sharp leather jackets, and to-die-for totes are perfect for any occasion. ✉ *Av. Alvear 1751, Recoleta* ☎ *11/4811–1066* ⊕ *www.ladolfina.com* Ⓜ *D to Tribunales (12 blocks away).*

Cora Groppo. A queen of the porteño haute-couture scene, Cora Groppo made her name designing flirty cocktail dresses with lots of cleavage and short flared or bell-shaped skirts. These continue to be the main attraction at her Recoleta branch. The lower-key Palermo store at El Salvador 4657 sells skinny pants and shorts best accompanied by draped tops, although the whisper-thin cotton jersey that most are made of doesn't do much for clients without catwalk figures. ✉ *Uruguay 1296, Recoleta* ☎ *11/4815–8516* ⊕ *www.coragroppo.com* Ⓜ *D to Tribunales (8 blocks away)* ✉ *El Salvador 4696, Palermo Viejo* ☎ *11/4833–7474.*

Evangelina Bomparola. Evangelina takes her clothes very seriously, and it's easy to see why. Top-of-the-line materials and detailed attention to the way they hang translate into designs that are simple but never dull. This is *the* place to come for a little (or long) black dress; wilder items—such as a '60s-style funnel-neck coat or a colorful raw-silk jumpsuit—also line the minimalist boutique's racks. ✉ *Alvear 1920, Recoleta* ☎ *11/4802–8807* ⊕ *www.evangelinabomparola.com* Ⓜ *D to Callao (12 blocks away).*

Luz Ballestero. Each collection by Luz Ballestero has a different inspiration: summer might reflect contemporary dance while winter takes shelter and protection as its muse. The result is a simple yet eclectic brand that is both modern and urban. Blushing brides should make an appointment to check out her gowns, too. ✉ *Vicente López 1661, Pasaje del Correo #5, Recoleta* ☎ *11/4812–2670* ⊕ *www.luzballestero. com* Ⓜ *D to Tribunales (8 blocks away).*

Tramando, Martín Churba. The name of this hushed town-house store means both "weaving" and "plotting"—and designer Martín Churba is doing plenty of both. Unique evening tops made of layers of draped and pleated sheer fabric adorned with circular beads and irregular embroidery look fit for an urban mermaid. Asymmetrical shrugs, screenprinted tees, and even vases are some of the other woven wonders that represent a fusion of art and fashion. ✉ *Rodríguez Peña 1973, Recoleta* ☎ *11/4811–0465* ⊕ *www.tramando.com* Ⓜ *C to Retiro (10 blocks away).*

Trosman. Highly unusual beadwork is the only adornment on Trosman designs. There's nothing small and sparkling about it: beads are smooth, inch-wide acrylic orbs that look futuristic yet organic. You might balk at the price tags, considering that most of the clothes are made of T-shirting, but that hasn't stopped Tokyo or Paris from stocking wares. Note that the brand is now under new ownership: you can check out original designer Jessica Trosman's latest, more urban offerings at JT in Palermo. ✉ *Patio Bullrich Mall, Av. del Libertador 750, Store 1, Recoleta* ☎ *11/4814–7414* ⊕ *www.trosman.com* Ⓜ *C to Retiro (8 blocks away)* ✉ *Armenia 1998, Palermo Viejo* ☎ *11/4833–3058.*

Varanasi. The structural perfection of Varanasi's clothes is a clue that the brains behind them trained as architects. Find A-line dresses built from silk patchwork and unadorned bias cuts, some of the night-out joys that local celebs shop for. ⊠ *Juncal 1280, Recoleta* ☎ *11/4812–4282* ⊕ *www.varanasi-online.com* Ⓜ *C to Retiro.*

JEWELRY AND ACCESSORIES

Celedonio. Local design hero Celedonio Lohidoy has created pieces—often with frothy bunches of natural pearls—for Kenzo and Emanuel Ungaro; his work has even been slung around Sarah Jessica Parker's neck on *Sex in the City.* He favors irregular semiprecious stones, set in asymmetrical, organic-looking designs such as butterflies and daisies. ⊠ *Uruguay 1223, #8, Recoleta* ☎ *11/4803–7598* ⊕ *www.celedonio. com.ar* ☉ *Closed weekends* Ⓜ *D to Tribunales (6 blocks away).*

Fahoma. This small boutique has enough accessories to make the rest of your outfit a mere formality. Berry-size beads go into chunky but affordable necklaces, which take flora and fauna as their inspiration, while all manner of handbags line the back wall. Need a royal seal of approval? Queen Máxima of the Netherlands has been photographed wearing their fun, oversize earrings. ⊠ *Libertad 1169, Recoleta* ☎ *11/4813–5103* ⊕ *www.fahoma.es* Ⓜ *D to Tribunales (5 blocks away).*

Homero. Previously known for innovative, beautifully designed necklaces and rings, Homero has taken a new turn by adding heirloom pieces to its selection: choose from jewels (including complete sets), watches, and other unique items—each with its own story. ⊠ *Patio Bullrich, Av. Libertador 750, #2007, Recoleta* ☎ *11/4812–9881* ⊕ *www.homero compra.com* Ⓜ *C to Retiro (7 blocks away).*

MARKETS

Feria de Artesanos de Plaza Francia (*Feria Plaza Francia*). The sprawling open-air market winds through several linked squares outside the Recoleta Cemetery. Each weekend, artisans sell handmade clothes, jewelry, and housewares as well as traditional crafts. ⊠ *Avs. Libertador and Pueyrredón, La Recoleta* ⊕ *www.feriaplazafrancia.com* ☉ *Weekends 11–dusk.*

SHOES, HANDBAGS, AND LEATHER GOODS

Guido. In Argentina loafers mean Guido, whose retro-looking logo has been the hallmark of quality footwear since 1952. Try on timeless handmade Oxfords and wing tips; there are also fun items like a tomato-red handbag or a cow-skin tote. Accessories include simple belts and suede wallets. ⊠ *Av. Quintana 333, Recoleta* ☎ *11/4811–4567* ⊕ *www.guido mocasines.com.ar* Ⓜ *C to San Martín (10 blocks away).*

Lonte. There's something naughty-but-oh-so-nice about Lonte's shoes. Chunky gold peep-toe heels are a dream, and the outré animal-print numbers are a favorite of local diva, TV presenter Susana Giménez. For more discreet feet there are patent-leather boots or classic heels in straightforward colors. ⊠ *Quintana 470, Recoleta* ☎ *11/4806–7083* ⊕ *www.lonteshoes.com.ar* Ⓜ *D to Callao (11 blocks away).*

Zapatos de María. María Conorti was one of the first young designers to set up shop in this swanky part of town, and she's still going strong.

Wedge heels, satin ankle-ties, and abundant use of patent leather in pumps and boots are the trademark touches of her quirky designs. Head to the basement at the back of the store for discounted footwear from past seasons. ⊠ *Libertad 1665, Recoleta* ☎ *11/4815–5001* ⊕ *www. zapatosdemaria.com.ar* Ⓜ *C to Retiro (6 blocks away).*

WINE

Grand Cru. Incredibly savvy staff, some trained as sommeliers, will guide you through Grand Cru's peerless selection; the vast range is dominated by high-end wines from small vineyards. ⊠ *Rodríguez Peña 1886, Recoleta* ☎ *11/4816–3975* ⊕ *www.grandcru.com.ar* Ⓜ *D to Callao.*

Ligier. Ligier has a string of wine stores across town and lots of experience guiding bewildered drinkers through their impressive selection. Although they stock some boutique-vineyard wines, they mostly carry big names such as Rutini, Catena, and Luigi Bosca, as well as more modest mass-produced wines. ⊠ *Callao 1111, Recoleta* ☎ *11/5353–8050* ⊕ *www.ligier.com.ar* Ⓜ *C to San Martín.*

ALMAGRO

MALLS

FAMILY **Abasto Shopping.** The soaring art deco architecture of what was once the city's central market is as much a reason to come here as the 250 shops spread over its three levels. Although Abasto has many top local chains, it isn't as exclusive as other malls, so relative bargains await at retailers like Ver, Yagmour, and Markova. Women can dress up at Paula Cahen d'Anvers, Akiabara, and Rapsodia; while men can hit trendy shops such as Bensimon, Prototype, and Old Bridge, or go for the *estanciero* look with smart La Martina polo wear. When you need a break, there's a top-floor food court beneath the glass panes and steel supports of the building's original roof. The mall is also home to Museo de los Niños (a hands-on children's museum) and a 12-screen cinema; you can pick up tickets for entertainment elsewhere in town at the Ticketek booth near the food court, too. ⊠ *Av. Corrientes 3247, Almagro* ☎ *11/4959–3400* ⊕ *www.abasto-shopping.com.ar* Ⓜ *B to Carlos Gardel.*

PALERMO

CLOTHING

BlackMamba. Rarely deviating from the house color (you guessed it, black), the collection here appeals to tough chicks and tougher guys: imagine mohair spider-web sweaters and stylish goth-meets-sexy vampire garments that fuse leather with natural fibers. ⊠ *Soler 4502, Recoleta* ☎ *11/4832–5083* ⊕ *www.beblackmamba.com* Ⓜ *D to Scalabrini Ortiz (6 blocks away).*

Nadine Zlotogora. Bring a sense of humor to Nadine Zlotogora, where you fight your way through giant knitted cacti to peruse way-out designs which are playful yet exquisitely put together. Sheer fabrics are embroidered with organic-looking designs, then worn alone or over thin cotton. Even the menswear gets the tulle treatment: military-look shirts come with a transparent top layer. ✉ *El Salvador 4638, Palermo Viejo* ☎ *11/4831–4203* ⊕ *www.nadinez.com* Ⓜ *D to Plaza Italia.*

CLOTHING: MEN

Félix. Hipster alert: waxed floorboards, worn rugs, exposed brick, and aging cabinets set the tone for the cool clothes at Félix. Beat-up denim, crisp flower-power shirts, and knits that look like a loving granny whipped them up are among the many delights. A kids' collection lets Mini-Me duplicate dad's look. ✉ *Honduras 4916, Palermo Viejo* ☎ *11/4832–2164* ⊕ *www.felixba.com.ar* Ⓜ *D to Plaza Italia.*

CLOTHING: WOMEN

Benito Fernández. Eye-popping colors, big prints, and unusual texture combinations characterize the light-hearted looks of Benito Fernández. Fans of his dramatic dresses include Sarah Jessica Parker, who requested that his Etnia collection be included in the *Sex and the City 2* wardrobe. ✉ *Armenia 1460, Palermo Viejo* ☎ *11/4833–0303* ⊕ *www. benitofernandez.com.ar/en* Ⓜ *D to Scalabrini Ortiz.*

Cecilia Gadea. The simple, almost stark, cuts Gadea favors are the perfect canvas for riotously pretty texture work—a dress, for instance, might be adorned with hundreds of hand-embroidered petals. Feast further on her skirts, suits, and well-cut cotton tops. The high-heeled Mary Janes here, specially designed by Belocca, are part girly, part sophisticated. ✉ *Serrano 1536, Palermo Viejo* ☎ *11/4831–5930* ⊕ *www.ceciliagadea. com* Ⓜ *D to Plaza Italia.*

Didi Bandol. The A-line coats, shiny fabrics, and blocks of primary colors are clearly a nod to the '60s, but the look is very now when they're combined with perfect drainpipe pants and an overlength T-shirt. The deal maker? Quality that's higher than many places in Palermo, at prices that are lower. ✉ *Gurruchaga 1767, Palermo* ☎ *11/4831–8041* ⊕ *www. bandol.com.ar* Ⓜ *D to Plaza Italia.*

Seco. Singing in the rain is encouraged at Seco, where all the clothes are designed to get wet but keep you dry. See-through plastic numbers come with matching rain hats worth risking a soaking for. Pick up a pretty umbrella that will weather any unexpected shower; the bright, beautiful bikinis are also tempting. ✉ *Armenia 1646, Palermo Viejo* ☎ *11/4833–1166* ⊕ *www.secorainwear.com* Ⓜ *D to Plaza Italia.*

GIFTS AND SOUVENIRS

Elementos Argentinos. A fair-trade agreement links this luminous Palermo town house to a team of craftswomen in northwest Argentina who spin, dye, and weave the exquisite woolen goods sold here. Some of the handmade rugs, blankets, and throws follow traditional patterns and use only natural pigments (such as *yerba mate* or beetroot juice); others are contemporary designs using brighter colors. Packable souvenirs include sheep-wool table runners, alpaca scarves, and knitted cacti. Ask about designing your own rug. ✉ *Gurruchaga 1881, Palermo Viejo* ☎ *11/4832–6299* ⊕ *www.elementosargentinos.com.ar* Ⓜ *D to Plaza Italia.*

Tienda Palacio. The slogan here is "Cool Stuff," and it's spot-on. From dress-up refrigerator magnet sets of Evita and El Che to traditional penguin-shape wine jugs, Tienda Palacio is full of the nifty Argentine paraphernalia with a heavy emphasis on kitsch meeting tongue-in-cheek. ✉ *Honduras 5272, Palermo Viejo* ☎ *11/4833–9456* ⊕ *www. tiendapalacio.com.ar/esp* Ⓜ *D to Palermo* ✉ *Defensa 926, San Telmo* ☎ *11/4361–4325.*

JEWELRY AND ACCESSORIES

Infinit. Infinit's signature thick acrylic eyeglass frames are favored by graphic designers and models alike. If the classic black rectangular versions are too severe for you, the same style comes in a range of candy colors and two-tones. Bug-eye shades and oversize '70s-inspired designs are other options. ✉ *Thames 1602, Palermo Viejo* ☎ *11/4831–7070* ⊕ *www.infinit.la* Ⓜ *D to Plaza Italia.*

María Medici. Industrial-looking brushed silver rings and necklaces knitted from fine stainless-steel cables are some of the attractions at this tiny shop. Architect and sculpturist María Medici also combines silver with primary-color resin to make unusual-looking rings. ✉ *Niceto Vega 4619, Palermo Viejo* ☎ *11/4773–2283* ⊕ *mariamedici.blogspot.com.ar* Ⓜ *B to Malabia.*

SHOES, HANDBAGS, AND LEATHER GOODS

28Sport. These leather bowling sneakers and boxing-style boots are the heart and, er, "sole" of retro. All the models are variations on a classic round-toed lace-up, but come with different-length legs. Plain black or chestnut uppers go with everything, but equally tempting are the two-tone numbers—in chocolate and orange, or black with curving white panels, for example. Even the store is a nod to the past, kitted out like a 1950s living room. ✉ *Gurruchaga 1481, Palermo Viejo* ☎ *11/4833–4287* ⊕ *www.28sport.com* Ⓜ *D to Plaza Italia (10 blocks away).*

Divia. Step out in a pair of limited-edition Divias and it doesn't really matter what else you've got on. Designer Virginia Spagnuolo draws inspiration from travels to India, her own vintage shoe collection, and even her cat. The results are leather collages—suede, textured metallic, or patent leathers—in colors such as teal, ruby, or plum. Really go to town and order a custom-made pair. ✉ *Armenia 1489, Palermo Viejo* ☎ *11/4831–9090* ⊕ *www.diviashoes.com* Ⓜ *D to Plaza Italia.*

Doma. Doma's leather jackets are both hard-wearing and eye-catching. Military-style coats in olive-green suede will keep you snug in winter, while collarless biker jackets in silver, electric blue, or deep red offer a cooler summer option. ✉ *El Salvador 4693, Palermo Viejo* ☎ *11/4831–6852* ⊕ *www.doma-leather.com* Ⓜ *D to Plaza Italia.*

Fodor's Choice ★ **Humawaca.** Thanks to its innovative shapes and funky colors, Humawaca is the hippest leather name in town. Cowhide is a favorite here, as are lively combinations like chocolate-brown leather and moss-green suede, or electric blue nubuck with a floral lining. Along with the expected bags and purses, you can pick up stylish laptop or travel totes. Price tags will make you gulp, but there are wallets, gloves, and pencil cases for more demure budgets. ✉ *El Salvador 4692, Palermo Viejo* ☎ *11/4832–2662* ⊕ *www.humawaca.com* Ⓜ *D to Plaza Italia* ✉ *Posadas 1380* ☎ *11/4811–5995.*

Mishka. At this longtime Palermo favorite, your feet will go to the ball in high-heel lace-ups, kick some butt in metallic boots, or feel like a princess sporting ballet pumps. Footwear comes in leather as well as in fabrics like brocade; most styles run narrow. You can also check out the San Telmo location at Balcarce 1011. ⊠ *El Salvador 4673, Palermo Viejo* 🕾 *11/4833–6566* ⊕ *www.mishkashoes.com.ar* Ⓜ *D to Scalabrini Ortiz.*

Uma. Light, butter-soft leather takes very modern forms here, with geometric stitching the only adornment on jackets and asymmetrical bags that might come in rich violet in winter and aqua-blue in summer. The top-quality footwear includes teetering heels and ultrasimple boots and sandals with, mercifully, next to no elevation. Ultra-tight jeans, leather boots and tops are also on offer. ⊠ *Paseo Alcorta Mall, Shop 1049, Jerónimo Salguero 3172, at Av. Figueroa Alcorta, Palermo* 🕾 *11/5777–6535* ⊕ *www.uma.com.ar* Ⓜ *D to Bulnes* ⊠ *Galerías Pacífico Mall, Shop 229, Calle Florida 753, at Av. Córdoba, Microcentro* 🕾 *11/5555–5229.*

WINE

Terroir. Wine lovers' dreams come true inside this white-stone town house. Expert English-speaking staffers are on hand to help you make sense of the massive selection of Argentine wine, which includes collector's gems such as the 1999 Angélica Zapata Cabernet Sauvignon. They even arrange private wine-tasting courses to get you up to speed on local vintages: call a week or two before you arrive. ⊠ *Buschiazzo 3040, Palermo* 🕾 *11/4778–3443* ⊕ *www.terroir.com.ar* Ⓜ *D to Palermo.*

SIDE TRIPS FROM BUENOS AIRES

WELCOME TO SIDE TRIPS FROM BUENOS AIRES

TOP REASONS TO GO

★ **Wall of Water:**
Nothing can prepare you for the roaring, thunderous Cataratas del Iguazú (Iguazú Falls). We think you'll agree.

★ **Cowboy Culture:**
No visit to the *pampas* (grasslands) is complete without a stay at an *estancia*, a stately ranch house, like those around San Antonio de Areco. Sleep in an old-fashioned bedroom and share meals with the owners for a true taste of the lifestyle.

★ **Delta Dreaming:**
Speeding through the Paraná River Delta's thousands of kilometers of rivers and streams, we'll forgive you for humming "Ride of the Valkyries"—it does feel very Mekong.

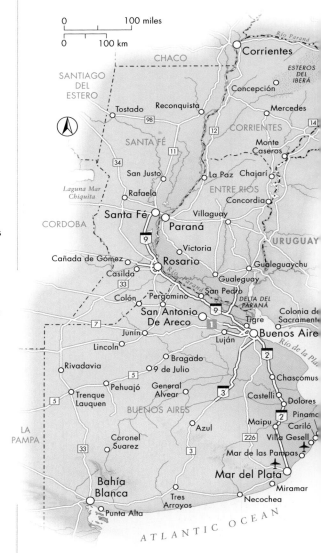

GETTING ORIENTED

3

Argentina's famous pampas begin in Buenos Aires Province—an unending sea of crops and cattle-studded grass that occupies nearly one-quarter of the country's landscapes. Here are the region's most traditional towns, including San Antonio de Areco. Suburban trains connect Buenos Aires to Tigre, close to the labyrinthine waterways of the Paraná Delta, explorable only by boat. On Argentina's northeastern tip, readily accessible by plane, are the jaw-dropping Cataratas del Iguazú.

1 Buenos Aires Province. An hour's drive from Buenos Aires leads to varied sights. The gaucho town of San Antonio de Areco lies northwest of other sites, such as the semitropical delta of the Paraná River, near the town of Tigre, and the provincial capital La Plata.

2 Iguazú Falls (Cataratas del Iguazú). The grandeur of this vast sheet of white water cascading in constant cymbal-banging cacophony makes Niagara Falls and Victoria Falls seem sedate. Allow at least two full days to take in this magnificent sight.

Updated by
Allan Kelin

To hear *porteños* (inhabitants of Buenos Aires) talk of their city, you'd think Argentina stops where Buenos Aires ends. Not far beyond it, however, the skies open up and the *pampas*—Argentina's huge flat grasslands—begin. Pampean traditions are alive and well in farming communities that still dot the plains that make up Buenos Aires Province.

The best known is San Antonio de Areco, a well-preserved provincial town that's making a name for itself as gaucho central. You can ride across the pampas and get a taste of country life (and lots of grass-fed beef) by visiting—or staying at—a traditional *estancia* (ranch).

Ranchland gives way to watery wonders. The quiet suburban town of Tigre is the gateway to the network of rivers and tributaries that form the delta of the Paraná River, lined with luscious tropical vegetation. Low wooden launches speed along its waterways to the houses, restaurants, and lodges built on stilts along the riverbanks.

If you like your natural wonders supersized, take a short flight or a long bus ride to Iguazú Falls, northeast of Buenos Aires in semitropical Misiones Province. Here, straddling the border between Argentina and Brazil, two natural parks contain and protect hundreds of roaring falls and a delicate jungle ecosystem. The spectacle caused Eleanor Roosevelt to exclaim "Poor Niagara!" but most people are simply left speechless by the sheer size and force of the Garganta del Diablo, the grandest falls of them all.

PLANNING

WHEN TO GO

Temperatures in Buenos Aires Province rarely reach extremes. Note that some hotels and restaurants in areas popular with local tourists open *only* on weekends outside of peak season—this coincides with school holidays in summer (January and February), winter (July), and the Easter weekend. You'll get great discounts at those that open midweek in winter.

Early November's a good time to visit San Antonio de Areco, which holds its annual gaucho festival then. Like Buenos Aires, it feels curiously empty in January, when everyone decamps to the coast.

Though Iguazú Falls is thrilling year-round, seasonal rainfall and upstream Brazilian *barrages* (minidams) can affect the amount of water. If you visit between November and March, booking a hotel with airconditioning and a swimming pool is as essential as taking mosquito repellent.

BORDER CROSSINGS

Crossing into Brazil from Argentina can be a thorny issue. By law, all U.S. citizens need a visa to enter Brazil. Visas can sometimes be issued in as little as three hours from the Brazilian consulate in Puerto Iguazú (as opposed to the three days they take in Buenos Aires) but can take up to two days. So it's best to secure your visa, which costs $160, well before you expect to cross. The Buenos Aires consulate also has a reputation for refusing visas to travelers who don't have onward tickets from Brazil.

If you stay in Foz do Iguaçu, travel on to other Brazilian cities, or do a day trip to Brazil by public bus or through an Argentine company, you'll need a visa. There have been reports of getting around this by using a Brazilian travel agent or by using local taxis (both Argentine and Brazilian) that have "arrangements" with border control. Though the practice is well established (most hotels and travel agents in Puerto Iguazú have deals with Brazilian companies and can arrange a visa-less visit), it *is* illegal. Enforcement of the law is generally lax, but sudden crackdowns and on-the-spot fines of hundreds of dollars have been reported.

CAR TRAVEL

Argentina has one of the world's worst records for traffic accidents, and the busy highways of Buenos Aires Province are often where they happen. January and February are the worst times, when drivers anxious to get to and from their holiday destination speed, tailgate, and exercise illegal maneuvers even more alarmingly than usual. If you're driving, do so very defensively and avoid traveling on Friday and Sunday, when traffic is worst.

Expressways and interprovincial routes tend to be atrociously signposted, so take a map. Getting a GPS-equipped rental car costs an extra 35 pesos or so per day: devices usually work well in cities, but the calibration is often a couple of hundred yards off in rural areas. Major routes are usually privately owned, which means frequent tolls. There are sometimes alternative roads to use, but they're generally smaller, slower, and in poor condition. On main roads the speed limit is 80 kph (50 mph), while on highways it's 130 kph (80 mph), though Argentinean drivers rarely pay heed to this.

SAFETY

Provincial towns like San Antonio de Areco are usually extremely safe, and the areas visited by tourists are well patrolled. Puerto Iguazú is fairly quiet in itself, but mugging and theft are common in nearby Foz do Iguaçu in Brazil, especially at night, when its streets are deserted.

WHAT IT COSTS IN ARGENTINE PESOS				
	$	**$$**	**$$$**	**$$$$**
Restaurants	under 30 pesos	30–50 pesos	51–75 pesos	over 75 pesos
Hotels	under 300 pesos	301–500 pesos	501–800 pesos	over 800 pesos

Restaurant prices are per person for a main course at dinner. Hotel prices are for a standard double room in high season.

BUENOS AIRES PROVINCE

Plains fan out where the city of Buenos Aires ends: this is the beginning of the pampas, which derive their name from the native Quechua word for "flat field." All over this fertile earth are signs of active ranch life, from the grazing cattle to the modern-day gauchos. The region is also noted for its crops, although these days the traditional alfalfa, sunflowers, wheat, and corn have largely been replaced by soy.

While Argentina was still a Spanish colony, settlers gradually began to force indigenous tribes away from the pampas near Buenos Aires, making extensive agriculture and cattle breeding possible. (In 1880, during the bloody Campaign of the Desert, the southern pampas were also "cleared" of indigenous tribes.) By the latter half of the 19th century the region had become known as the grain supplier for the world. From 1850 to 1950 more than 400 important estancias were built in Buenos Aires Province alone. Some of these have been modified for use as guest ranches and provide the best glimpse of the fabled pampean lifestyle.

TIGRE AND THE PARANÁ DELTA

30 km (19 miles) northwest of Buenos Aires on the Ruta Panamericana, 35 km (22 miles) northwest of Buenos Aires on Avenida Libertador.

A coastal train ride or a drive through the shady riverside suburbs of Buenos Aires takes you to the riverport town of Tigre, the embarkation point for boats that ply the Delta del Paraná. A couple of hours is plenty of time to visit the town itself from Buenos Aires; allow a whole day if you also plan to explore the delta—a vast maze of canals, tributaries, and river expanding out like the veins of a leaf. Heavy vegetation and rich birdlife (as well as clouds of mosquitoes) make the network of rivers feel tropical. The delta's many islands hide peaceful luxury getaways and cozy riverside restaurants accessible only by boat.

The waterways and close-packed islands that stretch northwest of Tigre are the most accessible part of the 14,000 square km (5,400 square miles) that make up the delta, where roads are replaced by rivers. Churning brown waters and heavy vegetation are vaguely reminiscent of Southeast Asia, though the chic houses and manicured gardens that line the rivers of the Primera Sección (closest to Tigre) are a far cry from Mekong River settlements.

Buenos Aires Area

If you want to take in more of the delta than a short boat trip allows, do as porteños do and combine it with a day's wining and dining at an island restaurant or a weekend at one of the hotels or luxury lodges a little farther afield. Many offer private transportation. The delta gets very hot and humid in summer, and the mosquitoes are ferocious, so bring insect repellent.

GETTING HERE AND AROUND

The cheapest way to get to Tigre by train is on the suburban commuter train from Estación Retiro to the central Estación Tigre. There are about four departures an hour on the Ramal Tigre (Tigre Branch) of the Línea Mitre; round-trip tickets cost 2.70 pesos. Alternatively, take the slick, tourist-oriented Tren de la Costa. It meanders through some of Buenos Aires' most fashionable northern suburbs and along the riverbank, stopping at nine stations before arriving at Estación Delta, near the Río Luján and Puerto de Frutos market. It starts halfway between Buenos Aires and Tigre, so you'll have to first take Línea Mitre, Ramal Mitre from Retiro to Estación Bartolomé Mitre, where you can change to the Tren de la Costa's Maipú Station. Round-trip fare is 40 pesos. The center of Tigre is small enough to walk around easily, but there are also taxis outside both train stations.

The most comfortable—and the most touristy—way to travel the delta's waterways is aboard the two-story catamarans that leave from docks on the Luján River, inside the Puerto de Frutos market. Rio Tur catamarans meander through 14 miles of waterways in about 90 minutes. They're a great way to glimpse delta life, and you'll see houses on stilts and boats piled high with provisions for towns upriver. ■TIP→ The last boat of the day usually catches the sunset.

The low-slung wooden *lanchas col-ectivas* (boat buses) are the cheaper and more authentic way to explore the waterways; locals use them to get around the delta. These leave from the Estación Fluvial (Boat Station), on the other side of the round-about from Estación Tigre, the main train station. The main transport company for the delta is Interisleña, which serves all of the closest islands to the Tigre. Round-trip tickets start at 56 pesos. Líneas Delta Argentino uses similar boats but also runs one-hour tourism-oriented trips every couple of hours on weekends and holidays, which cost 60 pesos. Buy tickets from Booth 6, opposite the jetty. Touts offering private boat trips loiter outside the Tigre tourist board offices at the train and boat stations, but it's best to stick with recognized companies. As the boats leave the delta, they pass the magnificent turn-of-the-20th-century buildings of Tigre's heyday and colorfully painted houses built on stilts to protect them from floods.

ESSENTIALS

Boat Contacts Interisleña. Located within the Estación Fluvial, Inter-isleña runs a fleet of lanchas colectivas. Tell the ticket agent where you're visiting on the delta, and he'll tell you which boat will take you. Round-trip fares start at 56 pesos. ✉ *Estación Fluvial, Mitre 345, Tigre* 🕾 *11/4749–0900.* **Líneas Delta Argentino.** This lanchas colectivas company runs transportation to various islands on the delta but also offers one-hour excursions on weekends and holidays. It's well worth the 60 pesos to get an idea of this aquatic community. ✉ *Estación Fluvial, Mitre 345, Tigre* 🕾 *11/4731–1236* ⊕ *www.lineasdelta.com.ar.*

Train Contacts Línea Mitre 🕾 *11/3220–6300* ⊕ *www.mininterior.gov.ar/sofse.* **Tren de la Costa** 🕾 *11/4002–6000* ⊕ *www.omnilineas.com.ar/buenos-aires/colectivo/linea-tren-de-la-costa.*

Visitor and Tour Info Rio Tur ✉ *Sarmiento and Buenos Aires, on the Río Luján, Tigre* 🕾 *11/4731–0280* ⊕ *www.rioturcatamaranes.com.ar* 🎟 *100 pesos* 🕓 *Weekdays noon–4, weekends 11–6.* **Tigre Tourist Board** ✉ *Estación Fluvial, Bartolome Mitre 305, Tigre* 🕾 *11/4512–4497* ⊕ *www.vivitigre.gov.ar* 🕓 *Daily 8–6.*

EXPLORING

TOP ATTRACTIONS

Museo de Arte de Tigre. An arcade of Doric columns leads from the Luján River to this ornate building, built in 1909 to house a social club and casino. It contains a modest collection of Argentine paintings by artists like Quirós, Castagnino, Soldi, and Quinquela Martín, as well as works portraying life in the delta. The real showstopper, however, is the beautifully restored architecture: a sweeping marble staircase, stained-glass windows, gilt-inlaid columns, and soaring ceilings conspire to form a microcosm of the fin-de-siècle European style adored by the porteño elite. A trim sculpture garden and flower-filled park surround the museum, which is best reached by walking along Paseo Victorica. ⊠ *Paseo Victorica 972, Tigre* ☎ *11/4512–4528* ⊕ *www.mat. gov.ar* ✉ *20 pesos* ⊙ *Wed.–Fri. 9–7, weekends noon–7.*

Museo Del Mate. Maté drinking in Argentina is even more deeply culturally rooted than coffee in the U.S. or even tea in the U.K. The maté gourd and the accompanying flask of hot water is ubiquitous throughout all social classes and age groups, whether one is sipping alone or sharing with a group of friends. The Museo del Mate is a great place to learn about the history of yerba maté —the shrub the bitter tea is made from—and the sometimes very stylish matés it's drunk from. Many of the matés, both antique and modern, are made from beautifully crafted porcelain or metal. Tours are available in English. ⊠ *Lavalle 289, Tigre* ☎ *11/4506–9594* ⊕ *www.elmuseodelmate.com* ✉ *20 pesos* ⊙ *Wed.– Sun. and holidays 11–6.*

Museo Naval de la Nación. Although most of its visitors are into naval, military, or nautical history, this museum's collection will fascinate even those whose interests point elsewhere. The interior of the building, which looks like a hangar-size Victorian barn, is filled with paintings, statues, uniforms, and beautifully crafted model ships. On the grounds are long-retired planes from Argentina's aviation history, including a great example of a North American AT-6 "Texan" from 1939. ⊠ *Av. Victorica 602, Tigre* ☎ *011/4749–0608* ✉ *10 pesos* ⊙ *Tues.–Fri. 8:30– 5:30, weekends and holidays 10:30–6:30.*

Puerto de Frutos. The center of the action at Tigre is its picturesque market. Hundreds of stalls selling furniture, handicrafts, and reasonably priced souvenirs fill the area around the docks along the Río Luján. It's particularly busy on weekends (indeed, many stalls are closed midweek). Grab a quick lunch from stands selling steak and chorizo sandwiches. ⊠ *Sarmiento at Buenos Aires, Tigre* ⊕ *www.puertodefrutos-arg. com.ar* ⊙ *Weekdays 10–6, weekends 10–7.*

WORTH NOTING

FAMILY **Parque de la Costa.** This is Argentina's largest and most modern amusement park. Its main attractions are the two side-by-side roller coasters, El Boomerang and El Desafío. There's also a splashy river ride, swinging inverter ship, and a host of milder thrills, including a petting zoo. Admission is often heavily discounted in winter. ⊠ *Vivanco 1509, Tigre* ☎ *11/4002–6000* ⊕ *www.parquedelacosta.com.ar* ✉ *101 pesos* ⊙ *Jan. and Feb., Tues.–Sun. 11–8; Mar.–Nov., weekends and holidays 11–7.*

Paseo Victorica. Italianate mansions, museums, restaurants, and several rowing clubs dot this paved walkway and waterside park that curves alongside the Río Luján for about 10 blocks. To reach it, cross the bridge next to the roundabout immediately north of Estación Tigre, then turn right and walk five blocks along Avenida Lavalle, which runs along the Río Tigre. ✉ *Along Río Luján between Río Tigre and Río Reconquista, Tigre.*

> **WORD OF MOUTH**
>
> "My brother-in-law had heard such great things about Tigre that he made us go there. It was a really good choice. After a surprisingly easy train ride out, we took a day-long boat tour. It was a beautiful day, and the islands were peaceful and nice to look at." —Messifan

WHERE TO EAT

$$$$ MODERN ARGENTINE 🍴 **Almacén de Flores.** Just about 100 yards west of the Estación Fluvial, this cozy eatery is seemingly miles away from the automobile and boat traffic. In a quiet quarter among a scattering of shops and cafés with bohemian flair, it's a great place to get away from the weekend crowds and enjoy a freshly made salad or sandwich. Aside from the tasty food and friendly staff, you're sure to enjoy being surrounded by freshly cut flowers, as the place is also a florist. [$] *Average main: 120 pesos* ✉ *Blvd. Saenz Peña 1336, Tigre* ☎ *11/5197–4009* 🕒 *Closed Mon. and Tues.*

$$$$ ARGENTINE 🍴 **Il Novo María del Luján.** An expansive terrace overlooking the river is the appropriate backdrop for Tigre's best fish dishes. The kitchen favors elaborate preparations: some are so packed with unlikely ingredients that the fish gets lost; others, such as the sole in lemon-infused cream, are spot-on. Land-based offerings like pork belly braised in beer are equally well executed. Both the terrace and the sunny, peach-colored inside room fill up on weekends, when harried waitstaff often take a long time to bring your orders or even the check. [$] *Average main: 200 pesos* ✉ *Paseo Victorica 611, Tigre* ☎ *11/4731–9613* 🌐 *www.ilnovomariadellujan.com* ✍ *Reservations essential.*

WHERE TO STAY

The city of Tigre is so close to Buenos Aires that there's little reason to stay overnight there. However, a night or two in the Paraná Delta is a rewarding experience.

$$$$ B&B/INN ALL-INCLUSIVE 🏨 **Bonanza Deltaventura.** Thick vegetation surrounds the tomato-red 19th-century country house that's the center of the eco-action at Bonanza Deltaventura. **Pros:** very back-to-nature; great home cooking; lots of sports. **Cons:** rooms get hot in summer; no pool; minimal luxury. [$] *Rooms from: 1175 pesos* ✉ *Arroyo Rama Negra, Tigre* ☎ *11/5603–7176* 🌐 *www.deltaventura.com* 🛏 *4 rooms, 3 guesthouses* 💳 *No credit cards* 🍽 *All-inclusive.*

$$$$ RESORT ALL-INCLUSIVE 🏨 **La Becasina Delta Lodge.** Wooden walkways connect the luxurious bungalows—each with a private riverside deck. **Pros:** total peace and quiet; lots of creature comforts; wild delta surroundings. **Cons:** expensive rates; there's nothing else nearby; lots of mosquitoes. [$] *Rooms*

from: 2400 *pesos* ⊠ *Arroyo las Cañas, San Fernando* ☎ *11/4328–2687* ⊕ *www.labecasina.com* ↝ *15 bungalows* ⊟ *No credit cards* ⦿ *All-inclusive.*

SAN ANTONIO DE ARECO

110 km (68 miles) west of Buenos Aires.

There's no better place to experience traditional provincial life in the pampas than this well-to-do farming town. Grand estancias dot the land in and around San Antonio. Many of the families that own them, which form a sort of local aristocracy, mix lucrative soy farming with estancia tourism. The gauchos who were once ranch hands now cook up huge *asados* (barbecues) and lead horseback expeditions for the ever-growing numbers of foreign tourists. You can visit one for a day—*un día de campo*—or immerse yourself with an overnight visit.

Porteño visitors tend to base themselves in the town itself, which is becoming known for its B&Bs. The fiercely conservative inhabitants have done a good job of preserving the turn-of-the-20th-century Italianate buildings that fill the sleepy *casco histórico* (historic center). Many contain bars and general stores, which maintain their original fittings; others are the workshops of some of the best craftspeople in the country.

In summer the banks of the Río Areco (Areco River), which runs through town, are teeming with picnickers—especially near the center of town, at the Puente Viejo (Old Bridge), which is overlooked by the open-air tables of various riverside parrillas. Nearby is the Museo Gauchesco y Parque Criollo Ricardo Güiraldes, which celebrates historical gaucho life. During the week surrounding November 10, the Día de la Tradición (Day of Tradition) celebrates the gaucho with shows, community barbecues, riding competitions, and a huge crafts fair. It's more fun to visit San Antonio on weekends, as many restaurants are closed Monday to Thursday.

GETTING HERE AND AROUND

To drive to San Antonio de Areco, leave Buenos Aires on RN9, crossing to RN8 when it intersects at Km 35 (total tolls of 15.60 pesos). There are more than 20 buses daily from Buenos Aires' Retiro Station to San Antonio; most are run by Nueva Chevallier, and some by Pullman General Belgrano. Each company operates from its own bus stop in San Antonio. Once you've arrived, the best way to get around is on foot, but you'll need a *remis* (radio taxi) to get to most estancias, though some have their own shuttle service.

ESSENTIALS

Bus Contacts Chevallier ☎ *11/4000–5255* ⊕ *www.nuevachevallier.com.*
Pullman General Belgrano ☎ *11/4018–0010* ⊕ *www.gralbelgrano.com.ar.*
Terminal de Ómnibus Retiro ☎ *11/4310–0700* ⊕ *www.tebasa.com.ar.*

Taxi Contacts Remis Centro ☎ *2326/456–225.*

Visitor Info San Antonio de Areco Tourist Board ⊠ *Blvd. Zerboni at Arellano, San Antonio de Areco* ☎ *2326/453–165* ⊕ *www.sanantoniodeareco.com* ⊙ *Weekdays 8–7, weekends 8–8.*

San Antonio
de Areco

KEY

❶   *Exploring sights*

①   *Hotels & Restaurants*

EXPLORING

TOP ATTRACTIONS

Museo Gauchesco y Parque Criollo Ricardo Güiraldes. Gaucho life of the past is celebrated—and idealized—at this quiet museum on a small estate just outside town. Start at the 150-year-old *pulpería* (the gaucho version of the saloon), complete with dressed-up wax figures ready for a drink. Then head for the museum proper, an early-20th-century replica of a stately 18th-century *casco de estancia* (estancia house). Polished wooden cases contain a collection of traditional gaucho gear: elaborately decorated knives, colorful ponchos, and all manner of elaborate saddlery and bridlery. The museum is named for local writer Ricardo Güiraldes (1886–1927), whose romantic gaucho novels captured the imagination of the Argentinean people. Several rooms document his life in San Antonio de Areco and the real-life gauchos who inspired his work. ⊠ *Camino Ricardo Güiraldes, San Antonio de Areco* ☎ *2326/455–839* ⊕ *www.museoguiraldes.com.ar* ⊠ *Free* ⊙ *Weekdays 10–5.*

Museo Las Lilas de Areco. Although iconic Argentinean painter Florencio Molina Campos was not from San Antonio de Areco, his humorous paintings depict traditional pampas life. The works usually show red-nose, pigeon-toe gauchos astride comical steeds, staggering drunkenly outside taverns, engaged in cockfighting or folk dancing, and taming bucking broncos. The collection is fun and beautifully arranged, and your ticket includes coffee and croissants in the jarringly modern café, which also does great empanadas and sandwiches. Behind its curtained walls lie huge theme park–style re-creations of three paintings. The lively and insightful voiceover explaining them is in Spanish only. ✉ *Moreno 279, San Antonio de Areco* ☎ *2326/456–425* 🌐 *www.museolaslilas.org* 🎟 *65 pesos* 🕒 *June–Sept., Thurs.–Sun. 10–6; Oct.–May, Thurs.–Sun. 10–8.*

3

WORTH NOTING

Museo Taller Draghi. San Antonio is famed for its silversmiths, and the late Juan José Draghi was the best in town. This small museum adjoining his workshop showcases the emergence and evolution of the Argentine silver-work style known as *platería criolla.* The pieces are mostly ornate takes on gaucho-related items: spurs, belt buckles, knives, stirrups, and the ubiquitous matés, some dating from the 18th century. Also on display is the incredibly ornate work of Juan José Draghi himself; you can buy original pieces in the shop. His son and a host of disciples keep the family business alive—they're often at work shaping new pieces at the back of the museum. ✉ *Lavalle 387, San Antonio de Areco* ☎ *2326/454–219* 🌐 *www.draghiplaterosorfebres.com* 🕒 *Daily 9–1 and 4–8.*

WHERE TO EAT

$$$$ ARGENTINE

🍴 **Almacén de Ramos Generales.** Airy and charming, this eatery's classic Argentine fare is consistently good. You can snack on cheeses, olives, prosciutto, salami, and eggplant *en escabeche* (pickled). The *bife de chorizo* (sirloin steak), meanwhile, is perfectly juicy, tender, and flavorful, all the more so when accompanied by wondrous french fries with basil. The country-store-meets-elegant-restaurant atmosphere is just right. No wonder locals and visiting porteños alike vie for tables—on weekends, reservations are essential. [$] *Average main: 120 pesos* ✉ *Zapiola 143, between Lavalle and Sdo. Sombra, San Antonio de Areco* ☎ *2326/456–376* 🌐 *www.ramosgeneralesareco.com.ar* 🕒 *Open daily for lunch and dinner.*

$$$$ MODERN ARGENTINE

🍴 **Café de las Artes.** The charismatic owner of this intimate restaurant clearly gets a kick out of breaking the rules. Instead of the country-style décor favored by most San Antonio eateries, the walls here are painted bordello red and are cluttered with artworks, photos, and souvenirs from all over the world. Pasta dishes are the specialty: expect unusual combinations like duck ravioli in a saffron and walnut sauce or tenderloin and carrot ravioli in spiced tomato. Only the wine list comes up short—literally so—though the few options are very reasonably priced, as is the food. [$] *Average main: 140 pesos* ✉ *Bolívar 70, San Antonio de Areco* ☎ *2326/456–398* 💳 *No credit cards* 🕒 *Closed Mon.–Thurs. No lunch Fri.*

$$$$ ARGENTINE

🍴 **Puesto la Lechuza.** Your first difficult decision at this waterfront eatery is where to sit: one of the breezy outside tables overlooking the river, or in the rustic yellow-painted interior hung with historic pictures of gauchos. Let gaucho-diet principles guide your order—go for the beef asado or *vacío* (on or off the bone, respectively), slow-cooked over hot coals. The little stage where folky guitar players perform in the evenings

Continued on page 149

THE COWBOYS at WORLD'S END

by Victoria Patience

Along a country road, you may come across riders herding cattle. Dressed in baggy pants and shirts, a knife stuck in the back of their belts, these are the descendants of the gauchos, Argentina's cowboys. These men of few words symbolize honor, honesty, and courage— so much so that a favor or good deed is known locally as a *gauchada*.

WHAT'S IN A NAME?

No one can agree on where the word "gaucho" comes from. Some say it's derived from the native Quechua-language word *guachu*, meaning "orphan" or "outcast"; others attribute similar meanings to the French word *gauche*, another suggested source. Yet another theory traces it (via Andalusian Spanish) to the Arabic word *chaouche*, a kind of whip for herding cattle.

Gauchos were the cattle-herding settlers of the pampas (grasslands), renowned for their prowess as horsemen. Most were criollos (Argentina-born descendants of Spanish immigrants) or mestizos (of mixed Spanish and native Argentine descent). They lived in villages but spent much of their time riding the plains, much like North American cowboys.

With the establishment of big estancias (ranches) in the early- and mid-19th century, landowners began taking on gauchos as hired hands. The sheer size of these ranches meant that the gaucho's nomadic lifestyle remained largely unchanged, however.

In the 1860s Argentina's president Domingo Faustino Sarmiento encouraged massive settlement of the pampas, and branded gauchos as barbaric, potentially criminal elements. (Despite being of humble origins, Sarmiento as a snob about anything he saw as uncivilized.) Laws requiring travelers to carry passes ended the gaucho's right to roam. Many more than ever signed on as permanent ranch hands; others were drafted into military service, at times becoming deserters and outlaws.

Vindication came in the late-19th and early-20th century, when a wave of literary works like José Hernández's Martín Fierro and Ricardo Güiraldes's Don Segundo Sombra captured the national imagination with their dramatic, romantic descriptions of gauchos and their nomadic lifestyle. The gaucho—proud, brave, and melancholy—has been a national icon ever since.

Gaucho on an estancia near
El Calafate, Patagonia, Argentina

GAUCHO GEAR

SOMBRERO
Although a sombrero (flat-crowned, wide-brimmed hat) is the most typical style, conical felt hats (shown), berets, flat caps, and even top hats are also worn.

CAMISA
Traditionally smocked shirt with baggy sleeves. Modern gauchos wear regular long-sleeved cotton shirts.

BOMBACHA
Baggy pants cinched at the ankle; the story goes that after the Crimean War, surplus Turkish-style army pants were sold to Argentina by Britain and France. The fashion caught on: no gaucho is seen without these.

BOTAS
Early gauchos wore rough, rawhide boots with open toes or a flip-flop-style thong. Today, gauchos in colder parts of Argentina wear flat-soled, tapered boots, usually with a baggy pirate-style leg.

PAÑUELO
Large, brightly colored kerchief, worn knotted around the neck; some gauchos drape them under their hats to protect their necks from the sun or cold.

CHAQUETA
Jacket; often kept for special occasions, and usually worn short and unbuttoned, to better display the shirt and waistcoat underneath.

CHIRIPÁ
Before bombachas arrived, gauchos used to wind a large swathe of woven fabric (like an oversize loincloth) over thin, long underpants.

FAJA
A long strip of colorful woven fabric once worn to hold the pants up, now mainly decorative and often replaced by a leather belt. Either way, gauchos stick their knives in the back.

ESPUELAS
Spurs; most gauchos favor those with spiked wheel-like designs.

Gaucho traditionally dressed

SUPER GAUCHOS

REBENQUE
A short rawhide crop, often with a decorative metal handle.

PONCHO
Woven from sheep's or llama's wool, usually long and often vertically striped. Some colors denote certain provinces.

ALPARGATAS
Spanish immigrants in the 18th century popularized flat, rope-soled espadrilles in warmer parts of Argentina. Today, rubber-soled versions are more common.

BOLEADORAS
Gauchos adopted this native Argentinian device for catching animals. It's made of two or three stones wrapped in cowhide and mounted at the end of a cowhide cord. You whirl the boleadora then release it at the animal's legs.

LAZO
A braided rawhide lasso used for roping cattle.

CUCHILLO OR FACÓN
No gaucho leaves home without his knife. Indeed, most Argentine men have one to use at barbecues (early gauchos used theirs for fighting, too). Handles are made of wood or horn, blades are triangular.

Unsigned mural of Gauchito Gil, a saint-like character in popular Argentine belief (supposedly a Robin Hood-type outlaw called Antonio Mamerto Gil Núñez).

EL GAUCHITO GIL: legend has it that this gaucho from Corrientes Province was hunted down by a sheriff over a woman. He was hung by his feet from a tree but, just before his throat was cut, he predicted that the sheriff would find his son at home mortally ill and only able to recover if the sheriff prayed to Gil. The prediction came true, and the repentant sheriff spread the word. Today, roadsides all over Argentina are dotted with red-painted shrines to this folk saint. Superstitious locals leave offerings, hoping for help with their problems.

MARTÍN FIERRO: the fictional hero of an eponymous 19th-century epic poem written by José Hernández. Fierro is a poor but noble gaucho who's drafted into the army. He deserts and becomes an outlaw. His pride, independence, and love of the land embody the national ideal of what a man should be. Writer Jorge Luis Borges so loved the poem that he started a literary magazine with the same name.

JUAN MOREIRA: a real-life gaucho who married the daughter of a wealthy landowner, provoking the wrath of a jealous local judge. Wrongly accused of various crimes, Moreira became a fugitive and a famed knife-fighter, killing 16 men before eventually dying in a police ambush in 1874 in the town of Lobos in Buenos Aires Province. A 1973 biographical film by arty local director Leonardo Favio was a box-office smash.

3

IN FOCUS THE COWBOYS AT WORLD'S END

UN DIA DE CAMPO

In the late 19th century, well-to-do European families bought huge blocks of pampas land on which to build estancias, often with luxurious houses reminiscent of the old country. The advent of industrial agriculture has led many estancias to turn to tourism for income; others combine tourism with small-scale farming.

The gauchos who once herded cows now have a new sideline shepherding visitors, putting on riding shows or preparing large-scale *asados* (barbecues). You can visit an estancia for a *día de campo* (day in the country) or to stay overnight or for a weekend. There are estancias for most budgets: some are ultraluxurious bed-and-breakfasts, others are homey, family-run farms.

A day at an estancia typically involves a late breakfast; horseback riding or a long walk; a full-blown asado accompanied by Argentine red wine; and afternoon tea. Longer stays at upscale establishments might also include golf or other sports; at working farms you can feed

Gaucho on an estancia near El Calafate, Patagonia, Argentina

animals or help with the milking. Estancia accommodation generally includes all meals, and although some estancias are close to towns, it's rare to leave the grounds during a stay.

HORSEMANSHIP

During a visit to an estancia, you may see gauchos demonstrating traditional skills and games such as:

Zapateo Criollo: a complicated, rhythmic, foot-stomping dance.

Jineteada or Doma: rodeo, gaucho-style.

La Carrera de Sortija: riders gallop under a bar from which metal rings are hung, trying to spear a ring on a stick as they pass.

Carrera Cuadrera: a short horseback sprint that riders start from a standstill.

Boleadas and Pialadas: catching an animal using boleadoras or a lasso, respectively.

La Maroma: participants hang from a bar or rope and jump onto a horse that gallops beneath them.

GAUCHO GRUB

When gauchos were out on the pampas for weeks, even months, at a time, their diet revolved around one food—beef—and one drink—mate (a type of tea). Times may have changed, but most Argentinians still consume a lot of both.

MAKING THE MOST OF AN ASADO

Whether you're just at someone's home or out on an estancia, a traditional Argentinian asado is a drawn-out affair. All sorts of meats go on the grill initially, including chorizo sausage, black pudding, and sweetbreads. These are grilled and served before the larger cuts. You'll probably also be served a picada (cheese, salami, and other snacks). Follow the local example and go easy on these starters: there's lots more to come.

The main event is, of course, the beef. Huge, grass-fed chunks of it, roasted for at least two hours over hot coals and flavored with little more than salt. While the asador (barbecuer) does his stuff, it's traditional to admire his or her skills; interfering (criticism, touching the meat, or the like) is not part of this tradition. The first meat to be served is often thick-cut ribs, accompanied simply by a mixed salad and bread. Then there will be a pause for digestion, and the asador will serve the choicest cuts: flank or tenderloin, usually. All this is washed down with a robust red wine and, not surprisingly, followed by a siesta.

Gaucho *asado* (barbecue), Argentina

MATE FOR BEGINNERS

Mate (mah-tay) is a strong tea made from the dried leaves of *Ilex paraguariensis*, known as yerba. It's drunk from a gourd (also called a mate) through a metal straw with a filter on the end (the *bombilla*).

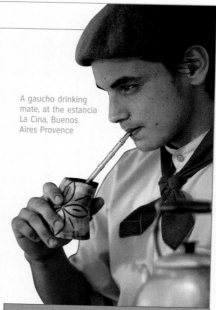

A gaucho drinking mate, at the estancia La Cina, Buenos Aires Provence

Mate has long been a traditional drink for the Guaraní people native to Argentina's northeast. They introduced it to Jesuit missionaries, who learned to cultivate it, and today, most yerba mate is still grown in Misiones and Corrientes provinces. The drink eventually became popular throughout Argentina, Uruguay, and southern Brazil.

Much like tea in England, mate serves as the basis of social interaction: people drink it at any hour of the day. Several drinkers share the same gourd, which is refilled and passed round the group. It's often extended to strangers as a welcoming gesture. If you're shown this hospitality be sure to wait your turn, drink all the mate in the gourd fairly quickly, and hand the gourd directly back to the *cebador* (server). Don't pour yourself a mate if someone else is the cebador, and avoid wiping or wiggling the straw around. Also, you don't say "gracias" until you've had your fill.

WHAT'S IN A MATE?

Caffeine: 30 mg per 8-oz serving (versus 47 mg in tea and 100 mg in coffee)

Vitamins:
A, C, E, B1, B2, B3, B5, B complex

Minerals:
Calcium, manganese, iron, selenium, potassium, magnesium, phosphorus, zinc

Antioxidant properties: similar to green tea

SERVING MATE

1) Heat a kettle of water to just before boiling (176°F/80°C)—boiling water ruins yerba.

2) Fill ⅔ of the gourd with yerba.

3) Without the bombilla in place, cover the gourd with your hand, and turn it quickly upside down (to get rid of any fine yerba dust that can block the bombilla).

4) For some reason, yerba never sits flat in the gourd; pour some hot water in the empty space left by the slightly slanting yerba leaves. Let the yerba swell a little, cover the top of the bombilla with your thumb, and drive it firmly into the leaves.

5) Finish filling the gourd with water, pouring it in slowly near the bombilla's base. (Some people also add sugar at this point.)

6) Drink all the mate in the gourd (the cebador traditionally drinks first, so the mate isn't so bitter when brewed for others) and repeat Step 5, passing the gourd to the next drinker—and so on—until the yerba mate loses its flavor.

might look touristy, but locals love the singsong here as much as visitors. Weekend reservations are essential. $ *Average main: 125 pesos* ✉ *Victorino Althaparro 423, San Antonio de Areco* ☎ *2326/1540–5745* 🚫 *No credit cards.*

WHERE TO STAY

$$$
B&B/INN
🔲 **Antigua Casona.** The brass bedsteads, antique wardrobes, and embroidered linens of this small B&B make you feel like you're staying in a Merchant-Ivory film. **Pros:** vintage furnishings; sunny patio; two blocks from the main square. **Cons:** high ceilings make some rooms drafty in winter; getting to the bathroom of one room involves crossing the (admittedly pretty) kitchen. $ *Rooms from: 700 pesos* ✉ *Segundo Sombra 495, at Bolívar, San Antonio de Areco* ☎ *2326/453–148* ⊕ *www. antiguacasona.com* ↩ *6 rooms* 🚫 *No credit cards* ❙◯❙ *Breakfast.*

$$$$
B&B/INN
🔲 **La Bamba de Areco.** Dating from the 1830s, the venerable La Bamba de Areco was once an important stop along the road from Buenos Aires to the northern reaches of Argentina. **Pros:** plenty of peace and quiet; gorgeous décor; great for outdoors lovers. **Cons:** might be too isolated for some. $ *Rooms from: US$700* ✉ *Ruta 31, San Antonio de Areco* ☎ *2326/454–895* ⊕ *www.labambadeareco.com* ↩ *11 rooms* ❙◯❙ *All meals.*

$$$$
HOTEL
🔲 **Patio de Moreno.** Being in the pampas doesn't mean you have to forget about slick design: this 1910 town house has been transformed into the coolest hotel around. **Pros:** two blocks from main street; beautifully designed rooms and lobby; spacious bathrooms. **Cons:** rooms overlooking street can be noisy; families might be uncomfortable with very adult vibe; service is professional but impersonal. $ *Rooms from: 1200 pesos* ✉ *Moreno 251, at San Martín, San Antonio de Areco* ☎ *2326/455–197* ⊕ *www.patiodemoreno.com* ↩ *11 rooms* ❙◯❙ *Breakfast.*

NIGHTLIFE

Pulpería, almacén (general store), and *despacho de bebidas* (drinks counter) are some of the labels you might find on San Antonio's many traditional bars. Some genuinely haven't changed in 50 years (neither have their clientele), and others are well-intentioned re-creations; all provide truly atmospheric surroundings for a coffee or a drink.

La Cervecería. Silver and leather aren't the only hand-crafted products in San Antonio. Seven varieties of artisanal beer, brewed on site, have made a name for La Cervecería. The amber-color Scottish ale packs a punch in winter; the paler pilsner's ideal for cooling off in summer. Pizzas, sandwiches, and other snacks accompany them. ✉ *Zapiola 76, San Antonio de Areco* ☎ *15/5163–6764.*

La Esquina de Mertí. Candy jars, old bottles, and a gleaming antique cash register sit atop the decades-old zinc-top bar of La Esquina de Mertí, a gorgeous old café on Plaza Arellano. The owners seem more preoccupied with the charm of the building than that of the waitstaff, so stick with drinks—mugs of icy beer or Cinzano and soda are the local favorites. ✉ *Arellano 149, at Segundo Sombra, San Antonio de Areco* ☎ *2326/456–705.*

SHOPPING

San Antonio de Areco is an excellent place to pick up high-quality hand-icrafts and gifts, especially traditional silverware and leather goods. Workshops that double as stores fill the old houses lining Calle Alsina and other streets leading off Plaza Arellano, the main square.

Cristina Giordano. The handwoven belts and ponchos Cristina Giordano creates in soft, naturally dyed fibers are fit to hang on the wall as art, and have justifiably made her San Antonio's best-known exponent of the traditional craft of weaving. ⊠ *Sarmiento 112, San Antonio de Areco* ☏ *2326/452–829* ⊕ *www.telarcriolloypampa.com.ar.*

Gustavo Stagnaro. Gustavo Stagnaro is a big name in San Antonio silversmithing. His majestic corner store sells gaucho knives, no-nonsense silver jewelry, and maté paraphernalia. ⊠ *Arellano at Matheu, San Antonio de Areco* ☏ *2326/454–801* ⊕ *www.stagnaro.com.ar.*

La Olla de Cobre. All of the mouthwatering chocolates and *alfajores* (dulce de leche sandwiched between two cookies) at La Olla de Cobre are handmade on the premises. Best of all, you can sample at leisure before you buy. ⊠ *Matheu 433, San Antonio de Areco* ☏ *2326/453–105* ⊕ *www.laolladecobre.com.ar* ⊙ *Closed Tues.*

Platería de Campo. All the gaucho accessories you can think of—including knives, belt buckles, and kerchief rings—are exquisitely made in silver at Platería del Campo. ⊠ *Alsina 86, San Antonio de Areco* ☏ *2326/456–825* ⊕ *www.plateriadecampo.com.ar* ⊙ *Closed Sun.*

IGUAZÚ FALLS

1,358 km (843 miles) north of Buenos Aires; 637 km (396 miles) west of Curitiba; 544 (338 miles) west of Vila Velha.

Iguazú consists of some 275 separate waterfalls—in the rainy season there are as many as 350—that plunge more than 200 feet onto the rocks below. They cascade in a deafening roar at a bend in the Iguazú River (Río Iguazú in Spanish, Rio Iguaçu in Portuguese) where the borders of Argentina, Brazil, and Paraguay meet. Dense, lush jungle surrounds the falls: here the tropical sun and the omnipresent moisture produce a towering pine tree in two decades instead of the seven it takes in, say, Scandinavia. By the falls and along the roadside, rainbows and butterflies are set off against vast walls of red earth, which is so ubiquitous that eventually even paper currency in the area turns red from exposure to the stuff.

The falls and the lands around them are protected by Argentina's Parque Nacional Iguazú (where the falls are referred to by their Spanish name, the Cataratas de Iguazú) and by Brazil's Parque Nacional do Iguaçu (where the falls go by the Portuguese name of Cataratas do Iguaçu).

To visit the falls, you can base yourself in the Argentine town of Puerto Iguazú, or its sprawling Brazilian counterpart, the city of Foz do Iguaçu. The two cities are 18 km (11 miles) and 25 km (15 miles) northwest

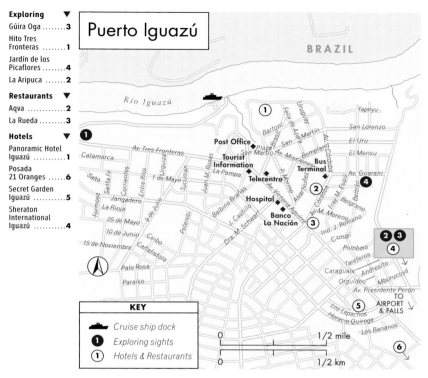

Puerto Iguazú

BRAZIL

Río Iguazú

Post Office
Plaza
Tourist
Information
Telecentro
Hospital
Banco
La Nación
Bus
Terminal

KEY

Cruise ship dock

❶ Exploring sights

① Hotels & Restaurants

0   1/2 mile

0   1/2 km

of the falls, respectively, and are connected by an international bridge, the Puente Presidente Tancredo Neves.

PUERTO IGUAZÚ, ARGENTINA

Originally a port for shipping wood from the region, Puerto Iguazú now revolves around tourism. This was made possible in the early 20th century when Victoria Aguirre, a wealthy visitor from Buenos Aires, funded the building of a road to the falls. Despite the constant stream of visitors from Argentina and abroad, Puerto Iguazú remains small and sleepy. Many of its secondary roads still aren't paved.

Many travelers to the falls—including those from Brazil—opt to stay on the Argentine side of the border because it's less expensive than the Brazilian side. The town is also a good place to wind down after a day or two of high-energy adventure before heading back to Buenos Aires. So spare some time to experience being surrounded by hummingbirds in a garden, or just grab some *helado* (ice cream) and meander to el Hito Tres Fronteras.

GETTING HERE AND AROUND

Aerolíneas Argentinas flies four to five times daily between Aeroparque Jorge Newbery in Buenos Aires and the Aeropuerto Internacional de Puerto Iguazú, which is about 20 km (12 miles) southeast of Puerto Iguazú; the trip takes 1¾ hours. LAN does the same trip two or three times daily. Normal rates start at about 800 pesos each way. Four Tourist Travel runs shuttle buses from the airport to hotels in Puerto Iguazú. They leave after every flight lands and cost 25 pesos. Taxis to Puerto Iguazú cost 100 pesos.

Vía Bariloche operates several daily buses between the Retiro bus station in Buenos Aires and the Puerto Iguazú Terminal de Omnibus in the center of town. The trip takes 16–18 hours, so it's worth paying the little extra for *coche cama* (sleeper) or *cama ejecutivo* (deluxe sleeper) services, which cost about 903 pesos one-way (regular semi-cama services cost around 410 pesos). You can travel direct to Rio de Janeiro (22 hours) and São Paolo (15 hours) with Crucero del Norte; the trips cost 1,035 and 904 pesos, respectively.

From Puerto Iguazú to the falls or the hotels along RN12, take El Práctico from the terminal or along Avenida Victoria Aguirre. Buses leave every 15 minutes from 7 to 7 and cost 20 pesos round-trip.

There's little point in renting a car around Puerto Iguazú: daily rentals start at 260 to 300 pesos, more than twice what you pay for a taxi between the town and the falls.

Crucero del Norte runs an hourly cross-border public bus service (60 pesos) between the bus stations of Puerto Iguazú and Foz do Iguaçu. Locals don't have to get on and off for immigration, but be sure you do so. To reach the Argentine falls, change to local minibus service El Práctico at the intersection with RN12 on the Argentine side. For the Brazilian park, change to a local bus at the Avenida Cataratas roundabout.

Argentinean travel agency Sol Iguazú Turismo organizes door-to-door transport to both sides of the falls, and can reserve places on the Iguazú Jungle Explorer trips.

Bus Contacts Crucero del Norte ☎ *11/4315–1652 in Buenos Aires, 3757/421–916 in Puerto Iguazú* ⊕ *www.crucerodelnorte.com.ar.* **Four Tourist Travel** ☎ *3757/420–681.* **Vía Bariloche** ☎ *0810/333–7575 in Buenos Aires, 3757/420–854 in Puerto Iguazú* ⊕ *www.viabariloche.com.ar.*

Visitor Info Cataratas del Iguazú Visitors Center ⊠ *Off Ruta Nacional 101, Puerto Iguazú* ☎ *3757/491–469* ⊕ *www.iguazuargentina.com* ☻ *Mar.–Aug., daily 8–6; Sept.–Feb., daily 8–8.* **Iguazú Tourist Information** ☎ *3757/491-469* ⊕ *www.iguazuargentina.com.* **Puerto Iguazú Tourist Office** ⊠ *Av. Victoria Aguirre 311, Puerto Iguazú* ☎ *3757/420–800* ⊕ *www.iguazuturismo.gov.ar* ☻ *Daily 7–1 and 2–9.* **Sol Iguazú Turismo** ☎ *3757/421–008* ⊕ *www.soliguazu. com.ar.*

EXPLORING

The falls are not the only sites to see in these parts, though few people actually have time (or make time) to go see others.

TOP ATTRACTIONS

Güira Oga. Although Iguazú Falls is home to around 450 bird species, the parks are so busy these days that you'd be lucky to see so much as a feather. It's another story at Güira Oga, which means "House of the Birds" in Guaraní. Birds that were injured, displaced by deforestation, or confiscated from traffickers are brought here for treatment. The large cages also contain many species you rarely see in the area, including the fearsome harpy eagle and the gorgeous red macaw. The sanctuary is in a forested plot just off RN12, halfway between Puerto Iguazú and the falls. The entrance price includes a 90-minute guided visit (in English and Spanish). ✉ *RN12, Km 5, Puerto Iguazú* ☎ *3757/423–980* 🌐 *www.guiraoga.com.ar* 🎟 *75 pesos* 🕘 *Daily 8:30–5.*

3

WORTH NOTING

Jardín de los Picaflores. With more than 400 species of birds in the national parks surrounding Iguazú Falls, bird-watchers will be kept happily busy. After trekking in the forest for a day or two, the sight of scores of hummingbirds in a more intimate setting might be a birder's dream. This tiny garden north of Puerto Iguazú serves as more of a feeding station than a refuge, but it's busy with the little powerhouses zipping about. ✉ *Fray Luis Beltran 150, Puerto Iguazú* ☎ *3757/424–081* 🎟 *30 pesos* 🕘 *Daily 8:30–6.*

Hito Tres Fronteras. This viewpoint west of the town center stands high above the turbulent reddish-brown confluence of the Iguazú and Paraná rivers, which also form the Triple Frontera, or Triple Border. A mini pale-blue-and-white obelisk reminds you you're in Argentina; across the Iguazú River is Brazil's green-and-yellow equivalent; farther away, across the Paraná, is Paraguay's, painted red, white, and blue. A row of overpriced souvenir stalls stands alongside it. ✉ *Av. Tres Fronteras, Puerto Iguazú.*

La Aripuca. It looks like a cross between a log cabin and the Pentagon, but this massive wooden structure—which weighs 551 tons—is a large-scale replica of a Guaraní bird trap. La Aripuca officially showcases different local woods, supposedly for conservation purposes—ironic, given the huge trunks used to build it and the overpriced wooden furniture that fills the gift shop. ✉ *RN12, Km 5, Puerto Iguazú* ☎ *3757/423–488* 🌐 *www.aripuca.com.ar* 🎟 *30 pesos* 🕘 *Daily 9–6.*

WHERE TO EAT

$$$$ MODERN ARGENTINE

🍴 **Aqva.** Locals are thrilled: finally, a date-night restaurant in Puerto Iguazú. Although the high-ceiling split-level cabin seats too many to be truly intimate, the owners make up for it with well-spaced tables, discreet service, and low lighting. Softly gleaming timber from different local trees lines the walls, roof, and floor. Local river fish like *surubí* and *dorado* are the specialty: have them panfried, or, more unusually, as pasta fillings. Forget being romantic at dessert time: the chef's signature dessert, fresh mango and pineapple with a torrontés sabayon, is definitely worth keeping to yourself. Reservations are essential on weekends. [$] *Average main: 220 pesos* ✉ *Av. Córdoba at Carlos Thays, Puerto Iguazú* ☎ *3757/422–064* 🌐 *www.aqvarestaurant.com.*

$$$$ ARGENTINE 🍴 **La Rueda.** This parrilla is so popular that it starts serving dinner as early as 7:30 pm—teatime by Argentine custom. The local beef isn't quite up to Buenos Aires standards, but La Rueda's perfectly cooked bife de chorizo is one of the best in town. Locally caught surubí is another house specialty, but skip the traditional Roquefort sauce, which overwhelms the fish's flavor. The surroundings stay true to the restaurant's rustic roots: hefty tree trunks hold up the bamboo-lined roof, and the walls are adorned by a curious wooden frieze carved by a local artist. [$] *Average main: 200 pesos* ✉ *Av. Córdoba 28, Puerto Iguazú* ☎ *3757/422–531* 🌐 *www.larueda1975.com.ar* ✍ *Reservations essential* 🕒 *No lunch Mon. and Tues.*

WHERE TO STAY

$$$$ HOTEL 🏨 **Panoramic Hotel Iguazú.** The falls aren't the only good views in Iguazú: half the rooms of this chic hotel look onto the churning, jungle-framed waters of the Iguazú and Paraná rivers. **Pros:** river views; great attention to detail; the gorgeous pool. **Cons:** the in-house casino makes the lobby noisy; staff can seem indifferent; in-house transportation is overpriced. [$] *Rooms from: 1627 pesos* ✉ *Paraguay 372, Puerto Iguazú* ☎ *3757/498–100, 3757/498–050* 🌐 *www.panoramic-hoteliguazu.com* 🛏 *91 rooms* 🍽 *Breakfast.*

$$$ B&B/INN 🏨 **Posada 21 Oranges.** Friendly owners Rémy and Romina give you a warm welcome at this rootsy B&B, which is surrounded by a lush garden. **Pros:** wonderfully helpful and attentive owners; peaceful surroundings; abundant homemade breakfasts served on a terrace in the garden. **Cons:** too far from the town center to walk to; low on luxury. [$] *Rooms from: 692 pesos* ✉ *Montecarlo s/n, near RN12, Km 5, Puerto Iguazú* ☎ *3757/494–014* 🌐 *www.21oranges.com* 🛏 *10 rooms* 💳 *No credit cards* 🍽 *Breakfast.*

$$$$ B&B/INN 🏨 **Secret Garden Iguazú.** Dense tropical vegetation overhangs the wooden walkway that leads to this tiny guesthouse's three rooms, tucked away in a pale-blue clapboard house. **Pros:** wood deck overlooking the back-to-nature garden; owner's charm and expert mixology; home-away-from-home vibe. **Cons:** the three rooms book up fast; no pool; comfortable but not luxurious. [$] *Rooms from: 936 pesos* ✉ *Los Lapachos 623, Puerto Iguazú* ☎ *3757/423–099* 🌐 *www.secretgardeniguazu.com* 🛏 *3 rooms* 💳 *No credit cards* 🍽 *Breakfast.*

$$$$ HOTEL 🏨 **Sheraton International Iguazú.** That thundering you hear in the distance lets you know how close this hotel is to the falls—the lobby opens right onto the park trails, and half the rooms have big balconies with fabulous falls views. **Pros:** the falls are on your doorstep; great buffet breakfasts; well-designed spa. **Cons:** rooms are in need of a complete makeover; mediocre food and service at dinner; other restaurants are an expensive taxi ride away. [$] *Rooms from: 3132 pesos* ✉ *Within Parque Nacional Iguazú, off RN101, Puerto Iguazú* ☎ *3757/491–800* 🌐 *www.sheraton.com* 🛏 *176 rooms, 4 suites* 🍽 *Breakfast.*

Continued on page 162

By Victoria Patience

IGUAZÚ FALLS

Big water. That's what *y-guasu*—the name given to the falls by the indigenous Guaraní people—means. As you approach, a thundering fills the air and steam rises above the trees. Then the jungle parts. Spray-soaked and speechless, you face the Devil's Throat, and it's clear that "big" doesn't come close to describing this wall of water.

Taller than Niagara, wider than Victoria, Iguazú's raging, monumental beauty is one of nature's most awe-inspiring sights. The Iguazú River, on the border between Argentina and Brazil, plummets 200 feet to form the Cataratas de Iguazú (as the falls are known in Spanish) or Foz do Iguaçu (their Portuguese name). Considered to be one waterfall, Iguazú is actually made up of around 275 individual drops, that stretch along 2.7 km (1.7 mi) of cliff-face. Ranging from picturesque cascades to immense cataracts, this incredible variety is what makes Iguazú so special. National parks in Brazil and Argentina protect the falls and the flora and fauna that surround them. Exploring their jungle-fringed trails can take two or three days: you get right alongside some falls, gaze down dizzily into others, and can take in the whole spectacle from afar. You're sure to come across lizards, emerald- and sapphire-colored hummingbirds, clouds of butterflies, and scavenging raccoonlike coatis. You'll also glimpse monkeys and toucans, if you're lucky.

GEOLOGY 101

Over 100 million years ago, lava surged up through cracks in the earth's crust near Iguazú. It spread out over the surrounding area, forming three layers of basalt (a dark, fine-grained rock) tens of meters high. The Iguazú River, which starts 1,200 km (745 mi) east, flowed over this. Later, the movement of tectonic plates raised parts of the surface, which became stepped. As the river flowed over these steps it eroded the rock surface it fell on even more, and over the next few million years, the waters carved out what are now the falls.

WHEN TO GO

Time of year	Advantages	Disadvantages
Nov.—Feb.	High rainfall in December and January, so expect lots of water.	Hot and sticky. December and January are popular with local visitors. High water levels stop Zodiac rides.
Mar.—Jun.	Increasingly cooler weather. Fewer local tourists. Water levels are usually good.	Too cold for some people, especially when you get wet. Occasional freak water shortages.
Jul.—Oct.	Cool weather.	Low rainfall in July and August—water levels can be low. July is peak season for local visitors.

WHERE TO GO: ARGENTINA VS. BRAZIL

Argentines and Brazilians can fight all day about who has the best angle on the falls. But the two sides are so different that comparisons are academic. To really say you've done Iguazú (or Iguaçu), you need to visit both. If you twist our arm, we'll say the Argentine side is a better experience with lots more to do, but (and this is a big "but") the Brazilian side gives you a tick in the box and the best been-there-done-that photos. It's also got more non-falls-related activities (but you have to pay extra for them).

	ARGENTINA	BRAZIL
Park Name	Parque Nacional Iguazú	Parque Nacional do Iguaçu
The experience	Up close and personal (you're going to get wet).	What a view!
The falls	Two-thirds are in Argentina including Garganta del Diablo, the star attraction.	The fabulous panoramic perspective of the Garganta do Diablo is what people really come for.
Timing	One day to blitz the main attractions. Two days to explore fully.	Half a day to see the falls; all day if you do other activities.
Other activities	Extensive self-guided hiking and Zodiac rides.	Organized hikes, Zodiac rides, boat rides, helicopter rides, rafting, abseiling.
Park size	67,620 hectares (167,092 acres)	182,262 hectares (450,379 acres)
Animal species	80 mammals/450 birds	50 mammals/200 birds

VITAL STATISTICS

Number of falls: 160—275*	Total length: 2.7 km (1.7 mi)	Average Flow: 396,258 gallons per second Peak Flow: 1,717,118 gallons per second
Major falls: 19	Height of Garganta del Diablo: 82 m (270 feet)	Age: 120—150 million years

*Depending on water levels

IGUAZÚ ITINERARIES

LIGHTNING VISIT. If you only have one day, limit your visit to the Argentine park. Arrive when it opens, and get your first look at the falls aboard one of Iguazú Jungle Explorer's Zodiacs. The rides finish at the Circuito Inferior: take a couple of hours to explore this. (Longer summer opening hours give you time to squeeze in the **Isla San Martín.**) Grab a quick lunch at the Dos Hermanas snack bar, then blitz the shorter Circuito Superior. You've kept the best

Tren Ecologico de la Selva

for last: catch the train from **Estación Cataratas** to **Estación Garganta del Diablo,** where the trail to the viewing platform starts (allow at least two hours for this).

BEST OF BOTH SIDES. Two days gives you enough time to see both sides of the falls. Visit the Brazilian park on your second day to get the panoramic take on what you've experienced up-close in Argentina. If you arrive at 9 AM, you've got time to walk the entire trail, take photos, have lunch in the Porto Canoas service area, and be back at the park entrance by 1 PM. You could spend the afternoon doing excursions and activities from Macuco Safari and Ma-

KEY

♿	Wheelchair-accessible
🍴	Restaurant
🌀	Scenic Viewpoint
---	Walking/Hiking Trails
🚢	Ferry Lines
⊢⊢⊢	Rail Lines

Estación Garganta del Diablo

Garganta del Diablo

Garganta del Diablo

ARGENTINA

Parque Nacional do Iguaçu

Isla San Martín

BRAZIL

Río Iguazú

cuco EcoAventura, or visiting the Itaipú dam. Alternatively, you could keep the visit to Brazil for the afternoon of the second day, and start off with a lightning return visit to the Argentine park and see the **Garganta del Diablo** (left) with the sun rising behind it.

SEE IT ALL. With three days you can explore both parks at a leisurely pace. Follow the one-day itinerary, then return to the Argentine park on your second day. Make a beeline for the Gar-

ganta del Diablo, which looks different in the mornings, then spend the afternoon exploring the **Sendero Macuco** (and Isla San Martín, if you didn't have time on the first day). You'll also have time to visit Güira Oga bird sanctuary or La Aripuca (both on RN 12) afterwards. You could spend all of your third day in the Brazilian park, or just the morning, giving you time to catch an afternoon flight or bus.

Walkway view at
Gargánta del Diablo

Estación
Central

Estación
Cataratas

Circuito
Superior

Parque Nacional
Iguazú

Circuito
Inferior

Dos Hermanas

VISITING THE PARKS

Visitors gaze at the falls in Parque Nacional Iguazú.

Argentina's side of the falls is in the **Parque Nacional Iguazú,** which was founded in 1934 and declared a World Heritage Site in 1984. The park is divided into two areas, each of which is organized around a train station: Estación Cataratas or the Estación Garganta del Diablo. (A third, Estación Central, is near the park entrance.)

Paved walkways lead from the main entrance past the **Visitor Center,** called *Yvyrá Retá*—"country of the trees" in Guaraní (☎ 3757/49-1469 ⊕ www.iguazuargentina. com ✉ 170 pesos ☉ Mar.–Aug. 8–6; Sept.–Feb. 8–8). Colorful visual displays provide a good explanation of the region's ecology and human history. To reach the park proper, you cross through a small plaza containing a food court, gift shops, and ATM. From the nearby Estación Central, the gas-propelled Tren de la Selva (Jungle Train) departs every 20 minutes.

In Brazil, the falls can be seen from the **Parque Nacional Foz do Iguaçu** (☎ 45/3521–4400 ⊕ www.cataratasdoiguacu.com.br ✉ R$40 ☉ Apr.–Sep 9–5; Oct.–Mar. 9–6). Much of the park is protected rain forest—off-limits to visitors and home to the last viable populations of panthers as well as rare flora. Buses and taxis drop you off at a vast, plaza alongside the park entrance building. As well as ticket booths, there's an ATM, a snack bar, gift shop, and information and currency exchange. Next to the entrance turnstiles is the small **Visitor Center,** where helpful geological models explain how the falls were formed. Double-decker buses run every 15 minutes between the entrance and the trailhead to the falls, 11 km (7 mi) away; the buses stop at the entrances to excursions run by private operators Macuco Safari and Macuco Ecoaventura (these aren't included in your ticket). The trail ends in the **Porto Canoas** service area. There's a posh linen-service restaurant with river views, and two fast-food counters the with tables overlooking the rapids leading to the falls.

VISAS

U.S. citizens don't need a visa to visit Argentina as tourists, but the situation is more complicated in Brazil. ⇨ See the planning section at the beginning of the chapter.

EXCURSIONS IN AND AROUND THE PARKS

A Zodiac trip to the falls.

Iguazú Jungle (☎ 3757/42–1696 ⊕ www.iguazujungle.com) runs trips within the Argentine park. Their standard trip, the Gran Aventura, costs 450 pesos and includes a truck ride through the forest and a Zodiac ride to San Martín, Bossetti, and the Salto Tres Mosqueteros (be ready to get soaked). The truck carries so many people that most animals are scared away: you're better off buying the 75-peso boat trip—Aventura Nautica—separately.

You can take to the water on the Brazilian side with **Macuco Safari** (☎ 045/3574–4244 ⊕ www.macucosafari.com.br). Their signature trip is a Zodiac ride around (and under) the Salto Tres Mosqueteros for R$170. You get a more sedate ride on the Iguaçu Explorer, a 3½ hour trip up the river.

It's all about adrenaline with **Iguazú Forest** (☎ 3757/42–1140 ⊕ www.iguazuforest.com). Their full day expedition involves kayaking, abseiling, waterfall-climbing, mountain-biking, and canopying all within the Argentine park.

In Brazil, **Cânion Iguaçu** (☎ 045/3529–6040 ⊕ www.campodedesafios.com.br) offers rafting and canopying, as well as abseiling over

the river from the Salto San Martín. They also offer wheelchair-compatible equipment.

Argentine park ranger Daniel Somay organizes two-hour Jeep tours with an ecological focus through his Puerto Iguazú–based **Explorador Expediciones** (☎ 3757/49–1469 ⊕ www.rainforest.iguazuargentina.com). The tours cost 260 pesos and include detailed explanations of the Iguazú ecosystem and lots of photo ops. A specialist leads the birdwatching trips, which cost 320 pesos and include the use of binoculars.

Macuco Ecoaventura (☎ 045/3529–9665 ⊕ www.macucoecoaventura.com.br) is one of the official tour operators within the Brazilian park. Their Trilha do Pozo Negro combines a 9-km guided hike or bike ride with a scary boat trip along the upper river (the bit before the falls for R$135). The aptly-named Floating trip is more leisurely; shorter jungle hikes are also offered.

ON THE CATWALK

You spend most of your visit to the falls walking the many trails and catwalks, so be sure to wear comfortable shoes.

FOZ DO IGUAÇU, BRAZIL

The construction of the Itaipú Dam (now the world's second largest) in 1975 transformed Foz do Iguaçu into a bustling city with seven times more people than nearby Puerto Iguazú. It's precisely because of the city's size that many visitors to the falls arrange accommodations in or near Foz do Iguaçu. After daytime adventures in the national park, the city's nightlife extends the fun. Aside from pubs, clubs, and all kinds of live music, there's even a samba show.

GETTING HERE AND AROUND

There are direct flights between Foz do Iguaçu and São Paulo (1½ hours; $230), Rio de Janeiro (2 hours; $260), and Curitiba (1 hour; $280) on TAM, which also has connecting flights to Salvador, Recife, Brasilia, other Brazilian cities, and Buenos Aires. Low-cost airline GOL operates slightly cheaper direct flights on the same three routes.

The Aeroporto Internacional Foz do Iguaçu is 13 km (8 miles) southeast of downtown Foz. The 20-minute taxi ride should cost R$40 to R$50; the 45-minute regular bus ride about R$2.60. Note that several major hotels are on the highway to downtown, so a cab ride from the airport to these may be less than R$30. A cab ride from downtown hotels directly to the Parque Nacional in Brazil costs about R$70.

Via bus, the trip between São Paolo and Foz do Iguaçu takes 15 hours (R$153). The Terminal Rodoviário in Foz do Iguaçu is 5 km (3 miles) northeast of downtown. There are regular buses into town; they stop at the Terminal de Transportes Urbano (local bus station, often shortened to TTU) at Avenida Juscelino Kubitschek and Rua Mem de Sá. From platform 2, Bus No. 120 (labeled "Parque Nacional") also departs every 15 minutes (from 7 to 7) to the visitor center at the park entrance; the fare is R$2.60. The buses run along Avenida Juscelino Kubitschek and Avenida Jorge Schimmelpfeng, where you can also flag them down.

There's no real reason to rent a car in Foz do Iguaçu, as you can't cross the border in a rental car. There are *pontos de taxi* (taxi stands) at intersections all over town. Hotels and restaurants can call you a cab, but you can also hail them on the street.

Bus Contacts Pluma ☏ *045/3522–2988 in Foz do Iguaçu* ⊕ *www.pluma.com.br.*

Visitor Info Foz do Iguaçu Tourist Office ✉ *Praça Getúlio Vargas 69* ☏ *45/3521–1455* ⊕ *www.iguassu.tur.br* ☉ *8–6.*

EXPLORING

TOP ATTRACTIONS

Itaipú Dam and Hydroelectric Power Plant. It took more than 30,000 workers eight years to build this 8-km (5-mile) dam, voted one of the Seven Wonders of the Modern World by the American Society of Civil Engineers. The monumental structure, which produces 25% of Brazil's electricity and 78% of Paraguay's, was the largest hydroelectric power plant in the world until China's Three Gorges Dam was completed.

You get plenty of insight into how proud this makes the Brazilian government—and some idea of how the dam was built—during the 30-minute video that precedes the hour-long guided panoramic bus

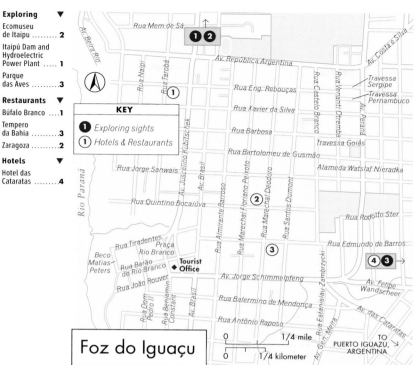

KEY

1 Exploring sights
① Hotels & Restaurants

Foz do Iguaçu

3

tours of the complex. Although commentaries are humdrum, the sheer size of the dam is an impressive sight. To see more than a view over the spillways, consider the special tours, which take you inside the cavernous structure and into the control room. Night tours—which include a light-and-sound show—begin at 8 on Friday and Saturday, 9 during the summer months (reserve ahead). ⊠ *Av. Tancredo Neves 6702, Foz do Iguaçu* ☎ *0800/645–4645* ⊕ *www.turismoitaipu.com.br* ✉ *Panoramic tour R$24, special tour R$64* ☉ *Regular tours daily 8–4 (on the hr). Special tours daily at 8, 8:30, 10, 10:30, 1:30, 2, 3:30, and 4*

Parque das Aves (*Bird Park*). Flamingos, parrots, and macaws are some of the more colorful inhabitants of this privately run park. Right outside the Parque Nacional Foz do Iguaçu, it's an interesting complement to a visit to the falls. A winding path leads you through untouched tropical forest and walk-through aviaries containing hundreds of species of birds. One of the amazing experiences is the toucan enclosure, where they are so close you could touch them. Iguanas, alligators, and other nonfeathered friends have their own pens. ⊠ *Rodovia das Cataratas, Km 17.1, Foz do Iguaçu* ☎ *045/3529–8282* ⊕ *www.parquedasaves. com.br* ✉ *R$28* ☉ *Daily 8:30–5.*

WORTH NOTING

Ecomuseu de Itaipú (*Itaipú Eco-Museum*). At the Ecomuseu de Itaipú you can learn about the geology, archaeology, and efforts to preserve the flora and fauna of the area since the Itaipú Dam was built. This museum is funded by the dam's operator, Itaipú Binacional, so the information isn't necessarily objective. ✉ *Av. Tancredo Neves 6731, Foz do Iguaçu* ☎ *045/3529–2892* 🌐 *www.turismoitaipu.com.br* 🎟 *R$10* 🕑 *Tues.–Sun 8–4:30.*

WHERE TO EAT

$$$$ BRAZILIAN 🍴 **Búfalo Branco.** The city's finest and largest churrascaria does a killer *rodizio* (all-you-can-eat meat buffet). The *picanha* (beef rump cap) stands out among the dozens of meat choices, but pork, lamb, chicken, and even bull testicles find their way onto the metal skewers they use to grill the meat. Never fear, vegetarians—the salad bar is also well stocked. The dining room is bright and cheerful, and bow-tied waiters serve your food. [$] *Average main: R$90* ✉ *Av. Rebouças 530, Foz do Iguaçu* ☎ *45/3523–9744* 🌐 *www.bufalobranco.com.br* 🕑 *Daily noon–11.*

$$$$ BRAZILIAN 🍴 **Tempero da Bahia.** If you're not traveling as far as Salvador and the state of Bahia, you can at least check out its flavors at this busy restaurant. It specializes in northeastern fare like *moquecas* (a rich seafood stew made with coconut milk and palm oil). The version here is unusual for mixing prawns with local river fish. Spicy panfried sole and salmon are lighter options. The flavors aren't quite so subtle at the all-you-can-eat seafood buffets served several times a week. At R$40, it certainly pulls in crowds. [$] *Average main: R$80* ✉ *Rua Marechal Deodoro 1228, Foz do Iguaçu* ☎ *45/3025–1144* 🌐 *www.restaurantetemperodabahia.com* 🕑 *Mon.–Sat. open from 6, Sun. from noon.*

$$$ SPANISH 🍴 **Zaragoza.** On a tree-lined street in a quiet neighborhood, this traditional restaurant's Spanish owner is an expert at matching Iguaçu's fresh river fish to authentic Spanish seafood recipes. Brazilian ingredients sneak into some dishes—the surubí à Goya (catfish in a tomato and coconut-milk sauce) definitely merits a try. [$] *Average main: R$50* ✉ *Rua Quintino Bocaiúva 882, Foz do Iguaçu* ☎ *045/3028–8084* 🌐 *www.restaurantezaragoza.com.br* 🕑 *Daily 11:30–3 and 7–midnight.*

WHERE TO STAY

$$$$ RESORT Fodor's Choice ★ 🏨 **Hotel das Cataratas.** Not only is this stately hotel *in* the national park, with views of the smaller falls from the frontside suites, but it also provides the traditional comforts of a colonial-style establishment: large rooms, terraces, vintage furniture, and hammocks. **Pros:** right inside the park, a short walk from the falls; serious colonial-style charm; friendly, helpful staff. **Cons:** rooms aren't as luxurious as the price promises; far from Foz do Iguaçu so you're limited to the on-site restaurants; only the most expensive suites have views of the falls. [$] *Rooms from: R$960* ✉ *Rodovia das Cataratas, Km 28, Foz do Iguaçu* ☎ *045/2102–7000, 0800/726–4545* 🌐 *www.hoteldascataratas.com.br* 🛏 *198 rooms, 5 suites* 🍽 *Breakfast.*

4

SIDE TRIPS TO URUGUAY

Montevideo, Colonia del Sacramento,
and Punta del Este

WELCOME TO SIDE TRIPS TO URUGUAY

TOP REASONS TO GO

★ **Bask in colonial splendor:** There's little that could be called old in this modern, progressive country—except for the once-walled 1680 Portuguese settlement of Colonia del Sacramento. Flowers spill over balconies, balladeers serenade their sweethearts, and lanterns illuminate the streets of this well-preserved colonial city.

★ **Frolic with the rich and famous:** One visit to Uruguay's tony Punta del Este, and Brazil's beaches will forever seem a tad too déclassé. From December through February, fun-in-the-sun crowds flock here.

★ **Ride 'em, cowboy:** The *gaucho* embodies the country's spirit, and these rugged cowboys still mount their trusty horses to round up livestock on vast ranges. If your time is limited, you don't even need to leave urban Montevideo to see the spectacle: the capital's El Prado district is the site of the best rodeos.

1 Montevideo. True to developing-country patterns, all roads, literal and figurative, lead to Montevideo. Uruguay's friendly capital strings for miles along the southern coast with an odd positioning that means you can walk south, north, or west from the center city to reach the water.

2 Colonia del Sacramento. It's hard not to fall in love with Colonia. The picturesque town has a six-by-six-block old city with wonderfully preserved architecture, rough cobblestone streets, and a sleepy grace. Tranquility reigns here—bicycles and golf carts outnumber cars.

3 Punta del Este. One of the world's trendiest beach communities, Punta del Este is a glitzy destination that doesn't sleep in peak season. Every summer, families and the celebrity jet-set flock to its shore for sun, good food, and luxury.

gas

Rivera

BRAZIL

Tacuarembo

26

DE HAEDO

5

Melo

6

CUCHILLA GRANDE

8

Lago Artificial
de Rincón del Bonete

Laguna
Merín

Treinta
Y Tres

Durazno

7

URUGUAY

Florida

8

San Jose De Mayo

Aguas Dulces

Minas

Rocha

Canelones

Las Piedras   Ciudad
de la Costa

San Carlos

ATLANTIC OCEAN

VIDEO ✪

1

Punta
Ballena

3

La Barra de Maldonado
Punta del Este

0 ——— 50 mi
0 ——— 50 km

GETTING
ORIENTED

4

Uruguay is one of South
America's smallest countries,
both in area (it's roughly the
size of England) and population. Montevideo anchors
the coast, and most of the
population and action hugs
the water line. Vast ranches
and farms fill the hilly,
sparsely developed interior.
Uruguay's elite beach destination Punta del Este attracts
beachgoers from across
South America and beyond
while historic Colonia del
Sacramento offers a quiet
getaway for many Buenos
Aires residents who take a
quick ferry ride across the
Río de la Plata. Ferries also
reach Montevideo from
Buenos Aires in a couple
hours, making Uruguay
a favorite and easy trip
from Argentina's capital.

Updated
by Karina
Martinez-Carter

It used to be that Uruguay missed out on the touristic attention it deserved, dwarfed by its larger neighbors Argentina and Brazil. That has changed dramatically in the past
years, though, as many around the world have turned their
attention to this serene, welcoming country. The government
has mounted concerted efforts to advertise Uruguay and
its offerings to international travelers, and there is plenty
to show: Colonia del Sacramento, one of South America's
most historic cities; tony resort town Punta del Este; and the
coastal capital city Montevideo. Many travelers come away
impressed and inspired with Uruguay's tranquil beauty and
laid-back vibe.

On a continent with a turbulent past, Uruguayans have parlayed their
human and natural resources into a history of success. A strong middle
class, a high standard of living, relative prosperity, and a long tradition of peace, good government, and democracy have defined Uruguay
(although that last feature did disappear for a dozen years in the last
century). The country has enacted landmark legislation that made it
the first in South America to sever relations between church and state,
to grant women the right to vote, to permit same-sex civil unions, to
legalize cannabis, and to enact a generous social-welfare system. The
Economist even named Uruguay its "country of the year in 2013" for
its landmark legislation.

Today about half the country's population lives in Uruguay's capital
city. The country takes pride in the number of famous artists it produces, and Uruguayans like to claim their country as the birthplace of
the internationally renowned tango singer Carlos Gardel, although the
Argentineans and French also vie for this honor. As in Argentina, the
legendary *gaucho* is Uruguay's most potent cultural fixture, and it's

difficult to pass a day without some reference to these cowboys who once roamed the country singing their melancholy ballads or, of course, to drive without seeing grazing cows or horses. You can still see remnants of the gaucho lifestyle on active ranches throughout the country.

PLANNING

WHEN TO GO

Between October and March the temperatures are pleasant—it's warm and the country is in bloom. Unless you're prepared to tangle with the multitude of tourists that overwhelm Punta del Este in January and February, late spring (November–December) and late winter (March) are the most appealing months to lounge on the beach.

Uruguay's climate has four distinct seasons. Summer (January–March) can be hot and humid, with temperatures as high as 90°F. Fall (April–June) is marked by warm days and evenings cool enough for a light sweater. Winter (July–September) is cold and rainy, with average temperatures generally below 50°F. Although it seldom reaches freezing, the wind off the water can give you quite a chill. Spring (October–December) is much like the fall, except that the trees will be sprouting, rather than dropping, their leaves.

GETTING HERE AND AROUND

AIR TRAVEL

Most international flights land at Montevideo's Aeropuerto Internacional de Carrasco, about 24 km (15 miles) east of downtown. Nearly all Montevideo-bound flights are routed through Buenos Aires. Aerolíneas Argentinas, LAN, GOL, TAM, and Avianca run regular flights to Latin American metropolises like Buenos Aires and São Paulo, and there also is a nonstop American Airlines flight from Miami as well as direct flights to Paris and Madrid.

If you fly a strictly Argentina–Uruguay itinerary, you'll likely depart from Buenos Aires' domestic airport, the Aeroparque Jorge Newbery. Through flights on American Airlines use the capital's international airport at Ezeiza.

Service to the Aeropuerto Internacional de Punta del Este is frequent from many South American cities during the resort's December–March high season, but almost nonexistent the rest of the year.

BOAT TRAVEL

Ferries cross the Río de la Plata between Argentina and Uruguay several times daily. They travel to Montevideo or Colonia, where you can get a bus to Montevideo and Punta del Este. The best companies are Aliscafos, Buquebus, Ferrylíneas Argentina, and Ferry Tur.

BUS TRAVEL

You can go almost anywhere in Uruguay by bus. Some are quite luxurious, with air-conditioning, movies, and snack service. Departures are frequent and fares low. Most companies are based in Montevideo and depart from its state-of-the-art Terminal Tres Cruces. The station's website (⊕ *www.trescruces.com.uy*) lists all bus schedules to and from Montevideo.

CAR TRAVEL

From Argentina you can transport your car across the Río de la Plata by ferry. Alternatively, you can cross the Argentina–Uruguay border in three places: Puerto Unzue-Fray Bentos, Colón-Paysandu, or Concordia-Salto.

Roads between Montevideo and Punta del Este or Colonia del Sacramento are quite good, as are the handful of major highways. In the countryside, roads are usually surfaced with gravel. If you want to leave the main roads, it's best to speak with locals about current conditions before setting off. Trips will often take longer than expected, so budget extra time. On the upside, country roads often have little traffic and spectacular scenery.

Car-rental rates are often higher in Uruguay than in the United States because of the value-added tax. For an economy-size car, expect to pay around US$55 per day. Uruguayans tend to drive carefully, but visitors from Argentina have the reputation of driving with wild abandon. Since almost all roads have only two lanes, keep an eye out for passing vehicles.

HEALTH AND SAFETY

It's a good idea to avoid tap water, as pipes in many older buildings are made of lead. Almost everyone drinks locally bottled *agua mineral* (mineral water), which is available *con gas* or *sin gas* (with or without carbonation).

Uruguay would win most "Safest South American Country" competitions, but standard travel precautions apply. Keep an eye on your purse or wallet, avoid unnecessary displays of wealth, and avoid wandering back streets of Montevideo at night.

RESTAURANTS

Argentina may leap to mind when discussing South American beef, but some 12 million cattle, primarily Hereford and Angus, graze Uruguay's open, vast grasslands—this in a nation of roughly 3 million people. Beef is the staple of the Uruguayan diet. It's quality, cheap, abundant, and often grilled in a style borrowed from the gauchos, and known as *parrillada*. A meal in a Uruguayan steakhouse should be on your agenda. Beef is also made into sausages, such as *chorizo* and *salchicha*, or is combined with ham, cheese, bacon, and peppers to make *matambre*.

Seafood is also popular here—and it's fresh and delicious, especially the *lenguado* (flounder), *merluza* (hake), and *calamar* (squid). Try the *raya a la manteca negra* (ray in blackened butter). If you are not up to a full meal, order what is often considered the national sandwich, *chivito*, a steak sandwich with thin strips of beef.

Uruguayan wines under the Bouza, Santa Rosa, and Calvinor labels are available in most restaurants. As Uruguayan wines also have raised their profile in the past decade, a vineyard visit or wine tasting is highly recommended. *Clericó* is a mixture of white wine and fruit juice, while *medio y medio* is part sparkling wine, part white wine.

Lunch is served between noon and 3; restaurants begin to fill around 12:30 and are packed by 1:30. Many restaurants do not open for dinner until 8 pm, and often don't start to get crowded until 9:30. Most pubs and *confiterías* (cafés) are open all day. Formal dress is rarely required. Smart sportswear is acceptable at even the fanciest establishments.

HOTELS

Hotels here are generally comfortable and good value for your money. Most include breakfast in their rates. All but the most basic hotels have air-conditioning—you'll appreciate it during the hot summers. *Hosterías* are country inns that not only offer modest rooms but are open for dinner as well. Menus tend to be limited, though the food served is unfailingly hearty.

Lodging at the beach requires reservations no matter what the time of year. Rooms fill up quickly (and prices increase dramatically) during the December–February high season. Rates go down during the shoulder months of November and March, but you can still count on good weather. Many hotels close for a few weeks between Easter and late May and/or in September. *Hotel reviews have been shortened. For full information, visit Fodors.com.*

WHAT IT COSTS IN URUGUAYAN PESOS				
	$	**$$**	**$$$**	**$$$$**
RESTAURANTS	Under 301	301–450	451–600	over 600
HOTELS	Under 1,501	1,501–3,000	3,001–4,500	over 4,500

Restaurant prices are the average cost of a main course at dinner or, if dinner is not served, at lunch. Hotel prices are the lowest cost of a standard double room in high season.

VISITOR INFORMATION

Contact Ministry of Tourism and Sport ✉ *Rambla 25 de Agosto 1825, Ciudad Vieja, Montevideo* ☎ *2/1885* ⊕ *www.uruguaynatural.com.*

MONTEVIDEO

Uruguay's capital city hugs the eastern bank of the Río de la Plata. A massive coastal promenade (*malecón*) that passes fine beaches, restaurants, and numerous parks recalls the sunny sophistications of the Mediterranean and is always dotted with Montevideans strolling, exercising, and lounging along the water. Montevideo has its share of glitzy shopping avenues and modern office buildings, balanced with its historic old city and sumptuous colonial architecture, as well as numerous leafy plazas and parks. It is hard not to draw comparisons to its sister city Buenos Aires across the river, and indeed Montevideo strikes many as a calmer, more manageable incarnation of Argentina's capital.

When the weather's good, La Rambla, a 22-km (14-mile) waterfront avenue that links the Old City with the eastern suburbs and changes names about a dozen times, gets packed with fishermen, ice-cream vendors, and joggers. Around sunset, volleyball and soccer games wind down as couples begin to appear for evening strolls. Polls consistently rate Montevideo as having the highest quality of life of any city in Latin America. After one visit here, especially on a lovely summer evening, you probably will agree.

GETTING HERE AND AROUND

AIR TRAVEL

Uruguay's principal airport, Aeropuerto Internacional de Carrasco (MVD), is 24 km (15 miles) east of Montevideo. A taxi to downtown costs about 550 pesos; plan on 620 pesos to reach the Ciudad Vieja. A city bus (marked Ciudadela) is cheap—about 26 pesos—but the drawback is that it takes an hour to get downtown.

BOAT AND FERRY TRAVEL

Buquebus operates ferry service between Buenos Aires and the ports at Montevideo and Colonia. The trip takes less than three hours to Montevideo and less than four hours to Colonia. A round-trip ticket between Buenos Aires and Montevideo costs about 3,000 pesos. A package that includes a round-trip ticket between Buenos Aires and Colonia and a shuttle bus to or from Montevideo costs about 2,000 pesos.

BUS TRAVEL

Montevideo's public buses are a great alternative to taxis, which can be difficult to find during peak hours. Buses crisscross the entire city 24 hours a day. You don't need exact change, and the price for any trip within Montevideo is only 213 pesos.

Colonia is serviced by several regional bus lines, including Cot and TURIL. The three-hour ride costs less than 400 pesos.

CAR TRAVEL

Because La Rambla, Montevideo's riverside thoroughfare, extends for dozens of miles, driving is a good way to see the city. Roads are well maintained and drivers obey the traffic laws—a rarity in South America. It's easy to rent a car, both downtown and at the airport. In Montevideo you can rent from several major international companies, including Avis, Budget, and Dollar, and from smaller companies such as Inter Car and Multicar.

TAXI TRAVEL

All cabs have meters that count *fichas,* or pulses, each 1/10 km (1/20 mile). When you arrive at your destination, the driver will take out an official chart that calculates the fare from the number of fichas elapsed. You can hail taxis on the street with ease, or call one to pick you up at your hotel. A ride to the airport from the Old City costs about 500 pesos.

SAFETY AND PRECAUTIONS

Although Montevideo doesn't have the problems with crime that larger cities in South America do, it's best to watch your wallet in crowded markets and to avoid walking down deserted streets at night. Most of Montevideo's residents stay up late, so the streets are usually full of people until 1 am. The city bus authority discourages boarding empty buses at night. Look for the helpful tourist police decked out in blue berets and yellow vests that say policía turística. They patrol Avenida 18 de Julio, the Ciudad Vieja, and the Mercado del Puerto.

ESSENTIALS

Air Contacts **Aerolíneas Argentinas** ☎ *0810/222–86527* ⊕ *www.aerolineas. com.ar.* **Aeropuerto Internacional de Carrasco** ⊠ *Ruta 101, Km 19.950, Ciudad de la Costa, Canelones* ☎ *2604–0329* ⊕ *www.aeropuertodecarrasco.com. uy.* **American Airlines** ☎ *800/437–300* ⊕ *www.aa.com.*

Boat Contacts **Buquebus** ☎ *4316–6500* ⊕ *www.buquebus.com.*

Bus Contacts **COT** ☎ *2409–4949 in Montevideo* ⊕ *www.cot.com.uy.* **Terminal Tres Cruces** ⊠ *Bulevar General Artigas 1825, Centro* ☎ *2401–8998* ⊕ *www. trescruces.com.uy.* **Turil** ☎ *477–1990 in Montevideo* ⊕ *www.turil.com.uy.*

Car-Rental Contacts **Avis** ☎ *5982–1700* ⊕ *www.avis.com.uy.* **Dollar** ☎ *2682– 8350 at Aeropuerto de Carrasco* ⊕ *www.dollar.com.uy.*

Taxi Contacts **Taxi Aeropuerto Internacional de Carrasco** ☎ *2604–0323* ⊕ *www.taxisaeropuerto.com.*

Visitor Information **Ministry of Tourism and Sport** ⊠ *Rambla 25 de Agosto 1825, Ciudad Vieja* ☎ *2/1885* ⊕ *www.uruguaynatural.com.* **Ministerio de Turismo** ⊠ *Rambla 25 de Agosto 1825, Ciudad Vieja* ☎ *2900–1078* ⊕ *www. uruguaynatural.com.*

EXPLORING

Modern Montevideo expanded outward from the peninsular Ciudad Vieja, the Old City, still noted for its narrow streets and mix of elegant colonial and art deco architecture. El Prado, an exclusive enclave a few miles north of the city center, is peppered with lavish mansions and grand parks. When you remember that these mansions were once summer homes for aristocratic Uruguayans who spent most of the year elsewhere, you'll get some idea of the wealth this small country once enjoyed.

CIUDAD VIEJA

Ciudad Vieja is fairly compact, and you could walk from one end to the other in about 15 minutes. Take care at night, when the area is fairly deserted.

TOP ATTRACTIONS

Fodor's Choice ★ **Mercado del Puerto.** For Montevideo's quintessential lunch experience, head to the old port market, a restored 1868 building of vaulted iron beams and colored glass, and a terrific example of urban renewal at its best. The market shields 14 stalls and eateries where, over large fires, the best *asado* (barbecue) in the city is cooked. It's a mix of casual

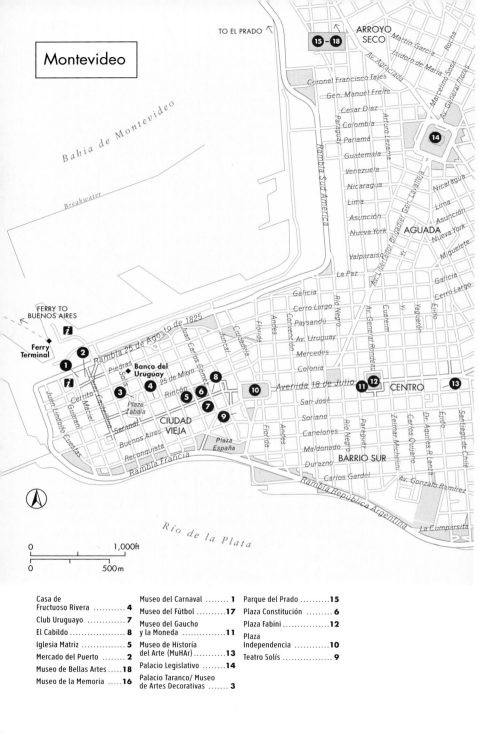

Montevideo

Bahía de Montevideo

Breakwater

TO EL PRADO ↖

15 – 18

ARROYO SECO

AGUADA

FERRY TO
BUENOS AIRES

Ferry
Terminal

Rambla 25 de Agosto de 1825

Banco del
Uruguay

CIUDAD
VIEJA

Plaza
Zabala

Plaza
España

CENTRO

Avenida 18 de Julio

BARRIO SUR

Rambla Francia

Rambla República Argentina

La Cumparsita

Río de la Plata

0   1,000ft
0   500m

lunch-counter places and sit-down restaurants. The traditional drink here is a bottle of medio y medio. Many other eateries congregate outside around the perimeter of the building and are open for dinner as well as lunch. ⊠ *Rambla 25 de Agosto, between Av. Maciel and Av. Pérez Castellano, across from port, Piedras 237, Ciudad Vieja* ⊕ *www.mercadodelpuerto.com.uy* ⊙ *Daily 11–6.*

CRIOLLAS

Also known as *jineteadas,* the Uruguayan-style rodeos called *criollas* are held all over the country, but the most spectacular one takes place in Montevideo's El Prado neighborhood every Easter. Gauchos from all over the country come to display their skill in riding wild horses.

Museo del Carnaval. Move over, Rio. Montevideo's annual Carnaval celebration may be more low-key than that of its northern neighbor, but it lasts for a full 40 days. This museum next to the Mercado del Puerto celebrates and honors the pre-Lenten festivities year-round with displays featuring the elaborate costumes and photos of processions. Guided tours are available. ⊠ *Rambla 25 de Agosto 1825, Ciudad Vieja* ☎ *2915–0807* ⊕ *www.museodelcarnaval. org* ⤳ *80 pesos* ⊙ *Tues.–Sun. 11–5.*

Fodor's Choice ★ **Plaza Independencia.** Connecting Cuidad Vieja and the Centro, Independence Square is the heart of Montevideo. All that remains of the original walls of the Spanish fort is the Puerta de la Ciudadela, the triumphal gate to the Old City. In the center stands a 30-ton statue of General José Gervasio Artigas, the father of Uruguay and the founder of its 19th-century independence movement. At the base of the monument, polished granite stairs lead to an underground mausoleum that holds Artigas's remains. The mausoleum is a moving memorial: bold graphics chiseled in the walls of this giant space detail the feats of Artigas's life. Two uniformed guards dressed in period uniforms stand at solemn attention beside the urn in this uncanny vault. There's a changing of the guard every Friday at noon.

Towering over the north side of the plaza, the 26-story **Palacio Salvo** was the tallest building in South America when it inaugurated in 1928 (it's still one of the tallest buildings in Uruguay). Today this emblematic art deco edifice is simply an office building. It was here where the palace now stands that Gerardo Matos Rodríguez composed *La Cumparsita,* a famous tango that transformed into a Uruguayan cultural hymn. You can still hear strains playing around the building twice a day.

WORTH NOTING

Casa de Fructuoso Rivera. Once the home of General Fructuso Rivera, Uruguay's first president, this neoclassical Rivera House from the early 1800s was acquired by the government in 1942 and opened as a national history museum. Exhibits inside this pale yellow colonial house with an octagonal cupola document the development of Uruguay and showcase daily life in Montevideo of the 1900s. ⊠ *Calle Rincón 437, Ciudad Vieja* ☎ *2915–1051* ⊕ *www.museohistorico.gub.uy* ⤳ *Free* ⊙ *Tues.–Fri. 11–4.*

The Plaza Independencia is the heart of Montevideo, a great place for history lovers and people-watchers.

Club Uruguay. Uruguay's most prestigious private social club, founded in 1888, is headquartered in this eclectic, three-story neoclassical national monument on the south side of Plaza Matriz. The club was formed for high society of European descent, but today is open to the public. Friendly, English-speaking guides happily bring visitors up the marble staircases so that they can marvel at the elegant salons. The club also hosts cultural events, including music performances and art shows, throughout the year. Nonmembers are welcome at the on-site bar and restaurant, but full access to the club's luxe facilities, including a library and billiards room, is reserved exclusively for its members. ⊠ *Calle Sarandí 584, Ciudad Vieja* ☎ *2915-7820* ⊕ *www.cluburuguay.com.uy* ⌹ *Free* ⊙ *Weekdays 9–8.*

El Cabildo. The original City Hall is where the Uruguayan constitution was signed in 1830. This two-story colonial edifice houses an impressive collection of paintings, antiques, costumes, and rotating history exhibits. Fountains and statuary line the interior patios. English-speaking guides are available. ⊠ *Calle Juan Carlos Gómez at Calle Sarandí, Ciudad Vieja* ☎ *2915-9685* ⊕ *www.cabildo.montevideo.gub.uy* ⌹ *Free* ⊙ *Wed.–Fri. noon–5:45, Sat. 11–4.*

Iglesia Matriz. It's officially the Cathedral of the Immaculate Conception and St. Phillip and St. James, but it is known to Montevideans as the Matriz ("head") Church, as well as the Catedral Metropolitana de Montevideo. The cathedral is the oldest public building in Montevideo, with a distinctive pair of dome-cap bell towers that stand guard over the plaza below. Besides its rich marble interior, colorful floor tiling, stained glass, and dome, the Matriz Church is notable as the final resting place of many of Uruguay's most important political and military figures. ⊠ *Calle Ituzaingó 1373, at Calle Sarandí, Ciudad Vieja* ☎ *2915–7018* ⊕ *www.arquidiocesis.net* ☉ *Daily 9–7; mass Sat. at 5, Sun. at 11 and 5.*

Palacio Taranco/Museo de Artes Decorativas. Built in 1907, the ornate Taranco Palace in the Ciudad Vieja is representative of the French-inspired architecture favored in fin-de-siècle Montevideo. Even the marble for the floors was imported from France. Today you can survey that bygone glory in the palace's new incarnation as the Museo de Artes Decorativas (Museum of Decorative Arts). Its rooms are filled with period furniture, statuary, draperies, clocks, and portrait paintings. A cultural center within has a calendar of performances and live music. ⊠ *Calle 25 de Mayo 376, Ciudad Vieja* ☎ *2915–6060* ⊕ *www.mec.gub. uy/museoartesdecorativas* ⊟ *Free* ☉ *Weekdays 12:30–5:40.*

Plaza Constitución. This plaza, also known as Plaza Matriz, is the heart of Montevideo's Ciudad Vieja. An ornate cantilever fountain in the center of this tree-filled square was installed in 1871 to commemorate the construction of the city's first water system.

Fodor's Choice ★ **Teatro Solís.** Named in honor of the discoverer of the Río de la Plata, Juan Díaz de Solís, the 1856 Solís Theater is famed for its fine acoustics. Informative guided tours of the building are offered in Spanish; call ahead to arrange one in English for a small extra cost. (The afternoon tours are occasionally canceled if the theater is in use for rehearsals.) The theater maintains an active calendar of concerts, dance, and plays, all in Spanish, and all for prices much lower than you'd pay for a comparable evening back home. ⊠ *Reconquista at Bartolomé Mitre, Ciudad Vieja* ☎ *1950–3323* ⊕ *www.teatrosolis.org.uy* ⊟ *Tours 20 pesos (free Wed.)* ☉ *Tours Tues. and Thurs. at 4, Wed., Fri., and Sun. at 11, noon, and 4, Sat. at 11, noon, 1, and 4.*

CENTRO

Montevideo's main street, the Avenida 18 de Julio, runs through the heart of the city's center. You'll find everything here—shops and museums, cafés and plazas, bustling traditional markets, chrome-and-steel office towers, and places to change money. The avenue runs east from Plaza Independencia, away from the Ciudad Vieja, passing through bustling Plaza Fabini and tree-lined Plaza Cagancha.

It's a 20-minute walk from Plaza Independencia to the Palacio Municipal. If shopping is your main interest, you may want to devote an entire afternoon to browsing and buying along the avenida.

TOP ATTRACTIONS

Fodor's Choice ★ **Museo del Gaucho y la Moneda** (*Cowboy and Coin Museum*). This museum is in a rococo 19th-century mansion near Calle Julio Herrera y Obes, four blocks east of Plaza Independencia. Here you'll find articles from the everyday life of the gauchos, from traditional garb to the detailed silver work on the cups used for maté (an indigenous herb from which tea is brewed). Ancient South American and European coins are on the first floor. Tours in English are available with a couple days' notice. ⊠ *Av. 18 de Julio 998, Centro* ☎ *2900–8764* ⊟ *Free* ☉ *Weekdays 10–4.*

Museo de Historia del Arte (MuHAr). In the Palacio Municipal (an ambitious name for this unremarkable brick city hall) you'll find the Museum of Art History, which has the country's best collection of pre-Columbian and colonial artifacts. You'll also find Greek, Roman, and Middle Eastern art, including ceramics and other antiquities. On the street level is the **Biblioteca de Historia del Arte** (Library of Art History), worth a stop if you're a student of the subject matter. ⊠ *Calle Ejido 1326, Centro* ☎ *1950–2191* ⊕ *www.muhar.montevideo.gub.uy* ☒ *Free* ⊗ *Museum Tues.–Sun. noon–5:30. Library weekdays 9:30–4:30.*

WORTH NOTING

Plaza Fabini. In the center of this lovely, manicured square is the Monumento del Entrevero, a large sculpture depicting a whirlwind of gauchos, *criollos* (mixed-blood settlers who are half native, half European), and native Uruguayans in battle. It's one of the last works by sculptor José Belloni (1882–1965). An open-air market takes place here every morning. ⊠ *Bounded by Av. 18 de Julio and Calles Río Negro, Colonia, and Julio Herrera y Obes, Centro.*

EL PRADO

The district known as El Prado lies roughly 6 km (4 miles) north of Plaza Independencia. You could make the long uphill walk along the busy Avenida Agraciada, but it's a lot easier in a taxi. It is pleasant to walk along Avenida Buschental in fall and spring when the trees are in full color. The Jardín Botánico (Botanical Garden) inside the Parque del Prado is a worthwhile stop, where you can admire thousands of plant species, many of which were brought to Uruguay in the 19th century by Charles Racine.

TOP ATTRACTIONS

Museo de Bellas Artes (*Museum of Fine Arts*). Known locally as the Blanes Museum, the Museum of Fine Arts is housed in an elegant colonial mansion that once belonged to Uruguay's foremost 19th-century painter, Juan Manuel Blanes. He was entirely self-taught, and did not begin painting until he was in his fifties. His realistic portrayals of gauchos and the Uruguayan countryside compose the core of the museum's collection. ⊠ *Av. Millán 4015, El Prado* ☎ *2336–2248* ⊕ *blanes. montevideo.gub.uy* ☒ *Free* ⊗ *Tues.–Sun. 12:15–5:45.*

Palacio Legislativo. Almost 50 different types of native marble were used in the construction of the Legislative Palace, the seat of Uruguay's bicameral legislature. Free Spanish- and English-language tours are available when the congress is in session; passes are available inside at the information desk. ⊠ *Av. Agraciada at Av. Flores, El Prado* ☎ *2200–1334* ☒ *US$3 for foreigners* ⊗ *Weekdays 9–6; tours at 10:30 and 3:30.*

Parque del Prado. The oldest of the city's parks is also one of the most popular. Locals come to see El Rosedal, the rose garden with more than 800 different varieties, and the fine botanical garden. Also in the 262-acre park you'll find the statue called *La Diligencia*, by sculptor José Belloni. ⊠ *Av. Carlos Brussa, El Prado* ⊗ *Daily 7–7.*

WORTH NOTING

Museo del Fútbol. "Other countries have their history," Helenio Herrera, Uruguay's most famous soccer coach once said. "We have our fútbol." Indeed, *fútbol*—that's "soccer" to U.S. readers—is played anywhere there's space, by kids of all ages. Uruguay both hosted and won the first World Cup competition in 1930 here at the Estadio Centenario. In the pits of the stadium is this museum dedicated to the country's soccer heritage. It's worth a detour if you're a big fan of the sport. ⊠ *Av. Ricaldoni s/n, El Prado* ☎ *2480–1259* ⊕ *www.auf.org.uy* ✉ *100 pesos* ☉ *Weekdays 10–5.*

Museo de la Memoria. The question still pains Uruguayans who remember the era: How did South America's strongest democracy dissolve into 12 years of brutal military dictatorship? This museum documents the history of the 1973–85 period that people here call simply the *dictadura*, during which an astounding 2% of the population experienced arrest for "political crimes" at some time or other. (The government did not begin investigating abuses by the military government until 2011.) The museum won't be a stop on most visitors' Montevideo itineraries, but if you're a student of Latin American history and politics, it's worth a look. ⊠ *Av. Las Instrucciones 1057, El Prado* ☎ *2355–5891* ⊕ *mume. montevideo.gub.uy* ✉ *Free* ☉ *Mon.–Sat. noon–6 (1–7 in summer).*

GREATER MONTEVIDEO

FAMILY

Fodor's Choice

★

Playa de los Pocitos. This stretch of sand is the city's most attractive beach, and surprisingly tranquil. Throughout the day you'll see locals running, biking, strolling, and rollerblading along the *rambla* (boardwalk) here. Snap a picture with the sculpture spelling out "Montevideo" for a classic tourist shot. **Amenities:** food and drink; lifeguards; showers; toilets. **Best for:** solitude; sunrise; sunset; swimming; walking. ⊠ *Rambla Perú at Gabriel A. Pereira, Pocitos.*

OFF THE
BEATEN
PATH

Bodega Bouza. Argentina and Chile grab all the attention in discussions of South American wines, but Uruguay has a number of impressive wineries of its own. It's worth stopping by the Bodega Bouza outside of Montevideo for a tour and sampling; it's one of the few wineries open for daily visits. For a real treat (US$80), reserve the works: a tour, tasting, and extravagant lunch with, of course, wines to accompany each course. It's worth visiting the winery for its standout restaurant alone. ⊠ *Camino de la Redención 7658* ☎ *2323–7491* ⊕ *www.bodegabouza. com* ✉ *Tours US$20, with sampling US$38* ☉ *Tours weekdays at 11, 1:30, and 4, weekends at 11 and 4.*

WHERE TO EAT

Montevideo was not long ago a city that almost exclusively subsisted on steak and potatoes and pastas, but the city's restaurant scene has experienced a slow-but-sure emergence the past decade. You still can find all the tasty steak you want, but offerings have diversified with an increasing number of international and fusion restaurants. From fine dining to quality chivito joints, you'll have your share of memorable meals in Montevideo.

CIUDAD VIEJA

$
SOUTH
AMERICAN

✕ **Café Bacacay.** This small and smartly designed restaurant facing Teatro Solís inhabits a building that dates to 1844 and attracts a young, hip crowd. The owner takes special care in preparing the excellent salads, such as the Bacacay (spinach, raisins, carrots, nuts, grilled eggplant) or the Sarandí (celery, chicken, apples, carrots). $ *Average main: 120 pesos* ✉ *Bacacay 1306, at Calle Buenos Aires, Ciudad Vieja* ☎ *2916–6074* ⊕ *www.bacacay.com.uy* ☉ *Closed Sun.*

$$
SOUTH
AMERICAN

✕ **Jacinto.** The smell of fresh-baked bread wafts through this pleasant, sunny spot off Plaza Zabala. Plates are fresh, inspired, and expertly prepared, from the soup of the day to desserts like panna cotta with red grapes and a sweet orange sauce. Jacinto is a favorite among the city's foodie crowd and stylish set. $ *Average main: 400 pesos* ✉ *Sarandí 349, Ciudad Vieja* ☎ *2915–2731* ⊕ *www.jacinto.com.uy* ☉ *Closed Sun. No dinner.*

$$$$
EUROPEAN

✕ **Rara Avis.** Located in the Teatro Solis theater building, Rara Avis is one of Montevideo's best restaurants. Both the food—such as a black-oyster risotto with smoked salmon or duck magret in baby greens with a pepper sauce—and the setting are sophisticated. It's a great option for the pre- and posttheater crowds. $ *Average main: 700 pesos* ✉ *Buenos Aires 652, Ciudad Vieja* ☎ *2915–0330* ⊕ *www.raraavis.com.uy* ☉ *Closed Sun. No lunch Sat.*

CENTRO

$$
SOUTH
AMERICAN

✕ **Corchos Bistro y Boutique de Vinos.** Uruguay's wines take center stage at this unpretentious restaurant located near Plaza Independencia. Wine is even incorporated into most dishes, including a salad with wine-soaked pears and white wine–infused chorizo. The fixed-price lunch menu is a hit with professionals who work nearby, and the prices won't hold you back from ordering another glass (or flight) of wine either. Corchos' staff also can arrange tastings and tours upon request. $ *Average main: 400 pesos* ✉ *25 de Mayo 651, Centro* ☎ *2917–2051* ⊕ *www.corchos. com.uy* ☉ *Closed weekends. No dinner Mon.–Thurs.*

GREATER MONTEVIDEO

$$
SOUTH
AMERICAN

✕ **Expreso Pocitos.** This classic and beloved diner-style establishment has been around for more than a century, and it is clear that some of the customers have been frequenting it for almost as long. Many congregate here for a coffee or beer, and the chivito, which is made with fresh, fluffy bread, is considered one of the best in town. $ *Average main: 350 pesos* ✉ *Benito Blanco at Av. Brasil, Pocitos* ☎ *2708–1828.*

$$$$
SOUTH
AMERICAN
Fodor'sChoice
★

✕ **La Casa Violeta.** Meats are the specialty at this beautiful restaurant facing Puerto del Buceo, one of the prettiest spots in the city. You can opt for a steak tasting menu that is served in the method called *espeto corrido,* with meat brought to your table on a long skewer. There's also a salad bar, which not many restaurants of this type can claim. There's a big deck shaded with umbrellas and with attractive views of the port and surrounding homes. $ *Average main: 900 pesos* ✉ *Rambla Armenia 3667, corner of 26 de Marzo, Puerto del Buceo, Pocitos* ☎ *2628–7626* ⊕ *www.lacasavioleta.com.*

$$$$ ✕ **Restaurant Francis.** This bright, upscale restaurant is a local favorite
MEDITERRANEAN and always filled, yet the efficient, friendly staff manages to keep up.
The menu is gourmet and extensive, ranging from sushi to paella to
cuts of meat on the grill. Everything is high quality and innovative, but
the seafood dishes in particular stand out, like the *chipirones* (baby
cuttlefish) in a garlic and parsley sauce with grilled onions. $ *Average
main: 700 pesos* ⊠ *Luis de la Torre 502, Punta Carretas* ☎ *2711–8603*
⊕ *www.francis.com.uy.*

$$$ ✕ **Tandory.** With Tandory, French-Uruguayan chef and owner Gabriel
INTERNATIONAL Coquel has created an intimate yet convivial restaurant with top-level
Fodor'sChoice service. Fusion dishes harmoniously blend Asian, Latin American,
★ and European flavors, and the eclectic décor includes heirlooms and
souvenirs from his travels around the world. Diplomats, tourists, and
well-traveled Uruguayans seeking cuisine more inspired than steak and
potatoes fill the tables here. The menu changes daily based on what's
fresh and in season, and don't worry if you can't decide what to order.
Coquel frequently pops by diners' tables to offer suggestions. $ *Average
main: 600 pesos* ⊠ *Ramon Masini at Libertad, Pocitos* ☎ *2709–6616*
⊕ *www.tandory.com.uy* ⊙ *Closed Sun.*

WHERE TO STAY

Many downtown hotels are grouped around the big three squares:
Plaza Independencia, Plaza Fabini, and Plaza Cagancha. In the weeks
before and after Carnaval in February, rooms become hard to come by.
Otherwise, rooms are plentiful in summer, when beach-bound residents
desert the city.

CENTRO

$$ 🏨 **Oxford Hotel.** Glass walls, broad windows, and mirrors give the small
HOTEL lobby an open but intimate feel, much like that of the hotel itself. **Pros:**
central location; attentive staff. **Cons:** some oddly configured rooms;
small bathrooms. $ *Rooms from: 1840 pesos* ⊠ *Calle Paraguay
1286, Centro* ☎ *2902–0046* ⊕ *www.hoteloxford.com.uy* ↘ *66 rooms*
†⊙† *Breakfast.*

$$$ 🏨 **Radisson Montevideo Victoria Plaza.** This luxurious glass-and-brick
HOTEL structure overlooks Plaza Independencia and blends harmoniously with
the surrounding architecture. **Pros:** great location for sightseeing; atten-
tive staff; many amenities. **Cons:** some reports of window frames that
rattle with temperature changes. $ *Rooms from: 4000 pesos* ⊠ *Plaza
Independencia 759, Centro* ☎ *2902–0111* ⊕ *www.radisson.com.uy*
↘ *190 rooms, 64 suites* †⊙† *Breakfast.*

$$$$ 🏨 **Sheraton Montevideo.** One of the city's biggest hotels is removed from
HOTEL the Old City, and, decidedly modern, feels a world away. **Pros:** attentive
staff; many amenities; shopping nearby. **Cons:** distant from downtown
and sights. $ *Rooms from: 6000 pesos* ⊠ *Victor Soliño 349, Punta
Carretas* ☎ *2710–2121* ⊕ *www.starwoodhotels.com/sheraton* ↘ *197
rooms, 10 suites* †⊙† *No meals.*

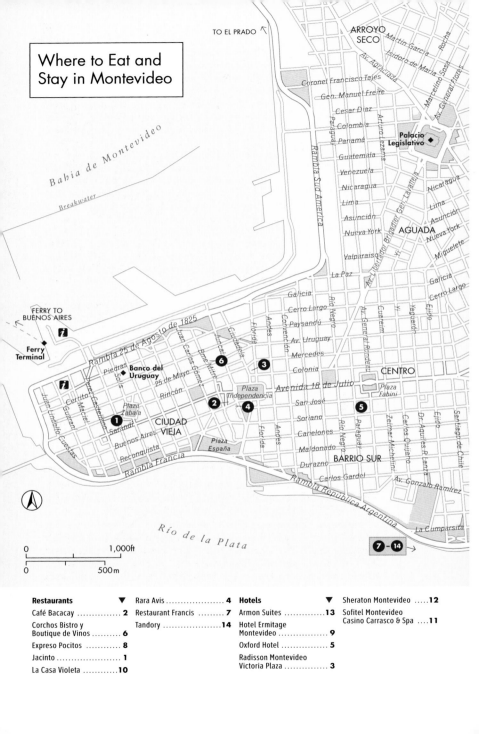

Where to Eat and Stay in Montevideo

TO EL PRADO

ARROYO SECO

Bahía de Montevideo

Breakwater

FERRY TO BUENOS AIRES

Ferry Terminal

Palacio Legislativo

AGUADA

CENTRO

CIUDAD VIEJA

Banco del Uruguay

Plaza Zabala

Plaza Independencia

Plaza Fabini

Plaza España

BARRIO SUR

La Cumparsita

Río de la Plata

0   1,000ft
0   500m

7 - 14

GREATER MONTEVIDEO

$$
HOTEL
Armon Suites. This hotel in a quiet neighborhood east of downtown is an all-suites hotel, and the spaces are huge. Pros: good value; ample-size suites. Cons: far from sights. $ *Rooms from: 2760 pesos* ⊠ *21 de Setiembre 2885, Pocitos* ☎ *2712–4120* ⊕ *www.armonsuites.com.uy* ↩ *40 rooms* ❙◯❙ *Breakfast.*

$$
HOTEL
Hotel Ermitage Montevideo. The Ermitage is in an unprepossessing, sandstone-front building overlooking the lovely Plaza Tomás Gomensoro, and is a good, affordable

choice if you want to be near the shore. Pros: great location in attractive Pocitos; wonderful historic building; good value. Cons: far from sights. $ *Rooms from: 2000 pesos* ⊠ *Calle Juan Benito Blanco 783, Pocitos* ☎ *2710–4021, 2711–7447* ⊕ *www.ermitagemontevideo.com* ↩ *100 rooms* ❙◯❙ *Breakfast.*

$$$$
HOTEL
Fodor's Choice
★
Sofitel Montevideo Casino Carrasco & Spa. Originally opened in 1921 as a summer escape for the Uruguayan elite, this stunning Belle Époque waterfront building, known as the "palace on the sand," underwent an intensive restoration process and reopened in splendor as part of the Sofitel chain. Pros: attractive casino, restaurant, and bar on site; inspired spa treatments. Cons: a lengthy taxi ride to the sights of Montevideo. $ *Rooms from: 6560 pesos* ⊠ *Rambla República de México 6451, Montevideo* ☎ *598/2604–6060* ⊕ *www.sofitel.com* ↩ *93 rooms, 23 suites* ❙◯❙ *No meals.*

NIGHTLIFE

Montevideo's nightlife scene is a smattering of pubs, bars, clubs, and tango and folk music venues. With few exceptions, bars and clubs come to life around 1 am and don't close until it's time for breakfast. Still, "after office" outings are popular, which is essentially happy hour with groups hitting the bars on an earlier-than-usual schedule.

BARS AND PUBS

La Pasiva. For an ice-cold beer, this popular beer house is a late-night favorite. The specialties are frankfurters, chivitos, and other bar food. In good weather you can socialize at the outdoor tables in Plaza Matriz. This Montevideo staple has franchises throughout the city, including a prominent location on Plaza Fabini. ⊠ *Calle Sarandí at Calle J. C. Gómez, Ciudad Vieja* ☎ *2915–7988* ⚠ *Reservations not accepted* ▭ *No credit cards.*

Shannon Irish Pub. This pub in the Old City is a classic Montevideo nightlife spot with good rock music and an unpretentious vibe. ⊠ *Mitre 1318, Ciudad Vieja* ☎ *2916–9585* ⊕ *www.theshannon.com.uy.*

Volvé Mi Negra. Lines form frequently outside this nightlife spot on weekends, where locals come for generous-sized drinks. While it's technically a pub complete with wood paneling, bar stools, and pool tables, live DJs get people dancing and give it a club vibe. ✉ *Francisco Muñoz 3177, Pocitos* ☎ *9708–7922* ⊕ *www.volveminegra.com.*

DANCE CLUBS

2 am. If you're itching to indulge in a full night out in Montevideo, make this *boliche* (club) your destination. Appropriately named, 2 am opens its doors at that hour to the city's young and stylish set, who dance into the morning to the beats of cumbia and Top 40. ✉ *Rambla Wilson at Requena y Garcia, Punta Carretas* ☉ *Closed Sun.–Thurs.*

Fodor's Choice ★ **Lotus Club.** Located in Montevideo's World Trade Center, this club for years has been considered one of Montevideo's best. The red-and-black color scheme gives the place an upscale feel, and Montevideans dance until the wee hours under shimmering disco balls. Get your night out started early on Wednesday at the "after-office" party. ✉ *Lecuender at Bonavita, Pocitos* ☎ *2628–1379* ⊕ *www.lotus.com.uy* ☉ *Closed Sun.–Tues.*

TANGO SHOWS

Joventango. If you're itching to try out your dance steps, Joventango is the best place in the city to learn tango. Shows are frequent; call or check the website for times. ✉ *Calle San José 1314, Centro* ☎ *2908–1550* ⊕ *www.joventango.org.*

SHOPPING

Let's face it: Montevideans head to Buenos Aires when they want to go on an extra-special shopping excursion. But quality and selection are decent here, and prices often are lower than in Argentina. Stores in Centro, along Avenida 18 de Julio, offer the standard selection of urban merchandise. The truly fun shopping experience is to be found in the city's markets, which are vibrant and numerous.

ANTIQUES

Calle Tristán Narvaja north of Avenida 18 de Julio is packed with antiques shops. In the Old City, the streets north of Plaza Constitución are also lined with such stores.

Louvre. This antiques store is the only source for handmade and painted trinket boxes—the perfect *recuerdos* (souvenirs). It also offers an impressive selection of jewelry and silver. ✉ *Calle Sarandí 652, Ciudad Vieja* ☎ *2916–2686* ⊕ *www.louvreantiguedades.com.uy.*

HANDICRAFTS

Fodor's Choice ★ **Manos del Uruguay.** With six locations total in Montevideo, Punta del Este, and Colonia del Sacramento, Manos del Uruguay stock a wide selection of woolen wear and locally produced ceramics crafted by women's artisan cooperatives around the country. ✉ *Punta Carretas Shopping, José Ellauri 350, Centro* ☎ *2710–6108* ⊕ *www.manos.com.uy.*

JEWELRY

Giamen. Giamen carries amethyst and topaz jewelry, agate slices, and elaborate objects made of precious gems. ✉ *Av. 18 de Julio 948, Centro* ☎ *2902–2572.*

LEATHER

Montevideo is a good source for inexpensive leather. Shops near Plaza Independencia specialize in hand-tailored coats and jackets made out of nutria (fur from a large semiaquatic rodent).

Casa Mario. Casa Mario has a particularly good selection of leather clothes. As a bonus, they offer free transportation, which your hotel can arrange. ✉ *Calle Piedras 641, Centro* ☎ *2916–2356* ⊕ *www.casa marioleather.com.*

MARKETS

Weekend ferias (open-air markets) are the best place for leisurely browsing among a warren of crafts stalls. Government regulations dictate that all ferias must close in the early afternoon, so make sure to arrive by 10 am.

El Mercado de la Abundancia. Dating back to 1836, El Mercado de la Abundancia is a fun indoor market in Centro, a few blocks from the Palacio Municipal. Inside are a tango dance center, a handful of good choices for a lunchtime parrillada, and a crafts fair. ✉ *Aquiles Lanza 1312, Centro.*

Fodor'sChoice
★
Feria Tristán Narvaja. Started in the early 1900s by Italian immigrants, Feria Tristán Narvaja is Montevideo's top attraction on Sunday and one of the city's largest and most popular fairs. (It operates only on Sunday, a day when all other markets, and much of the city, are closed. Hours run about 9–4.) The fair, a 5- to 10-minute walk from the Old City and in the Centro district, is plentifully stocked with secondhand goods and antiques. ✉ *Dr. Tristán Narvaja at Av. Uruguay, Centro.*

Plaza Cagancha. Between Avenida 18 de Julio and Calle Rondeau in Centro, Plaza Cagancha regularly has vendors set up in the area selling trinkets and crafts. ✉ *Av. 18 de Julio between Av. Gral Rondeau and Pasaje de los Derechos Humanos.*

SHOPPING CENTERS

Fodor'sChoice
★
Punta Carretas Shopping. Housed in a former prison, Punta Carretas Shopping is the city's largest and most upscale mall, measuring in at around 200 stores mixing local and international brands. It's in a pleasant residential area near the Sheraton Montevideo, a 10-minute cab ride from the Old City. ✉ *Calles Ellauri and Solano, Punta Carretas* ☎ *2711–6940* ⊕ *www.puntacarretasshopping.com.uy.*

COLONIA DEL SACRAMENTO

The peaceful cobbled streets of Colonia are just over the Río de la Plata from Buenos Aires, but they seem a world away. Charm might be an overused descriptor, but Colonia, with its old-world architecture, serenity, and water lapping at sandy shores is a place that redefines it.

The best activity in Colonia is walking through its peaceful Barrio Histórico (Old Town), a UNESCO World Heritage Site. Porteños come to Colonia for romantic getaways or for a break from the city. If you like to keep busy on your travels, a late-morning arrival and early-evening departure give you plenty of time to see the sights and wander at will.

To really see the city at its own pace, spend the night in one of its many colonial-style bed-and-breakfasts: This offsets travel costs and time and makes a visit here far more rewarding.

GETTING HERE AND AROUND

Hydrofoils and ferries cross the Río de la Plata between Buenos Aires and Uruguay several times a day. Boats often sell out, particularly on summer weekends, so book tickets at least a few days ahead. The two competing companies that operate services—Buquebus and Colonia Express—often wage a reduced-rates war in the low season.

Buquebus provides two kinds of service for passengers and cars: the quickest crossing takes an hour by hydrofoil and the slower ferry takes around three hours. The Buquebus terminal in Buenos Aires is at the northern end of Puerto Madero at the intersection of Avenida Alicia M. de Justo and Avenida Córdoba (which changes its name here to Bulevar Cecilia Grierson). It's accessible by taxi or by walking seven blocks from L. N. Alem subte station along Trinidad Guevara.

Colonia Express operates the cheapest and fastest services to Colonia but has only four daily services in each direction. There often are huge discounts on the 50-minute catamaran trip if you buy tickets in advance. The Colonia Express terminal in Buenos Aires is south of Puerto Madero on Avenida Pedro de Mendoza, the extension of Avenida Huergo. It's best reached by taxi, but Bus No. 130 from Avenidas Libertador and L. N. Alem also stops outside it.

The shortest way to the Barrio Histórico is to turn left out of the port parking lot onto Florida—it's a six-block walk. Walking is the perfect way to get around this part of town; equally practical—and lots of fun—are golf carts and sand buggies that you can rent from Thrifty.

ESSENTIALS

Ferry Contacts Buquebus ⊠ *Av. Antartida Argentina 821, Puerto Madero, Buenos Aires* ☎ *11/4316–6500* ⊕ *www.buquebus.com* ✉ *Av. Córdoba 867, Centro, Buenos Aires.* **Colonia Express** ⊠ *Av. Pedro de Mendoza 330, La Boca, Buenos Aires* ☎ *11/4317–4100 in Buenos Aires* ⊕ *www.coloniaexpress.com* ✉ *Av. Córdoba 753, Centro, Buenos Aires.*

Rental Cars Thrifty ⊠ *Av. Gral. Flores 172* ☎ *4522–2939* ⊕ *www.thrifty.com.uy.*

Taxi Contact Taxis Colonia ☎ *598/4522–2920.*

Visitor Information Colonia del Sacramento Tourism Office ⊠ *Manuel Lobo, between Ituzaingó and Paseo San Antonio* ☎ *4522–6886* ⊕ *www. coloniaturismo.com.*

Cobblestones abound in the Old Town section of Colonia del Sacramento, Uruguay.

EXPLORING

Begin your tour at the reconstructed Portón de Campo or city gate, where remnants of the old bastion walls lead to the river. A block farther is Calle de los Suspiros, the aptly named Street of Sighs, a cobblestone stretch of one-story colonials that can rival any street in Latin America for sheer romantic effect. It runs between a lookout point on the river, called the Bastión de San Miguel, and the Plaza Mayor, a lovely square filled with Spanish moss, palms, and spiky, flowering *palo borracho* trees. The many cafés around the square are ideal places to take it all in. Clusters of bougainvillea flow over the walls here and in the other quiet streets of the Barrio Histórico, many of which are lined with art galleries and antiques shops.

Another great place to watch daily life is the Plaza de Armas Manoel Lobo, where you can find the Iglesia Matriz, the oldest church in Uruguay. The square itself is crisscrossed with wooden catwalks over the ruins of a house dating to the founding of the town. The tables from the square's small eateries spill from the sidewalk right onto the cobblestones: they're all rather touristy, but give you an excellent view of the drum-toting *candombe* (a style of music from Uruguay) squads that beat their way around the Old Town each afternoon.

You can visit all of Colonia's museums with the same ticket, which you buy from the Museo Portugués or the Museo Municipal for about $2.50. Most take only a few minutes to visit, but you can use the ticket on two consecutive days.

TOP ATTRACTIONS

Faro (*Lighthouse*). Towering above the Plaza Mayor is the lighthouse, which was built in 1857 on top of a tower that was part of the ruined San Xavier convent. The whole structure was engulfed in flames in 1873 after a lighthouse keeper had an accident with the oil used in the lamp at the time. Your reward for climbing it are great views over the Barrio Histórico and the River Plate. ⊠ *Pl. Mayor* ☉ *Weekdays 1–sunset, weekends 11 am–sunset.*

Museo Portugués. The museum that's most worth a visit is this one, which documents the city's ties to Portugal. It's most notable for its collection of old map reproductions based on Portuguese naval expeditions. A small selection of period furnishings, clothes, and jewelry from Colonia's days as a Portuguese colony complete the offerings. Exhibits are well labeled, but in Spanish only. ⊠ *Pl. Mayor between Calle de los Suspiros and De Solís* ☉ *Thurs.–Tues. 11:15–4:45.*

WORTH NOTING

Museo del Azulejo. A small collection of the beautiful handmade French majolica tiles that adorn fountains all over Colonia are on display at the tile museum, housed in a small 18th-century building near the river. The 50-peso entry fee is good for all Colonia's museums. ⊠ *Misiones de los Tapies 104, at Paseo San Gabriel* ☎ *4522–1056* ⊕ *www.museoscolonia. com.uy* ☉ *Sat.–Wed. 11:15–4:45.*

Nacarello Museum. A colonial Portuguese residence has been lovingly re-created inside this 17th-century structure. The simple bedroom and kitchen furnishings are period pieces, but the real attraction is the house itself, with its thick, whitewashed walls and low ceilings. For 50 pesos you gain access to all Colonia's museums, including this one. ⊠ *Pl. Mayor at Henríquez de la Peña* ⊕ *www.museoscolonia.com.uy* ☉ *Wed.–Thurs. and Sat.–Mon. 11:15–4:45.*

OFF THE BEATEN PATH

Narbona Wine Lodge. For an upscale, indulgent Uruguayan wine experience, Narbona Wine Lodge is your place. The peaceful property includes a vineyard, a restaurant with exposed-brick walls that serves Italian-influenced dishes featuring the wines and products like cheeses made on site, and a luxurious tasting room. If you understandably find yourself unable to leave at the end of the day, book a stay at one of property's five sophisticated, bright, and homey rustic rooms named after varietals. Your stay includes a vineyard tour, mountain bikes for borrowing, and access to Narbona's private beach. ⊠ *Ruta 21, Km 268, Carmelo* ⊕ *www.narbona.com.uy.*

WHERE TO EAT

In Colonia, both dollars and Uruguayan pesos are accepted. Uruguayan food is as beef-based as Argentine fare, and also has a notable Italian influence. Here, enticing cafés and restaurants with plaza and riverfront views are numerous.

$$

SOUTH AMERICAN

✕ **El Drugstore.** The colorful, eclectic decor has turned this restaurant into a notorious spot in tranquil Colonia. You'll find Uruguayan standby dishes like pastas and chivito on the menu, all of which come in generous portions. People are drawn to this restaurant for its relaxed, funky ambience, which the open kitchen and frequent live musicians enhance. Outdoor tables on the plaza are prime real estate. [$] *Average main: 450 pesos* ✉ *Portugal 174* ☎ *4522–5241.*

$$ MEDITERRANEAN 🍴 **El Mesón de la Plaza.** Simple dishes—many steak-based—made with good-quality ingredients have made this traditional restaurant a favorite with porteño visitors to Colonia. The comprehensive wine list showcases Uruguayan vineyards hard to sample anywhere outside the country. Try to get one of the outside tables that sit right on the peaceful Plaza de Armas. Guitar-strumming musicians regularly play for diners, adding to the ambience. [$] *Average main: 400 pesos* ✉ *Vasconcellos 153* ☎ *598/4522–4807* ⌚ *No dinner Mon.*

$ SOUTH AMERICAN 🍴 **La Bodeguita.** This hip restaurant serves delicious, crispy pizza, sliced into bite-size rectangles. The backyard tables overlook the river, and inside is cozy, with warm walls. The terrace is a great spot for a bite and beer when it's warm. [$] *Average main: 150 pesos* ✉ *Calle del Comercio 167* ☎ *598/4522–5329* 🌐 *www.labodeguita.net* 💳 *No credit cards* ⌚ *Closed Mon. in winter. No lunch Tues.–Fri.*

$$$$ LATIN AMERICAN Fodor's Choice ★ 🍴 **La Florida.** The black-and-white photos, lace tablecloths, and quaint knickknacks that clutter this long, low house belie the fact that it was once a brothel. It still has private rooms, but it's dining that politicians and the occasional celeb rent them for these days. You, too, can ask to be seated in one, but consider the airy back dining room, which has views over the river. It's hard to say if it's the flamboyant French-Argentinean owner's tall tales that keep regulars returning or his excellent cooking. Specialties include kingfish, sole, and salmon cooked to order. You can suggest sauces of your own or go with house suggestions like orange-infused cream. [$] *Average main: 800 pesos* ✉ *Odriozola 215* ☎ *598/094 293–036* 🌐 *www.restoranlaflorida.com* 💳 *No credit cards* ⌚ *Closed Wed. Dinner by reservation only Apr.–Nov.*

$ CAFÉ Fodor's Choice ★ 🍴 **Lentes Maravillas.** There's no spot more perfect in Colonia to while away an afternoon with a leisurely lunch or tea than this café nestled along the water. The baked goods are not to be missed—the *redondos* (rich, round cheesecakes) are particularly heavenly. Lounge in the lush, enclosed yard, or cozy into the main dining room, which feels like a friend's welcoming living room, complete with a bookshelf for borrowing and perusing. [$] *Average main: 250 pesos* ✉ *Santa Rita 61* ☎ *4522–0636* 💳 *No credit cards* ⌚ *Closed Wed. No dinner.*

WHERE TO STAY

Since Colonia is the consummate day trip from Montevideo or Buenos Aires, few visitors actually spend the night here. Consider breaking that mold; there's no shortage of homey lodgings to choose from, and an overnight stay really gives you the opportunity to unwind and adopt the relaxed Colonia pace.

$$$$ RESORT Fodor's Choice ★ 🏨 **Four Seasons Carmelo.** Serenity pervades this harmoniously decorated resort an hour west of Colonia del Sacramento, reachable by car, boat, or a 25-minute flight from Buenos Aires. **Pros:** all rooms are spacious bungalows; fabulous, personalized service; on-site activities

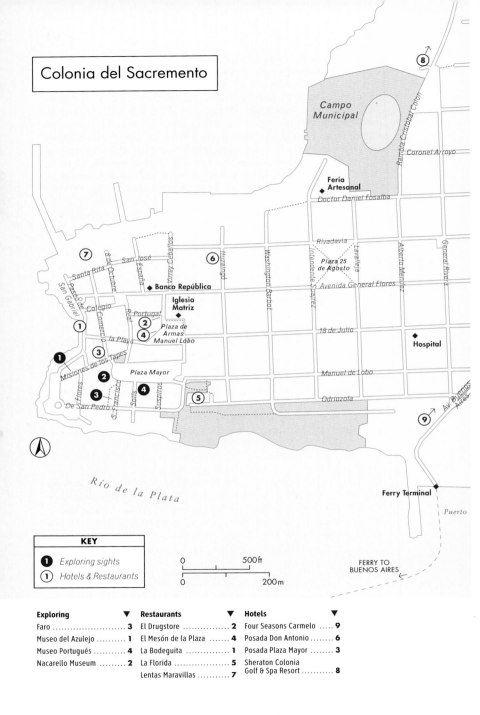

Colonia del Sacremento

Campo Municipal

Coronet Arroyo

Rambla Cristobal Colon

Feria Artesanal

Doctor Daniel Fosalba

Rivadavia

⑦

San José

Santa Rita

8 de Octubre

Virrey Cebatlos

Espana

⑥

Ituzaingó

Washington Barbot

Intendente Suárez

Plaza 25 de Agosto

Lavalleja

Alberto Mendez

General Rivera

Banco República

Avenida General Flores

Colegio

Comercio

Real

Portugat

Iglesia Matriz

Plaza de Armas Manuel Lobo

18 de Julio

Hospital

Paseo de San Gabriel

①

② ④

③

la Playa

①

Misiones de los Tapes

② Plaza Mayor

Manuel de Lobo

Flores

Solis

③ ④

San Francisco

Suspiros

⑤

Odriozota

De San Pedro

⑨

Av. Buenos Aires

Río de la Plata

Ferry Terminal

Puerto

KEY

❶ Exploring sights
① Hotels & Restaurants

| 0 | | 500 ft |
| 0 | | 200 m |

FERRY TO BUENOS AIRES

compensate for distance to sights and restaurants. **Cons:** despite copious netting and bug spray, the mosquitoes can get out of hand; food quality is erratic; noisy families can infringe on romantic getaways. [$] *Rooms from: 11500 pesos* ✉ *Ruta 21, Km 262, Carmelo* ☎ *4542–9000* 🌐 *www.fourseasons.com/carmelo* 🛏 *20 bungalows, 24 duplex suites* 🍴 *Breakfast.*

$$ HOTEL **Posada Don Antonio.** Long galleries of rooms overlook an enormous split-level courtyard at Posada Don Antonio, the latest incarnation of a large, elegant building that has housed one hotel or another for close to a century. **Pros:** sparkling turquoise pool, surrounded by loungers; two blocks from the Barrio Histórico; rates are low, but there are proper hotel perks like poolside snacks. **Cons:** ill-fitting doors let in courtyard noise; some rooms open onto the street. [$] *Rooms from: 2500 pesos* ✉ *Ituzaingó 232* ☎ *598/4522–5344* 🌐 *www.posadadonantonio.com* 🛏 *38 rooms* 🍴 *Breakfast.*

$$ B&B/INN **Posada Plaza Mayor.** A faint scent of jasmine fills the air at this lovely old hotel, where all the rooms open onto a large, plant-filled courtyard complete with a bubbling fountain. **Pros:** beautiful green spaces; on a quiet street of the Barrio Histórico; cheerful, accommodating staff. **Cons:** cramped bathrooms; the three cheapest rooms are small. [$] *Rooms from: 2865 pesos* ✉ *Calle del Comercio 111* ☎ *598/4522–3193* 🌐 *www.posadaplazamayor.com* 🛏 *17 rooms* 🍴 *Breakfast.*

$$$ RESORT **Sheraton Colonia Golf & Spa Resort.** This riverside hotel and spa is a favorite with porteños on weekend escapes. **Pros:** peaceful location with river views from many rooms; great spa; rooms are often discounted midweek. **Cons:** it's a 10-minute drive or taxi ride north of the Barrio Histórico; can be noisy on weekends. [$] *Rooms from: 3900 pesos* ✉ *Continuación Rambla de las Américas s/n* ☎ *4522–9000* 🌐 *www.sheraton.com* 🛏 *96 rooms, 8 suites* 🍴 *Breakfast.*

PUNTA DEL ESTE

Fodor's Choice ★

134 km (83 miles) east of Montevideo.

Often likened to the Hamptons or St-Tropez, Punta del Este is a flashy destination where parties run nonstop in peak season. But it is also a destination that draws a range of beachgoers to its shores, from summering families to the celebrity jet-set. There's a bustling city on the beach downtown, as well as quiet countryside populated solely with upscale ranches called *chacras* or *estancias,* and creative, buzzing hamlets like La Barra and José Ignacio. Though it's pricey and at times a logistical challenge to get around, everyone finds something about Punta to love.

The resort takes its name from the "east point" marking the division of the Río de la Plata on the west from the Atlantic Ocean to the east. It also lends its name to the broader region encompassing the nearby communities of Punta Ballena and La Barra de Maldonado. These days even José Ignacio, some 20 miles away, is grouped in. It's usually a given that Argentina's upper class spends at least part of the summer in Punta, soaking in the ample rays.

GETTING HERE AND AROUND

Most visitors headed to the beach fly into Montevideo's Aeropuerto Internacional de Carrasco (MVD). Flights arrive from many South American cities, in high season only, directly to the Aeropuerto Internacional de Punta del Este (PDP), about 24 km (15 miles) east of town.

Many bus lines travel daily between Montevideo's Terminal Tres Cruces and Punta del Este's Terminal Playa Brava. Two companies that serve the entire region are Copsa and Cot. Buquebus also offers flights, and ferries with a bus connection to Punta.

To get to Punta del Este from Montevideo, follow Ruta 1 east to the Ruta 93 turnoff. The road is well maintained and marked, and the trip takes about 1½ hours. Rental agencies, such as Avis, Budget, and Dollar, are in downtown Punta del Este.

SAFETY AND PRECAUTIONS

For such a touristy locale, Punta maintains a reassuring level of security. Nevertheless, it pays to watch your things. Swimming is not safe at several of the beaches, especially those on the Atlantic side of the point. Never swim alone, and gauge your abilities carefully.

ESSENTIALS

Airport Contact Aeropuerto Internacional de Punta del Este ⊠ *Ruta 93, Km 113* ☎ *4255–9777* ⊕ *www.puntadeleste.aero.*

Bus Contacts COT ☎ *2409–4949 in Montevideo* ⊕ *www.cot.com.uy.* **Copsa** ☎ *2902–1818* ⊕ *www.copsa.com.uy.* **Terminal de Omnibus** ⊠ *Rambla Artigas and Calle 32.*

Visitor and Tour Information Maldonado Tourist Office ⊠ *Parada 1, Calles 31 and 18* ☎ *4222–1921.* **Punta del Este Tourist Office** ⊠ *Av. Gorlero* ☎ *4244–8685* ⊕ *www.turismo.gub.uy.*

EXPLORING

TOP ATTRACTIONS

Avenida Gorlero. Punta del Este is circled by the Rambla Artigas, the main coastal road that leads past residential neighborhoods and pristine stretches of beach. You can find everything on Avenida Gorlero, Punta's main commercial strip. The thoroughfare runs northeast–southwest through the heart of the peninsula and is fronted with cafés, restaurants, boutiques, and casinos.

Casapueblo. A hotel and museum at the tip of a rocky point with tremendous views of the Río de la Plata is the main draw in Punta Ballena, east of Punta del Este. Uruguayan abstract artist Carlos Páez Vilaró created his work as a "habitable sculpture" and it defies architectural categorization. With allusions to Arab minarets and domes, cathedral vaulting, Grecian whitewash, and continuous sculptural flourishes that recall the traceries of a Miró canvas, this curvaceous 13-floor surrealist complex climbs up a hill and looks like nothing else in South America—or anywhere much else.

The spaces include an excellent series of galleries dedicated to the artist's work. Here you can see photos of him with friends like Picasso

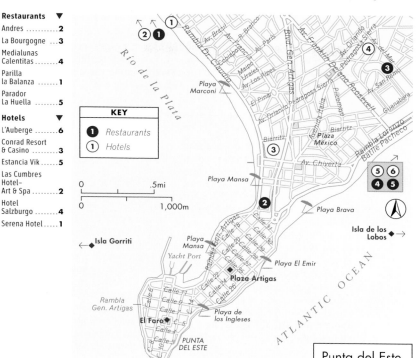

Punta del Este

and peruse copies of his books. One book tells the true story of his son Carlos Miguel, who survived a plane crash in the Andes, which was made into the 1993 film *Alive*. ⊠ *Punta Ballena* ☎ *4257–8611* ⊕ *www. clubhotelcasapueblo.com* ⊠ *180 pesos* ☉ *Daily 10–dusk.*

Isla de Lobos. This island is a government-protected natural reserve and national park home to one of the world's largest colonies of sea lions. You can view them from tour boats that leave regularly from the marina. Its 1907 lighthouse stands nearly 190 feet tall.

WORTH NOTING

Arboretum Lussich. Naturally perfumed with the scent of eucalyptus, this huge arboretum is one of the most important botanical gardens in the world. Its creation was the labor of love of Croatian-Uruguayan botanist Antonio Lussich (1848–1928). The approximate 474 acres contain more than 350 species of trees from outside Uruguay as well as 70 domestic species. Guided tours are in Spanish only. ⊠ *Av. Antonio Lussich* ☎ *4257–8077* ⊠ *Free* ☉ *Jan. and Feb., daily 8–8; Mar.–Dec., daily 9–6.*

Isla Gorriti. Once the site of a prison, Isla Gorriti now attracts a different type of exclusive crowd. High-end residents with their own boats often set Gorriti as their destination to play and party for the day. You can catch a ferry ride from the marina, though, and make a day trip of it.

Note that the island is reachable only by boat, (The *parador*, or beach club, has a good restaurant.)

Punta del Este Port. Punta's sunsets seem even more spectacular when witnessed over its port, with sails and boats dotting the bay. Stop for a drink at any one of the many restaurants lining the street, or make it your destination for a leisurely walk or scenic run. ⊠ *2 de Febrero at Mareantes.*

BEACHES

This stretch of coast has a dozen or so beaches, each with its own high-season personality. All bets are off on activity levels the rest of the year, and remember: what's hot one season may be so "last year" the next. Punta is that kind of place. Locals frequently shorthand things to the *mansa* (calm) side fronting the Río de la Plata—many sections are fine for swimming—and the *brava* (rough) side lining the Atlantic Ocean—its waves draw surfers but should make you think twice about going into the water. By law, all beaches in Uruguay are public.

RÍO DE LA PLATA SIDE

Playa Chihuahua. Uruguay's only sanctioned nude beach—look for the *playa naturista* ("naturalist beach") sign—sits out near the airport west of Punta Ballena and divides into a straight and a gay section. Be cool about it if you go: no cameras, no binoculars, no gawking. **Amenities:** none. **Best for:** nudists.

Playa El Chiringo. This beach, just east of Punta Ballena, can be a bit rough, with gritty sand and deep water. Chiringo catches full sun at midmorning, but shadows descend as the afternoon progresses, and the sun sets behind Punta Ballena. The wind and waves make swimming risky here. **Amenities:** lifeguards. **Best for:** solitude; sunrise.

FAMILY
Fodor's Choice
★

Playa Mansa. The waters are calm at Punta's longest beach and one of its most popular. Good sand, shallow water, many food stands, and proximity to the center of town make it the area's most family-oriented stretch of coast. Catch good sunset views here, and take in one of the late-afternoon beach aerobics classes, too. **Amenities:** food and drink; lifeguards; parking; showers; toilets; water sports. **Best for:** sunset; swimming; walking.

Playa Solanas. The famous Casapueblo museum and hotel sit above this calm beach, also called Portezuelo, at Punta Ballena. Its shallow water shielded from the wind makes it a favorite of families with small children. Great sunset views are a plus here, too. **Amenities:** lifeguards; showers; toilets. **Best for:** sunrise; sunset; swimming; walking.

A CAVALCADE OF STARS

Visitors to Punta del Este during its first heyday in the '50s and '60s rubbed shoulders with the likes of Ingmar Bergman and Yul Brynner. Even Brigitte Bardot, that then-icon of similarly themed St-Tropez, appeared here periodically. Recently celebrities such as Shakira, Madonna, Enrique Iglesias, Antonio Banderas, Ralph Lauren, Bob Dylan, Eric Clapton, and Leonardo DiCaprio have done the Punta circuit. You never know who you might see—in season, that is.

In high season, people come to see and be seen at Punta del Este's glamorous beaches.

ATLANTIC SIDE

Fodor's Choice ★ **La Barra.** The La Barra hamlet is both artistic and trendy, with a number of popular boutiques, restaurants, and nightlife spots. A mostly locally patronized beach sits here, too, where the Río Maldonado spills into the ocean. Keep in mind that swimming is risky. **Amenities:** food and drink; lifeguards; parking; toilets. **Best for:** partiers; sunrise; sunset; surfing; walking.

Fodor's Choice ★ **José Ignacio.** This hamlet with a vibrant art community and some of the most jaw-dropping properties for miles is the choice beach for Punta's most well-heeled and stylish. José Ignacio sits on a miniature peninsula and has beaches with both calm and rough waters. Because it's just enough outside the downtown Punta orbit, visiting is a day trip for most. **Amenities:** food and drink; lifeguards; toilets. **Best for:** partiers; sunrise; sunset; surfing; swimming; walking; windsurfing.

Playa de los Ingleses. While this beach has fine sand, the wind and waves are strong here. Venture into the water at your own risk. You're still close to the center of Punta, meaning this beach sees many nonswimming visitors. Restaurants lining this so-called "Englishmen's Beach" were the spots for afternoon tea in a bygone era. **Amenities:** none. **Best for:** walking.

Playa El Emir. This beach is named for an eccentric Middle Eastern emir who vacationed here and built a house near this stretch of sand.

SUNRISE, SUNSET

How many beach resorts let you enjoy spectacular sunrises *and* sunsets over the water? Punta's orientation on a narrow north–south peninsula allows you to take in both.

High waves make this beach popular with surfers but somewhat dangerous for swimmers. **Amenities:** food and drink; lifeguards; showers; toilets. **Best for:** surfing; walking.

Playa Brava. The golden sand and numerous food stands here draw a young crowd that mostly stays on the beach rather than braving the rough water. Brava is one of the most frequented beaches—largely thanks to *La Mano de Punta,* a giant sculpture with the fingers of an enormous hand appearing to reach out of the sand—where many visitors will surely be snapping photos. This work by Chilean artist Mario Irarrázabal gives the beach its colloquial name, Playa de los Dedos (Beach of the Fingers). **Amenities:** food and drink; lifeguards; showers; toilets. **Best for:** sunrise; sunset; walking.

Playa Montoya. Just east of La Barra beach (but still belonging to La Barra) is this stretch of sand, where a young, attractive crowd mostly stays dry but always seems to have a volleyball or soccer game going. Montoya also is the site of a number of surf competitions. **Amenities:** lifeguards; showers; toilets. **Best for:** partiers; sunset; surfing; swimming; walking,

Fodor's Choice ★ **Playa Manantiales.** Locals have dubbed this trendy stretch of sand Bikini Beach. The swimwear skews a tad more daring here, where people come to see and be seen, as well as swim or play volleyball. During peak season DJs often spin through sunset. If you're looking for a party beach, this is where you want to be. **Amenities:** food and drinks; lifeguards; parking; showers; toilets. **Best for:** partiers; sunrise; sunset; surfing; swimming; windsurfing.

WHERE TO EAT

$$$ EUROPEAN 🍴 **Andres.** Still bearing the name of its founder, this small restaurant on the Rambla Artigas, the oceanside promenade, offers fine dining at moderate prices—its successful recipe for attracting clientele for more than 40 years. You can't beat the view, and in the summer you can appreciate the excellent service while also enjoying the sea breeze. They are famous for their spinach and cheese soufflés, and their grilled meats and fish also are exquisite. [$] *Average main: 500 pesos* ✉ *Parada 1, Edificio Vaguardia* ☎ *4248–1804* 🌐 *www.restaurantandres.com.uy/en* 🕒 *Closed Mon.–Thurs. Mar.–Nov.*

$$$$ FRENCH Fodor's Choice ★ 🍴 **La Bourgogne.** A shaded terra-cotta terrace gives way to a breezeway with arched windows at this restaurant, considered one of the best in Latin America, and opens onto a large split-level dining room with antique sideboards. French chef Jean Paul Bondoux is at the helm, and the food, served by impeccably clad waiters who go about their business with cordial authority, is prepared with only the finest and freshest of ingredients. The breads are baked on the premises (an adjoining bakery sells them by the loaf), and the herbs and berries are grown in the backyard garden. The desserts are sublime—the sampler is a good way to try them all. [$] *Average main: 2500 pesos* ✉ *Av. del Mar at Calle Pedragosa Sierra* ☎ *4248–2007* ✍ *Reservations essential* 🕒 *Closed Mon.–Thurs. May–Nov.*

$ 🍴 **Medialunas Calentitas.** People flock to this classic Punta spot at all
CAFÉ hours for their piping-hot *medialunas,* which are crescent moon–shaped pastries that taste like fluffy croissants and come brushed with a sweet syrup. In fact, many patrons profess they're the best medialunas to be found anywhere. You can sit down or grab your medialunas (and other food, such as chivitos) to go. [$] *Average main: 200 pesos* ✉ *Ruta 10 at Camino del Cerro Eguzquiza* ☎ *4277–2347* 🌐 *www.medialunascalentitas.com.*
Fodor's Choice ★

$$$ 🍴 **Parador La Huella.** *Huella* means footprint, and this now-legendary
SOUTH AMERICAN restaurant certainly has left its mark. Built right on the sand, La Huella takes beach dining to an unrivaled level with exquisite grilled seafood and meats—the octopus is not to be missed—as well as fresh sushi, pastas, and pizzas. The restaurant epitomizes the best of beach culture and spirit, and while celebrity sightings are common, everyone seems to be relaxed and easygoing. Because the place is wildly popular, reservations in peak seasons are necessary. [$] *Average main: 550 pesos* ✉ *Calle de los Cisnes, Brava Beach* ☎ *4486–2779* 🌐 *www.paradorlahuella.com* ✍ *Reservations essential* ⏲ *Closed Apr.–Nov., Mon.–Thurs. No dinner Sun.*
Fodor's Choice ★

$$ 🍴 **Parrilla la Balanza.** It's a bit hard to believe a place as low-key and
SOUTH AMERICAN affordable as this traditional Uruguayan steakhouse exists in chic Punta del Este, but it does—and that's precisely why locals love it. Your best bet is to stick to steak and sides to share, including the platter of mini *provoleta* (baked, seasoned cheese) with a bottle of wine to wash it all down. Expect to wait for a table at prime mealtimes, but the friendly and fast waitstaff will have you feasting in no time. [$] *Average main: 450 pesos* ✉ *25 de Mayo y Santa Teresa* ☎ *4225–3909* 🌐 *www.parrillalabalanza.com.*

WHERE TO STAY

Punta hotels operate on a multitier rate system. Prices go through the roof during Christmas and Easter weeks. Standard high-season rates apply in January and go slightly lower in February. March and December see prices a bit lower still, and then November creeps down a bit more, with some real bargains to be found the rest of the year. On the "rest of the year" topic, lodgings may close for a few weeks in the off-season. Always check ahead. Renting also is popular for long-term stays, and listings are available on sites like 🌐 *www.apuntavamos.com.*

$$$$ 🏨 **L'Auberge.** At this hotel in the heart of Parque del Golf, one of Punta's
HOTEL chicest neighborhoods, a stone water tower, which now contains guest rooms, rises from a double-wing chalet and affords spectacular Punta panoramas. **Pros:** secluded neighborhood; great restaurant; friendly staff. **Cons:** not on beach. [$] *Rooms from: 6870 pesos* ✉ *Parada 19 Brava. Carnoustie y Av. del Agua* ☎ *4888–8888* 🌐 *www.laubergehotel.com* 🛏 *34 rooms, 2 suites* 🍽 *Breakfast.*

$$$$ 🏨 **Conrad Resort & Casino.** Spectacularly lit fountains and gardens, an
HOTEL abundant use of marble, and stunning artwork make this an extraordinary resort. **Pros:** always something going on; friendly staff; phenomenal shows. **Cons:** not a good choice if you crave intimate surroundings;

rooms have started to show some wear. $ *Rooms from: 9500 pesos* ✉ *Rambla Claudio Williman at Parada 4, Playa Mansa* ☎ *4249–1111* ⊕ *www.conrad.com.uy* ⤳ *253 rooms, 41 suites* ⦿ *Breakfast.*

$$$$ 🍽 **Estancia Vik.** This luxe yet bohemian 12-suite ranch property set on
HOTEL 4,000 acres in José Ignacio offers guests the best of both a countryside and beach retreat. **Pros:** tranquil; impressive amenities. **Cons:** one-mile walk to the beach. $ *Rooms from: 25000 pesos* ✉ *Camino Eugenio Saiz Martinez, Km 8* ☎ *9460–5212, 9460–5314* ⊕ *www.vikhotels.com* ⤳ *12 suites* ⦿ *Breakfast.*

$$$$ 🍽 **Las Cumbres Hotel–Art & Spa.** At this alluring, un-Punta-like lodging
HOTEL up a 160-meter (520-foot) hill north of Punta Ballena, you can expect great views and a wooded, away-from-it-all vibe. **Pros:** quiet location; attentive staff; cooler temperatures than in town. **Cons:** far from Punta; need car to stay here; open weekends only during off-season. $ *Rooms from: 5400 pesos* ✉ *Ruta 12, Km 3.5, Laguna del Sauce* ☎ *4257–8689* ⊕ *www.cumbres.com.uy* ⤳ *18 rooms, 10 suites* ☾ *Closed Mon.–Thurs. Apr.–Nov.* ⦿ *Breakfast.*

$$ 🍽 **Hotel Salzburgo.** This delightful hotel occupies a white-stucco,
HOTEL three-story chalet with polished slate floors and exposed beams. **Pros:** friendly owner; secluded neighborhood. **Cons:** removed from the beach. $ *Rooms from: 2000 pesos* ✉ *Calle Pedragosa Sierra at El Havre* ☎ *4248–8851* ⊕ *www.hotelsalzburgo.com* ⤳ *36 rooms* ⦿ *Breakfast.*

$$$$ 🍽 **Serena Hotel.** While few Punta hotels actually sit on the beach, this
HOTEL is the rare exception: a stay here puts you steps from tranquil Playa Mansa and all its amenities. **Pros:** right on beach. **Cons:** not an option for families with young children. $ *Rooms from: 6800 pesos* ✉ *Rambla Williman Parada 24* ☎ *4223–3441* ⊕ *www.serenahotel.com.uy* ⤳ *26 rooms, 6 suites* ⦿ *Breakfast.*

NIGHTLIFE

Nightlife and tastes change capriciously from season to season. Expect fast-paced evenings in bars and nightclubs that might open as late as 1 am and reach a fever pitch around sunrise. Many places are open only in high season and have steep covers.

BARS AND PUBS

Moby Dick. Punta del Este's most classic and popular pub sits right across from the city's port. While most other establishments close or slow in low season, Moby Dick keeps whistles wet year-round. ✉ *Rambla de Artigas 650* ☎ *4244–1230* ⊕ *www.mobydick.com.uy.*

Negroni. During peak season the sunset party at nearby Bikini Beach invariably migrates to Negroni, anchoring the Manantiales strip along Punta's main artery, Ruta 10. Bartenders serve up top-notch cocktails while DJs spin. ✉ *Ruta 10, Km 163.5* ☎ *4277–5451* ☾ *Closed Mar.–Nov.*

DANCE CLUBS

Tequila. This luxe Buenos Aires–based club opens in Punta del Este (La Barra, specifically) during peak summer season and is the place to see and be seen at night. Dress your best and expect to share the dance floor with South America's celebrities and well-heeled. ⊠ *Av. Eduardo Víctor Haedo at Las Espumas* ☉ *Mid-Mar.–Nov.*

LIVE ENTERTAINMENT

Conrad Resort & Casino. For many visitors, the Conrad Resort & Casino defines nightlife in Punta with its casino and a year-round slate of Las Vegas–style shows by some of the biggest stars in Latin entertainment. Even if you don't recognize the names, taking in a performance at the area's largest hotel is de rigueur. The hotel also has one of the city's best clubs on its premises, Ovo, which attracts top international DJs. ⊠ *Rambla Claudio Williman at Parada 4* ☏ *4249–1111.*

SPORTS AND THE OUTDOORS

Not everyone is in Punta for beach bumming—many spend their time in the water. Surfing is popular on the brava side, as is swimming on the mansa side.

GOLF

Cantegril Country Club. This country club has welcomed visitors to its golf course since 1947. At its main location on Salt Lake and Avenida Mauricio Litman, it offers tennis, and at Honorato de Balzac y Calderón de la Barca, it has rugby and soccer fields and tennis courts. ⊠ *Av. San Pablo s/n* ☏ *4222–3211* ⊕ *www.cantegrilcountryclub.com.uy* ☒ *$150 in high season; $50 in low season* ⸙. *18 holes, 6412 yds, par 71.*

Club del Lago Golf. You can play a round of golf at the challenging Club del Lago Golf, the only green in Punta del Este with 20 holes. As the course is popular in peak season, reservations are recommended, as well as confirming hours off-season. ⊠ *Ruta Interbalnearia, Km 116.5* ☏ *4257–8423* ⊕ *www.lagogolf.com* ☒ *$100* ⸙. *20 holes, 6823 yds, par 82.*

HORSEBACK RIDING

Estancias Gauchas. Montevideo-based Estancias Gauchas offers various trips to nearby estancias, where you can ride horses and take part in the gaucho life. There are English-, French-, German-, and Portuguese-speaking guides. ⊠ *Bacacay 1334, Montevideo* ☏ *2916–3011* ⊕ *www. estanciasgauchas.com.*

SHOPPING

Feria Artesanal. An essential part of visiting Punta is exploring the colorful Feria Artesanal on the town's central Plaza Artigas. It's open weekend evenings all year; between Christmas and Easter it's open weekday evenings as well. Popular items include gourds for sipping maté and leather and silver crafts. ⊠ *Pl. Artigas.*

THE NORTHWEST

WELCOME TO THE NORTHWEST

TOP REASONS TO GO

★ **The Quebrada:** In this vast, mountainous, color-splashed landscape, gaze up at an eternity of stars or the otherworldly carved walls of the gorge.

★ **Sports and the Outdoors:** Rivers deep, mountains high, valleys, lakes, and plains all play their part in tempting the adventurous to hike, ride, raft, fish, and rock climb. Take a spin in a kite buggy on the Salinas Grandes or try trekking with a llama.

★ **Folk Music:** Dive into the fabled Argentine folk scene by spending a night out at one of Salta's *peñas* (halls of food, music, and dancing). Wind instruments, diverse percussion, and soaring harmonies define the evocative high-Andean soundtrack.

★ **Wine:** Vintners from the Northwest—especially the Cafayate region of Salta—are gaining worldwide recognition for their *cépages* grown at great heights. The area is part of Argentina's Wine Trail and offers ample touring opportunities for oenophiles.

1 **Jujuy.** A province of varied histories and geographies, Jujuy (pronounced "hoo-hoo-wee") combines a respect for ancestral customs with stunning high-altitude landscapes—its most famous, the Quebrada de Humahuaca, is a UNESCO World Heritage Site.

2 **Salta.** The colonial city of Salta is a perfect base for exploring the wonders of the eponymous province. Chief among them is the Calchaquí Valley, which follows the Inca Trail and Ruta 40 through improbably charming towns in a dusty, cactus-studded wilderness. And in the midst of this are the world's highest vineyards.

GETTING ORIENTED

The landscape in Argentina's northwestern reaches is incredibly varied—from 22,000-foot Andean peaks to the high, barren plateau known as La Puna, from subtropical jungles to narrow sandstone canyons. Much of the area is desert, cut and eroded by raging brown rivers that wash away everything in sight during summer rains. The region's inhabitants have a tough, resilient quality. Here you'll find some of the country's most vibrant cities—but even they grind to a halt each afternoon for a siesta.

5

TREN A LAS NUBES

With a bird's-eye view of its passage over the 64-meter-high (210-foot-high) Viaducto La Polvorilla, the Tren a las Nubes (Train to the Clouds) is probably the Northwest's most famous attraction. This train ride takes you on a 16-hour journey to the high, desolate Puna and back.

(above) Approaching the tracks for the Tren a las Nubes, Salta Province (top right) Car and engine, Tren a las Nubes (bottom right) Famous Viaducto La Polvorilla, a highlight of the journey

The trip begins at 1,322 meters (4,336 feet) as the train climbs out of the Lerma Valley from Salta into the mountains. It rattles over steel bridges that span wild rivers, winding through many turns and tunnels to reach the 4,197-meter (13,770-foot) high viaduct just beyond San Antonio de los Cobres, the only town of any size in the Puna. Here, you can disembark to bargain with locals selling textiles and ceramics next to the railway line.

The 217-km (135-mile) round trip takes in 29 bridges, 21 tunnels, 13 viaducts, and a couple of hairpin bends and spirals, all of which are interpreted by the bilingual guides on board. Medical assistants ride with you to help with altitude sickness, while an ambulance follows the train's tracks. Stop in at the dining car; breakfast and an afternoon snack are included in the fare.

WHEN TO GO

The heavy rains of summer mean the train stops running completely from the end of November through March, and in winter those that mind the cold might want to think twice about committing to 16 hours' travel in the mountains. On August 1, the Festival of the Pachamama is celebrated in San Antonio de los Cobres.

WHAT'S OUT THE WINDOW

The infrastructure alone makes this trip incredible, as the rack-and-pinionless train uses all the tricks in the book to gain altitude while avoiding steep grades. The Tren a las Nubes isn't just for railway enthusiasts, though: an ethereal landscape offers view after spectacular view as the train twists and turns along the route. When it runs parallel with a road or passes through one of the infrequent villages, there are people to wave to. In San Antonio de los Cobres and on the lookout point at Viaducto La Polvorilla, locals gather round the train for a chat—and to sell handicrafts and trinkets. The guides in each carriage provide lots of information for each stage of the journey, backed up by videos; when there's nothing more to be seen out the window, or once the sun's gone down on the return journey, they screen movies.

SAN ANTONIO DE LOS COBRES

San Antonio, the highest town in Argentina, is as slow-moving as many of the country's small rural communities; it's also heavily battered by sun and wind, and there is little oxygen in the air. Essential accessories for visitors are sunscreen, extra clothes for warmth, and coca leaves—they're chewed as an aide to digestion (which helps with altitude sickness). All that saliva production promotes swallowing, too, which will pop your ears.

Only in the past couple of years have there been any lodging options: the basic **Hostal del Cielo** (✉ Belgrano at Comandante Goulu ☎ 387/490–9912 ⊕ www.vivirenloscobres.com. ar) and the smarter **Hosteria de las Nubes** (✉ RN51 s/n ☎ 387/490–9059 ⊕ www.hoteldelasnubes.com) are the best right now. Renting a room in someone's house is an option, too. A small ethnographic and archaeological museum, ANTAPU, fills in some detail on the town's background, but it's still very new and needs more work. The main business is making artesanías—handmade goods that can be sold to tourists.

RESERVATIONS

Reservations can be made at many agencies in Salta or with **Les Amis** (✉ Cerrito 844 ☎ 0810/345–3030 ⊕ www.lesamisviajes. com) in Buenos Aires and cost 1,300 pesos. ✉ Salta Station, Ameghino and Balcarce ☎ 0800/888–6823 ⊕ www. trenalasnubes.com.ar.

EXTENDING YOUR TRIP

Though you can buy only return tickets, there's nothing to stop you getting off in San Antonio and continuing north to the salinas (salt flats) and on to Purmamarca in Jujuy. There's no public transport; for the right price, however, drivers will take you in their own cars. Going south to Cachi isn't as easy; the road is narrow and dangerous. Make sure to tell the gendarmeria (border guards) in San Antonio if you're going to attempt this route.

Updated by
Sorrel Mose-
ley-Williams

This region flourished under the Inca, then attracted trea-sure-seeking Spaniards during colonial times; now it's luring an international contingent of tourists—and rightly so. The Northwest is notable for diverse locales, ranging from colonial towns to thriving vineyards and arid Andean deserts. It appeals to diverse types of travelers, too. Hikers converge on colorful canyons; oenophiles satisfy their wine cravings in Cafayate; and history buffs get their fix at ancient ruins and archaeology museums. Visitors who swoon over scenery, meanwhile, ascend to the clouds on the Tren a las Nubes: a day-long trip that's literally and figuratively breathtaking.

Despite their proximity, the provinces of Jujuy and Salta are at opposing ends of the cultural and geographical spectrum. The capital of the former is San Salvador de Jujuy. A quiet business-oriented city with a historic center, it serves as the provincial gateway. To the north is the Quebrada de Humahuaca, a stunning UNESCO-designated valley poised 3,000 meters (9,843 feet) above sea level; colorful mineral deposits make its sandstone walls particularly photogenic, and small towns like Purmamarca, Tilcara, and Humahuaca that are rich in indigenous culture as well as natural beauty give it added appeal. Llama-trekking through the foothills and a visit to a well-preserved pre-Inca settlement are among the highlights here. The Quebrada is also a great base for exploring the vast salt flats known as Salinas Grandes.

Salta Province, to the south, is anchored by its capital city—also called Salta. The jewel in Argentina's colonial crown is blessed with bright, beautiful religious architecture, interesting museums, and atmospheric streets. More sophisticated than San Salvador de Jujuy but still a world away from Buenos Aires, the city has an array of restaurants specializing in local dishes, plus a lively nightlife scene led by folk-music peñas. Continuing south to the vineyard-studded Calchaquí Valley, you can sample wares at the bodegas in and around Cafayate, where wine tourism opportunities abound. This region is proud of its own spectacular canyon, dubbed Quebrada de Las Conchas. Looping back from it to Salta on fabled Ruta 40, you'll encounter the picturesque Andean villages of Cachi and Molinos, as well the cactus-capped hills of Parque Nacional Los Cardones.

PLANNING

WHEN TO GO
January and February are Argentina's summer vacation months, meaning hotels get booked up and prices rise. Ironically, these two months coincide with rainy season, when flooding and/or landslides can block mountain roads. (The Salta–Cachi route is notorious for this.) Other busy times are winter break (July), Easter week, and moveable feasts such as Carnaval in the Quebrada de Humahuaca. Most facilities remain open year-round.

GETTING HERE AND AROUND
AIR TRAVEL
Aerolíneas Argentinas/Austral (⊕ *www.aerolineas.com.ar*) has direct flights from Buenos Aires to Jujuy and Salta, as well as connecting flights between Salta and Iguazú or Mendoza. LAN (⊕ *www.lan.com*) and Andes Líneas Aéreas (⊕ *www.andesonline.com*) fly from Buenos Aires to Salta. All flights between Buenos Aires and the Northwest use the capital's Aeroparque Jorge Newbery, about 15 minutes north of downtown.

BUS TRAVEL
Buses are reliable, affordable, and well used, though certain routes require a little advance planning. Some companies offer roadside pickup; others have luxury double-decker vehicles offering overnight services and maybe even a glass of sparkling wine and a game of bingo. Tourist offices can advise which companies go where. In peak season, buy tickets a day or two in advance.

CAR TRAVEL
Traveling outside of urban centers is often easiest by car. However, picking up a rental vehicle in one city and dropping it off in another incurs significant extra costs, so plan to drive for only parts of your journey or commit to a round trip. Roads are generally good and not very crowded, but be prepared for paved roads turning *ripio* (unpaved) and bumpy for long stretches. Very few routes require a 4X4 (apart from wet weather).

Two main roads cross the area: the legendary Ruta 40, winding its unpaved way through small towns nearly 3,000 miles to the country's southern tip, and Ruta 9, the ancient road of the Incas, which takes you from Bolivia through San Salvador de Jujuy, Salta, and on toward Córdoba. Before you set out, visit an Automóvil Club Argentino

(⊕ *www.aca.org.ar*) office for maps and information, especially during the January–March rainy season.

REMIS TRAVEL

For short trips (e.g., Salta to Cafayate), consider taking a *remis* (a hired car with driver). Some routes have shared services, where you split the cost with others making the same journey. You can find a remis at airports, bus stations, and on main plazas—or your hotel can call one for you. Be sure to agree on a price before setting off.

HEALTH AND SAFETY

Visitors unaccustomed to traveling at great heights may be susceptible to *soroche*, or altitude sickness, resulting in shortness of breath and headaches. Walk slowly, eat light meals, and drink plenty of fluids (but avoid alcohol). Locals swear by the *coqueando* remedy: sucking on coca leaves (sold at corner groceries and street vendors for around 10 pesos). Tear off the stems and stuff several leaves into the space between your teeth and cheek; leave them in for an hour or so, neither chewing nor spitting, but swallowing when you salivate.

Aside from being sold an overpriced tour (recommended rates are listed in Salta's tourism office), you're unlikely to encounter crime, and local people are happy to receive visitors. Many hotels pride themselves on not needing safety deposit boxes.

The many roadside shrines marking car accidents, especially on winding mountain routes, are a reminder to check your speed. Also take care on the many bumpy, unpaved roads. And wear your seatbelt, as it is the law.

RESTAURANTS

The Northwest's indigenous heritage still influences its cuisine: corn, grains, beans, and potatoes are common ingredients stemming back to the days of the Inca. Dishes worth trying include *locro*, a spicy soup with corn, beans, and red peppers that becomes a rich stew when meat is added; *tamales*, ground corn baked with potatoes and meat and tied up in a corn husk; and *humita*, grated corn with melted cheese cooked in a corn husk. Grilled *cabrito* (goat) is also a regional specialty. For dessert you may come across *cayote,* an interesting concoction of green-squash marmalade served with nuts and local goat cheese.

HOTELS

Hotels in the Northwest's major cities tend to be modern and comfortable. Most accept credit cards; if you are paying in cash, however, do ask whether a discount is offered. Many *estancias* (ranches) in the foothills welcome guests and are listed with local tourist offices. Although the whole region has really started to open up to local and foreign tourism, chain hotels are few and far between. Instead, take advantage of a dazzling array of boutique hotels and estancias built—or reinvented—to reflect history and ever mindful of their location. *Hotel reviews have been shortened. For full information, visit Fodors.com.*

WHAT IT COSTS

	$	$$	$$$	$$$$
Restaurants (in Pesos)	Under 65 pesos	65 pesos–99 pesos	100 pesos–150 pesos	over 150 pesos
Hotels (in USD)	Under $116	$116–$200	$201–$300	over $301

Restaurant prices are the average cost of a main course at dinner or, if dinner is not served, at lunch. Hotel prices are the lowest cost of a standard double room in high season.

SAN SALVADOR DE JUJUY

1,643 km (1,020 miles) northwest of Buenos Aires; 92 km (57 miles) north of Salta on RN9.

Founded by Spaniards in 1593, San Salvador de Jujuy (known as Jujuy to most Argentineans and as "S.S. de Jujuy" on signs) is a compact city. Its focal point is Plaza General Belgrano, in the city center between the Río Grande and Río Xibi Xibi. The square is home to a number of key sights, the 18th-century cathedral and grand Casa de Gobierno among them.

The city's quarter-million inhabitants—including a large indigenous population—busy themselves with administering the province's main sources of income (tobacco, mining, and sugarcane), although more are beginning to deal with tourism. Jujuy may lack nearby Salta's colonial dreaminess and ample hotel selection, but it has a laid-back, unadulterated local culture plus a touch of frontier-town charm. It also makes a great stop-off point and touring base. Just outside town you can ride horses along mountain paths in the jungle or go boating in valley waterways.

GETTING HERE AND AROUND

Aerolíneas Argentinas (⊕ *www.aerolineas.com.ar*) flies six times a day from Buenos Aires, making the trip in two hours and 15 minutes. Jujuy's Aeropuerto Dr. Horacio Guzmán is 30 km (19 miles) southeast of town. La Veloz del Norte, Balut, and Panamericano buses travel between Salta and Jujuy; the latter two continue north to Purmamarca, Tilcara, Humahuaca, and La Quiaca at the Bolivian border. La Quiaqueño buses also depart for La Quiaca nine times a day. Other bus companies serving Jujuy include Andesmar, Atahualpa, and La Estrella.

ESSENTIALS

Bus Contacts Andesmar ☎ *388/423–3293.* **Atahualpa** ☎ *388/155–815–298.* **Balut** ☎ *388/422–2134* ⊕ *www.balutsrl.com.ar.* **La Estrella** ☎ *388/424–3218.* **La Quiaqueño** ☎ *388/428–0041.* **La Veloz del Norte** ☎ *388/423–4409.* **Panamericano** ☎ *388/425–4336.* **Terminal de Omnibus** ✉ *Dorrego 365* ☎ *388/422–1374.*

Rental Cars Hertz ✉ *San Martín 900* ☎ *388/491–1505* ⊕ *www.hertz.com.*

Taxis Parada Uno ☎ *388/425–6500.*

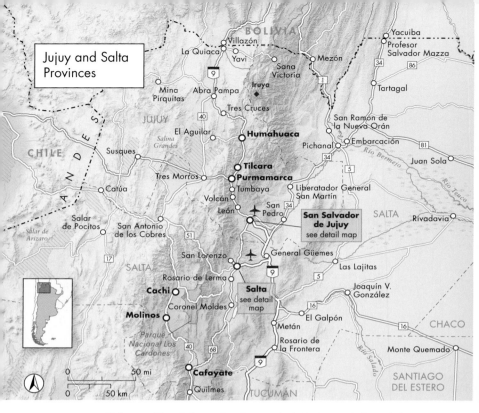

Jujuy and Salta Provinces

Visitor and Tour Information Secretaría de Turismo y Cultura de la Provincia de Jujuy ✉ *Gorriti 295* ☎ *388/422–1325* ⊕ *www.turismo.jujuy.gov.ar* ☉ *Daily 9–9.*

TOURS

NASA. You can arrange airport pickups, city tours, eco-oriented trips, and rural excursions around Jujuy through NASA, a family-owned and -operated travel office with two generations of experience. ✉ *Av. Senador Pérez 154* ☎ *388/422–3938* ⊕ *www.nasa.tur.ar* ☎ *From 380 pesos.*

Paisajes del Noroeste. This Jujuy specialist runs a range of tours and day trips, including minibus outings to the remote village of Iruya and excursions to Hornocal (an impressive 21-color hill near Humahuaca). ✉ *San Martín 132* ☎ *388/423–7565* ⊕ *www.paisajesdelnoroeste.tur.ar* ☎ *From 350 pesos.*

Tawantinsuyo. The efficient, friendly Tawantinsuyo agency can organize local transfers and custom tours. ✉ *Belgrano 566* ☎ *388/424–4658* ⊕ *www.evttawantinsuyo.tur.ar* ☎ *From 380 pesos per person for day tour of the Quebrada.*

EXPLORING

TOP ATTRACTIONS

Fodor's Choice ★ **Casa de Gobierno.** The 1907 Casa de Gobierno (Government House) fronts the plaza on San Martín and contains the provincial government offices. A first-floor hall, the Salón de la Bandera, displays the original Argentine flag donated by General Belgrano in 1813, a gift to the city after it cooperated with the Belgrano-headed Exodus of Jujuy during the War of Independence. Entry is on Calle Sarmiento. The flag was replaced a few years later by the current white and sky-blue stripe version, and the one here is now used as the national coat of arms. ⊠ *San Martín 450* 🕾 *388/423–9400* ⊕ *www.jujuy.gov.ar* 🎫 *Free* 🕙 *Daily 8 am–9 pm.*

Catedral de Jujuy. The cathedral dates from 1765 and was the first building constructed in the city; however, it has been augmented and remodeled so many times that it's now a hodgepodge of architectural styles. The interior contains an ornately carved, gold-plated pulpit, said to be the finest in South America. A close look reveals an intricate population of carved figures, biblical and otherwise. It was inspired by the Cusqueña school of art from Cuzco, Peru, as were the building's ornate doors and confessionals. The cathedral museum next door houses a wealth of religious art. ⊠ *West side of Pl. General Belgrano* 🕾 *388/423–5333* 🎫 *Free; museum 5 pesos* 🕙 *Weekdays 10–noon and 5–10, weekends 7–noon and 5–10; museum Tues.–Fri 9:30–12:30, Sat. 10–1.*

Centro Cultural y Museo Pasquini López. Elevated on a natural balcony overlooking the city and with its own small patch of regenerated jungle, this mansion has a little museum of centuries-old ceramics and other artifacts found locally. Better still, botanists have been developing a mile-long nature trail that buzzes with cicadas. Knowledgeable guides can enlighten you on the flora. Call ahead to organize tours in English. ⊠ *Victor Hugo 45, Alto la Viña* 🕾 *388/15–439–2548* ⊕ *www.grupoyavi.com.ar* 🎫 *5 pesos* 🕙 *Weekdays 9:30–12:30 and 4:30–7:30.*

Iglesia de San Francisco. An ornate 18th-century wooden pulpit with dozens of figures of monks is the centerpiece of the Church of St. Francis, two blocks west of Plaza General Belgrano. There's some debate about who carved the pulpit: it may have been local artisans, or the pulpit may have been transported from Bolivia. Although the church and bell tower look colonial, they date from 1930. ⊠ *Lavalle 325* 🎫 *Free* 🕙 *Daily 10–1 and 5–9.*

Museo Arqueológico Provincial. The Provincial Archaeological Museum houses such treasures as a 2,600-year-old ceramic goddess and the 700-year-old mummy of a teen boy found in Tilcara. Ancient bones are on display, too—including the skeleton of a cap-wearing shaman buried with his medical kit. Ceramic pots painted with geometric designs from Yavi and Humahuaca are constantly being added to the collection. ⊠ *Lavalle 434* 🕾 *388/422–1343* 🎫 *5 pesos* 🕙 *Weekdays 8–8.*

Fodor's Choice ★ **Plaza General Belgrano.** Orange trees and vendors populate the central square, which is surrounded by colonial buildings—including the imposing government palace. It's empty by day, but starts to fill with

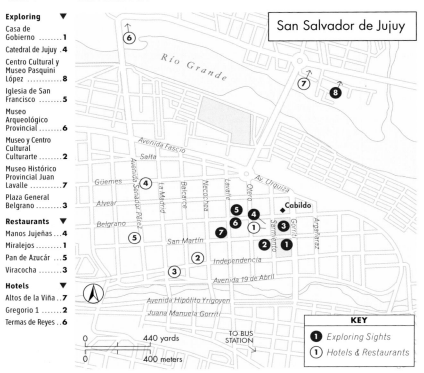

San Salvador de Jujuy

KEY

❶ Exploring Sights

① Hotels & Restaurants

gossiping *jujeños*, old and young, by late afternoon. ■TIP→ **The plaza benefits from free Wi-Fi.**

WORTH NOTING

Museo Histórico Provincial Juan Lavalle. Arms, trophies, and military memorabilia collected from the 25 years of fighting for independence are on display at the Juan Lavalle Provincial History Museum. In this adobe building General Juan Lavalle, a hero of the War of Independence and an enemy of the dictator Juan Manuel de Rosas, was assassinated. A replica of the door through which Lavalle was shot in 1746 is part of the exhibit. ⊠ *Lavalle 256* 🕾 *388/422–1355* 🎟 *4 pesos* ⊙ *Weekdays 8–8, Sat. 9–1 and 4–8.*

Museo y Centro Cultural Culturarte. Drop into Culturarte to get a quick hit of contemporary art and photography. After seeing the exhibits, you can order a coffee and pull up a breezy balcony seat for a different side-on view of Government House. ⊠ *Sarmiento and San Martín* 🕾 *388/424–9548* 🎟 *Free* ⊙ *Weekdays 9–1, 3–5:30, and 6–9, Sat. 10–1 and 5–9, Sun. 5–8.*

WHERE TO EAT

$$ ARGENTINE 🍴 **Manos Jujeñas.** Ponchos on the walls, old paintings, native artifacts, stucco archways, and Andean background music are clues that this might be one of the best places to sample authentic Northwestern cuisine. Try the *locro*: a stew of maize, white beans, beef, chorizo, pancetta, and a wonderful red pepper–oil glaze, all of which come together in a mélange of savory, starchy flavors. Ask for a table at the back for a more authentic and less hurried dining experience. [$] *Average main: 90 pesos* ✉ *Senador Pérez 379* ☎ *388/424–3270* 💳 *No credit cards* 🕓 *Closed Mon.*

$$ ARGENTINE 🍴 **Miralejos.** With a great location on the main square nestling between the cathedral and the handicrafts market, Miralejos serves both Argentine standards and regional dishes with a view of the bustling activity. Enjoy them with a home-brewed beer. [$] *Average main: 90 pesos* ✉ *Sarmiento 268* ☎ *388/422–4911.*

$$ ARGENTINE 🍴 **Pan de Azucár.** For jujeña classics with an eclectic twist, head to Pan de Azucár, where an ample menu offers original concoctions of the local staple, llama—think curry, carpaccio, grilled filet, or stuffed in ravioli. House specialties also include quinoa, pork, and pasta. [$] *Average main: 86 pesos* ✉ *Senador Perez 110* ☎ *388/423–2392* 💳 *No credit cards.*

$$ ARGENTINE Fodor's Choice ★ 🍴 **Viracocha.** The menu at this unassuming *picanteria* (restaurant specializing in spicy foods) has everything from trout to rabbit, but llama or quinoa are the dishes to try: give them a go as an *empanada* starter. Less adventurous eaters can have one of the pasta dishes. Named after an Andean god, Viracocha's staff is helpful, and the atmosphere amid the yellow walls and arches is happily relaxed. [$] *Average main: 72 pesos* ✉ *Independencia 994, corner of Lamadrid* ☎ *388/423–3554* 💳 *No credit cards* 🕓 *Closed Tues. No dinner Sun.*

WHERE TO STAY

$$ HOTEL FAMILY Fodor's Choice ★ 🏨 **Altos de la Viña.** This former state-owned hotel, a short ride out of town, has comfortable rooms and recreational facilities that invite you to linger; the view from the swimming pool takes in most of the city and the mountains beyond. **Pros:** great pool; good for families; helipad. **Cons:** very little within walking distance. [$] *Rooms from: US$139* ✉ *Pasquini López 50, Alto la Viña* ☎ *388/426–2626* 🌐 *www.altosdelavina.com.ar* 🛏 *60 rooms* 🍽 *Breakfast.*

$ HOTEL 🏨 **Gregorio 1.** This downtown boutique hotel has sober rooms with parquet floors and all the modern conveniences. **Pros:** close to everything; attentive service. **Cons:** few in-hotel services. [$] *Rooms from: US$70* ✉ *Independencia 829* ☎ *388/424–4747* 🌐 *www.gregoriohotel.com* 🛏 *18 rooms, 1 suite* 🍽 *Breakfast.*

$$ HOTEL 🏨 **Termas de Reyes.** Built on the edge of a spectacular river valley, this countryside complex has natural thermal baths—both indoor and out—that bubble up from underground hot springs. **Pros:** the chance to take the cure and find inner peace; great views. **Cons:** located 19 km (12 miles) outside of Jujuy on a partially paved road. [$] *Rooms from: US$195* ✉ *R4, Km 19* ☎ *388/492–2522* 🌐 *www.termasdereyes.com* 🛏 *60 rooms* 🍽 *Breakfast.*

5

Head to Jujuy Province to see Puna architecture—like this church in Tafna—as stark as the landscape.

NIGHTLIFE

El Bodegón. This popular downtown peña with hundreds of vinyl records on the walls calls itself "the cathedral of Jujuy folklore." It's predominantly filled with a young crowd of locals who have no qualms about taking to the small stage. ⊠ *Güemes, corner of Ramirez de Velazco* ☎ *388/423–0802.*

Punta Norte. Check out this peña on the main plaza for live regional music and local bands. ⊠ *Bolivar and Belgrano, Tilcara.*

Urquiza Bar. Pop into this buzzing downtown bar for live music and happy hours most nights of the week. ⊠ *Alvear 441, corner of Gral. Urquiza* ☎ *388/15–582–2129* ⊙ *Closed Mon. and Tues.*

SHOPPING

Annuar Shopping. The shiny Annuar Shopping mall may stock regular high-street fare, but it's worth popping into for two reasons: first, to cool off with an ice cream and some AC on a hot summer's day, and, second, for a different perspective of the Cathedral's steeple from the top floor. ⊠ *Belgrano 563* ☎ *388/423–6178* ⊕ *www.annuarshopping. com.ar.*

Paseo de los Artesanos. The modest Paseo de los Artesanos on Plaza General Belgrano has reasonable prices on all kinds of woven and handcrafted souvenirs. And those *coca* tea bags, imported from Bolivia, are a curiosity that's hard to resist. ■ TIP→ **The small café at the back is ideal for a quick empanada pitstop.** ⊠ *Sarmiento 240* ⊙ *9 am–9:30 pm.*

SPORTS AND THE OUTDOORS

With its jungles, lakes, waterfalls, and wild rivers, the area around San Salvador de Jujuy is great for hiking and horseback riding. There are a number of companies offering excursions, but only a handful have an online presence, which makes things hard, as most trips must be booked a few days in advance. Check the Jujuy tourism board's website (⊕ *www.turismo.jujuy.gov.ar*) for a complete list of operators.

JUJUY PROVINCE

San Salvador de Jujuy is both the capital of Argentina's northernmost province and the region's gateway; the star attraction here, however, is the 161-km (100-mile) Quebrada de Humahuaca, which has been used as a trade route for more than 10,000 years. The gorge is breathtaking, and each of its three noteworthy towns—Purmamarca, Tilcara, and Humahuaca—has a unique feel. Most of the region's attractions are within day-trip distance of these bases; in fact, there are few visitor facilities elsewhere.

By far the largest part of Jujuy is the area known as the Puna: vast, high-altitude desert plains that merge into the Andes. Except for some villages built around exquisite adobe churches (most notably Yavi, near the Bolivian border), this area is pristine and tough, baked by day and chilly at night. The easiest way to experience it is on a trip to the Salinas Grandes (Great Salt Plains) from Purmamarca, a two-hour drive offering spectacular views as you scale the Cuesta de Lipan range.

For an otherworldly adventure, head to Laguna de los Pozuelos, with its exotic year-round colony of pink flamingos. Note, though, that it's a long way from the nearest hotel. The best approach is via Abra Pampa, the town where Ruta 9 and Ruta 40 meet, a 97-km (60-mile) drive from Humahuaca.

PURMAMARCA

65 km (40 miles) north of San Salvador de Jujuy.

Nestled in the shadow of craggy rocks and multicolored, cactus-studded hills—with the occasional low-flying cloud floating by—the colonial village of Purmamarca is one of the best bases from which to explore the Quebrada. Its 2,195-meter (7,200-foot) altitude, dry air, and dearth of artificial light also make it a great spot for stargazing.

Here blazing red adobe replaces the white stucco used in architecture elsewhere, and the simple, square buildings play off the matching red rock. Come quick, before it's completely transformed from a two-horse town with basic stores and artisans selling their wares in the pleasant, tree-shaded plaza into a more exclusive destination.

GETTING HERE AND AROUND

Located on Ruta 52, Purmamarca is just a 3-km (2-mile) detour from Ruta 9. Balut buses traveling between Jujuy and Humahuaca run through about 10 times a day. Almost no place here has its own

Continued on page 225

TOURING THE
QUEBRADA DE HUMAHUACA

by Andy Footner, updated by Sorrel Moseley-Williams

This rugged, windswept canyon connects Argentina's desert-like Puna near Bolivia with the city of San Salvador de Jujuy 150 km (93 mi) further south. It's a natural passage through the surrounding mountains, so it's no surprise that thousands of years of history have played out between its sandstone walls. For many, those very walls are the main attraction: colorful minerals, seismic activity, and a powerful river continue to shape one of Argentina's most fascinating geological formations.

Cardones, or cacti, and sandstone formations are a major part of the landscape in Argentina's northwest

HISTORY OF THE QUEBRADA

Jujuy Province, Quebrada de Humahuaca landscape near Purmamarca village

The Quebrada de Humahuaca continues to be carved into existence by the ever-changing Rio Grande. A roaring, splashing force in summer, the river in winter reduces to barely a trickle in its wide, dry riverbed. You'll have a good view wherever you are in the main canyon of the Quebrada; Route 9, the main north-south road through here, runs parallel to it. Like the river, people have come through this canyon in both trickles and torrents over the centuries—but unlike the river, the sense of history is strong whenever you visit.

PRE-INCAN TO THE CAMINO INCA

Ten thousand years ago, the first humans to inhabit the Southern Cone came from the north through this very canyon. Some stayed, becoming this area's original indigenous peoples. In the 15th and 16th centuries, the Incan Empire left its mark on the valley and the culture; the single road through this protected canyon became part of the hugely important Camino Inca—

PEÑAS

Clubs, restaurants, and *peñas* attract both locals and tourists, who come to hear regional folk bands give it their all on small, cramped stages. Adding to the rowdy, dinner-theater atmosphere are the local dancers who entice (and often entrap) foreigners into strutting their stuff on stage; it's always a good laugh, no matter what language you speak.

the Inca Trail, a system of roads used to travel through the empire which eventually spanned much of the Andes. Because of this unique Andean history, the culture here can seem to share more with those of Bolivia and Peru than with other parts of Argentina; keep your ears open in town squares: in this part of Argentina you can still hear people speaking Quechua and Aymara, two of the main languages of the Incas.

Tilcara, Children's carnival, Quebrada de Humauaca

JESUITS AND VICEROYALTIES

The Incans weren't the only conquering force that found the protected valley appealing: in the 17th century, Jesuit priests used Aymara and Quechua to convert the locals to Catholocism, which helped the Spanish eventually use the Quebrada to connect the Viceroyalties (administration center) of Peru in Lima and La Plata in what would later become Buenos Aires. Today, the local mix of pre-Incan, Incan, and Christian traditions and symbols are reflected in everything from dress to architecture to the kinds of items you'll find for sale.

WORLD HERITAGE

Traditions and festivals celebrated along the Quebrada include a unique combination of ancient Andean rites and European religious celebrations. In 2003, UNESCO added the Quebrada to its World Heritage list for its continued legacy of pre-Hispanic and pre-Incan settlements in the area.

SHOPPING CULTURE

The best shopping is in Humahuaca. Numerous small shops sell tourist trinkets, and there's a daily handicrafts market on the steps leading up the hill to the monument. Most of the items for sale will be familiar to anyone who has traveled in the central Andean region, and there are a few artisans making jewelery and other items in more modern Argentine styles.

GEOLOGICAL COLORS: A TIMELINE

| white composed of limestone | | purple/violet colored by lead and calcium | yellow composed of iron hydroxides |

The hills in the Quebrada de Humahuaca are famous for their colors—caused by mineral deposits formed from 1 to 400 million years ago. The two best places to see the colors are the Paleta del Pintur (Painter's Palette, pictured) and the Cerro de los Siete Colores (Hill of Seven Colors).

red composed of clay and iron oxide

light orange composed of red clay, mud, and sand

green colored by copper oxides

brown colored by manganese oxides and hydroxides

3–4 MILLION YEARS

1–2 MILLION YEARS

ITINERARY

Salinas Grandes

DAY ONE

MORNING: Purmamarca

The smallest and most picturesque town in the Quebrada, Purmamarca is about two hours north of Salta or over an hour north of San Salvador de Jujuy on R9. The turnoff (left side) onto RA52 is well marked. Arrive as early as possible for the morning light. Get your bearings with a view of the Cerro de Los Siete Colores (Hill of Seven Colors) from a popular viewpoint on the north side of RA52; the trailhead is on your right as you approach town. You can also walk along Paseo de los Colorados, a dirt road (watch for vehicles) that winds around the base of hill itself; to get to it from Plaza 9 de Julio, head west on Florida for 3 blocks.

AFTERNOON: Siesta or Salinas Grandes

Purmamarca goes from quiet to dead during the afternoon siesta; take a siesta yourself, or head out on a half-day side trip. Drive farther west on RA52 as it winds its way up the **Cuesta de Lipan** (the Lipan Slope, the Quebrada's mountainous western barrier) and on to the **Salinas Grandes** (Big Salt Flats). If you're without your own transport, there are plenty of taxis, remises, or guides to take you. Technically, the Salinas Grandes themselves are outside of the Quebrada, but the drive there takes you through a dramatic mountain pass—and the highest driveable point in the Quebrada; look for a sign marking your altitude of 4170 m (13,681 ft). After an hour or two (depending on your vehicle's horsepower and photo stops), you'll take unpaved EX-RN40 south to the turnoff (right side) for the Salinas Grandes. Drive until you're on the salt flats themselves—this is the parking lot. This is a working salt flat; don't miss gazing into the clear blue harvesting pools.

NIGHT: Purmamarca

Once back in Purmamarca, explore some nouveau Andean cuisine in town. After dinner, head to a peña where musicians offer renditions of folk songs about the Quebrada.

DAY TWO

MORNING: Tilcara

Set out early and take R9 north to Tilcara; head straight to the **Pucará de Tilcara**. This partially reconstructed pre-Columbian fort shows one of the most complex ruins in Argentina. Make time to visit the botanical garden next door. Wander through the central square's market, one of the best in the region. Leave to arrive in Humahuaca before noon.

AFTERNOON: Humahuaca to Maimara

Every day at noon at San Francisco Solano church, a statue of the church's namesake pops out of the clock tower and, as the story goes, delivers a blessing. Catch this if you can, then have lunch and explore the market near the monument steps. Stop in at the small yet atmospheric folklore museum. On your way back to Salta or Jujuy, make brief photo stops at the **Tropic of Capricorn** at Huacalera, the church at Uquia (known for its Cuzco School angel paintings), and the photogenic cemetery of the town of Maimara. If sunset is approaching, however, simply head straight for Maimara—visible behind the cemetary is the Painter's Palette. This flat segment of the east canyon wall contains colored layers of mineral deposits that attain stunningly rich hues as the light shines in from the west.

Pucará de Tilcara

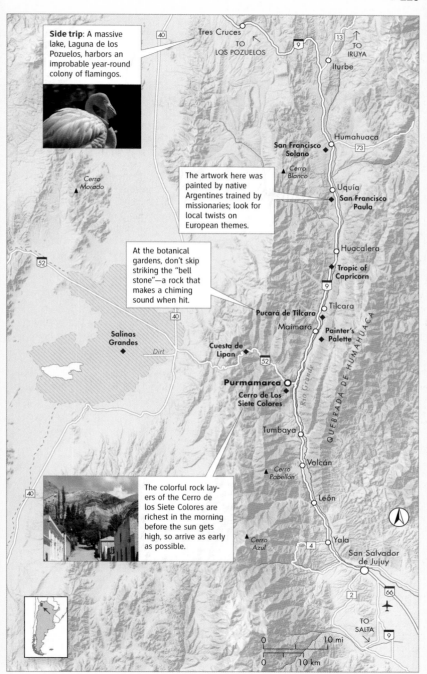

Side trip: A massive lake, Laguna de los Pozuelos, harbors an improbable year-round colony of flamingos.

The artwork here was painted by native Argentines trained by missionaries; look for local twists on European themes.

At the botanical gardens, don't skip striking the "bell stone"—a rock that makes a chiming sound when hit.

The colorful rock layers of the Cerro de los Siete Colores are richest in the morning before the sun gets high, so arrive as early as possible.

Tres Cruces

TO LOS POZUELOS

TO IRUYA

Iturbe

Humahuaca

San Francisco Solano

Cerro Blanco

Cerro Morado

Uquía
San Francisco Paula

Huacalera

Tropic of Capricorn

Pucará de Tilcara

Tilcara

Maimará

Painter's Palette

Salinas Grandes

Dirt

Cuesta de Lipan

Purmamarca
Cerro de Los Siete Colores

Río Grande

QUEBRADA DE HUMAHUACA

Tumbaya

Volcán

Cerro Pabellón

León

Cerro Azul

Yala

San Salvador de Jujuy

TO SALTA

0   10 mi

0   10 km

PLANNING YOUR VISIT

PUBLIC TRANSIT

A good and frequent bus system and shared taxis between the main towns mean hitchhiking isn't common or necessary. However, although buses reach all destinations described, renting a car or going with a guide mean you can stop at any point to explore, take pictures, and admire the views.

SELF-DRIVE LOGISTICS

Cars can be rented in Salta and Jujuy. Check the conditions for off-road driving and the options for crossing a pass into Chile—these are not automatically included in the rental.

Good to Know:

■ Car hire agencies like to calculate the price on the spot and there's little transparency in their calculations. Many destinations from Salta and San Salvador de Jujuy involve unpaved roads that are punishing on cars, so it might help to let them know your itinerary if you're only visiting the Quebrada (where all the roads are paved). Pricing systems favor round trips (i.e. there's a big surcharge for dropping off a car in another city).

■ Gas stations can be found in most of the towns, but they don't all take credit cards. Except for in Humahuaca (ACA—the Automovil Club Argentino) and San Salvador de Jujuy, plan for cash only. As well as providing gas and good maps, ACA is the Argentine equivalent of the AAA and can help you out if your car breaks down somewhere.

■ The roads in the Quebrada are better than most in the area—they're well marked and have clear passing lanes—but during the rainy season (between October and February), falling rocks or mudslides can block the roads.

GUIDED TOURS

Personal guides, with their own cars or ones owned by their companies, can be found through the tourism offices of Salta and Jujuy.

For Indigenous Culture:

When you pull into the town of Humahuaca, you'll see a group of locals waiting under the main sign. These are tour guides; if you know a little Spanish, they're a wealth of information on how Wichí and other indigenous peoples live and work in Humahuaca today. Even if you're here with a tour guide of your own, he or she might hire one of these guides—they're part of an initiative to provide career alternatives in a place where drug smuggling (Bolivia is just a few clicks north, after all) has in the past been one of the only decent-paying jobs available.

For Getting Out Into the Landscape:

Caravana de Llamas (☎ 0388/408–8000 ⊕ www.caravanadellamas.com.ar), out of Tilcara, offers an experience you won't get at home: llama treks along trails that have been used for thousands of years. You lead the llamas along; they carry everything you need for trips that can last from 1 to 10 days. On overnight excursions, you're hosted by the inhabitants of remote mountain huts.

Crias, or baby llamas, Jujuy Province

street number (they're marked "*s/n*" or "*sin número*" ["no number"] in addresses), but the town is so small that everything is either on or within one block of the main square, Plaza 9 de Julio. There's no bank or hospital, but there is a cash machine next to the tourist information office.

ESSENTIALS

Bus Contacts Balut ☏ *388/423–1157* ⊕ *www.balutsrl.com.ar.*

Taxi Contacts Taxi ☏ *388/490–8030.*

Visitor and Tour Information Tourist Office ✉ *Florida near Rivadavia* ☏ *388/490–8443.*

EXPLORING

Bodega Fernando Dupont. On the lovely grounds of this bodega, cardon cacti mingle with Malbec, Cabernet Sauvignon, and Syrah vines, which thrive at 2,500 meters (8,202 feet) thanks to hot days and very cool nights. The Paleta del Pintor hills provides a stunning backdrop. You can call ahead for a brief yet interesting tour. Reaching the winery is impossible when the river floods in summer, though a new bridge is being planned. ✉ *RN9, Km 1776, Maimará, 5 km (3 miles) north of Purmamarca* ☏ *388/154–731–918* ⊕ *www.bodegafernandodupont. com* 🍷 *Free tour* ☉ *Mon.–Sat. 9–6.*

Fodor's Choice ★ **Cerro de Siete Colores.** Looming above Purmamarca is the brightly tinted Cerro de Siete Colores (Hill of Seven Colors). Look closely and see if you can find all seven—most people can pick out only four. The best way to see the hill is by walking a 3-km (2-mile) loop called the **Paseo de Siete Colores,** which starts to the left of the church on the main square. This one-lane gravel road winds through bizarre, humanlike formations of bright, craggy, red rock, before passing a series of stark, sweeping, Mars-like vistas with stands of trees in the river valley. The road then passes a few family farms and ends with a striking view of the Cerro itself before bringing you back to the center of Purmamarca. ■ TIP➔ The colors are most clearly visible in the morning. The tourist office on Florida Street has a map showing the best points for photos.

Iglesia de Santa Rosa de Lima. The most notable landmark downtown on the central plaza is Iglesia de Santa Rosa de Lima. Dating from 1648, it was constructed from adobe and thistle wood. ✉ *Pl. 9 de Julio.*

Salinas Grandes. West of Purmamarca you can ogle one of the area's most eye-popping sights: the Salinas Grandes, more than 200 square km (80 square miles) of dazzling salt flats at the top of a mountain. Take the sinuous Ruta 52 for 64 km (40 miles) over the majestic Cuesta de Lipan (Lipan Rise)—which tops out at 4,170 meters (13,700 feet) above sea level—and cross Ruta 40. The salty landscape is surreal, and it's made even more so by a building constructed entirely out of slabs of salt turned a brownish color and salt furniture set up like church pews, complete with lectern. A series of small pools have been cut out of the salt flats' surfaces, revealing a layer of water and freshly forming crystals underneath. ■ TIP➔ Remember to carry a camera, a hat, some water, and sunblock.

WHERE TO EAT

$$ ARGENTINE Fodor's Choice ★ 🍴 **El Churqui.** For a more contemporary spin on regional delicacies, head to El Churqui. The llama in Malbec, fresh grilled trout, and succulent goat stew are all noteworthy picks; this busy spot also cooks up a sizzling barbecue worth ordering for its smell alone. Reservations are a good idea. ■ **TIP→ Check out El Churqui's wine cellar—it stocks only wines made at high altitudes.** [$] *Average main: 90 pesos* ✉ *Salta s/n* ☎ *388/490–8063* 💳 *No credit cards* 🕒 *Daily noon–3:30 and 7:30–10:30.*

$$ ARGENTINE 🍴 **La Posta.** Empanadas, llama dishes, and other regional specialties dominate the menu at this eatery on the main square. Take a seat by the window and watch the scene at the market stalls outside while enjoying jujeño staples such as *picante de pollo* (spicy chicken) or regional stews. [$] *Average main: 80 pesos* ✉ *Rivadavia s/n, on Pl. 9 de Julio* ☎ *388/490–8040* 🌐 *www.terrazasdelaposta.com.ar* 💳 *No credit cards* 🕒 *Closed Mon.*

WHERE TO STAY

$ B&B/INN 🏨 **El Cardon.** It's small and no-frills, but if you're just looking for a place to sleep in between excursions, this friendly lodging a short walk from the main square is a good bet. **Pros:** a reliable, in-town option. **Cons:** few facilities; often booked in high season. [$] *Rooms from: US$48* ✉ *Belgrano s/n* ☎ *388/490–8672* 🌐 *www.hostal-elcardon.com* 🛏 *7 rooms* 💳 *No credit cards* 🍽 *Breakfast.*

$ HOTEL Fodor's Choice ★ 🏨 **El Manantial del Silencio.** At this tranquil retreat, weeping willows, red rocks, and gardens filled with birdsong are hemmed in by the craggy Quebrada and its utter calm; inside the colonial-style stucco mansion, local artifacts and earth tones make things warm and harmonious throughout. **Pros:** one of the grandest lodgings in the Quebrada; great gardens, restaurant, spa, and pool. **Cons:** one of the most expensive lodgings in the area. [$] *Rooms from: US$107* ✉ *RN52, Km 3.5* ☎ *388/490–8080* 🌐 *www.hotelmanantialdesilencio.com.ar* 🛏 *18 rooms, 1 suite, 1 house* 🍽 *Breakfast.*

$$ RENTAL 🏨 **La Comarca.** The various rooms, cabins, and houses here surround a garden of flowers and cacti; all accommodations are built with traditional local materials—adobe, cane, wood—and are decorated with a contemporary eye. **Pros:** quiet; well decorated; good restaurant; houses can sleep up to six guests. **Cons:** showers not designed for tall people. [$] *Rooms from: US$190* ✉ *RN52, Km 3.8* ☎ *388/490–8098* 🌐 *www.lacomarcahotel.com.ar* 🛏 *12 rooms, 2 houses, 2 cabins, 1 suite* 🍽 *Breakfast.*

$$ B&B/INN 🏨 **Los Colorados.** All the reddish adobe walls of the cabins at Los Colorados, on the Cerro de Siete Colores, have rounded corners, giving the whole place a look of having been sculpted straight from the earth; it's a perfect spot for kicking back, whether you're curled up by the fireplace in your room or stargazing on the common terrace. **Pros:** quiet retreat; a six-person Jacuzzi. **Cons:** small bathrooms. [$] *Rooms from: US$120* ✉ *El Chapacal 511* ☎ *388/490–8182* 🌐 *www.loscoloradosjujuy.com.ar* 🛏 *7 rooms/cabins* 🍽 *Breakfast.*

"Rectangles have been dug out [of Salinas Grandes] to allow the water to seep through and salt to crystallize. . . . The clearest water and the whitest salt I have ever seen." —Clive Ellston, Fodors.com member

NIGHTLIFE

Don Heriberto. You'll meet a good mix of locals and visitors at the town's only late-night bar. In high season, it opens at 10 pm and closes at 5 am or when the last customer leaves—whichever comes first. ✉ *Sarmiento s/n, close to corner of Libertad* ☎ *388/490–8026.*

SPORTS AND THE OUTDOORS

Purmamarca Trekking. Local guide Carlos Prado leads excursions in and around the Quebrada. Choices include a half-day trip to see 10,000-year-old cave paintings near Humahuaca and a full-day outing that involves driving to the Salinas Grandes, then hiking back down to Purmamarca. ✉ *Maimará* ☎ *388/590–7100* ⊕ *www.purmamarcatrekking.com.ar* 🖭 *From 150 pesos.*

TILCARA

85 km (53 miles) north of San Salvador de Jujuy; 18 km (11 miles) northeast of Purmamarca via RN9.

Founded in 1600 and witness to many battles during the War of Independence, Tilcara is on the eastern side of the Río Grande at its confluence with the Río Huasamayo. Purveyors of local crafts crowd the main plaza, and artists and musicians escaping the big cities fill the cafés and bars. There are several reasons to stop off in this 2,469-meter-high (8,100-foot-high) Quebrada town: an interesting museum; nearby Inca ruins, caves, and waterfalls; and a good selection of accommodations and restaurants.

GETTING HERE AND AROUND

Tilcara is well served by buses running between Jujuy and Humahuaca or La Quiaca. Taking a shared taxi from San Salvador de Jujuy's bus station is another option; the cost is about the same. Arriving from the south, look out for the surprisingly large cemetery of Maimará, which sprawls on either side of the road outside town.

ESSENTIALS

Bus Contacts Atahualpa ☏ *387/155–815–298.* **Balut** ☏ *388/423-1157* ⊕ *www.balutsrl.com.ar.*

Visitor Information Tourist Office ✉ *Belgrano s/n, at Padilla.*

EXPLORING

La Garganta del Diablo. Seven km (4 miles) west of town is La Garganta del Diablo (The Devil's Throat), a red-rock gorge with waterfalls (the number depends on the season). The tourist office in Tilcara can point you in the right direction; ask about the path that knocks about half the distance off the journey. Ask, too, for directions to the wind-eroded caves that are a similar distance east of town.

Museo Arqueológico. Exhibits at the Museo Arqueológico, run by the University of Buenos Aires, can be a little confusing due to a lack of explanatory labels. The two mummies here are considerably less well cared for than those in Salta's MAAM (Museum of High Altitude Archaeology), but no less fascinating. The clothes, hair, and skin of the first, which was found in San Pedro de Atacama in Chile, are well preserved. Other rooms display Nazca, Inca, Moche, and other remains from the past 2,000 years. ■TIP➔ **Keep your ticket stubs, as they'll get you in to the nearby Pucará de Tilcara ruins, where some of this museum's artifacts were discovered.** ✉ *Belgrano 445* ☏ *388/495–5006* ⊕ *tilcara.filo.uba.ar* 🎫 *50 pesos* ⊙ *Daily 9–6.*

Fodor's Choice ★ **Museo en los Cerros.** You'll find this surprising photograph gallery by following a stony road that runs alongside the River Huichaira up into the mountains. The brainchild of photographer Lucio Boschi, the "museum in the hills" opened in 2012 and has two spaces displaying permanent collections as well as a temporary exhibit room. For the ultimate in artsy tranquility, kick back in the library while browsing coffee-table books. ✉ *Huichaira, 4 km (2½ miles) off R9* ☏ *388/155–250–240* ⊕ *www.museoenloscerros.com.ar* 🎫 *Free* ⊙ *Daily 10–2 (call to confirm).*

Fodor's Choice ★ **Pucará de Tilcara.** Set on a hill above the left bank of the Río Grande, this fortified, pre-Inca *pucará* (settlement) is the best-preserved of several in the Quebrada de Humahuaca and the only one that can be visited. Its different areas (some of which have been rebuilt) can be clearly discerned. Allow at least 90 minutes to walk around the site, where an estimated 2,000 Omaguaca once lived, worshipped, and kept their animals. On your way out, turn right at the entrance to the fort for the Jardín Botánico (Botanical Garden): inside you can admire a large array of cacti and other plants. Don't miss the chance to strike the Piedra Campana with a mallet disguised as a stick—true to its name (Bell Stone) it rings like a bell. ■TIP➔ **Ticket stubs from a visit to the Museo Arqueológico in town get you free entrance to both the ruins and the**

botanical garden. ✉ *About 1½ km (1 mile) south of Tilcara* 🎫 *50 pesos* ⊙ *Daily 9–12:30 and 2–6.*

WHERE TO EAT

$$

ARGENTINE

Fodor'sChoice

★

✕ **El Nuevo Progreso.** The food is superb; the wine list is fairly priced; and the wooden floors, whimsical lights, and artwork make the space appealing. What's more, every evening around 9:30 there's live music, generally performed by friends of the owners. El Nuevo Progreso is right in the center of town, with windows looking out across the small plaza. $ *Average main: 80 pesos* ✉ *Lavalle 351* ☎ *388/495–5237.*

$$

ARGENTINE

✕ **El Patio.** With three dining rooms, a patio out back, a location just yards from the central plaza, and well-priced regional cuisine, El Patio is one of Tilcara's most-recommended restaurants. The menu is an unpretentious yet delectable mix of regional specialties and standard Argentine fare, and service is friendly. $ *Average main: 70 pesos* ✉ *Lavalle 352* ☎ *388/495–5044* ⊙ *Closed Tues.*

$$

ARGENTINE

✕ **Los Puestos.** A poetic narrative in the menu describes this place as "a haven for parched travelers," along the lines of the watering holes used for centuries by local shepherds. Top picks include empanadas baked in the oven right by the entrance and a llama filet served with orange sauce and Andean new potatoes. $ *Average main: 95 pesos* ✉ *Belgrano, corner of Padilla* ☎ *388/495–5100* ⊙ *Closed Mon.*

$$

ARGENTINE

✕ **Q'omer.** Located at the back of a small shopping arcade, Q'omer dishes up simple, healthy fare with regional flair. Order one of the creative, generously sized salads or opt for a llama stir-fry. Service (though slightly slow) is friendly, and reliable Wi-Fi is an added bonus. This spot is open daily from early morning to midnight, so you can drop in for breakfast or a late snack. $ *Average main: 70 pesos* ✉ *Belgrano 417* ☎ *388/15–473–0588* ⊕ *www.qomer.com.ar.*

$$

ARGENTINE

✕ **Yacón.** The warm service, wooden tables and chairs, cane roof, and stone walls all suggest tradition. Yet Yacón's kitchen shows some innovation by serving up llama meat on skewers and a shepherd's pie made with quinoa. It's just a block from the main square. $ *Average main: 95 pesos* ✉ *Rivadavia 222* ☎ *388/495–5611* ⊙ *No dinner Sun.*

WHERE TO STAY

$$

HOTEL

Fodor'sChoice

★

⌂ **Hotel Huacalera.** This hotel, on the main road in the heart of the Quebrada de Humahuaca, has recently undergone a substantial refit; the result is a stunning colonial-style property, complete with a spa, an outdoor swimming pool, and spacious, well-appointed guest rooms. **Pros:** courteous staff; good on-site restaurant; large breakfast. **Cons:** the peace and tranquility can be disturbed by trucks on the main drag. $ *Rooms from: US$170* ✉ *R9, Km 1790, Huacalera* ☎ *388/155–813–417* ⊕ *www.hotelhuacalera.com* ⇆ *32 rooms* ⦙⊙⦙ *Breakfast.*

$$

B&B/INN

⌂ **Las Terrazas.** A few blocks from the square in a quieter area, Las Terrazas has nine spacious rooms, each with its own balcony. **Pros:** good-size rooms and bathrooms; great views; great breakfast. **Cons:** not very central. $ *Rooms from: US$150* ✉ *Calle de la Sorpresa s/n, at San Martín* ☎ *388/495–5589* ⊕ *www.lasterrazastilcara.com.ar* ⇆ *9 rooms* ⦙⊙⦙ *Breakfast.*

5

Cardones (cacti) grow amid the ruins of the Pucará de Tilcara in Jujuy Province.

$
HOTEL
Refugio del Pintor. The building that houses this hotel was formerly used by the painter Medardo Pantoja from Jujuy, hence the name (Refuge of the Painter) and the artworks adorning the walls. **Pros:** attentive staff; great views; plenty of common spaces; good breakfast with homemade bread. **Cons:** small rooms. $ *Rooms from: US$75* ✉ *Alverro s/n, between Jujuy and Ambroseti* ☎ *388/495–5695* ⊕ *www. elrefugiodelpintor.com* ⤳ *13 rooms* ⦿ *Breakfast.*

$
B&B/INN
Uwa Wasi. The name of this B&B means "a house with grapes," and it does, indeed, have a few vines in its rambling back garden, where there's also space to relax and get to know your hosts (one of whom works for the tourism office). **Pros:** good location; friendly service; nice garden and communal areas. **Cons:** compact rooms; some shared bathrooms; few facilities. $ *Rooms from: US$67* ✉ *Lavalle 564* ☎ *388/495–5368* ⊕ *www.uwawasi.com.ar* ⤳ *6 rooms* ⦿ *Breakfast.*

$$
HOTEL
Viento Norte. This long, thin, adobe boutique hotel overlooks a decent-size swimming pool; inside, rooms have simple decorations and low lighting. **Pros:** central yet quiet; a good breakfast; great bathrooms. **Cons:** pool is visible from the street. $ *Rooms from: US$120* ✉ *Jujuy 536* ☎ *388/495–5605* ⊕ *www.hotelvientonorte.com.ar* ⤳ *11 rooms* ⦿ *Breakfast.*

SHOPPING

The central plaza is lined with stalls selling Andean-type souvenirs and gifts, some handcrafted by the owner, others imported from Bolivia. The best of the local stuff includes knitted hats and scarves. On Saturday afternoons there are also carts selling *chicha*—an alcoholic drink made from fermented corn. You won't want a lot, but this is a rare opportunity to try it.

SPORTS AND THE OUTDOORS

Fodor's Choice
★

Caravana de Llamas. For an unforgettable trekking experience, sign on with Caravana de Llamas. You'll lead a team of llamas along trails that have been used for thousands of years. Trips run the gamut from half-day picnics to 10-day adventures: on overnight excursions, you're hosted by the inhabitants of remote mountain huts. ⊠ *Calle Corte and Viltipoco* ☎ *388/495–5326* ⊕ *www.caravanadellamas.com.ar* ✉ *From 200 pesos.*

HUMAHUACA

126 km (78 miles) north of San Salvador de Jujuy; 42 km (26 miles) north of Tilcara on RN9.

Humahuaca—at an altitude of 2,957 meters (9,700 feet)—is the gateway to the Puna. Its narrow stone streets hark back to pre-Hispanic civilizations, when aboriginals fought Incan marauders from the north. The struggle for survival continued into the 16th century, when the Spanish arrived.

Given its location, the village feels a bit touristy today—especially at midday, when an automated carving of Saint Francisco Solano emerges like a cuckoo from a clock to bless the folks gathered in the main plaza with his mechanized arm. More visitor amenities are slowly becoming available, too: however, the tourist board is less than organized (if you find it open) and lodgings are predominantly hostels. That said, if you're near Humahuaca around the time of Carnaval (40 days before Easter), it's worth putting up with whatever accommodations you can find to participate in the wonderful festivities that are a complicated mix of Catholicism and paganism.

GETTING HERE AND AROUND

Most people visit Humahuaca either on a day trip from Tilcara, Purmamarca, Jujuy, or Salta; or as a stopover en route to Iruya. If you're not coming by car or with a tour group, you can catch a bus. Balut, Panamericano, and other lines serving the San Salvador de Jujuy-to-La Quiaca route have buses running through almost every hour during the day.

ESSENTIALS

Bus Contacts Balut ☎ *388/424–2883* ⊕ *www.balutsrl.com.ar.* **Panamericano** ☎ *388/423–7330.*

Visitor Information Tourist Office ⊠ *Cabildo, central plaza* ☎ *388/421–375.*

EXPLORING

Cabildo. Humahuaca's *cabildo* (town hall), the most striking building in the village, has a beautifully colored and richly detailed clock tower. Each day at noon crowds fill the small main square outside to watch a life-size mechanized statue of San Francisco Solano pop out of the tower—it's kitschy fun and one of the world's few clock performances. You can't enter the cabildo, but you can peer into the courtyard. ⊠ *Central plaza.*

5

Iglesia de la Candelaria. The 1631 Iglesia de la Candelaria contains fine examples of Cusqueño art, most notably paintings depicting elongated figures of Old Testament prophets by 18th-century artist Marcos Zapaca. ✉ *Calle Buenos Aires, west side of central plaza.*

Museo Folklórico Regional. At first glance the Museo Folklórico Regional appears to be a dusty collection of stones and strange objects, but allow a guide to show you around (arrange in advance for an English-speaking one), and you'll learn a lot about the indigenous population. The museum was founded by Sixto Vázquez Zuleta, who has invested a huge amount of passion and imagination, and each exhibit—from dolls made of dried apricots to musical instruments made from armadillos—provides a new insight into the carnival spirit of the area. Note that it is only open to groups of three or more. ✉ *Buenos Aires 447* ☎ *388/421–064* 🎟 *10 pesos* 🕐 *Daily 8–8.*

OFF THE BEATEN PATH

Iruya. If you can endure a harrowing five-hour, 50-km (31-mile) ride east from Humahuaca on an unpaved cliffside road, you'll be rewarded with one of Argentina's most stunning settings. (Take the bus from Humahuaca rather than driving yourself; you really have to know the road, as the bus drivers do, to negotiate it safely.) This cobblestoned town, which clings to sheer rock, has become an increasingly popular stop despite its small size. It has just a couple of accommodations, the **Hotel Iruya** (☎ *3887/482–002*) and **Hostal Milmahuasi** (☎ *3887/445-7994*), but many villagers offer rooms for rent. The busiest times to visit are at Easter and during the first and second weekends in October, when the village holds its festival. There are some good hikes from Iruya to even more remote towns like San Isidro, three hours away through the mountains. For more information and guide recommendations, call Adelina López at the **Tourist Office** (☎ *3887/155–094–799*).

WHERE TO EAT

$$ ARGENTINE

🍴 **K'allapurca.** At lunch the best tables are taken by groups of tourists being serenaded by a band of minstrels, but don't let that put you off. The food is simple, well-presented Andean fare, and the prices are very reasonable. The kitchen can accommodate vegetarians, too. $ *Average main: 75 pesos* ✉ *Belgrano 210* ☎ *3887/421–318.*

SHOPPING

The shops just east of the plaza are full of the same ponchos, bags, hats, and shirts sold elsewhere in the Quebrada. Though things are reasonably priced, they're more expensive than they would be in Bolivia, which is where most of the stock originates. There are also some interesting original articles on sale in the main plaza.

SALTA

92 km (57 miles) south of San Salvador de Jujuy on RN9 or 311 km (193 miles) south of San Salvador de Jujuy on R34 (La Cornisa Road).

It's not just "Salta" to most Argentineans, but "Salta la Linda" ("Salta the Beautiful"). That nickname is actually redundant: "Salta" already comes from an indigenous Aymara word meaning "beautiful." But for the country's finest colonial city, it's worth stating twice. Walking among

its well-preserved 18th- and 19th-century buildings, single-story houses, and narrow streets, you could easily forget that this is a city of more than half a million people. But the ever-increasing traffic, the youthful population, and the growing number of international itinerants also give Salta a cosmopolitan edge. All in all, it's a hard place to leave. For its friendliness, its facilities, its connections, and its central location, Salta is also the best base for a thorough exploration of the Northwest. Do make good use of the tourist office, which has a helpful staff armed with a wealth of maps and information.

GETTING HERE AND AROUND

Salta is two hours by air from Buenos Aires. Aerolíneas Argentinas flies the route six times a day, LAN twice a day, and Andes once a day. From Aeropuerto El Aybal, it's a 10-km (6-mile) drive southeast into Salta; the trip costs 80 pesos by taxi or 2.50 pesos (small change required) by bus. Balut buses connect Salta to Jujuy (15 trips daily) and Humahuaca (six trips daily). El Indio has two daily buses to Cafayate, while Marco Rueda has at least one to Cachi. Buy tickets the day before, as most buses leave early in the morning.

Most city sights are within walking distance of one another, and taxis are cheap and easy to find. Note that some visitors opt to stay in the quieter hillside suburb of San Lorenzo, 10 km (6 miles) northwest and a cooler 299 meters (980 feet) higher. It's a great place if you have a car or are prepared to rely on the half-hourly bus to and from Salta.

ESSENTIALS

Bus Contacts Balut ☎ *388/422–9393* ⊕ *www.balutsrl.com.ar.* **El Indio** ☎ *387/432–0846.* **Marcos Rueda** ☎ *387/421–4447.* **Terminal de Omnibus** ✉ *Av. Hipólito Yrigoyen 339* ☎ *387/401–1143* ⊕ *www.terminalsalta.com.*

Rental Car Contacts Hertz ✉ *Caseros 374* ☎ *387/424–0113* ⊕ *www. hertz.com.* **Perfil Rent a Car** ✉ *Buenos Aires 189* ☎ *387/422–7855* ⊕ *www. perfilrentacar.com.*

Taxi Contacts Taxi Car ☎ *387/439–0530.*

Visitor and Tour Information Tourist Office ✉ *Buenos Aires 93* ☎ *0800/222–3752* ⊕ *www.turismosalta.gov.ar.*

TOURS

MoviTrack. This Northwest specialist offers excursions around Salta but is best known for its Bus to the Clouds, an oxygen-equipped vehicle that follows the same route as the Tren a las Nubes. Trips last 16 hours; they depart daily in winter and nearly every day in summer. Check the website for schedules and prices. ✉ *Buenos Aires 68* ☎ *387/431–1223* ⊕ *www.movitrack.com.ar* ✉ *From 970 pesos.*

Uma Travel. The knowledgeable, English-speaking guides at Uma lead day trips to Cafayate or through the Quebrada de Humahuaca. Rafting, riding, and biking tours are also available; if you're more into local culture, there's a folklore circuit as well. ✉ *Güemes 569* ☎ *387/421–5971* ⊕ *www.umatravel.com.ar* ✉ *From 390 pesos.*

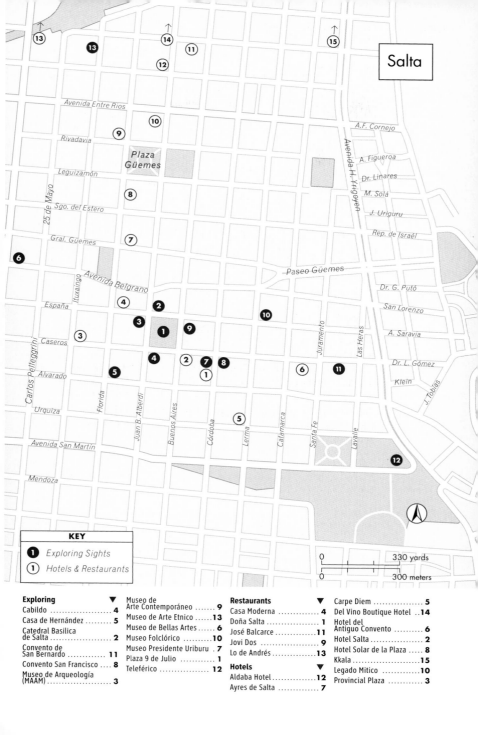

Salta

KEY

① Exploring Sights

① Hotels & Restaurants

0 ——— 330 yards
0 ——— 300 meters

EXPLORING

TOP ATTRACTIONS

Basílica Menor y Convento San Francisco. Every *salteño*'s soul belongs to the landmark St. Francis Church and Convent, with its white pillars and bright terra-cotta-and-gold facade. The first sanctuary was built in 1625; the second, erected in 1674, was destroyed by fire; the present version was completed in 1882. A 53-meter (173-foot) belfry houses the Campaña de

la Patria. This bell, made from the bronze cannons used in the War of Independence, sounds once a day at 7:30 pm. In the sacristy, the Museo Convento San Francisco displays religious art. ⊠ *Córdoba 33* ☎ *387/432–1445* ⌨ *Church free, museum 30 pesos* ⊙ *Church daily 8– noon and 5–9; museum weekdays 9:30–noon and 5–6:30.*

Cabildo. The whitewashed town hall, first rebuilt in 1582 and rebuilt many times since, used to house Salta's municipal government. Not only a colonial gem in itself, the Cabildo—the most well-preserved council building in Argentina—is home to the Museo Histórico del Norte, which includes a relevant collection of pre-Hispanic stone sculptures, as well as religious artifacts and a rather obscure assortment of vintage cars in the back garden. ⊠ *Caseros 549* ☎ *387/421–5340* ⊕ *www.museonor.gov.ar* ⌨ *15 pesos (free Tues.–Fri. 9–10)* ⊙ *Tues.– Sat. 9–6.*

Catedral Basílica de Salta. The city's 1882 neoclassical cathedral fronts the central plaza. It's notable for the enormous frescoes portraying the four gospel writers on the portico around the altar and its impressive stained glass windows. Inside the entrance is the Panteón de las Glorias del Norte, enclosing the tombs of General Martín Miguel de Güemes and other heroes from the War of Independence. Wander to the back of the rose-color cathedral for a peek at the beautiful, jasmine-infused garden. ⊠ *España 558* ☎ *387/431–8206* ⊕ *www.catedralsalta.org* ⌨ *Free* ⊙ *Weekdays 6:30–12:30 and 4:30–8:30, Sat. 7:30–12:30 and 5–8:30, Sun. 7:30–1 and 5–9:30. No mass in Jan.*

Convento de San Bernardo. Salta's oldest religious building served as a chapel first, then a hospital. Today it is home to a cloistered order of Carmelite nuns. The wooden rococo-style door, carved by indigenous craftsmen in 1762, contrasts markedly with the otherwise stark exterior of this 1625 structure. ⊠ *Caseros 73* ☎ *387/431–0092* ⌨ *Free* ⊙ *Chapel Mon.–Sat. 7–8:30 am, Sun. 8–10 am; Mass daily at 7:45 am.*

Museo de Árqueología de Alta Montaña. The fascinating Museum of High Mountain Archaeology (MAAM) holds the mummified remains of three children born into nobility—ages 6, 7, and 15—and the 146 objects buried with them in Incan sacrificial services some 600 years ago. They were discovered at the summit of the 22,058-foot Volcán Llullaillaco, on the Argentine–Chilean border, in 1999. The high altitude and freezing temperatures kept their skin, hair, hands, and clothes in impeccable condition, although the face of one was damaged by lightning. The museum also contains an exhibition about the Qhapaq Ñan Inca trading route from southern Colombia to Mendoza and another mummy, the Reina del Cerro (Queen of the Mountain), which for decades was illegally in the hands of private collectors. ✉ *Mitre 77* ☎ *387/437–0592* ⊕ *www. maam.gob.ar* 🖃 *40 pesos* ☉ *Tues.–Sun. 11–7:30.*

Museo de Arte Etnico Americano Pajcha. The small, private Museum of Ethnic American Art Pajcha contains interesting artifacts and illustrations from the pre-Columbian world and later. Enthusiastic tour guides explain exhibits, using religious objects, furniture, jewelry, and the like to illuminate indigenous culture. A new addition is devoted to a well-curated textile collection. There's enough reason to linger here for hours; when you're done, relax with a coffee on the back terrace. ✉ *20 de Febrero 831* ☎ *387/422–9417* ⊕ *www.museopajchasalta.com. ar* 🖃 *30 pesos (guided tour an additional 10 pesos)* ☉ *Mon.–Sat. 10–1 and 4–8.*

Museo Folclórico Pajarito Velarde. The two rooms of this museum are stuffed with curiosities and background information pertaining to Guillermo "Pajarito" Velarde Mors—the consummate bohemian who brought tango to Salta and lived here from 1930 to 1965. The space is brimming with his trinkets, artworks, and possessions. Take a look at the hat that Carlos Gardel gave him and the rosewood bed that folk singer Atahualpa Yupanki slept on. Even if you're not well versed in Argentine culture from that period, the museum is a delightful tribute to a real character. ✉ *Pueyrredón 106* ☎ *387/421–2921* 🖃 *10 pesos, includes 20-minute guided tour* ☉ *Weekdays 10:30–2 and 3:30–6.*

Plaza 9 de Julio. The heart of Salta is quintessential Latin America: a leafy central plaza named after the date of independence. Arcaded buildings line the streets surrounding it, and some have been converted into cafés, providing perfect spots to while away a warm afternoon. Popular with families who take shade under the palm and jacaranda trees, the square is dotted with craftsmen selling their wares and teens canoodling by the bandstand.

Teleférico a Cerro San Bernardo. The Cerro San Bernardo rises east of downtown Salta, a cool 268 meters (880 feet) higher than the city center. This cable car takes you up the hill from a station across from Parque San Martín in 10 minutes. Views of the entire Lerma Valley await at the top; you can also wander the breezy garden and browse around a small crafts market. ■TIP→ If you're in the mood for a little light exercise, take the winding road back down. ✉ *San Martín and H. Yrigoyen* ☎ *387/431–0641* ⊕ *www.telefericosanbernardo.com* 🖃 *70 pesos* ☉ *Daily 10–7.*

WORTH NOTING

Casa de Hernández/Museo de la Ciudad. The City Museum is in Casa de Hernández, an 1879 neocolonial house. The ground floor displays an exceptional collection of musical instruments. Rooms upstairs document the history of Salta through paintings and photographs. ✉ *Florida*

97 ☎ 387/437–3352 ⊕ *www.museociudadsalta.gov.ar* ✉ *Voluntary donation* ☉ *Mon.–Sat. 9–1 and 4–8:30.*

Museo de Arte Contemporáneo. In a privileged position on a corner of Plaza 9 de Julio, the Contemporary Art Museum has a "Museum of the Year" award from the Association of Argentine Art Critics under its belt. It rotates the shows on both floors; expect photography, installations, and traveling exhibitions from other Argentine galleries. ✉ *Zuviria 90* ☎ *387/437–0498* ⊕ *www.macsaltamuseo.org* ✉ *2 pesos* ☉ *Tues.–Sat. 9–8, Sun. 4–8.*

Museo de Bellas Artes. The Fine Arts Museum's collection of colonial-era religious works includes figures from Argentina's Jesuit missions as well as Cuzco-style paintings from Peru and Bolivia. Another part of the museum highlights 20th-century pieces by salteño artists. ✉ *Belgrano 992* ☎ *387/431–8562* ✉ *5 pesos* ☉ *Weekdays 9–7, Sat. 11–7, holidays 10–2.*

Museo Presidente José Evaristo Uriburu. Fine examples of late-colonial architecture—an interior courtyard, thick adobe walls, a reed-and-tile roof—abound in this simple building, the 19th- and 20th-century home of the Uriburu family, which gave Argentina two presidents. Furniture, costumes, paintings, and family documents are on display across six rooms. ✉ *Caseros 417* ☎ *387/421–8174* ⊕ *www.museonor.gov.ar* ✉ *15 pesos* ☉ *Tues.–Fri. 9–7, Sat. 9–1:30.*

WHERE TO EAT

SALTA

$$$
DELI

✕ **Casa Moderna.** *Picadas*—assorted cured meats and local cheeses, accompanied by home-baked breads—are the star attractions here (be sure to try the smoked boar and trout). Although this deli–wine bar hybrid does get busy, the staff is generally friendly, and you can escape the bustle by retreating to the back terrace. ■ TIP➔ **Wash down your meal with one of the hearty Los Morros–brand reds, produced by Casa Moderna's own small winery.** $ *Average main: 100 pesos* ✉ *España 674* ☎ *387/422–0066* ▭ *No credit cards.*

$$
ARGENTINE

✕ **Doña Salta.** This warm, festive, family-friendly locale serves dishes quite typical of Salta and the Northwest. You'll dine in a room steeped in local tradition, amid wine jugs and old wooden implements. Try classics like *humita* (steamed corn husks filled with cheese) or the local locro stew, with beans and hunks of beef. Empanadas and meats are also reliable; the pastas are unremarkable, though. The location, across from Iglesia San Francisco, couldn't be more central. $ *Average main: 80 pesos* ✉ *Córdoba 46* ☎ *387/432–1921* ▭ *No credit cards.*

$$$
MODERN
ARGENTINE
Fodor's Choice
★

✕ **José Balcarce.** A group of chefs launched a restaurant and catering service with high Andean cuisine as its goal—"high" referring to both the altitude and the gourmet techniques. The result is José Balcarce, in a brick-and-wood building with large windows just two blocks from bustling Balcarce Street. The menu is short, and the service can be slow, but the creative dishes—using local ingredients such as quinoa and llama—are delicious. $ *Average main: 130 pesos* ✉ *Necochea 590*

☎ 387/421–1628 🌐 *www.cocinadealtura.com.ar/jose-balcarce.php* ▭ *No credit cards* ⏲ *No lunch. Closed Sun.*

$$ ARGENTINE 🍴 **Jovi Dos.** A great-value restaurant on a bustling downtown corner, Jovi Dos has several airy, high-ceiling rooms with wood beams and plate-glass windows. At lunchtime it's filled with businesspeople. Noteworthy starters include marinated eggplant and baked beef empanadas. Grilled meats, seafood, pizza, and pasta have equal billing on the ridiculously long menu. Dishes such as the *ravioles mixtas* (ravioli filled with spinach and cheese, then topped with a creamy sauce) are big enough for two people. The waitstaff is attentive, and the wine list is solid. [$] *Average main: 90 pesos* ✉ *Balcarce 601* ☎ *387/432–9438* 🌐 *www.jovidos.com.ar.*

SAN LORENZO

$$ ARGENTINE 🍴 **Lo de Andrés.** Folks from Salta and San Lorenzo favor this bright, semi-enclosed brick-and-glass building with a vaulted ceiling for weekend dining. Lo de Andrés prepares a lightly spiced Argentine-style parrillada, but if you're not up for a full-on feast, there are empanadas and *milanesas* (breaded steak), as well as regional dishes like humita. [$] *Average main: 90 pesos* ✉ *Juan Carlos Dávalos and Gorriti* ☎ *387/492–1600* 🌐 *www.saltaonline.com/andres* ⏲ *No lunch Mon. No dinner Tues.–Thurs.*

WHERE TO STAY

SALTA

$ HOTEL 🏨 **Aldaba Hotel.** This 19th-century home now operates as a small and tranquil hotel close to the nocturnal action on Balcarce. **Pros:** friendly service; large, pastry-based breakfast. **Cons:** walls are a little thin. [$] *Rooms from: US$69* ✉ *Mitre 910* ☎ *387/421–9455* 🌐 *www.aldabahotel.com* 🛏 *10 rooms* 🍽 *Breakfast.*

$$ HOTEL 🏨 **Ayres de Salta.** Conveniently located between the main plaza and Balcarce Street, Ayres de Salta has a small pool and fitness center on the roof and a good little restaurant on the ground floor; rooms are large and well equipped. **Pros:** efficient, professional staff; good location; buffet breakfast. **Cons:** some rooms look into the windows of other rooms. [$] *Rooms from: US$125* ✉ *General Güemes 650* ☎ *387/422–1616* 🌐 *www.ayresdesalta.com.ar* 🛏 *40 rooms* 🍽 *Breakfast.*

$ B&B/INN Fodor's Choice ★ 🏨 **Carpe Diem.** Run by a German-Italian couple, this B&B in a heritage home has an eclectic mix of singles and doubles; rooms fuse antiques sourced from Buenos Aires with ethnic art, and period details with modern amenities (free Wi-Fi among them). **Pros:** homemade bread and cakes at breakfast; friendly welcome; quiet, convenient location. **Cons:** no children under 14; guests with cat allergies will need to ask the owners to relocate their pets to the garden, which they'll happily do. [$] *Rooms from: US$87* ✉ *Urquiza 329* ☎ *387/421–8736* 🌐 *www.bedandbreakfastsalta.com* 🛏 *8* 🍽 *Breakfast.*

$$ HOTEL 🏨 **Del Vino Boutique Hotel.** Oenophiles will appreciate the décor at Del Vino—a remodeled, Spanish-style villa where the airy guest rooms are painted in grape tones (Malbec red among them) and decorated with wine-themed artworks. **Pros:** two blocks from theTren a las Nubes

railway station, welcome glass of wine on arrival. **Cons:** it can be chilly going up and down the exposed stairway. [$] *Rooms from: US$122* ✉ *Ameghino 555* ☎ *387/432–0092* 🌐 *www.hoteldelvinosalta.com.ar* 🛏 *18 rooms* 🍴 *Breakfast.*

$ HOTEL 🏨 **Hotel del Antiguo Convento.** This charming property in a former convent is run by a cheerful, attentive young staff; rooms are clean, bright, and well priced. **Pros:** staffers go out of their way to be helpful; convenient location. **Cons:** small courtyard and pool. [$] *Rooms from: US$82* ✉ *Caseros 113* ☎ *387/422–7267* 🌐 *www.hoteldelconvento.com.ar* 🛏 *15 rooms* 💳 *No credit cards* 🍴 *Breakfast.*

$ HOTEL 🏨 **Hotel Salta.** Designated as a National Historic Monument, the Salta occupies a handsome neocolonial building in the heart of the city; antique furniture and views of either the plaza or the surrounding mountains make every room attractive. **Pros:** ideal location; access to Salta Polo Club; free Wi-Fi; spa; breakfast buffet. **Cons:** rooms facing the plaza can be noisy. [$] *Rooms from: US$90* ✉ *Buenos Aires 1* ☎ *387/426–7500* 🌐 *www.hotelsalta.com* 🛏 *99 rooms* 🍴 *Breakfast.*

$ B&B/INN 🏨 **Hotel Solar de la Plaza.** The exterior of this beautiful old house belies the modern comforts within; an elegant lobby leads to a tastefully appointed sitting room, an airy courtyard, and a good (though expensive) restaurant. **Pros:** high comfort level; rooftop pool; buffet breakfast. **Cons:** costly in-house dining. [$] *Rooms from: US$90* ✉ *Leguizamón 669* ☎ *387/431–5111* 🌐 *www.solardelaplaza.com.ar* 🛏 *28 rooms, 2 suites* 🍴 *Breakfast.*

$$$ B&B/INN Fodor's Choice ★ 🏨 **Kkala.** This elegant 10-room abode represents Salta, right down to the cardon cactus door panels and hand-stitched headboards depicting Andean landscapes. **Pros:** delightful bilingual staff; stylish rooms; honesty bar. **Cons:** not that close to main attractions. [$] *Rooms from: US$240* ✉ *Las Higueras 104, Los Cerritos* ☎ *387/439–6590* 🌐 *www.hotelkkala.com.ar* 🛏 *10* 🍴 *Breakfast.*

$$$ B&B/INN Fodor's Choice ★ 🏨 **Legado Mítico.** Sister to the Buenos Aires hotel of the same name, the family-run Legado Mítico attends to every detail—right down to the welcome glass of wine. **Pros:** warm and pleasing spaces; the living room and terrace are comfy spots for a moment of relaxation; attractive décor. **Cons:** located on a rather busy main drag; street-facing rooms can be noisy. [$] *Rooms from: US$275* ✉ *Bartolomé Mitre 647* ☎ *387/422–8786* 🌐 *www.legadomitico.com* 🛏 *11 rooms* 🍴 *Breakfast.*

$ HOTEL 🏨 **Provincial Plaza.** This hotel is on a corner, just blocks from Plaza 9 de Julio; standard rooms have had recent renovations—superior and executive floors are spruced up and have good facilities. **Pros:** central location; full buffet breakfast. **Cons:** lower floors get street noise. [$] *Rooms from: $75US* ✉ *Caseros 786* ☎ *387/432–2000* 🌐 *www.provincialplaza.com.ar* 🛏 *88 rooms* 🍴 *Breakfast.*

SAN LORENZO

$ B&B/INN 🏨 **Eaton Place.** Despite appearances, this striking Georgian-style mansion only dates from the 1980s, when it was built as a private home; it still feels like one, with bright and airy rooms in the main house and in a guesthouse with huge windows, hardwood floors, and period furniture. **Pros:** well appointed; large breakfast; lovely property with pool and gardens. **Cons:** a long way from the center of town. [$] *Rooms from:*

US$100 ✉ *San Martín 2457* ☎ *387/492–1347* ⊕ *www.eatonplacesalta.com.ar* ⇴ *8 rooms, 1 suite* ▭ *No credit cards* †◎| *Breakfast.*

NIGHTLIFE

Salta is a young and lively city, with a bar district along a few blocks of Balcarce Street that can get quite busy. Clubs, restaurants, and peñas attract both locals and tourists, who come to hear regional folk bands perform on small, cramped stages. Adding to the rowdy, dinner-theater atmosphere are the local gaucho dancers who entice (and often entrap) foreigners into strutting their stuff on stage; it's always a good laugh, no matter what language you speak. For a more authentic musical experience, head to La Casona del Molino.

Fodor'sChoice
★
La Casona del Molino. Twenty-odd blocks down Caseros Street from the main plaza, La Casona del Molino is an authentic gem renowned for nightly folk performances; join in by clapping or dancing. It also serves great regional food at extremely decent prices. ✉ *Luis Burela 1* ☎ *387/434–2835.*

La Vieja Estación. The self-proclaimed "home of folklore" stages nightly shows; it's a top spot for regional music, gaucho dancing, and the like. ✉ *Balcarce 885* ☎ *387/421–7727* ⊕ *www.la-viejaestacion.com.ar.*

Macondo. Blues and beer are always on tap at this raucous pub, where you're as likely to meet backpacking Aussies as you are local law students. ✉ *Balcarce 980* ☎ *387/431–7191.*

Peña Gauchos de Güemes. One of the oldest and most traditional venues in the city, this peña retains a genuine gaucho spirit. It's been hosting folkloric nights for more than 50 years. ✉ *Uruguay 750* ☎ *387/421–0820* ⊕ *www.gauchosdeguemes.org.ar.*

SHOPPING

En lo de Carmén. Although it stocks a far smaller selection of products than the Mercado Artesanal, artist Carmén Clerici de Dominguez's store does house a workshop for craftsmen. Pick up reasonably priced ceramic dishes, hand-knitted alpaca socks and gloves, and paintings by local artists. ✉ *Ameghino 529* ☎ *387/421–3207.*

Feria de la Balcarce. Every Sunday, on Balcarce street between Entre Ríos and Ameghino, around 200 local artisans get together for this weekly handicrafts market. It's considered to be the most important in the north. Pick up ceramics, knitwear, rugs, shawls, and even furry llama toys. ✉ *Balcarce 700 between Entre Ríos and Ameghino* ⊘ *Sun. 10 am–10:30 pm.*

Mercado Artesanal. Although Salta has all the usual high-street shops where you can stock up on sundries, provincial villages are a better bet for souvenirs and regional products. There are, however, a few proud exceptions to that rule—including the huge 1882 Jesuit monastery that holds the Mercado Artesanal and the open stalls across the street. Look for red-and-black salteño ponchos, alpaca knitwear and weavings, leather goods, wooden masks, carved animals, and fine silver from around the province. Everything is open daily 9–9. ⊠ *Av. San Martín 2555* ☎ *387/434–2808.*

SPORTS AND THE OUTDOORS

Salta has just a few outfitters, but the options they offer feel fresh and exciting. Horseback riding is growing in popularity, as is rafting.

HORSEBACK RIDING

Finca Lesser. Fifteen km (10 miles) west of Salta, Finca Lesser provides horseback-riding tours on a huge private estate. Trips can last anywhere from a few hours to two days. They can also organize a folk-music performance and a tour showing gauchos at work. ⊠ *4 km (2½ miles) past Castellanos, San Lorenzo* ☎ *387/492–1155* ⊕ *www.fincalesser.com.ar.*

MacDermott's Argentina. Despite being told by local gauchos that he and his horse Pancho wouldn't make it across the Andes, Hugh Mac-Dermott proved the cynics wrong. Now he shares his expertise by leading horse-riding holidays across the northwest, with options ranging from short breaks to two-week treks. ☎ *11/5354–0487* ⊕ *www. macdermottsargentina.com* ☜ *From $100.*

Sayta. Rural tourism specialist Sayta offers stays out at a ranch in Chicoana, 40 km (24 miles) south of Salta, and horseback treks lasting from one to five days for riders of all levels. ⊠ *Chicoana* ☎ *387/156–836–565* ⊕ *www.saltacabalgatas.com.ar* ☜ *From 400 pesos.*

RAFTING

Salta Rafting. This company specializes in whitewater rafting, operating from a base 35 km (21 miles) south of Salta by the Cabra Corral dam. Kayaking excursions, 4X4 adventures, and tandem paragliding are also available. For a breathtaking canopy surfing experience, try its "death slide"—a network of zip-line cables that crosses high above the Río Juramento. ⊠ *Caseros 117* ☎ *387/421–3216* ⊕ *www.saltarafting. com* ☜ *From 350 pesos.*

EN ROUTE When the road to Cachi starts ascending toward Piedra de Molina—a lookout point 3,353 meters (11,000 feet) above sea level—it winds up the spectacular Cuesta del Obispo (Bishop's Rise) and, shortly before the top, reaches the **Parque Nacional Los Cardones.** Almost nothing other than thousands of *cardones* (the cardon cacti, for which the park is named) can thrive here, and even they've been threatened. (People were chopping them down for use as "wood" at a faster rate than they could grow back; they're now protected.) Try to make the journey in the morning, as clouds descend in the afternoon and the road becomes difficult to navigate; never drive the route at night, and seek advice before setting out in the rainy season. Halfway through the park the road splits: the quicker route is via Payogasta to the north, but Ruta 42 takes you on a fantastic but unpaved road through red mountains nicknamed Los Colorados.

SALTA PROVINCE

The city of Salta, unofficial capital of the Argentine north, is known for its colonial architecture and its unassuming provincial appeal. It's also a hot spot for international visitors and, compared with its neighbors, really has its act together in terms of tourist infrastructure. The surrounding province of the same name, however, is only slowly being discovered by outsiders. Even the main circuit, the Valles Calchaquíes (Calchaquíes Valleys), involves long drives on unpaved roads with few other vehicles in sight.

Only the central third of the province has much in the way of population (the east and the west being vast, uninhabitable wilderness), but within that there's plenty of variety. Although new circuits are being opened up that take in the Cabra Corral dam and thermal waters of Rosario de la Frontera, the main destinations outside the city of Salta are Cafayate for its wine, Cachi for its landscape and archaeological sites, and San Antonio de las Cobres—the destination of the Tren a las Nubes.

CACHI

157 km (97 miles) southwest of Salta.

This small colonial village on Ruta 40 is fast becoming a base for exploring the north of Calchaqui Valley. Cachi itself has a charming church, a small archaeological museum, and a couple of decent hotels and restaurants, although there is nothing in the way of nightlife. Watching over it all is the 6,340-meter (20,800-foot) Nevado de Cachi, a few miles away.

The surrounding area is loaded with archaeological sites that have scarcely been explored. El Tero contains the remains of pre-Inca dwellings, and within 15 km (10 miles) are two more important sites: Puerta La Paya to the southwest and Las Pailas to the north (at the foot of the Nevado de Cachi). A little farther north, en route to La Poma, are the Graneros Incaicos, stunning cave-carved granaries from the Inca era.

GETTING HERE AND AROUND
Just one bus company, Marcos Rueda, serves Cachi from Salta. You're advised to buy tickets for the journey (which takes just over four hours) a day in advance. For more flexibility, Remis San José runs a fixed-price taxi service four times daily; the cost is about 300 pesos. It also offers area sightseeing tours, plus transfers to Cafayate and the villages in between.

ESSENTIALS
Bus Contacts Marcos Rueda ☎ *387/421-1327.*

Taxi Contacts Remis San José ☎ *3868/491-907.*

Visitor Information Tourist office ✉ *General Güemes s/n* ☎ *3868/491-902.*

TOURS
Turismo Urkupiña. From two-hour walking trips around Cachi to day-long excursions deep into the Salta countryside, this tour company covers most areas from its Cachi base. ✉ *Benjamin Zorrilla s/n* ☎ *387/155-118-396* ⊕ *www.aventuracalchaqui.wix.com/cachi* 🖅 *From 120 pesos.*

THE NORTHWEST SHOPPING EXPERIENCE

Throughout the Northwest, almost every town has an area where vendors sell *artesenías*—emblematic crafts using local materials and incorporating the culture. Spending time at these markets, which may simply be set up around the main plaza, isn't just a great way to find the perfect souvenir; it's also a real opportunity to interact with locals.

Andean artesanías come in two forms: mass-produced products (generally imported from Bolivia) and locally produced handmade items. Often, stall owners will sell a mix of the two; ask which fall into the latter category and opt for them, as they do more to support the local community. Bolivian goods get cheaper the farther north you go. Some towns such as Humahuaca and Tilcara have shops that are exclusively fair trade, so look out for the signs reading, "*Comercio justo.*"

Also, you'll see lots of dimpled *cardon* (cactus) wood carved into all manner of souvenirs, but there's no system right now for verifying the origin of the wood (only souvenirs carved from already-dead cardones are legal). We encourage you to ask your guide or another local for vendor recommendations.

Alpaca knits. Alpacas look like a cross between a llama and a sheep with a glossy, silky fleece. Textiles from them feel lovely and are unmistakably Andean, with the traditional designs.

Coca. Freely available, coca here is a medicine rather than a narcotic. Coca tea is neatly packaged and doesn't taste too bad. But don't try taking it home without checking customs regulations first.

Leather. Unless there's an item that particularly catches your eye, save your leather purchases for the pampas. They do use leather in the Quebrada, but not in the decorative ways of elsewhere in the country.

Masks. If you don't experience Humahuaca at carnival time, you might be surprised by the number of masks—of humans and animals, made of wood or pottery—among the stalls. If you do go during carnaval, it'll make more sense.

Musical instruments. Panpipes are easy to play (though harder to play well) and instantly evocative of the windswept Quebrada. There are more intricate instruments available for musicians or the curious. For some tips on how to play, take it to a peña one evening and corner one of the performers.

Ponchos. Made from sheep or llama wool, ponchos go with everything, are useful against the cool cloudless nights in the Quebrada, and make great souvenirs (just resist the temptation to wear one out in Buenos Aires if you want to blend in). You can also pick up hats and gloves in matching patterns.

Silver. It was its position on the road to the Potosí silver mines that made the Quebrada so important in colonial days, but don't count on the silver on sale now being locally sourced. Look for traditional motifs and symbols cast into silver as jewelry and, borrowing traditions from elsewhere, tableware.

5

WHERE TO STAY

$ HOTEL
ACA Hosteria. For most of the past 40 years this Argentine Automobile Club hosteria was the only decent place to stay in Cachi. **Pros:** lovely pool views; buffet breakfast; large play area. **Cons:** compact rooms. [$] *Rooms from: US$99* ✉ *Av. Automóvil Club Argentino s/n* ☎ *3868/491–904* 🌐 *www.aca.tur.ar/hoteles/vinculados/salta/cachi/index.htm* 🛏 *33 rooms* 🍴 *Breakfast.*

$ B&B/INN
El Cortijo. Converted from a vintage villa, this boutique hotel stands out for its rustic-chic style and friendly service; the 12 guest rooms are tastefully decorated with traditional antiques and art. **Pros:** artistic décor; buffet breakfast; free Wi-Fi. **Cons:** rooms vary in terms of size and views. [$] *Rooms from: US$85* ✉ *Av. Automóvil Club Argentino s/n* ☎ *387/439–9771* 🌐 *www.elcortijohotel.com* 🛏 *12 rooms* 🍴 *Breakfast.*

$$ HOTEL Fodor's Choice ★
La Merced del Alto. Although this stately white-adobe building looks like it's been here forever, it was in fact built in 2006; inside, rooms are huge and comfortable with tasteful wood and iron furniture. **Pros:** expansive grounds with great views; attention to detail; accessible for people with disabilities; buffet breakfast. **Cons:** 3 km (2 miles) from Cachi; echoing corridors. [$] *Rooms from: US$134* ✉ *Fuerte Alto s/n* ☎ *3868/490–030* 🌐 *www.lamerceddelalto.com* 🛏 *12 rooms, 1 suite* 🍴 *Breakfast.*

MOLINOS

206 km (128 miles) southwest of Salta (via Cachi); 50 km (31 miles) south of Cachi.

Molinos, a village with about 5,000 inhabitants, has a photogenic 17th-century church and a small vicuña-breeding farm (*vicuñas* are similar to llamas but their fur makes a much finer, more expensive wool). The main draw, however, is its location on the way to Argentina's oldest winery (Bodega Colomé) and to many more in Cafayate.

Molinos is also just a few miles from Seclantás' Camino de Artesanos (Road of the Artisans), where weavers make ponchos and scarves by the roadside on contraptions improvised from wood and old bicycle parts. The Laguna de Brealito, 10 km (6 miles) due west of Seclantás, is a picturesque lake in the middle of nowhere. Eight km (5 miles) east of Molinos are the pre-Columbian ruins of Chicoana.

GETTING HERE AND AROUND

Ale Hermanos offers bus service five times a week between Salta and Molinos.

ESSENTIALS

Bus Contacts Ale Hermanos ☎ *387/423–1811* 🌐 *www.alehnos.com.ar.*

EXPLORING

Fodor's Choice ★
Bodega Colomé. Remote wineries are one thing, Bodega Colomé is something else altogether. Yet finally arriving at this world-class spot puts the miles of driving along bumpy, unpaved roads firmly into perspective. Established in 1831 and owned by the Swiss Hess Group since 2001, Colomé is Argentina's oldest winery. A visitor center runs daily tours and offers tastings, while a terrace restaurant serves delectable lunches with views of one of the world's highest vineyards. Since 2009, Colomé

has also been home to the breathtaking and unexpected James Turrell Museum. It showcases five decades of the artist's works with light and space, and includes a fun tunnel of color (advance reservations recommended). **TIP→ Turrell's contemporary art installations are at their most striking at sunset.** ✉ *RP53, Km 20, 20 km (13 miles) west of Molinos* ☎ *387/439–4009* 🌐 *www.bodegacolome.com* 🎟 *Winery free, tastings from 40 pesos; museum free* 🕓 *Winery daily 10:30–6; museum Tues.–Sun. 2–6.*

WHERE TO EAT

$$ ARGENTINE 🍴 **Inti Raymi.** It's an honest little restaurant in Seclantás, with some fine old photos on the walls and good, oven-baked empanadas. Other attractions include a delicious goat stew, corn-based dishes, regional breads, and a warm welcome from your host, Alejandro Diaz. [$] *Average main: 80 pesos* ✉ *Abraham Cornejo s/n, opposite police station, Seclantás* ☎ *3868/498–009* 💳 *No credit cards.*

5

CAFAYATE

185 km (115 miles) southwest of Salta via RN68; 340 km (211 miles) southwest of Salta via R40.

Thanks to a microclimate and fertile soil, Cafayate and the surrounding area is one of Argentina's booming wine regions. The town itself is civilized and orderly, with various bodegas offering tours and tastings, lots of good restaurants, and some exquisite hotels. But wander a couple of blocks from the central plaza and you're back on unpaved roads. Take a bit of a hike, and you're in the mountains—probably enjoying a wine-tasting session at a tiny *finca* and trying hard to get your camera to do justice to the view.

GETTING HERE AND AROUND

Chevallier and Balut both run about 10 buses a day from Salta. It's best to buy your ticket for the four-hour trip a day in advance, especially in summer. In Cafayate, many agencies and hotels rent bikes, which can come in handy when visiting bodegas and sights within a few miles of town.

ESSENTIALS

Bus Contacts Balut ☎ *0387/422–9393* 🌐 *www.balutsrl.com.ar.* **Chevallier** ☎ *387/491–3548* 🌐 *www.nuevachevallier.com.*

Visitor Information Tourist Office ✉ *Pl. 20 de Febrero* ☎ *3868/422–224* 🌐 *www.turismosalta.gov.ar.*

EXPLORING

Museo de la Vid y del Vino. This museum, located in a warehouse dating from 1881, has undergone an extensive refurbishment to include more flash and 3D exhibits. You can learn about winemaking in the Calchquíes valleys. Machinery, agricultural implements, and old photographs also tell the history of winemaking in this area. ✉ *Guemes Sur and Fermín Perdiguero* ☎ *3868/422–322* 🌐 *www.museodelavidyelvino.gov.ar* 🎟 *30 pesos* 🕓 *Tues.–Sun. 10–7:30.*

Museo Regional y Arqueológico Rodolfo Bravo. For 66 years, Rodolfo Bravo collected and catalogued funerary and religious objects from local excavations. These objects, made of clay, ceramic, metal, and textiles, are on display at the private Museo Regional y Arqueológico Rodolfo Bravo (Rudolfo Bravo Regional and Archaeological Museum). Artifacts from the Incas and Diaguitas of the Calchaqui Valley also form part of the collection. ☒ *Colón 191* ☎ *3868/421–054* 🖃 *Voluntary contribution* ⊙ *Daily 11–2 (call ahead to confirm).*

NEED A BREAK?

Helados Miranda. For wine-tasting with a difference, be sure to stop at Helados Miranda in Cafayate. In 1994, at the age of 60, Ricardo Miranda decided that he wasn't going to succeed as a painter. So he turned his creative energy to making wine sorbets, taking two years to perfect the recipe. Sweet yet tangy torrontés arguably makes sense as a sorbet; the cabernet makes a good match for his fruit-flavored ice creams. All are made organically on the premises. ☒ *Av. Güemes Norte 170* ☎ *3868/421–106.*

Quebrada de las Conchas. The first 50 km (30 miles) of the direct road to Salta (or the last stretch if you don't come via Cachi and Molinos) is known as the Gorge of the Shells, and breathtaking scenery makes it an attraction in its own right. Various rock formations have been eroded into wildly different shapes that have been nicknamed the Windows, the Castles, the Frog, the Friar—each name seems fanciful, that is until the road winds around the corner and you're actually confronted by the formation itself. The climax is the Amphitheater, sometimes used as a venue for proper orchestras thanks to its outstanding natural acoustics; wandering minstrels offer impromptu performances. ☒ *RN68, Km 6–Km 46.*

WINERIES

Although Salta makes only 1.5% of Argentina's wine, the province accounts for 8% of the country's exports. Most of the production is in or around Cafayate, which has a dozen bodegas, ranging from boutique family businesses to small branches of multinational concerns.

Bodega José L. Mounier. In 1996 there was nothing on the land of Bodega José L. Mounier in El Divisadero, 4 km (2 miles) outside of town. Now this is one of Salta's best boutique wineries. Almost half its small line of red, white, rosé, and sparkling wine is sold in the bodega itself. The tour includes sampling three wines, and lunch on the verandah is available if you book ahead. ☒ *El Divisadero, Km 4* ☎ *3868/422–129* ⊕ *www. bodegamounier.com.ar* 🖃 *20 pesos* ⊙ *Weekdays 9:30–5, Sat. 9:30–1.*

Bodega Nanni. Nanni has been in the same family and in the same building—just a block from the main square—since 1897. Thanks to its organic certification, much of its small production of Torrontés, Malbec, Cabernet Sauvignon, and Tannat is exported to the United States. ☒ *Silverio Chavarria 151* ☎ *3868/421–527* ⊕ *www.bodegananni.com* 🖃 *20 pesos for tour and 3-wine tasting* ⊙ *Daily 9:30–1 and 2:30–6.*

Domingo Molina. About 2 km (1 mile) north of Cafayate, Domingo Molina has been making Torrontés, a Malbec, and various blends since 2000. Tastings are available, and you can book in advance for a *picada* or

asado. A drive leads you high up into the hills, offering stunning views of the wine lands to the east.
■ TIP→ Take a look at Domingo Molina's oldest vine—a 100-year-old malbec, still providing drinkable grapes. Domingo Hermanos, a sister winery in town, is one of Cafayate's biggest operations, producing three million liters a year. ⊠ *RN40, Km 6, Yacochuya Norte* ☏ *3868/1545–2887* ⊕ *www.domingomolina.com.ar* 🎫 *40 pesos, refundable with wine purchase* ⊙ *Wed.–Mon. 10–5 (tastings at 4).*

El Porvenir de Cafayate. Old blends with new at Bodega El Porvenir. Founded at the turn of the 20th century by Italian immigrants, the winery was bought by the Romero Marcuzzi family in the 1990s and brought up to date. The result is a small yet sleek facility surrounded by old oak casks and presses. Drop by the tasting room to sample the Laborum-label Malbec and Torrontés, as well as the high-end Amauta three-grape red blend. ⊠ *Córdoba 32* ☏ *3868/422–007* ⊕ *www.elporvenirdecafayate.com* 🎫 *45 pesos* ⊙ *Sun. and Mon. 9–1, Wed.–Sat. 9–1 and 3–6.*

El Transito. A contemporary building in the center of town houses El Transito's bodega and visitor center, a business run by a family that shares common ancestors with the folks at Bodega Nanni across the street. Pop in for a short tour and the chance to sample Malbec, Cabernet Sauvignon, and Torrontés. ⊠ *Belgrano 102* ☏ *3868/422–385* ⊕ *www.bodegaeltransito.com* 🎫 *Free* ⊙ *Mon.–Sat. 9–1 and 3–6:30, Sun. 10–1 and 3:30–6:30.*

Fodor's Choice **Piattelli Vineyards.** The first winery in Cafayate to be constructed with tour-
★ ism in mind, Piattelli caused a bit of a flurry with locals when it opened in 2013 thanks to the modern aesthetic conceived by its American owners. The state-of-the-art bodega, halfway up the foothills towards Yacochuya, promises tastings, tours, and fabulous valley views. Kick back on one of the two terraces with a refreshing torrontés before tucking into slow-roasted lamb or pan-fried salmon at the winery's restaurant. ⊠ *R2, on the way to Yacochuya* ☏ *3868/1540–5881* ⊕ *www.piattellivineyards.com* 🎫 *50 pesos for tour and 4-wine tasting, 100 pesos for premium tasting* ⊙ *Daily 9:30–5:30; tours in English at 11, 1, and 3.*

San Pedro de Yacochuya. Head 8 km (5 miles) northwest of town toward the hills to find Arnaldo Etchart's boutique winery. He established it in 1988, collaborating with star oenologist Michel Rolland to create a trio of award-winning wines. Visits don't require a reservation, so you can simply drop by to sample the Coquena or San Pedro de Yacochuya lines

5

Drying chilies near Cachi, Calchaquí Valley

while enjoying stunning views over the valley. ☎ *3868/421–233* ⊕ *www. sanpedrodeyacochuya.com.ar* ✉ *Tastings 50–150 pesos* ☉ *Weekdays 10–5, Sat. 10–1.*

Vasija Secreta. Occupying a grand 1850s building on the northern edge of town, Vasija Secreta has a small museum displaying imported oak barrels and machinery for pumping and bottling wine. Short tours give a historical overview and show how production methods have changed. Tasty local dishes are served at the rustic on-site restaurant. ✉ *RN40 s/n* ☎ *3868/421–850* ⊕ *www.vasijasecreta.com* ✉ *Free* ☉ *Daily 9–1 and 2:30–7 (9–6:30 in summer).*

WHERE TO EAT

$$
ARGENTINE
✗ **El Rancho.** Facing the main plaza, this big barn of a restaurant serves regional specialties (like baked rabbit and roasted kid goat), as well as pastas and classic Argentine steaks. Expect generous portions, a bustling atmosphere, live folk music, and wines from the owner's Bodega Río Colorado, just a block away. $ *Average main: 90 pesos* ✉ *Vicario Toscano 4* ☎ *3868/421–256* ⊕ *www.elranchocafayate.com.ar* 🚫 *No credit cards* ☉ *Closed Mon.*

$$$
ARGENTINE
✗ **Peña y Parrillada de la Plaza.** This place makes the list for its music rather than its food—though the barbecued meats and empanadas are good deals. Singers, musicians, and sometimes dancers bring Peña y Parrillada de la Plaza to life each night. $ *Average main: 130 pesos* ✉ *Nuestra Señora del Rosario 96* ☎ *3868/421–043* ⊕ *www.laplaza restaurante.com.ar.*

$$ ARGENTINE Fodor's Choice ★ 🍴 **Macacha Gourmet.** A 100-year-old converted school building houses one of Cafayate's more ambitious restaurants. Overseen by the friendly owner Matías, it has three dining rooms themed after the Nanni, Domingo Hermanos, and Etchart bodegas, with wine displays and special cutlery. The decoration is from all around the world, but the food is strictly local—llama, quinoa, rabbit, kid, and Andean potatoes feature prominently on the menu. A convivial wine bar stays open late to serve vino from every bodega in town. ■ **TIP→ There's live music and dancing some weekends.** [$] *Average main: 90 pesos* ✉ *Av. Güemes Norte 28* ☎ *3868/422–319* ▭ *No credit cards* ⏲ *Closed Sun.*

WHERE TO STAY

$$$ HOTEL 🏨 **Altalaluna Boutique Hotel & Spa.** This gorgeous boutique hotel in the village of Tolombón, 14 km (9 miles) south of Cafayate, occupies an 1892 colonial mansion; there's a wine bar and cellar, an excellent restaurant, a reading room complete with fireplace, and a peaceful spa overlooking endless vines. **Pros:** great facilities; perfect for star-spotting. **Cons:** the pitter-patter of small feet running past rooms can sound very loud; a bit far from the town center. [$] *Rooms from: US$205* ✉ *RN40, Km 4326* ☎ *3868/461–0283* 🌐 *www.altalaluna.com* 🛏 *14 rooms, 6 suites* 🍴 *Breakfast.*

$$ RESORT 🏨 **Cafayate Wine Resort.** Three km (2 miles) from the plaza on a straight dusty road lined with vineyards and in the shadow of San Isidro is a large white adobe building with 22 rooms built around a wide courtyard. **Pros:** spacious shared areas and access to veranda from all rooms; vineyards right up to the hotel; buffet breakfast. **Cons:** a little isolated from the town; only the 10 "superior" rooms (added in 2013) have TVs and minibars. [$] *Rooms from: US$180* ✉ *25 de Mayo s/n, Camino al Divisadero* ☎ *3868/422–272* 🌐 *www.cafayatewineresort.com* 🛏 *22 rooms* 🍴 *Breakfast.*

$$$$ HOTEL Fodor's Choice ★ 🏨 **Grace Cafayate.** A contemporary offering in the area, Grace Cafayate isn't just a step away from the local style—it's a whole welcome world away. **Pros:** efficient staff; super-comfy king beds; spacious communal areas. **Cons:** breakfast is on the small side. [$] *Rooms from: US$420* ✉ *RN40, Km 4340* ☎ *3868/427–000* 🌐 *www.gracehotels.com/cafayate* 🛏 *52 rooms* 🍴 *Breakfast.*

$ HOTEL 🏨 **Hotel Asturias.** The swimming pool is terrific, the garden is ample, and this—the biggest and oldest hotel in town—is quite comfortable. **Pros:** great garden and pool; two art galleries; close to the center; buffet breakfast. **Cons:** restaurant open only in high season. [$] *Rooms from: US$105* ✉ *Av. Güemes Sur 154* ☎ *3868/421–328* 🌐 *www.cafayateasturias.com* 🛏 *63 rooms* 🍴 *Breakfast.*

$$ HOTEL 🏨 **La Casa de la Bodega.** Carob wood and local boulders from the Quebrada de las Conchas were used to construct the little Casa de la Bodega. **Pros:** total peace and quiet in a beautiful setting; friendly staff. **Cons:** can be windy; the piped '80s music gets a bit much. [$] *Rooms from: US$164* ✉ *RN 68, Km 18.5, 18 km (11 miles) from Cafayate center* ☎ *3868/492–056* 🌐 *www.lacasadelabodega.com.ar* 🛏 *8 rooms* 🍴 *Breakfast.*

5

$$$$ HOTEL Fodor's Choice ★ 🏨 **Patios de Cafayate Wine Hotel.** Creature comforts, a fine restaurant, and rustic-chic rooms overlooking the vineyards make this luxury property a top choice. **Pros:** exclusive; afternoon tea and breakfast included; fabulous facilities. **Cons:** pricey. [$] *Rooms from: US$306* ✉ *R40 at RN68, 3 km (2 miles) from Cafayate center* ☎ *3868/422–229* 🌐 *www.patiosdecafayate.com* 🛏 *30 rooms* 🍴 *Some meals.*

$$ B&B/INN 🏨 **Portal del Santo.** Just two blocks from the plaza but already on the edge of town, this place feels like a hideaway; behind the large colonial-style building, with its big guest rooms and its fireplace-warmed common area, is a garden with a blue-and-white swimming pool and great views. **Pros:** both central and quiet; good bathrooms; big breakfast. **Cons:** many guests are families, which tends to disturb the peace. [$] *Rooms from: US$120* ✉ *Silvero Chavarria 250* ☎ *3868/422–500* 🌐 *www.portaldelsanto.com.ar* 🛏 *13 rooms* 🍴 *Breakfast.*

SHOPPING

Cesteria (weaving with cane), *tejidos* (weaving with fabric), and *cerámica* (pottery) are the local specialties. Find these goods in the Paseo de Artesanos on the main plaza or in individual workshops. The tourist office opposite the Paseo de Artesanos has details. Cafayate has also seen a boom in wine stores selling products from local bodegas.

Calchaquitos. Just next to the plaza, Calchaquitos sells cookies and chocolates, local jams, wine, and clothes. ✉ *Güemes Sur 118* ☎ *3868/421–799* 🌐 *www.fabricacalchaquitos.com.ar.*

La Última Pulpería. For a time-warp trip, just step into this store. La Última Pulpería, which has barely changed since opening in 1923, is an "Aladdin's Cave" selling loose herbs and spices, animal hides, and produce. If you can pry owner Miguel Dioli away from his regular Salta-brand beer-drinking customers at the makeshift bar, he's good for a chat in Spanish. ✉ *Mitre 20* ☎ *3868/421–629.*

Vinoteca La Escalera. Plenty of wine stores have popped up of late in Cafayate but Vinoteca La Escalera is one of the more established ones. It carries a solid selection from around the valley. ✉ *San Martín 63* ☎ *3868/421–142.*

SPORTS AND THE OUTDOORS

Getting active in Cafayate involves the gentler end of adventure tourism: there are lots of opportunities for hikes, horseback rides, and bike excursions, but nothing too extreme. The waterfalls in the Río Colorado make a good excursion on a bike or on foot.

Los Toneles. Biking is a pleasant way to access some of the farther-afield wineries or to explore the countryside. You can rent cycles from Los Toneles hostel. ✉ *Camila Quintana de Niño 38* ☎ *3868/422–301* 🌐 *www.lostoneleshostal.com.ar* 🎟 *From 40 pesos.*

6

MENDOZA AND THE WINE REGIONS

WELCOME TO MENDOZA AND THE WINE REGIONS

TOP REASONS TO GO

★ **Scenic Wonders:** Wherever you go—over the pass to Chile, north to San Juan, south to San Rafael—the sight of those towering Andean peaks never ceases to amaze.

★ **Fun in the Sun:** This sun-soaked land will delight, whether you pedal a bike along flat vineyard roads, ride a horse along Andean trails, or ski down challenging slopes.

★ **Bed and Bodega:** Country inns with gourmet restaurants, vineyard visits and tastings, cooking classes, and discussions with oenologists make wine touring a pure pleasure.

★ **Food and Wine:** Some of Argentina's premier chefs have left coastal resorts and Buenos Aires' bistros behind, choosing to relocate to wine-country inns and bodegas.

★ **Unique Terroir:** All the big-name wineries have planted in the high-altitude region of the Valle de Uco, where grapes ripen slowly and varietals show tremendous fruitiness.

1 **Gran Mendoza.** Gran, or greater, Mendoza refers to the city and the surrounding *departments* (urban areas) of Godoy Cruz, Guaymallén, Maipú, Junín, Luján de Cuyo, and Las Heras—most of which have vineyards, bodegas, small hotels, and restaurants.

2 **Valle de Uco.** At the foot of the Cordón del Plata, between the towns of Ugarteche and Pareditas, the valley spreads its green mantle of vineyards and fruit orchards for 125 km (78 miles). The Río Tunuyán and its many *arroyos* (streams) create an oasis in this otherwise dry desert region.

3 **San Rafael Region.** The vineyards and olive groves that ring this burgeoning agricultural town in the southern portion of Mendoza Province are irrigated by the Ríos Atuel and Diamante, which flow from the nearby Andes.

4 **San Juan Region.** From this historic town surrounded by three important wine-producing valleys—Tulum, Ullum, and Zonda—you can travel west up the Río San Juan into a landscape of mountains, valleys, and desert.

GETTING ORIENTED

The provinces of Mendoza and San Juan, in the central-west portion of Argentina, lie at the foot of the highest Andean ranges along the border with Chile. The city of Mendoza and its surrounding departments are in Mendoza Province's northern portion, 1,040 km (646 miles) from Buenos Aires but only 360 km (224 miles) from Santiago, Chile. The east–west Ruta Nacional 7 (RN7, part of the Ruta Panamericana or Pan-American Highway) crosses the Andes from Mendoza to Chile and links Argentina and neighboring countries (Brazil, Uruguay, Paraguay) with Pacific ports. Ruta Nacional 40 runs north–south the length of the country, passing through San Juan and down to Mendoza, the Valle de Uco, and San Rafael.

6

La Rioja
38
Desagues
de los
Colorados
Patquía
510
Chamical
38
San Ramón
Milagro
32
Chepés
141
Salina de
Mascasín
Ulapes
San Jorge
Quines
20
San Antonio
San Francisco
del Monte
de Oro
147
146
San Gerónimo
San Luís
SAN
LUÍS
7
146
TRAVESÍA PUNTANA
Río Salado
188
PAMPA DE LA VARITA
0   50 miles
0   50 km

CERRO ACONCAGUA VIA THE USPALLATA PASS

At 6,957 meters (22,825 feet), Cerro Aconcagua is the highest mountain in both the Western and the Southern hemispheres. The so-called Giant of America towers over the Andes with its five glaciers gleaming in the sun; and every year, late November through March, thousands try to conquer it.

However, you don't have to be a mountaineer to enjoy the wild beauty here. Although guided climbing expeditions require two weeks of hiking and acclimating, a worthy alternative is to park at the rangers' cabin right off Ruta Nacional 7 just beyond the Puente del Inca, pay the park fee, and hike three hours from the Río Horcones to a lagoon. If this seems like a short hike for such a drive out, relax knowing that the journey to this place is as breathtaking as Aconcagua itself.

While fauna isn't thick, sight lines are unobstructed, and you might see foxes or shy guanacos; look up for condors, too. Alpine meadows bloom in the spring, and lichen are up to 500 years old.

(above) Sunset on Aconcagua from Plaza de Mulas base camp (top right) Poplar trees en route to the pass (bottom right) Look up: condor sightings are common in this area.

DRIVE SAFELY

Ruta Nacional 7 is the only road that connects the Pacific ports of Chile with Argentina, Brazil, and Uruguay. Be prepared for heavy truck traffic.

In winter, icy roads can close for days; mudslides can cause closures in all seasons. The altitude jumps from 762 meters (2,500 feet) in Mendoza to 3,184 meters (10,446 feet) at the top of the pass; winds can sometimes be brutal.

ALONG THE USPALLATA PASS (RN7, THE PANAMERICAN HIGHWAY)

Leaving Mendoza, green vineyards give way to barren hills and scrub brush as you follow the river for 30 km (19 miles). If you find yourself engulfed in fog and drizzle, don't despair: you'll likely encounter brilliant sunshine when you reach the Potrerillos Valley 39 km (24 miles) away. The road passes a long dam and then follows the Río Mendoza for 105 km (65 miles) to Uspallata, the last town before the Chilean frontier.

Along the way, the ríos Blanco and Tambillos rush down from the mountains into the Río Mendoza, and remnants of Inca *tambos* (resting places) marked by signs en route remind you that this was once an Inca trail; if you're traveling with a guide, she or he will stop for you to check them out. At Punta de Vacas, corrals that held cattle on their way to Chile lie abandoned alongside defunct railway tracks. Two km (1 mile) beyond the army barracks and customs office three valleys converge. Looking south, the region's third-highest mountain— Cerro Tupungato, an inactive volcano (6,800 meters/22,310 feet)—reigns above the Valle de Uco.

After passing the ski area at Los Penitentes, you arrive at Puente del Inca (2,950 meters/9,680 feet). Legend has it that long before the Spaniards arrived, an Inca chief traveled here to cure his paralysis in the thermal waters. Today, in addition to the thermal springs, you'll see a natural bridge of red rocks encrusted with yellow sulfur that spans the Río Cuevas; what's left of a spa hotel, built in the 1920s and destroyed in a 1965 flood, is covered in copper and gold sediment below the bridge. A few miles farther west, past the Argentine customs check, are the entrance to the park and the ranger's cabin. Fifteen km (9 miles) farther along, the highway passes Las Cuevas, a settlement where the road forks right to Chile or left to the statue of Cristo Redentor (Christ the Redeemer), commemorating the 1902 peace pact between the two countries.

HIKING GUIDES AND LOGISTICS

November through March, you can sign on for two- or three-day guided treks to the Plaza de Mulas base camp at 4,260 meters (13,976 feet), where there's a *refugio* (cabin with bunk beds).

Guides will often take care of the necessary paperwork (⇨ *Hiking and Mountaineering in Uspallata*); otherwise, you can purchase a permit at the **Parque San Martín Visitor's Center** in Mendoza City (✉ *Las Tipas at Los Robles* ☉ *Week-days 8–6, weekends 9–1*). Trekking permits cost US$110–$280, depending on the season, level, and number of days; ascent permits cost US$500–$800. Day permits, available at the entrance to Aconcagua Park, cost about US$2.

INTO CHILE

Some tour groups and independent travelers continue on through to Chile to explore the vintages there. Visas, required of U.S. citizens, can be obtained at the border.

Updated
by Amanda
Barnes

Exceptional wine, top-quality cuisine, exhilarating outdoor activities, and the skyscraping Andes framing almost every view: it's easy to see why people come here, and why many stay longer than they'd planned. The provinces of Mendoza and San Juan might just have it all. In the center of Argentina, this region is often referred to as the Cuyo; and the name—passed down from the early indigenous Huarpe people, who called it Cuyum Mapu (Land of Sand)—is a reminder that the terrain is naturally semi-arid.

It is only because of carefully managed snowmelt from the mountains that the provinces are so green and, through irrigation, able to produce around 90% of the country's wine. *Acéquias* (canals) built by the Huarpes and improved upon by the conquering Incas and Spaniards, as well as by modern engineers, continue to capture the flow of the region's great rivers and channel it along the shady streets of the major cities: Mendoza, San Juan, and San Rafael.

Jesuit missionaries crossed the Andes from Chile to plant the first grape vines in 1556. Today more than 200,000 hectares (494,200 acres) of vineyards bask in the sun from the suburbs of Mendoza City south through the Valle de Uco to San Rafael. The grapes are protected from the humid winds of the Pacific by the Andes, and grow at altitudes between 609 and 1,700 meters (2,000 to 5,500 feet), where they ripen slowly during long, hot summer days, while cool nights maintain acidity for long-lasting taste. Indeed, many vineyards could be classified as organic, as chemicals are seldom used or needed, and vintages are very consistent.

Many bodegas offer tours and tastings; some also have atmospheric restaurants that pair fine wine with inspired food. But beyond the wineries, active adventures await. With more than 330 days of annual sunshine, this region is a four-season destination for outdoor enthusiasts. Ski resorts like Las Leñas attract snow bunnies in winter, and Aconcagua, the highest peak outside of the Himalayas, lures ambitious hikers and climbers in summer. At lower altitudes, there are less dizzying activities for all ages year-round, including horseback riding, whitewater rafting, and soaking in thermal baths.

PLANNING

WHEN TO GO

The wine harvest ends in autumn and is celebrated with festivities that culminate in the *vendimia* (wine festival). In Mendoza this takes place during the last days of February and first week of March. A parade circles the Plaza Independencia and ends in San Martín Park with a grand finale of music, dancing, and religious ceremonies to ensure a good harvest. People shop and graze at food stands in the parks and plazas.

Winter is time for pruning and tying vines. Ski season begins in mid-June. July, the month with the best weather, is most favored by Argentineans and Brazilians. August usually has plenty of snow, and September offers spring conditions. Weather in the Andes is unpredictable, though; pack clothes for all conditions, and get up-to-date reports from ski areas. Springtime in the Valle de Uco brings trees covered in pink and white blossoms and new life in the vineyards. The snowcapped Andes form a spectacular backdrop, so bring your wide-angle lens.

GETTING HERE AND AROUND

There are direct flights from Buenos Aires to Mendoza (about two hours), San Juan (1¾ hours), and San Rafael (1½ hours). Comfortable buses between the three major cities are cheap, and bus stations are centrally located. On arrival, you'll find that all three cities have car-rental agencies and *remises* (hired cars with drivers), as well as wine-oriented tour companies that will take care of local transportation for you.

Hiring a remis for a full or half day is a good use of money, as frequent detours, road construction or washed-out roads, and misleading (or nonexistent) signs can make driving yourself frustrating. Further, finding wineries on your own requires not only a good map (most are off the GPS grid) but also a working knowledge of Spanish. That said, if you have the time and the temperament for it, exploring on your own—stopping to snap photos and chat with locals—has its rewards. Driving to Andean villages and the border with Chile is a particularly remarkable experience.

If you are using Mendoza City as a base for independent winery visits, just bear in mind that Maipú is about a 30-minute drive away; reaching Luján de Cuyo by car takes 45 minutes and the Uco Valley can take upwards of an hour. In San Rafael, you can reach many wineries by bike. In San Juan, some are within cycling distance, while others are on quiet, pretty roads that are best accessed by car; driving onward from San Rafael is also a practical solution if you're combining wine tours with a ski vacation in Las Leñas.

6

RESTAURANTS

Most of the region follows national culinary trends—think beef, lamb, chicken, and pork *a la parrilla* (grilled). Malargüe, southwest of San Rafael, famously adds *chivito* (goat) to the mix—whether cooked a la parrilla or *al asador* (skewered on a metal cross stuck in the ground aslant a bed of hot coals). But you don't have to be a carnivore to eat well; after all, more than grapes grow in this part of Argentina. The vineyards are matched by olive groves, vegetable fields, and fruit orchards, which provide local chefs with an abundance of fresh ingredients. You'll taste them in the side dishes served at old-school *asados* (barbecues); in the hearty Spanish-style stews and casseroles that are an edible connection to the region's past; and in the innovative gourmet fare prepared at next-generation winery restaurants.

HOTELS

Like the altitude, the types of accommodations available here vary widely, so tourist offices can recommend all kinds of lodgings. As you'd expect, Mendoza City has the largest selection, with options including basic hostels, practical "apart-hotels" (furnished units with kitchen facilities), stylish boutique hotels, plus a healthy handful of luxury properties. In the countryside, you'll find everything from traditional *estancias* (ranches) that offer horseback riding and other outdoorsy activities to rustic *cabañas* (cabins), homey *residenciales* (bed-and-breakfasts), and modern ski lodges—all of which are generally well maintained and well priced. Vacationing hedonists can also choose between several posh resorts and *posadas* (country inns), where the on-site amenities include top-notch restaurants, extensive wine cellars, and soothing spas. *Hotel reviews have been shortened. For full information, visit Fodors.com.*

WHAT IT COSTS				
	$	**$$**	**$$$**	**$$$$**
Restaurants in Pesos	Under 65 pesos	65 pesos–99 pesos	100 pesos–150 pesos	over 150 pesos
Hotels in USD	Under $116	$116–$200	$201–$300	over $300

Restaurant prices are the average cost of a main course at dinner or, if dinner is not served, at lunch. Hotel prices are the lowest cost of a standard double room in high season.

WINE TOURS

Most wineries require reservations, so it's easiest to arrange visits through your hotel, a tourist office, or a local tour operator. Organized tours are particularly good if there's a specific bodega you wish to see or if you're traveling with a group and/or during the harvest. Most last a full day and include transportation from city hotels. If you do head out yourself, remember that many wineries charge for tastings; be sure to ask about fees when making your reservation.

ORGANIZED TOURS

Ampora. This well-established outfit runs full-day group tours (maximum eight people) to Luján de Cuyo and the Uco Valley. Ampora also has a private wine bar above the booking office. ✉ *Sarmiento 647, Mendoza* ☎ *261/429–2931* ⊕ *www.mendozawinetours.com* ✎ *From $185.*

Aventura and Wine (Bacchus Tours). Over the last 10 years this company has been creating private tours for individuals and groups. ☎ *261/420–4230 in Mendoza* ⊕ *www.aventurawine.com* ✎ *From $195.*

Aymará Turismo. In business for 20-plus years, Aymará offers a variety of tours—the most popular of which includes two Maipú wineries and an olive oil producer. Prices are cheap but groups are large. ☎ *261/420–2064 in Mendoza* ⊕ *www.aymaramendoza.com.ar* ✎ *From $25.*

Malbec Symphony. Directed by a sommelier, this agency offers tours in Mendoza and the San Juan region. Each itinerary is custom-made, so you can take a more thematic approach (like organic wine tastings) if you'd like. ☎ *261/429–3696* ⊕ *www.malbecsymphony.com* ✎ *From $180.*

Mendoza Viajes. This big agency offers all sorts of excursions (usually in large groups and in Spanish); wine-themed options include half- or full-day tours. Prices are reasonable, but the service is less personal. ☎ *261/461–0210 in Mendoza* ⊕ *www.mdzviajes.com.ar* ✎ *From $50.*

Mendoza Wine Camp. This company has full- or multiday tours to Luján de Cuyo and Uco Valley. You can also sign on for an asado master class to practice your Argentine BBQ skills. ☎ *261/423–6958* ⊕ *www.mendozawinecamp.com* ✎ *From $195.*

San Rafael Wine Tours. Veronica and her small team lead hands-on experiences at a local winery; transfers and reservations for unguided visits to wineries in San Rafael or the Valle de Uco can also be arranged. ☎ *260/442–0155* ⊕ *www.sanrafaelwinetours.com.ar* ✎ *From $170.*

Trout & Wine Tours. Owned by a cheery Irish expat, one of the longest-running, high-end operators in Mendoza offers full-day group tours (eight people maximum) to Luján de Cuyo and the Valle de Uco. Private tours are available, too. ☎ *261/425–5613, 261/15–541–3892 (cell)* ⊕ *www.troutandwine.com* ✎ *From $185.*

Uncorking Argentina. This custom-package creator will book the wineries and driver for you. Most clients opt to visit the Valle de Uco or Luján de Cuyo, but the choice is yours. ☎ *261/429–6955 in Mendoza* ⊕ *www.uncorkingargentina.com* ✎ *From $140.*

SELF-GUIDED TOURS

Each area has its own unique *caminos del vino* (wine routes), and the Caminos del Vino de Argentina's Spanish-language website is a valuable trip planning tool (⊕ *www.caminosdelvino.org.ar*). Wineries in San Juan Province have pooled their resources to print a booklet, *Ruta del Vino*, with maps, photos, and information in Spanish. In Mendoza Province, you can pick up the free WINEMAP at bookstores and wineries; it consists of four maps and a guidebook in Spanish. DIY types based in Mendoza City can also take advantage of the convenient, cost-effective Vitivinicola bus service.

Bus Vitivinicola. Mendoza's hop-on, hop-off Vitivinicola bus is the most affordable way to reach area wineries without your own transportation. Wednesday through Saturday, the comfy, air-conditioned vehicle picks up passengers at various points in the city and then starts its run to select venues. ■ TIP→ Because you'll be going without a guide, you'll need to make your own advance reservations for the wineries you wish to visit and pay your own way at each once you arrive. Bus tickets can be purchased online or on board; they're also sold at visitor information centers and participating hotels. ⊕ *www.busvitivinicola. com* ✉ *Full-day ticket $15.*

INSIDER INFORMATION
Vines of Mendoza. Before heading out to the wineries, stop by the Vines of Mendoza's Tasting Room, where you can sample the wares from a vast number of smaller producers. It's owned by an American entrepreneur, Michael Evans, and Pablo Gimenez-Riili, a third-generation winemaker from Mendoza. Their intention was to create a gathering place where English-speaking visitors could explore the region's wineries with an insider's perspective. More than 100 boutique wines are available by the glass and flight; and each Wednesday in high season winemakers present their products during a public Q&A tasting session. You can also learn from sommeliers in the Vines' private blending lab. ✉ *Belgrano 1194, Mendoza* ☎ *0261/438–1031* ⊕ *www.vinesofmendoza.com* ⟳ *Mon.–Sat. 3–10.*

GRAN MENDOZA

Mendoza Province, its eponymous capital, and the capital's departments are home to about 1,750,000 people, roughly 130,000 of whom live in Mendoza City. Most of the major vineyards and bodegas are in departments south of the city (such as Maipú and Luján de Cuyo) and farther south across the Río Mendoza, in the regions of Agrelo and Perdriel. Still more vineyards are farther south in the Valle de Uco. Each department has its own commercial areas, with shopping centers, hotels, and restaurants.

MENDOZA CITY

1,060 km (659 miles) southwest of Buenos Aires; 250 km (155 miles) east of Santiago, Chile.

Mendoza's streets are shaded from the summer sun by a canopy of poplars, elms, and sycamores. Water runs along its sidewalks in acéquias, disappears at intersections, then bursts from fountains in the city's 74 parks and squares. Many acéquias were built by the Huarpe Indians and improved upon by the Incas long before the city was founded in 1561 by Pedro del Castillo.

Thanks to the booming wine and tourism industries, Mendoza bustles with innovative restaurants and lodgings that range from slick highrises with conference rooms for serious wine tasting to low-key inns and B&Bs for serious relaxing. Low-rise colonial buildings with their lofty ceilings, narrow doorways, and tile floors house restaurants and shops.

In the afternoon shops close, streets empty, and siesta-time rules—until around 5, when the city comes back to life and goes back to work.

GETTING HERE AND AROUND

Mendoza's Aeropuerto Internacional Francisco Gabrielli is 6 km (4 miles) north of town on Ruta Nacional 40. Flights from Buenos Aires operated by Aerolíneas Argentinas (⊕ *www.aerolineas.com.ar*) take about two hours; flights from Santiago, Chile, operated by LAN (⊕ *www.lan. com*) take 55 minutes. Bus Terminal del Sol is in Guaymallén, an eastern suburb about a 10-minute drive from town. From here buses provide daily service to San Juan (3 hours), Buenos Aires (14 hours), Santiago (8 hours) and other destinations. Never cut it close on timing when it comes to bus connections. If the bus company says a trip will take 10 hours, it may, unfortunately, take 12 or 13. So leave a decent amount of time for extenuating circumstances—especially if you're crossing the Chilean border and have to account for customs queues.

Driving from Buenos Aires (on lonely but paved Ruta Nacional 7, aka the Panamerican Highway) or Santiago (again, on Ruta Nacional 7, which is sometimes closed along this stretch in winter) is an option, provided you have plenty of time and speak some Spanish. There's little need for a car in town, and it can be hard to find wineries in outlying areas on your own—even when you *do* speak Spanish. Furthermore, mendocinos are known for their cavalier attitude toward traffic rules. Pay attention to weather and road information. If you fear getting lost or breaking down in remote areas, hire a remis or arrange a tour. ⚠ Downtown streets have ankle-breaking holes, steps, and unexpected obstacles, so watch where you're going.

Bus Contacts Andesmar ☎ *261/429–9501, 261/413–6000* ⊕ *www.andesmar. com*. **CATA Internacional** ☎ *261/524–1699* ⊕ *www.catainternacional.com*. **Chevallier** ☎ *261/431–0235, 261/431–3900* ⊕ *www.nuevachevallier.com*. **El Rápido** ☎ *261/405–4344* ⊕ *www.elrapidoint.com.ar*. **Terminal de Ómnibus** ✉ *Av. Gobernador Videla at Av. Acceso Oeste* ☎ *261/431–5000*.

Car Rentals Avis ✉ *Primitivo de la Reta 914* ☎ *261/420–3178* ⊕ *www.avis. com.ar*. **Hertz** ✉ *Espejo 391* ☎ *261/423–0225* ⊕ *www.hertz.com*. **Localiza** ✉ *Primitivo de la Reta 936* ☎ *261/429–6800* ⊕ *www.localiza.com*.

Taxi Contacts La Veloz del Este ✉ *Alem 439* ☎ *261/429–9999*.

ESSENTIALS

Visitor Information Mendoza Tourist Board ✉ *Av. San Martín 1143, at Garibaldi* ☎ *261/413–2101* ⊕ *www.turismo.mendoza.gov.ar* ⊙ *Daily 8 am–9 pm*.

EXPLORING

After a devastating earthquake in 1861, Mendoza was reconstructed on a grid, making it easy to explore on foot. Four small squares (Chile, San Martín, Italia, and España) radiate from the four corners of Plaza Independencia, the main square. Their Spanish tiles, exuberant fountains, shaded walkways, and myriad trees and flowers lend peace and beauty. Avenida San Martín, the town's major thoroughfare, runs north–south out into the southern departments and wine districts. Calle Sarmiento intersects San Martín at the tourist office and becomes a *peatonal* (pedestrian mall) with cafés, shops, offices, and bars. It crosses the

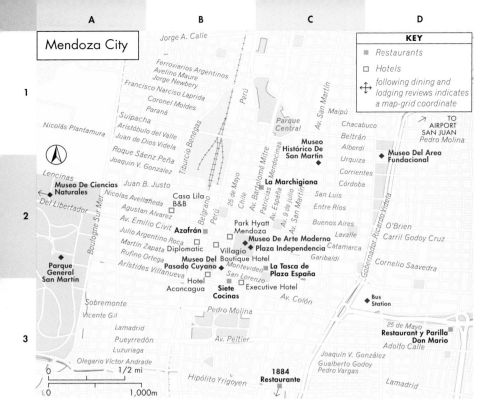

Mendoza City

KEY
- ■ Restaurants
- □ Hotels

following dining and lodging reviews indicates a map-grid coordinate

TO AIRPORT SAN JUAN Pedro Molina

Plaza Independencia, stops in front of the Park Hyatt, then continues on the other side of the hotel to a busy restaurant strip.

TOP ATTRACTIONS

Parque General San Martín. Dating back to 1896, this 971-acre park has more than 50,000 trees from all over the world. Fifteen km (9 miles) of paths meander through it. You can stop and smell the roses (a dedicated garden contains about 500 varieties), observe aquatic competitions from the rowing club's balcony restaurant, visit the zoo to see monkeys running loose, or set the kids free on the numerous playgrounds. Scenes of the 1817 Andes crossing by José de San Martín and his army during the campaign to liberate Argentina are depicted on a monument atop Cerro de la Gloria (Glory Hill), a steep 20-minute walk up from the park's center. The stadium here (built for the 1978 World Cup, which Argentina won) hosts popular soccer matches; and the amphitheater (capacity 22,500) fills to the brim during vendimia, the annual harvest festival.

Plaza Independencia. In Mendoza's main square you can sit on a bench in the shade of a sycamore tree and watch children playing in the fountains, browse the stands at the daily artisan fair, or stroll past the historic Plaza Hotel (now the Park Hyatt) on your way to the shops and outdoor cafés on pedestrian-only Calle Sarmiento, which bisects the square.

Museo Arte Moderno (*Museum of Modern Art*). Right in Plaza Independencia, this museum displays regularly changing paintings, ceramics, sculptures, and drawings by Mendocino artists from 1930 to the present. ⊠ *Pl. Independencia* ☎ *261/425–7279* 💵 *16 pesos (free Wed.)* ⏱ *Tues.–Fri. 9–8, weekends 2–8.*

TOURING TIPS

In high season, a hop-on, hop-off tour bus loops around the city daily, taking in the most historically important and interesting parts of Mendoza. Tickets are valid for 24 hours and cost around US$8; they can be purchased from the stand in front of the Park Hyatt in Plaza Independencia, the Tourist Office, or most hotels.

NEED A BREAK?

Bonafide. Caffeine fans can get their espresso fix at Bonafide. The Bonafide brand was the first to bring a coffee roasting machine to Argentina in 1917, and it now has locations citywide. On the corner of Sarmiento and 9 de Julio near the central plaza, enjoy a steaming cup of joe with *medialunas* (sweet croissants) and *alfajores* (cookies with *dulce de leche*, sweet caramelized milk). ⊠ *Peatonal Sarmiento 102* ☎ *261/423–7915* ⊕ *www.bonafide.com.ar* ⏱ *Closed Sun.*

WORTH NOTING

Bodega Escorihuela. The closest winery to the city—and the oldest working one in the province—is Bodega Escorihuela. Located in Godoy Cruz (about a 15-minute cab ride from Mendoza center), it was founded in 1884 by Spaniard Miguel Escorihuela Gascón and purchased in 1993 by a group of investors led by pioneer vintner Nicolás Catena. Today it includes the handsomely refurbished shell of the old winery as well as modern buildings. On-site superlatives include Mendoza's largest barrel (it can hold 63,000 liters) and arguably its finest restaurant (*1884 Restaurante Francis Mallman.*) ⊠ *Belgrano 1188, Godoy Cruz* ☎ *261/424–2282* ⊕ *www.escorihuelagascon.com.ar* ⏱ *Weekdays by appointment only.*

Museo de Ciencias Naturales (*Museum of Natural Sciences*). At this writing, Museo de Ciencias Naturales is closed for renovation; however, it is expected to reopen by early 2015, enabling visitors to again peruse its interesting collection devoted to anthropology, mineralogy, paleontology, archaeology, and zoology. ⊠ *Parque General San Martin, at Av. de las Tipas and Av. de Circunvalacion* ☎ *261/428–7666* 💵 *2 pesos* ⏱ *Weekdays 8–1 and 2–7, weekends 3–7.*

Museo del Area Fundacional (*Foundational Museum*). On the site of the original *cabildo* (town hall), the Foundation Museum explains the region's social and historical development. Of note is the display of a mummified child found on Aconcagua, with photos of his burial treasures. Excavations, made visible by a glass-covered viewing area, reveal layers of pre-Hispanic and Spanish remains. ⊠ *Beltrán and Videla Castillo* ☎ *261/425–6927* 💵 *16 pesos* ⏱ *Tues.–Sat. 8–8, Sun. 3–8.*

Museo del Pasado Cuyano (*Museum of Cuyo's Past*). Home of former governor and senator Emilio Civit, this 26-bedroom 1873 mansion was the gathering place of the Belle Époque elite. Today it's the Museum of the Cuyo's Past. Exhibits include paintings, antiques, and weaponry used in Argentina's War of Independence. A library contains more than 5,000 volumes relating to the history of Mendoza. ✉ *Montevideo 544* ☎ *261/423–6031* 🎟 *Suggested donation 10 pesos* ⏲ *Tues.–Sat. 9–1.*

Museo Histórico de San Martín (*San Martin Historical Museum*). This museum has a decent library and a token collection of artifacts, including uniforms and journal entries from campaigns of the Great Liberator. ✉ *Remedios de Escalada de San Martin 1843* ☎ *261/425–7947* 🎟 *10 pesos* ⏲ *Weekdays 10–4, Sat. 10–1:30.*

NEED A BREAK?

Soppelsa. More than 40 ice-cream flavors, including traditional Argentine staples such as dulce de leche with *granizado* (chocolate chip) and many fruit and wine concoctions, merit a visit (or two) to Soppelsa. ✉ *Emilio Civit 2 at Belgrano* ☎ *261/422–9000* 🌐 *www.soppelsahelados.com.*

WHERE TO EAT

$$$$ MODERN ARGENTINE Fodor's Choice ★

🍴 **1884 Restaurante Francis Mallman.** Still on top of its game, the province's most famous restaurant promises good service, handsome surroundings, and tasty fare that you might recognize from Francis Mallmann's many cookbooks. The master of fire, Mallmann focuses on grilled meats and fish; a host of Patagonian dishes and succulent salads (including a delicious salt-baked pear with burrata cheese) are served as well. The restaurant, located in Godoy Cruz, takes understandable pride in its wine list: choose something from the historic Escorihuela and Caro wineries next door or let the friendly sommelier lead you through the 500-plus choices. ■ TIP→ **If you are booking in the summer, try to reserve a table in the pretty garden.** [$] *Average main: 220 pesos* ✉ *Belgrano 1188, Godoy Cruz* ☎ *261/424–2698* 🌐 *www.1884restaurante.com.ar* ✍ *Reservations essential* ⏲ *No lunch* ✣ *C3.*

$$$ MODERN ARGENTINE

🍴 **Azafrán.** This character-filled spot is more than just a restaurant. Grocery shelves are stocked with local olive oils, dried herbs, smoked meats, and homemade jams; and over 80 wineries are represented by more than 400 labels in the wine bar, where an old press has been converted into a tasting table. There is no wine list, but a sommelier will help you choose the perfect pairing for your meal order. Offering a welcome break from parrilla, the food is fresh, nicely presented, and gives traditional Argentine cuisine a creative twist. Try the empanada selection with the accompanying wine flight or opt for the beef filet with blue cheese and spinach wrapped in filo. ■ TIP→ **The fixed-price lunch menu is an excellent value.** [$] *Average main: 120 pesos* ✉ *Sarmiento 768* ☎ *261/429–4200* 🌐 *www.azafranresto.com* ✣ *B2.*

$$ ITALIAN

🍴 **La Marchigiana.** They've been serving homemade pasta at La Marchigiana since 1950, and many of the recipes were passed down from founder Nonna Fernanda; today her descendants carry on the tradition in the kitchen. The original venue burned down in 2006, but a modern version with underground parking is just as popular with mendocinos looking for a reasonably priced meal (and a great lasagna). [$] *Average* *main: 90 pesos* ✉ *Patricias Mendocinas 1550* ☎ *261/423–0751* 🌐 *www.marchigiana.com.ar.*

$$$ ARGENTINE 🍴 **Restaurant y Parilla Don Mario.** Mendocinos have been coming here for years to get their basic beef fix. Bife de lomo and bife de chorizo are grilled to perfection at this comfortable country-style restaurant, which also promises pastas, grilled vegetables, and a good wine list. [$] *Average main: 110 pesos* ✉ *25 de Mayo 1324* ☎ *261/431–0810* ✥ *D3.*

$$$$ MODERN ARGENTINE 🍴 **Siete Cocinas.** In a beautiful old house in the city center, chef Pablo del Rio prepares modern Argentine cuisine inspired by the country's seven different food regions. The menu is slightly more daring than most in Mendoza, so you can order interesting cuts and meats (like brains and wild boar) in addition to tasty river fish and enormous steaks. The wine list, organized by flavor profile, is presented on iPads. Although the atmosphere here is a bit sterile, the visible kitchen adds interest to an otherwise plain white room. ■ **TIP→ If you want to go all out, try the four- or seven-course tasting menu.** [$] *Average main: 170 pesos* ✉ *Av. Bartolomé Mitre, 794* ☎ *261/423–8823* 🌐 *www.sietecocinas.com.ar* ⏲ *Closed Sun.* ✥ *B3.*

WHERE TO STAY

$$ B&B/INN 🏨 **Casa Lila Bed and Breakfast.** With only four rooms, this handsome B&B guarantees personalized service within walking distance of the city center, lots of restaurants, and Parque General San Martin. **Pros:** charming, quiet home base; spacious en-suite bathrooms. **Cons:** meals upon request, but no on-site restaurant. [$] *Rooms from: US$140* ✉ *Nicolás Avellaneda 262* ☎ *261/429–6349, 261/15–510–2476* 🌐 *www.casalila.com.ar* 🛏 *4 rooms* 🍴 *Breakfast* ✥ *B2.*

$$$ HOTEL 🏨 **Diplomatic.** One of the city center's large top-end hotels, the Diplomatic has plenty of room for meetings, parties, wine tastings, and events. **Pros:** good location with parking; all the amenities; big picture windows in rooms. **Cons:** pricey; small swimming pool; artwork or rugs in rooms would make them a little friendlier. [$] *Rooms from: US$220* ✉ *Belgrano 1041* ☎ *261/405–1900, 0810/122–5000 for reservations* 🌐 *www.diplomatichotel.com.ar* 🛏 *156 rooms* 🍴 *Breakfast* ✥ *B2.*

$$ HOTEL 🏨 **Executive Hotel.** The tall, elegant tower of this slick downtown hotel looks out on the Plaza Italia. **Pros:** sauna, good value in city center. **Cons:** windowless bar-restaurant. [$] *Rooms from: US$120* ✉ *San Lorenzo 660* ☎ *261/524–5000* 🌐 *www.executive.parksuites.com.ar* 🛏 *74 rooms* 🍴 *Breakfast* ✥ *B3.*

$$$ HOTEL Fodor's Choice ★ 🏨 **Park Hyatt Mendoza.** The Hyatt has preserved the landmark Plaza Hotel's 19th-century Spanish colonial facade: a grand pillared entrance and a wide veranda that extends to either side of the street. **Pros:** ideal location; staff accustomed to accommodating foreign guests; special wine-tasting dinners. **Cons:** pool area can get a lot of noise from the street; some rooms look onto the public wine bar patio, so keep blinds pulled (unless you want to put on a show!). [$] *Rooms from: US$200* ✉ *Calle Chile 1124* ☎ *261/441–1234* 🌐 *www.mendoza.park.hyatt.com* 🛏 *171 rooms, 15 suites* 🍴 *Breakfast* ✥ *B2.*

$$ HOTEL 🏨 **Villaggio Hotel Boutique.** If you want to stay right in the city but prefer to sidestep the big hotel chains, the modern Villaggio offers an intimate alternative; located just one block from the main plaza, its attractive

Difficult choices at Mendoza City's Mercado Central

guest rooms are done in earthy tones and feature original artwork.
Pros: central location; free Wi-Fi; spa with sauna and Jacuzzi with
mountain view. **Cons:** some guests complain of thin walls and noise
from neighbors; some rooms have views of air shaft. $ *Rooms from:
US$130* ✉ *25 de Mayo 1010* ☎ *261/524–5200* ⊕ *www.hotelvillaggio.
com* ↝ *26 rooms, 2 apartments* ⧆ *Breakfast* ✚ *B2.*

NIGHTLIFE

BARS AND PUBS

Avenida Arístedes Villanueva. Full of bars and cafes, this avenida begins to
wake up around 10 pm (don't even bother going earlier). As the evening
progresses, crowds get bigger, and the music—rock, tango, salsa—gets
louder. Action peaks at midnight.

Ayayay. This resto-bar combines a supercasual atmosphere with Euro-
chic design. Ayayay also takes reservations, making it a convenient
option if you want to dine, drink, and dance on busy weekends. ✉ *Aris-
tides Villanueva 240* ☎ *261/429–9061.*

Believe Irish Pub. Sick of wine? Satisfy your craving for pub grub and
beer at this popular Irish pub; it's open until 2 am daily. ✉ *Av. Colon
241* ☎ *261/429–5567.*

El Mercadito. A pretty bar with a nice patio on busy Arístides Street, El
Mercadito plays good music and even serves a decent salad. ✉ *Arístides
Villanueva 521* ☎ *261/463–8847* ⊘ *Closed Sun.*

CASINOS

Regency Casino. Inside the Park Hyatt, this casino has blackjack, stud poker, roulette tables, slot machines, and a bar. ✉ *25 de Mayo and Sarmiento* ☎ *261/441–1234.*

MUSIC CLUBS

Por Acá. This two-story bar/pizzeria attracts both locals and tourists. Sometimes featuring live music or DJs, Por Acá can get packed after 1 am and is good fun all night long. ✉ *Arístedes Villanueva 557* ☎ *261/420–0346.*

SHOPPING

Pick up leather goods, shoes, and clothing along Sarmiento and its cross streets, or on Avenida Las Heras, where you'll find regional products to eat, drink, wear, or decorate your house with. On summer evenings and weekends Plaza Independencia becomes an artisan market, with stands selling jewelry, handmade sweaters, ponchos, maté gourds, olive oil, and other regional wares.

CLOTHES AND ACCESSORIES

La Matera. Mendocinos shop at La Matera for boots, vests, belts, scarves, and riding gear. ✉ *Villanueva 314* ☎ *261/425–3332.*

FOOD AND WINE

Juan Cedrón. Before your picnic, grab a bottle of Malbec at Juan Cedrón. The store also stocks many older vintages of wine worth collecting (or drinking!). ✉ *Sarmiento 278* ☎ *261/423–9450.*

La Casa del Vino. There's a huge selection of very affordable wine and olive oil at La Casa del Vino. ✉ *Aristedes Villanueva 160* ☎ *261/423–6862* ⊕ *www.casadelvinomendoza.com.ar.*

Sol y Vino. Billing itself as "Mendoza's best in just one place," this spot has a great stock of wines and gourmet edibles. Handcrafts and other local items are sold as well. ✉ *Sarmiento 664* ☎ *261/425–6005* ⊕ *www. solyvinomendoza.com.ar* ☉ *Daily 10–10.*

MALLS

La Barraca Mall. The newest mall on the block is only a 10-minute drive from Mendoza City; it has lots of local brands, a 3-D cinema, a children's playground, restaurants, and a pharmacy. ✉ *Las Cañas 1833, Dorrego* ☎ *261/459–8019* ⊕ *www.labarracamall.com.*

Mendoza Plaza Shopping Center. Located 10 minutes from town, this mall in Guaymallén has more than 160 stores, including Falabella, an American-style department store, plus cafés, and a bookstore (Yenny) with English titles. If shopping isn't your thing, the property also has a movie theater, bowling lanes, plus an indoor amusement park complete with a roller coaster, carousel, and games. ✉ *Lateral Accesso Este 3280, Guaymallén* ☎ *261/449–0100* ⊕ *www.mendozaplazashopping.com.*

Palmares Open Mall. A 15-minute drive south of Mendoza, the Palmares Open Mall has 120 stores, lots of restaurant options, and 10 movie theaters (including one in 3-D). There is a lack of big-name North American brands, but you can check out local favorites like La Martina. ✉ *Panamericano 2650, Godoy Cruz* ☎ *261/413–9100* ⊕ *www. palmares.com.ar.*

MARKET

Mercado Central. For more than 120 years the Mercado Central has been selling local foods and handcrafts. Stock up on souvenirs while noshing on dried fruits, homemade empanadas, and fresh cheeses. ⊠ *Av. Las Heras and Patricias Mendocinas* ⊙ *Daily 9–1:30 and 4:30–9.*

SPORTS AND THE OUTDOORS

The high peaks of the Andes provide a natural playground, with slopes to ski down in winter, mountains to climb up in summer, and miles of trails to hike, bike, or ride on horseback. Rivers roar out of the mountains in spring, inviting rafters and kayakers to test the water. Some of the wildest and most remote mountain areas are made accessible by the Ruta Nacional 7, which crosses the Andes right by Parque Provincial Aconcagua.

HORSEBACK RIDING

Cabalgata (horseback riding) is an enjoyable and natural way to explore the mountains west of Mendoza. You can ride to the foot of Aconcagua or Tupungato, or follow the hoofprints of General San Martín on a seven-day trip over the Andes.

Cordon del Plata. Horseback experiences, ranging from one-day treks to week-long tours, are organized by Cordon del Plata; combination riding/hiking/rafting trips and mountain-biking excursions are available, too. ☎ *261/423–7423* ⊕ *www.cordondelplata.com.*

Trekking Travel. Offering everything from one-day excursions to 11-day trips that take you across the Andes, this outfitter can accommodate beginner and expert riders alike. ☎ *261/421–0450, 261/15–306–8707* ⊕ *www.horseriding.com.ar.*

MULTISPORT TOUR OPERATORS

Argentina Rafting. Whether you want to go rafting, kayaking, climbing, or zip-lining, this company can set you up. Two-day multisport packages that combine rafting, horseback riding, and mountain biking with a night in a refugio are also available. ☎ *262/429–6325* ⊕ *www. argentinarafting.com.*

Aymará Turismo. Guided horseback riding, trekking, mountain climbing, and river rafting can be arranged through Aymará Turismo. Tours are very affordable, though they often cater to large Spanish-speaking groups. ☎ *261/420–2064* ⊕ *www.aymaramendoza.com.ar.*

Turismo TrasAndino. With operations in Mendoza City and in the mountains, Turismo TrasAndino organizes treks to a base camp at Aconcagua as well as 15-day ascents. Mountain biking, rock climbing, rappelling, paragliding, rafting, and horseback riding are other options. ☎ *261/423–7993* ⊕ *www.trasandinoturismo.com.ar.*

SKIING

Argentina Ski Tours. Whether you are a beginner or a backcountry expert, this small personalized agency can help plan your ski trip to Las Leñas or (if you want to stick closer to Mendoza) Los Penitentes. ☎ *261/15–630–0026* ⊕ *www.argentinaskitours.com.*

MAIPÚ

16 km (10 miles) southeast of Mendoza City.

Lying south and slightly east of Mendoza City, Maipú—the province's oldest wine region—is spread over the districts of General Gutierrez, Coquimbito, and Cruz de Piedra. While not as glamorous as neighboring Luján de Cuyo, on the other side of the Acceso Sur, Maipú does have its virtues. Thirty-odd bodegas are open to tourism and they, together with local tour operators, provide some of the province's most affordable wine-themed experiences.

GETTING HERE AND AROUND

Acceso Sur (Ruta Nacional 40), the main highway south, is the fastest way to get to the area. Driving yourself here can be a bit of a headache, though, given Maipú's notorious road works and diversions. If you're on a tight budget, you can catch a public bus from Mendoza City, and then rent a bike to visit wineries; alternately, you come by cab (most wineries are only a 20-minute taxi ride from Mendoza City). If you want to drink, the best options are to hire a remis for a day or sign on for a wine tour.

WINERIES

Bodega la Rural. In 1855, Felipe Rutini left the hills of Italy to found a winery in the raw land of Coquimbito, Argentina. His descendants planted the first grapes (Chardonnay and Merlot) in the now-popular Tupungato District of the Valle de Uco. Today, Bodega la Rural is still family-owned and -operated. The winery's well-known San Felipe label was created by Alejandro Sirio, a famous Spanish artist. Inside the original adobe barns the Museo del Vino (Wine Museum) displays leather hoppers, antique pressing machines, vintage carriages, 100-year-old tools, and even an amazing mousetrap. ⊠ *Montecaseros 2625, Coquimbito, Maipú* ☎ *261/497–2013* ⊕ *www.bodegalarural.com.ar* ☉ *Mon.– Sat. 9–1 and 2–5.*

Bodegas y Viñedos López. Wines up to 60 years old are stored in the main cellar of this traditional winery, established in 1898 and still owned by the same family. Tours are followed by a tasting; more extensive programs—which can include hands-on harvesting in season—are also available. An upstairs restaurant serves à la carte and fixed-menu lunches. ⊠ *Ozamis 375, Maipú* ☎ *261/497–2406* ⊕ *www.bodegaslopez. com.ar* ☉ *Weekdays tours hourly 9–5, Sat. tours at 9:30, 10:30, 11:30, and 12:30.*

Carinae. This boutique spot is run by a charming French couple, Philippe and Brigitte, who came to Mendoza to start a new life in wine-making. You can turn up for a tour without booking—there is always someone on hand to take you through the small facility and offer a tasting. ⊠ *Videla Aranda, 2899, Cruz de Piedra, Maipú* ☎ *261/499–0470* ⊕ *www. carinaevinos.com* ☉ *Daily 10–5.*

Di Tomasso. A family business in a gorgeous 1869 building, Di Tomasso maintains the best of old and new. Although the roof is made of mud and cane, the machinery inside is shiny and modern. This is one of the few bodegas that do not require advance reservations. The casual

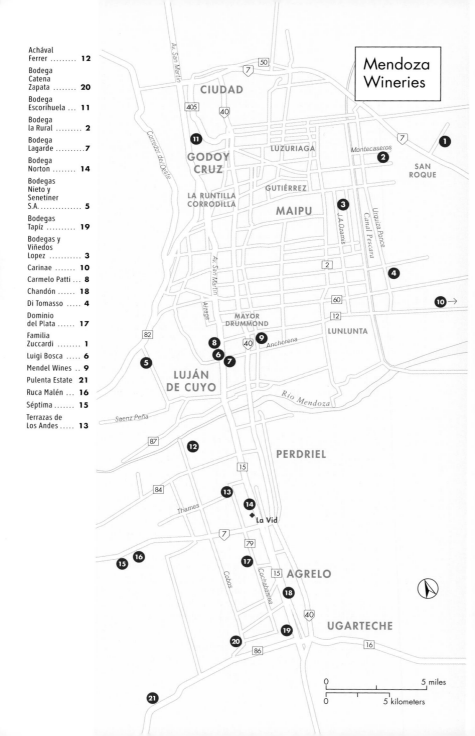

Mendoza
Wineries

CIUDAD

GODOY
CRUZ

LUZURIAGA

Montecaseros

SAN
ROQUE

LA RUNTILLA
CORRODILLA

GUTIÉRREZ

MAIPU

MAYOR
DRUMMOND

LUNLUNTA

Anchorena

LUJÁN
DE CUYO

Río Mendoza

Saenz Peña

Thames

PERDRIEL

La Vid

AGRELO

UGARTECHE

Av. San Martín

Corredor del Oeste

Av. San Martín

J.A.Ozamis

Urquiza Ponce

Canal Pescara

Arzaga

Saenz Peña

Cobos

Cochabamba

0   5 miles

0   5 kilometers

on-site restaurant, La Chiase, serves salads, sandwiches, and Italian-influenced foods, with tables outside overlooking the vines. ✉ *Carril Urquiza 8136, Maipú* ☎ *261/524–1829* 🌐 *www.familiaditommaso.com* 🕒 *Mon.–Sat. 10–6.*

Fodor's Choice ★ **Familia Zuccardi.** In 1950 Don Alberto Zuccardi, a civil engineer, developed a more modern system of irrigation for his vineyards in Maipú and later in Santa Rosa. He and his son Sebastian (both of whom have been ranked among the top five most influential personalities in Argentine wine by *Decanter* magazine) continue to push boundaries and play with new approaches to viticulture. The extensive tourist offerings here include harvest experiences and olive oil–making sessions in season, as well as vineyard rides, cooking classes, and even hot-air-balloon trips. There are two restaurants on site: one is based entirely on olive oil–infused dishes (including a rich olive oil–chocolate tart), while the other serves a popular all-you-can-eat asado, or a 12-course tasting menu. ✉ *RP33, Km 7.5, Maipú* ☎ *261/441–0000* 🌐 *www.familiazuccardi.com* 🕒 *Daily.*

WHERE TO STAY

$$ HOTEL 🏨 **Club Tapiz.** Surrounded by vineyards and centered on a 19th-century governor's mansion, Club Tapiz feels like a private villa; guests can lounge on the enclosed patio and gaze at the Andes from the outdoor pool or indoor Jacuzzi, then sample wines from Bodega Tapiz at an evening tasting. **Pros:** great restaurant; complimentary perks include Wi-Fi, daily wine tasting, and a visit to Bodega Tapiz (20 minutes away). **Cons:** close to vineyards but far from shops or town; rooms a bit outdated. [$] *Rooms from: US$170* ✉ *Pedro Molina (RP60) s/n, Maipú* ☎ *261/496–3433* 🌐 *www.club-tapiz.com.ar* 🛏 *11 rooms* 🍴 *Breakfast.*

NIGHTLIFE

CASINOS

Arena Maipú Casino Resort. Opened in 2011, the huge Arena Maipú Casino Resort features more than 480 slots, 40 electronic roulette tables, five traditional roulette tables, and six card tables. An on-site stadium, cinema, and hotel—plus several bars and restaurants—make this complex popular with nongamblers, too. ✉ *Emilio Civit y Maza, Maipú* ☎ *261/481–9800* 🌐 *www.arenamaipu.com.ar.*

DANCE CLUBS

Black Jagger. Late-night dancing and a fun crowd make for good times at the Black Jagger. It's part of the Arena Maipú Casino complex. ✉ *Emilio Civit y Maza, Maipú* ☎ *261/481–9800* 🌐 *www.arenamaipu.com.ar/black-jagger.*

SHOPPING

Historias & Sabores (*Histories and Flavors*). Inside a lovely old country house, Historias & Sabores conducts guided tours and offers tastings of fruits, olives, chocolates, and liquors. Learn how chocolate-covered cordials are made, and grab some goodies to take home as souvenirs. ✉ *Carril Gómez 3064, Coquimbito* ☎ *261/15–574–6400 for reservations* 🕒 *Mon.–Sat. 11–6.*

SPORTS AND THE OUTDOORS

BIKING

Many of Mendoza's back roads lead through the suburbs and vineyards into the Andean foothills and upward to mountain villages—or all the way to Chile.

Bikes and Wines. You can rent mountain bikes for full- or half-day self-guided tours in the wine district of Maipú and Chacras de Coria from Bikes and Wine. Trips include a map, a water bottle, and a glass of Malbec to get you started off right. Medical and mechanical assistance is also provided. ✉ *Urquiza 1606, Maipú* ⊕ *www.bikesandwines.com.*

Mr. Hugo Wineries and Bikes. Genial Mr. Hugo owns one of the longest-running bike-rental spots on the Maipú wine route. He'll provide water and maps before you head out and lots of wine when you return. ✉ *Urquiza 2288, Maipú* ☎ *261/497–4067* ⊕ *www.mrhugobikes.com.*

LUJÁN DE CUYO

20 km (12 miles) south of Mendoza City.

Bordering both banks of the Mendoza River, Luján de Cuyo is known as the home of Malbec because it was here that the variety first started showing great potential. With more than 50 bodegas, ranging from the traditional to the ultramodern, this is one of the largest wine regions in Mendoza—and one of the province's best pastimes is hopping between them (you can expect to visit three or four a day), enjoying tours and tasting great vino along the way. Luján also has a smattering of luxury resorts and boutique hotels should you wish to extend your stay.

GETTING HERE AND AROUND

Some wineries are accessible by public transport (you can catch a bus to ones in Chacras de Coria or on the main San Martín road); however, the large majority—and often the cream of the crop—are best visited by car. A self-driving tour is doable, provided you carry a good map, but hiring a remis or joining a tour group is more convenient.

WINERIES

Achával Ferrer. With a past score of 97 from *Wine Spectator* for its Malbec, Santiago Achaval's winery on the banks of the Mendoza River continues to score consistently high points for reds. Guided visits include barrel and bottle tastings. Try the Quimera—a delicious blend of red grapes (Malbec, merlot, Cabernet Sauvignon, and Cabernet Franc) grown on three different *fincas*, including one in the Valle de Uco; quantities of each grape are adjusted according to their quality. ✉ *Calle Cobos 2601, Perdriel* ☎ *261/553–5565* ⊕ *www.achaval-ferrer. com* ☉ *Daily.*

Bodega Catena Zapata. A faux Mayan pyramid rising from the vineyards fronts the towering Andes at this landmark winery where the architecture rivals the wine. You descend from a crystal cupola through concentric spaces to the tasting room, which is surrounded by 400 oak barrels. Founding father Nicola Catena arrived in 1898 and planted his first vineyard of Malbec in 1902. Sons Domingo and Nicolás manage the vineyards planted at varying altitudes, blending varieties from

Bodega Catena Zapata, Luján de Cuyo

these different microclimates to create complex, distinctive wines. Special tastings with meals can be arranged for groups with prior notice. ⊠ *Calle J. Cobos s/n, Agrelo* ☎ *261/490–0214* ⊕ *www.catenawines.com* ⊙ *Daily tours at 9:30, 11, and 3.*

Bodega Lagarde. Built in 1897, Lagarde is one of the oldest and most traditional wineries in Mendoza. The third generation of the Pescarmona family now cultivates the grapes, producing limited quantities of quality wine and searching for ways to improve while avoiding fleeting trends. At lunchtime, enjoy an asado-based tasting menu in the 19th-century *casona* (farm house) or order a picnic in the gardens. ⊠ *San Martín 1745, Mayor Drummond* ☎ *261/498–0011* ⊕ *www.lagarde. com.ar* ⊙ *Mon.–Sat.*

Bodega Norton. In 1895 English engineer Sir Edmund Norton built the first winery in the valley south of the Mendoza River. Part of the old adobe house and a wing of the winery demonstrate the traditional construction of beamed ceilings with bamboo reeds under a zinc roof. In 1989 an Austrian businessman purchased the already huge company, and his son continues to modernize and expand the production of the 100-year-old vineyards. Tours with tastings and other vineyard experiences are available with advance reservations, though these are typically limited to groups of two or more. A stylish on-site restaurant, La Vid, welcomes lunch guests from all over Mendoza, with or without a wine tour. Order the five-course tasting menu or opt for à la carte dishes, including rabbit lasagna and salmon ravioli. ⊠ *RP15, Km 23.5, Perdriel* ☎ *261/490–9700* ⊕ *www.norton.com.ar* ⊙ *Daily 9:30–4:30.*

Bodegas Nieto y Senetiner S.A. White adobe walls, flowerbed-lined walkways, and huge shade trees welcome you to this historic bodega. Visits typically include a walk through the winery and either a wine tasting or a chocolate-and-wine pairing. Perhaps the most unusual tour is a three-hour, 2-km (1-mile) horseback ride to a hilltop for a view of the mountains and vineyards; during a maté and muffin break, an oenologist explains the varietals growing around you. Most activities finish with an asado lunch at the bodega. ⊠ *Guardia Vieja, between RN7 and Rosque Sáenz Peña s/n, Vistalba* ☎ *261/496–9099* ⊕ *www.nietosenetiner.com. ar* ⊗ *Mon.–Sat.*

Bodegas Tapíz. When the Ortiz family bought this modern bodega from Kendall Jackson in 2003, CEO Patricia Ortiz and oenologist Fabián Valenzuela decided to make wines that are easier to drink and more food-friendly. Tours begin in the vineyard, followed by tank, barrel, and bottle tastings. In summer, a two-horse carriage driven by a local gaucho takes you on a learning tour of the vineyard. ⊠ *RP15, Km 32, Agrelo* ☎ *261/490–0202* ⊕ *www.bodega-tapiz.com.ar* ⊗ *Weekdays 9–4, Sat. 10–12.*

Carmelo Patti. Carmelo—a legendary old-school winemaker—is the passionate owner of this operation. He answers the phone, greets you at the door, and personally conducts tours (in Spanish only), drawing wine from the barrel and entertaining guests with anecdotes and fascinating facts about everything from growing grapes to preserving corks. Famous for his Cabernet Sauvignon, his top-quality wines have a cultlike following (only 10,000 bottles are produced at a time). The bodega is nothing fancy, but as Carmelo likes to point out, he puts all of his energy where he feels it needs to go: into making incredible wines, not into building and maintaining a flashy facility. ⊠ *San Martín 2614* ☎ *261/498–1379* ⊗ *By appointment only.*

Chandon. The president of Moët & Chandon was so impressed by Agrelo's *terroir* (the soil, climate, and topography that contribute to making each wine unique) that he decided to build the first foreign branch of his family's company here. Today the winery is producing *vino spumante* (sparkling wine) in great quantities. Chandon is popular, so book ahead for private tours. The pretty restaurant serves a tasting menu paired exclusively with sparkling wine. ⊠ *RN40, Km 29, Agrelo* ☎ *261/490–9968* ⊕ *www.chandon.com.ar* ⊗ *Mon.–Sat. (reservations required for Sat. tours).*

Dominio del Plata. Susana Balbo—Argentina's first licensed female oenologist and an internationally known wine-making consultant—has been making a name for herself since 2001. Combining the newest technology with a passion for the land, Balbo pioneered the making of a high-quality Torrontés. Taste it here, then linger over lunch in her winery's relaxed Osadía de Crear Restó & Deli; picnics are also available. ⊠ *Cochabamba 7801, Agrelo* ☎ *261/498–9200* ⊕ *www.dominiodelplata. com* ⚑ *Reservations essential* ☉ *Daily.*

Luigi Bosca. Alberto, Raul, and Roberto Arizú—descendants of Leoncio Arizú, who brought the original vines from Spain in 1890—continue the family legacy at this large winery, which has both a big domestic following and impressive exports. A tourist circuit takes in all the production areas; the bodega itself is an architectural gem, with tile floors, inlaid wood ceilings, painted arches, and 14 carved reliefs depicting the history of winemaking in Argentina. ⊠ *San Martín 2044, Mayor Drummond* ☎ *261/498–1974* ⊕ *www.luigibosca.com.ar* ☉ *Daily.*

Mendel Wines. Mendel's Malbec and Malbec–Cabernet Sauvignon blend (Unus) regularly receive scores above 90 from both *Wine Spectator* and Robert Parker's *Wine Advocate.* This is a testimony to the skill of one of Argentina's best-known winemakers, Roberto de la Mota, and to the dedicated owners of this limited-production winery, where quality, not quantity, is the mantra. Informal tours of the unassuming 80-year-old adobe building highlight the loving care grapes receive—from hand-picking to hand-crushing to storage. ⊠ *Terrada 1863* ☎ *261/524–1621* ⊕ *www.mendel.com.ar* ☉ *Weekdays by reservation only.*

Fodor'sChoice ★ **Pulenta Estate.** Two brothers from one of the most iconic wine families in Mendoza—the Pulentas—started their own premium winery in 2002. The attractive, modern facility runs excellent tours through the production line; visitors can taste the end results (including one of Argentina's best Cabernet Francs) and even take a sensory aroma class. ⊠ *RP 86, Km 6.5, Alto Agrelo* ☎ *261/15–507–6426* ⊕ *www.pulentaestate.com* ☉ *Mon.–Sat.*

Fodor'sChoice ★ **Ruca Malén.** Business has been booming at Ruca Malén ever since the Great Wine Capitals network dubbed its winery restaurant the "world's best" in 2014, but lunch here is still a relaxed experience; two smaller dining rooms and outdoor tables keep it intimate. Chef Lucas Bustos and winemaker Pablo Cuneo masterfully pair colorful dishes with Ruca's predominantly red wines. The well-run tourism department leads interesting tours around the modern facility and offers an option of wine flights, which can include vertical tastings of different vintages or a fun blending session. As an added bonus, the winery has stunning views throughout. ⊠ *RN7, Km 1059, Agrelo* ☎ *261/15–454–1236* ⊕ *www.bodegarucamalen.com* ☉ *Daily 10–3 (reservations required).*

Séptima. When the Spanish wine group Codorniú decided to invest in Argentina, they constructed their winery in the *pirca* style of the Huarpe natives by piling stones one atop the other. The end result is both practical (it helps keep the winery naturally cool) and visually arresting. Tours of Séptima's state-of-the-art interior, with its sleek wood and glass corridors, are available. The highlight of the winery is the large terrace, which has a panoramic view over the vineyards and mountains; enjoy it to the fullest by ordering lunch at the terrace restaurant. ⊠ *RN7, Km 6.5, Agrelo* ☎ *261/498–9550* ⊕ *www.bodegaseptima.com* ⚑ *Reservations essential* ☉ *Mon.–Sat. 10–4.*

6

DID YOU KNOW?

There are two main pruning methods for grape vines. Spur (or head) pruning involves allowing only two shoots per branch to bear grapes; this is most common in older vineyards or in the warmest growing climates. Cane pruning trains up to 4 shoots per branch along a trellis so that up to 16 new shoots will bear fruit along the trellis the next season.

Terrazas de Los Andes. Four vineyards situated at different heights—syrah at 800 meters (2,600 feet), Cabernet Sauvignon at 980 meters (3,200 feet), Malbec slightly higher, and Chardonnay at 1,200 meters (3,900 feet)—take advantage of different microclimates, allowing each varietal to develop to its maximum potential. Bare brick walls, high ceilings, and a labyrinth of soaring arches shelter premium wines in stainless-steel tanks and oak barrels. Built in 1898 and restored in the mid-1990s, everything in the tasting room—from the bar to the tables to the leather chairs—is made with recycled barrels. The restaurant serves a well-paired tasting menu. ✉ *Thames and Cochabamba, Perdriel* ☎ *261/490–9862* 🌐 *www.terrazasdelosandes.com* 🕒 *Weekdays (reservations required).*

WHERE TO EAT

$$$$ INTERNATIONAL Fodor's Choice ★ 🍴 **Brindillas.** Partners in life and in the kitchen, Mariano and Florencia traveled the world working in restaurants; they've brought that experience to bear in their own intimate eatery, which is one of the best dinner spots in Mendoza. The sophisticated space may be small (it sits only 18 people), but you can expect diverse culinary creations with consistently appealing flavors and presentation. Staff can recommend wines by the glass or bottle to match the seasonally changing five- or seven-course menus. [$] *Average main: 285 pesos* ✉ *Guardia Vieja 2898* ☎ *261/496–3650* 🌐 *www.brindillas.com* 🕒 *Closed Sun., Mon., and month of Jun.*

WHERE TO STAY

$$$$ HOTEL Fodor's Choice ★ 🏨 **Cavas Wine Lodge.** Surrounded by mountains and vineyards, this hotel makes a positive first impression. **Pros:** luxurious and private; attentive, personalized service. **Cons:** very expensive; reservations needed at least 24 hours ahead for most activities. [$] *Rooms from: US$804* ✣ *RN40 south, west on RN7, turn off onto Costa Flores just before Ruca Malen Winery. Follow signs for 2.2 km (1½ miles)* ☎ *261/410–6927* 🌐 *www.cavaswinelodge.com* 🛏 *17 rooms and villas* 🍽 *Breakfast.*

$$$$ HOTEL 🏨 **Entre Cielos.** Set in the middle of vineyards, this stunning modern resort is a great place to relax. **Pros:** the Swiss founders have impeccable taste; terrific spa; good sunset view. **Cons:** nothing in close vicinity; expensive. [$] *Rooms from: US$420* ✉ *Guardia Vieja 1998, Vistalba* ☎ *261/498–3377* 🌐 *www.entrecielos.com* 🛏 *16 rooms* 🍽 *Breakfast.*

$$$ HOTEL 🏨 **Lares de Chacras.** This long-running boutique hotel is in the heart of little Chacras de Coria. **Pros:** good value; pleasant, small-town location with wineries nearby. **Cons:** some street noise from residential neighborhood. [$] *Rooms from: US$260* ✉ *Larrea 1266, Chacras de Coria* ☎ *261/496–1061* 🌐 *www.laresdechacras.com* 🛏 *10 rooms* 🍽 *Breakfast.*

SPORTS AND THE OUTDOORS

FAMILY **Parque de Agua.** Like its sister property, Termas Cacheuta, Parque de Agua takes advantage of the area's hot springs; this spot, though, is focused on family fun rather than adult-only activities. On peak days, more than 1,000 visitors come to frolic in its naturally heated water (65–102°F). Slide into the wave pool, swim along the 270-meter (886-foot) canal through a tunnel and under a waterfall, or just loll about in the myriad indoor and outdoor pools. Even toddlers will enjoy the shallow ones with age-appropriate slides. In addition to an on-site restaurant, the park has covered eating areas with picnic tables, and you can grill your own bife in the many parrillas provided. ✉ *RP82, Km 38, Cacheuta, 24 km (15 miles) west of Luján de Cuyo* ☎ *2624/490–139* ⊕ *www.termascacheuta.com* ✉ *75 pesos* ☉ *Daily 10–6:30.*

Fodor's Choice ★ **Termas Cacheuta.** Locals have been soaking in the natural hot springs here for centuries; these days they're joined by day-tripping tourists, who come to enjoy both the thermal waters and an attractive spa. The latter features hot and cool indoor and outdoor pools, a steamy grotto sauna, a thermal mud bath, and high-powered showers. Day passes include a huge lunch buffet, with countless salads and all the cuts of a traditional Argentine asado. Dedicated spa-goers can spend the night in one of the 16 all-inclusive rooms at Hotel Termas Cacheuta ($$$).■ TIP→ **Unlike the Parque de Agua next door, this is a child-free zone.** ✉ *RP82, Km 38, Cacheuta, 24 km (15 miles) west of Luján de Cuyo* ☎ *261/490–153* ⊕ *www.termascacheuta.com* ✉ *From $40* ☉ *Daily 10–6:30.*

USPALLATA

125 km (78 miles) west of Mendoza City.

At the crossroads of three important routes—Ruta Nacional 7 from Mendoza across the Andes, Ruta 57 from Mendoza via Villavicencio, and Ruta 39 from San Juan via Barreal—this small town lies in the Calingasta Valley between the foothills and the front range of the Andes. Although most people will use Uspallata only as a food- and petrol-refill point, it's also a good base for memorable excursions into the mountains by 4X4 or on horseback. Metals have been forged at **Las Bóvedas,** the pointed adobe cupolas a few miles north of town, since pre-Columbian times. Weapons for San Martín's army were made here, and some of them were melted down to create the Cristo Redentor monument on the Chilean border; other big Andean attractions in the vicinity include Parque Provincial Aconcagua and Puenta del Inca.

GETTING HERE AND AROUND

From Mendoza City, head south on Avenida San Martín to the Ruta Nacional 7 and turn west. You can make this 125-km (78-mile) journey in two to three hours by bus or rental car; the easiest option, though, is to visit Uspallata and nearby attractions on a guided day trip from Gran Mendoza.

SAFETY

An adventurous way to explore the dramatic landscape around Uspallata is by driving yourself. There are things to keep in mind, though, if you want to have a safe, stress-free time. Always leave town with a full tank of gas, as there are few services available, and traffic is minimal. Carry a flashlight if you leave late in the day, and be mindful of weather conditions (the drive is not recommended in winter snowstorms). Good maps are available from the ACA (Automóvil Club Argentino) in Mendoza and at the tourist office.

6

Hikers traverse a low portion of the south face of Cerro Aconcagua.

EXPLORING

Cristo Redentor de los Andes. A steep, bumpy ascent off of Ruta 7 leads to a stunning view of the Andes and a large statue of Christ that was erected to mark the end of the war between Chile and Argentina. Made from melted weaponry when peace was declared in 1902, it's poised right on the border at an altitude of 4,206 meters (13,800 feet). There are two food spots up here: one selling Chilean churros, the other Argentine *alfajores* (filled cookies). The gravel path is not for the faint-hearted but can just about be done in a hired car; the drive up from the road takes half an hour. ■ TIP➔ **Bring a jacket!** ✉ *RN7, Puente del Inca.*

Fodor's Choice ★ **Parque Provincial Aconcagua.** Extending 66,733 hectares (164,900 acres) over wild, high country, this provincial park has few trails other than those used by expeditions ascending the impressive Cerro Aconcagua (Aconcagua Mountain). You can get multiday permits for climbing it either through your tour operator or on your own at the Mendoza Tourist Board Visitor's Center in Parque San Martín; it's open weekdays 8–6 and weekends 9–1. Day permits (to visit as a tourist, not trekker) are available at the entrance to Aconcagua Park itself. ✉ *San Martín Park Office, Las Tipas at Los Robles, Mendoza* ⊙ *Weekdays 8–6, weekends and holidays 9–1* 🎫 *Day permits $2; trekking permits $110–$280, depending on season, permit level, and number of hiking days; ascent permits $500–$800.*

Puente del Inca. Spanning the Río Cuevas, Puente del Inca is natural rock bridge that was formed over thousands of years. The abandoned hotel below is a more recent addition, built in the 1920s to accommodate guests who came to soak in the therapeutic hot springs here. Both are now covered in bright yellow sulfur deposits, giving the surreal site an eerie appeal. An artisan market sells unusual souvenirs like healing stones and sulfur-coated bottles or shoes. ⊠ *RN7, 3 km (2 miles) east of Parque Provincial Aconcagua, Puente del Inca.*

SCENIC DRIVES AND LOOKOUTS

Camino del Año. From Mendoza traveling 47 km (29 miles) north on Ruta Provincial 52, passing through Canota, you arrive at Villavicencio, the source of mineral

WORD OF MOUTH

"[Mendoza to Aconcagua] is an amazing drive, and if you drive yourself you can stop where and when you what. It is approximately 4–5 hours each way. Go for the drive, it is awesome. It was the first time I saw purple mountains, yellow mountains, green mountains, and snow-covered mountains together."
—sandiej

water sold throughout Argentina. The nearby Hosteria Villavicencio offers a simple lunch menu.

Farther up the road, the Camino del Año begins its ascent around 365 turns to El Balcón atop the pass at Cruz de Paramillo (3,000 meters/9,840 feet). Look for the ruins of a Jesuit mine, the Arucarias de Darwin (petrified trees found by Darwin in 1835), and the 1,000-year-old petroglyphs on Tunderqueral Hill. From the top of the pass you can see three of the highest mountains outside of Asia, all over 6,000 meters (20,000 feet): Aconcagua to the west, Tupungato to the south, and Mercedario to the north.

At Km 67, the road straightens and descends into Uspallata, where you can continue west on Ruta Nacional 7 to Chile or take the lonely road north on Ruta 39 (which turns into Ruta 412) onward to Barreal in San Juan Province, 108 km (67 miles) away. The road to Barreal crosses a high desert valley, where the only sign of life is an occasional ranch obscured by a grove of alamo trees.

At Los Tambillos, about 40 km (25 miles) north of Uspallata, the route is intersected by the Inca road that ran from Cusco, Peru, through Bolivia and into northern Argentina. The site is surrounded by a fence that protects traces of the original road and remains of an Inca *tambo* (resting place). A map shows the route of the Incas.

The mountains to the west get higher and more spectacular as you approach Barreal. At the San Juan Province border, the road becomes Ruta 412, and is paved the remaining 50 km (31 miles) to Barreal.

Uspallata Pass on Ruta Nacional 7 (*Panamerican Highway*). This route heads west on R13 and then RN7 (also known as the Panamerican Highway) and takes you straight into the mountains. You'll go from vineyards to barren hills until you reach the Potrerillos Valley, then head farther west on R7 into the heart of the Andes. This was a major Inca route, so keep your eyes peeled for Inca tambos. You'll pass the Puente del Inca ancient thermal springs and the ruins of a spa from the 1920s. This is the only route between Chile and Argentina for miles and miles, so if you're self-driving be ready to share the road with cargo trucks.

WHERE TO EAT AND STAY

$$
ARGENTINE

✕ **El Rancho.** This spit-and-sawdust style eatery has monster-size steaks, irresistible BBQ smells, and cheap wine by the jug. If you've had a long day in the mountains and need a place to refuel, old-school El Rancho is your best bet: open daily for lunch and dinner, it also serves coffee and snacks outside mealtimes. $ *Average main: 82 pesos* ✉ *RN7, Km 1147* ☎ *2624/420–134* ☼ *Daily.*

$$
HOTEL

🖳 **Hotel Uspallata.** In spite of the cavernous hallways, minimal décor, barren walls, and dim lighting (legacies of the Perón era, when the government built hotels for its employees), this grand old hotel offers comfortable refuge en route to Aconcagua, Chile, or Barreal in the opposite direction. **Pros:** big rooms; proximity to outdoor activities including skiing. **Cons:** impersonal décor. $ *Rooms from: US$115* ✉ *RN7, Km 1149* ☎ *2624/420–003* ⊕ *www.granhoteluspallata.com. ar* ⌨ *74 rooms* ⦿ *Breakfast.*

$$$
HOTEL

🖳 **Hotel Valle Andino.** Approaching Uspallata on Ruta Nacional 7, you'll see this wood-trimmed brick building with a pitched tile roof by the roadside. **Pros:** family-friendly; practical base; scenic vistas in all directions. **Cons:** rooms could use updating; facilities are spread out; you need a car to visit nearby sights and town. $ *Rooms from: US$230* ✉ *RN7* ☎ *2624/420–095, 261/15–597–7858* ⊕ *www.hotelvalleandino. com* ⌨ *25 rooms* ⦿ *Breakfast.*

SPORTS AND THE OUTDOORS

HORSEBACK RIDING

El Rincón de los Oscuros. Gentle horses and experienced guides make riding at this ranch near Potrerillos a pleasure. Two-hour and full-day outings take you to high-altitude sites where condors and guanacos are often seen. ✉ *Av. Los Cóndores s/n, Potrerillos, 50 km (30 miles) southeast of Upsallata* ☎ *2624/483–030* ⊕ *www.rincondelososcuros.com.*

HIKING AND MOUNTAINEERING

November through March is the best time for hiking and climbing. You can arrange day hikes with area tour operators. Of the longer treks, the most popular lasts four to seven days and begins at Puente del Inca (2,950 meters/9,680 feet), where you spend a night to get acclimated, and then set out for Aconcagua's base camp. On the first day, a steady climb takes you to Confluencia, where most people spend two nights and enjoy a day hike to the south wall and its incredible glacier. The hike continues to the Plaza de Mulas (4,260 meters/13,976 feet) and ends at the base camp for climbers making a final ascent on Cerro Aconcagua.

Fernando Grajales. Guiding since 1976, Fernando Grajales is a veteran of many Aconcagua ascents. His company leads 18-day excursions to the summit in season. ☎ *261/15–658–8855 (cell), 800/516–6962* ⊕ *www. grajales.net.*

Inka Expeditions. This outfit has 20 years of experience leading tours both to the base camp and to Aconcagua's summit. Other treks in the area can also be organized. ☎ *261/425–0871* ⊕ *www.inka.com.ar.*

SKIING

Los Penitentes. Named for the rock formations that resemble penitent monks, this medium-size ski area attracts mostly Argentineans and is a popular day-trip destination for mendocinos. Despite the elevation— 2,580 meters (8,465 feet) at the base and 3,194 meters (10,479 feet) at the top—the snow here is often thin, so check weather reports before coming. When it does snow, the danger of avalanches is severe. The base village has hotels, restaurants, bars, discos, medical services, a ski school, and guides.

Facilities: 700-meter (2,300-foot) vertical drop; 300 hectares (741 acres); 20% beginner, 30% intermediate, 50% advanced; two double chairs, one T-bar, five surface lifts. Cross-country ski trails, extreme and off-piste snocat skiing, sledding, and *pato* (snow polo).

Lessons and Programs: Ski school, mountain guides, and a children's school and day care.

Lift Tickets: From 300 pesos a day in high season

Rentals: Rental shops at the base area. ✉ *153 km (95 miles) northwest of Mendoza on RN7* ☎ *261/429–9953, 262/442–0356* ☉ *Winter (depending on snow conditions).*

6

VALLE DE UCO

The Valle de Uco extends south of Mendoza along the foothills of the Cordón de Plata and the Andes, whose two highest peaks—Tupungato Volcano and El Plata—rise over 580 meters (19,000 feet) on the western horizon. Horseback riding, climbing, trekking, and simply savoring the quietude are all popular pastimes here; however, most people are drawn by the prospect of indulging in fabulous wine and fresh food while admiring up-close views of the Andes.

The Ríos Tunuyán in the north and Las Tunas in the south bring mineral-rich melted snow from the glaciers to the garlic fields, apple and cherry orchards, olive groves, and, of course, the vineyards that are planted across this immense valley. Old family ranches that once extended all the way to Chile are being sold off or converted to vineyards in what is now the country's fastest-growing wine area. It's also one of the world's highest wine regions, with approximately 81,000 hectares (200,000 acres) planted at altitudes between 900 and 1,700 meters (2,952 and 5,577 feet). Cool nights and warm days allow grapes to ripen slowly while developing excellent fruit flavor, good acidity in white wines, and the formation of strong tannins in reds.

Wineries vary from traditional family-run spots to ultramodern facilities operated by big international names. Since they tend to be scattered about in infrequently traveled areas, reservations are highly recommended. The easiest way to see them is to take a tour or stay in a local lodge that offers excursions.

Continued on page 294

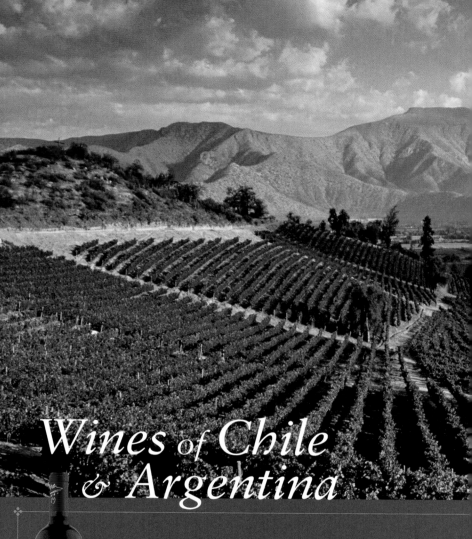

Wines *of* Chile *&* Argentina

The wine regions of both Chile and Argentina are set against the backdrop of the Andes. And while these mountains do play an important role in the making of wine in both countries, Chile and Argentina have very different traditions and strengths.

Although wine-loving Spaniards settled both countries in the 16th century, only Chile's wine industry developed quickly, largely because the land around Santiago was particularly good for growing grapes. Buenos Aires, on the warm and humid Atlantic coast, however, was hardly an ideal place for viticulture. Mendoza, Argentina's present-day wine wonderland, was impossibly far away to be a reliable supplier of wine to the capital until the railroad united it with the coast in the mid-19th century.

Chile also experienced a boom in the 19th century as new, French-inspired wineries sprang up. Both countries continued without significant change for more than 100 years, until the 1990s international wine boom sparked new interest in South American wines. Big investments from France, Spain, Italy, the United States, and elsewhere—plus some extraordinary winemakers—have made this an exciting place for oenophiles to visit.

(left) Bottle of Maradona red wine;
(above) Errazuriz Winery, Chile

NEIGHBORS ACROSS THE ANDES

CHILE

In the early days, the emphasis was on growing cheap wine to consume domestically. Then, in the middle of the 20th century, Chile's political turmoil caused the business to stagnate. It wasn't until the 1980s that wine exports became a major business, and today Chile exports more than it imports.

Chile's appellation system names its valleys from north to south, but today's winegrowers stress that the climatic and geological differences between east and west are more significant. The easternmost valleys closest to the Andes tend to have less fog, more hours of sunlight, and greater daily temperature variations, which help red grapes develop deep color and rich tannins while maintaining bright acidity and fresh fruit characteristics. On the other hand, if you're after crisp whites and bright Pinots, head to the coast, where cool fog creeps inland from the sea each morning and Pacific breezes keep the vines cool all day.

Viña Cousiño Macul, Chile

Interior areas in the Central Valley are less prone to extremes and favor varieties that require more balanced conditions, such as Merlot, and Chile's own rich and spicy Carmenère. Syrah, a relatively new grape in Chile, does well in both cold and warm climates.

Miguel Torres, Chile

BE SURE TO TASTE:

Sauvignon Blanc: Cool-climate vineyards from Elqui to Bío Bío are producing very exciting Sauvignon with fresh green fruit, crisp acidity, and often an enticing mineral edge.

Carmenère: Chile's signature grape arrived in Chile during the mid-19th century from France, where it was usually a blending grape in Bordeaux. Over time Chileans forgot about it, mistaking it for Merlot, but during the Chilean boom times of the 1990s they realized that they had a very unique grape hidden among the other vines in their vineyards.

Cabernet Sauvignon: The king of reds grows well almost anywhere it's planted, but Cabernets from the Alto Maipo are particularly well balanced, displaying elegance and structure.

Syrah: Chile produces two distinct styles of this grape. Be sure to try both: luscious and juicy from Colchagua or enticingly spicy from coastal areas, such as Elqui or San Antonio.

Malbec: True, this is Argentina's grape, but Chile produces award-winning bottlings that have appealing elegance and balance.

Bodega Tres Erres, Chile

ARGENTINA

Unlike Chile, Argentina exports far less wine than it consumes, and much of its wine is produced in accordance with local tastes and wallets. The 1990s wine boom sparked a greater emphasis on export, and following new investments, the country is now widely recognized for the quality of its red wines, particularly its signature Malbec.

Monteviejo Winery, Clos de los Siete, Mendoza

Broad-shouldered Argentina looks west to the Andes for a life-giving force. Its wine regions receive no cooling maritime influence, as Chile's do, and its vineyards rely on the mountain altitudes not only to irrigate its lands, but also to attenuate the effects of the blazing sun. The climate here is capricious, so producers must be ever-prepared for untimely downpours, devastating hailstorms, and scorching, dehydrating Zonda winds.

Estancia San Pablo Tupungato

BE SURE TO TASTE:

Malbec: Just one sip of Argentina's most widely known wine evokes gauchos and tangos. Deep, dark, and handsomely concentrated, this is a must-try on its home turf.

Cabernet Sauvignon: Argentine Cabs are big, bold, and brawny, as is typical of warmer climates. They're perfect with one of those legendary Argentine grilled steaks.

Red Blends: The red blends here may be mixtures of classic Bordeaux varietals with decidedly Argentine results, or audacious combinations that are only possible in the New World.

Torrontés: Argentina's favorite white has floral overtones, grown most often in Cafayate, in the northwestern province of Salta.

Colome Winery, Molinos, Salta

TASTING TIPS ON BOTH SIDES OF THE BORDER

1. Make reservations! Unlike wineries in the U.S., most wineries are not equipped to receive drop-in visitors.

2. Don't expect wineries to be open on Sunday. Winery workers need a day off too.

3. The distances between wineries can be much longer than they look on the map. Be sure to allot plenty of travel time, and plan on no more than three or four wineries per day.

4. Do contact the wine route offices in the region you're visiting. They can be extremely helpful in coordinating visits to wineries and other local attractions.

5. Hire a driver, or choose a designated driver.

6. Know what you are walking into. Some wineries offer free tours and tastings, others can charge upwards of 150 pesos per person.

GREAT WINE ITINERARIES

SEE CHAPTER FOR WINERY CONTACT INFORMATION

Chile and Argentina are wine paradises in terms of the climate they usually enjoy. On the Argentine side, Mendoza is blessed with over 330 days of sunshine, a dry climate, and a low risk of mold or disease. On the other side of the Andes, Chile enjoys great light and air purity, and a cooling Humboldt current. Its natural fortunes are balanced with natural disasters, though. Chile has been ravaged by some of the world's worst earthquakes; the devastating 2010 quake and tsunami wiped out more than 130 million liters of wine. The greatest frustration for winemakers in Mendoza is the infamous zonda (a burning and dusty foehn wind that burns grapes and tears vines down) and occasional hail storms. Even paradise has its share of difficulties!

Crossing the Andes will be one of the highlights of your trip, especially the series of switchbacks that wind into the mountains just before the border crossing.

Haras de Pirque. Horses are the owners' first love. You'll pass the breeding farm and the race track on the way to this horseshoe-shaped winery tucked up into the Andean hills.

COLCHAGUA ITINERARY

If it's Saturday, book a ride on the Wine Train, which travels from San Fernando to the heart of the Colchagua Valley in Santa Cruz.

Viña Bisquertt. This family-run winery houses several 15-foot-tall wooden casks from the 1940s.

Lapostolle. Viña Casa Lapostolle built this gravity-flow wonder exclusively for their red blend, Clos Apalta.

Viña Santa Cruz. More than just a winery, this is an entire wine complex. Take the a cable car to the "indigenous village."

ALTO MAIPO ITINERARY

Plenty of wineries are a day trip from Santiago. You can go solo and hire a taxi ($70 for a half day), but for around US$160 (full day) a guide provides better access.

Concha y Toro. Start the day at one of Chile's oldest and best known wineries, located just outside of the capital in Pirque.

Antiyal. One of Chile's first boutique-garage wineries, Antiyal only makes two red blends, both of which are organic and biodynamic.

Bodegas Salentein

ARGENTINA ITINERARY

The charming city of Mendoza is the logical home base for exploring Argentine wine country, and the country's finest wineries surround the city.

Ruca Malén. The fame of Ruca Malen's award-winning restaurant has overtaken that of the winery. However, no great meal in Mendoza works without good wines, so it's best to walk off the five-course lunch here with a tour afterward.

Pulenta Estate. Owned by the renowned Pulenta wine dynasty, this modern winery makes a fabulous Cabernet Franc and has a great boutique feel to it. Tours can include a sensory aroma game.

Bodega Catena Zapata. Rising like a Mayan temple from the fertile soil, this winery produces some of Argentina's most memorable blended wines.

Familia Zuccardi, Mendoza

Harvest time at Andeluna

WINERY-ARCHITECTURE ITINERARY

Fans of spectacular architecture will enjoy visiting Argentina's wineries. Big, modern, sometimes whimsical, and often surprising, many of these enormous high-tech facilities have restaurants and even lodgings to make the long distances between them bearable. Plan for a long day in the beautiful Valle de Uco visiting some striking examples.

Salentein. A perfect example of the "winery-plus" experience in South American wine tourism, this property is a work of art set against a natural backdrop of the Andes, complete with an art gallery, restaurant, chapel, and award-winning wines.

Andeluna. With a stellar view of Tupungato and the Cordon del Plata, this stellar winery draws your eyes to the mountains and your nose to the open-plan kitchen serving great food to pair with their full-bodied wines.

O. Fournier. End your day at this highly unusual building that looks, from a distance, like a city of Oz for the new millennium. An enormous, flat roof seems to hover over the building, and the large U-shaped ramp accommodates gravity-flow winemaking.

CROSSING THE ANDES

Mendoza, Argentina; Andean foothills, wine harvest.

■ If you're coming all the way to South America to taste wine, be sure to visit both sides of the Andes. There are frequent hour-long jet flights between Santiago and Mendoza for US$200–$300 that provide a spectacular condor's-eye view of the craggily snow-covered peaks below.

■ If you are visiting in the summer months and have time for the day-long 250 km (155 miles) overland route, by all means take it. Know that you will most likely have to get a roundtrip car rental. Most companies will not allow one-way international crossings. Better to rent a car in Santiago or Mendoza to see the wineries in each country, then fly or catch a bus to cross the border. On the Argentina side, a flight from Buenos Aires to Mendoza can save time.

■ Roads are well-maintained and reasonably marked. Take Ruta 57 north from Santiago to the small city of Los Andes, then head east on Ruta 60 toward the mountains and the Argentine border, where the highway's name changes to Ruta 7, to Mendoza.

■ Crossing the Andes will be one of the highlights of your trip, especially the series of switchbacks that wind into the mountains just before the border crossing some 8,200 feet above sea level. Be aware that the Libertadores Pass is often closed for days at a time during the winter months, so don't risk it unless you're willing to spend several days sleeping in your car while you wait for things to clear up. Be sure to bring a jacket any time of year, as it can be very chilly at that altitude.

■ Plan a couple of stops along the way; make the Portillo Ski Resort your last stop on the Chilean side, where you can visit the Laguna del Inca at nearly 10,000 feet. The ski resort is a great place to stop for lunch. On the Argentine side, stop for gas and a bite to eat in Upsallata, about 100 km (65 miles) before reaching Mendoza.

WINE TASTING PRIMER

Ordering and tasting wine—whether at a winery, bar, or restaurant—is easy once you master a few simple steps.

LOOK AND NOTE

Hold your glass by the stem and look at the wine in the glass. Note its color, depth, and clarity.

For whites, is it greenish, yellow, or gold? For reds, is it purplish, ruby, or garnet? Is the wine's color pale or deep? Is the liquid clear or cloudy?

SWIRL AND SNIFF

Swirl the wine gently in the glass to intensify the scents, then sniff over the rim of the glass. What do you smell? Try to identify aromas like:

- **Fruits**—citrus, peaches, berries, figs, melon

- **Flowers**—orange blossoms, honey, perfume

- **Spices**—baking spices, pungent, herbal notes

- **Vegetables**—fresh or cooked, herbal notes

- **Minerals**—earth, steely notes, wet stones

- **Dairy**—butter, cream, cheese, yogurt

- **Oak**—toast, vanilla, coconut, tobacco

- **Animal**—leathery, meaty notes

Are there any unpleasant notes, like mildew or wet dog that might indicate that the wine is "off?"

SIP AND SAVOR

Prime your palate with a sip, swishing the wine in your mouth. Then spit in a bucket or swallow.

Take another sip and think about the wine's attributes. Sweetness is detected on the tip of the tongue, acidity on the sides of the tongue, and tannins (a mouth-drying sensation) on the gums. Consider the body—does the wine feel light in the mouth, or is there a rich sensation? Are the flavors consistent with the aromas? If you like the wine, try to pinpoint what you like about it, and vice versa if you don't like it.

Take time to savor the wine as you're sipping it—the tasting experience may seem a bit scientific, but the end goal is your enjoyment.

TUPUNGATO

78 km (48 miles) south of Mendoza.

Tupungato is a sleepy agricultural town most of the year. During harvest (February and March), though, the roads in and around it overflow with carts and tractors loaded with grapes from many surrounding vineyards. The population doubles from its official number of nearly 30,000 as pickers arrive.

GETTING HERE AND AROUND

The most direct route from Mendoza to the Valle de Uco is south on Ruta Nacional 40 for 37 km (23 miles) to Ugarteche, where you turn west onto Ruta 86 for another 37 km (23 miles), passing through the village of San José just before arriving in Tupungato. Although buses arrive several times a day from Mendoza, the best way to get around the area is to join a tour or rent a car. If you're driving north, turn off Ruta Nacional 40 onto Ruta Provincial 88 at Zapata.

If you have some time and aren't put off by driving on a dirt road, a scenic way here is south on Ruta Nacional 40 from Mendoza and west on Ruta Nacional 7 to the dam at Potrerillos; exiting at the dam, take the unpaved Ruta Provincial 89 south through the villages of Las Vegas and El Salto, where clusters of vacation cottages brim with flowers in summer and are covered with snow in winter. The road climbs steeply out of the canyon and over a pass, then crosses a high valley with a magnificent view of the Andes. Soon the great expanse of the Valle de Uco lies before you, with its miles of vineyards and orchards of peaches, almonds, and chestnuts, adding wide swaths of pink and white blossoms in spring (late September–October). This drive is equally impressive in reverse.

ESSENTIALS

Visitor Information Oficina de Turismo de Tupungato ✉ *Av. Belgrano 348* ☎ *2622/488–016* ⊕ *www.tupungato.gov.ar.*

WINERIES

Fodor's Choice
★

Andeluna. Surrounded by miles of vineyards, with the majestic Andes as a backdrop, this red brick bodega blends beautifully into the scenery. Inside, the large reception and tasting room—with leather furnishings and high ceiling of reeds and open beams—evokes an old mendocino mansion. The open kitchen at one end serves fine tasting menus and conducts cooking classes with two days' notice. ✉ *R89, Km 11* ☎ *2622/423–226* ⊕ *www.andeluna.com.ar* ☉ *Tours daily at 10:30, 12:30, and 3:30 (reservations required).*

Bodega Atamisque. The gray adobe building with its uneven slate roof, reminiscent of houses in Spain and France, almost disappears against the background of bushes and mountains. But once inside this boutique winery, visitors quickly see the dedication to detail and the creation of fine wines that is the mission of its French owners. They bought this enormous estancia property (the boundaries of which date back to 1658, when the Jesuits owned it) and named it after a native tree. In addition to the winery, Atamisque includes a trout farm, a 9-hole golf

Valle de Uco Wineries

course, a restaurant, and accommodations. ✉ *RP86, Km 30* ☎ *261/15–518–1786* 🌐 *www.atamisque.com* 🕒 *Daily 9:30–4:30.*

Bodega Salentein. On a knoll with an Andean backdrop, this ultramodern winery is built in the shape of a cross. Each of its four arms operates as a separate winery with two divisions: one at ground level housing stainless-steel tanks and one belowground where wine matures in oak barrels. The four wineries meet at a circular atrium where tastings, sales, and large events are held. This complex also contains an art museum, a wine bar, a sculpture garden, a pretty chapel, and two restaurants, making it easy to spend a leisurely afternoon here. ✉ *R89 at Elias Videla, Los Árboles, 15 km (9 miles) south of Tupungato* ☎ *2622/429–500* 🌐 *www.bodegasalentein.com* 🕒 *Daily 10–4.*

La Azul. Exporters of wine as well as peaches, plums, cherries, and apples, this agro-wine complex's vineyard tours demonstrate the different vine-growing methods used over the centuries. Nice lunch options are served at the rustic-chic restaurant. ✉ *R89* ☎ *2622/423–593* 🕒 *Weekdays 9–5, by reservation.*

WHERE TO EAT

$$ ARGENTINE 🍴 **Restaurante Valle de Tupungato.** Traditional grilled meats, homemade pastas, and appetizers featuring locally made cold cuts make up the hearty fare at this friendly family-style restaurant. On Sunday you can help yourself to steak, lamb, chicken, and goat at the open grill. Crowds of locals show up on weekends, overflowing onto the Astroturf lawn. [$] *Average main: 80 pesos* ✉ *Belgrano 542* ☎ *2622/488–421* 💳 *No credit cards.*

WHERE TO STAY

$ B&B/INN 🏨 **Don Romulo.** This hotel is run with warmth and enthusiasm; guest rooms are basic but clean, and the food served at its on-site eatery is pure *criollo* (country cooking)—think empanadas, grilled meat, sausages, and salads. **Pros:** good price; local flavor. **Cons:** low-tech; needs renovating; staff speak little English. [$] *Rooms from: US$50* ✉ *Almirante Brown 1200* ☎ *2622/489–020* 🌐 *www.donromulo.com.ar* 🛏 *6 rooms* 💳 *No credit cards.*

$$$ HOTEL 🏨 **Posada Salentein.** Located behind Bodega Salentein, this posada has smaller, modern rooms and larger cottages all looking onto the vineyards and swimming pool. **Pros:** peaceful vineyard setting; pretty pool; complimentary bikes available. **Cons:** impersonal service; newer rooms are a tight fit. [$] *Rooms from: US$240* ✉ *RN89 at Elias Videla, Los Árboles, 15 km (9 miles) south of Tupungato* ☎ *2622/429–090* 🌐 *www.bodegasalentein.com* 🛏 *16 rooms (8 in cottages)* 🍽 *Multiple meal plans.*

$$ B&B/INN Fodor's Choice ★ 🏨 **Tupungato Divino.** Architect Sergio Viegas and economist Pablo Cerutti traded Buenos Aires for the tranquility of the Valle de Uco, and the popular posada they opened is now in the heart of Uco wine country. **Pros:** serene retreat; gorgeous mountain views; superlative restaurant; attentive owners; good value. **Cons:** the pool isn't very private when the restaurant fills up at lunchtime. [$] *Rooms from: US$150* ✉ *RP89 and Calle Los Europeos s/n* ☎ *2622/1544–8948* 🌐 *www.tupungatodivino.com.ar* 🛏 *4 rooms* 💳 *No credit cards* 🍽 *Breakfast.*

SHOPPING

KDS Hecho a Mano. Five members of the da Silva family have been designing and selling handmade knives and leather cases at KDS Hecho a Mano since the 1970s. You can watch the process and choose the right knife for your next asado from many designs in their showroom. ✉ *Ruta 92, KM 5* ☎ *2622/488–852* ⊕ *www.kdscuchillos.com.ar.*

SPORTS AND THE OUTDOORS

HORSEBACK RIDING

You can ride in the foothills of the Andes for a day or cross the Andes on a six-day trip to Chile that takes you through a treeless landscape of rocky trails, roaring rivers, tiny green meadows, and lofty peaks. Argentine horses aren't allowed in Chile, so you'll have to either change horses at the border or return.

Estancia El Puesto. This five-bedroom ranch offers accommodations, meals, and assorted excursions—most notably horseback riding. The owner, Raúl Labat, has made more than 30 crossings to Chile and still finds each trip rewarding. He leads riders there on six-day journeys each summer. ✉ *Los Árboles, off R89* ☎ *261/428–8541* ⊕ *www. estanciaelpuesto.com.ar* ⌧ *From $150 (reservations essential).*

Parque Provincial Volcán Tupungato. Tupungato Volcano rises 6,800 meters (22,310 feet) in snowbound splendor, looming above the high peaks that march along the border between Chile and Mendoza Province. The park that's named for it covers 110,000 hectares (272,000 acres) in the western portion of the departments of Luján de Cuyo, Tupungato, and Tunuyán. There are no roads into the park, but local tour companies lead horseback rides and hikes into the area. Some offer six-day horseback rides to the Chilean border. Mules can be hired to climb to South Glacier at 2,000 meters (6,562 feet).

TUNUYÁN

81 km (50 miles) south of Mendoza.

Twice the size of Tupungato, Tunuyán makes a good base for touring the Valle de Uco wineries. Downtown consists of two traffic circles on either side of two blocks, where most of the shops are geared to local agricultural pursuits. Along with grape growing, said pursuits include growing cherries, pears, and apples, and making apple cider.

GETTING HERE AND AROUND

There's bus service here from Mendoza, but you'll have a hard time getting around without a car unless you're on a tour. From Mendoza City you can take Ruta Nacional 40 directly to Tunuyán, then use Ruta 88, 89, 90, or 96 to reach Tupungato (your choice will depend on which wineries you want to visit).

Bodega Piedra Negra is on the road to Manzano Histórico, while Clos de los Siete is south of Tunuyán, in the district of Vista Flores. Although San Carlos, a dusty agricultural town 25 km (15 miles) south of Tunuyán, isn't yet on the tourist map, it does have several noteworthy wineries near it—including O. Fournier, the southernmost bodega in the Valle de Uco.

ESSENTIALS

Tourist Information Oficina de Turísmo ✉ *San Martín at Dalmau* ☎ *2622/425–810, 2622/422–193* ⊕ *www.tunuyan.gov.ar.*

WINERIES

TUNUYÁN AND NEARBY

Bodega Piedra Negra. Jacques and François Lurton began searching for an Argentine vineyard in 1992. Three years later they planted their grapes in Vista Flores, where low yields and a wide temperature range would ensure premium wines with a defined varietal identity. The arched doorways of their wood-and-stucco colonial-style winery lead into three functional areas—one for wine-making, one for storage, and one for sales and tastings. ✉ *Camino al Manzano, RP94, Km 21* ☎ *261/441–1134* ⊕ *www.francoislurton.com* ⊗ *Weekdays 9–4:30.*

Clos de los Siete: Monteviejo, Flecha de Los Andes, Cuvelier de Los Andes, Bodega Diamandes, Bodega Rolland. It's been called "the most ambitious winery project ever attempted." Five architecturally impressive wineries owned by seven respected partners, under the expert supervision of Michel Rolland, share these vineyards. Each chooses a particular type of grape (these are planted at different altitudes so that they mature at different times); each then makes their own wine and also contributes grapes to create a blend of them all, thereby bringing together the best grapes of some of the world's best winemakers. Of the five wineries, four receive visitors. ■TIP→ **A BBQ-style lunch is available at Monteviejo.** ✉ *Clodomiro Silva s/n, Vistaflores* ☎ *2622/1540–3692* ⊕ *www.clos7.com.ar* ⊗ *Daily (by reservation only).*

Gimenez Riili. You can often get Federico Gimenez-Riili or his father to take you around this family-owned boutique operation and offer you a taste of their Torrontés straight from the barrel. If you want to stay for lunch, they'll organize a traditional asado in the vineyard. ✉ *Ruta 94, Vistaflores* ☎ *261/424–5973* ⊕ *www.gimenezriili.com* ⊗ *Mon.–Sun. (by reservation only).*

SAN CARLOS VICINITY

Finca La Celia. Built by Eugenio Bustos in 1890, this winery flourished under his daughter Celia's leadership, producing an excellent Malbec. Now it's owned by a Chilean company that has invested in the latest technology. Tastings, traditional lunches, and tours of the winery and experimental garden are available with advance booking. In season, pruning and harvesting programs are offered in the vineyard as well. ■TIP→ **There is a rustic posada on site for anyone interested in spending the night.** ✉ *Circunvalación Celia Bustos de Quiroga 374, San Carlos* ☎ *2622/451–010* ⊕ *www.fincalacelia.com.ar* ⊗ *Weekdays 9–4 (by reservation only).*

Fodor's Choice
★

O. Fournier. Approaching this ultramodern winery on a lonely dirt road, you could be forgiven for thinking you'd discovered a flying saucer instead. But, as your tour guide will tell you, every part of the futuristic building has a function—whether it's to make the best use of gravity or to direct the sometimes brutal winds that whip through. Using both local and international expertise, the Spanish Ortega Gil-Fournier family aims to produce the highest-quality wines here. Their

Bodegas in Argentina's wine region often have restaurants with dedicated chefs and stellar cuisine. Some prepare food using traditional methods, like this charcoal grill.

grapes—planted in rocky, sandy soil on three estates at an altitude of 1,200 meters (3,940 feet)—are delivered by truck to rolling vats on the roof; after being hand sorted, they slide down to the first floor, where they are gently crushed; they then go down into fermenting tanks, and finally to the basement to age in oak barrels. If you need a further incentive to come, consider Urban, the on-site restaurant: at lunchtime, chef Nadia de Ortega creates innovative entrées that pair gracefully with the many wines served. ✉ *Los Indios s/n, La Consulta* ☎ *2622/451–579* 🌐 *www.ofournier.com* 🕓 *Daily 9:30–4:30 (by reservation only).*

WHERE TO EAT AND STAY

$$$ BARBECUE 🍴 **La Juntada.** Serving a buffet of salads and starters followed by a main course straight from the grill, La Juntada updates the classic *pulperia* (tavern) atmosphere with a good wine list and a fresh lick of paint. Expect typical Argentine fare that's well prepared and well presented. [$] *Average main: 140 pesos* ✉ *R92, Vista Flores* ☎ *262/266–6355.*

$$ ARGENTINE 🍴 **Posada del Jamon.** It doesn't matter if you're a world-famous winemaker (many are hugely loyal fans of this place and show up often), a local, or a tourist who speaks no Spanish—you will get the same warm service at the casual, family-run Posada del Jamon. It serves ham cooked up every way imaginable (and some ways you have probably never imagined). There are also a surprising number of vegetarian options available, and all of the wines offered are from the neighborhood wineries. A little shop onsite sells unique artisanal items, such as hand-knit sweaters, blankets, and artwork. **TIP→ If you like the place so much you don't want to leave, there are very reasonably priced cabañas for**

rent behind the restaurant. $ *Average main: 80 pesos* ✉ *Ruta 92, Km 14* ☎ *2622/492–053* ⊕ *www. laposadadeljamon.com.ar.*

$$$$
HOTEL
☂ **Casa Antucura.** Next to Vista Flores village, the stately Casa Antucura has comfortable, individually decorated rooms; stellar views; and the best library in Mendoza. **Pros:** intimate and exclusive; private home feel; beautiful gardens and art. **Cons:** expensive; not much to do without your own transport; staff speak little English. $ *Rooms from: US$450* ✉ *Barandica, Vista Flores* ☎ *261/15–339–1440* ⊕ *www.casaantucura. com* ⤳ *8 rooms* ¶◎¶ *Breakfast.*

TRIUMPHAL MARCH

Manzano Histórico. Forty km (25 miles) west of Tunuyán, the Manzano Histórico is the site of an apple tree under which General San Martín camped during his return from liberating Chile in 1823. Several local outfitters offer horseback rides that follow the hoofprints of San Martín's triumphal march across the Andes. During the weekends the area is filled with local families who pack into the handful of restaurants nearby.

SAN RAFAEL REGION

Numerous dams and acres of irrigated land have created a vigorous agro-industrial oasis in the department of San Rafael, one of the country's smallest wine regions to claim a Denominación de Origen (DOC). This is a point of pride for local vintners, and the quality of wine produced here speaks for itself. San Rafael has a nearly perfect climate for growing grapes: low humidity, cold and dry winters, ample temperature variation, and plenty of water from the Ríos Diamante and Atuel. But into every vineyard a little rain must fall—and when it comes in the form of hail (*granizo*), it can be devastating, destroying one year's crop and the next year's tiny buds in one short shower. Most vineyards now protect their crops with expensive heavy netting that lets the water drip through and shades the grapes, aiding ripening.

SAN RAFAEL

240 km (150 miles) south of Mendoza.

San Rafael (population 175,000) is the second largest city in Mendoza. Wide avenues lined with leafy sycamores and tall poplars fed by streetside canals give it a bucolic charm, but the bodegas are reason enough for many visitors to make the trip. Winemaking took off here in the late 19th century when immigrants from Italy, Switzerland, and France came with advanced viticulture skills and new grape varieties. When the railroad arrived in 1903, the fledgling industry was connected to Buenos Aires and the rest of the world. Today the city has about 100 wineries. Although most are small, family-owned operations, a number do have tourist-friendly facilities within walking or cycling distance of the center. If you're looking for more active alternatives, local tour operators can arrange rafting, riding, and hiking excursions in the surrounding

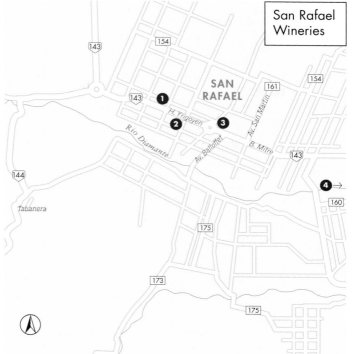

San Rafael
Wineries

mountains and lakes. About 75 km (47 miles) west of San Rafael, the Cañón del Atuel (aka the "other" Grand Canyon) can also be explored.

GETTING HERE AND AROUND

Three Aerolíneas Argentinas flights per week make the 1½-hour trip from Buenos Aires to San Rafael's airport, located about 15 minutes west of downtown on Ruta 150. But since Mendoza has daily flights, many visitors fly there instead and carry on by road: if you plan to do the same, take Ruta Nacional 40 south from Mendoza to Pareditas, where you pick up Ruta Nacional 143 to San Rafael. Coming on an overnight bus from Buenos Aires is another option, as it's less expensive than flying.

San Rafael is flat and laid out on a grid, which makes it easy to tour on foot. At Km 0, Avenida Yrigoyen crosses the downtown area (north–south) and becomes Bartolomé Mitre. At this same intersection (east–west), Avenida El Libertador becomes San Martín—the main shopping street. Hotels are scattered on the edge of residential areas, but you can still walk (or take a short cab ride) to downtown. ⚠ **Beware of the acéquias—canals between the sidewalks and streets. At night people riding bicycles with no lights or reflectors on narrow dirt roads can also be a hazard.**

San Rafael's wineries are mainly within cycling distance (or a cheap taxi ride) of the city center; if you're driving, note that road signs are scarce in the region, though the municipality is working to correct that. Before heading for the wineries, it's wise to make an appointment as owners are often busy in the vineyard, working in the bodega, testing wine with the oenologist, or tending to customers.

Bus Contacts Andesmar ☎ *2627/427–720* ⊕ *www.andesmar.com.* **Iselin** ☎ *2627/425–441* ⊕ *www.iselin.com.ar.* **Terminal de Ómnibus** ✉ *Colonel Suarez and Avellaneda.*

ESSENTIALS

Visitor and Tour Information San Rafael Tourist Board ✉ *Av. H. Yrigoyen 745, at Balloffet* ☎ *260/422–4217* ⊕ *www.sanrafaelturismo.gov.ar.*

WINERIES

Goyenechea. One of the country's oldest wineries, Goyenechea was founded in 1868 by a Basque immigrant family that had the foresight to build not only a solid brick winery, but also 60 houses for the working families, a school for their children, a repair shop, and a chapel. Today fifth-generation families live in the homes, and the school still rings with the laughter of their children. As you pass through the arched caves where wine ages in bottles, you can see the *piletas,* huge concrete vats that held 8,976 gallons of wine when the industry was focused on quantity, not quality. Family members often lead tours (call ahead or email ✎ *visitas@goyenchea.com* to reserve one in English), and visitors are sometimes invited for wine tastings next door on the family's patio. ✉ *Sotero Arizú s/n, Villa Atuel* ☎ *262/547–0181* ⊕ *www.goyenechea. com* ☾ *Mon.–Sat. 10–5:30.*

Jean Rivier. The Swiss-French brothers who own this winery produce a limited quantity of quality wines from their own grapes. Tours of the spotless facility include crushing, fermentation, and tasting areas. ✉ *Hipólito Yrigoyen 2385, Rama Caída* ☎ *260/443–2675* ⊕ *www. jeanrivier.com* ☾ *Mon.–Sat.*

La Champañera Valentín Bianchi. After a variety of entrepreneurial endeavors, Valentin Bianchi realized in 1928 that he wanted to do nothing else except make great wine. He struggled until 1934, when one of his wines won a gold medal in Mendoza and high praise in Buenos Aires. His legacy of hard work continues La Champañera. This is one of the most organized and commercial bodegas in the area, receiving more than 100,000 visitors per year to its lush, garden setting, which is just a little over 5 km (3 miles) from the center of San Rafael. The fact that La Champañera focuses solely on the production and tasting of sparkling wine also sets it apart. The wine shop sells all of Bianchi's other lines of wines if fizz isn't what you are looking for. Free tours are run often throughout the day, and end with a sparkling wine tasting. ✉ *R143 at Valentin Bianchi, Las Paredes* ☎ *260/444–9600* ⊕ *www. vbianchi.com* ☾ *Daily.*

Suter. In 1900 the Suter family journeyed to Argentina from Switzerland and planted the first Riesling variety in the country. Today the fourth generation of the family continues to produce fine white wines, reds like Malbec and Cabernet Sauvignon, and Espumante. A winery tour leads you through a labyrinth of underground caves filled with huge oak casks—used more to evoke atmosphere than to store wine. ⊠ *Hipólito Yrigoyen 2850, near the airport, El Toledano* ☎ *2627/421–076* ⊕ *www. sutersa.com.ar* ⊙ *Mon.–Sat. 9–6 (by reservation only).*

WHERE TO EAT

$

CAFÉ

✕ **Bonafide.** A popular gathering place for both locals and visitors just one block from Km 0 (the very center of town), Bonafide serves up freshly ground coffees, a wide range of sandwiches, plus lots of chocolates and other goodies to buy for the road. Grab one of the window seats with leather couches and take advantage of the Wi-Fi. $ *Average main: 40 pesos* ⊠ *San Martín 102* ☎ *260/4442–0420* ⊕ *www.bonafide.com.ar.*

$$$

ARGENTINE

✕ **Chez Gaston at Algodón.** Nestled between a golf green and tennis courts, Chez Gaston is the center of culinary activity at the luxe Algodón Wine Resort. Surrounded by ancient olive groves and vineyards, you can sit outside on the brick patio where pine-log tables are surrounded by comfy couches with puffy white cushions. Here you listen to birds singing while you sip Algodón wine and dine on high-quality (but never pretentious) regional dishes. Many of the products used, such as the olives, fruits, and walnuts, are harvested right on the property, and bread is baked daily in a clay oven. $ *Average main: 130 pesos* ⊠ *RN144, Km 674, Cuadro Benegas* ☎ *260/442–9020* ⊕ *www. algodonwineestates.com.*

$$$$

ARGENTINE

Fodor's Choice

★

✕ **L'Obrador-Casa de Campo.** Daniel Ancina, his wife Graciela, and a team of cooks will greet you at this typical ranch house, about 20 minutes from town; then they'll fill your wineglass, introduce you to the other guests, and seat you family-style at a long table. Little pots of spreads and sauces for dipping or spreading on *pan casero* (homemade bread) line the center of the table. Out of the mud-brick oven comes a platter of crisp baked empanadas followed by some type of meat— goat, lamb, beef, chicken, or chorizo. Everything is cooked on the spot, and there couldn't be a better (or warmer) introduction to the region's traditional cuisine. ■ TIP→ **Don't even try to find this place on your own: call to be picked up or inquire at the tourist office for directions and reservations.** $ *Average main: 190 pesos* ⊠ *Camino Bentos 50* ☎ *260/460–1347* ⚒ *Reservations essential* ▤ *No credit cards* ⊙ *Tues., Thurs., Fri., or by appointment.*

WHERE TO STAY

$$$

RESORT

Fodor's Choice

★

🛏 **Algodón Wine Resort.** Country casual meets luxury at the Algodón Wine Resort, a sister to the gorgeous Algodón Mansion in Buenos Aires. **Pros:** between sunset views, birds singing, and availability of Algodón wine around every corner, it's hard not to feel profoundly relaxed here. **Cons:** about 20 minutes from downtown San Rafael; closed in winter. $ *Rooms from: US$229* ⊠ *RN144, Km 674, Cuadro Benegas* ☎ *260/4429–020* ⊕ *www.algodonwineestates.com* ⤴ *8 rooms* ⊙ *Closed in winter* ❋ *Breakfast.*

$$

HOTEL

🛏 **Hotel Tower Inn and Suites.** Across the street from the tourist office, this modern hotel has spacious accommodations with big picture windows that fill the rooms with natural light and provide views of the main street and the mountains in the distance. **Pros:** large rooms with plenty of places to stow your stuff; helpful staff who are very used to dealing with foreigners. **Cons:** on a busy street at the edge of town.

6

A Recreational Drive

Cañón del Atuel (Atuel Canyon). This has been called the world's second Grand Canyon, as they were both formed at the same time, and their coloring is quite similar. To traverse the photogenic, 160-km (99-mile) route with its four hydroelectric stations along the Atuel River, start at the top of the canyon in the village of El Nihuel, 75 km (47 miles) west of San Rafael. Take Ruta Provincial 144 from San Rafael in the direction of Malargüe, turning south at El Desvío onto 180. At the dam, Ruta 173 descends into a labyrinth of red, brown, and gray sandstone rock formations. Unfortunately, the river disappears into underground pipes—supplying energy for the growing population and the vineyards of Mendoza Province. At Valle Grande the water is collected behind a large dam, after which the river runs freely between sandstone cliffs, beneath shady willows and poplar trees. Swimming holes, sheltered picnic spots, and rafting adventures offer escape from the city on hot summer days. Small hotels, cottages, campsites, and shops that rent rafting and kayaking equipment line the road before it returns across the desert to San Rafael.

$ *Rooms from: US$140* ⊠ *H. Irigoyen 774* ☎ *260/442–7190* ⊕ *www. towersanrafael.com* ⤷ *89 rooms, 11 suites* ❙○❙ *Breakfast.*

$ **HOTEL** ⌂ **San Martín Hotel & Spa.** At the quiet end of downtown's main street, this hotel caters to wine-business travelers. **Pros:** owner-manager makes you feel welcome; good restaurant. **Cons:** small rooms. $ *Rooms from: US$110* ⊠ *San Martín 435* ☎ *260/4420–400, 260/4433–363* ⊕ *www. sanmartinhotelspa.com* ⤷ *32 rooms, 2 apartments* ❙○❙ *Breakfast.*

$$ **RENTAL** ⌂ **Tierra Mora.** This apart-hotel is a compact three-story building overlooking a large park; it's about 14 blocks from downtown but within walking distance of an up-and-coming area with restaurants and shops. **Pros:** large rooms; in a nice part of town with park. **Cons:** not a lot of amenities. $ *Rooms from: US$120* ⊠ *Ameghino 350* ☎ *260/4447–222* ⊕ *www.tierramora.com* ⤷ *19 apartments, 17 rooms* ❙○❙ *Breakfast.*

SHOPPING

FOOD

Ketobac. Wines, jams, and homemade goodies (such as chocolate-covered figs, raisins, and dried apricots from the region) are all sold at Ketobac. ⊠ *San Martín 175* ☎ *260/4422–082.*

Yancanelo. An olive oil factory that offers tastings, Yancanelo also sells local olive oil and other regional foods. ⊠ *Hipólito Yrigoyen 4030* ☎ *2604/423–879* ⊙ *Mon.–Sat. 9–7, Sun. 10–2.*

LAS LEÑAS

200 km (124 miles) south of San Rafael.

Las Leñas is the largest ski area served by lifts in the Western Hemisphere—bigger than Whistler/Blackcomb in British Columbia, and larger than Vail and Snowbird combined. Although it should be thriving, the area has suffered bankruptcies, absentee owners, and several management teams. You must go through tour operators and travel agents to book into area hotels, all of which have minimum-stay requirements. Accommodations range from dorm-style houses and apart-hotels—some in disrepair—to hotels with indoor/outdoor pools, decent restaurants, bars, and a ski concierge. Travel offices in Buenos Aires, Mendoza, and San Rafael sell ski packages with lift tickets, equipment, and, in some cases, transportation—which may involve a combination of bus rides and charter flights.

The ski season runs June through October, depending on the year's snow. Most South Americans take their vacation in July, the month to avoid if you don't like crowds and high prices, although the weather is more benign. August has the most reliable snow conditions, September the most varied. Prices for lifts and lodging are lowest in June and from September to closing; rates are highest in July.

GETTING HERE AND AROUND

In high season (July and August) there are two charter flights a day from Buenos Aires to Malargüe, a town 80 km (50 miles) from the resort. A more reliable alternative is to take a 90-minute flight from Buenos Aires to San Rafael, then a three-hour drive onward to Las Leñas. From San Rafael, follow Ruta Provincial 144 for 141 km (88 miles) to El Sosneado, then pick up Ruta Nacional 40 to the turnoff onto Ruta Provincial 222 that passes through Los Molles, 20 km (12 miles) from Las Leñas. This is a dramatically beautiful drive, but carry chains and be aware of weather conditions.

If you want to save your pesos for lift tickets and good lodgings, consider taking the Las Leñas "Coche-cama" from Buenos Aires. This sleeper bus departs on Friday and Sunday evenings, making the trip in 11 hours; return tickets (bookable directly through the resort) cost about US$230.

ESSENTIALS

Visitor Information Malargüe Tourism Office ⊠ *Hipólito Yrigoyen 774, San Rafael* ☎ *2604/471–659* ⊕ *www.malargue.gov.ar* ✉ *San Martin s/n, Malargüe* ☎ *2604/471–659.*

WHERE TO STAY

$$$
HOTEL
Aries. This slopeside luxury hotel has plenty of diversions for stormy days—including a space for children's games and activities, a piano bar in the lobby, a wine bar serving cheese and regional smoked meats, a movie theater, a pool, and a sauna. **Pros:** proximity to slopes and non-ski alternatives. **Cons:** no direct reservation service and two-night minimum stay. $ *Rooms from: US$260* ⊠ *Las Leñas Ski Resort* ☎ *11/4819–6060 in Buenos Aires (off-season), 2627/471–1000 in Mendoza (ski season)* ⊕ *www.laslenas.com* ⊷ *100 rooms* ❧*Breakfast.*

$$
HOTEL
Escorpio. This small, intimate ski lodge is right on the slopes; you can watch the action from the terrace while having lunch, or hit the cozy piano bar for après-ski board games with tea or cocktails. **Pros:** proximity to slopes. **Cons:** difficult to make reservations directly at times. $ *Rooms from: US$175* ⊠ *Las Leñas Ski Resort* ☎ *11/4819–6060 in*

Buenos Aires (off-season), 2627/471–1000 in Mendoza (ski season) 🌐 *www.laslenas.com* 🛏 *47 rooms, 1 suite, 2 apartments* 🍴 *Some meals.*

$$$ HOTEL 🏨 **Piscis.** This deluxe hotel pampers its guests with spa services, ski-equipment delivery, and an indoor/outdoor pool. **Pros:** loads of services. **Cons:** difficult to make direct reservations; two-night minimum stay [$] *Rooms from: US$295* ✉ *Las Leñas Ski Resort* ☎ *11/4819–6060 in Buenos Aires (off-season), 2627/471–1000 in Mendoza (ski season)* 🌐 *www.laslenas.com* 🛏 *90 rooms* 🍴 *Some meals.*

SPORTS AND THE OUTDOORS

SKIING

Las Leñas Ski Resort. From the top (3,429 meters/11,250 feet), a treeless lunar landscape of white peaks extends in every direction. There are steep, scary, 610-meter (2,000-foot) vertical chutes for experts; machine-packed routes for beginners; and plenty of intermediate terrain. A terrain park for snowboarders has jumps and a half pipe. There's also a free-style slope. Off-piste skiing can be arranged through the ski school.

Facilities: 3,300 hectares (8,154 acres) skiable terrain; 1,230-meter (4,035-foot) vertical drop; 64 km (40 miles) of groomed runs, the longest is 8 km (5 miles); 15% beginner, 40% intermediate, 45% expert; 1 quad, 6 double chairs, 5 surface lifts. There are no detachable quad chairs or high-speed lifts.

Seasonal Rate Information: Low: September 13–closing. Medium: June 28 –July 10 and August 2–August 29. High: July 11–August 1. Special: June 14–27 and August 30–September 12. Prices below in pesos.

Lessons and Programs: Multilingual ski and snowboard instructors give 2½-hour classes or two-hour private lessons for all levels. Good intermediate skiers to experts can experience untracked slopes with heli-ski and off-piste skiing accompanied by trained guides and avalanche experts.

One-Day Adult Lift Tickets: Low: 395 pesos, Special: 450 pesos, Medium: 510 pesos, High: 585 pesos

Rentals: The following one-day rental packages are for skis or snowboards, boots, and poles. Low and Special: 180 pesos, Medium: 236 pesos, High: 280 pesos. To rent just one of these items, you must inquire at the shop. "Fat skis" for deep-powder and off-piste skiing are scarce, so bring your own. ☎ *11/4819–6060 in Buenos Aires* 🌐 *www.laslenas.com* 🕒 *June–late Sept., weekdays 9–6, depending on snow.*

SAN JUAN REGION

In the foothills of the Andes, the city of San Juan lies in an oasis of orchards and vineyards, surrounded by mountains to the west and monotonous desert in every other direction. People here work hard in the fields during the day, take long siestas in the afternoon, and head back to the fields until sundown. Although San Juan wineries have been slow to make the shift from quantity to quality, some 160 facilities have converted (or are converting) from producing bulk wine, and a new generation of oenologists and vintners is taking the lead. The province

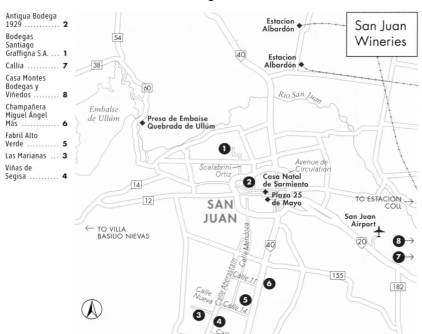

produces more wine than Napa and Sonoma combined, and you'll likely find the fine cabernets, bonardas, and syrahs—as well as the whites and sparkling wines—of San Juan on the world's wine lists in short order.

The Ullum, Tulum, and Zonda valleys are the principal wine-growing areas close to the city of San Juan, and the Río San Juan flows from the mountains into 2,000 km (1,243 miles) of canals to irrigate about 48,500 hectares (120,000 acres) of vineyards. Other growing areas include El Perdenal, southeast near the Mendoza border, and Jachal, to the north.

SAN JUAN

167 km (104 miles) northwest of Mendoza.

Easygoing San Juan makes a good base if you want to combine active pursuits (a good selection of which can be found in and around the Ullum Valley Dam Reservoir) with visits to local bodegas. This small city was founded in 1562 as part of the Chilean viceroyalty, and *sanjua-ninos* began making wine almost immediately; however, it wasn't until the 1890s, when Graffigna and other major operations put down roots here, that production increased. At that point wineries began offering varieties other than the sweet white table wines, sherries, and ports that the area had been known for. Today, although the city remains steeped in history and awash in wine, it is surprisingly modern. San Juan was devastated by earthquakes in 1944 and 1977 (the first of these helped establish Juan Perón, who led the relief effort, as a national figure): all of the low-rise buildings, tree-lined plazas, and pedestrian walkways you see are the results of reconstruction.

GETTING HERE AND AROUND

San Juan is a 1½-hour drive from Mendoza on Ruta Nacional 40. The trip from Buenos Aires takes 10 hours by car, slightly longer by bus, but daily flights on Aerolíneas Argentinas (⊕ *www.aerolineas.com.ar*) take just 1¾ hour. The Chacritas Airport is 11 km (7 miles) southeast of San Juan; a taxi in takes about 15 minutes and costs about 100 pesos. The city is easy to negotiate: there's one main shopping area in a three-block radius around the Plaza 25 de Mayo, and most hotels are within walking distance of it. Some wineries are within cycling distance, whereas others are drive-to destinations. Always try to reserve visits ahead of time.

Bus Contacts Andesmar ☎ *264/422–2871* ⊕ *www.andesmar.com.* **Autotransportes** ☎ *264/431–1000 for San Juan office* ⊕ *www.atsj.com.ar.* **CATA Internacional** ☎ *264/427–7600, 800/122–2282* ⊕ *www.catainternacional. com.* **Chevallier** ☎ *264/422–2871* ⊕ *www.nuevachevallier.com.* **Terminal de Ómnibus** ✉ *Estados Unidos 492, between Santa Fe and España 985* ☎ *264/422–1604.*

Car Rentals Avis ✉ *Domingo Sarmiento Sur 164* ☎ *264/420–0571, 264/15–499–1472* ⊕ *www.avis.com.ar.*

Taxis Argentina Remise ✉ *Gral. Mariano Acha Norte 989* ☎ *264/422–5522, 264/421–3837.* **Radio Taxi** ☎ *264/422–3561, 264/426–5555.*

ESSENTIALS

Visitor Information San Juan Secretaria de Turismo ✉ *Sarmiento 24 Sur* ☎ *264/421–0004, 264/427–5946* ⊕ *www.sanjuan.gov.ar.*

TOURS

Dante Montes Turismo. Anna Maria de Montes and her partners at Dante Montes Turismo are experienced local agents with a full-service agency for lodging and transportation. They offer guided tours to bodegas, Valle Fertí (where they own their own cabins), Ischigualasto Park, and beyond. ✉ *Santa Fe 58 Este, Galeria Estornell, Loc 31* ☎ *264/422–9019, 264/421–5198* ⊕ *www.agenciamontes.com.ar.*

Moneytur. This outfit conducts tours of local bodegas; outings to Ischigualasto, Talampaya, Las Quijades, and Jachal; plus rafting trips on the Río San Juan and horseback trips in the Calingasta Valley. ✉ *Santa Fe 202* ☎ *264/420–1010* ⊕ *www.moneytur.com.ar.*

EXPLORING

Casa Natal de Sarmiento (*Sarmiento's Birthplace*). This modest house was the birthplace of Domingo Faustino Sarmiento (1811–88), known to Argentines as the Father of Education. Sarmiento was a prolific writer, a skilled diplomat, and a successful politician who served as governor of San Juan Province from 1862 to 1864 and as president of the country from 1869 to 1874. During this time he passed laws establishing public education. Today Casa Natal de Sarmiento—Argentina's first designated National Historic Landmark—pays tribute to his achievements. ⊠ *Sarmiento 21 Sur* ☎ *264/422–4603* ⊕ *www.casanatalsarmiento.com. ar* ⊠ *15 pesos* ☼ *Weekdays 9–7, weekends 10– 4.*

Presa de Embalse Quebrada de Ullum *(Ullum Valley Dam Reservoir).* Fifteen km (9 miles) west of San Juan, this huge hydroelectric complex—also known as the Ullum Valley Dam Reservoir—offers grand views of the Río San Juan. Windsurfing, sailing, swimming, rowing, fishing, and diving keep sanjuaninos cool on hot summer days. You can rent boating equipment at the Bahía Las Tablas sports complex, just beyond the dam, where you'll also find a café and change cabins. There's a public beach at the Embarcadero turnoff. You can go white-water rafting and kayaking on the San Juan, Los Patos, and Jachal rivers. Fishing in Las Hornillas River can be arranged through local tour companies.

WINERIES

Antigua Bodega 1929. At this landmark bodega and museum, great concrete wine-storage tubs are exposed in a cavernous old building that survived three earthquakes and now functions as part of the museum. Wine and espumante are served in the lovely garden or at a wine bar in the front room. ⊠ *Salta 782 Norte, Capital* ☎ *264/421–2722* ⊕ *www. antiguabodega.com* ☼ *Mon.–Sat. 11–1 and 6–9.*

Bodegas Santiago Graffigna S.A. Italian wine expert Don Santiago Graffigna, who planted Tulum Valley's first vines, founded this winery in 1870. You can learn the history of his family and their vineyard in the excellent museum on the premises. Today the company is owned by Allied Domecq, and grapes arrive at the winery from vineyards in many valleys. An enormous barrel serves as a sitting area in the tasting room. ⊠ *Colón 1342 Norte, Desamparados* ☎ *264/421–4227* ⊕ *www. graffignawines.com* ☼ *Mon.–Sat. 9–5; daily 9–5 in April, July, and Sept.*

Callia. In a hot, dry, wide open valley 35 km (22 miles) from town and with vineyards planted in every direction, Callia produces some of Argentina's best syrah. The winery looks modern, but inside its superstructure is the old bodega (albeit with all new equipment). It's owned by Salentein, a formidable Dutch company that also makes wine in the Valle de Uco. ⊠ *Calle de los Ríos s/n, Caucete* ☎ *264/496–0000* ⊕ *www. bodegascallia.com* ☼ *Weekdays (by appointment only).*

Casa Montes Bodegas Y Viñedos. Across the road from Callia, in a white cube surrounded by vineyards, Don Francisco Montes cultivates high quality grapes. His Ampakama label is widely distributed in Argentina and abroad, including the U.S. Appointments for tours must be made two days in advance. ⊠ *Pozo de los Algarrobos, Calle Colón y Caseros Caucete* ☎ *264/423–6632* ⊕ *www.casamontes.com.ar* ☼ *Weekdays (by reservation only).*

Champañera Miguel Ángel Más. There's a lot going on at this unassuming little winery. It doesn't run fancy tours, but workers will stop to show you how they make sparkling wine, turning the bottles slowly on the many racks. Everything is certified organic—from the wine to the garlic and tomatoes that grow out back. ⊠ *Calle 11 s/n, 300 meters (984 feet) east of RN40* ☎ *264/422–5807* ☼ *Daily 10–5.*

Taking a rest at Cerro Aconcagua's Camp Two

Fabril Alto Verde. Grapes from this spotless winery are grown organically, and the wine and espumante are stabilized without preservatives or additives. They are made in small quantities, and a great deal of care and control go into the production. ⊠ *RN40, between calles 13 and 14* ☎ *264/492–1905* ⊕ *www.fabril-altoverde.com.ar* ☉ *Weekdays 9–1 and 2:30–5:30, Sat. 9–1.*

Las Marianas. Founded in 1922, this winery is a fusion of tradition and technology. Gold adobe walls, arched doorways, and wine casks filled with flowers give it an Old Spanish air, but inside everything is state-of-the-art. Lots of care goes into irrigation, growing the grapes on *espalderas altos* (espaliers) or *parrales* (trellises), selecting grapes on the vine, hand harvesting, and hand crushing. The owner leads some of the tours. ⊠ *Calle Nueva s/n, La Rinconada, Pocito* ☎ *264/15–463–9136* ⊕ *www. bodegalasmarianas.com.ar* ☉ *Tues.– Sat. 10–1 and 3–6.*

Viñas de Segisa. Segisa claims to be the first boutique winery in San Juan. In 1925 Don Vicente Perez Ganga settled here and quickly became one of the region's best winemakers. Earthquakes ensued, destroying most of the original buildings; in 1995, however, new owners resurrected what they could and built a new, anti-seismic facility with thick brick walls and a traditional high ceiling of bamboo canes held in place by crossed timbers. ⊠ *Aberastain at Calle 15, La Rinconada, Pocito* ☎ *264/492–2000* ⊕ *www.saxsegisa.com.ar* ☉ *Mon.–Sat. 10–7, Sun. 10–2.*

WHERE TO EAT

$$

ECLECTIC

✕ **de Sanchez Libros y Discos.** What fun to find a gourmet restaurant with good books (*libros*) and old CDs (*discos*) lining one wall, larger-than-life photos of Rita Moreno on the other, and beaded chandeliers lighting the open booths. The menu's unlikely yet delicious fusions include lots of seafood and fresh vegetables like asparagus, artichoke hearts, and green beans—a welcome relief in this country of carnivores. The vibe is hip and healthy; wine glasses (and pours) are large. You can browse and/or buy the books and CDs. $ *Average main: 99 pesos* ⊠ *Rivadavia 61 Oeste* ☎ *264/420–3670* ⊕ *www.desanchezrestoran.com.ar* ⊗ *Closed Sun. No lunch Sat.*

$$

ARGENTINE

✕ **Remolacha.** Delicious smells from the outdoor grill lure locals off the streets and into this popular smoke-free restaurant in the center of town. Saffron-yellow tablecloths throughout brighten the low-ceiling dining room and add a splash of color to the outdoor patio. A variety of typical dishes—including grilled goat, beef, chicken, and vegetables—are served for lunch and dinner. $ *Average main: 90 pesos* ⊠ *Av. José de la Roza 199 Oeste, at Sarmiento* ☎ *264/422–7070.*

$$

MEDITERRANEAN

✕ **Restaurante Palito—Club Sirio Libanés.** Tiled walls that look straight out of the Middle East mark the entrance to this eatery. Don't be dismayed by the bright lights and TV showing soccer games; just order a bottle of Malbec, head for the table of appetizers, and fill your plate with crab brochettes, pickled eggplant, fresh tomatoes, and sliced tongue. Entrées include pastas, chicken, and beef prepared with a Middle Eastern touch. $ *Average main: 90 pesos* ⊠ *Entre Ríos 33 Sur* ☎ *264/422–3841* ⊕ *www.hostaldepalito.com.ar* ⊗ *No dinner Sun.*

$

VEGETARIAN

✕ **Soychu.** Dedicated to natural foods, this buffet-style restaurant has lots of vegetarian and even vegan options. The atmosphere is laid-back, and your meal—which is priced by weight—can be eaten in or taken out. ■TIP→ **Be sure to try the fresh-squeezed fruit and vegetable juices.** $ *Average main: 50 pesos* ⊠ *Av. Ignacio de la Roza 223* ☎ *264/422–1939* ⊗ *No dinner Sun.*

WHERE TO STAY

$

HOTEL

🏨 **Albertina.** Bright white walls with colorful art, glass partitions, and slick modern furniture have rejuvenated this venerable four-story hotel on the main square in the center of town. **Pros:** convenient location; affordable rates; on-site eatery. **Cons:** tiny windows; stairway down to entrance is inconvenient (although elevator access from street to second floor is available). $ *Rooms from: US$70* ⊠ *Mitre 31 Este* ☎ *264/421–4222* ⊕ *www.hotelalbertina.com* ⤳ *36 rooms* ⦿*Breakfast.*

$

HOTEL

🏨 **Alkazar.** Polished granite floors, chrome, and glass lend this hotel's lobby a businesslike air. **Pros:** professional staff; good location and business amenities. **Cons:** rooftop pool is small; bedroom décor is a bit dated. $ *Rooms from: US$75* ⊠ *Laprida 82 Este* ☎ *264/421–4965* ⊕ *www.alkazarhotel.com.ar* ⤳ *96 rooms, 8 suites* ⦿*Breakfast.*

$$

HOTEL

🏨 **Del Bono Park.** Light shines from a skylight four stories above the registration area, lobby, bar, and gathering spaces, and a third-floor glass bridge connects rooms by spanning the atrium, with a circular staircase winding around a glass cylinder down into the basement bar, restaurant, and casino. **Pros:** San Juan's sleekest, most modern hotel. **Cons:** just off the Circunvalación (Ring Road). $ *Rooms from: US$150* ⊠ *Av. José de la Roza 1946* ☎ *0800/333–5266, 264/426–2300* ⊕ *www.delbonohotels.com* ⤳ *100 rooms* ⦿*Breakfast.*

$ RENTAL **La Deolinda.** The helpful owners of this apart-hotel have created a cheery complex of cabins with outdoor patios, backyard grills, and a swimming pool. **Pros:** friendly staff; spacious grounds with open-air pool; good for families. **Cons:** 15-minute drive from town; no public transportation. [$] *Rooms from: US$65* ✉ *25 de Mayo and Lateral Este* ☎ *264/422–2923* 🌐 *www.ladeolinda.com.ar* 🛏 *4 rooms, 20 apartments* 🍴 *Breakfast.*

$ HOTEL FAMILY **Villa Don Tomás.** If you're tired of downtown streets with traffic, crowds, and noise or if you're traveling with active children who need to get out and play, consider this resortlike hotel on the outskirts of town. **Pros:** huge lawn; pool; dedicated staff; low rates. **Cons:** 15-minute drive from town; no nearby shops or restaurants. [$] *Rooms from: US$55* ✉ *Comandante Cabot Oeste 568* ☎ *264/428–3842* 🌐 *www.villadontomas.com.ar* 🛏 *32 rooms, 11 cottages, 8 apts* 🍴 *Breakfast.*

BARREAL

136 km (85 miles) northwest of San Juan.

Beyond the streets of Barreal, hiding in the shade of *sauce llorones* (weeping willows) and alamos, lie apple orchards, vineyards, and fields of mint, lavender, and anise. Using this tranquil village as your headquarters, you can mountain bike, horseback ride, hike, climb, or drive a 4X4 east into the Sierra Tontal, where at 3,999 meters (13,120 feet) you can see the highest peaks in the Andes, including Aconcagua (6,957 meters/22,825 feet) and Mercedario (6,770 meters/22,211 feet).

GETTING HERE AND AROUND

You can reach Barreal by bus or car in about three hours. Leave San Juan on Ruta Nacional 40 driving north, then veer west on 436 to Talacasto, which becomes 149 to the Calingasta Valley and then continues south to Barreal. Another option is the long, lonely but scenic drive from Uspallata (⇨ *Scenic Drives in Uspallata*) on north–south Ruta 39 (which turns into Ruta 412) all the way to Barreal. The optimal way to explore the surrounding area is by car, using a 4X4 for forays into the mountains, or by joining a tour.

ESSENTIALS

Visitor Information Tourist Office ✉ *Municipalidad, Presidente Roca* ☎ *264/844–1066.*

EXPLORING

Reserva Natural El Leoncito. Twenty-two km (14 miles) south of Barreal on Ruta 412 toward Uspallata, a dirt road turns off into Reserva Natural El Leoncito (Little Lion Natural Reserve), a vast, rocky area with little vegetation. You can continue on this road for 17 km (11 miles) to the CASLEO observatory, known for its exceptional stargazing.

Near the turnoff, on the western side of Ruta 412 at Pampa Leoncito, the sport of *carrovelismo* (land-sailing) is practiced during summer months in wheeled sand cars called wind yachts that can travel up to 150 kph (93 mph) across a cracked-clay lake bed.

An all-day drive (160 km/100 miles round-trip) in a 4X4 to Las Hornillas at 3,300 meters (9,500 feet) takes you along the Río Los Patos into a red rock–wall canyon. The road narrows, clinging to the canyon walls, as it winds around closed curves, eventually opening into a small valley where, in 1817, General San Martín's troops gathered before crossing the Andes over the Los Patos Pass on one of his historic liberation campaigns.

A brief glimpse of Aconcagua looming in solitary splendor about 160 km (100 miles) south is a preview of coming attractions: four peaks over 6,000 meters (20,000 feet) tall are visible in the Ramada Range to the northwest: Polaco, Alma Negra, La Ramada, and Mercaderio. The last of these—rising to 6,770 meters (22,211 feet)—is the fourth highest peak in the Americas. As the road winds ever higher, herds of guanacos graze on the steep slopes, pumas prowl in the bush, and condors soar above. ⊠ *Cordillera de Ansilta.*

WHERE TO STAY

$
B&B/INN

⬚ **El Mercedario.** This 1928 adobe farmhouse on the main street is a gathering place for like-minded lovers of all that Barreal has to offer. **Pros:** local flavor; reasonable price; bike and 4X4 excursions can be arranged. **Cons:** yard is a work in progress. Ⓢ *Rooms from: US$70* ⊠ *Av. Presidente Roca and Calle Los Enamorados* ☎ *264/15–509–0907* ⊕ *www.elmercedario.com.ar* ↩ *7 rooms* ✵ *Breakfast.*

$
B&B/INN

⬚ **La Querencia.** Situated just beyond the south end of town, this Southwest-style inn looks west to the Andes and east to the pre-Cordillera. **Pros:** big backyard; mountain views and magnificent sunsets. **Cons:** you'll need a car, bike, or horse to get around. Ⓢ *Rooms from: US$85* ⊠ *Florida s/n* ☎ *264/15–436–4699 (cell), 264/15–504–6958 (cell)* ⊕ *www.laquerenciaposada.com* ↩ *6 rooms* ⊟ *No credit cards* ✵ *Breakfast.*

$
B&B/INN
Fodor's Choice
★

⬚ **Posada San Eduardo.** A yellow adobe house with green shutters sits on the shady corner of Calle Los Enamorados (Lover's Lane); inside, spacious rooms decorated with local weavings and rustic pine furniture open on to a colonial patio. **Pros:** peaceful setting; attentive staff and owners; good base for mountain forays. **Cons:** rooms are dark. Ⓢ *Rooms from: US$90* ⊠ *Av. San Martín at Los Enamorados* ☎ *2648/441–046 in Barreal* ↩ *14 rooms* ⊟ *No credit cards* ✵ *Breakfast.*

SPORTS AND THE OUTDOORS

Tour offices in Barreal, San Juan, and as far away as Mendoza City offer assorted activities—including hikes or horseback rides of varying lengths—in the Reserva Natural El Leoncito and the high mountain ranges of the Cordillera Ansilta.

Fortuna Viajes. In business for more than 30 years, this outfit arranges horseback trips lasting from one to nine days—including ones to Valle Colorado, where you'll see six peaks over 6,000 meters (20,000 feet). Hiking, mountaineering, fishing, and 4X4 excursions are also offered. ⊠ *Presidente Roca s/n* ☎ *264/15–404–0913* ⊕ *www.fortunaviajes. com.ar.*

THE LAKE DISTRICT

WELCOME TO THE LAKE DISTRICT

TOP REASONS TO GO

★ **The Great Outdoors:** Hikers following well-marked trails in the national parks will encounter atmospheric forests, camera-ready cascades, and magnificent vistas. Waterways can carry rafters and kayakers all the way to Chile.

★ **Water, Water Everywhere:** 40 different lakes, seven major rivers flowing into two oceans, and you can spend days just staring at Nahuel Huapi Lake with its shoreline disappearing under distant peaks and volcanoes.

★ **Summer Skiing:** In the northern Lake District of Patagonia, June through September is ski season on the slopes of Cerro Catedral, near Bariloche, and Cerro Chapelco, near San Martín de los Andes.

★ **Savage Beauty:** One day a lake is silent, a mirror of the surrounding mountains. Another day waves are crashing on its shores, with wind tearing limbs from trees.

1 Bariloche. Full of sightseers, shoppers, and skiers in winter, this unashamedly touristy city on the southeastern shore of Nahuel Huapi Lake welcomes the world with all levels of lodgings, restaurants, and tour offices. The best part of Bariloche is beyond the city limits.

2 San Martín de los Andes and Nearby. Tourist amenities, combined with the alpine setting and distinctive architecture, make San Martín both a pretty and practical base for exploring Parque Nacional Lanín. The town's location also makes it a logical stopover on the Seven Lakes Route.

3 Ruta de los Siete Lagos (Route of the Seven Lakes). The highlight of this 105-km (65-mile) drive is the scenic leg between Villa La Angostura and San Martín de los Andes, where the road winds up and around lake after lake—all of them different in shape, size, and setting.

4 Parque Nacional Nahuel Huapi. Founded in 1934, Argentina's oldest national park covers more than 7,050 square km (2,720 square miles): 800,000-plus visitors per year come to explore its high mountain glaciers, endless lakes, and enticing trails in buses, boats, and private vehicles.

5 El Bolsón and Nearby. Known as a refuge for hippies and ex-urbanites, amiable little El Bolsón is a valley town that straddles Ruta Nacional 40 just north of Parque Nacional Lago Puelo on the Chilean border. Hops and berry farms thrive in the microclimate along the Río Azul.

GETTING ORIENTED

The Lake District lies in the folds of the Andes along the Chilean border in the provinces of Neuquén, Río Negro, and Chubut, where myriad glacial lakes lap at the forest's edge beneath snowcapped peaks.

The area includes three national parks, with towns in each. Bariloche is the base for exploring Parque Nacional Nahuel Huapi, and the departure point for the lake crossing to Chile. North of Bariloche is Parque Nacional Lanín, which contains the town of San Martín de los Andes. South of Bariloche and El Bolsón is Parque Nacional Lago Puelo in the Pacific watershed.

7

RUTA DE LOS SIETE LAGOS

To fully experience the Lake District, head north of Bariloche past Nahuel Huapi Lake to the Ruta de los Siete Lagos (Route of the Seven Lakes). This excursion has it all: lake after lake, mountains, wildflowers, waterfalls, hiking trails, and small towns along the way.

(above) You'll pass lots of big-leaf lupine, or *Lupus polyphyllus*—an invasive species here. (top right) Rainbow trout (bottom right) One of many stunning views along the way

The route itself links Bariloche and San Martín de los Andes. Start in Bariloche and follow the Circuito Grande along Ruta 237 and Ruta 231 to Villa La Angostura, then pass Lagos Espejo and Correntoso on Ruta 231 to get to mostly unpaved Ruta 234; take this north to San Martín.

For a day trip, return from San Martín de los Andes through Junín de Los Andes and Alicura (rutas 234, 40, and 237) on 260 km (161 miles) of paved road. If you have the time, though, overnight in San Martín de los Andes, take Ruta Provincial 63 to Confluencia, and then join Ruta 237 south along the Río Limay to Bariloche.

Renting a car is best, but even on a group tour it's spectacular. Buses are available from Bariloche or Villa La Angostura; you can also rent bicycles in these towns and take to the road on two wheels instead of four.

TIPS

Ask about road conditions before you leave Villa La Angostura; the route's unpaved portion north of there is often closed during heavy rains, winter storms, or construction. Best bets for picnic spots or campsites are the beaches of lakes Villarino, Falkner, and Hermoso. For maps, pick up *Guía Busch* and *Viajar Hoy* (tour pamphlets in English and Spanish). There are no gas stations on the Ruta de los Siete Lagos.

HIGHLIGHTS OF THE DRIVE

Rivers. Just past Villa La Angostura, the **Río Correntoso**—one of the world's shortest rivers at 300 meters (984 feet)—flows from the lake of the same name into Nahuel Huapi. This is a classic mouth-of-the-river fishing spot; you can watch the action from the glassed-in deck at the Hotel Correntoso *(see Where to Stay in Villa La Angostura)* or from the old fishing lodge on the shore of Nahuel Huapi Lake.

Lakes. Traveling north from Villa Angostura to San Martín de los Andes is the most scenic part of the drive, and it's no coincidence that this is where you'll find the region's most scenic namesake natural features—lakes. **Lago Correntoso** (Rapid Water Lake) is the first one you'll pass, and you'll do so immediately after you cross over the Río Correntoso. Drive along its northern shore to arrive at an abandoned hotel site; from here you'll see a road that leads to **Lago Espejo Chico** (Little Mirror Lake), with a beach, a campground, and trails. Return to the main road and you'll come to **Lago Espejo** (Mirror Lake)—head to the viewpoint for a good lunch spot, or use the camping area's tables. **Lago Falkner** (east side of the road) has sandy beaches and a popular campground. It is linked by a stream and an isthmus, which you will cross to **Lago Villarino** (west side of the road). **Lago Hermoso** (Beautiful Lake) is a small sheltered lake. A sunny beach faces west, with nearby camping and a few cabins. Finally, before you reach San Martín de los Andes, enjoy **Lago Machónico's** dry landscape via the scenic overlook, or take the short walk to the shore.

Waterfalls. Between Lakes Villarino and Falkner, **Cascada Vulignanco,** a 20-meter (66-foot) waterfall, is visible on the left-hand side of the road, where you can pull off at the *mirador* (overlook).

DETOURS

Four km (2½ miles) south of Lago Villarino, jade-green **Lago Escondido** (Hidden Lake) lies veiled in a thick forest. You'll need to park and walk in.

At Pichi Traful, turn east onto a bumpy road for 2 km (1 mile) and walk to the sandy beach at **Pichi Traful Lake** (aka Brazo Norte of Lago Traful). Fishermen, bikers, and hikers enjoy camping or picnicking here.

About 30 km (18 miles) north of the junction of Ruta Provincial 234 and Ruta Provincial 65, look on your left for a sign indicating the trail to **Casacada Ñivinenco** (Whispering Falls). The 2-km (1-mile) trail crosses a river (in November and December the river is high; check conditions ahead of time), then follows the river into a silent forest.

If you pass through **Confluencia,** take Ruta Provincial 65 along the Traful River west a few km to **Cuyín Manzano,** a dirt road that continues along the river into a world of strange caves and limestone rock formations.

CIRCUITO CHICO Y CIRCUITO GRANDE

If you're in Bariloche, get out of town to take in some of the spectacular scenery and old-school resort feel of the area on either the Circuito Chico (Small Circuit) or Circuito Grande (Large Circuit) by rental car, hired driver, or tour group.

(above) "We drove the Circuito Chico and stopped at this overlook." —HappyTrvlr (top right) "With flowers in full bloom it couldn't get much better." —Josh Roe (bottom right) Peninsula Llao Llao

The Circuito Chico is a 70-km (43½-mile) half-day round-trip from Bariloche along the southern shore of Lago Nahuel Huapi. Visitors head out to the Llao Llao Peninsula to ski or take in the lake views and waterfalls without ever being too far from a cup of tea.

The Circuito Grande covers 250 km (155 miles) and is an all-day excursion across the lake from Bariloche. This drive is more about wooded hikes and hidden lakes, and includes two towns where you could spend a night.

You can do the Circuito Chico on one tank of gas. Circuit Grande, however, has longer unpopulated spans. Leave Bariloche with a full tank and refuel at Confluencia or Villa La Angostura.

WEATHER TIPS

The Circuito Chico has lots of traffic but is otherwise an easy drive whatever the weather. The Circuito Grande is another story. The roads to Villa La Angostura and Confluencia are good, but Ruta Provincial 65 past Lago Traful is unpaved and can be treacherous in bad weather. Always check road conditions with the Automóvil Club Argentino (⊕ www.aca.org.ar), the park office, or your hotel.

CIRCUITO CHICO

From Bariloche's Centro Cívico (Km 0), follow the shore of Lago Nahuel Huapi west on Ruta 237. At Km 7, stop at **Playa Bonita**'s sandy beach. At Km 10, take the chairlift or climb to the top of **Cerro Campanario**. When you reach the Península Llao Llao (Km 25.5), bear right to **Puerto Pañuelo,** where boats embark on lake excursions to Isla Victoria, Puerto Blest, and the boat crossing to Chile. Across from the Puerto Pañuelo, the **Llao Llao Hotel & Resort** (See Where to Stay in Bariloche) sits on a lakeside knoll with a backdrop of sheer cliffs and snow-covered mountains. Continue following Ruta 77 to **Bahía Lopez**; you'll approach through a forest of ghostly, leafless *lenga* trees. After Bahía Lopez, the road crosses **Arroyo Lopez** (Lopez Creek); stop to hike to the waterfall or continue on Ruta 77 to **Punto Panorámico**, one of the most scenic overlooks on the peninsula. Just before you cross the Moreno Bridge, an unmarked dirt road off to the right leads to the rustic village of Colonia Suiza, a perfect stop for tea or lunch. Backtrack to cross Moreno Bridge, then leave Ruta 77 for Ruta 237 back to Bariloche.

CIRCUITO GRANDE

Leaving Bariloche on Ruta 237 heading east, follow the Río Limay into the **Valle Encantado** (Enchanted Valley), with its magical red rocks. Before crossing the bridge at Confluencia (where the Río Traful joins the Limay), turn left onto Ruta 65 to Lago Traful. Five km (3 miles) beyond the turnoff, a dirt road to Cuyín Manzano leads to **astounding sandstone formations**. Return to Ruta 65 and follow Lago Traful's shore. When you see the sign indicating a mirador, stop and climb the wooden stairs to one of the loveliest views in the region. Descend to Villa Traful, follow the lakeshore, then dive into a dense forest of *caña colihue* and lenga trees. At the intersection with Ruta 237, turn left and follow the shore of Lago Correntoso to the paved road down to Villa La Angostura. The road skirts Lago Nahuel Huapi back into Bariloche.

NEED A BREAK?

Circuito Chico: Chiado (✉ Av. Bustillo [R237], Km 18 ☎ 2944/448–152 ⊙ Closed Wed.) is a log house with a corrugated metal roof, a stone terrace, and colorful plants hanging out over the lake. Views are through the gnarly branches of a giant *coihué* tree to blue water and mountains. The brie sorrentinos in pear and port sauce are as good as the view.

Circuito Grande: If you visit Lago Traful in the morning, chances are you'll hit Villa Traful in time for lunch at Nancu Lahuen (✉ Village center, opposite chapel ☎ 294/447–9017), a casual spot in the middle of town with home cooking. If you've brought a picnic, continue on past the town to the beach, where the road leaves the lake for Ruta 234 and Villa La Angostura. In Villa La Angostura, head to La Casita de la Oma (✉ Cerro Inacayal 303 ☎ 2944/494–602), which serves homemade cakes, pies, and scones. Any dulce de leche item is a sure bet.

7

Updated by
Melissa Kitson

The northern Lake District has become Patagonia's most popular tourist region. Spread over three states and encompassing more than a million hectares (2½ million acres) of nature preserves, it offers more than natural beauty. The hundreds of sapphire lakes here allow visitors to experience an array of outdoor activities. Lakes such as Lago Nahuel Huapi and Lago Puelo are the focal points of eponymous national parks; at both you can choose between fishing, boating (whether in a kayak, raft, or motor launch), and swimming from a pretty playa.

Back on dry land other recreational opportunities await. In the warmer months, horseback riding, mountain biking, and hiking are popular pastimes; climbing Volcán Lanín for a wraparound view of the sublime landscape is another memorable option. In winter, conversely, snow-sport enthusiasts head for the hills. Cerro Catedral (the continent's oldest ski area) is notable for its size, terrain, and superb setting, while smaller areas like Chapelco attract mostly vacationing Argentineans and Brazilians.

A broad range of accommodations—ranging from rustic refugios and classic ranches to luxe destination hotels—cater to these travelers year-round. Yet despite growing popularity and heightened accessibility from developed towns like San Martín de los Andes and Bariloche, first-time visitors are constantly amazed at how easy it is to lose yourself in a silent forest, on a rugged mountaintop, or by one of the district's beautiful namesake lakes.

PLANNING

WHEN TO GO

June through September the weather is typical of any ski region—blowing snowstorms, rain, and fog punctuated by days of brilliant sunshine. August and September are the best months for skiing, as the slopes are crowded with vacationers in July.

In December the weather can be cool, breezy, overcast, or rainy, but the rewards for bringing an extra sweater and raingear are great: an abundance of wildflowers and few tourists. January and February are the peak summer months, with days that are warm and long (the sun sets at 10 pm). March and April are good months to visit; the leaves of lenga and *ñire* trees brighten the rolling green forests with splashes of yellow and red, but rainy, cloudy days and cold nights can curtail some excursions.

GETTING HERE AND AROUND

The most efficient way to get here is by air from Buenos Aires or Calafate. The most scenic way to arrive is from Puerto Montt, Chile, by boat through the lakes. Buses are the new trains—fast, inexpensive, with varying degrees of luxury, including beds, meals, and attendants. A car or bus is the best way to travel between cities in the Lake District, and once you've settled in a destination, you can use local tours, buses, taxis, or a *remis* (a hired car with driver).

AIR TRAVEL

Aerolíneas Argentinas (⊕ *www.aerolineas.com.ar*) flies from Buenos Aires to Bariloche, Esquel, San Martín de los Andes, and Neuquén; it also connects Bariloche and Calafate. LAN (⊕ *www.lan.com*) flies to Bariloche from Buenos Aires, as well as from Santiago, Chile.

BOAT TRAVEL

Traveling between Bariloche and Puerto Montt, Chile, by boat is one of the most popular excursions in Argentina. It requires three lake crossings and various buses, and can be done in a day or overnight. Travel agents and tour operators in Bariloche and Buenos Aires can arrange this trip.

BUS TRAVEL

Buses arrive in Bariloche from every corner of Argentina—from Jujuy in the north, Ushuaia in the south, and everywhere in between.

CAR TRAVEL

Driving to the Lake District from Buenos Aires is a long haul: the trip takes at least three days, and the route—extending for more than 1,500 km (930 miles)—has interminable stretches with few hotels, gas stations, or restaurants. In Bariloche, unless you're on a tour or a ski-only vacation, renting a car gives you the freedom to stop when and where you want. The Ruta de los Siete Lagos closes when weather is bad; for winter travel, rent a 4X4. Hiring a remis is another option.

RESTAURANTS

Restaurant reservations are seldom needed except during school, Easter, and summer holidays (July, January, and February). Attire is informal, and tipping is the same as in the rest of the country (about 10%). Most menus will feature regional dishes such as *trucha,* the salmon-like trout commonly found in the lakes and rivers of the district, as well as *cordero* (lamb), *ciervo* (venison), and *jabalí* (wild boar).

HOTELS

Idyllic lake-view lodges, cozy *cabañas* (cabins), vast *estancias* (ranches), and inexpensive *hospedajes* or *residenciales* (bed-and-breakfasts) are found in towns and in the countryside throughout northern Patagonia. Superluxurious hotels in Bariloche and Villa La Angostura attract outdoor enthusiasts from all over the world, as do small family-run hostels where backpackers squeeze five to a room. Fishing lodges in the San Martín de los Andes area and the Cholila Valley are not only for anglers; they make great headquarters for hiking, boating, or just getting away. Most of them include all meals. Guides are extra. "Apart-hotels" have small, furnished apartments with kitchenettes. Local tourist offices are helpful in finding anything from a room in a residence to a country inn or a downtown hotel. Advance reservations are highly recommended if you're traveling during peak times (December–March; July for the ski resorts). Note: lodging prices include tax (IVA—which is 21%) unless otherwise noted. *Hotel reviews have been shortened. For full information, visit Fodors.com.*

WHAT IT COSTS			
$	**$$**	**$$$**	**$$$$**
Restaurants (in Pesos)	Under 65 pesos	65 pesos–99 pesos	100 pesos–150 pesos	over 150 pesos
Hotels (in USD)	Under $116	$116–$200	$201–$300	over $300

Restaurant prices are the average cost of a main course at dinner or, if dinner is not served, at lunch. Hotel prices are the lowest cost of a standard double room in high season.

TOURS

Alunco. Everything from hour-long tours in Bariloche to week-long excursions in the surrounding countryside can be arranged by Alunco. The company works with local guides who know the area well and have partnerships with many estancias and restaurants. Adventure and ski package are also available. ⊠ *Moreno 187, 1st fl., Bariloche, Río Negro* ☎ *2944/422–283* ⊕ *www.aluncoturismo.com.ar* ⊠ *From 150 pesos* ⊙ *Daily 9–8.*

Causana Viajes. The team at Causana Viajes takes pride in providing tours that respect the natural surroundings. They've been offering excursions through Nahuel Huapi National Park for more than 25 years. ⊠ *Paulina Escardo 148, Puerto Madryn, Chubut* ☎ *2965/452–769* ⊕ *www.causanaviajes.com.ar* ⊙ *Weekdays 9–1 and 4:30–8.*

El Claro Turismo. For more than 20 years, El Claro Turismo has been leading excursions to Cerro Chapelco and Parque Nacional Lanín. Visitors can choose a half- or full-day tour to nearby attractions like Villa Quila Quina, or opt for a week-long package that includes accommodations, airport transfers, and some meals. ⊠ *Colonel Diaz 751, San Martín de los Andes, Neuquén* ☎ *2972/428–876, 2972/425–876*

⊕ *www.elclaroturismo.com.ar* ✉ *From 300 pesos for day trips; from 4,000 pesos for packages* ⊙ *Daily 9–1 and 4–8.*

Siete Lagos Turismo. This outfit provides a comprehensive range of tourism services including guided excursions, vehicle rentals, airport transfers, plus bus and hotel reservations. Its rafting adventures are particularly popular. ✉ *Villegas 313, San Martín de los Andes, Neuquén* ☎ *2972/427–877* ⊕ *sietelagosturismo.com.ar/empresa.html* ✉ *From 350 pesos* ⊙ *Mon.–Sat. 9–1 and 4–8.*

VISITOR INFORMATION

The comprehensive InterPatagonia website (⊕ *www.interpatagonia. com*), covering every city and region in Patagonia, is an excellent resource for travelers. Local tourist offices (Direcciónes de Turismo) are helpful, easy to find, and usually open late every day.

BARILOCHE

1,615 km (1,001 miles) southwest of Buenos Aires (2 hours by plane); 432 km (268 miles) south of Neuquén on R237; 1,639 km (1,016 miles) north of Río Gallegos; 876 km (543 miles) northwest of Trelew; 357 km (221 miles) east of Puerto Montt, Chile, via lake crossing.

Bariloche is the gateway to all the recreational and scenic splendors of the northern Lake District and the headquarters for Parque Nacional Nahuel Huapi. Although planes, boats, and buses arrive daily, you can escape on land or water—or just by looking out a window—into a dazzling wilderness of lakes, waterfalls, mountain glaciers, forests, and meadows.

The town of Bariloche hugs the southeastern shore of Lago Nahuel Huapi, expanding rapidly east toward the airport and west along the lake toward Llao Llao, as Argentineans and foreigners buy and build without any apparent zoning plan. Being the most popular vacation destination in Patagonia has not been kind to the town once called the "Switzerland of the Andes." Traffic barely moves on streets and sidewalks during holidays and the busy months (January, February, March, July, and August).

Nevertheless, the Centro Cívico (Civic Center) has not lost its architectural integrity. Designed by Alejandro Bustillo (1889–1982), the landmark square is as handsome as ever; and the buildings around it—with their gray-green local stone, brightly varnished wood, and decorative gable ends—are prime examples of the region's signature alpine style. With its view of the lake and mountains, the Centro Cívico is a good place to begin exploring Bariloche.

GETTING HERE AND AROUND

Many travelers choose to come via the Chilean Lakes crossing. If you're flying from Buenos Aires, regular nonstop flights take about two hours; by contrast, long-distance sleeper buses from the capital can take up to 23 hours. The airport is 30 minutes from the Centro Cívico, the bus terminal is 15; in either case, you can take a public bus into town (rutas 72 and 10, respectively) or grab a cab.

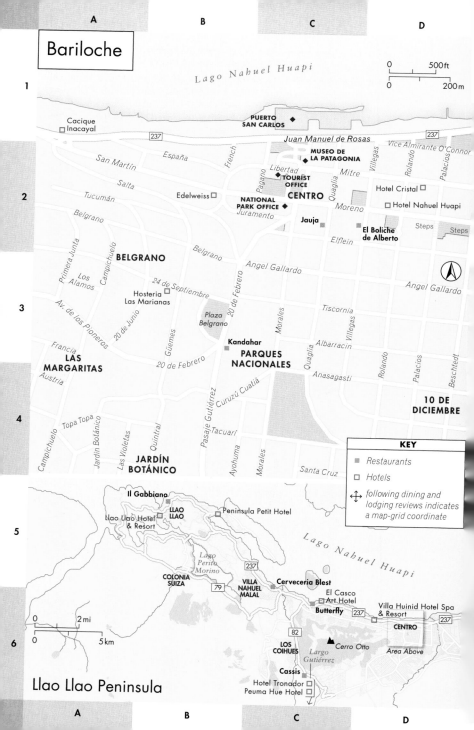

Bariloche

Lago Nahuel Huapi

0 — 500ft
0 — 200m

| | A | B | C | D |

1

Cacique □ Inacayal

PUERTO SAN CARLOS ◆

237

Juan Manuel de Rosas

237

Vice Almirante O'Connor

España

San Martín

French

Pagano

Libertad

MUSEO DE LA PATAGONIA ◆

Mitre

Villegas

Rolando

Palacios

2

Salta

Tucumán

Edelweiss □

TOURIST OFFICE ◆

NATIONAL PARK OFFICE ◆

Juramento

CENTRO

Quaglia

Moreno

Hotel Cristal □

□ Hotel Nahuel Huapi

Belgrano

Jauja ■

El Boliche de Alberto ■

Elflein

Steps

Steps

BELGRANO

Primera Junta

Los Álamos

Campichuelo

24 de Septiembre

Hostería Las Marianas □

Belgrano

Angel Gallardo

20 de Febrero

Angel Gallardo

3

Av. de los Pioneros

20 de Junio

Güemes

Plaza Belgrano

Kandahar ■

Morales

Tiscornia

Villegas

Albarracín

Quaglia

Rolando

Palacios

Beschtett

Francia

LAS MARGARITAS

Austria

20 de Febrero

PARQUES NACIONALES

Anasagasti

10 DE DICIEMBRE

4

Campichuelo

Topa Topa

Jardín Botánico

Las Violetas

Quintral

Pasaje Gutiérrez

Curuzú Cuatiá

Tacuarí

Ayohuma

Morales

Santa Cruz

JARDÍN BOTÁNICO

KEY

■ *Restaurants*

□ *Hotels*

↔ *following dining and lodging reviews indicates a map-grid coordinate*

Il Gabbiano ■

LLAO LLAO ■

Llao Llao Hotel & Resort □

□ Peninsula Petit Hotel

Lago Nahuel Huapi

5

Lago Perito Moreno

COLONIA SUIZA

237

79

VILLA NAHUEL MALAL

Cervecería Blest ■

El Casco Art Hotel □

Butterfly ■

237

Villa Huinid Hotel Spa & Resort □

CENTRO

237

0 — 2 mi
0 — 5 km

82

▲ Cerro Otto

Largo Gutiérrez

LOS COIHUES

Cassis ■

Hotel Tronador □

Peuma Hue Hotel □

Area Above

6

Llao Llao Peninsula

| | A | B | C | D |

For long excursions, such as the Ruta de los Siete Lagos, Circuito Grande, or Tronadór, sign up for a tour through your hotel or with a local tour agency. The *Guía Busch,* available at car-rental agencies, kiosks, and hotels, has listings of the latter along with good maps. Fishing, rafting, and biking trips typically include transportation from your hotel; skiers can reach the slopes by public bus, although many hotels also have private shuttles. If you prefer the independence of figuring out maps and driving yourself, rent a car.

Bus Contacts Andesmar ☏ *0261/405–0600* ⊕ *www.andesmar.com.* **Bariloche Bus Terminal** ⊠ *Av. 12 de Octubre* ☏ *2944/430–211.* **Don Otto** ☏ *2944/437–699* ⊕ *www.donotto.com.ar.* **El Valle** ☏ *0810/333–7575* ⊕ *www.elvalle.com.ar.* **Via Bariloche** ☏ *2944/432–444* ⊕ *www.viabariloche.com.ar.* **VIATAC** ☏ *2944/421–235* ⊕ *www.viatac.com.ar.*

Rental Cars Baricoche ⊠ *Moreno 115, 1st fl., office 14* ☏ *2944/427–638* ⊕ *www.baricoche.com.ar* ⊗ *Daily 9–6.*

SAFETY AND PRECAUTIONS

Driving in Bariloche requires total attention to blind corners, one-way streets, and stop signs where no one stops. Be wary of road construction as avenues such as Bustillo regularly undergo maintenance work. Don't leave anything in your car. Bariloche's challenging sidewalks are riddled with uneven steps, broken pavement, and unexpected holes—all potential ankle breakers.

ESSENTIALS

Visitor and Tour Information Oficina Municipal de Turismo ⊠ *Centro Cívico, across from clock tower* ☏ *2944/422–484* ⊕ *www.barilochepatagonia.info* ⊗ *Daily 9–9.*

EXPLORING

TOP ATTRACTIONS

Cerro Otto. For an aerial view of the area around Bariloche, ascend 1,405 meters (4,608 feet) to the top of Cerro Otto. A little red cable car owned by **Teleférico Cerro Otto** will carry you there in about 12 minutes, and all ticket proceeds go to local hospitals. ■ TIP→ **A free shuttle bus leaves from the corner of Mitre and Villegas, and Perito Moreno and Independencia.** You can also hike or bike to the top, or drive up from Bariloche on a gravel road. In winter, cross-country skis and sleds are for rent at the cafeteria. In summer, hiking and mountain biking are the main activities. There is a revolving restaurant on the summit. For a real thrill, try soaring out over the lake in a paraplane. ⊠ *Av. de los Pioneros, 5 km (3 miles) west of Bariloche* ☏ *2944/441–035 for info on schedules and equipment rental* ⊕ *www.telefericobariloche.com.ar* ⊠ *30 pesos* ⊗ *Daily 10–5:30* ⊗ *Mt. Otto.*

Museo de la Patagonia. This small museum explains the social and geological history of northern Patagonia through displays of Indian and gaucho artifacts and exhibits on regional flora and fauna. The stories of the Mapuche and the Conquista del Desierto (Conquest of the Desert)

Chilean Lakes Crossing

Cruce a Chile por Los Lagos (*Chile Lake Crossing*). This unique excursion by land and lakes can be done in one or two days in either direction.

Travelers boarding the boat at Puerto Pañuelo, west of Bariloche, will stop for lunch in Puerto Blest, then travel by bus up to Laguna Frías, a cold glacial lake frozen in winter. After crossing that lake to Puerto Fríos, you pass Argentine customs, then board another bus that climbs through lush rain forest over a pass before descending to Peulla. Clear Chilean customs just before a lodge by Lago Todos los Santos. You may spend the night at the lodge (recommended) or head straight to Chile by catamaran from Peulla, with volcano views. An overnight stay is mandatory in winter. The boat trip ends at the port of Petrohué. Your final bus ride skirts Lago Llanquihue, stopping at the Petrohué waterfalls, passing the town of Puerto Varas, and arriving, at last, at Puerto Montt. Guides on the Argentina side speak little English, and passenger literature in English isn't available; if your Spanish is shaky, do this trip with a tour group. ⊠ *Mitre 219* 🕾 *2944/426–228* ⊕ *www. cruceandino.com* ⊠ *US$280* ⊗ *Daily 8–1 and 4–9.*

If you're pressed for time, return to Bariloche by paved road via Osorno, crossing at Cardenal Samoré (aka Paso Puyehue) to Villa La Angostura, which is 125 km (78 miles) from the border to Bariloche on Ruta Nacional 231.

OTHER CROSSINGS

Paso Hua Hum is the only crossing open year-round. It may be the shortest route—only 47 km (29 miles) from San Martín de los Andes on Ruta Provincial 48—as the condor flies, but it's the longest journey by road, after factoring in the 1½-hour ferry ride across Lake Pirehueico on the Chilean side. There are three ferries daily, and buses leave regularly from San Martín de los Andes. You can also make this crossing by raft on the river Hua Hum.

Farther north, and accessible via Junín de los Andes, are two passes that require a longer excursion. Mamuil Malal (aka Paso Tromen) is 67 km (41½ miles) northwest of Junín de los Andes on Ruta Provincial 60. This dirt road crosses Parque Nacional Lanín and passes through a forest of ancient araucaria trees as it heads for the foot of Volcán Lanín. Just before the park office, a road leads to good picnic spots and campsites on Lago Tromen. If you continue on to Chile, you'll see the Villarrica and Quetupillán volcanoes to the south and Pucón to the north.

Paso Icalma is 132 km (82 miles) west of Zapala on Ruta Nacional 13. Villa Pehuenia, 10 km (6 miles) before the pass, is a small village on the shore of Lake Alluminé with modern accommodations and restaurants. Rafting, fishing, or horse, bike, and raft rentals might tempt you to stay awhile.

No fresh fruits, meats, dairy products, or vegetables are allowed across the border, so bring a snack for long stretches without food. Lake crossings are not fun in driving rain and high waves. Snow may close some passes in winter. If driving, double-check with your rental agent that you have all the necessary paperwork. It's also good to have some Chilean pesos with you; it can be expensive to change them at the border.

are told in detail. ✉ *Centro Cívico, next to arch over Bartolomé Mitre* ☎ *2944/422–309* 🌐 *www.bariloche.com.ar/museo* 🎟 *15 pesos* 🕑 *Tues.–Fri. 10–12:30 and 2–7, Sat. 10–4.*

WHERE TO EAT

$$$$ INTERNATIONAL 🍴 **Butterfly.** For an indulgent meal and direct views of Lake Nahuel Huapi, consider Butterfly. At this intimate, modern restaurant every element is carefully thought out—from the tiny handmade salt spoons to the sublime degustation menu, which moves from a light foie gras to a rich sous-vide lamb. Spanish chef Andres Lopez's training under renowned pastry chef Ramon Morato is particularly evident in the beautifully presented desserts. Wine lovers will appreciate the intelligent choice of accompanying blends. [$] *Average main: 340 pesos* ✉ *Hua Huan 7831, Bariloche* ☎ *294/446–1441* 🌐 *www.butterflypatagonia.com.ar* ✍ *Reservations essential* 💳 *No credit cards* ✥ *C6.*

$$$$ CONTEMPORARY Fodor's Choice ★ 🍴 **Cassis.** Chef Mariana Wolf combines the freshest seasonal ingredients, many from her own rural garden, in beautifully presented dishes that are both elegant and comforting. Meat eaters will love the ribeye in shortcrust pâté brisée pastry, loaded with its own juices and port wine, and served with baked edible lilies and wild pine mushrooms. Mariana's husband Ernesto can recommend the perfect wine pairing from the restaurant's impressively stocked cellar. Desserts here are art. Try the Fruits of the Forest with Cointreau and cardamom ice cream served with oranges. Cassis's forest location near the shores of Lago Gutierrez is worth the drive. [$] *Average main: 400 pesos* ✉ *Ruta 82, Km 5.5, Lago Gutiérrez* ☎ *2944/467–747* 🌐 *www.cassis.com.ar* ✍ *Reservations essential* 💳 *No credit cards* ✥ *C6.*

$$$ ARGENTINE 🍴 **Cerveceria Blest.** This lively spot claims that it was the first brewpub in Argentina, and its relaxed bustle hits the spot after a day on the slopes. Don't miss the excellent bock beer, with a toasty coffee flavor, or if you prefer hard cider, the Fruto Prohibido. You can come in just for an après-ski beer sampler or stay for dinner, which might include *costillitas de cerdo ahumadas con chucrut* (smoked pork chops with sauerkraut—is there a more classic beer food than that?). Pizzas, steak potpies, and other Anglophile options round out the menu. [$] *Average main: 150 pesos* ✉ *Av. Bustillo, Km 11.6* ☎ *2944/461–026* 🌐 *www.cervezablest.com.ar* 🕑 *Daily noon–midnight* ✥ *C5.*

$$ STEAKHOUSE 🍴 **El Boliche de Alberto.** Leather placemats, calfskin menus, and the smell of beef all hint heavily at steakhouse. Alberto has the best beef in Bariloche. Grilled beef, chicken, lamb, and chorizos all arrive sizzling on a wooden platter, accompanied by empanadas, *provoleta* (fried provolone cheese), salad, fried potatoes, and chimichurri sauce (slather it on the bread). [$] *Average main: 80 pesos* ✉ *Villegas 347* ☎ *2944/43–1433* 🌐 *www.elbolichedealberto.com* ✥ *C2.*

$$ ITALIAN 🍴 **Il Gabbiano.** Staff at this cozy but elegant, candlelit house on the Circuito Chico near Llao Llao boast, "we don't serve lunch because preparing dinner takes all day." It's hard to argue with that after you sample the exquisite pastas, which change daily. Look for pumpkin ravioli or tortelli stuffed with wild boar. They also have a way with fresh trout. Friendly, bow-tie-wearing waiters provide an ingredient-by-ingredient

explanation of each dish. A beautiful wine cellar is open to guests. [$] *Average main: 80 pesos* ✉ *Av. Bustillo, Km 24.3* ☎ *2944/448–346* 🌐 *www.gabbiano.com.ar* ✍ *Reservations essential* 💳 *No credit cards* 🕒 *Closed Tues. No lunch* ✥ *B5.*

$$ ARGENTINE

🍴 **Jauja.** Locals come to this friendly restaurant for its outstanding pastas and variety of entrées listed on an eight-page menu: expect meats from Patagonia to the pampas, fish from both oceans, local game, and fresh vegetables. Hearty portions make this an ideal place to end a long day on the slopes. **TIP→ Empanadas and take-out items can be ordered at the entrance.** [$] *Average main: 90 pesos* ✉ *Elflein 148* ☎ *2944/422–952* 🌐 *www.restaurantejauja.com.ar* 🕒 *Daily 11:30–3 and 7:30–midnight* ✥ *C2.*

$$ ARGENTINE

🍴 **Kandahar.** A rustic wood building with a woodstove and cozy windowseats provide the perfect setting for sipping a pisco sour and savoring a plate of smoked trout or salmon. Start with the *tarteleta de hongos* (mushroom tart) and *rosa mosqueta* (rose hip) soup, followed by wild game and profiteroles with hot chocolate sauce. [$] *Average main: 75 pesos* ✉ *Av. 20 de Febrero 698* ☎ *2944/424–702* ✍ *Reservations essential* 🕒 *8 pm–11 pm* 🕒 *Closed Sun., and May 25–June 10* ✥ *B3.*

WHERE TO STAY

If you don't have a car, finding a place in town may be the most convenient option. That said, local buses run regularly and choosing a hotel or cabin en route to the Llao Llao Peninsula will give you better access to hiking trails and lake views. Many of the restaurants with the best views are also located away from the city center. Distances listed for out-of-town dining and lodging properties are measured in kilometers from the Bariloche Centro Cívico.

$$$$ HOTEL

🏨 **Cacique Inacayal.** The waterside Cacique Inacayal has a reception area, a bar, and an outdoor patio on the top floor; a fine dining room for hotel guests down one floor; and lakeview rooms on the three floors below. **Pros:** impressive views; central location; free shuttle to Cerro Catedral in season. **Cons:** five rooms on the east side of the building (next to the disco) throb to the beat until late at night during holidays. [$] *Rooms from: US$330* ✉ *Juan Manuel de Rosas 625* ☎ *2944/433–888* 🌐 *www.hotelinacayal.com.ar* 🛏 *67 rooms* 🍽 *Breakfast* ✥ *A1.*

$$$$ HOTEL Fodor's Choice ★

🏨 **El Casco Art Hotel.** This stunning modern hotel is the area's most stylish option. **Pros:** art everywhere; activities galore; self-contained luxury; close to activities. **Cons:** very pricey; perhaps too extravagant for some. [$] *Rooms from: US$670* ✉ *Av. Bustillo, Km 11.5* ☎ *2944/463–131* 🌐 *www.hotelelcasco.com* 🛏 *33 suites* 🍽 *Breakfast* ✥ *C6.*

$ B&B/INN

🏨 **Hosteria Las Marianas.** On a quiet street surrounded by well-tended gardens, this perfectly proportioned Tyrolean villa in Barrio Belgrano (Bariloche's nicest neighborhood) is only four blocks from the city center, but it feels a world away. **Pros:** sunny hillside location; away from the crowds; multilingual staff. **Cons:** uphill haul from city center. [$] *Rooms from: US$110* ✉ *Av. 24 de Septiembre 218* ☎ *2944/439–876* 🌐 *www.hosterialasmarianas.com.ar* 🛏 *16 rooms* 🍽 *Breakfast* ✥ *B3.*

$$ HOTEL 🏨 **Hotel Cristal.** A basic businesslike hotel, this old standby in the center of Bariloche has been greatly improved, thanks to updated furnishings and facilities. **Pros:** central location on a popular downtown street; good value. **Cons:** small bathrooms; desultory reception; frequented by tour groups. [$] *Rooms from: US$160* ✉ *Mitre 355* ☎ *2944/422–442* 🌐 *www.hotel-cristal.com.ar* 🛏 *50 rooms* 🍴 *Breakfast* ✥ *D2.*

$$$ HOTEL 🏨 **Hotel Edelweiss.** Fresh flowers from the owner's nursery are a tradition throughout this medium-size hotel, which is within walking distance of everything in town. Rooms on the upper floors have lake views from bay windows. **Pros:** great location; spacious rooms. **Cons:** bar has no windows; so-so streetside restaurant. [$] *Rooms from: US$205* ✉ *Av. San Martín 202* ☎ *2944/445–500* 🌐 *www.edelweiss.com.ar* 🛏 *95 rooms, 4 suites* 🍴 *Breakfast* ✥ *B2.*

$ HOTEL 🏨 **Hotel Nahuel Huapi.** This slick hotel on a busy downtown street in Bariloche has a spacious lobby with a wine bar in one corner and a sit-around fireplace in another. Textured beige wallpaper in the large bedrooms show off the deep oranges of the woven bedspreads and upholstered chairs. **Pros:** central location; good accessibility for people with disabilities. **Cons:** rooms overlooking street might be noisy. [$] *Rooms from: US$90* ✉ *Moreno 252* ☎ *2944/433–635* 🌐 *www.hotelnahuelhuapi.com.ar* 🛏 *74 rooms* 🍴 *Breakfast* ✥ *D2.*

$$ HOTEL 🏨 **Hotel Tronadór.** Named for the mountain that towers above the wild landscape only 25 km (15½ miles) up the road, this stone-and-log lodge on Lago Mascardi has been owned by the Vereertbrugghen family since 1929. **Pros:** practically in the lap of the region's highest mountain glacier; amenities include a games rooms, organic garden, and private beach. **Cons:** the road here is one-way heading towards the hotel 10:30 am–2 pm, one-way heading away from 4 pm–7:30 pm, and two-way from 7:30 pm–10:30 am only. [$] *Rooms from: US$120* ✉ *RN40 west from Bariloche 66 km, past Villa Masacardi, turn right on dirt road to west end of Lago Mascardi* ☎ *2944/490–550* 🌐 *www.hoteltronador.com* 🛏 *29 rooms, 7 apartments* 🕑 *Closed mid-Apr.–mid-Nov.* 🍴 *All meals* ✥ *C6.*

7

$$$$ RESORT Fodor's Choice ★ 🏨 **Llao Llao Hotel & Resort.** This masterpiece by architect Alejandro Bustillo sits on a grassy knoll surrounded by three lakes with a backdrop of cliffs and snow-covered mountains. **Pros:** gorgeous setting; dramatic lake views; helpful staff; lots of activities; variety of rooms. **Cons:** public tours of the landmark building come through Wednesday at 3 pm. [$] *Rooms from: US$478* ✉ *Av. Bustillo, Km 25* ☎ *2944/448–530* 🌐 *www.llaollao.com* 🛏 *205 rooms, 12 suites, 1 cabin* 🍴 *Breakfast* ✥ *B5.*

$$ HOTEL 🏨 **Península Petit Hotel.** Combining the amenities of a hotel with the warmth of a home, this handsome lodge is a great getaway spot for couples. **Pros:** great views; friendly staff; homemade breakfast. **Cons:** limited capacity. [$] *Rooms from: US$131* ✉ *Av. Campanario 493, Bariloche* ☎ *294/444–8537* 🌐 *www.peninsulapetithotel.com.ar* 🛏 *11 rooms* 💳 *No credit cards* 🕑 *Closed May* 🍴 *Breakfast* ✥ *B5.*

$$$$ HOTEL FAMILY 🏨 **Peuma Hue.** Inside Peuma Hue, a sense of rustic luxury prevails: picture pine beams overhead, kilim rugs on wood floors, a lace tablecloth on the dining table, and guests gathered around the stone fireplace. Outside, Lago Gutiérrez shimmers through the trees across the lawn.

Evening shoppers on Avenida Bartolomé Mitre, Bariloche

Pros: lovely grounds; massage, yoga, and wine tastings are just the tip of the activities iceberg. **Cons:** remote location. [$] *Rooms from: US$410* ✉ *R40, Km 2014* ✣ *Enter dirt road, 1½ mile to Lago Gutiérrez* ☎ *2944/501–030* 🌐 *www.peuma-hue.com* 🛏 *14 rooms, 2 cabins* 🕓 *Closed June* 🍴 *Multiple meal plans* ✣ *C6.*

$$ HOTEL 🏨 **Villa Huinid.** This peaceful complex consists of a grand hotel and older two-story log-and-stucco cottages on the lawns below. **Pros:** cabins have one to four bedrooms, combining privacy with hotel amenities; lake-view pool and spa. **Cons:** outdoor hike from cabins to breakfast in hotel. [$] *Rooms from: US$180* ✉ *Av. Bustillo, Km 2.6* ☎ *2944/523–523* 🌐 *www.villahuinid.com.ar* 🛏 *70 rooms, 21 cabins* 🍴 *Breakfast* ✣ *D6.*

SHOPPING

Along Bariloche's main streets, Calles Mitre and Moreno, and the cross streets from Quaglia to Rolando, you can find shops selling sports equipment, leather goods, hand-knit sweaters, and gourmet food like homemade jams, dried meats, and chocolate.

Ahumadero Familia Weiss. Come here to buy delicious pâtés, cheeses, smoked fish, and wild game. ✉ *Mitre 131* ☎ *2944/435–874* 🌐 *www.ahumaderoweiss.com* 🕓 *Daily 9–noon and 5–8.*

Mamuschka. Crowned by giant mamuschka dolls, this renowned chocolate store is famous for its range of high quality, if slightly more expensive, chocolate and pastry products. Ask for the house specialty (a chocolate mousse "Timbal") or simply admire the beautifully decorated *bombones* (chocolate balls). ✉ *Mitre 298* ☎ *0294/442–3294* ⊕ *www. mamuschka.com* ⊙ *Daily 8:30 am–10 pm.*

Rapa Nui. A Willy Wonka wonderland overflowing with chocolate, sweets, and ice cream, Rapa Nui has treats to delight adults and children alike. Established in 1939, it is one of the longest-running *chocolaterías*. ✉ *Mitre 202* ☎ *0294/442–3779* ⊕ *www.chocolatesrapanui. com.ar* ⊙ *Daily 9 am–10 pm.*

Tito Testone. Local artisan and sculptor Tito Testone sells finely crafted bronze ornaments and decorations. ✉ *Av. Bustillo 5709* ☎ *0294/452–5418* ⊙ *Weekdays 10–7, Sat. 10–noon and 1–6, Sun. 10–noon and 1–7.*

SPORTS AND THE OUTDOORS

FISHING

Fishing season runs November 15–April 15 (extended through May in certain areas), and guides are available by the day or the week. Nahuel Huapi, Gutiérrez, Mascardi, Correntoso, and Traful are the most accessible lakes in the Lake District. If you're seeking the perfect pool or secret stream for fly-fishing, you may have to do some hiking, particularly along the banks of the Chimehuín, Limay, Traful, and Correntoso rivers. Near Junín de los Andes the Malleo and Currihué rivers, and Lakes Huechulafquen, Paimún, and Lácar are good fishing grounds. Note that catch-and-release is usually compulsory.

Baruzzi Deportes. Oscar Baruzzi at Baruzzi Deportes is a good local fishing guide. ✉ *Urquiza 250* ☎ *2944/424–922* ⊕ *www.barilochefishing. com* ⊙ *Daily 9–1 and 4:30–8:30.*

Direcciones Provinciales de Pesca. Fishing licenses allowing you to catch brown, rainbow, and brook trout as well as perch and *salar sebago* (landlocked salmon) are obtainable in Bariloche at the Direcciones Provinciales de Pesca. You can also get licenses at the Nahuel Huapi National Park office and at most tackle shops. Nonresident license fees are $180/day, $540/week, $720/season. ✉ *Elfleín 10* ⊕ *www.maa.gba. gov.ar/pesca.*

Martín Pescador. This shop carries fishing and hunting equipment. ✉ *Rolando 257* ☎ *2944/422–275* ⊙ *Mon.–Sat. 10–1 and 6–9.*

Patagonia Fly Shop. Ricardo Almeijeiras, also a guide, owns the Patagonia Fly Shop. ✉ *Quinchahuala 200, at Av. Bustillo, Km 6.7* ☎ *2944/441–944.*

HIKING

For day hikes along the shores of Nahuel Huapi Lake, try the trails of the Circuito Chico in Parque Municipal Llao Llao. For altitude and grand panoramas, take the ski lift to the top of Cerro Catedral and follow the ridge trail to Refugio Frey, returning down to the base of the ski area. West of Bariloche, turn right at Villa Mascardi onto the dirt road to Pampa Linda; from there you can take a day-long hike to the Otto Meiling Refuge or make shorter forays to the glacier and nearby waterfalls. A three-day trek will take you right past Tronadór and its glacier, along the Alerce River, and over the Paso de los Nubes (Cloud Pass) to Puerto Blest, returning to Bariloche by boat.

Parque Municipal Llao Llao. Llao Llao Municipal Park has two main trails, each approximately 3 km (2 miles) long. One takes you through the mixed forest of coihués and mountain cypresses to the top of Cerro Llao Llao for a stunning view of Lago Nahuel Huapi. The other continues on to the small coastal beaches of Villa Tacul (Tacul Village), where you can paddle in the lake or explore the ruins of what is thought to be an abandoned World War II bunker. Access the park by taking the Route 20 bus to the end of the line or driving along Avenida Ezequiel Bustillo until you reach the beginning of the Circuito Chico. ☒ *Av. Bustillo, Km 27.5.*

Paseo de los Duendes. Looking for a child-friendly excursion? The 1-km (½-mile) Paseo de los Duendes (Walk of the Gnomes) in Villa Los Coihues leads to a small but pretty waterfall. You can also hike onward for a view of the nearby Lago Gutiérrez or follow the 7½- km (4½-mile) trail to Playa Muñoz. Once a campground, this area is still regenerating, and while wide paths make it easy to navigate, it does not have the same impact as other hiking trails. ☒ *Perito Moreno, Villa Los Coihues, San Carlos de Bariloche*

HORSEBACK RIDING

Carol Jones. The granddaughter of an early pioneering family, Carol Jones's ranch north of town does day rides and overnights from the Patagonian steppes into the mountains. ☒ *Modesta Victoria 5600* ☎ *2944/426–508* ⊕ *www.caroljones.com.ar* ☛ *From 500 pesos (cash only), includes transfers/pick-up.*

El Manso. This outfitter combines riding and rafting over the border to Chile. ☒ *Av. Bustillo, Km 13.491, Bariloche* ☎ *2944/441–378* ⊕ *www. bastiondelmanso.com* ☛ *From 950 pesos, includes transfers/pick-up.*

Tom Wesley. Located at the Club Hípico Bariloche, Tom Wesley offers rides lasting from one hour to several days. ☒ *Av. Bustillo, Km 15.5* ☎ *2944/448–193* ⊕ *www.cabalgatastomwesley.com* ☛ *From 200 pesos (cash only)* ☉ *Daily 10–6. Closed May and June.*

SKIING

Cerro Catedral (*Mount Cathedral*). Named for its Gothic-looking spires, Cerro Catedral is the oldest ski area in South America, with 38 lifts, 1,820 hectares (4,500 acres) of mostly intermediate terrain, and a comfortable altitude of 2,050 meters (6,725 feet). The runs are long, varied, and scenic. One side of the mountain has a vertical drop of 914 meters (3,000 feet), mostly in the fall line. Near the top of the highest chairlift at 2,250 meters (7,385 feet) is Refugio Lynch, a small restaurant on the edge of an abyss with a stupendous 360-degree view of Nahuel Huapi Lake. To the southwest, Monte Tronadór, an extinct volcano straddling the border with Chile, towers above lesser peaks that surround the lake. Other on-site facilities include a terrain park and picturesque cross-country ski trails. ■ TIP➔ **August and September are the best months to hit the slopes; avoid the first three weeks of July (school vacation).**

Villa Catedral, at the base of the mountain, has numerous equipment retail and rental shops, information and ticket sales, ski-school offices, restaurants, and even a disco. Frequent buses transport skiers from Bariloche to the ski area. For information and trail maps, contact

La Secretaría de Turismo de Río Negro (✉ *Av. 12 de Octubre 605*
☏ *2944/429–896*). **Club Andino Bariloche** (✉ *Av. 20 de Febrero 30*
☏ *2944/422–266*) also has information and trail maps. ✉ *46 km (28½*
miles) west of Bariloche on R237; turn left at Km 8.5 just past Playa
Bonita ☏ *2944/409–000* 🌐 *www.catedralaltapatagonia.com* 🖰 *Day*
pass 585 pesos (high season) ⊙ *Daily 9–5 (depending on conditions).*

SAN MARTÍN DE LOS ANDES AND NEARBY

SAN MARTÍN DE LOS ANDES

260 km (161 miles) north of Bariloche on R237, R40, and R234 via
Junín de los Andes (a four-hour drive); 158 km (98 miles) north of Bari-
loche on R237 and R63 over the Córdoba Pass (less than half of which
is unpaved); 90 km (56 miles) northeast of Villa La Angostura on R234
(Ruta de los Siete Lagos, partly unpaved and closed for much of winter).

Surrounded by lakes, dense forests, and mountains, San Martín de los
Andes lies in a natural basin at the foot of Lago Lácar. It's a small, easy-
going town, much like Bariloche was many decades ago, with hotels and
houses reflecting the distinctive Andean alpine architecture of Bustillo.
Wide, flat streets lined with rosebushes run from the town pier on the
eastern shore of Lago Lácar to the main square, Plaza San Martín,
where two parallel streets—San Martín and General Villegas—teem
with block after block of ski and fishing shops, chocolatiers, souvenir
stores, clothing boutiques, and cafés.

The Mapuche lived in the area long before immigrants of Chilean,
French, Dutch, and Italian descent founded the town in 1898. Because
all of the water from this area runs into the Pacific, the territory was
disputed by Chile, which claimed it as its own until 1902, when it was
legally declared Argentine.

After Parque Nacional Lanín was established in 1937 and the ski area
at Chapelco developed in the 1970s, tourism replaced forestry as the
main source of income. Today San Martín is the major tourist center
in Neuquén Province—the midpoint in the Ruta de los Siete Lagos and
the gateway for exploring the Parque Nacional Lanín.

GETTING HERE AND AROUND

Aerolíneas Argentina and LAN make the two-hour flight from Buenos
Aires up to three times a day, but most people arrive from Bariloche
via Junín de los Andes or along the Ruta de los Siete Lagos. El Valle
buses make frequent daily trips between Bariloche and San Martín;
the first typically leaves at 6 am and the last at 6 pm. The picturesque
journey takes four hours with a brief stopover in Villa La Angostura.
The centrally located San Martín bus terminal is within walking distance of most hotels.

Being flat, the town is pleasant for pedestrians. To access nearby
beaches, hiking trails, or the ski area in winter, you need to rent a car,
join a tour, or be an energetic cyclist. Taxis are inexpensive, and remises
can be arranged through your hotel.

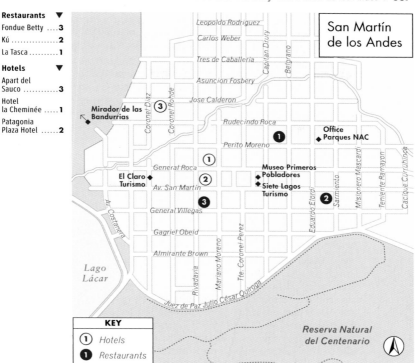

San Martín
de los Andes

KEY

① Hotels

❶ Restaurants

Lago
Lácar

Reserva Natural
del Centenario

Bus Contacts **El Valle** ☎ 0810/333–7575 ⊕ www.elvalle.com.ar. **San Martín de los Andes Bus Terminal** ✉ Villegas 251 ☎ 2972/427–044.

Remis Del Oscar ✉ Av. San Martín 1254 ☎ 2972/428–774.

ESSENTIALS

Visitor and Tour Information Dirección Municipal de Turismo ✉ J. M. Rosas 790, at Av. San Martín ☎ 2972/427–347 ⊕ www.sanmartindelosandes.gov.ar ☽ Daily 8 am–9 pm.

EXPLORING

Mirador de las Bandurrias (*Bandurrias Overlook*). From town you can hike, mountain bike, or drive 5 km (3 miles) up a steep hill through a dense forest of cypress and oak to the Mirador de las Bandurrias, where you'll be rewarded with a view of San Martín and the lake. The chance to visit **Paraje Trompul**—a Mapuche community that's home to about 40 families—is an added bonus. After taking a snack break in the *quincho* (café) and perusing the weavings and wood carvings sold here, you can continue another 5 km (3 miles) to see **Playa La Islita**, a small, rocky island in the middle of Lácar Lake.

If you're walking, take Avenida San Martín to the lake, turn right, cross the bridge behind the waterworks plant over Puahullo Creek, and then head uphill on a path around the mountain. By car, leave town on Ruta

Provincial 48 and drive about 4 km (2½ miles) to a turnoff (no sign) on your left. Take the turn and continue to Comunidad Mapuche Curruhuinca, where you pay a fee for the lookout. 🎟 *5–10 pesos.*

Museo Primeros Pobladores (*Pioneer Museum*). Next to the tourist office, this museum occupies the tiny building that served as the original city council lodge. It is mainly dedicated to Mapuche ceramics and weavings; a collection of 13,000-year-old tools and fossils gives an idea of ancient life in the region. ✉ *J. M. de Rosas 700* ☎ *2972/428–676* 🎟 *Free* 🕒 *Mon. 10–12:30, Wed.–Fri. 10–4, Sat. 10–8.*

BEACHES

FAMILY **Playa Catrite.** Easy access and a family-friendly atmosphere have made Playa Catrite one of the most popular beaches in San Martín. On the south side of Lago Lácar, 4 km (2½ miles) from the town center, it's a great spot to enjoy a dip in the calm, clear lake waters and admire the view of the Cerro Bandurrias. Oak trees provide shade for picnics, and water activities for children are available. A Mapuche-run campground is nearby. **Amenities:** food and drink; water sports. **Best for:** swimming; walking. ✉ *4 km (2½ miles) from San Martin on R234.*

Playa Quila Quina. Situated in a Mapuche village, this small lakeside beach is a tourist hotspot with ferries bringing visitors from San Martín five times a day. It's possible to arrive by car, but be prepared for a steep descent to the rocky beach. Although busy, Playa Quila Quina is perfect for swimming and enjoying the panoramic views of Lago Lácar. Not far from the shore, a trail leads to a small waterfall, Arroyo Grande. To reach Playa Quila Quina, turn off Ruta 234 2 km (1 mile) before the road to Catrite and get on Ruta 108. **Amenities:** food and drink; parking; toilets. **Best for:** swimming; walking. ✉ *18 km (11 miles) from San Martín on R108.*

WHERE TO EAT

$$ ARGENTINE FAMILY
🍴 **Fondue Betty.** It wouldn't be a ski town without a fondue restaurant, and this one is particularly appealing. The cheese fondue is smooth and rich, while the meat version comes with cubes of Argentine beef in assorted cuts and up to 12 condiments. Vegetable fondues are a bit limp. Steaks and pasta are also served, plus there's a fantastic wine list. The service is warm, and the restaurant's two rooms—adorned with wooden panels and rustic tables— are equally well suited to children and honeymooners. [$] *Average main: 70 pesos* ✉ *Villegas 586* ☎ *2972/422–522* 💳 *No credit cards* 🕒 *Daily 7:30 pm–11 pm. Closed May.*

$$$ ARGENTINE Fodor's Choice ★
🍴 **Kú.** Cozy dark-wood tables and booths, a friendly staff, a chalkboard listing tempting special—these are good building blocks for a restaurant. Order the smoked-meat plate with venison, boar, trout, salmon, and cheese as a starter; then try the Patagonian lamb *al asador* (on the open fire). Assorted parrilla classics are paired with a fine wine list. **TIP→ Kú has a second location on Ruta 234, just outside of town.** [$] *Average main: 100 pesos* ✉ *Av. San Martín 1053* ☎ *2972/427–039* 🌐 *www.kudelosandes.com.ar* ✍ *Reservations essential.*

$$$ ARGENTINE
🍴 **La Tasca.** This is one of the traditional high-end choices in town for locals and tourists alike. With tables scattered about the blackstone floor, and wine barrels, shelves, and every other imaginable

surface stacked with pickled vegetables, smoked meats, cheese rounds, dried herbs, olive oils, and wine bottles, you might think you're in a Patagonian deli. Diners should try local wild game dishes; the "La Tasca" appetizer platter of smoked salmon, venison, boar, and trout pâté is especially good. $ *Average main: 100 pesos* ✉ *Moreno 886* ☎ *2972/428–663* ✍ *Reservations essential.*

WHERE TO STAY

$$
RENTAL

🏠 **Apart del Sauco.** Accommodating up to eight guests, these clean, well-equipped apartments are a practical option for families and for any travelers considering longer stays. **Pros:** comfortable; full kitchen; basic hotel services. **Cons:** bland décor; little ambience. $ *Rooms from: US$160* ✉ *Calderón 364* ⊕ *www.apartdelsauco.com.ar/en/index.htm* ↘ *15 rooms* ⓘⓄ *Breakfast.*

$$$
HOTEL
Fodor's Choice
★

🏠 **Hotel la Cheminée.** Two blocks from the main street, this comfortable inn has finely carved wooden staircases, a small art gallery, and warm, familiar service; all rooms have been renovated and turned into suites. **Pros:** great breakfast; convenient location; attentive service. **Cons:** on a somewhat busy street. $ *Rooms from: US$240* ✉ *M. Moreno at General Roca* ☎ *2972/427–617* ⊕ *www.lachemineehotel.com* ↘ *11 suites* ⓘⓄ *Breakfast.*

$$
HOTEL

🏠 **Patagonia Plaza Hotel.** Good-bye genteel rusticity, hello modern downtown hotel with all the amenities. **Pros:** central location; big rooms with modern bathrooms. **Cons:** atmosphere deficient in restaurant. $ *Rooms from: US$125* ✉ *Av. San Martín at Rivadavia* ☎ *2972/422–280* ⊕ *www. hotelpatagoniaplaza.com.ar* ↘ *90 rooms* ⓘⓄ *Breakfast.*

SPORTS AND THE OUTDOORS

Tour agencies can arrange rafting trips on the Hua Hum or Aluminé rivers, guided mountain biking, horseback riding, and fishing tours, plus excursions to lakes in both Lanín and Nahuel Huapi national parks.

El Refugio. Active travelers can join this full service tour company and travel agency for rafting, trekking, mountain biking, fly-fishing, and skiing excursions. Overland road tours are available for the less intrepid. El Refugio can also book accommodations. ✉ *Villegas 698* ☎ *2972/425–140* ⊕ *www.elrefugioturismo.com.ar* ✉ *From 350 pesos* ☉ *Daily 9–1 and 5–11.*

BOATING

Lacar Nonthue. You can rent small boats, canoes, and kayaks at the pier from Lacar Nonthue. You can also rent a bicycle and take an all-day excursion to the other side of Lago Lácar, where there is a nice beach and woods to explore. Another option is the boat tour to Hua Hum at the western end of the lake, where the river of the same name runs to the Chilean border. ✉ *Av. Costanera* ☎ *2972/427–380.*

FISHING

During the fishing season (November 15–April 15, extended to the end of May in certain areas) local guides will take you to their favorite spots on lagos Lácar, Lolog, Villarino, and Falkner and on the ríos Caleufu, Quiquihue, Malleo, and Hermoso, or farther afield to the Chimehuín River and Lakes Huechulafquen and Paimún.

Intendencia de Parque Nacional Lanin. Permits for fishing are available at the Lanín National Park Office or any licensed fishing store along Avenida San Martín. Most stores and tour operators can suggest guides. ✉ *Emilio Frey 749* ☎ *2972/420–664* ⊕ *www.parquenacionallanin.gov.ar.*

Jorge Cardillo. Since opening his small Fly Shop in 1994, this well-known local guide has gained a reputation for his friendly, familial fishing trips to nearby rivers like Meliquina, Filo Hua-Hum, and Caleufu. ✉ *Villegas 1061, behind the casino* ☎ *2972/428–372* ⊕ *www.jorgecardillo.com.*

HORSEBACK RIDING

Cabalgatas Abuelo Enrique. These folks offer rides with a guide for two hours or all day, asado included. To get there, take Avenida Dr. Koessler (R234) toward Zapala, turn left at the polo field, and head toward Lago Lolog, then take a right past the military barracks to Callejón Ginsgins. ✉ *Callejón Ginsgins, Campo 9* ☎ *2972/426–465* 🍴 *From 300 pesos* 🕙 *Tours at 10 and 3:30. Closed Sun.* ☞ *Reservations required.*

MOUNTAIN BIKING

HG Rodados. San Martín itself is flat, but from there everything goes up. Dirt and paved roads and trails lead through forests to lakes and waterfalls. You can rent bikes in town at HG Rodados. ✉ *Av. San Martín 1061* ☎ *2972/427–345* 🍴 *From 70 pesos per day* 🕙 *Daily 9–noon and 4–8:30.*

SKIING

Cerro Chapelco (*Chapelco Ski Resort*). The Chapelco Ski Resort is ideal for families and beginner-to-intermediate skiers. It has modern facilities and lifts, including a high-speed *telecabina* (gondola) from the base. On a clear day almost all the runs are visible from the top—a height of 1,991 meters (6,534 feet)—and Lanín Volcano dominates the horizon. Lift tickets cost from 165 pesos per day in low season to 285 pesos in high season. Equipment rental facilities are available at the base camp (130–270 pesos per day for skis, boots, and poles). On some days cars need chains to get up to the mountain, so call and check the latest conditions before driving up. Taxis can also take you up or down for about 45 pesos each way. ■TIP➡ In summer, the Adventure Center has mountain biking for experts and classes for beginners, plus horseback rides, hiking, archery, a swimming pool, an alpine slide, and children's activities. ✉ *Information Office, San Martín at Elordi, 23 km (14 miles) southeast of San Martín de los Andes* ☎ *2972/427–845* ⊕ *www.cerrochapelco.com* ☞ *5 km (3 miles) of the road is unpaved.*

WHITE-WATER RAFTING

El Claro Turismo. Offering both short and long trips in the area, El Claro Turismo is a good rafting choice. ✉ *Col. Diaz 751* ☎ *2972/428–876, 2972/425–876* ⊕ *www.elclaroturismo.com.ar* 🍴 *From 200 pesos.*

Siete Lagos Turismo. An all-day rafting trip that crosses into Chile on either Río Aluminé or Río Hua Hum can be arranged by Siete Lagos Turismo. Owner Fernando Aguirre, a lifelong resident of the area, also offers two- to four-day camping trips with combinations of rafting, hiking, riding, biking, and kayaking. ✉ *Villegas 313* ☎ *2972/427–877* ⊕ *www.sietelagosturismo.com.ar* 🍴 *From 450 pesos* 🕙 *Daily 9–1 and 4–8:30.*

PARQUE NACIONAL LANÍN

The dramatically beautiful Parque Nacional Lanín contains 35 mountain lakes, countless rivers, ancient forests, and the Volcán Lanín. Tucked into the folds of the Andes along the Chilean border, it stretches 150 km (93 miles) north to south, covering 4,120 square km (1,590 square miles). The area is home to the Mapuche, and you can learn about their history and buy their handicrafts in one of the 50 communities throughout the park.

GETTING HERE AND AROUND

Three towns have access to the park. The northernmost section is reached from Aluminé: 145 km (90 miles) west of Zapala on Ruta Provincial 46, it's a typical Andean community with no paved streets but an abundance of nearby lakes (including Aluminé, Quillén, and Mohquehue). Junín de los Andes, in the middle section, is at the end of the paved road from Bariloche. Another paved road leads 41 km (25 miles) to San Martín, the park's major town, in the southern section. Daily buses run from San Martín and Junín to Lago Huechulafquen and Volcán Lanín; however, service can be unreliable and timetables change depending on the season. In Aluminé, public transport is largely nonexistent, so cars or remises are the only option. Note that all three of these towns have roads leading to the border with Chile *(See Chilean Lakes Crossing box)*.

ESSENTIALS

Intendencia de Parques Nacionales (*National Park Office*). For information on the park, go to the Intendencia de Parques Nacionales in San Martín. The office has maps and information on all the parks and trails in the region, as well as fishing permits. ⊠ *Emilio Frey 749, San Martín de los Andes* ☏ *2972/427–233* ⊕ *www.parquesnacionales.gob. ar* ⊗ *Weekdays 8–1:30.*

EXPLORING

Araucaria Araucana. Found only in this part of the Andes, the ancient Araucaria Araucana tree grows to 30 meters (100 feet) and has long spiny branches. Cones the size of bowling balls are full of piñon nuts that provided nourishment to the Mapuche, who call these trees *pehuenes*. The northern portion of the park near Lago Huechulafquen and Aluminé is one of the best places to view these peculiar giants. ⊠ *Lago Huechulafquen.*

Volcán Lanín. Rising 3,773 meters (12,378 feet) in solitary snow-clad splendor on the western horizon, Volcán Lanín towers over the area and is visible from every direction. It sits on the Chilean border, with Parque Nacional Lanín on one side and Chile's Parque Nacional Villarica on the other. The closest Argentine access is from Junín, but the northern route to Paso Tromen also offers endless photo ops through the tangled branches of the araucaria trees. You can climb Lanín in three to four days round-trip with a guide or, November through April, fly over it with **Aero Club de Los Andes** (⊠ *Chapelco in San Martín de los Andes* ☏ *2972/426–254*). ⊕ *www.parquenacionallanin.gov.ar* ⊠ *Flights 1,500 pesos.*

7

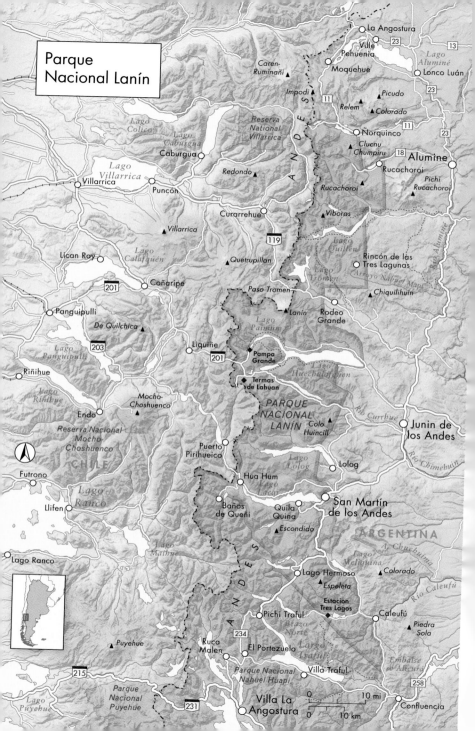

Parque Nacional Lanín

La Angostura
Ville Pehuenia
Moquehue
Lago Aluminé
Lonco Luán
23
13
23
11
Caren-Rumiñañi
Impodi
Picudo
Relem
Colorado
11
Ñorquinco
Clucnu Chumpiru
18
Aluminé
23
Reserva Nacional Villarrica
Rucachoroi
Pichi Rucachoroi
Lago Colico
Lago Caburgua
Caburgua
Redondo
Rucachoroi
Lago Villarrica
Villarrica
Puncón
Villarrica
Viboras
Curarrehue
119
Lago Quillén
Rincón de las Tres Lagunas
Lican Ray
Lago Calafquén
Quetrupillan
Arroyo Ñahuel Mapi
Río Aluminé
Lago Tromen
Chiquilihuín
Coñaripe
201
Paso Tromen
Lanín
Rodeo Grande
Panguipulli
De Quilchica
Lago Paimún
203
Liquiñe
201
Pampa Grande
Lago Huechulafquen
Lago Panguipulli
Riñihue
Termas de Lahuan
Lago Riñihue
Mocho-Choshuenco
Río Currhué
Junín de los Andes
Endo
PARQUE NACIONAL LANÍN
Colo Huincill
Reserva Nacional Mocho-Choshuenco
Río Chimehuín
Futrono
CHILE
Puerto Pirihueico
Lago Lolog
Lolog
Lago Ranco
Llifen
Húa Hum
Lago Lácar
San Martín de los Andes
ARGENTINA
Baños de Queñi
Quila Quina
Escondido
A. Chachuma
Lago Maihue
Lago Meliquina
Colorado
Lago Ranco
Lago Hermoso
Espeleta
Puyehue
Estación Tres Lagos
Caleufú
Río Caleufú
Piedra Sola
Ruca Malen
234
Pichi Traful
Brazo Norte
Lago Traful
El Portezuelo
Parque Nacional Nahuel Huapi
Villa Traful
258
Embalse o Alicurá
215
231
Parque Nacional Puyehue
Puyehue
Villa La Angostura
Confluencia
Lago Puyehue

0 10 mi
0 10 km

SPORTS AND THE OUTDOORS

BOATING

You'll only find piers or marinas at designated resorts. At Puerto Canoa on Lago Huechulafquen a catamaran takes about 50 passengers on a three-hour excursion to Lago Epulafquen, where you can view huge deposits of lava covered with vegetation at the end of the lake. The culprit, a large volcano minus its cone, looms in the distance. The fishing lodge at Lago Paimún has a dock, and in Villa Pehuenia you can rent boats and kayaks. It's best to organize an excursion at the dock (arrive early) or through a tour operator.

FISHING

Professional fishing guides operating in the park have their favorite fishing spots, and they offer excursions by the day or week. To contact a guide, go to ⊕ *www.neuquentur.gov.ar*. Fishing lodges lie concealed along the Chimihín River near Junín de los Andes and deeper into the lakes at Paimún. Smaller rivers such as the Malleo, Quillén, Meliquina, and Hua Hum are ideal for wading. In larger rivers like the Aluminé, Chimihuín, and Caleufu, guides provide rubber float boats.

HIKING

Besides climbing the Lanín Volcano, trails throughout the park wind around lakes and streams, mostly at lower elevations. Signs are intermittent, so hiking with a guide is recommended. The best hikes are out of Lago Paimún to a waterfall, Lago Quillén near Aluminé, and Lácar near San Martín. For information, check out ⊕ *www.sendasybosques. com.ar*.

RAFTING

You can run the Caleufu River October through November, and then move on to the Hua Hum December through March. Both are Class II rivers. *Aluminé* in the Mapuche language means "clear," and this wide river in the northern section of the park provides a thrilling descent through dense vegetation and a deep canyon.

VILLA TRAFUL

60 km (37 miles) north of Villa La Angostura on R231 and R65; 39 km (23 miles) from Confluencia on R65; 100 km (60 miles) northwest of Bariloche on R237 and R65.

If there were a prize for the most beautiful lake in the region, Lago Traful would win for its clarity, serenity, and wild surroundings. Small log houses peek through the cypress forest along the way to Villa Traful, a village of about 500 inhabitants.

The tiny community consists of log cabins, horse corrals, shops for picnic and fishing supplies, a school, a post office, and a park ranger's office. Well-maintained campgrounds border the lake, and ranches and private fishing lodges are hidden in the surrounding mountains. By day swimmers play on rocky beaches, kayakers cut the still blue water, and divers go below to explore the mysteries of a submerged forest. Night brings silence, stars, and the glow of lakeside campfires.

Continued on page 350

FLY FISHING

Chile and Argentina are the final frontier of fly fishing. With so many unexplored rivers, lakes, and spring creeks—most of which are un-dammed and free flowing to the ocean—every type of fishing is avail-able for all levels of experience. You'll find many species of fish, including rainbow trout, browns, sea-run browns, brooks, sea trout, and steelhead.

Above: Flyfishing in Torres del Paine National Park, Patagonia, Chile

The Southern Cone has endless—and endlessly evolving—rivers, streams, and lakes, which is why they're so good for fly fishing. These waterways formed millions of years ago, as volcanic eruptions and receding glaciers carved out the paths for riverbeds and lakes that feed into the Pacific or Atlantic Oceans. With more than 2,006 volcanoes in Chile alone (including South America's most active mountain, Volcano Llaima, outside of Temuco), the Lake Districts of both countries are still evolving, creating raw and pristine fishing grounds.

Why choose Chile or Argentina for your next fly fishing adventure? If you're only after huge fish, stick to California. What these two South American countries offer is a chance to combine fishing, culture, and food in a unique package during the northern hemisphere's off season. With the right guide, you just might find yourself two hours down a dirt road, fishing turquoise water in the shadow of a glacial peak, with not a soul in sight but the occasional gaucho or huaso. It's an experience you will find nowhere else.

WHAT TO EXPECT ON THE GROUND

Fishing, Chile

LOGISTICS

You'll probably fly into Bariloche, Argentina, or Puerto Montt, Chile. You won't need more than two weeks for a good trip, and hiring a guide can make a big difference in the quality of your experience. Since most rivers are un-dammed, you'll need the extra help managing your drift boat or locating foot access for wading that stream you've spotted around the bend.

GUIDES VS. LODGES

You can purchase your trip package through either an independent guide or a specific lodge property. In both cases, packages usually last one week to 10 days, and include breakfast, lunch, and dinner. If you opt to purchase through a lodge, you have the benefit of property-specific guides who know every nook and cranny of stream surrounding the lodge. On the other hand, hiring an independent guide will give you more power to customize your trip and go farther afield.

TIMING

Contact your guide or lodge in October or November, during the southern hemisphere's spring; the upcoming season's peak fishing times depend on snow melt. Plan on traveling in February or March.

CHOOSING YOUR GUIDE

What type of fishing suits you best? Do you like to fish from a boat, or do you prefer wading the river as it rushes by? Ask guides these questions to find the best one for you.

WHAT TO ASK A GUIDE

- How early do you start in the morning?
- Do you mainly spin cast or fly fish?
- How long have you been in business?
- Do you always catch and release?
- Will I fish with you or another guide?
- Can I see pictures of your raft or drift boat?
- Do you supply the flies?
- Where do you get your flies?
- Can we fish a river twice if we like it?
- Which rivers and lakes do you float?
- Can we set an itinerary before I arrive?

WHAT TO BRING

5 to 7 Weight Rod: at least 9 foot (consider bringing 9½ foot for larger rivers, windy days, lakes, and sink-tip streamer fishing).

Floating Lines: for dry fly fishing and nymphing.

Streamers: for use while wading to or from the drift boat.

Lines: 15 to 20 foot sink-tip lines with a sink rate of 5.5 to 8 inches per second. It's good to carry two to four different sink rate lines.

Intermediate sink lines: for lakes and shallow depth fishing.

Line Cleaner: because low-ozone areas (the hole in the ozone is close to Antarctica) will eat up lines if you don't treat and clean the lines daily.

Hook sharpener: most guides don't have this very important item.

Small gifts: for the people you meet. Gift-giving can help you gain access to private rivers and lakes. Chocolates, such as Hershey Kisses, or some unique fly pattern, such as a dragon fly, always go over well.

Good map: Turistel, in Chile, puts out the best maps and internal information for that country (⊕ www.turistel.com). Check Argentina Tourism (⊕ www.turismo.gov.ar) for help with that country.

Coffee: Chile has Nescafé instant coffee just about everywhere you go. So if you like a good cup of joe, bring a filter and your favorite coffee. That way all you need is a cup and hot water, and you're all set for your morning fishing.

FLIES

■ Ask your guide where he or she gets flies. Those bought at a discount in countries outside of the United States are often sub-par, so get good guidance on this.

■ If you can, get a list of flies for the time of year you're scheduled to arrive and buy them in the United States before you go. Pay particular attention to the size as well type of insect.

■ The big fish and the quality catches are fooled by the flies that are tied by the guides

themselves, because the guides know the hatches and the times they occur.

■ Flies are divided up into similar categories in Chile and Argentina since South America has many of the same insects as we do in North America. Check and see what time each insect is hatching. Note their sizes and colors. **You'll need both dry and nymph versions of the following, in a variety of sizes, colors, and patterns:**

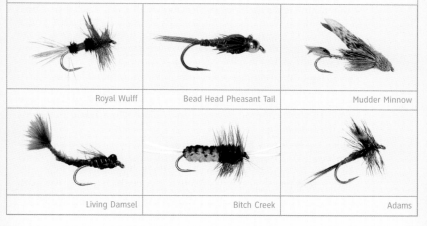

| Royal Wulff | Bead Head Pheasant Tail | Mudder Minnow |
| Living Damsel | Bitch Creek | Adams |

GETTING HERE AND AROUND

On the Ruta de los Siete Lagos, Villa Traful can be reached by bus from Bariloche, San Martín, and Villa la Angostura (the nearest town); bus operators include Via Bariloche. Otherwise you can come by car or with a tour group. The waterside hamlet is contained within a single circuit, and most stores are in walking distance of the pier.

Bus Contacts Via Bariloche ✉ *Villa Traful, Neuquén* ☎ *2944/432–444* 🌐 *www.viabariloche.com.ar.*

ESSENTIALS

Visitor Information Oficina Municipal de Turismo ✉ *Across from municipal pier, RP65* ☎ *2944/479–099* 🌐 *www.villatraful.gov.ar.*

WHERE TO STAY

$$ RENTAL 🏠 **Cabañas Ruca Lico.** Intimate Ruca Lico hits the sweet spot between ranch and resort; the quaint, rustic interiors are very cozy, and you can admire views of Lago Traful from a private balcony or hot tub. **Pros:** close to lake, trails, and town center; self-catering facilities; price includes airport transfers. **Cons:** limited services. [$] *Rooms from: US$145* ✉ *RP65, Km 35, Villa Traful, Río Negro* ☎ *2944/479–004* 🌐 *www.interpatagonia.com/rucalico* 🛏 *1 house, 1 cabin, 1 loft* 🍴 *No meals.*

SPORTS AND THE OUTDOORS

HIKING

Arroyo Blanco and Arroyo Coa Có. Drive, walk, or pedal about 3 km (2 miles) up from the village to the trailhead at Pampa de los Alamos, a clearing where the trail to Arroyo Blanco descends into a forest of 1,000-year-old coihué trees with ghostly naked trunks, gigantic *lenga* (deciduous beech), and ñires that grow only at high altitudes. The trail leads to a wooden walkway along a steep cliff—the only way one could possibly view the waterfall tumbling 20 meters (66 feet) into a dark chasm. Follow the wooden trail along the cliff for increasingly amazing glimpses of this wild gorge, then return up the same route. Arroyo Coa Có is in the opposite direction, with a view of both the waterfall and Lago Traful.

Casacada Co Lemú. At the end of an arduous trail, the Casacada Co Lemú thunders down 20 meters (67 feet) with a deafening roar. Drive 8 km (5 miles) west toward the Ruta de los Siete Lagos to the bridge over Arroyo Cataratas. Before you cross the stream, on your left, the trail—covering 19 km (12 miles), round-trip—climbs slowly at first, then straight up to the falls.

Cerro Negro. A strenuous seven-hour hike from the village to Cerro Negro climbs up through forests of cypress, coihué, lenga, and ñire, passing strange rock formations en route to the top. The summit (1,829 meters [6,000 feet]) promises a splendid view of Lago Traful and across the Andes all the way to Lanín.

Laguna Las Mellizas y Pinturas Rupestres (*The Twins Lagoon and Cave paintings*). A 15-minute boat trip across the lake from the wharf takes you to a sandy beach on the northern shore. A two-hour walk down a trail into a steep gully leads to the pools. Nearby caves with

Lanín Volcano, an ice-clad, cone-shaped stratovolcano, in Parque Nacional Lanín

600-year-old Tehuelche cave paintings are worth exploring. The area is protected and registration with national park officials is required.

SCUBA DIVING

Bosque Sumergido. In 1975 a violent earthquake caused half a mountain and its forest of cypress trees to slide to the bottom of the lake, creating the Bosque Sumergido. You can dive to 30 meters (98 feet) in crystal-line water and explore this sunken forest. Boat trips can be arranged at **Cabañas Aiken** (☎ 2944/479–048 ⊕ *www.aiken.com.ar*).

VILLA LA ANGOSTURA

81 km (50 miles) northwest of Bariloche (an hour's drive on R231 around the east end of Lago Nahuel Huapi; also accessible by boat from Bariloche); 90 km (56 miles) southwest of San Martín de los Andes on R234 (the Ruta de los Siete Lagos, partly unpaved and closed for much of winter).

Sitting on a narrow *angostura* (isthmus) on the northern shore of Lake Nahuel Huapi, Villa La Angostura was once a mere hamlet. But, having benefited from thoughtful planning and strict adherence to business codes, it's now the second most popular tourist area in the Lake District. Its first hotel was built in 1923, 10 years before the town was founded, and today some of the most luxurious accommodations in Patagonia look out on the lake from discreet hiding places along its wooded shores.

Shops and restaurants line the Avenida Arrayanes, where you can stop for homemade ice cream or cakes while window-shopping in the three-block-long commercial zone. The tourist office and municipal buildings are at El Cruce (the Crossroads), where Ruta 231 from Bariloche to the Chilean border intersects with the road to the port and the Ruta de los Siete Lagos (Ruta 234) to San Martín de los Andes.

GETTING HERE AND AROUND

Fast and frequent El Valle buses make the two-hour trip from Bariloche at least six times a day; however, you'll want a car to get around the environs, which are creeping slowly from Lago Correntoso to Puerto Manzano.

Bus Contacts El Valle ☎ 0810/333-7575 ⊕ www.elvalle.com.ar. **Villa La Angostura Bus Terminal** ⊠ Av. 7 Lagos 3 ☎ 294/494-961.

ESSENTIALS

Visitor and Tour Information Secretaría de Turismo y Cultura ⊠ Av. Arrayanes 9 ☎ 2944/494-124 ⊕ www.villalaangosturaturismo.blogspot.com.

WHERE TO EAT

$$
ARGENTINE
✕ **Australis.** This is one of the best microbreweries in Patagonia. The excellent cuisine integrates beer all the way through to dessert—a memorable flan is made with chocolate and a delicious stout. ■TIP→ The restaurant will cook up your own fresh-caught fish if you bring it in. $ *Average main: 90 pesos* ⊠ *R231, Km 60, Av. Arrayanes 2490* ☎ *2944/495-645* ⊕ *www.cerveceriaaustralis.com.ar* ▭ *No credit cards* ⊗ *Closed May and June.*

$
ARGENTINE
✕ **La Casita de la Oma.** Between the bay and the main street, this teahouse, with its award-winning garden, serves homemade cakes, pies, and scones. Moist chocolate brownie cake with dulce de leche is a winner, as is a pile of filo leaves with dulce de leche and meringue on top. Jars of jam line the shelves. $ *Average main: 35 pesos* ⊠ *Cerro Inacayal 303* ☎ *2944/494-602* ⊗ *Daily 4–6. Closed Easter–July.*

WHERE TO STAY

$$$
HOTEL
FAMILY
⊡ **Costa Serena.** Every room at this complex in Puerto Manzano has a lake view; A-frame *cabañas* (cabins) with decks, kitchens, and outdoor barbecues sleep up to seven, while suites have huge wooden Jacuzzis with views to the water. **Pros:** good family reunion spot. **Cons:** far from town and tourist attractions. $ *Rooms from: US$225* ⊠ *Los Pinos 435, Puerto Manzano* ☎ *2944/475-203* ⊕ *www.costaserenavla.com.ar* ⤒ *7 rooms, 4 cabins* ⑩ *Breakfast.*

$$
HOTEL
Fodor'sChoice
★
⊡ **Hotel Correntoso.** Perched on a hill where the Correntoso River runs into Nahuel Huapi Lake, this landmark hotel celebrates its place in history with old photos, light fixtures made from colihue branches, hand-woven Mapuche fabrics, and custom furniture. **Pros:** great location, food, and spa facilities; well-organized excursions; the bar often has live music. **Cons:** expensive. $ *Rooms from: US$175* ⊠ *RN231, Km 86, Puente Correntoso* ☎ *2944/15–619–728, 11/4803–0030 in Buenos Aires* ⊕ *www.correntoso.com* ⤒ *49 rooms* ⑩ *Breakfast.*

$$
HOTEL
Fodor'sChoice
★
⊡ **Puerto Sur.** Stone and wood merge throughout the angular space of this hillside hotel in Puerto Manzano, which has views of the lake and mountains from enormous windows; every room also has a lake view, as well as a Jacuzzi and restrained modern art. **Pros:** quiet,

secluded spot. **Cons:** far from town and tourist activities. $ *Rooms from: US$180* ⊠ *Los Pinos 221, Puerto Manzano* ☎ *2944/475–399* ⊕ *www.hosteriapuertosur.com.ar* ⊙ *Closed mid-May–June 30* ⤳ *14 rooms* ⦿| *Breakfast.*

SHOPPING

En El Bosque. Follow your nose to En El Bosque, where the scent of delicious artisanal sweets wafts out onto the sidewalk. It ranks among the best of the many chocolate shops here. ⊠ *Av. Arrayanes 218* ☎ *2944/495–738.*

SPORTS AND THE OUTDOORS

Visitors will be delighted at how well the region has recovered following the 2011 eruption of the Puyehue volcano, just across the Chilean border from Villa La Angostura. Most restaurants, hotels, and tour operators have reopened after the clean-up effort; a trip to the Secretaría de Turismo y Cultura will give you a good overview of the many outdoor activities available.

BOATING

Patagonia Infinita. Full- and half-day kayaking tours of the Nahuel Huapi, Correntoso, and Espejo lakes are organized by Patagonia Infinita. Lunch is included in full-day trips, and snorkeling is available in summer. ⊠ *Arrayanes 204* ⊕ *www.patagoniainfinita.com* ⊠ *From 400 pesos.*

HORSEBACK RIDING

Cabalgatas Montahue. Short- and long-distance riding adventures can be arranged through Cabalgatas Montahue. Opt for a two-hour trip to the Lake Correntoso lookout point or a four-day excursion to Villa Traful. ⊠ *Av. 7 Lagos 402* ☎ *154–511–345* ⊕ *www.cabalgatasmontahue.com. ar* ⊠ *From 200 pesos* ⊙ *Daily 11 am–sunset.*

MOUNTAIN BIKING

Alquiles Rental & Outdoors. Mountain bikes can be rented by the day from Alquiles Rental & Outdoors. You can easily ride from the village to Laguna Verde, near the port, or off the Ruta de los Siete Lagos to Mirador Belvedere and on to the waterfalls at Inacayal. Kayaks and ski gear are also available. ⊠ *Av. Arrayanes 96* ⊕ *www.aquilesrental.com. ar/mountain.html* ⊠ *From 50 pesos.*

PARQUE NACIONAL NAHUEL HUAPI

Created in 1934, Parque Nacional Nahuel Huapi is the oldest national park in Argentina. It's also one of the largest, encompassing more than 7,050 square km (2,720 square miles) along the eastern side of the Andes in the provinces of Neuquén and Río Negro, on the frontier with Chile. Since much of the park is covered by lakes—Lago Nahuel Huapi being the most sizable one—some of your exploration will be by boat to islands, down narrow fjords, or to distant shores on organized excursions. Multiple hiking trails also wind through the park, leading visitors from the thick undergrowth to open lakeside beaches. Nearby destinations such as the Circuito Chico, Circuito Grande, Tronadór, or the ski area at Catedral can be done in a day.

GETTING AROUND

The easy way to get around is to rent a car, hire a remis, or sign on with a local tour operator. When planning all-day or overnight trips, remember that distances are long and unpaved roads slow you down.

ESSENTIALS

Visitor Information Intendencia del Parque Nacional Nahuel Huapi
✉ *Av. San Martín 24, at the Centro Cívico, Bariloche* ☎ *2944/423–111* ⊕ *www. nahuelhuapi.gov.ar* ☉ *Park Office weekdays 8–4.*

EXPLORING

Parque Nacional Nahuel Huapi. This national park is notable for having the highest concentration of lakes in Argentina. The largest of them, Lago Nahuel Huapi, covers 897 square km (346 square miles) and has seven arms—the longest of which is 96 km (60 miles) long and 12 km (7 miles) wide—reaching deep into forests of coihue (a native beech), cypress, and lenga (deciduous beech) trees. Intensely blue across its vast expanse and aqua green in its shallow bays, the lake meanders into distant lagoons and misty inlets where the mountains, covered with vegetation at their base, rise straight up out of the water.

Inside the park, nearly every water sport invented can be arranged through local travel agencies, tour offices, or hotels. Boating is particularly popular, with options ranging from a placid Isla Victoria outing to challenging white-water-rafting adventures. Information offices throughout the park can also offer tips about tackling the miles of mountain and woodland trails. Small towns like Villa La Angostura and Villa Traful are excellent destinations for further explorations on foot or horseback. Since most of the park is at a low elevation (under 1,829 meters or 6,000 feet), getting around in winter is not difficult—just cold. Fall foliage, long, warm summer days, and spring flowers are the rewards of other seasons. ✉ *Av. San Martín 24, San Carlos de Bariloche* ☎ *2944/423–111, 2944/423–121* ⊕ *www.nahuelhuapi.gov. ar* ☜ *12 pesos* ☉ *Park Office weekdays 8–4.*

Isla Victoria. The most popular excursion on Lago Nahuel Huapi is the 30-minute boat ride from Puerto Pañuelo on the Península Llao Llao to Isla Victoria, the largest island in the lake. A grove of redwoods transplanted from California thrives in the middle of it. Walk on trails that lead to enchanting views of emerald bays and still lagoons; then board the boat to sail on to the Parque Nacional los Arrayanes. Boats go daily at 10 am and 2 pm (more frequently in high season). The earlier departure includes time for lunch on the island in a cafeteria-style restaurant. The later departure is a shorter trip. Vessels are run by **Cau Cau** (✉ *Mitre 139, Bariloche* ☎ *2944/431–372* ⊕ *www.islavictoriayarrayanes.com*) and **Turisur** (✉ *Mitre 219, Bariloche* ☎ *2944/426–109* ⊕ *www.turisur.com.ar*). ✉ *Nahuel Huapi National Park.*

Monte Tronadór (*Thunder Mountain*). A visit to Monte Tronadór requires an all-day outing, covering 170 km (105 miles) round-trip from Bariloche. This 3,658-meter (12,000-foot) extinct volcano—the highest mountain in the northern Lake District—straddles the frontier with Chile, with one peak on either side. Take Ruta 258 south along the

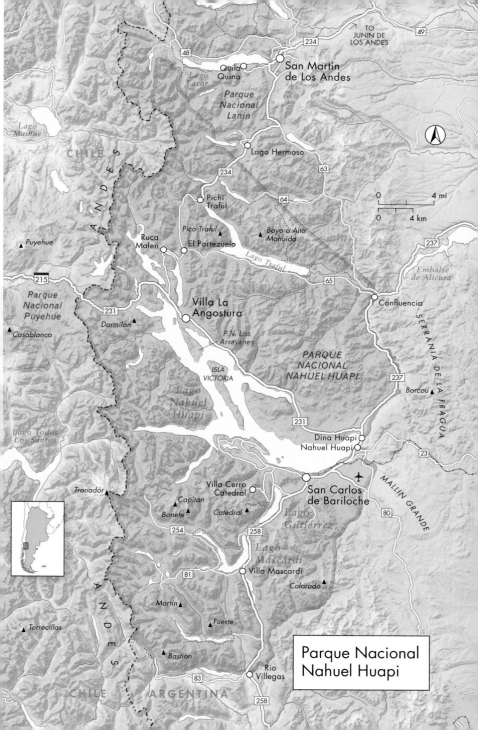

Parque Nacional
Nahuel Huapi

shores of Lago Gutiérrez and Lago Mascardi. Between the two lakes the road crosses from the Atlantic to the Pacific watershed. At Km 35, turn off onto a road marked "Tronadór" and "Pampa Linda" and continue along the shore of Lago Mascardi, passing a village of the same name. Just beyond the village the road forks, and you continue on a gravel road, Ruta 254. Near the bridge the road branches left to Lago Hess and Cascada Los Alerces—a detour you might want to take on your way out.

As you bear right after crossing Los Rápidos Bridge, the road narrows: note that it's one-way heading up from 10:30 am–2 pm, one-way heading down from 4 pm–7:30 pm, and two-way from 7:30 pm–10:30 am only. The lake ends in a narrow arm (Brazo Tronadór) at the Hotel Tronadór, which has a dock for tours arriving by boat. The road then follows the Río Manso to Pampa Linda, which has a lodge, restaurant, park ranger's office, campsites, and the trailhead for the climb up to the Refugio Otto Meiling at the snow line. Guided horseback rides are organized at the lodge. The road ends 7 km (4½ miles) beyond Pampa Linda in a parking lot that was once at the tip of the receding Glaciar Negro (Black Glacier). As the glacier flows down from the mountain, the dirt and black sediment of its lateral moraines are ground up and cover the ice. At first glance it's hard to imagine the tons of ice that lie beneath its black cap.

Parque Nacional los Arrayanes. Lago Nahuel Huapi's entire Quetrihue Peninsula, with its unique forest of *arrayanes* (myrtle trees), is protected by the Parque Nacional los Arrayanes. These trees absorb so much water through their thin skins that all other vegetation around them dies, leaving a barren forest of peeling cinnamon-color trunks. A stroll up and down wide wooden steps and walkways is a memorable experience, as light filters through the twisted naked trunks, reflecting a weird red glow. You can make this excursion from the pier at Bahía Brava in Villa La Angostura (or by boat from Bariloche via Isla Victoria). In summer, you can walk (three hours) or cycle, after registering at the *guardaparque* (ranger station) near the pier. ■TIP→ Leave in the morning, as the park entrance closes at 2 pm. A nice combination is to go by boat and return by bike (it's all downhill that way). If returning by boat, buy your return ticket at the pier before you leave. ⊠ *12 km (7½ miles) along a trail from the Península Quetrihué* ☎ *2944/423–111* ⊕ *www.parquesnacionales.gob.ar.*

WHERE TO STAY

$$$$ 🏨 **Isla Victoria Lodge.** Poised dramatically on a cliff overlooking the lake
RESORT   and forests, this classic stone-and-wood lodge enjoys one of the most beautiful settings on earth. **Pros:** facilities include a heated outdoor pool and hiking trails; rates cover meals, alcoholic drinks, and on-site activities (including horseback riding). **Cons:** nightlife consists of stargazing. $ *Rooms from: US$305* ⊠ *IslaVictoria CC 26, Parque Nacional Nahuel Huapi* ☎ *11/43–949–605* ⊕ *www.islavictoria.com* 🛏 *20 rooms, 2 suites* ᵀ⊚ʅ *All meals.*

Take in the view of Lago Nahuel Huapi on your way to Villa La Angostura.

$ **Río Mel Lodge.** Taking "off the beaten track" to a whole new level,
HOTEL this homey lodge sits on the banks of the Meliquina River in the middle
of Parque Nacional Lanín and is a favorite with both fly fishermen
and families. **Pros:** beautiful setting; friendly service. **Cons:** difficult to
reach without a car. *$ Rooms from: US$25 ⊠ Río Meliquina, 42 km
(26 miles) south of San Martín de los Andes ☎ 02972/427–199 ⊕ www.
riomellodge.com ➴ 4 suites, 2 cabins ▭ No credit cards ⊗ Closed May
¡⊙¡ Some meals.*

SPORTS AND THE OUTDOORS

Intendencia del Parque Nacional Nahuel Huapi. For information on mountain climbing, trails, refugios, and campgrounds, visit the Intendencia
del Parque Nacional Nahuel Huapi. *⊠ Av. San Martín 24, at the Centro
Cívico, Bariloche ☎ 2944/423–111 ⊕ www.nahuelhuapi.gov.ar ⊗ Park
Office weekdays 8–4.*

HIKING

Nahuel Huapi National Park has many forest trails near Bariloche, El
Bolsón, and Villa La Angostura. Hiking guides can be recommended by
local tour offices. For trail maps and information on all of the Lake District, look for the booklet (in Spanish) *Guía Sendas y Bosques* (*Guide
to Trails and Forests*) sold at kiosks and bookstores.

Club Andino Bariloche. For ambitious treks, mountaineering, or information about mountain huts and climbing permits, contact Club Andino
Bariloche. Click "*mapas*" on the website. *⊠ 20 de Febrero 30, Bariloche
☎ 2944/422–266 ⊕ www.clubandino.org.*

MOUNTAIN BIKING

The entire park is ripe for all levels of mountain biking. Popular rides go from the parking lot at the Cerro Catedral ski area to Lago Gutiérrez and down from Cerro Otto. Local tour agencies can arrange guided tours by the hour or day and even international excursions to Chile. Rental agencies provide maps and suggestions and sometimes recommend guides.

Dirty Bikes. Day trips all over the Lake District (including long-distance ones to Chile and back) are organized by Dirty Bikes. Options for many ages and ability levels are available. ⊠ *Bariloche* 🕿 *2944/444–2743* ⊕ *www.dirtybikes.com.ar* 🖃 *100 pesos per hr* ☯ *Weekdays 9–1 and 4–8.*

WHITE-WATER RAFTING

Thanks to all of its interconnected lakes and rivers, the national park offers rafters everything from a basic family float down the swift-flowing, scenic Río Limay to a wild and exciting ride down Río Manso (Class II), which carries you 16 km (10 miles) in three hours. If you're really adventurous, you can take the Manso all the way to Chile (Class IV).

Aguas Blancas. This outfit specializes in the Manso River and offers an overnight trip to Chile with asado and return by horseback. They also run guided inflatable kayak trips. ⊠ *Morales 564, Bariloche* 🕿 *2944/432–799* ⊕ *www.aguasblancas.com.ar* 🖃 *790 pesos* ☯ *Mon.– Sat. 8:30 am–9 pm.*

Alunco. October through May, Alunco arranges rafting trips in the area. ⊠ *Moreno 187, 1st fl., Bariloche* 🕿 *2944/422–283* ⊕ *www. aluncoturismo.com.ar* 🖃 *From 700 pesos (includes transfers, guide, lunch, and equipment)* ☯ *Daily 9–8.*

Extremo Sur. Trips on the Ríos Limay and Manso are arranged by Extremo Sur. ⊠ *Morales 765, Bariloche* 🕿 *2944/427–301* ⊕ *www. extremosur.com* 🖃 *From 550 pesos.*

EL BOLSÓN AND NEARBY

EL BOLSÓN

131 km (80 miles) south of Bariloche via R40.

El Bolsón ("the purse") lies in a valley enclosed on either side by the jagged peaks of two mountain ranges. You catch your first glimpse of the valley about 66 km (41 miles) from Bariloche, with the glaciers of Perito Moreno and Hielo Azul—both more than 1,980 meters (6,500 feet) high—on the horizon south and west.

The first in Argentina to declare their town a non-nuclear zone, El Bolsón's residents have preserved the purity of its air, water, and land. In spring (late November–December), the roads are lined with ribbons of lupine in every shade of pink and purple imaginable. Red berry fruits, which are exported in large quantities, thrive on hillsides and in backyard *chacras* (farms); and huge fields of green hops support the exploding Patagonian microbrew industry.

Beer Sampling

This region has long been the biggest producer of hops in Argentina, and with a local population dedicated to agricultural pursuits, it's logical that entrepreneurial *cervecerías artesanales* (artisanal breweries) would become a growing industry.

Cervecería El Bolsón. About 2 km (1 mile) north of town, Cervecería El Bolsón is the brewery that started the Patagonian "cerveza artesanal craze," and even if it is now the least artisanal of the bunch, it's still a local landmark. Every night December through March, and Friday and Saturday for the rest of the year, the brewery's tasting room turns into a hopping bar and restaurant, where *picadas* (kind of like tapas), pizzas, sausages with sauerkraut, and a hearty goulash are listed on one side of the menu with suggested beers on the other. For instance, black beer is

recommended with smoked meats; chocolate beer with dessert. There are 14 types of brew for you to taste, and descriptions of their ingredients are provided. A large campground is conveniently located by the river in back. ■ TIP→ There is now a second location (Cervecería El Bolsón Centro) in town at the corner of San Martín and Juez Fernandez. ✉ *R258, Km 123.9* ☎ *2944/492–595* ⊕ *www.cervezaselbolson.com* ◷ *Tues.–Sun. noon–midnight.*

Otto Tipp. Herr Tipp was a German immigrant who opened the first local brewery in 1890. Beers here include the classic triumvirate of blonde, red, and black—plus nonalcoholic malt beer and a fruity wheat beer. You can watch them being brewed and bottled from a bar stool. ✉ *Islas Malvinas at Roca* ☎ *2944/493–700* ◷ *Tues.–Sun. 11 am–midnight.*

GETTING HERE AND AROUND

Most travelers come from Bariloche by car or bus; if you choose the latter, El Valle and Via Bariloche make the three-hour journey multiple times per day and deposit passengers downtown. The main street, San Martín, has shops, restaurants, and some lodgings within a two- to three-block area. A grassy plaza next to the tourist office is the center of activities; trails along the Río Azul or to nearby waterfalls and mountaintops are a short taxi or bike ride from it.

Bus Contacts El Valle ☎ *0810/333–7575* ⊕ *www.elvalle.com.ar.* **Via Bariloche** ✉ *El Bolsón* ☎ *2944/432–444* ⊕ *www.viabariloche.com.ar.*

ESSENTIALS

Visitor and Tour Information Secretaría de Turismo ✉ *Pl. Pagano at Av. San Martín* ☎ *2944/492–604, 2944/455–336* ⊕ *www.turismoelbolson.gob.ar.*

EXPLORING

Bolsón International Jazz Festival. In February, the Bolsón International Jazz Festival brings music to streets and restaurants around town. The Fiesta Nacional de Lúpolo (National Hop Festival) is celebrated the same month. ⊕ *www.elbolsonjazz.com.ar.*

Bosque Tallado (*Carved Forest*). About 1 km (½ mile) from the base of Piltriquitrón, you'll find fire-damaged beech trees that have been carved over the years by 13 notable Argentinean artists. Thirty-one

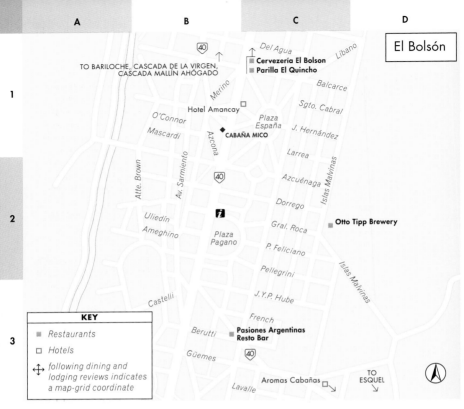

KEY

■ *Restaurants*

□ *Hotels*

⟊ *following dining and lodging reviews indicates a map-grid coordinate*

monumental sculptures transform the dead forest into a living gallery. Tours can be arranged through Maputur. ☎ *2944/491–440 for Maputur* ⊕ *www.maputur.com.ar.*

Cabaña Mico. Don't leave the El Bolsón area without a jar of jam! Not to be outdone by the beer tasting offered next door at Otto Tipp, Cabaña Mico has a long table lined with little jam pots (and disposable sticks), so you can sample the 40 different flavors before making your purchase. ⊠ *Islas Malvinas at Roca* ☎ *2944/492–691* ⊕ *www.mico.com.ar* ☉ *Weekdays 9–7, Sat. 9–6.*

Cascada de la Virgen (*Waterfall of the Virgin*). Venture 15 km (9 miles) north of El Bolsón to see the Cascada de la Virgen. It's most impressive in spring, when the runoff from the mountain falls in a series of three cascades visible from the road coming from Bariloche. Nearby is a campground (☎ *2944/492–610 for info*) with cabins, grills, and a restaurant.

Cascada Mallín Ahogado (*Drowned Meadow Waterfall*). Four km (2½ miles) north of El Bolsón on Ruta 258, the Cascada Mallín Ahogado makes a great picnic spot.

WHERE TO EAT

$$$$ ✕ **Parrilla El Quincho.** About 10 minutes north of town, on the bank of the river Arroyo del Medio, Parrilla El Quincho is the primo place to try *cordero patagónico al asador* (lamb roasted slowly on a metal cross over a fire), along with sizzling platters of beef. Vegetarian options are also available. From El Bolsón, take RN40 north and get off at the left exit for Cascada Mallín Ahogado. Follow that winding road north, then follow signs for El Quincho; once you arrive at the Cascada you will find the restaurant 500 meters to the left (if you hit the Iaten K'aik museum, you've gone too far). $ *Average main: 200 pesos* ✉ *Mallín Ahogado* ☎ *2944/492–870* ⊕ *elquincho.guiapatagonia.net/* ➡ *No credit cards* ☉ *Daily noon–midnight. Closed in winter* ✛ *C1.*

ARGENTINE

CRAFTS FAIR

A **mercado artesanal** (crafts fair) takes place on the main plaza each Tuesday, Thursday, Saturday, and Sunday from 10 to 5. Artisans sell ceramics, leather goods, wood items, objects made from bone and clay—plus the famous local beers. Agricultural products are also available (December through March, be sure to sample the delicious small strawberries El Bolsón is known for).

$$ ✕ **Pasiones Argentinas Resto Bar.** Paintings of passionate tango dancers enliven the brick walls of this popular restaurant near the Villa Turismo. Vegetarian dishes, homemade pastas, pizzas, and even Asian items their fill the menu, but the *cordero con salsa de hongos* (lamb in mushroom sauce) is the standout. Patagonian wine, local beer, Wi-Fi, and take-out food are added attractions $ *Average main: 70 pesos* ✉ *Av. Belgrano at Berutti* ☎ *2944/483–616* ⊕ *www.pasionesrestobar.com.ar* ➡ *No credit cards* ☉ *Tues.–Sun. noon–4 and 8–midnight* ✛ *B3.*

ECLECTIC

WHERE TO STAY

The hotel selection in downtown El Bolsón is woefully inadequate. Numerous guesthouses take small groups, but the Hotel Amancay is the only full-service hotel worth "recommending." You'll find more choices in **Villa Turismo,** a hillside community of cabins, bed-and-breakfasts, and small inns located about 2 km (1½ miles) south of town, off Avenida Belgrano. Lodges in the surrounding mountains open for fishing season in summer (November–April) and close in winter (May–October).

$ ⛱ **Aromas Cabañas.** Perched higher than all the other cabin complexes, these modern cottages have plenty of room and all the accoutrements of a vacation home. **Pros:** lots of space; easy walk up to Piltriquitrón. **Cons:** far from restaurants and downtown shops. $ *Rooms from: US$66* ✉ *Villa Turismo, Subida Los Maitenes* ☎ *2944/492–073* ⊕ *www.aromascabanias.com.ar* ➡ *6 cabins* ➡ *No credit cards* ⛌*No meals* ✛ *C3.*

RENTAL

$ ⛱ **Hotel Amancay.** A rose garden and masses of flowers greet you at the door of this yellow-stucco hotel three blocks from the center of town. **Pros:** walking distance to restaurants; clean rooms. **Cons:** rooms and bathrooms are small and slightly run-down. $ *Rooms from: US$60* ✉ *Av. San Martín 3207* ☎ *2944/492–222* ⊕ *www.hotelamancayelbolson.com* ➡ *15 rooms* ⛌ *Breakfast* ✛ *C1.*

HOTEL

7

Cerro Lindo, near El Bolsón, is a hiker's dream.

SPORTS AND THE OUTDOORS
HIKING
There are 10 refugios with beds and meals in the mountains around Bolsón. A few easy hikes begin a short taxi ride from the center of town. The Río Azul (Blue River) drops down from the high mountains north of town and runs through the valley to Lago Puelo. Most of the hiking trails are in this area. To reach the Mirador Azul, about 5 km (3 miles) from the town center, ride or drive west on Azuénaga Street, then cross the bridge over the River Quemquemtreu and follow the signs. From here you can look down the valley to Lago Puelo and up at the snow-covered mountains to the west.

A 6-km (4-mile) walk will take you to the **Cabeza del Indio** (Indian Head) and **Cascadas Escondidas** (Hidden Falls). A strenuous two-day trek to the **Hielo Azul** (Blue Glacier) climbs through forests to a refugio next to the glacier. Another overnight hike through the forest and past hidden lagoons is to the refugio by the glacier at **Cerro Lindo.** Easier to climb than to say, the summit of **Cerro Piltriquitrón** (pronounced pill-tree-quee-tron, from a Mapuche word meaning "hanging from the clouds") offers stupendous views of lakes and mountains all around you, including Tronadór on the Chilean border near Bariloche. There's a refugio at the top with beds and meals.

HORSEBACK RIDING
Cabalgatas en Azul. Javier Eduardo offers guided horseback tours to the Azul Canyon, a gorge named for the river's deep blue waters. He also leads tours around Cascada Mallín Ahogado; more adventurous riders

can opt to go all the way to the glaciers. ☎ *2944/483–590* 🖥 *From 350 pesos* ☉ *Daily (reservations required).*

MOUNTAIN BIKING

Maputur. You can rent a mountain bike through Maputur and pedal off on your own or join one of its guided group tours. Both half- and full-day options are offered. ✉ *Av. San Martín and P. Hube* ☎ *294/449– 1440* ⊕ *www.maputur.com.ar* 🖥 *From 90 pesos* ☉ *Weekdays 9–1 and 4–8, weekends 9–1 and 6–8.*

SKIING

Cerro Perito Moreno. Used mainly by local families, the ski area at Cerro Perito Moreno is owned and operated by Club Andino Piltriquitrón, which also runs a restaurant at the base where you can rent skis, snowboards, and sleds. Four short tows for beginners and one T-bar access the 750 meters (2,460 feet) of skiable terrain on east-facing slopes. ■TIP→ **Since storms approach from the west, snowfall can be minimal; it's best to call the tourist office or Club Andino before you go.** ✉ *25 km (15 miles) northwest of El Bolsón* ☎ *2944/492–600* ⊕ *www.cerroperitomoreno.com, www.capiltriquitron.com.ar* 🖥 *Day passes from 190 pesos* ☉ *Mid-June–mid-Oct.*

PARQUE NACIONAL LAGO PUELO

18 km (11 miles) south of El Bolsón on RN40 and RP16.

Parque Nacional Lago Puelo is one of the smallest national parks in the southern Andes and one of the warmest spots in the region. The oh-so-blue lake for which it's named (glacial sediment creates the distinctive color) offers a host of recreational opportunities. The land around it, meanwhile, is ideal for hiking and threaded with trails that lead all the way to the Chilean border.

GETTING HERE AND AROUND

To come by car, follow Ruta 16 to Villa Lago Puelo; from there, a 4-km (2½-mile) gravel trail leads to the park entrance. If you don't have your own vehicle, your hotel will happily arrange transport with a local remis driver. You can get information on the park at the tourist office in El Bolsón; picnic and fishing supplies can be purchased in a roadside store at the turnoff to the trail.

EXPLORING

Parque Nacional Lago Puelo. Set more than 200 meters (656 feet) above sea level, this park's titular lake has warm water for swimmers, plentiful fish stocks for anglers, plus a selection of on-the-water excursions for boaters. Hiking options abound in the area as well—the most interesting of which are at the west end of the lake on the Chilean border. ✉ *18 km (11 miles) south of El Bolsón on R16, Chubut* ⊕ *www.lagopuelo. gov.ar.*

SPORTS AND THE OUTDOORS

BOAT EXCURSIONS

Three launches, maintained by the Argentine navy, wait at the dock to take you out on Lago Puelo. The trip to El Turbio, an ancient settlement at the southern end of the lake on the Chilean border, is the longest.

One side of the lake is inaccessible, as the Valdivian rain forest grows on steep rocky slopes right down into the water. Campgrounds are at the park entrance by the ranger's station, in a bay on the Brazo Occidental, and at the Turbio and Epuyén river outlets.

Juana de Arco. Board the *Juana de Arco*, a vintage 1931 naval ship, for either a 45-minute boat trip through Parque Nacional Lago Puelo or a 2½-hour one to the Chilean border. At the helm is Javier, who has 25 years of experience and offers lots of local insight. ⊠ *Perito Moreno 1364, El Bolsón* ☏ *2944/498–946, 2944/15–633–838* ⊕ *www. interpatagonia.com/juanadearco* ⊒ *From 150 pesos.*

HIKING

Arriving at the water's edge, you have three trails to explore: one is an easy stroll in the woods on a wooden walkway; another involves a steep climb to an overlook; and the third is an all-day trek (eight hours round-trip) to **Los Hitos** on the Chilean border, where you can admire the rapids on the Río Puelo. It's possible to camp there at **Arroyo Las Lágrimas** and continue on for five or six days across Chile to the Pacific Ocean. You can also take a boat to **El Turbio** at the other end of the lake, where a tough two- to three-day trek climbs to Lago Esperanza. Another option would be to hike to El Turbio from **El Desemboque** on **Lago Epuyén**. For a guide, contact one of the tour offices in El Bolsón.

PATAGONIA

WELCOME TO PATAGONIA

TOP REASONS TO GO

★ **Glaciers and Mountains:** Set yourself opposite an impossibly massive wall of ice and contemplate the blue-green-turquoise spectrum trapped within. Meanwhile, stark granite peaks planted like spears in the Cordillera beckon extreme mountain climbers and casual trekkers alike.

★ **Marine Life:** Península Valdés is home to breeding populations of sea lions, elephant seals, orcas, and the star of the local sea show, the southern right whale. Punta Tombo is the world's largest Magellanic-penguin colony.

★ **Estancia Stay:** Visit an estancia, a working ranch where you can ride horses alongside tough-as-nails *gauchos* (cowboys) and dine on spit-roasted lamb under the stars.

★ **Earth, Sea, and Fire:** Patagonian cuisine has some of the most exquisite natural flavors in the world. Specialties include sumptuous king crab; flavorful Patagonian lamb; and indulgent Welsh teacakes.

1 **Puerto Madryn and Península Valdés.** Puerto Madryn provides easy access to Península Valdés, one of the world's best places for marine wildlife viewing.

2 **Trelew, Gaiman, and Punta Tombo.** Gaiman and Trelew's teahouses and rose gardens date back to the original 19th-century Welsh settlers. Head south to Punta Tombo, the largest penguin rookery in South America.

3 **Sarmiento.** This small, friendly town is a green oasis. Nearby are stunning petrified forests and a paleontology "park" with life-size dinosaur replicas.

4 **El Calafate, El Chaltén, and Parque Nacional los Glaciares.** The wild Parque Nacional los Glaciares dramatically contrasts with nearby boomtown El Calafate. North is El Chaltén, base camp for hikes to Cerros Torre and Fitzroy.

5 **Puerto Natales and Torres del Paine, Chile.** Border town Puerto Natales is the last stop before one of the finest national parks in South America, Parque Nacional Torres del Paine.

6 **Ushuaia and Tierra del Fuego.** This rugged, windswept land straddles Chile and Argentina. Ushuaia, in Argentina, is the world's southernmost city.

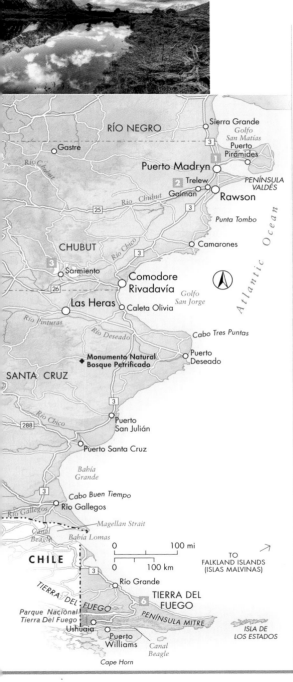

GETTING ORIENTED

Most of Patagonia is windswept desert steppe inhabited by rabbits, sheep, *guanacos* (a larger, woollier version of the llama), and a few hardy human beings. The population centers—and attractions—are either along the coast or in a narrow strip of land that runs along the base of the Andes mountain range, where massive glaciers spill into large turquoise lakes. In nearby Chile, Puerto Natales is the gateway town to Parque Nacional Torres del Paine. At the bottom end of the continent, separated by the Magellan Strait, lies Tierra del Fuego. The resort town of Ushuaia, Argentina, base camp for explorations of the Beagle Channel and the forested peaks of the Cordillera Darwin mountain range, is the leading tourist attraction of the region.

8

CALENDAR OF FAUNA ON PENINSULA VALDES

Although few wildlife-viewing experiences are as grandiose as seeing whales breach or witnessing orcas charge the beaches in a hunt for sea lions, there are numerous special moments throughout the yearly cycles of all Atlantic Patagonian fauna. Regardless of what time you visit, you'll be witnessing something memorable.

(above) Elephant seal bull with Snowy Sheathbill (top right) Dolphin Gull (bottom right) Southern Right Whale off Puerto Pirámides

Since practically everyone who visits Península Valdés is here for the wildlife, any guide we recommend will know where to go for the best views of the wildlife that's most active. Renting a car is a possibility, but going with a guide service makes things easier—your guide will be able to navigate the unpaved roads while you scan the land and water for creatures.

Here is a Península Valdés wildlife primer to get you acquainted with what you'll see when.

WHEN TO GO

Birds: June–Dec.

Whales: May–Dec.

Dolphins: Dec.–Mar.

Elephant Seals: year-round

Sea Lions: year-round

Orcas: Sept.–Apr.

Penguins: Sept.–Mar.

SCOPE IT OUT

Consider purchasing or renting binoculars or a scope.

LOOK TO THE WATER FOR . . .

Southern Right Whales. The first southern right whales arrive in Golfo Nuevo between the end of April and the beginning of May, and can be observed from beaches in and along Puerto Madryn as well as the Península Valdés. Your best chance of seeing them will be from a whale-watching point at Puerto Pirámides. These whales are between 36 and 59 feet long, and have several endearing behaviors such as "sailing," where they hold their fins up in the air, and when a mother uses her flippers to teach calves how to swim.

Elephant Seals. Elephant seals are larger mammals than sea lions, and have a different way of moving—using their flippers to waddle along on land, whereas sea lions use both front and back flippers to thrust themselves forward. Adult males can reach up to 6 meters (20 feet) in length and weigh up to 4 tons, and after four years develop a proboscis, or elephant-like appendage on their noses, which inflates to help produce sounds. The biggest elephant-seal colonies are in Península Valdés, at Punta Cantor and Punta Delgada.

Sea Lions. In January and February sea lions begin to form "harems," with each dominant male taking up to a dozen females. The fights to maintain these harems can be violent, and it's possible to witness an invading male drag off one of the females from the harem with his teeth. Most of the year, however, sea-lion colonies appear peaceful: the animals sun themselves or swim, and the pups are curious and playful. They can be observed year-round all along the Atlantic Coast. Summertime (which in the Southern Hemisphere begins on December 21) up until April is when sea lions and elephant seals are reproducing and raising pups.

Orcas. It's possible to see the black fins of orcas cutting through the water along the coastline, occasionally storming the beach in violent and spectacular chases. The best place to see orcas is at the extreme northern tip of Península Valdés, Punta Norte, in April.

LOOK TO THE AIR AND LAND FOR . . .

Seabirds. Among the many seabirds found in Patagonia—including dolphin gulls, kelp geese, southern giant petrels, rock and blue-eyed cormorants, snowy sheathbills, blackish oystercatchers, and steamer ducks—one species, the arctic tern, has the longest migration—it flies over 21,750 miles annually from the Arctic to Antarctica and back.

Penguins. Along Atlantic Patagonia—most notably Punta Tombo—there are large rookeries of Magellanic penguins, with up to 500,000 of these flightless birds. The males arrive from the sea each August. A month later the females arrive and the males begin fighting territorial battles. In October and into November the nesting pairs incubate the eggs. Once the chicks hatch in November, the parents make continual trips to the ocean for food. In January the chicks leave the nest, learning to swim in February. Their plumage matures throughout the fall, when the penguins begin migrating north to Brazil.

Updated
by Amanda
Barnes

Patagonia is a wild and rugged land filled with breathtaking landscapes and eye-catching wildlife. There are few other places in the world where you can feel such a great isolation and vast emptiness and yet see waters teeming with wildlife; visit gauchos living on windswept estancias; and get so close to ancient glaciers that you can actually walk inside these ice cathedrals. Spanning over a million square kilometers Patagonia has many worlds to discover.

Atlantic Patagonia is where the low pampas meet the ocean. It's a land of immense panoramic horizons and a coastline of bays, inlets, and peninsulas abounding with birds and marine wildlife. The region is most famous for Península Valdés, a UNESCO Natural World Heritage Site with southern right whales, orcas, elephant seals, and sea lions. There are seemingly endless dirt roads where you won't see another person or vehicle for hours—only guanacos, rheas, and other animals running across the steppe.

Farther south and inland to the Andes, the towns of El Calafate and El Chaltén come alive in summer (December through March) with the influx of visitors to the Parque Nacional los Glaciares, and climbers headed for Cerro Torre and Cerro Fitzroy. Imagine sailing across a blue lake full of icebergs, or traversing an advancing glacier in the shadow of the Andes mountain range, watching a valley being formed before your eyes. The Perito Moreno glacier attracts tourists continuously to this region.

Experiencing Patagonia, however, still means crossing vast deserts to reach isolated population centers, taking deep breaths of mountain air and draughts of pure stream water in the shadow of dramatic snow-capped peaks. Most of all, it means being embraced by independent, pioneering souls beginning to understand the importance of tourism as traditional industries—wool, livestock, fishing, and oil—are drying up.

PLANNING

WHEN TO GO

Late September to March—spring and summer in the Southern Hemisphere—is high season in Patagonia. Reservations are advised, especially in September and October in Atlantic Patagonia and December through February in Southern Patagonia. Although the summer sun can be strong, the winds whistle year-round, so always bring extra layers and a windbreaker. In Atlantic Patagonia many properties close in April and May to prepare for the first whale-watchers in June and July. While most of Southern Patagonia grinds almost to a halt from May to September, the ski season in Ushuaia is increasingly popular.

GETTING HERE AND AROUND

AIR TRAVEL

Flying is the best way to reach Patagonia from Buenos Aires (through which flights from most other parts of the country also pass). Always allow some buffer time when traveling to Patagonia: bad weather, heavy fog, and strikes can cause common delays on either side of the journey.

Aerolíneas Argentinas (⊕ *www.aerolineas.com.ar*) and LAN (⊕ *www. lan.com*) have regular, direct flights to Trelew, Comodoro Rivadavía, Río Gallegos, El Calafate, and Ushuaia from Buenos Aires.

LADE (Líneas Aéreas del Estado ⊕ *www.lade.com.ar*) connects Trelew and Comodoro Rivadavía to other parts of Patagonia, including Bariloche, El Calafate, and Ushuaia. Andes Líneas Aéreas (⊕ *www. andesonline.com*) has direct flights between Buenos Aires and Puerto Madryn three times per week.

BUS TRAVEL

Comfortable overnight sleeper buses connect Patagonia to Buenos Aires (and other major cities). However, as getting to even the closest city in Atlantic Patagonia, Puerto Madryn, takes 20 hours, most travelers feel it's worth the price to fly. All the same, buses are a major form of transportation between destinations up to about 600 km (370 miles) apart. Don Otto (⊕ *www.donotto.com.ar*) is a reliable carrier.

CAR TRAVEL

If you truly enjoy the call of the open road, there are few places that can rival the vast emptiness and jaw-dropping beauty of Patagonia. Be prepared for miles and miles of semi-desert steppes with no gas stations, towns, or even restrooms. Always carry plenty of water, snacks, a jack, and tire-changing tools, with at least one spare. Take extra care when driving on *ripios* (gravel roads): it's easy to flip small cars at speeds over 80 kph (55 mph). Fill your tank at every opportunity. If you're not driving, consider simply paying for a *remis* (car with driver) for day excursions.

RESTAURANTS

With so many miles of coastline, it's not surprising that Atlantic Patagonia is famous for its seafood, notably sole and salmon, *mejillones* (mussels), and *pulpo* (octopus). *Centolla* (king crab) is another specialty, especially south of Comodoro Rivadavía. Most restaurants are sit-down-and-take-your-time affairs that don't open for dinner until at

8

least 8, and despite all the seafood on offer, steak still reigns supreme. The other carnivorous staple in the area is *cordero patagónico*, local lamb, usually served barbecued or stewed. Dining prices in most Patagonian cities rival those of upper-end Buenos Aires restaurants. Thankfully, so do the skills of local chefs, although expect more basic offerings of pizza, milanesas, and empanadas in smaller towns. Whenever possible, accompany your meal with a bottle of wine from one of the increasing number of Patagonian wineries.

Huge numbers of foreign visitors mean that vegetarian options are getting better; *woks de verdura* (vegetable stir-fries) are a newly ubiquitous option. Most cafés and bars serve quick bites known as *minutas*. The region is also famous for its stone fruits, which are used in various jams, preserves, sweets, and *alfajores* (a chocolate-covered sandwich of two cookies with jam in the middle). When in El Calafate, be sure to nibble on some calafate berries (or drink them in cocktails like the Calafate Sour)—legend has it if you eat them in El Calafate you are destined to return one day soon.

HOTELS

There aren't many budget options accommodations in Patagonia; the luxury market, on the other hand, is booming. Patagonia is a "once-in-a-lifetime" destination that most people are happy to splurge on, and the increasing cruise culture doesn't ease accommodation prices. In most cities and towns you'll find a mix of big, expensive hotels with comfortable resorts, local flavor estancias, and small B&B-style *hosterías*.

The terms *hospedaje* and *hostal* are used interchangeably in the region, so don't make assumptions based on the name. Many *hostals* are fine hotels—not youth hostels with multiple beds—just very small. By contrast, some *hospedajes* are little more than a spare room in someone's home. Campsites in the national parks often have shelter and can offer some of the best views in Patagonia. *Hotel reviews have been shortened. For full information, visit Fodors.com.*

WHAT IT COSTS IN U.S. DOLLARS			
$	$$	$$$	$$$$
Restaurants: Under $9	$9–$12	$13–$18	over $18
Hotels: Under $116	$116–$200	$201–$300	over $300

Restaurant prices are the average cost of a main course at dinner or, if dinner is not served, at lunch. Hotel prices are the lowest cost of a standard double room in high season.

HEALTH AND SAFETY

Most mountains are not high enough to induce altitude sickness, but the weather can turn nasty quickly. Sunglasses and sunscreen are essential. Although tap water is safe to drink throughout the region, most travelers still choose to drink bottled water. Do not approach or let your children approach sea lions, penguins, or any other animals, no matter how docile or curious they might seem.

Border Crossing

The border between Chile and Argentina is still strictly maintained, but crossing it doesn't present much difficulty beyond getting out your passport and waiting in a line to get the stamp. Most travelers end up crossing the border by bus, which means getting out of the vehicle for 30–45 minutes to go through the bureaucratic proceedings, then loading back in.

Crossing by car is also quite manageable (check with your car-rental company for restrictions on international travel). Chilean customs officers are extremely strict about bringing food into the country, especially compared with their Argentinean counterparts. Always declare food products (they are usually flexible once items are declared); otherwise, you face a hefty fine.

Emergency Services Coast Guard ☎ *106.* **Fire** ☎ *100.* **Forest Fire** ☎ *103.* **Hospital** ☎ *107.* **Police** ☎ *101.*

CRUISING IN PATAGONIA

Cruising is a leisurely and comfortable way to take in the rugged marvels of Patagonia and the southernmost region of the world. Sailing through remote channels and reaching islands virtually untouched by man, you'll witness fjords, snowcapped mountains and granite peaks, and glacial lakes. You'll get a close look at elephant seals, migrating whales, colonies of Magellanic penguins, and cormorants from the comfort of your vessel and during shore excursions taken in Zodiacs (small motorized boats) led by naturalist guides. Far from the beaten path, you'll visit small fishing villages accessible only by sea, explore fantastic temperate rain forests, and enjoy the freshest seafood and local wines.

Most short cruises depart from Ushuaia, Argentina, or Punta Arenas, Chile. Longer and more luxurious itineraries typically depart from either Buenos Aires or Santiago.

WHEN TO GO

In the Southern Hemisphere, where the seasons are reversed, November through March is considered high season. However, the weather in Patagonia is unpredictable: strong winds and sudden storms are common. Summertime (December through February) is the best time to visit. Shoulder months—October, November, March, and April—tend to have cooler temperatures but also less wind. In winter, cruise companies all but hibernate for the season.

October (late spring). Best time to witness the whale migration and the immense colonies of elephant seals and sea lions in Península Valdés.

November (early summer). The natural nesting cycle of Magellanic penguins is November to February. Penguins arrive at the rookeries at the beginning of the month. Spring flowers are in full bloom. This is the best time to catch the bird nesting of finches, sparrows, condors, albatrosses, and other species.

December and January (high summer). The warmest months see penguin chicks hatch in Tierra del Fuego. Long daylight hours also mean great photography opportunities all over Patagonia.

February and March (late summer). Receding ice allows for easier exploration farther south. Whale-watching is at its best. Penguin colonies are very active, as the adults feed the chicks.

BOOKING YOUR CRUISE

The majority of cruisers plan their trips four to six months ahead of time. Book a year ahead if you're planning to sail on a small adventure vessel, as popular itineraries may be full six to eight months ahead.

Consider booking shore excursions when you book your cruise to avoid disappointment later. You can even book your spa services pre-cruise to have your pick of popular times, such as sea days.

Although most travel is booked over the Internet nowadays, for cruises, booking with a travel agent who specializes in Patagonia cruises is still your best bet. Agents have strong relationships with the lines and have a better chance of getting you the cabin you want, possibly even a free upgrade. Cruise Lines International Association (⊕ *www.cruising.org*) lists recognized agents throughout the United States.

CRUISE ITINERARIES

Choosing an itinerary is as important as choosing a cruise line or tour operator that fits your tastes and budget. We highlight possibilities that focus on specific areas, as well as typical departure points, and the tour operators that can take you there.

ANTARCTIC CRUISES

Founded to promote environmentally responsible travel to Antarctica, the **International Association of Antarctica Tour Operators** (☎ *970/704–1047* ⊕ *www.iaato.org*) is a good source of information, including suggested readings. Most companies operating Antarctica trips are members of this organization and display its logo in their brochures.

Season: November–March.

Location: Most cruises depart from Ushuaia, in Argentine Patagonia.

Cost: From \$5,495 from Ushuaia; prices can get quite high.

Tour Operators: Abercrombie & Kent; Adventure Center; Big Five Tours & Expeditions; ElderTreks; G Adventures; Lindblad Expeditions; Mountain Travel-Sobek; Quark Expeditions; Travcoa; Wilderness Travel; Zegrahm Expeditions.

Overview: Ever since Lars-Eric Lindblad operated the first cruise to the "White Continent" in 1966, Antarctica has exerted an almost magnetic pull for serious travelers. From Ushuaia, the world's southernmost city, you'll sail for two (often rough) days through the Drake Passage. Most visits are to the Antarctic Peninsula, the continent's most accessible region. Accompanied by naturalists, you'll travel ashore in motorized rubber crafts called Zodiacs to view penguins and nesting seabirds. Some cruises visit research stations, and many call at the Falkland, South Orkney, South Shetland, or South Georgia islands. Certain operators offer sea kayaking and, at an extra cost, the chance to camp for a night on the ice.

Expedition vessels have been fitted with ice-strengthened hulls; many originally were built as polar-research vessels. It's wise to inquire about the qualifications of the onboard naturalists and historians, the maximum number of passengers carried, the ice-readiness of the vessel, onboard medical facilities, whether there is an open bridge policy, and the number of landings attempted per day.

CRUISING THE TIP OF SOUTH AMERICA

Cruising the southern tip of South America and along Chile's western coast north to the Lake District reveals fjords, glaciers, lagoons, lakes, narrow channels, waterfalls, forested shorelines, fishing villages, and wildlife. While many tour operators include a one- or two-day boating excursion as part of their Patagonia itineraries, the companies listed below offer 4 to 12 nights aboard ship.

Season: September–April.

Locations: Chilean fjords; Puerto Montt and Punta Arenas, Chile; Tierra del Fuego and Ushuaia, Argentina.

Cost: From $2,200 for a four-day, three-night cruise between Punta Arenas and Ushuaia.

Tour Operators: Abercrombie & Kent; Adventure Life; Big Five Tours & Expeditions; Cruceros Australis; International Expeditions; Lindblad Expeditions; Mountain Travel-Sobek; Wilderness Travel; Wildland Adventures.

Overview: Boarding your vessel in Punta Arenas, Chile, or Ushuaia, Argentina, you'll cruise the Strait of Magellan and the Beagle Channel, visiting glaciers, penguin rookeries, and seal colonies before heading north along the fjords of Chile's western coast. With Abercrombie & Kent and Wildland Adventures, you'll savor the mountain scenery of Torres del Paine National Park for several days before or following the cruise, while Lindblad Expeditions, Mountain Travel-Sobek, and International Expeditions visit Tierra del Fuego National Park. Cruceros Australis and some other companies also include Cape Horn National Park. Most itineraries begin or end in Santiago or Punto Arenas in Chile, or Buenos Aires, El Calafate, or Ushuaia in Argentina.

OCEAN CRUISES

Some ships set sail in the Caribbean and stop at one or two islands before heading south; a few transit the Panama Canal en route. West Coast (U.S.) departures might include one or more Mexican ports before reaching South America. Fourteen- to 21-day cruises are the norm. Vessels vary in the degree of comfort or luxury as well as in what is or isn't included in the price. Guided shore excursions, gratuities, dinner beverages, and port taxes are often extra.

Season: October–April.

Locations: Many itineraries visit Argentina (Buenos Aires and Ushuaia), Brazil (Belém, Fortaleza, Rio de Janeiro, and Salvador), and Chile (Antofagasta, Arica, Cape Horn, Coquimbo, Puerto Montt, Punta Arenas, and Valparaíso).

Cost: Prices vary according to the ship, cabin category, and itinerary.

MAJOR CRUISE LINES

Celebrity Cruises: Fjords, glaciers, and emerald lakes are the highlight of a cruise down the west coast of Chile and back up the Atlantic Coast to Buenos Aires. The 15-day cruise is offered December through February. ☎ 800/647–2251 ⊕ www.celebrity.com.

Fred.Olsen Cruise Lines: Their February cruise from Buenos Aires to Lima prides itself on being intimate, friendly, and catering to retired couples. ☎ 845/421–3663 ⊕ www.fredolsencruises.com.

Oceania Cruises: Patagonia (Buenos Aires to Valparaíso in January, and Lima to Buenos Aires in March) voyages with Oceania are as relaxed and elegant as a private country club—mahogany décor, plush carpeting and grand, sweeping staircases. ☎ 800/254–5067 ⊕ www.oceaniacruises.com.

Princess Cruises: Trips (in January and February) on this cruise line include eight ports of call in the Argentine and Chilean Patagonia regions. ☎ 800/774–6237 ⊕ www.princess.com.

Seabourn Cruise Line: Patagonia cruises with Seabourn include visits to the Beagle Channel and the Chilean fjords; a couple cruises run November through February. ⊕ www.seabourn.com.

Silversea Cruises: Voyages with Silversea dock in Uruguay, the Falkland Islands, and Ushuaia, among others, running November through January. ☎ 877/276–6816. ⊕ www.silversea.com.

PUERTO MADRYN AND PENÍNSULA VALDÉS

Visiting populations of whales, orcas, sea lions, elephant seals, and penguins all gather to breed or feed on or near the shores of this unique peninsula, which comprises one of the lowest points in South America. The wildlife isn't only water-based; wandering the Patagonian scrub are guanacos, gray foxes, *maras* (Patagonian hares), skunks, armadillos, and rheas, while myriad bird species fill the air. There are also three inland salt lakes, and the curving gulf at Puerto Pirámides is one of the few places in Argentina where the sun sets over the water, not the land. With nature putting on such a generous display, it's not surprising that the 3,625-square-km (1,400-square-mile) peninsula has been designated a UNESCO World Heritage Site and is the main reason visitors come to Atlantic Patagonia.

Puerto Madryn is where you'll head first for organized excursions onto the peninsula. While a major part of the town's identity is as a staging ground for these trips, it's also well worth exploring and has an interesting history. The first economic boom came in 1886, when the Patagonian railroad was introduced, spurring port activities along with the

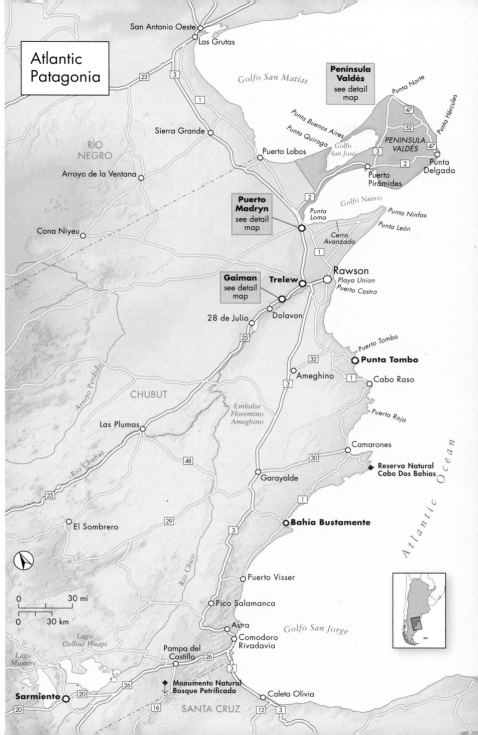

Atlantic Patagonia

San Antonio Oeste
Las Grutas
Golfo San Matías

Península Valdés
see detail map

Punta Norte
Punta Buenos Aires
Punta Quiroga
Golfo San José
PENÍNSULA VALDÉS
Puerto Pirámides
Punta Hércules
Punta Delgada

[23] [3]
[1]

RÍO NEGRO

Sierra Grande

Arroyo de la Ventana

Puerto Lobos

[47]
[52]
[47]
[2]

Puerto Madryn
see detail map

[2]
Punta Loma
Golfo Nuevo
Punta Ninfas
Punta León
Cerro Avanzado
[1]

Cona Niyeu

Gaiman
see detail map

Trelew

Rawson
Playa Unión
Puerto Castro

28 de Julio
Dolavon

[25]

Puerto Tombo
Punta Tombo
[32]
Ameghino
[1]
Cabo Raso
[3]

CHUBUT

Embalse Florentino Ameghino

Puerto Roja

Las Plumas

Río Chubut

[48]

[30]
Camarones

Reserva Natural Cabo Dos Bahías

[25]

Garayalde

Arroyo Perdido

El Sombrero

[29]

[3]

[1]

Bahía Bustamente

Puerto Visser

Pico Salamanca

Río Chico

Astra
Comodoro Rivadavia

Golfo San Jorge

Pampa del Castillo
[26]
[3]

Lago Colhué Huapi

Lago Musters

Sarmiento
[20]
[26]
[16]

◆ **Monumento Natural**
↓ **Bosque Petrificado**

Caleta Olivia
[12] [3]

SANTA CRUZ

[20]

0   30 mi
0   30 km

Atlantic Ocean

salt and fishing industries. Although it isn't likely that the original Welsh settlers who arrived here in 1865 could have imagined just how much Puerto Madryn would evolve, a large part of the town's success is owed to their hardworking traditions, which continue with their descendants today. The anniversary of their arrival is celebrated every 28th of July here and in other Chubut towns. Only a statue—the Tehuelche Indian Monument—serves as a reminder of the indigenous people who once lived here and who helped the Welsh survive.

PUERTO MADRYN

67 km (41½ miles) north of Trelew; 104 km (64 miles) west of Puerto Pirámides.

Approaching from Ruta 3, it's hard to believe that the horizon line of buildings perched just beyond the windswept dunes and badlands is the most successful of all coastal Patagonia settlements. But once you get past the outskirts of town and onto the wide coastal road known as the Rambla, the picture begins to change. Ranged along the clear and tranquil Golfo Nuevo are restaurants, cafés, dive shops, and hotels, all busy—but not yet overcrowded—with tourists from around the world.

Puerto Madryn is more a base for visiting nearby wildlife-watching sites like Península Valdés and Punta Tombo than a destination in its own right. The town's architecture is unremarkable, and beyond a walk along the coast there isn't much to do. Indeed, even the few museums serve mainly to introduce you to the fauna you'll see elsewhere. The exception is the beginning of whale season (May through July), when the huge animals cavort right in the bay before heading north—you can even walk out alongside them on the pier. During these months it's worth the extra expense for a room with a sea view.

The many tour agencies and rental-car companies here make excursion planning easy. Aim to spend most of your time here on one- or two-day trips exploring the surroundings. ⚠ Note that competition is fierce between tourism operators in destinations such as Puerto Madryn and Puerto Pirámides on Península Valdés. Take information that tour operators and even the tourism office give you about these with a grain of salt: they often exaggerate Madryn's virtues and other areas' flaws.

GETTING HERE AND AROUND

Madryn is just small enough to walk around in, and many hotels are on or near the 3½-km-long (2-mile-long) Avenida Almirante Brown—often referred to as "La Rambla"—which runs alongside the bay and has a wide pedestrian walkway. Renting a bicycle is a great way to reach the EcoCentro and (if you're feeling fit) the Punta Loma nature reserve. Otherwise, to get to either of these, to El Doradillo beach north of town, and to Península Valdés and Punta Tombo, you'll need to either rent a vehicle, travel with a tour, or take a remis. Mar y Valle also run two daily bus services between Puerto Madryn's bus terminal and Puerto Pirámides on the Península Valdés.

For those flying in and out of Trelew, Transportes Eben-Ezer operates a shuttle service direct to any hotel in Puerto Madryn (about US$13). The

Continued on page 388

INTO THE PATAGONIAN WILD

Patagonia will shatter your sense of scale. You will feel very small, surrounded by an epic expanse of mountains and plains, sea, and sky. Whether facing down an advancing wall of glacial ice, watching an ostrich-like rhea racing across the open steppe, or getting splashed by a breaching right whale off the Valdez Peninsula, prepare to gasp at the majesty of the Patagonian wild.

GLACIERS OF PATAGONIA

Cruise on Lago Argentino, Santa Cruz province, Glaciers National Park, Argentina

The Patagonia ice field covers much of the southern end of the Andean mountain range, straddling the Argentina–Chile border. The glaciers that spill off the high altitude ice field are basically rivers of slowly moving ice and snow that grind and push their way across the mountains, crushing soft rock and sculpting granite peaks.

Most of Patagonia's glaciers spill into lakes, rivers, or fjords. Chunks of ice calve off the face of the glacier into the water, a dramatic display of nature's power that you can view at several locations. The larger pieces of ice become icebergs that scud across the water surface like white sailboats blown by the wind.

TRAVEL SHRINKS

The link between high-impact activities—such as air travel—and climate change is clear, leading to a disturbing irony: the more people come to see the glaciers of Patagonia, the more carbon is released into the atmosphere, and the more the glaciers shrink.

WEATHER
Weather is unpredictable around glaciers: it's not uncommon to experience sunshine, rain, and snow squalls in a single afternoon.

ICE COLORS
Although clear days are best for panoramas, cloudy days bring out the translucent blue of the glacial ice, creating great opportunities for magical photographs. You'll also see black or gray streaks in the ice caused by sediment picked up by the glacier as it grinds down the mountain valley. When that sediment is deposited into lakes, it hangs suspended in the water, turning the lake a pale milky blue.

ENVIRONMENTAL CONCERN
There's no question that human-induced climate change is taking its toll on Patagonia's glaciers. Although the famous Perito Moreno glacier is still advancing, nearly all the others have shrunk in recent years, some dramatically. You can find out more about the effects of climate change and their impact on the glaciers at Calafate's Glaciarium museum.

Right: Glacier Grey, Paine Circuit, Torres del Paine National Park, Chile

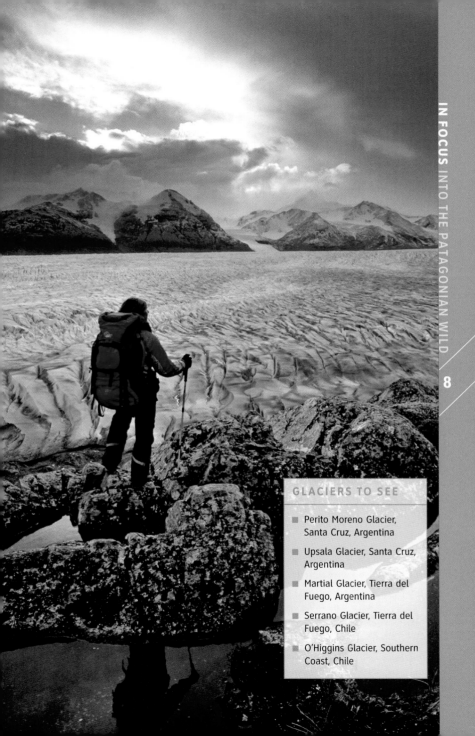

GLACIERS TO SEE

- Perito Moreno Glacier, Santa Cruz, Argentina

- Upsala Glacier, Santa Cruz, Argentina

- Martial Glacier, Tierra del Fuego, Argentina

- Serrano Glacier, Tierra del Fuego, Chile

- O'Higgins Glacier, Southern Coast, Chile

FIRE AND ICE: MOUNTAINS OF PATAGONIA

A trekker takes in the view of Cerro Torre (left) and Fitz Roy in Los Glaciares National Park, Patagonia.

In Patagonia, mountains mean the Andes, a relatively young range but a precocious one that stretches for more than 4,000 miles. The Patagonian Andes are of special interest to geologists, who study how fire, water, and ice have shaped the mountains into their present form.

CREATION

Plate tectonics are the most fundamental factor in the formation of the southern Andes, with the oceanic Nazca plate slipping beneath the continental South American plate and forcing the peaks skyward. Volcanic activity is a symptom of this dynamic process, and there are several active volcanoes on the Chilean side of the range.

GLACIAL IMPRINT

Glacial activity has also played an important role in chiseling the most iconic Patagonian peaks. The spires that form the distinctive skylines of Torres del Paine and the Fitzroy range are solid columns that were created when rising glaciers ripped away weaker rock, leaving only hard granite skeletons that stand rigid at the edge of the ice fields.

MOUNTAIN HIGH BORDERS

Because the border between Chile and Argentina cuts through the most impenetrable reaches of the ice field, the actual border line is unclear in areas of the far south. Even in the more temperate north, border crossings are often located at mountain passes, and the officials who stamp visas seem more like mountain guides than bureaucrats.

MOUNTAINS OF THE SEA

Tierra del Fuego and the countless islands off the coast of southern Chile were once connected to the mainland. Over the years the sea swept into the valleys, isolated the peaks, and created an archipelago that, viewed on a map, looks as abstract as a Jackson Pollack painting. From the water these island mountains appear especially dramatic, misty pinnacles of rock and ice rising from the crashing sea.

Right: Mt. Fitzroy

PROMINENT PEAKS AND RANGES

- Mt. Fitzroy and Cerro Torre, Santa Cruz, Argentina
- Cuernos of Torres del Paine, Chile
- Beagle Channel Mountains, Tierra del Fuego, Chile/Argentina
- Cerro Piltriqitron, El Bolson, Argentina
- Osorno Volcano, Lake District, Chile

PENGUINS OF PATAGONIA

Magellanic Penguin walking to his nest in Peninsula Valdes

Everyone loves penguins. How could you not feel affection for such cute, curious, and loyal little creatures? On land, their awkward waddle is endearing, and you can get close enough to see the inquisitive gaze in their eyes as they turn their heads from side to side for a good look at you. In the water, penguins transform from goofballs into Olympic athletes, streaking through the waves and returning to the nest with mouthfuls of fish and squid for their chicks.

TYPES
Most of the penguins you'll see here are Magellanic penguins, black and white colored birds that gather in large breeding colonies on the beaches of Patagonia in the summer and retreat north to warmer climes during winter. Also keep an eye out for the red-beaked Gentoo penguins that nest among the Magellanics.

If your image of penguins is the large and colorful Emperor penguins of Antarctica that featured in the documentary *March of the Penguins*, you might be slightly underwhelmed by the little Magellanics. Adults stand about 30 inches tall and weigh between 15 and 20 pounds. What they lack in glamour, Patagonia's penguins make up in vanity—and numbers. Many breeding sites are home to tens of thousands of individuals, all preening and strutting as if they were about to walk the red carpet at the Academy Awards.

PENGUIN RELATIONS
Male and female penguins form monogamous pairs and share the task of raising the chicks, which hatch in small burrows that the parents return to year after year. If you sit and observe a pair of penguins for a little while you'll notice how affectionate they appear, grooming each other with their beaks and huddling together on the nest.

HUMAN CONTACT
Although penguins are not shy of humans who keep a respectful distance (about 8 feet is a good rule of thumb), the history of penguin-human relations is not entirely one of peaceful curiosity. Early pioneers and stranded sailors would raid penguin nests for food, and in modern times, oil spills have devastated penguin colonies in Patagonia.

Magellanic Penguins

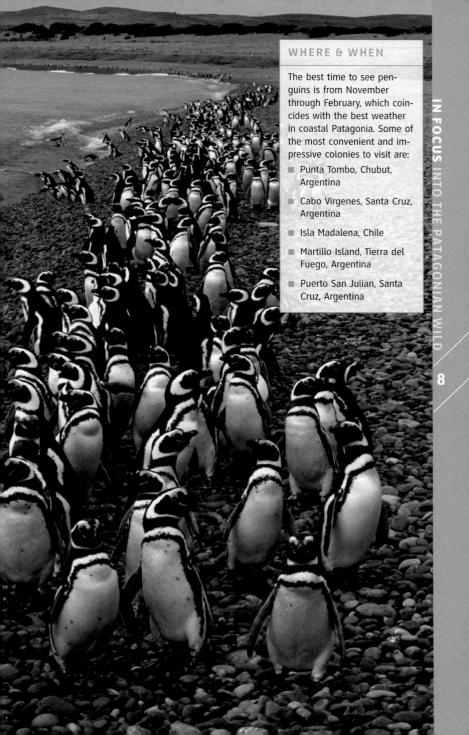

WHERE & WHEN

The best time to see penguins is from November through February, which coincides with the best weather in coastal Patagonia. Some of the most convenient and impressive colonies to visit are:

- Punta Tombo, Chubut, Argentina

- Cabo Virgenes, Santa Cruz, Argentina

- Isla Madalena, Chile

- Martillo Island, Tierra del Fuego, Argentina

- Puerto San Julian, Santa Cruz, Argentina

IN THE SEA

The Patagonian coast teems with marine life, including numerous "charismatic megafauna" such as whales, dolphins, sea lions, and seals.

❶ Seals and Sea Lions

In the springtime massive elephant seals and southern sea lions drag themselves onto Patagonian beaches for mating season—hopefully out of range of hungry orcas. These giant pinnipeds form two groups in the breeding colonies. Big, tough alpha bulls have their own harems of breeding females and their young, while so-called bachelor males hang out nearby like freshman boys at a fraternity party, hoping to entice a stray female away from the alpha bull's harem.

❷ Orcas

Orcas aren't as common as dolphins, but you can spot them off the Valdez Peninsula, Argentina, hunting seals and sea lions along the shore. Sometimes hungry orcas will chase their prey a few feet too far and beach themselves above the tide line, where they perish of dehydration.

❸ Whales

The Valdez Peninsula is also one of the best places to observe right whales, gentle giants of the ocean. Although the name right whale derives from whalers who designated it as the "right" whale to kill, the right whale is now protected by both national legislation and international agreements.

❹ Dolphins

Dolphins are easy to spot on tours, because they're curious and swim up to the boat, sometimes even surfing the bow wake. Commerson's dolphins are a common species in coastal Argentina and the Straights of Magellan. Among the world's tiniest dolphins, their white and black coloring has earned them the nickname "skunk dolphin" and prompted comparisons with their distant cousins, orcas.

IN THE AIR

Patagonia is a twitcher's paradise. Even non-bird-lovers marvel at the colorful species that squawk, flutter, and soar through Patagonia's skies.

❺ Albatross

You can spot several species of albatross off the Patagonian coast, gliding on fixed wings above the waves. The albatross lives almost entirely at sea, touching down on land to breed and raise its young. Unless you're visiting Antarctica or the Falklands, your best bet for seeing an albatross is to take a cruise from Punta Arenas or Ushuaia.

❻ Andean Condor

You probably won't see a condor up close. They nest on high-altitude rock ledges and spend their days soaring in circles on high thermals, scanning mountain slopes and plains for carrion. With a wing span of up to 10 feet, however, the king of the Andean skies is impressive even when viewed from a distance. Condors live longer than almost any other bird. Some could qualify for Social Security.

❼ Magellanic Woodpecker

You can hear the distinctive rat-tat of this enormous woodpecker in nothofagus forests of Chilean Patagonia and parts of Argentina. Males have a bright red head and a black body, while females are almost entirely black.

❽ Rhea (Nandu)

No, it's not an ostrich. The rhea is an extremely large flightless bird that roams the Patagonian steppe. Although they're not normally aggressive, males have been known to charge humans who get too close to their partner's nests.

❾ Kelp Goose

As the name implies, kelp geese love kelp. In fact, kelp is the only thing they eat. The geese travel along the rocky shores of Tierra del Fuego in search of their favorite seaweed salad.

buses are timed to leave after the arrival of each Aerolíneas Argentinas flight. They fill up fast, so call ahead to book your seat. There are services every half hour between Puerto Madryn and Trelew and Gaiman with the bus company 28 de Julio. Andesmar and Don Otto connect Puerto Madryn to Buenos Aires, Bariloche, Río Gallegos, and Puerto Montt in Chile. Numerous car rental agencies are along Avenida Roca.

CRUISE TRAVEL TO PUERTO MADRYN

Cruise ships land right next to the city center in Puerto Madryn, where it's only a short walk off the pier to the town's restaurants and tourism center. Most cruise companies will already have paid the port tax for you, so simply bring your ID and some layered clothing when exploring Puerto Madryn by foot.

If you have a full day here you should head to the Península Valdés (100 km northeast). If you have only a couple of hours, head out to the Sea Lion Reserve (17 km southeast) or simply enjoy the city and try spotting whales from the coastline.

ESSENTIALS

Bus Contacts 28 de Julio ⊠ *Terminal de Ómnibus, Doctor Ávila 350* ☎ *2804/472–056.* **Andesmar** ⊠ *Terminal de Ómnibus* ☎ *0280/447-3764* ⊕ *www.andesmar.com.* **Don Otto** ⊠ *Terminal de Ómnibus* ☎ *0280/445-1675* ⊕ *www.donotto.com.ar.* **Mar y Valle** ⊠ *Terminal de Ómnibus* ☎ *0280/445-0600.* **Transportes Eben-Ezer** ⊠ *RN250* ☎ *2804/472-474.*

Visitor Information Puerto Madryn ⊠ *Av. Roca 223* ☎ *0280/445-3504* ⊕ *www.madryn.gov.ar/turismo.*

TOURS

Puerto Madryn is a useful base for exploring nearby wildlife sites such as Península Valdés and Punta Tombo. If time is tight, or you don't feel like driving the several hundred kilometers round-trip, consider taking an organized day tour. The regular services offered by the many agencies around town vary little in price and content. Try to book a couple of days ahead if you can, although midweek many companies accept bookings the night before the tour leaves.

Note that the English spoken by most guides can vary wildly, so read up on the area first. Drinks, snacks, and meals are never included: bring plenty of your own along, and be prepared to spend a long, long time on your minibus.

Standard tours to Península Valdés typically include a stop at the visitor center, a whale-watching boat trip (June through December), and a visit to two other wildlife spots on the peninsula. Time is often tight, and tours can feel more like working through a fauna checklist than getting close to nature. Companies can drop you off in Puerto Pirámides on the way back if you've decided to stay there overnight.

Day trips to Punta Tombo stop off at Rawson for dolphin-watching (not always included in the tour price), then continue south to the penguin reserve, where you get a scant hour or so. They usually return via Gaiman (with a visit to a Welsh teahouse) or Trelew (to see the dinosaur museum). Most companies are happy to drop you at the Trelew airport on the way back if you have an evening flight.

For more information, see the Getting Here and Around sections for Península Valdés and Punta Tombo.

Argentina Vision. With more than 35 years of experience, this tour company offers excursions including visiting Península Valdés, kayaking and diving with seals in Punta Loma, bird-watching boat tours, whale-spotting, and horseback riding. They also do a half-day 4X4 outing to Punta Loma. ✉ *Av. Roca 536* ☎ *0280/445–5888* ⊕ *www. argentinavision.com* ✆ *From US$60.*

Bottazzi. One of the first whale-watching operators in Puerto Madryn, Bottazzi specializes in whale-watching from its own fleet of 20-, 50-, and 80-passenger boats from Puerto Pirámides. Guided trips last about an hour and a half. When it isn't whale season, they offer dolphin-watching trips at Puerto Rawson, where you can watch *toninas*, the world's smallest dolphins, at play. One of the most popular tours combines a full-day Punta Tombo excursion (which includes transport from Puerto Madryn) to see penguins with dolphin-watching. Bottazzi also offers snorkeling, scuba diving, full-day Península Valdés tours, 4X4 excursions, and a host of other custom tours. ✉ *Complejo La Torre, Martin Fierro 85 at Blvd. Brown* ☎ *0270/447–4110* ⊕ *www. titobottazzi.com* ✆ *From US$65.*

Causana Viajes. Custom-tour operator Causana Viajes will organize the tour or schedule you want with your own chauffeur and guide. The most requested tours are full-day excursions to Península Valdés with whale-watching, and full-day tours to Punta Tombo for penguins and dolphin-spotting. ✉ *Paulina Escardo 148, Ste. 12, 3rd fl.* ☎ *0280/445–5044* ⊕ *www.causanaviajes.com.ar* ✆ *From US$300.*

Miras del Mar. Popular tours through this outfitter are the full-day Punta Tombo excursions, which include a stopover for Welsh tea at Gaiman and Trelew's paleontology museum; the full-day Península Valdés excursion with an hour on the water whale-watching; and a full day at the Florentino Ameghino dam combined with Trelew's paleontology museum. All tours include transport from Puerto Madryn. ✉ *Moreno 38* ☎ *0280/447–4316* ⊕ *www.mirasdelmar.com* ✆ *From US$50.*

Nievemar. As well as full-day tours to Punta Tombo and Península Valdés, Nievemar offers private day tours to the Petrified Forest, half days visiting the toninas, and whale-spotting visits from Playa el Doradillo. You can book tours from their Puerto Madryn and Trelew offices. ✉ *Av. Roca 493* ☎ *0280/445–5544* ⊕ *www.nievemartours.com.ar* ✆ *From US$55.*

EXPLORING

FAMILY **EcoCentro.** From its perch on a windswept outcrop 4 km (2½ miles) south of the town center, this museum and research center affords excellent views of Madryn's bays and desolate coastline. Inside, thoughtful, well-translated displays introduce you to the area's ocean fauna and seek to promote marine conservation. An invertebrates "touch pool" and a whale-sounds exhibit—which you reach by walking through a curtain imitating baleen plates—are especially good for kids. All the same, the exhibits are a bit scant to justify the astronomical entrance price. A slick gift shop and café are also on site. ✉ *Julio Verne 3784*

Puerto Madryn

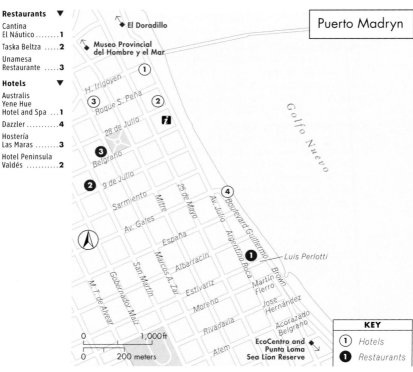

☏ 0280/488–3173 ⊕ www.ecocentro.org.ar ☑ Approx. US$12
◷ Wed.–Mon. 3–7.

El Doradillo. Following the coastal road 14 km (9 miles) north from Puerto Madryn brings you to this whale-watching spot. The ocean floor drops away steeply from the beach, so between June and mid-December you can stand on the sand almost alongside southern right whales, usually mothers teaching their young to swim. During the rest of the year it's just a regular beach. It's a pleasant 1½ hours' bike ride from Puerto Madryn. Alternatively, taxis charge about US$25 for the round trip, including a 45-minute stay.

Fodor'sChoice **Museo Provincial del Hombre y el Mar (Ciencias Naturales y Oceanografía).**
★ This whimsical collection of taxidermied animals, shells, skeletons, and engravings examines humankind's relationship with the sea. Housed in a restored 1915 building, the beautifully displayed exhibits evoke the marine myths of the Tehuelche (the area's indigenous people), imagined European sea monsters, the ideas of 19th-century naturalists, through to modern ecology. It's more about experience than explanation, so don't worry about the scarcity of English translations, although the excellent room on orca behavior is a welcome exception. Finish by looking out over the city and surrounding steppes from the tower. ⊠ Domecq García at José Menéndez ☏ 0280/445–1139 ☑ About US$1 ◷ Mar.–Nov.,

weekdays 9–7, Sat. 3–7; Dec.–Feb., weekdays 9–8, Sat. 4–8.

Punta Loma Sea Lion Reserve. Some 600 South American sea lions lounge on the shore below a tall, crescent bluff at Punta Loma, 17 km (10½ miles) southeast of the city. Aim to visit during low tide. You can reach the reserve by car (follow signs toward Punta Ninfas); by bicycle, if the wind is not too strong; or by taxi—expect to pay about US$25 for the return trip, including a 45-minute stay. ✉ *Punta Loma* 🎫 *Approx. US$8* 🕐 *Daily 8–8.*

LITERARY PATAGONIA

The British writer Bruce Chatwin achieved widespread acclaim with his work *In Patagonia* (1977), a lyrical journey many consider among the greatest travel books of all time, despite criticism related to Chatwin's embellishments. Much of Charles Darwin's classic *Voyage of the Beagle* (1839) takes place in Patagonia, where the young naturalist marveled at the region's stark geology during a boat trip up the Río Santa Cruz.

WHERE TO EAT

$$ INTERNATIONAL 🍴 **Cantina El Náutico.** Photos of visiting Argentinean celebrities mingle with the marine-theme doodads that cover the walls at this local favorite. Run by three generations of a French Basque family, it specializes in simple fish and seafood dishes and homemade pasta, all served in huge portions. [$] *Average main: US$10* ✉ *Av. Roca 790* ☎ *0280/447–1404* 🌐 *www.cantinaelnautico.com.ar.*

$$$$ MODERN ARGENTINE 🍴 **Unamesa Restaurante.** This intimate restaurant focuses on fresh, flavorful cuisine, with vegetables, fruit, and herbs used from the owners' garden. Predinner you can tuck into a fresh batch of hummus and sweet-potato chips while you peruse the small and daily changing menu, which might include Patagonian lamb, shellfish casserole, Argentine steak, or the catch of the day. [$] *Average main: US$21* ✉ *Belgrano 346* ☎ *0280/447–4479* 🕐 *Closed Sun.–Thurs. Mar.–Dec. No lunch.*

WHERE TO STAY

$$ HOTEL 🏨 **Australis Yene Hue Hotel and Spa.** This self-styled luxury hotel gets off to a good start with its cavernous lobby with cascading water garden and luminous breakfast room overlooking the bay; with their textured gray and yellow walls, boxy TV sets, and small beds, the rooms are rather less impressive, but at least they're spacious. **Pros:** the terrace pool, small gym, and spa make it a well-equipped hotel in Puerto Madryn. **Cons:** service is rough around the edges; bland rooms aren't up to the price, especially those not facing the ocean. [$] *Rooms from: US$147* ✉ *Av. Roca 33* ☎ *0280/447–1214* 🌐 *www.hotelesaustralis.com.ar* 🛏 *71 rooms* 🍽 *Breakfast.*

$ HOTEL 🏨 **Dazzler.** Right on the beachfront in the city center, Dazzler couldn't have a better location—the sea views will keep you eagerly hunting for whales—but the comfy beds and generous amenities will pull you away from the window for just a little while. **Pros:** central beachfront location; friendly staff. **Cons:** rooms can get a bit hot; no bathtubs. [$] *Rooms from: US$95* ✉ *Blvd. Almirante Brown 637* ☎ *0280/447–5758* 🌐 *www.dazzlerpuertomadryn.com* 🛏 *95 rooms* 🍽 *Breakfast.*

$ HOTEL 🏨 **Hostería Las Maras.** Sofas, potted plants, warm lighting, and polished wooden tables bring a homey feel to the lobby of this small redbrick hotel; beds with crisp white covers make the rooms snug, though consider the newer superior doubles if you're after a bit more space. **Pros:** peaceful; central. **Cons:** not on the waterfront; Wi-Fi doesn't reach bedrooms; breakfast disappointing. [$] *Rooms from: US$103* ✉ *Marcos A. Zar 64* ☎ *0280/445–3215* 🌐 *www.hosterialasmaras.com.ar* 🛏 *30 rooms* 🍴 *Breakfast.*

$$ HOTEL 🏨 **Hotel Península Valdés.** The minimal gray-and-taupe lobby and slick, wooden-walled breakfast bar are the result of the gradual renovation of this well-established hotel; some rooms are cramped and still outdated but the *panorámicos* have bigger beds and fabulous views of the bay, and the Peninsula Suite has an outdoor balcony and a Jacuzzi tub with a bay view. **Pros:** oceanfront location; good service; disabled access. **Cons:** older rooms not worth the price; gym is tiny; cramped spaces. [$] *Rooms from: US$194* ✉ *Av. Roca 155* ☎ *0280/447–1292* 🌐 *www.hotelpeninsula.com.ar* 🛏 *76 rooms* 🍴 *Breakfast.*

SPORTS AND THE OUTDOORS

BICYCLING

Escuela Windsurf Na Praia. Cycling is a great way to reach El Doradillo and Punta Loma. You can rent mountain bikes by the hour or the day from Escuela Windsurf Na Praia, next to Vernadino Club Mar. ✉ *Av. Almirante Brown 860* ☎ *0280/445–5633* 🌐 *www.grupovds.com.ar.*

DIVING

Lobo Larsen. Dive shops line Puerto Madryn's beachfront, but you'd do well to detour a block inland to talk to Lobo Larsen. Their English-speaking dive masters offer snorkeling and introductory dives and courses to nondivers, and wreck and reef outings to certified divers. Best of all is the chance to dive or snorkel with sea lions who swim right up to you. The company is specially permitted to interact with the pinnipeds, and everybody gets a training session before getting in the water. Equipment and transport from Puerto Madryn is provided; special polar dry suits allow for winter diving. ✉ *Av. Roca 885* ☎ *0280/447–0277* 🌐 *www.lobolarsen.com* 🎫 *From US$130.*

KAYAKING AND WINDSURFING

FAMILY **Escuela Windsurf Na Praia.** This outfit rents sea kayaks and Windsurfers, and runs guided nature-watching kayak tours to nearby bays. During their summer Sea School, local instructors work with children ages 6–14 on snorkeling, windsurfing, bait and lure fishing, basic nautical and fishing knots, and identification of local fauna, as well as offering motor and sailboat excursions. There is also a windsurfing school for adults and kayaking activities. ✉ *Av. Almirante Brown 860* ☎ *0280/445–5633* 🌐 *www.napraclub.com, www.escueladelmar.com.ar.*

PENÍNSULA VALDÉS

Puerto Pirámides is 104 km (64 miles) northeast of Puerto Madryn.

Fodor's Choice ★ The biggest attraction in Península Valdés is the *ballena franca* (southern right whale) population, which feeds, mates, and gives birth here.

Experienced divers might be lucky enough to swim near a right whale calf like the one in the foreground here.

The protected mammals attract more than 120,000 visitors every year from June, when they first arrive, through December. Especially during the peak season of September and October, people crowd into boats at Puerto Pirámides to observe at close range as the 30- to 35-ton whales breach and blast giant V-shaped spouts of water from their blowholes.

GETTING HERE AND AROUND
About 60 km (37 miles) northeast along the coast on Ruta 2 from Puerto Madryn, the land narrows to form an isthmus. A ranger's station here marks the entrance to the Península Valdés Area Natural Protegida (Protected Natural Area), where you pay a park entry fee of about US$20. A further 22 km (14 miles) down the road is the remodeled Centro de Visitantes Istmo Ameghino (Ameghino Isthmus Visitor Center). A series of rather dry displays provides a basic introduction to the marine, coastal, and continental flora and fauna ahead of you. More exciting are the complete skeleton of a southern right whale and the views over the isthmus from the lookout tower.

From the visitor center it's another 24 km (15 miles) to the junction leading to Puerto Pirámides, 2 km (1.2 miles) to the south. By following the road 5 km (3 miles) east, you reach the start of the circuit of the interconnected 32- to 64-km (20- to 40-mile) dirt roads around the peninsula.

There are different ways to explore the peninsula. If you prefer natural surroundings to cityscapes and really want to see all the area has to offer, plan on spending at least a night or two here rather than using Puerto Madryn as your base. The accommodations in Puerto Pirámides easily rival those in town, and when the tour parties leave, you get the rugged, windswept coastal landscape to yourself. Hearing whales splashing offshore at night is a particularly magical experience. By staying you also have time to do an additional whale-watching trip at sunset, and to go hiking, kayaking, or snorkeling with sea lions.

However, if your schedule is tight, consider one of the many organized day trips that operate out of Puerto Madryn. A minibus typically picks you up at your hotel around 8 am, stops briefly at the visitor center, then continues to Puerto Pirámides for whale-watching (June through December only) and lunch. During the afternoon you visit two other spots on the peninsula before returning to Puerto Madryn by about 7 pm. These tours are reasonably priced (at this writing, prices started at US$65 per person) and pack a lot in. However, you spend most of the day crammed in the minibus, don't get to visit the entire peninsula, and have little time to linger at wildlife spots.

To visit the peninsula more extensively at your own pace, you need to rent a car and stay overnight. Having your own wheels also gives you the freedom to stay in the beautiful but remote lodgings at Punta Delgada and Punta Norte. Bear in mind, though, that you'll have to drive several hundred kilometers on dirt and gravel roads in varying states of repair. Stock your vehicle well with drinks, snacks, and gas (the only station is at Puerto Pirámides), and don't try to overtake the tour buses: cars are much lighter, and flipping is unfortunately a common accident here. Economy vehicle rental starts at about US$60 per day; the nearest place to rent from is Puerto Madryn—there are numerous car rentals along Avenida Roca.

If all you want to do is whale-watch, you can reach Puerto Pirámides on the daily public bus service from Puerto Madryn run by Mar y Valle (in high season they shuttle back and forth twice a day). Tickets cost around US$7 each way.

For the freedom of having your own car without the responsibility of driving, arrange for a remis. You can do this as a day trip from Puerto Madryn through most local tour operators (prices vary), or from Puerto Pirámides, if you're staying there, with El Gauchito. Expect to pay about US$120 for a full day (six hours) exploring the peninsula.

Finally, you can combine some of the above approaches and get an overview of the peninsula on a tour, but then get off at Puerto Pirámides on the way back and stay overnight, do other excursions, and then return on the public bus.

ESSENTIALS

Bus Contacts **Mar y Valle** ✉ *Terminal de Ómnibus* ☎ *0280/445–0600.*

Remis Tours **El Gauchito** ☎ *0280/449–5014.*

Visitor Information **Centro de Visitantes Istmo Ameghino (Ameghino Isthmus Visitor Center)** ✉ *At the entrance to the Peninsula* ☉ *Daily 8–8.*

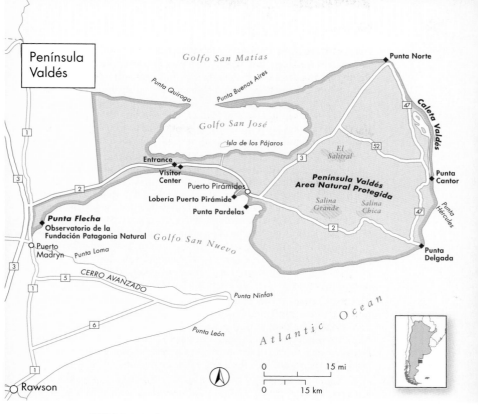

Península Valdés

Golfo San Matías

Punta Norte

Punta Quiroga

Punta Buenos Aires

Golfo San José

Isla de los Pájaros

El Salitral

Caleta Valdés

47

52

Entrance

Visitor Center

Puerto Pirámides

Lobería Puerto Pirámide

Punta Pardelas

3

Península Valdés
Area Natural Protegida

Salina Grande

Salina Chica

Punta Cantor

47

Punta Hércules

Punta Flecha
Observatorio de la
Fundación Patagonia Natural

O Puerto
Madryn

Punta Loma

Golfo San Nuevo

2

Punta Delgada

1

3

3

5

CERRO AVANZADO

1

6

Punta Ninfas

Punta León

A t l a n t i c   O c e a n

1

O Rawson

0   15 mi

0   15 km

EXPLORING

PUERTO PIRÁMIDES

The only settlement on Península Valdés is tiny Puerto Pirámides, which transforms into Argentina's whale-watching capital between June and December. The main street, Avenida de las Ballenas, runs parallel to the shore about 200 meters inland, and is lined with pretty tin-roofed buildings among dunes and scrubby flowers. Two streets run down from it to the sea; all the whale-watching operations are clustered around the first of these, known as La Primera Bajada.

For ecological reasons, only 350 people are allowed to live here permanently, but there is a good selection of hotels and restaurants. ■TIP→ **Bring plenty of money with you, as the one ATM may be out of cash.** In addition to whale-watching and lounging around with a beer while looking out on the pyramid-shape cliffs that gave the town its name, you can go scuba diving or snorkeling with sea lions, kayaking, sand boarding, and mountain biking.

Lobería Puerto Pirámides. Some 4 km (2½ miles) from Puerto Pirámides lies the Lobería Puerto Pirámides, a sea-lion colony which is also a great bird-watching spot. A signposted turnoff from the main road into town leads here, or you can follow the coastal path on foot.

PUNTAS DELGADA, CANTOR, AND NORTE

Gravel-surfaced Ruta Provincial 2 continues 70 km (43 miles) east from Puerto Pirámides toward the edge of the peninsula. About halfway along are the **Salina Grande** and **Salina Chica,** two salt lakes you walk near. On the southeastern tip of Península Valdés lies **Punta Delgada,** marked by an old lighthouse. It now houses a luxury hotel: both the lighthouse and the surrounding beaches—home to a colony of elephant seals—are open only to hotel guests or those who dine at its restaurant.

Elephant seals also gather at **Punta Cantor,** a farther 35 km (22 miles) north along the eastern coast of the island (on Ruta Provincial 47, though it's unmarked). A well-maintained cliffside walkway leads you from the restrooms and restaurant near the road to a viewing area above the seals. The breeding season starts in August, when the males compete for beach space. Then the females arrive, form harems, give birth, and fatten up their cubs before heading out to sea in November. From Punta Cantor Ruta Provincial 52 crosses back across the peninsula, reconnecting with Ruta Provincial 3 to return to Puerto Pirámides. Alternatively, another 22 km (14 miles) north up the coast is **Caleta Valdés,** a long cove with turquoise waters beside which Magellanic penguins often gather.

The northeastern corner of the peninsula, **Punta Norte,** has the largest sea lion settlement of all, and is also the best place to spot orcas in December. Magellanic penguins also roam the land from October through March. From Punta Norte Ruta Provincial 3 is an inland shortcut that heads straight back southwest to Pirámides, passing by **El Salitral,** the largest of the peninsula's three salt-lake ecosystems.

WHERE TO EAT

PUERTO PIRÁMIDES

For quick sandwiches or burgers before a whale-watching trip, try one of the snack bars that are interspersed with the tour operators on the Primera Bajada. All close at about 7 pm. Aside from the food joints on the main drag, check out the hotel restaurants for good options, too.

$$
ARGENTINE
╳ **La Estación Pub.** The coolest bar in Pirámides is also the town's best seafood restaurant. Amid the nets and nautical gear hangs a motley collection of soccer-team flags, glam-rock posters, and LPs. Equally eye-catching are the tables—painted tomato-red, tangerine, or sea-green—and the menus, illustrated with pictures of David Bowie. As well as the requisite fish and steak dishes, offerings include a great range of pizzas and homemade pastas: try the garlicky mussel sauce. [$] *Average main: US$12* ⊠ *Av. de las Ballenas s/n* ☎ *0280/449–5047* ⊘ *Closed Tues.*

WHERE TO STAY

PUERTO PIRÁMIDES

$
RENTAL
▢ **Cabañas en el Mar.** Skip the aging A-frame cabins and try to book one of the apartments—their living rooms look down the street to the ocean and include fully equipped kitchens, making them popular with families and biologists here on extended stays. **Pros:** stylish; good value, especially for groups. **Cons:** located near all the whale-watching operators, so may be noisy during the day; cabins are much less attractive than apartments. [$] *Rooms from: US$103* ⊠ *Av. de las Ballenas s/n*

General Julio Argentino Roca

Look at the street signs in any Patagonian city and you're sure to spot the name General Julio Argentino Roca. (To see what he looks like, whip out your wallet: he's riding along the 100-peso note, too). But look a little closer and you may well find stickers or stencils changing the street's name to "Pueblos Originarios" ("First Peoples").

The history books celebrate Roca as the man who "civilized" Patagonia and extended Argentine territory south, but the real story is much darker. In the late 1870s the bottom half of Argentina was still largely controlled by various indigenous peoples who resisted the European colonization of their territory. Funded by rich landowners from Buenos Aires anxious to extend their estates, war minister Roca led a series of brutal military attacks—euphemistically known as the "Desert Campaigns"—which led to the massacre of over a thousand Mapuche, Tehuelche, and Ranquel warriors and the enslavement of countless indigenous women and children.

Despite repeated attempts by indigenous rights groups to rename the streets and reprint the banknotes, for the time being these continue to honor the man behind the massacre.

📠 *0280/449–5049* ⊕ *www.piramides.net* ➔ *2 cabañas, 4 apartments* ⏐○⏐ *No meals.*

$$$
HOTEL
Fodor'sChoice
★

🛏 **Hostería Ecológica del Nómade.** When you're staying in a wildlife reserve, taking care of Mother Nature seems only right; although this eco-friendly hotel uses solar panels and low-energy fittings and recycles its grey water, they haven't skimped on style or luxury. **Pros:** eco-awareness at no loss to comfort; detailed local information from staff and library of nature books; fabulous breakfasts. **Cons:** slightly removed from the restaurants on the main drag. $ *Rooms from: US$210* ⊠ *Av. de las Ballenas s/n* 📠 *0280/449–5044* ⊕ *www.ecohosteria.com.ar* ➔ *8 rooms* ⊗ *Closed mid-Apr.–mid-Aug.* ⏐○⏐ *Breakfast.*

$$$
HOTEL

🛏 **Las Restingas.** The powder-blue clapboard facade of Puerto Pirámides's most upmarket hotel stretches along the beachfront: squint and you can see whales from the huge picture windows in the front-facing rooms and lobby lounge. **Pros:** excellent restaurant with a deck overlooking the sea; sea (and whale) views from some rooms. **Cons:** rooms facing the village are very overpriced; tiny bathrooms. $ *Rooms from: US$231* ⊠ *Primera Bajada at the beach* 📠 *0280/449–5101* ⊕ *www.lasrestingas. com* ➔ *12 rooms* ⊗ *Closed Apr. and May* ⏐○⏐ *Breakfast.*

PUNTA DELGADA

$$
HOTEL
Fodor'sChoice
★

🛏 **Faro Punta Delgada.** This remote complex of buildings on the tip of Península Valdés offers luxuries that are simple and old-fashioned: comfortable beds with chintz covers, a pleasant pub with pool and darts, board games, and utter tranquility under starry night skies. **Pros:** peaceful; private beaches afford great wildlife experiences; guided nature walks; fabulous food. **Cons:** rooms don't have water views; very isolated for some; busy with tour buses at midday. $ *Rooms from: US$144* ⊠ *Punta Delgada, Península Valdés* 📠 *0280/445–8444*

8

⊕ *www.puntadelgada.com* ↩ *27 rooms* ☉ *Closed Apr.–June* ❍ *Multiple meal plans.*

SPORTS AND THE OUTDOORS

From June to December the main attractions at Puerto Pirámides are whale-watching boat trips into the Golfo Nuevo to see southern right whales. Experienced captains pilot the boats between the huge mammals while bilingual guides tell you about their habits and habitats. Expect to use up lots of your camera memory as the graceful creatures dive, spout water, and salute you with their tails.

Most whale-watching companies operate several trips a day while the whales are in town, especially during the peak months of September and October. Standard daytime excursions last about 1¼ hours, and the price is set each year by the municipality (at this writing it was about US$35). Trips in smaller boats and longer tours are usually more expensive. Although no boat is allowed closer than 15 meters to the whales (the animals themselves sometimes break the rules by diving under your boat), you certainly feel closer from smaller vessels. On clear days the magical sunset tours are definitely worth paying extra for: you see the whales frolic as the sun sets over the water around them. It's best to call a day or two ahead to reserve, although many companies will fit you in if you show up on the day.

BOAT TOURS

Bottazzi. Although trips tend to be more expensive with Bottazzi, they tend to be longer than other companies' and have excellent English-speaking guides. The sunset trips are on very small boats, and include wine and cheese back at their office afterwards. ⊠ *Primera Bajada* ☎ *0280/449–5050* ⊕ *www.titobottazzi.com.*

Hydrosport. Ecological commitment is the foremost priority at Hydrosport, a reliable, long-running operator with three different boat sizes. ⊠ *Primera Bajada* ☎ *0280/449–5065* ⊕ *www.hydrosport.com.ar.*

Southern Spirit. This outfitter allows you not only to see but also to hear the whales, thanks to their underwater sound-detection system. They use large but fairly low boats and operate up to five 90-minute trips a day, including a sunset outing. ⊠ *Av. de las Ballenas at La Primera Bajada* ☎ *0280/15–4572–551* ⊕ *www.southernspirit.com.ar.*

KAYAKING

Patagonia Explorers. Kayaking in the Golfo Nuevo and the Golfo San José is offered by Patagonia Explorers, who also have English-speaking guides. ⊠ *Av. de las Ballenas at La Primera Bajada* ☎ *0280/15–4340–619* ⊕ *www.patagoniaexplorers.com.*

TRELEW, GAIMAN, AND PUNTO TOMBO

When the Welsh settlers landed on the desertlike Patagonian coast in 1865, they realized they would need to move inland to find suitable land for farming. Some 25 km (15 miles) inland, in the fertile Chubut River valley, they founded Trelew and Gaiman. Both retain Welsh traditions to this day: Trelew holds an Eisteddfod (festival of Welsh poetry, song,

Trelew's Museo Paleontológico Egidio Feruglio, or Paleontology Museum, is bursting with fossil treasures.

and dance) each October, and Gaiman is the largest Welsh settlement outside of Wales.

With almost 100,000 inhabitants, Trelew is now a large city by Patagonian standards, and its airport is the gateway to Atlantic Patagonia. Beyond the excellent dinosaur museum, however, the dusty, windswept center is of little interest to tourists. With its teahouses, rose gardens, and chapels, Gaiman retains a country-town feel. Indeed, farms and stone-fruit orchards still fill the countryside surrounding it.

On the coast 120 km (74 miles) south of Trelew lies the Punta Tombo penguin reserve, which you can easily visit on a day trip from Trelew, Gaiman, or Puerto Madryn.

TRELEW

11 km (6 miles) east of Gaiman; 67 km (41½ miles) south of Puerto Madryn.

Trelew (pronounced Tre-*leh*-ew) is a commercial, industrial, and service hub that contains the region's main airport. Its biggest attractions are its paleontology museum (with the largest dinosaur fossils in the world on exhibit) and its proximity to the Punta Tombo reserve (though both can also be reached on day trips from Gaiman and Puerto Madryn). Otherwise, the city has little to recommend it: its mediocre hotels are notoriously overpriced, and aside from rental-car firms its tourism infrastructure is far less organized than Puerto Madryn's. If you come in the second half of October you can watch part of the Eisteddfod, a Welsh literary and music festival first held in Patagonia in 1875.

Trelew was founded in 1886 as a result of the construction of the now-defunct Chubut railway line, which connected the Chubut River valley with the Atlantic coast. The town is named after its Welsh founder, Lewis Jones (*Tre* means "town" in Welsh, and *Lew* stands for Lewis), who fought to establish this railroad.

GETTING HERE AND AROUND

If you're driving, from the Ruta Nacional 3, take Ruta Nacional 25 to Avenida Fontana. The long-distance bus terminal is at Urquiza and Lewis Jones, along the Plaza Centenario. Most of what you'll visit is found in the half-dozen blocks between Plaza Centenario and Plaza Independencia, which is also where you'll find the tourist office.

ESSENTIALS

Bus Contacts Andesmar ⊠ *Terminal de Ómnibus, Urquiza and Lewis Jones* ☎ *0280/443-3535.* **Don Otto** ⊠ *Terminal de Ómnibus, Urquiza and Lewis Jones* ☎ *0280/442-9496.* **TAC** ⊠ *Terminal de Ómnibus, Urquiza and Lewis Jones* ☎ *0280/443-9207.*

Car Rental Hertz ⊠ *Aeropuerto de Trelew* ☎ *0280/442-4421* ⊕ *www.hertzargentina.com.ar.*

Visitor and Tour Information Tourist Office ⊠ *Mitre 387* ☎ *0280/442-0139* ⊕ *www.trelew.gov.ar.*

EXPLORING

FAMILY
Fodor'sChoice
★
Museo Paleontológico Egidio Feruglio (MEF). Trelew's star attraction is the paleontology museum, where four hushed and darkened galleries of fossils both real and replica take you back in time. You start among the South American megafauna (giant armadillos and the like) that may have cohabited with the first humans here, then plunge back to a time before the Andes existed. Back then Patagonia was a subtropical rain forest filled with dinosaurs, including one of the largest creatures ever to walk the earth: the 70-ton, 120-foot-long Argentinosaurus. Replicas of its massive leg bones are on display, along with countless other dino skeletons, including the latest discovery of the largest dinosaur in the world—a 130-foot-long herbivore. Other highlights include a 290-million-year-old spider fossil with a 3-foot leg span and the 70-million-year-old petrified eggs of a Carnotaurus. The visit ends with a peek into the workshop where paleontologists study and preserve newly unearthed fossils. Tours in English are available—they're a good idea, as only the introductions to each room are translated. ⊠ *Av. Fontana 140* ☎ *0280/443-2100* ⊕ *www.mef.org.ar* ⊠ *About US$7* ⊗ *Apr.–Sept., weekdays 10–6, weekends 10–7; Oct.–Mar., daily 9–7.*

Museo Regional Pueblo de Luis (*Trelew Regional Museum*). Across the street from MEF is Trelew's old train station, which now contains a small museum of the town's history. Photos, clothing, and objects from local houses, offices, and schools form the mishmash of displays on the European influence in the region, the indigenous populations of the area, and wildlife. ⊠ *Av. 9 de Julio at Av. Fontana* ☎ *0280/442-4062* ⊠ *About US$0.25* ⊗ *Weekdays 8–8, weekends 2–8.*

WHERE TO EAT AND STAY

$$ ITALIAN Fodor's Choice ★ 🍴 **Miguel Angel.** With its paneled walls, sleek black tables, and vintage photos, this stylish Italo-Argentine restaurant is the happy exception to a dining scene that's as bleak as the steppes surrounding the town. Deferential waitstaff help you pick which of their pasta specialties to go for. Options include squash ravioli in wild mushroom sauce, spinach and Parma ham agnolotti, or—most indulgent of all—stuffed gnocchi. Lunching professionals come for the set menus, which often include thick steaks and roast potatoes. [$] *Average main: US$11* ✉ *Av. Fontana 246* ☎ *0280/443–0403* ⏲ *Closed Mon.*

$$ CAFÉ 🍴 **Touring Club.** Legend has it that Butch Cassidy and the Sundance Kid once stayed here—search long enough and you might find them among the old photos cluttering the walls. This cavernous old *confitería* (café) was founded in 1895, and became Chubut's first hotel in 1926. Its vintage tiles and molded ceiling don't seem to have changed much since, except that you can now use Wi-Fi from your scuffed table. The hotel's rooms are too shabby to recommend, but a toasted sandwich and a coffee or beer here is tantamount to a trip back in time. [$] *Average main: US$9* ✉ *Av. Fontana 240* ☎ *0280/443–3997.*

$ HOTEL 🏨 **Hotel Libertador.** This big hotel has definitely seen better days, though rooms are clean (if worn around the edges)—the faded bedcovers, textured wallpaper, and scuffed furnishings of the standard rooms really aren't up to the price, although it still remains one of the best of the rather limited options in town. **Pros:** on-site parking; amenable staff. **Cons:** only the superior rooms are worth the price. [$] *Rooms from: US$93* ✉ *Av. Rivadavía 31* ☎ *0280/442–0220* 🌐 *www.hotellibertadortw.com.ar* 🛏 *90 rooms* 🍽 *Breakfast.*

8

GAIMAN

17 km (10½ miles) west of Trelew.

The most Welsh of the Atlantic Patagonian settlements, sleepy Gaiman (pronounced *Guy*-mon) is far more charming than nearby Trelew and Rawson. A small museum lovingly preserves the history of the Welsh colony, and many residents still speak Welsh (although day-to-day communication is now in Spanish). A connection to Wales continues with teachers, preachers, and visitors going back and forth frequently (often with copies of family trees in hand). Even the younger generation maintains an interest in the culture and language.

Perhaps the town's greatest draws are its five Welsh teahouses (*casas de té*)—Ty Gwyn, Plas-y-Coed, Ty Nain, Ty Cymraeg, and Ty Té Caerdydd. Each serves a similar set menu of tea and home-baked bread, scones, and a dazzling array of cakes made from family recipes, although the odd dulce de leche–filled concoction is testament to Argentine cultural imperatives. Most teahouses are open daily 3–8 and charge about US$15 per person for tea (the spreads are generous enough to replace lunch or dinner, and you can usually take away a doggy bag of any cake you don't finish). Each establishment has its own family history and atmosphere, and there's healthy competition between them as to which is the most authentically Welsh.

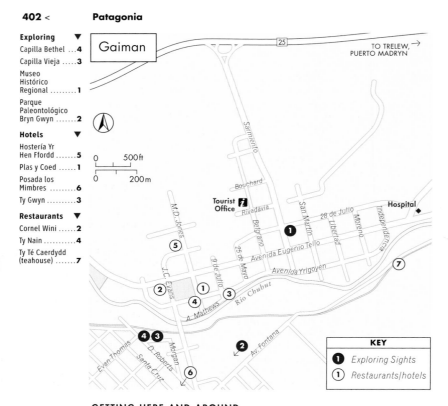

GETTING HERE AND AROUND

Gaiman is easily walkable: nearly all the teahouses and other attractions are within a five-block radius of the town square at Avenue Eugenio Tello and M. D. Jones. If you don't have a car, you can access the few sites outside of town—such as the Bryn Gwyn Paleontology Park—by taking an inexpensive remis from one of the *remiserías* on the square.

Although their English isn't great, the friendly young staff at the tourist office give enthusiastic advice on what to visit in Gaiman and hand out detailed maps of the town and its surroundings.

ESSENTIALS

Visitor and Tour Information Tourist Office ⊠ *Belgrano 574, at Rivadavía* 🕾 *0280/449–1571* ⊘ *May–Sept., weekdays 9–6; Oct.–Apr., weekdays 9–8.*

EXPLORING

Capilla Bethel. Throughout the Chubut Valley there are three dozen or so chapels where the Welsh settlers prayed, went to school, and held meetings, trials, and social events. Two of these simple brick chapels stand alongside each other just over the river from Gaiman—they're usually closed to the public, but are interesting to see from the outside. Built in 1914, Capilla Bethel is used today by Protestants for Sunday service. To reach the chapels, walk south from the square on J. C. Evans and cross the pedestrian bridge. Locals take a shortcut by ducking through

Gaiman's Teahouses

Gaiman's Welsh teahouses have been famous among travelers for decades. The first teahouse, Plas y Coed, opened in 1944, and figured in Bruce Chatwin's *In Patagonia.*

Each of Gaiman's teahouses serves up its own unique family recipes for all manner of baked goodies, including *torta galesa* (a rich dried-fruit cake), seasonal fruit tarts, buns and sponges, *torta de crema* (a rich baked cream cake), as well as homemade bread, scones, and jam. The tea is always served in big china pots dressed for the occasion in deliciously kitsch hand-knitted tea cozies to ensure your brew stays warm.

Just as the recipes and tastes differ slightly from teahouse to teahouse, so do their interiors. But common to all the teahouses are tapestries and ornamental tea towels, often inscribed with Welsh words and with intricate Celtic designs around the borders. Hanging from the walls—and often for sale, too—are heart-shape wooden spoons with intricately carved handles. Known as love spoons, they're a Welsh tradition that dates to the 16th century: a young man would carve a spoon from a single piece of wood and give it to the girl he wished to marry.

Most of Gaiman's teahouses are owned and run by descendants of the original Welsh settlers, who are happy to recount their family history if you ask about it. There's a strong sense of appreciation for how easy things are today compared to just a couple of generations ago. Ana, of Plas y Coed, whose great-grandmother was featured in Bruce Chatwin's book, told us, "Imagine making everything from scratch and running this place without refrigerators."

There's an Alice in Wonderland effect as you nibble various cakes and look out on the vast Atlantic Patagonian steppe (which would make anyone feel small).

the fencing where the bridge ends and walking 100 meters to the right along the riverside. Otherwise take the first right into Morgan and follow the dirt road around several bends.

Capilla Vieja (*Old Chapel*). The aptly named Capilla Vieja, next to Capilla Bethel, was built in 1880 and is used each year for the traditional Welsh Eisteddfod, when townspeople gather to celebrate—and compete with each other in—song, poetry, and dance under the chapel's wooden vaulted ceiling.

Museo Histórico Regional (*Regional Historical Museum*). Photographs and testimonies of Gaiman's original 160 Welsh settlers are on display in the Museo Histórico Regional, along with household objects they brought with them or made on arrival. The staff are passionate about their history and will happily show you round the tiny building, which used to be Gaiman's train station. ✉ *28 de Julio 705, at Sarmiento* 🖼 *About US$1* ⏲ *Daily 3–7.*

Parque Paleontológico Bryn Gwyn (*Bryn Gwyn Paleontology Park*). Just south of Gaiman the green river valley gives way to arid steppes where clearly visible strata reveal over 40 million years of geological history. Some 600 acres of these badlands—many of them bursting with fossils—make up the Parque Paleontológico Bryn Gwyn, a branch of the Museo Paleontológico Egidio Feruglio in Trelew. Guides lead you along the fossil trail, then you're left to wander freely through the botanical gardens of native Patagonian plants. ✉ *8 km (5 miles) south of town* ☎ *0280/443–2100* 🌐 *www.mef.org.ar/mef/en/institucional/geoparque.php* 🎟 *About US$2* 🕒 *Tues.–Sun. 10–4.*

WHERE TO EAT

$$ ARGENTINE 🍴 **Cornel Wini.** For decades the Jones family, owners of this stately red-brick corner building, ran a hotel and bar (complete with a boxing ring in the basement) here, but switched to serving steaks, pizzas, and pasta. The decision has been a success: on weekends, locals from as far afield as Puerto Madryn pack themselves round the wooden tables of the bright, high-ceiling dining room to devour their generous *parrilladas* (mixed grills). We love the presence of Gaiman's traditional dark fruit cake in the Postre Wini, in combination with ice cream, nuts, whipped cream, and liqueurs. [$] *Average main: US$10* ✉ *Av. Eugenio Tello 199* ☎ *0280/449–1397* 💳 *No credit cards* 🕒 *Closed Tues., and Wed. in winter.*

$$$ CAFÉ Fodor's Choice ★ 🍴 **Ty Nain.** The matriarch who presides over the kitchen here, Mirna Jones, is a proud descendant of the first woman born in Gaiman. Her ivy-covered teahouse on the main square looks like a knickknack shop: it's stuffed with doodads and hung with crochet, and there are gramophones, carriage lamps, and antique radios on display above the four original chimneys, which date to 1890, although Formica paneling detracts slightly from the Old World style. [$] *Average main: US$16* ✉ *Hipólito Yrigoyen 283* ☎ *0280/449–1126* 💳 *No credit cards* 🕒 *Closed weekdays in winter.*

$$$$ CAFÉ Fodor's Choice ★ 🍴 **Ty Té Caerdydd.** A short way out of town lies Gaiman's largest teahouse, surrounded by cypress trees, sculpted gardens, and a giant tea pot. It stands apart from its rivals culturally, too: it's run by descendants of a Spanish family, which shows in the sprawling colonial-style architecture. Otherwise you'd never know they weren't Welsh, as they do the most impressive spread of traditional cakes in town. Better yet, this was where Princess Diana took her tea during her visit to Gaiman in the early 1990s (Scotland Yard liked the security of its rural location). The cup she used, numerous photos, and other memorabilia form a shrine-like display in her honor. [$] *Average main: US$20* ✉ *Finca 202, Zona de Chacras* ☎ *0280/449–1510.*

WHERE TO STAY

$ B&B/INN 🏨 **Hostería Yr Hen Ffordd.** Gaiman's best budget accommodation is this family-run B&B, where rooms are simple but spacious and warm, with comfy beds, bright feather quilts, good bathrooms, and free Wi-Fi (quite a find in Gaiman). **Pros:** great breakfasts; friendly owners give spot-on advice on Gaiman's sights and restaurants. **Cons:** drab carpets detract from the century-old building's charm. [$] *Rooms from: US$43* ✉ *Michael Jones 342* ☎ *0280/449–1394* 🌐 *www.yrhenffordd.com.ar* 🛏 *5 rooms* 💳 *No credit cards* 🍽 *Breakfast.*

$ B&B/INN 🏨 **Plas y Coed.** Gaiman's oldest teahouse has also been a bed-and-breakfast since 1997, and a stay here is rather like visiting with a favorite

CLOSE UP

Pandas of the Sea

You've watched the whales, seen the seals, and admired the penguins. But how about *toninas* (dolphins)? The southern coast of Argentina is home to a particularly attractive species, *Cephalorhynchus commersonii*, whose black-and-white coloring has earned them the nickname "pandas of the sea." **Toninas Adventure** (✉ *Av. Marcelino González at the docks, Puerto Rawson* ☎ *2965/498–372* 🌐 *www.enpuertorawson.com.ar/toninas* 🎫 *Boat-trip 120 pesos* 🕘 *Daily 9–6*), the only dolphin-watching enterprise in the area, operates hour-long boat trips from the port at Rawson. They guarantee sightings of their playful namesake creatures, who love to race alongside the boats in packs of three or four, regularly jumping up in perfect arcs. Puerto Rawson is on the coast 30 km (20 miles) east of Trelew, and is an easy detour on trips south to Punta Tombo or beyond. Most organized tours to Punta Tombo stop here.

aunt: The rooms are simple but immaculate, have polished wooden floors and pastel bedspreads, and there's a comfy lounge area for relaxing in. **Pros:** an inclusive, family-friendly atmosphere. **Cons:** not much room for groups larger than six. [$] *Rooms from: US$61* ✉ *M. D. Jones 123* ☎ *0280/449–1133* 🌐 *www.plasycoed.com.ar* 🛏 *5 rooms* 💳 *No credit cards* 🍴 *Breakfast.*

$$$ B&B/INN 🏨 **Posada Los Mimbres.** Wandering the nature trail alongside the Chubut River is one of the joys of staying on this working farm; picking fruit from the orchard and helping at milking time are others. **Pros:** variety of rooms to choose from; the option of lunch and dinner means you don't need to go back into town for meals; most ingredients are sourced from the farm; beautiful rural setting. **Cons:** isolated from town if you don't have a vehicle. [$] *Rooms from: US$200* ✉ *Chacra 211* ☎ *0280/449–1299* 🌐 *www.posadalosmimbres.com.ar* 🛏 *7 rooms, 1 cottage* 💳 *No credit cards* 🍴 *Multiple meal plans.*

$ B&B/INN Fodor's Choice ★ 🏨 **Ty Gwyn.** The soaring ceilings, wooden rafters, and cobbled white walls of this cavernous teahouse make it seem like you're eating in a medieval dining hall; an interior garden leads to the staircase that takes you to four lovely bedrooms with wood floors, heavy drapes, and dressers fashioned from antique sewing-machine tables. **Pros:** rooms overlook the river; generous breakfasts include fruit and eggs. **Cons:** cruise-ship groups arrive regularly in high season. [$] *Rooms from: US$61* ✉ *Av. 9 de Julio 149* ☎ *0280/449–1009* 🌐 *www.tygwyn.com.ar* 🛏 *4 rooms* 🍴 *Breakfast.*

PUNTA TOMBO

120 km (74 miles) south of Trelew.

This protected area is home to one of the world's biggest colonies of Magellenic penguins; they come for the season to lay eggs and feed their newly hatched young. The park is also a great spot for observing other seabirds along with guanacos, seals, and hares.

EXPLORING

Area Natural Protegido Punta Tombo (*Punta Tombo Protected Natural Area*). From the middle of September through March, up to half a million penguins live in the Area Natural Protegido Punta Tombo, the world's largest colony of Magellanic penguins and one of the most varied seabird rookeries. From the park entrance, a series of trails, boardwalks, and bridges lead you 3.5 km (2¼ miles) through the scrubby landscape where the penguins nest to the sea. The quizzical creatures seem unafraid of humans, and peer up at you from under the bushes where, between September and November, both males and females incubate eggs, often right beside the trail. Look for the bald vertical strips on the penguins' abdomens: they pluck out feathers so the eggs can sit warm against their skin. Come December, the ground is teeming with fluffy gray young, and the adult penguins waddle back and forth from the sea to feed them. They may move comically on land, but once you reach the rocky outcrops overlooking the water you'll see how graceful and powerful these creatures become when they enter the water. You may also spot guanacos, seals, and Patagonian hares in the reserve, as well as cormorants and a host of other seabirds.

■TIP→ The last 22 km (13½ miles) of the road from Trelew is fairly bumpy gravel. If you're not driving, you can easily reach Punta Tombo on a day tour from Trelew, Gaiman, or Puerto Madryn, although note that these often give you a scant 1½ hours in the reserve. A small restaurant next to the carpark serves good lamb empanadas and also has burgers, coffee, cakes, and cold beverages. ⊕ *www.puntatombo.com* 🖃 *About US$7* ⊙ *Daily 8–6.*

SARMIENTO AND THE BOSQUE PETRIFICADO

545 km (339 miles) southwest of Gaiman.

Built in a fertile valley formed by the Río Senguer and its two interconnected lakes, Lago Musters and Lago Colhué Huapi, the Sarmiento area is a green oasis in the middle of the hard Patagonian steppe. The town itself—home to about 13,000 people—is relatively unattractive, but a visit here gives you a taste of what is undeniably and unpretentiously the "real Patagonia." Relatively few foreign travelers come here, even though the lakes and river, petrified forest, and paleontology park are great attractions, and the rolling farmland outside of town is truly striking, with its tall windbreaks of Lombardy poplars twisting in the strong wind.

GETTING HERE AND AROUND

There are several daily bus services between Sarmiento and Comodoro Rivadavia run by ETAP and Don Otto. The latter also has services to Esquel and Bariloche. Buses arrive at the bus station at 12 de Octubre and Avenida San Martín, which runs through the center of town.

Sarmiento is only 15 blocks long and 8 blocks wide, and can be walked easily, but if you get tired or would like to arrange a trip outside of town, there are various remiserías along Avenida San Martín.

You're not the only visitor to Punta Tombo: guanacos might join you as you scope out the Magellanic penguins.

ESSENTIALS

Bus Contacts Don Otto ⊠ *Terminal de Ómnibus* ☎ *297/489–4749* ⊕ *www. donotto.com.ar.* **ETAP** ⊠ *Terminal de Ómnibus* ☎ *297/489–3058.*

Visitor and Tour Infornation Sarmiento ⊠ *Av. Regimiento de Infanteria 25 at Pietrobelli* ☎ *297/489–2105* ⊕ *www.sarmientochubut.gov.ar.*

EXPLORING

Monumento Natural Bosque Petrificado Sarmiento (*Sarmiento Petrified Forest Natural Monument*). An eerie and vast landscape scattered with hundreds of petrified trees takes you more than 75 million years back in time. The palm and conifer trees originally arrived here by river when the area was a tropical delta, although now the sun-bleached and striated badlands are anything but tropical. Dry, parched, and whipped by winds, this place requires a jacket any time of year. Entrance is free, but consider paying for a guide to help you understand exactly what you are looking at. The Monumento Natural Bosque Petrificado Sarmiento is about 30 km (19 miles) from Sarmiento following Ruta 26 until you reach the access road on the right. If you don't have your own vehicle, book a remis from Sarmiento: most will charge you for the return trip, including an hour's waiting time. ⊠ *30 km (19 miles) from Sarmiento* ☎ *297/489–8282* ⊠ *20 pesos* ⊗ *Apr.–Aug., daily 10–6; Oct.–Mar., daily 9–7.*

Parque Paleontológico Valle de los Gigantes (*Valley of the Giants Paleontology Park*). Walk among life-size and scientifically accurate replicas of a dozen different dinosaurs whose fossils were discovered in the region. Guided visits in English leave directly from the tourist office every hour on the hour—arrive 10 minutes ahead to get your ticket. ✉ *200 meters from the tourist office* ☎ *297/489–2105* 💲 *US$1* 🕐 *Mon.–Sun. 10–8.*

While you're in the area, stop at **Lago Musters,** 7 km (4 miles) from Sarmiento, and **Lago Colhué Huapi,** a little farther on. At Lago Musters you can swim, and there's fishing year-round.

> **TO SPELUNK?**
>
> Unique in the region, **spelunking,** or cave exploration, is possible at the **Túnel de Sarasola,** a natural basalt tunnel 45 km (28 miles) west of Sarmiento. Agencia Santa Teresita (☎ *297/489–3238*) can arrange expeditions there.

WHERE TO STAY

$$
B&B/INN
Fodor's Choice
★

🏨 **Hostería Labrador.** You get a taste of Patagonian country life when you stay on this working *chacra* (farm) as wife-and-husband team Annelies Geritsen (who speaks Dutch and English) and Nicolás Ayling (who speaks English) welcome guests, tend the land, produce homemade fruit preserves and honey, and cook huge breakfasts for their guests. **Pros:** homey atmosphere; Nicolás can arrange local guided tours. **Cons:** far out of town—you need your own vehicle. 💲 *Rooms from: US$100* ✉ *R20, 10 km (6 miles) from Sarmiento, 1 km (½ mile) before the Río Senguer* ☎ *2974/893–329* ⊕ *www.hosterialabrador.com* 🛏 *5 rooms* ▬ *No credit cards* 🕐 *Closed Apr.–Sept.* 🍴 *Breakfast.*

$
HOTEL

🏨 **Los Lagos.** This small, affordable hotel has updated carpets, furnishings, and bathrooms; the staff doesn't speak much English but they're friendly and helpful and there's a decent on-site restaurant. **Pros:** affordable; free Wi-Fi. **Cons:** can get hot in summer. 💲 *Rooms from: US$59* ✉ *Av. Roca at Alberdi* ☎ *2974/893–046* ⊕ *www.hotelloslagos.com.ar* 🛏 *20 rooms* ▬ *No credit cards* 🍴 *Breakfast.*

EL CALAFATE, EL CHALTÉN, AND PARQUE NACIONAL LOS GLACIARES

The Hielo Continental (Continental Ice Cap) spreads its icy mantle from the Pacific Ocean across Chile and the Andes into Argentina, covering an area of 21,700 square km (8,400 square miles). Approximately 1½ million acres of it are contained within the Parque Nacional los Glaciares (Glaciers National Park), a UNESCO World Heritage Site. The park extends along the Chilean border for 350 km (217 miles), and 40% of it is covered by ice fields that branch off into 47 glaciers feeding two enormous lakes—the 15,000-year-old **Lago Argentino** (Argentine Lake, the largest body of water in Argentina and the third largest in South America) at the park's southern end, and **Lago Viedma** (Lake Viedma) at the northern end near **Cerro Fitzroy,** which rises 11,138 feet.

Plan on a minimum of two to three days to see the glaciers and enjoy El Calafate—more if you plan to visit El Chaltén or any of the other lakes. Entrance to the southern section of the park, which includes Perito Moreno Glacier, costs around US$20 for non-Argentineans.

Near Parque Nacional Los Glaciares and El Calafate you'll find some of the most remote-feeling estancias in Argentina.

EL CALAFATE

320 km (225 miles) north of Río Gallegos via R5; 253 km (157 miles) east of Río Turbio on Chilean border via R40; 213 km (123 miles) south of El Chaltén via R40.

Founded in 1927 as a frontier town, El Calafate is the base for excursions to the Parque Nacional Los Glaciares, which was created in 1937 as a showcase for one of South America's most spectacular sights, the Glaciar Perito Moreno. Because it's on the southern shore of Lago Argentino, the town enjoys a microclimate much milder than the rest of southern Patagonia.

To call El Calafate a boomtown would be a gross understatement. In the first decade of this millennium the town's population exploded from 4,000 to more than 25,000, and it shows no signs of slowing down; at every turn you'll see new construction, with many luxury and boutique hotels cropping up. As a result, the downtown has a new sheen to it, although most buildings are constructed of wood, with a rustic aesthetic that respects the majestic natural environment. One exception is the casino in the heart of downtown, the facade of which seems to mock the face of the Glaciar Perito Moreno. Farther out of the city is another glacier lookalike, the brand new Glaciarium museum, architecturally modeled on Perito Moreno and with Argentina's only ice bar.

Now with a paved road between El Calafate and the glacier, the visitors continue to flock in to see the creaking ice sculptures. These visitors include luxury-package tourists bound for handsome estancias in the park surroundings, backpackers over from Chile's Parque Nacional

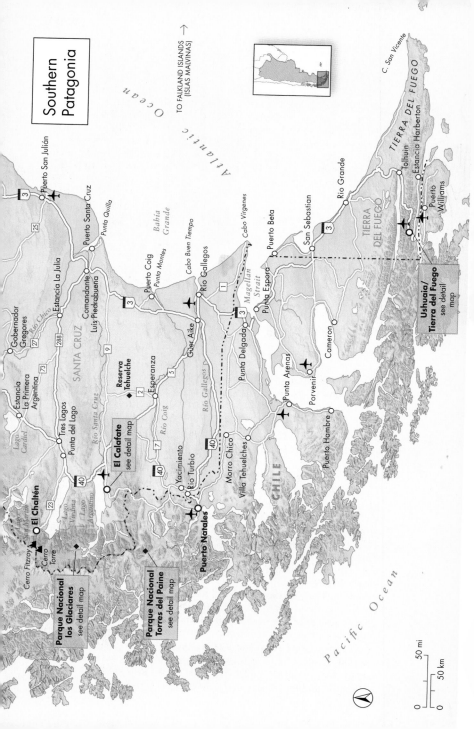

CASH WOES

For a town that lives and dies on tourism, one of the most infuriating elements of the boom is the cash shortage that strikes El Calafate every weekend during high season. The four ATMs in town frequently run out of money starting as early as Friday evening, and there's often no respite until midday Monday.

The shortage is compounded by tour companies who offer steep discounts for cash on combined glacier, ice-trekking, and estancia tours. Apart from stocking up during the week, the best plan to ensure that you won't run out is to bring all the cash you'll need for your stay here. If worse comes to worst, most hotels and many restaurants will accept credit cards, or exchange dollars.

Torres del Paine, and *porteños* (from Buenes Aires) in town for a long weekend.

GETTING HERE AND AROUND

Daily flights from Buenos Aires, Ushuaia, and Río Gallegos, and direct flights from Bariloche transport tourists to El Calafate's 21st-century glass-and-steel airport with the promise of adventure and discovery in distant mountains and glaciers. El Calafate is so popular that the flights sell out weeks in advance, so don't plan on booking at the last minute.

If you can't get on a flight or are looking for a cheaper option, there are daily buses between El Calafate, El Chaltén, Río Gallegos, Ushuaia, and Puerto Natales in Chile—all of which can be booked at the bus terminal. El Calafate is also the starting (or finishing) point for the legendary Ruta 40 journey to Bariloche. If you can bear the bus travel for a few days, you'll pass some exceptional scenery, and most operators allow you to hop on and hop off at canyons, lakes, and the famous handprint-covered caves en route.

Driving from Río Gallegos takes about four hours across desolate plains enlivened by occasional sightings of a gaucho, his dogs, and a herd of sheep, and *ñandú* (rheas), shy llama-like guanacos, silver-gray foxes, and fleet-footed hares the size of small deer. Esperanza is the only gas, food, and bathroom stop halfway between the two towns. Driving from Puerto Natales is similar, although snow-topped mountains line the distance; arriving by road from Ushuaia requires four border crossings and more than 18 hours.

Avenida del Libertador San Martín (known simply as Libertador) is El Calafate's main street, with tour offices, restaurants, and shops selling regional specialties, sportswear, camping and fishing equipment, and food.

A staircase ascends from the middle of Libertador to Avenida Julio Roca, where you'll find the bus terminal and a very busy Oficina de Turismo with a board listing available accommodations and campgrounds; you can also get brochures and maps, and there's a multilingual staff to help plan excursions. The tourism office has another location on the corner of Rosales and Libertador; both locations are open daily from 8 to 8 (during high season). The Oficina Parques Nacionales, open week-days 8 to 4, has information on the Parque Nacional Los Glaciares, including the glaciers, area history, hiking trails, and flora and fauna.

TIMING

During the long summer days between December and February (when the sun sets around 10 pm), and during Easter vacation, tens of thou-sands of visitors come from all corners of the world and fill the hotels and restaurants. This is the area's high season, so make reservations well in advance. October, November, March, and April are less crowded and less expensive periods to visit, although some estancias might still be closed. March through May can be rainy and cool, but it's also less windy and often quite pleasant, and the autumn colors can be quite stunning. The only bad time to visit is winter, particularly May, June, July, and August, when many of the hotels and tour agencies are closed.

TOURS

In El Calafate, each tour has to be approved by the local government and is assigned to one tour operator only. On the upside you'll never fall foul of a shady operator, but on the downside there is no compe-tition to keep prices low. Whether you book a tour directly with the operator who leads it, with another operator, or through your hotel or other tour agency, the price should remain the same. Take note that most tour prices do not include the park entrance fee, an extra US$30 for foreigners.

ESSENTIALS

Bus Contacts Cal Tur ⊠ *Terminal Ómnibus* ☎ *2902/493–801* ⊕ *www.caltur. com.ar* ⊠ *Av. Libertador 1080* ☎ *2902/491–842* ⊕ *www.caltur.com.ar.* **Freddy** ☎ *2902/492–127.* **TAQSA** ⊠ *Bus terminal* ☎ *2902/491–843* ⊕ *www.taqsa.com. ar.* **Turismo Zaahj** ⊠ *Bus terminal* ☎ *2902/491–631* ⊕ *www.turismozaahj.co.cl.*

Currency Exchange Casa de Cambio Thaler ⊠ *Av. del Libertador 963* ☎ *2902/493–245.*

Remis El Calafate ⊠ *Av. Roca 1004* ☎ *2902/492–005.*

Rental Cars Fiorasi ⊠ *Av. Libertador 1319* ☎ *2902/495–330.* **Hertz** ⊠ *Av. del Libertador 1822* ☎ *2902/493–033.* **ServiCar** ⊠ *Av. Libertador 695* ☎ *2902/492–541.*

Visitor and Tour Information Oficina de Turismo ⊠ *Rosales at Libertador* ☎ *2902/491–090* ⊕ *www.elcalafate.gov.ar* ⊠ *Bus terminal* ☎ *2902/491–476.* **Oficina Parques Nacionales** ⊠ *Av. Libertador 1302* ☎ *2902/491–005, 2902/491–545* ⊕ *www.parquesnacionales.gov.ar.*

EXPLORING

Glaciarium. This out-of-town glacier museum gives you an educational walk through the formation and life of glaciers (particularly in Pata-gonia) and the effects of climate change, as well as temporary art exhi-bitions. A 3-D film about the national park and plenty of brightly lit displays, along with the stark glacier-shaped architecture, give it a mod-ern appeal. Don't miss the Glaciobar —the first ice bar in Argentina— where you can don thermal suits, boots, and gloves, and where a whisky on the rocks means 200-year-old glacier rocks from Perito Moreno.

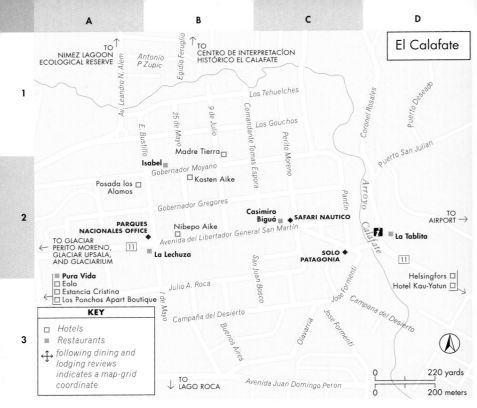

☒ *R7, Km 6* ✛ *Arrive by taxi (US$10 each way), 1 hr walking, or by the shuttle service from the tourism office leaving every hr (US$5 return)* ☎ *2902/497–912* ⊕ *www.glaciarium.com* ☒ *Museum US$18; bar US$14 for 25 mins, includes 1 drink* ☉ *Daily 9–8 (shorter hrs in winter), bar daily noon–6:30.*

Fodor's Choice
★

Glaciar Perito Moreno. Eighty km (50 miles) away on Ruta 11, the road to the Glaciar Perito Moreno has now been entirely paved. From the park entrance the road winds through hills and forests of lenga and ñire trees, until all at once the glacier comes into full view. Descending like a long white tongue through distant mountains, it ends abruptly in a translucent azure wall 5 km (3 miles) wide and 240 feet high at the edge of frosty green Lago Argentino.

Although it's possible to rent a car and go on your own (which can give you the advantage of avoiding large tourist groups), virtually everyone visits the park on a day trip booked through one of the many travel agents in El Calafate. The most basic tours start at US$50 for the round-trip and take you to see the glacier from a viewing area composed of a series of platforms wrapped around the point of the Península de Magallanes. The platforms, which offer perhaps the most impressive view of the glacier, allow you to wander back and forth, looking across the Canal de los Tempanos (Iceberg Channel). Here you listen and wait for nature's number-one ice show—first, a cracking sound, followed by tons of ice breaking away and falling with a thunderous crash into the lake. As the glacier creeps across this narrow channel and meets the land on the other side, an ice dam sometimes builds up between the inlet of Brazo Rico on the left and the rest of the lake on the right. As the pressure on the dam increases, everyone waits for the day it will rupture again. The last time was in July 2008, when the whole thing collapsed in a series of explosions, heard as far away as El Calafate, that sent huge waves across the lake.

In recent years the surge in the number of visitors to Glaciar Perito Moreno has created a crowded scene that is not always conducive to reflective encounters with nature's majesty. Although the glacier remains spectacular, savvy travelers would do well to minimize time at the madhouse that the viewing area becomes at midday in high season, and instead encounter the glacier by boat or on a mini-trekking excursion. Better yet, rent a car and get an early start to beat the tour buses, or visit Perito Moreno in the off-season when a spectacular rupture is just as likely as in midsummer and you won't have to crane over other people's heads to see it.

Glaciar Upsala. The largest glacier in South America, Glaciar Upsala is 55 km (35 miles) long and 10 km (6 miles) wide, and accessible only by boat. Daily cruises depart from Puerto Banderas (40 km [25 miles] west of El Calafate via R11) for the 2½-hour trip. Dodging floating icebergs (*tempanos*), some as large as a small island, the boats maneuver as close as they dare to the wall of ice that rises from the aqua-green water of Lago Argentino. The seven glaciers that feed the lake deposit their debris into the runoff, causing the water to cloud with minerals ground to fine powder by the glacier's moraine (the accumulation of earth and stones left by the glacier). Condors and black-chested buzzard eagles build their nests in the rocky cliffs above the lake. When the boat stops for lunch at Onelli Bay, don't miss the walk behind the restaurant into a wild landscape of small glaciers and milky rivers carrying chunks of ice from four glaciers into Lago Onelli. Glaciar Upsala has diminished in size in recent years. ✉ *Cruises start from US$50.*

Nimez Lagoon Ecological Reserve. A marshy area on the shore of Lago Argentino just a short walk from downtown El Calafate, the Nimez Lagoon Ecological Reserve is home to many species of waterfowl, including black-necked swans, buff-necked ibises, southern lapwings, and flamingos. Road construction along its edge and the rapidly advancing town threaten to stifle this avian oasis, but it's still a haven for birdwatchers and a relaxing walk in the early morning or late afternoon. Strolling along footpaths among grazing horses and flocks of birds may not be as intense an experience as, say, trekking on a glacier, but a trip to the lagoon provides a good sense of the local landscape. During high season the nature reserve is open from 8 am until 9 pm. Don't forget your binoculars and a telephoto lens. ✉ *1 km (½ miles) north of downtown, just off Av. Alem* ☎ *2902/495–536* ✉ *About US$3.*

VISITING LAGO ROCA

Lago Roca. This little-visited lake is inside the national park just south of Brazo Rico, 46 km (29 miles) from El Calafate. The area receives about five times as much annual precipitation as El Calafate, creating a relatively lush climate of green meadows by the lakeshore, where locals come to picnic and cast for trophy rainbow and lake trout. Don't miss a hike into the hills behind the lake—the view of dark-blue Lago Roca backed by a pale-green inlet of Lago Argentino with the Glaciar Perito Moreno and jagged snowcapped peaks beyond is truly outstanding.

Camping Lago Roca. There are gorgeous campsites, simple cabins, fishing-tackle rentals, hot showers, and a basic restaurant at Camping Lago Roca. Make reservations in advance if visiting over the Christmas holidays; at other times the campground is seldom crowded. In high season Cal Tur offer shuttles from Lago Roca to Perito Moreno. For more comfortable accommodations, you can arrange to stay at the Nibepo Aike Estancia at the western end of Lago Roca, about 5 km (3 miles) past the campground. The national park entrance fee is collected only on the road to Glaciar Perito Moreno or at Puerto Banderas, where cruises depart, so admission to the Lago Roca corner of the park is free. ☎ *2902/499–500* ⊕ *www. losglaciares.com/campinglagoroca* ☽ *Closed May–Sept.*

WHERE TO EAT

$$$$
ARGENTINE

✕**Casimiro Biguá.** This restaurant and wine bar boasts a hipper-than-thou interior and modern menu serving such delights as Patagonian lamb with *calafate* sauce (calafate is a local wild berry). The **Casimiro Biguá Parrilla,** down the street from the main restaurant, has a similar trendy feel but you can recognize the parrilla by the *cordero al asador* (spit-roasted lamb) displayed in the window. A third branch, also on Libertador, offers Italian dishes in a less formal setting. Each closes periodically during winter. Ⓢ *Average main: US$25* ✉ *Av. Libertador 963* ☎ *2902/492–590* ⊕ *www.casimirobigua.com* ✛ *C2.*

$$$
ARGENTINE
Fodor'sChoice
★

✕**Isabel.** It takes a lot of moxie to open a restaurant not serving cordero, barbecue, or pizza in Patagonia, and former "fancy" chefs José and Leandro show they have just that with their homely restaurant, Isabel. They use vintage plow wheels to cook a traditional and ultimately delicious stew-style dish known as *al disco*. The al disco menu offers all sorts of meats and veggies cooked in beer, red wine, or white wine; more creative and quasi-modern options like Bife al Napolitana; or you can create your own. And you've got to love a restaurant that tells you not to bother with starters but rather just dunk your bread in the disco sauce. Great atmosphere, laid-back charm, and effortlessly tasty food have made this one of the most popular new additions in town. Ⓢ *Average main: US$14* ✉ *Gobernador Moyano 1226, at 25 Mayo* ☎ *2902/489–000* ✛ *B2.*

$$
ARGENTINE

✕**La Lechuza.** This bustling joint is known for having some of the best pizza in town. The brick oven and thin crust make for a more authentic, Italian-style taste and texture than at most spots. Their empanadas are just as good—pick up a few and you have the perfect pastry pick-me-up during a long day's exploring. With two other branches on the main strip (one with a kids' playground and the other for more Patagonian-style dishes), the secret is out, but stick with the original pizzeria, as the locals do. If it's not crowded, you're in the wrong one. $ *Average main: US$12* ⊠ *Av. Libertador at 1 de Mayo* ☎ *2902/491–610* ✛ *B2.*

$$$
ARGENTINE

✕ **La Tablita.** It's a couple of extra blocks from downtown and across a little white bridge, but this parrilla is where the locals go for a special night out. You can watch your food as it's cooking: Patagonian lamb and beef ribs roasting gaucho-style on frames hanging over a circular asador, and an enormous grill along the back wall is full of steaks, chorizos, and *morcilla* (blood sausage). The whole place is filled with a warm glow despite the lackluster décor. It's slightly more expensive than other parillas in the center of town—and almost always fully booked—but has a classier atmosphere that will make you want to linger for dessert, if you have room. $ *Average main: US$14* ⊠ *Coronel Rosales 28* ☎ *2902/491–065* ⊕ *www.la-tablita.com.ar* ✛ *D2.*

$$
ARGENTINE

✕ **Pura Vida.** Bohemian music, homey cooking, and colorful patchwork cushions set the tone for this unpretentious, vegetarian-friendly restaurant several blocks from downtown. You'll be surrounded by funky artwork, couples whispering under low-hung lights, and laid-back but efficient staff as you try to decide which big-enough-to-share dish you'll order while working your way through a great dome of steaming bread. Choose between soups, pies, and bakes; the stew served inside a *calabaza* (pumpkin) is the signature dish. The cooking isn't quite up to the rest of the restaurant's charms, and the wine list is thin, but Pura Vida is more than the sum of its parts, attracting a curious blend of diners. $ *Average main: US$12* ⊠ *Av. Libertador 1876* ☎ *2902/493–356* ⊘ *Closed Wed. No lunch* ✛ *A3.*

WHERE TO STAY

$$$$
HOTEL
ALL-INCLUSIVE

⌂ **Eolo.** A luxury lodge on the road to Perito Moreno, Eolo offers full-board stays in handsome accommodations where you can take in the beauty of Patagonia's vast, empty lands and see Lago Argentino in the distance. **Pros:** beautiful location; luxury service. **Cons:** expensive; no drinks included; far from town or any services. $ *Rooms from: US$950* ⊠ *RP11 N, Km 23* ☎ *2902/492–042* ⊕ *www.eolo.com.ar* ⇱ *12 rooms, 5 suites* ⊘ *Closed mid-Apr.–mid-Oct.* ⏉ *All-inclusive* ✛ *A3.*

$$$$
HOTEL
ALL-INCLUSIVE

⌂ **Estancia Cristina.** Boarding a catamaran for the four-hour journey across Lago Argentino, you pass a field of giant icebergs in front of the Glaciar Upsala—as spectacular as Perito Moreno, minus the crowds—then disembark at Punta Bandera for a short drive up to the three guest lodges, their stark green roofs mirroring the mountain ridges beyond. **Pros:** combines a glacier visit with a stay in a genuine estancia; gourmet packed lunches; knowledgeable guides; incredible mountain views from comfortable, well-appointed rooms. **Cons:** long boat journey to get here; pricey for a one-night stay. $ *Rooms from: US$620* ⊠ *Punta Bandera* ☎ *2902/491–133* ⊕ *www.estanciacristina.com* ⇱ *20 rooms* ⊘ *Closed mid-Apr.–mid-Nov.* ⏉ *All-inclusive* ✛ *A3.*

8

$$$$ HOTEL ALL-INCLUSIVE Fodor's Choice ★ 🏨 **Helsingfors.** This luxurious converted ranch house has an absolutely spectacular location in the middle of the national park on the shore of Lago Viedma. **Pros:** unique location; wonderful staff; comfy atmosphere; beautiful blue lake. **Cons:** three hours by dirt road from El Calafate; expensive. [$] *Rooms from: US$725* ✉ *Lago Viedma* ☎ *11/5277–0195 in Buenos Aires* 🌐 *www.helsingfors.com.ar* 🛏 *9 rooms (max. 20 guests)* ⏲ *Closed May–Sept.* 🍴 *All-inclusive* ✥ *D3.*

$$ HOTEL FAMILY 🏨 **Hotel Kau-Yatun.** From the homemade chocolates and wildflower bouquets that appear in the rooms each evening to the sweeping backyard complete with swing sets for the kids, there are many thoughtful details in this converted ranch. **Pros:** good food; nice details; central location. **Cons:** water pressure is only adequate; lost a bit of personality from chain takeover. [$] *Rooms from: US$180* ✉ *25 de Mayo s/n* ☎ *2902/491–059* 🌐 *www.kauyatun.com* 🛏 *44 rooms* ⏲ *Closed Apr.–Sept.* 🍴 *Breakfast* ✥ *D3.*

$$$ HOTEL 🏨 **Kosten Aike.** Lined with wooden balconies, high beamed ceilings, and a slate floor, this hotel is a paragon of Andean Patagonian architecture. **Pros:** large rooms; central location; great views from the spa; good value at this price point. **Cons:** dining room décor is uninspired. [$] *Rooms from: US$208* ✉ *G. Moyano 1243, at 25 de Mayo* ☎ *2902/492–424* 🌐 *www.kostenaike.com.ar* 🛏 *78 rooms, 2 suites* ⏲ *Closed May–Sept.* 🍴 *Breakfast* ✥ *B2.*

$$$ B&B/INN 🏨 **Los Ponchos Apart Boutique.** Cozy and handsomely designed two-floor apartments in this boutique complex have beautiful views over Lago Argentino and offer some independence and privacy with a self-catering kitchen and homey, gaucho-chic decoration. **Pros:** warm service; cozy; private. **Cons:** a bit of a walk from town. [$] *Rooms from: US$220* ✉ *Los Alamos 3321* ☎ *2902/496–330* 🌐 *www.losponchosapart.com.ar* 🛏 *8 rooms, 2 duplex apartments, 1 cabin* ⏲ *Closed June–mid-Sept.* 🍴 *Breakfast* ✥ *A3.*

$$ B&B/INN 🏨 **Madre Tierra.** The friendly welcome from the owners makes staying at this B&B feel like visiting a friend's home (with great attention to detail in design and well-chosen furnishings). **Pros:** personalized and friendly service; central location; authentic. **Cons:** accept cash payments only; walls are thin and noise travels. [$] *Rooms from: US$165* ✉ *9 de Julio 239* ☎ *2902/489–880* 🌐 *www.madretierrapatagonia.com* 🛏 *7 rooms* 🍴 *Breakfast* ✥ *B1.*

$$$$ RESORT 🏨 **Nibepo Aike.** This lovely estancia is an hour and a half from El Calafate in a bucolic valley overlooking Lago Roca and backed by snow-capped mountain peaks. Sheep, horses, and cows graze among purple lupine flowers, and friendly gauchos give horse-racing and sheep-shearing demonstrations. **Pros:** spectacular scenery; yummy food; welcoming staff. **Cons:** long drive by dirt road from downtown; two-night minimum stay; no Wi-Fi. [$] *Rooms from: US$340* ✉ *For reservations: Av. Libertador 1215* ☎ *11/5031–0755 for reservations (Buenos Aires), 2902/492–797 for day visits (El Calafate)* 🌐 *www.nibepoaike.com.ar* 🛏 *10 rooms* ⏲ *Closed May–Sept.* 🍴 *Multiple meal plans* ✥ *B2.*

$$$ HOTEL 🏨 **Posada los Alamos.** Surrounded by tall, leafy alamo trees and constructed of brick and dark *quebracho* (ironwood), this enormous complex incorporates a country manor house, half a dozen convention

"We walked from our hotel in the center of town to the Laguna Nimez Reserve. Wild horses grazed lazily amid the white wildflowers. It was a magical moment . . . So unexpected!" —Lois Zebelman, Fodors.com member

rooms, a spa, indoor swimming pool, and minigolf course to offer all the trappings of a top-notch hotel. **Pros:** modern and distinctive reception and public areas; beautiful gardens; long breakfast hours. **Cons:** it's easy to get lost in the maze of corridors; rooms are indifferently furnished; overly formal staff. $ *Rooms from: US$245* ✉ *Moyano at Bustillo* ☎ *2902/491–144* ⊕ *www.posadalosalamos.com* ⤴ *144 rooms* ❖| *Breakfast* ✛ *A2.*

SPORTS AND THE OUTDOORS

BOAT TOURS

Glaciares Gourmet. If fine dining and sipping wine while admiring the glaciers is more your style, this is the no-effort-required cruise for you. With a maximum of 28 passengers, the deluxe cruise liner is never overcrowded. You get a full day of cruising around the Spegazzini and Upsala glaciers, a short leg-stretching walk at beauty spot Puesto de las Vacas, and a six-course gourmet lunch with wine. If a full day isn't enough, you can opt for the two-night cruise option where you'll visit four glaciers (Spegazzini, Upsala, Perito Moreno, and Mayo) and access views that no one else can. ✉ *Cruceros Marpatag, 9 de Julio (Local 4, Galleria de los Pajaros)* ☎ *2902/492–118* ⊕ *www.crucerosmarpatag. com* ✉ *From US$288.*

Safari Náutico. Boats depart from a small port 7 km (4 miles) from Perito Moreno glacier and take tourists on an hour-long cruise around the glacier's south face for a closer inspection of the advancing glacier and floating icebergs. On a good day, you can stand on the deck for the best up-close photo opportunities. Tours run year-round and can be reserved at the port or in advance in the downtown office or other

Great views of Cerro Fitzroy seem to wait at every bend on the trail in Parque Nacional Los Glaciares.

tour agencies. ⊠ *Hielo y Aventura, Av. Libertador 935* ☎ *2902/492–205* ⊕ *www.hieloyaventura.com* ✉ *From US$50.*

Solo Patagonia. With two different full-day boat excursions, Solo Patagonia has been navigating the milky waters for years. Their fleet of large cruisers offers access to some of the best views of the Perito Moreno, Upsala, and Spegazzini glaciers from October to March. ⊠ *Av. Libertador 867* ☎ *2902/491–155* ⊕ *www.solopatagonia.com* ✉ *From US$70.*

HIKING

Although it's possible to find trails along the shore of Lago Argentino and in the hills south and west of town, these hikes traverse a rather barren landscape and are not terribly interesting. The mountain peaks and forests are in the park, an hour by car from El Calafate. If you want to lace up your boots in your hotel, walk outside, and hit the trail, go to El Chaltén—it's a much better base than El Calafate for hikes in the national park. Good hiking trails are accessible from the camping areas and cabins by Lago Roca, 50 km (31 miles) from El Calafate.

HORSEBACK RIDING AND ESTANCIAS

Alta Vista. Convenient to El Calafate, Alta Vista is a solid choice for the standard estancia activites (horses, sheep, asados) and offers good guidance for local hikes. ⊠ *R15, 33 km (20 miles) from El Calafate* ☎ *2902/499–902* ⊕ *www.hosteriaaltavista.com.ar.*

Estancia El Galpón del Glaciar. This estancia welcomes guests overnight or for the day—for a horseback ride, bird-watching, or an afternoon program that includes a demonstration of sheep dogs working, a walk to the lake with a naturalist, sheep-shearing, and dinner in the former sheep-shearing barn served right off the asador by knife-wielding gauchos.

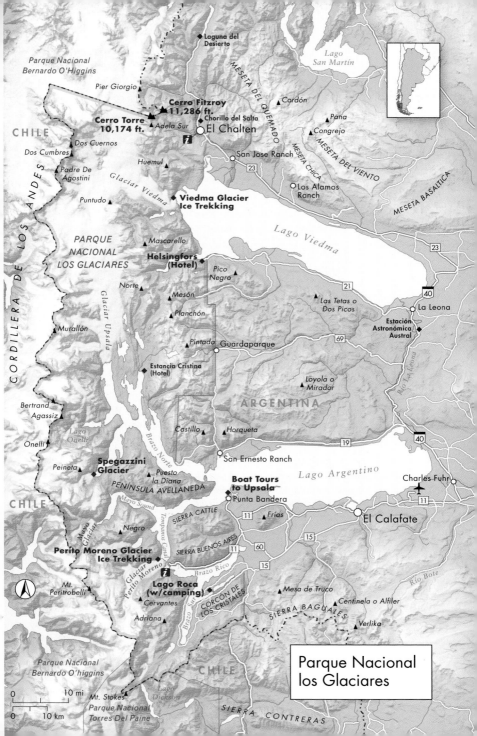

Parque Nacional
los Glaciares

⊠ *R11, Km 22* ☎ *2902/497–793–503, 11/5217–6719* ⊕ *www.el galpondelglaciar.com.ar.*

Nibepo Aike. This pretty estancia an hour and a half from El Calafate offers a range of horseback experiences from hour-long excursions to full-day, nine-hour rides to view glaciers in the distance. It's possible to visit Nibepo Aike by booking a day trip at the office in downtown El Calafate, or you can stay overnight at the estancia. ⊠ *R15, 53 km (31 miles) from El Calafate near Lago Roca* ☎ *2902/492–797, 2902/492–859* ⊕ *www.nibepoaike.com.ar.*

> ## ESTANCIAS TURÍSTICAS
>
> **Provincial Tourist Office.** *Estancias turísticas* (tourist ranches) are ideal for a combination of horseback riding, ranch activities, and local excursions. Information on all the estancias can be obtained from Estancias de Santa Cruz in Buenos Aires, or on the website. ⊠ *Reconquista 642, Buenos Aires* ☎ *11/5237–4043* ⊕ *www. estanciasdesantacruz.com.*

ICE TREKKING

Hielo y Aventura. For the most unusual and up-close-and-personal experience with Glaciar Perito Moreno, book yourself an ice-trekking day trip where you'll don crampons and walk over the glacier studying crevasses and ice lakes before finishing with a whiskey on the rocks using ice from the glacier. The Mini Trekking excursion is a 10-hour trip and includes a 90-minute ice trek, a short hike in the forest, a 20-minute boat ride, and a transfer to the park from your hotel. You'll have to pay your own park entrance, bring a packed lunch, and wear the right clothing (crampons are provided), but you also get over an hour to enjoy the view of Perito Moreno from the park. For a more in-depth and challenging ice day, Hielo y Aventura also offers the Big Ice trek, which includes more time on the ice and ducking through bright-blue ice tunnels. This excursion has around seven hours' walking in total and is a longer day (ages 18–50 only). During high season, tours can get a bit crowded, but with a glacier the size of Buenos Aires, there is plenty of white space to feel true isolation. Ice trekking is available May through mid-September. ⊠ *Av. Libertador 935* ☎ *2902/492–205* ⊕ *www.hieloyaventura.com* ✉ *From US$100.*

KAYAKING

Viva Patagonia. Those brave enough to get in the milky ice waters can get dropped off by a boat on the glacier's edge and take a two-hour guided kayaking excursion with this outfitter. Available November through March, weather permitting. ⊠ *Calafate Mountain Park (Viva Patagonia), Av. Libertador 1037* ☎ *2902/491–446* ⊕ *www. calafatemountainpark.com* ✉ *From US$30.*

LAND ROVER EXCURSIONS

MIL Outdoor. If pedaling uphill sounds like too much work, check out the Land Rover expeditions offered October through April. These trips use large tour trucks to follow dirt tracks into the hills above town for stunning views of Lago Argentino. On a clear day, you can even see the peaks of Cerro Torre and Cerro Fitzroy on the horizon. MIL's Land Rovers are converted to run on vegetable oil, so environmentalists can enjoy bouncing up the trail with a clean conscience. During the winter, the same company (also known as Calafate Mountain Park) runs a children's snow park with sledding, beginners' slopes, and more advanced off-piste skiing, snowshoeing and tearing around on snowmobiles. Open Winter only, the snow park is 15 km (9 miles) from El Calafate. ⊠ *MIL Aventura (Calafate Mountain Park/Viva Patagonia), Av. Libertador 1037* ☎ *2902/491–446* ⊕ *www.calafatemountainpark. com* ⤳ *From US$50.*

MOUNTAIN BIKING

Alquiler de Bicicletas. Mountain biking is popular along the dirt roads and mountain paths that lead to the lakes, glaciers, and ranches. Rent bikes and get information at Alquiler de Bicicletas. ⊠ *HLS, Perito Moreno 65* ☎ *2902/493–806.*

EL CHALTÉN

222 km (138 miles) north of El Calafate (35 km [22 miles] east on R11 to R40, then north on R40 to R23 north).

Founded in 1985, El Chaltén is Argentina's newest town, and it's growing at an astounding rate. Originally just a few shacks and lodges built near the entrance to Parque Nacional Los Glaciares, the town is starting to fill a steep-walled valley in front of Cerro Torre and Cerro Fitzroy, two of the most impressive peaks in Argentina.

Famous for the exploits of rock climbers who started their pilgrimage to climb some of the most difficult rock walls in the world in the 1950s, the range is now drawing hikers whose more earthbound ambitions run to dazzling mountain scenery and unscripted encounters with wildlife including condors, Patagonian parrots, red-crested woodpeckers, and the *huemul*, an endangered deer species.

GETTING HERE AND AROUND

The three-hour car or bus trip to El Chaltén from El Calafate makes staying at least one night here a good idea. The only gas, food, and restroom facilities en route are at La Leona, a historically significant ranch 110 km (68 miles) from El Calafate where Butch Cassidy and the Sundance Kid once hid from the long arm of the law.

Before you cross the bridge into town over Río Fitzroy, stop at the Parque Nacional office. It's extremely well organized and staffed by bilingual rangers who can help you plan your mountain treks and point you to accommodations and restaurants in town. It's an essential stop; orientation talks are given in coordination with arriving buses, which automatically stop here before continuing on to the bus depot.

There's only one ATM in town (it's in the bus station), and it's in high demand; because of servicing schedules, on the weekend El Chaltén runs into the same cash availability problems that El Calafate does, though on a smaller scale. ⚠ **During the week, stockpile the cash you'll need for the weekend, or bring it with you if you're arriving between midday Friday and midday Monday.**

ESSENTIALS

Visitor Information Parque Nacional Office ✉ *Av. M.M. de Güemes 21* ☎ *2962/493–004* 🌐 *www.losglaciares.com/en.*

EXPLORING

Cerro Torre and Cerro Fitzroy. You don't need a guide to do the classic treks to Cerro Torre and Cerro Fitzroy, each about 6 to 8 hours round-trip out of El Chaltén. If your legs feel up to it the day you do the Fitzroy walk, tack on an hour of steep switchbacks to Mirador Tres Lagos, the lookout with the best views of Cerro Fitzroy and its glacial lakes. Both routes, plus the Mirador and various side trails, can be combined in a two- or three-day trip.

Chorillo del Salta (*Trickling Falls*). Just 4 km (2½ miles) north of town on the road to Lago del Desierto, the Chorillo del Salta waterfall is no Iguazú, but the area is extremely pleasant and sheltered from the wind. A short hike uphill leads to secluded river pools and sun-splashed rocks where locals enjoy picnics on their days off. If you don't feel up to a more ambitious hike, the short stroll to the falls is an excellent way to spend the better part of an afternoon. Pack a bottle of wine and a sandwich and enjoy the solitude.

Laguna del Desierto (*Lake of the Desert*). A lovely lake surrounded by lush forest, complete with orchids and mossy trees, the Laguna del Desierto is 37 km (23 miles) north of El Chaltén on R23, a dirt road. Hotels in El Chaltén can arrange a trip for about US$40 for the day. Locals recommend visiting Lago del Desierto on a rainy day, when more ambitious hikes are not an option and the dripping green misty forest is extra mysterious.

WHERE TO EAT AND STAY

$$$ ARGENTINE 🍴 **Aonikenk.** In a dark wooden dining hall you'll share hearty steaks, warming soups, and wine poured from penguin-shape ceramic jugs, in a family restaurant that includes a hostel upstairs. It's rustic, and the food is not spectacular, but you can't beat the friendly atmosphere in what is easily El Chaltén's largest and most popular restaurant. It's also the only one that's consistently open for lunch and dinner in the off-season. [$] *Average main: US$13* ✉ *Av. M. M. de Güemes 23* ☎ *2962/493–070* 💳 *No credit cards.*

$$ ARGENTINE Fodor's Choice ★ 🍴 **La Cervecería.** While El Chaltén is still building all it needs to become a full-fledged town, it already has a successful microbrewery. The owners of this restaurant and bar pride themselves on handmade beers, with the stout, or *negra,* not to be missed. They call the place a "Hausbrauerei," but it's not just the hops bringing in the crowds: they also cook up delicious soups, snacks, empanadas, and a great *locro* (hearty traditional northern Argentine stew). [$] *Average main: US$10* ✉ *San Martin 320* ☎ *2962/493–109* ⏲ *Closed May–Oct.*

$$$$ HOTEL 🏨 **Aguas Arriba Lodge.** Accessible only by boat or a three-hour trek, Aguas Arriba has a privileged location right on the Lago del Desierto, with a glimmer of Cerro Fitzroy in the distance. **Pros:** fantastic location; attended by owners. **Cons:** noise travels between rooms; private shuttle to lake required in addition to walk/boat; no phone signal. [$] *Rooms from: US$375* ✉ *Lago del Desierto* ☎ *11/4152–5697 (Buenos Aires)*

🌐 *www.aguasarribalodge.com* 🛏 *6 rooms* 🕒 *Closed mid-Apr.–Sept.* 🍴 *Breakfast.*

$ B&B/INN 🏨 **Nothofagus.** A simple B&B off the main road, Nothafagus is named after the southern beech tree, and the lodge has a rough-hewn, woodsy feel with exposed beams and leaves stamped into the lampshades. **Pros:** great views; bright and sunny breakfast room. **Cons:** staff energy too low for some; spartan rooms and bathrooms, some of which are shared. [$] *Rooms from: US$85* ✉ *Hensen, at Riquelme* ☎ *2962/493–087* 🌐 *www.nothofagusbb.com.ar* 🛏 *9 rooms* 💳 *No credit cards* 🕒 *Closed June–Sept.* 🍴 *Breakfast.*

$$ HOTEL 🏨 **Posada Lunajuim.** A traditional A-frame roof keeps the lid on a funky, modern lodge filled with contemporary artwork, exposed brick masonry, and a spacious lounge and dining room complete with a roaring fireplace and a library stacked with an intriguing mix of travel books. **Pros:** you could spend all day in the common areas; staff and owners are pleasantly energetic and will make you a packed lunch for hikes. **Cons:** not all rooms have views; baths are quite small; a little pricey compared to the rest of town. [$] *Rooms from: US$165* ✉ *Trevisan 45* ☎ *2962/493–047* 🌐 *www.lunajuim.com* 🛏 *26 rooms* 🍴 *Breakfast.*

SPORTS AND THE OUTDOORS

El Chaltén owes its existence to those who wanted a base for trekking into this corner of Los Glaciares National Park, specifically Cerro Torre and Cerro Fitzroy. It's no surprise that nearly everyone who comes here considers hiking up to those two mountains to be the main event—though the locro and microbrews at the end of the day are a plus.

HIKING

Both long and short hikes on well-trodden trails lead to lakes, glaciers, and stunning viewpoints. There are two main hikes, one to the base of Cerro Fitzroy, the other to a windswept glacial lake at the base of Cerro Torre. Both hikes climb into the hills above town, and excellent views start after only about an hour on either trail. The six-hour round-trip hike to the base camp for Cerro Torre at Laguna Torre has (weather permitting) dramatic views of Torres Standhart, Adelas, Grande, and Solo.

Trails start in town and are very well marked, so if you stick to the main path there is little danger of getting lost. Just be careful of high winds and exposed rocks that can get slippery in bad weather. The eight-hour hike to the base camp for Cerro Fitzroy passes Laguna Capri and ends at Laguna de los Tres, where you can enjoy an utterly spectacular view of the granite tower. If you have time for only one ambitious hike, this is probably the best choice, though the last kilometer of trail is very steep. At campsites in the hills above town, hardy souls can pitch a tent for the night and enjoy sunset and dawn views of the mountain peaks. Ask about current camping regulations and advisories at the national park office before setting off with a tent in your rucksack. Finally, use latrines where provided, and under no circumstance should you ever think about starting a fire—a large section of forest near Cerro Torre was devastated several years ago when a foolish hiker tried to dispose of toilet paper with a match.

Picadas, or light snacks, reach a new level of delicious after an excursion in the wilds of Patagonia; a selection may include peanuts, pistacios, marinated baby onions, or a local cheese.

MOUNTAIN CLIMBING

Casa de Guias. A guide is required if you want to enter the ice field or trek on any of the glaciers in Parque Nacional Los Glaciares. Casa de Guias is a group of professional, multilingual guides who offer fully equipped multiday treks covering all the classic routes in the national park, and longer trips exploring the ice field. They even offer a taste of big-wall climbing on one of the spires in the Fitzroy range. ⊠ *Av. San Martin 310* ☎ *2962/493–118* ⊕ *www.casadeguias.com.ar.*

El Chaltén Mountain Guides. Five mountain guides offer expeditions in and around El Chaltén, as well as many other destinations in Argentina. One-day and multiday treks and ascents to rock and ice-climbing expeditions are available. In the winter they also offer backcountry skiing tours. ⊠ *San Martín 187* ☎ *2962/493–329* ⊕ *www.ecmg.com.ar.*

PUERTO NATALES AND TORRES DEL PAINE, CHILE

Serious hikers often come to this area and use Puerto Natales as their base for hiking the classic "W" or circuit treks in **Torres del Paine**, which take between four days and a week to complete. Others choose to spend a couple of nights in one of the park's luxury hotels and take in the sights during day hikes.

If you have less time, however, it's possible to spend just one day touring the park, as many people do, with Puerto Natales as your starting point. In that case, rather than drive, you'll want to book a one-day

Torres del Paine tour with one of the many tour operators here. Most tours pick you up at your hotel between 8 and 9 am and follow the same route, visiting several lakes and mountain vistas, seeing Lago Grey and its glacier, and stopping for lunch in Hostería Lago Grey or one of the other hotels inside the park. These tours return around sunset. A budget option is the daily bus tour (year-round) from the bus station with Transportes María José, which also offers hop-on, hop-off options for hikers and campers.

While visiting Torres del Paine remains the most popular excursion, nearby Parque Bernardo O'Higgins is also ripe for exploration with popular boat tours to glaciers with companies Turismo 21 de Mayo (year-round) and Agunsa (September through April).

Argentina's magnificent **Glaciar Perito Moreno,** near El Calafate, can be visited on a popular (but extremely long) one-day tour, leaving at the crack of dawn and returning late at night—don't forget your passport. It's a four-hour-plus trip in each direction; some tours sensibly include overnights in El Calafate.

Please note, if calling outside of Chile, you will require the international dialing code (+56). From within Chile you need to add 0 before dialing any local code.

Prices for restaurants and hotels in Puerto Natales and Torres del Paine are given in Chilean pesos. As of this writing, the exchange rate was US$1 to 595 Chilean pesos.

PUERTO NATALES, CHILE

242 km (150 miles) northwest of Punta Arenas.

Puerto Natales has become the main base for exploring a number of southern Patagonia's top attractions, including Parque Nacional Torres del Paine and Parque Nacional Bernardo O'Higgins. The medium-sized fishing town offers picturesque views of the Seno Última Esperanza (Last Hope Sound) channel, which was named so by Spanish navigator Juan Ladrillero in the 16th century as it was his last hope to reach the Straight of Magellan.

As a launching point for many touristic sites, Puerto Natales has recently seen a large increase in tourism and development with a new surge of luxury accommodation offering all-inclusive stays with excursions. The town has added a string of hip eateries, cafés, and boutique hotels recently, and is starting to challenge the more staid larger city of Punto Arenas as a hub for exploring the entire region.

GETTING HERE AND AROUND

The trip to Puerto Natales from El Calafate is a beautiful journey through color-washed Patagonian landscapes with white peaked mountains in the distance and picturesque estancias and cattle ranches dotted along the way.

Puerto Natales centers on the Plaza de Armas, a lovely, well-landscaped sanctuary. A few blocks west of the plaza on Avenida Bulnes you'll find the small Museo Histórico Municipal. On a clear day, an early morning walk along Avenida Pedro Montt, which follows the shoreline of the

Seno Última Esperanza (or Canal Señoret, as it's called on some maps), can be a soul-cleansing experience. The rising sun gradually casts a glow on the mountain peaks to the west.

ESSENTIALS

Bus Contacts Buses Fernández ⊠ *Eleuterio Ramirez 399* ☎ *612/411–111* ⊕ *www.busesfernandez.com.* **Cootra** ⊠ *Baquedano 456* ☎ *612/412–785.* **Transportes María José** ⊠ *Av. España 1455* ☎ *61/414–312.*

Rental Cars Avis ⊠ *Eberhard 577* ☎ *612/614–388.*

Visitor and Tour Information Tourism Office (Senatur) ⊠ *Pedro Montt and Phillipi* ☎ *61/241–2125* ⊕ *www.patagonia-chile.com* ☉ *Summer weekdays 8:30–7, weekends 10–1 and 2:30–6; winter weekdays 8:30–5.*

EXPLORING

Iglesia Parroquial. Across from the Plaza de Armas is the squat little Iglesia Parroquial. The ornate altarpiece in this church depicts the town's founders, indigenous peoples, and the Virgin Mary all in front of the Torres del Paine. ⊠ *Arturo Prat and Eberhard.*

Museo Historico Municipal. A highlight in the small but interesting Museo Historico Municipal is a room filled with antique prints of Aonikenk and Kaweshkar indigenous peoples. Another room is devoted to the exploits of Hermann Eberhard, a German explorer considered the region's first settler. Check out his celebrated collapsible boat. In an adjacent room you will find some vestiges of the old Bories sheep plant, which processed the meat and wool of over 300,000 sheep a year. ⊠ *Av. Bulnes 285* ☎ *61/220–9548* 🖀 *1,000 pesos* ☉ *Weekdays 8–7, Sat. 10–1 and 3–7.*

Monumento Natural Cueva de Milodón. In 1896, Hermann Eberhard stumbled upon a gaping cave that extended 200 meters (650 feet) into the earth. Venturing inside, he discovered the bones and dried pieces of hide (with deep red fur) of an animal he could not identify. It was later determined that what Eberhard had discovered were the extraordinarily well-preserved remains of a prehistoric herbivorous mammal, *mylodon darwini*, about twice the height of a man, which they called a *milodón*. The discovery of a stone wall in the cave, and of neatly cut grass stalks in the animal's feces led researchers to conclude that 10,000 years ago a group of Tehuelche Indians captured this beast. The cave is at the Monumento Natural Cueva de Milodón. The cathedral-sized space was carved out of a solid rock wall by rising waters. It was the final destination for Bruce Chatwin in research for his book *In Patagonia*, but its dusty floor and barren walls are unspectacular, and the tacky life-size fiberglass model at the cave mouth is useful only as a reference to the size of the gigantic animal that lived here. ⊠ *5 km (3 miles) off R9 signpost, 28 km (17 miles) northwest of Puerto Natales* 🖀 *4,000 pesos* ☉ *Oct.–Apr., daily 8–8; May–Sept., daily 8:30–6.*

Plaza de Armas. A few blocks east of the waterfront overlooking Seno Última Esperanza is the not-quite-central Plaza de Armas. An incongruous railway engine sits prominently in the middle of the square. ⊠ *Arturo Prat at Eberhard.*

WHERE TO EAT

$$$$ CHILEAN 🍴 **Asador Patagónico.** This bright spot in the Puerto Natales dining scene is zealous about meat. So zealous, in fact, that there's no seafood on the menu. Incredible care is taken with the excellent *lomo* and other grilled steaks, and the room is filled with the smell of roasting meat. The place used to be a pharmacy, and much of the furniture is still labeled with the remedies (*catgut crin* anyone?) they once contained. There's lively music, dim lighting, an open fire, and a friendly buzz; wear removable layers since it can get warm when the grill is cranking. [$] *Average main: 10000 pesos* ✉ *Prat 158* ☎ *61/241–3553* 🕒 *Closed June.*

$$$ SEAFOOD 🍴 **Cangrejo Rojo.** Although it requires a taxi drive to the other side of town, this nautical-chic café is worth it for its maritime feel, good music and atmosphere, and the tasty, feel-good food prepared lovingly by the marine-biologist owners, Francisco and Nuriys. As well as a plethora of sea dwellers, you'll find lamb and other meats on the contemporary menu. Add organic wine, homemade waffles, and nice looseleaf teas, and you are onto a winner. [$] *Average main: 7000 pesos* ✉ *Santiago Bueras Av. 782* ☎ *612/412–436* 🕒 *Closed Sun.*

$$ CAFÉ Fodor's Choice ★ 🍴 **The Coffee Maker.** A coffee bar with steaming espressos and some of the best views in town, right on the water's edge and facing the mountains in the distance, the Coffee Maker serves some of the best java in Chile. In the trendy lodge Kau, its breakfasts, cakes, and afternoon nibbles make it a good spot to enjoy the view and take advantage of the Wi-Fi. [$] *Average main: 4000 pesos* ✉ *Kau, Pedro Montt 161* ☎ *61/241–4 611* 🌐 *www.kaupatagonia.com* 🕒 *No lunch in winter.*

$$ VEGETARIAN 🍴 **El Living.** This bohemian, loft-style café offers comfy couches and tables covered in gossip magazines and tour info. The gluten-free and vegetarian options on the menu will tick the box in comfort and health. Fresh juices, warming hot drinks, and hearty breakfasts make this a good option during the summer, right in front of Plaza de Correo with a garden in the back. [$] *Average main: 6000 pesos* ✉ *Arturo Prat 156* 🌐 *www.el-living.com* 🕒 *Closed Apr.–Oct.*

$$$ CHILEAN 🍴 **Espacio Ñandu.** Right on the corner of the plaza, this modern artisan shop doubles as a restaurant, bar, café, post office, and the best Wi-Fi spot in town, where you can surf on your own computer or rent one of theirs. With empanadas, tacos, seafood, and salads, you've got all bases covered for lunch, dinner, or just coffee and a snack. In addition to hot beverages, the bar also stocks local beers and a decent wine selection. [$] *Average main: 5000 pesos* ✉ *Eberhard and Arturo Prat* ☎ *61/241–4382.*

$$$ CHILEAN 🍴 **Kosten.** You'll watch the wind whip the Seno Ultima Esperanza from a comfortable lounge in front of the fireplace at this modern café and bar attached to Indigo Hotel. With a well-stocked bar upstairs, this is a nice spot for a Calafate Sour, and if you are feeling lazy, just amble downstairs to the small restaurant where they serve simple, modern Chilean cuisine. [$] *Average main: 7000 pesos* ✉ *Indigo Hotel, Ladrilleros 105* ☎ *612/613–450* 🌐 *www.indigopatagonia.cl/en* 🕒 *Closed winter; months vary.*

$$$$ CHILEAN 🍴 **Restaurant Ultima Esperanza.** Named for the strait on which Puerto Natales is located, it is perhaps your last chance to try Patagonian

8

seafood classics in a town being overrun by hip eateries. This traditional restaurant is well known for attentive if formal service, and top-quality, typical dishes. Poached conger eel in shellfish sauce, king crab stew, and cordero are specialties—dishes served with plenty of flavor and little fuss. The room is big and impersonal, and for this reason alone the restaurant may be losing ground to new arrivals more focused on atmosphere and comfort. $ *Average main: 9000 pesos* ⊠ *Av. Eberhard 354* ☏ *61/241–3626* ⊕ *Closed July.*

WHERE TO STAY

$$
B&B/INN

☐ **Hostal Lady Florence Dixie.** Named after an aristocratic English immigrant and tireless traveler, this long-established hotel with an alpine-inspired facade on the town's main street; its bright, spacious upstairs lounge is a good people-watching perch. **Pros:** convenient location; relaxed atmosphere. **Cons:** not quite the boutique hotel it purports to be; rooms have a dowdy feel in a town that's rapidly modernizing. $ *Rooms from: 70000 pesos* ⊠ *Av. Bulnes 655* ☏ *612/411–158* ⤴ *19 rooms* ❙◎❙ *Breakfast.*

$$$
HOTEL

☐ **Hotel CostAustralis.** Designed by a local architect, this venerable three-story hotel is one of the most distinctive buildings in Puerto Natales; its peaked, turreted roof dominates the waterfront. **Pros:** great views from bay-facing rooms; good restaurant; courteous and professional staff; startlingly low off-season rates. **Cons:** rooms are somewhat bland; endless corridors a little impersonal. $ *Rooms from: 155000 pesos* ⊠ *Av. Pedro Montt 262, at Av. Bulnes* ☏ *612/412–000* ⊕ *www.hoteles-australis.com* ⤴ *105 rooms, 5 suites* ❙◎❙ *Breakfast.*

$$
HOTEL

☐ **Hotel Martín Gusinde.** Part of Chile's modern AustroHoteles chain, this intimate inn has retained an aura of sophistication even as it has grown to accommodate the surge in visitors to Puerto Natales. **Pros:** atmosphere is urbane. **Cons:** staff language barrier; seedy casino neighbor; absence of bathtubs in this style of hotel is a mystery. $ *Rooms from: 110000 pesos* ⊠ *Carlos Bories 278* ☏ *612/412–770* ⊕ *www.hotelmartin gusinde.com* ⤴ *28 rooms* ❙◎❙ *Breakfast.*

$$$
HOTEL
Fodor'sChoice
★

☐ **Índigo.** Chilean architect Sebastian Irarrazabel was given free rein by a multinational trio of owners to redesign this building along a nautical theme; inside, a maze of gangplanks, ramps, and staircases shoot out across cavernous open spaces, minimalist wood panels line walls and ceilings, and water burbles down a waterfall that borders the central walkway. **Pros:** steeped in ultramodern luxury; at the forefront of Puerto Natales's efforts to attract the hip young traveler market; rooftop spa; great views; excellent guided excursions. **Cons:** ultramodern aesthetic not for everyone; standard rooms do not have bathtubs (though the showers are excellent). $ *Rooms from: 158200 pesos* ⊠ *Ladrilleros 105* ☏ *612/413–609* ⊕ *www.indigopatagonia.cl* ⤴ *29 rooms* ❙◎❙ *Breakfast.*

$$
B&B/INN

☐ **Kau Lodge.** This modern and attractive B&B offers great value with an intimate setting, some of the best sea views and certainly the best coffee in town, and excellent touring tips from the mountain-guide owner, Hernan, who also runs a tourism agency offering customized trips and activities. **Pros:** great views; excellent value; good Wi-Fi. **Cons:** rooms are all facing the coast and the windows can get a bit battered during strong winds; small breakfast. $ *Rooms from: 61000* *pesos* ✉ *Pedro Montt 161* ☎ *612/414–611* 🌐 *www.kaulodge.com* 🛏 *9 rooms* 🍴 *Breakfast.*

OUTSIDE PUERTO NATALES

Several lodges have been constructed on a bluff overlooking the Seno Ultima Esperanza, about a mile outside of town. The views at these hotels are spectacular, with broad panoramas and unforgettable sunsets. While some might complain about the 10- to 30-minute trek into town, it is an easy walk along the seafront. A taxi will set you back around 2,000–2,500 Chilean pesos.

$$ HOTEL 🏨 **Altiplanico Sur.** This is the Patagonian representative of the Altiplánico line of thoughtfully designed eco-hotels, and nature takes center stage: the hotel blends so seamlessly with its surroundings, it's almost subterranean. **Pros:** couldn't be closer to nature; stellar views of the fjords and mountains, even from a low vantage point; outdoor Jacuzzi on request. **Cons:** staff speaks little English; few technological amenities. [$] *Rooms from: 110000 pesos* ✉ *R9 N, Km 1.5, Huerto 282* ☎ *61/241–2525* 🌐 *www.altiplanico.cl* 🛏 *22 rooms* ⏲ *Closed mid-May–mid-Sept.* 🍴 *Breakfast.*

$$$$ HOTEL ALL-INCLUSIVE Fodor's Choice ★ 🏨 **Remota.** For most guests the Remota experience begins with the safari-esque transfer from Punta Arenas Airport, during which the driver stops to point out animals and other items of interest; on arrival, you meet what seems like the entire staff, check into your ultramodern room, have a drink from a top-shelf open bar, and run off to the open-air Jacuzzis and impossibly serene infinity pool. **Pros:** after a few days the staff feels like family; restaurant uses the freshest locally sourced ingredients; inspiring design. **Cons:** all-inclusiveness discourages sampling local restaurants; views not as good as those from hotels inside Torres Del Paine National Park. [$] *Rooms from: 195000 pesos* ✉ *R9 N, Km 1.5, Huerto 279* ☎ *612/414–040* 🌐 *www.remota.cl* 🛏 *72 rooms* 🍴 *All-inclusive.*

$$$ HOTEL 🏨 **Weskar Patagonian Lodge.** Weskar stands for "hill" in the language of the indigenous Kaweskar, to whom owner Juan José Pantoja, a marine biologist, pays homage in creating and maintaining this cozy lodge, which is high on a ridge overlooking the Ultima Esperanza fjord. **Pros:** great views from your room; cozy log-cabin décor. **Cons:** less luxurious than neighbors for similar price; from the dining room you can really hear the wind when it's howling, or the traffic; bathrooms are so-so. [$] *Rooms from: 117000 pesos* ✉ *R9 N, Km 1* ☎ *612/414–168* 🌐 *www.weskar.cl* 🛏 *30 rooms* ⏲ *Closed mid-May–Sept.* 🍴 *Breakfast.*

PARQUE NACIONAL TORRES DEL PAINE, CHILE

80 km (50 miles) northwest of Puerto Natales.

A top global destination for hikers and nature spotters, Torres del Paine National Park is, quite simply, outstanding. With breathtaking mountains, glaciers, and lakes, along with wildlife like guanacos, rheas, and pumas, the Park offers plenty of picture-perfect moments. Frequently changeable Patagonian weather is the only blemish in this UNESCO World Heritage Site, which attracts more than 150,000 visitors a year.

the Hostería Las Torres, 7 km (4½ miles) to the west. Alternatively, you can walk approximately two hours before reaching the starting point of the hiking circuits.

Although considerable walking is necessary to take full advantage of Parque Nacional Torres del Paine, you need not be a hard-core trekker. Many people choose to hike the **"W" route,** which takes four days, but others prefer to stay in one of the comfortable lodges and hit the trails in the morning or afternoon. **Glaciar Grey,** with its fragmented icebergs, makes a rewarding and easy hike; equally rewarding is the spectacular boat or kayak ride across the lake, past icebergs, and up to the glacier, which leaves from Hostería Lago Grey (⇨ *below).* Another great excursion is the 900-meter (3,000-foot) ascent to the sensational views from **Mirador Las Torres,** four hours one way from Las Torres Patagonia (⇨ *below).* Even if you're not staying at the Hostería, you can arrange a morning drop-off there, and a late-afternoon pickup, so that you can see the Mirador while still keeping your base in Puerto Natales or elsewhere in the park; alternatively, you can drive to the Hostería and park there for the day.

If you do the "W," you'll begin (or end, if you reverse the route) at Laguna Amarga and continue to Mirador Las Torres and Los Cuernos, then continue along a breathtaking path up Valle Frances to its awe-inspiring and fiendishly windy lookout (hold on to your hat!) and finally Lago Grey. The W runs for 100 kilometers (62 miles), but always follows clearly marked paths, with gradual climbs and descents at relatively low altitude. The challenge comes from the weather. Winds whip up to 90 mph, and a clear sky can suddenly darken with storm clouds, producing rain, hail, or snow in a matter of minutes. An even more ambitious route is the "Circuito," which essentially leads around the entire park and takes from a week to 10 days. Along the way some people sleep at the dozen or so humble *refugios* (shelters) evenly spaced along the trail, and many others bring their own tents.

Driving is an easy way to enjoy the park: a new road cuts the distance to Puerto Natales from a meandering 140 km (87 miles) to a more direct 80 km (50 miles). Inside the national park more than 100 km (62 miles) of roads leading to the most popular sites are safe and well maintained, though unpaved. ■ TIP➡ **If you stick to the road, you won't need four-wheel drive.**

You can also hire horses from the Hostería Las Torres and trek to the Torres, the Cuernos, or along the shore of Lago Nordenskjold (which offers the finest views in the park, as the lake's waters reflect the chiseled massif). Alternatively, many Puerto Natales–based operators offer multiday horseback tours. Water transport is also available, with numerous tour operators offering sailboat, kayak, and inflatable Zodiac speedboat options along the Río Serrano toward the Paine massif and the southern ice field. Additionally, the Hostería Lago Grey operates the *Grey II,* a large catamaran making a three-hour return trip to Glaciar Grey four times daily as well as dinghy runs down the Pingo and Grey rivers. Another boat runs between Refugio Pudeto and Refugio Lago Pehoé.

Erratic Rock. For anyone seriously contemplating trekking the W or the full Circuit around Torres del Paine, the Erratic Rock hostel in Puerto Natales offers a free seminar on how best to make the journey. Rustyn Mesdag, the hostel's Oregonian co-owner, is a rambunctious, opinionated guide who gives the not-to-be-missed "Three O'Clock Talk," describing all the routes, tips, and tricks you need to complete one of South America's most challenging treks. His hour-long presentation to a room full of eager hikers starts promptly at 3 pm every day of the high season, and is full of advice on camping, equipment, food, and provisions, including the latest reports on weather and trail conditions inside the park. It's a great introduction to possible trekking partners, as CONAF doesn't allow you to complete the walk on your own. The irrepressible Mr. Mesdag also publishes the ubiquitous *Black Sheep* newspaper in English. ⊠ *Baquedano 719, Puerto Natales* ☎ *61/414–317* ⊕ *www.erraticrock.com.*

WHERE TO STAY

$$$$
HOTEL
☂ **Hostería Lago Grey.** The panoramic view from the restaurant and bar, past the lake dappled with floating icebergs to the glacier beyond, is worth the journey here; however, that doesn't change the fact that this older hotel is almost scandalously overpriced and not very attractive, with plain, dark rooms (only a few of which have a view). **Pros:** great views and comfortable seating in the well-stocked bar; location; heated bathroom floors; some rooms have a view—be sure to ask for one. **Cons:** thin walls in summer camp cottages; staggering price; staff speak very little English. $ *Rooms from: 154000 pesos* ⊠ *Lago Grey* ☎ *612/712–100* ⊕ *www.lagogrey.com* ↝ *60 rooms* ❤ *Breakfast.*

$$
HOTEL
☂ **Hostería Tyndall.** A boat ferries you from the end of the road the few minutes around the meandering bends of the Serrano River to this wooden lodge, often surrounded by flocks of snow geese and other wild birds; inside, the simple rooms in the main building are small but cute and spotless, with attractive wood paneling. **Pros:** cheaper lodging and dining options than other places in the park; great views to Los Cuernos (the Horns) on a clear day. **Cons:** hallways are poorly lit; the lodge itself can get noisy, frayed around the edges. $ *Rooms from: 92000 pesos* ⊠ *Lago Tyndall* ☎ *612/614–682* ⊕ *www.hosteriatyndall.com* ↝ *36 rooms, 6 cottages* ☉ *Closed Apr.–Oct. 1* ❤ *Multiple meal plans.*

$$$$
HOTEL
ALL-INCLUSIVE
Fodor's Choice
★
☂ **Hotel Explora—Salto Chico.** Next to a gently babbling waterfall on the southeast corner of Lago Pehoé, this lodge is one of the most luxurious—and most expensive—in Chile; outside, the shimmering lake is offset by tiny rocky islets, and although there may be some debate about the aesthetics of the hotel's low-slung minimalist exterior, the interior is impeccable, with a Scandinavian style using local woods throughout. **Pros:** the grande dame of Patagonian hospitality and one of the best hotels in the country; heart-stopping views from the center of the national park. **Cons:** a bank breaker; not a stunning building from the outside. $ *Rooms from: 1110000 pesos* ⊠ *Lago Pehoé, Parque Nacional Torres Del Paine* ☎ *2/239–5280 in Santiago* ☎ *2/395–2580 in Lake Pehoé* ⊕ *www.explora.com* ↝ *49 rooms* ❤ *All-inclusive.*

\$\$\$\$ ⬛ **Hotel Río Serrano.** What used to be a fairly humble posada has com-
HOTEL pleted a successful transformation into a grand hotel; the main draw
is the view from rooms on the third floor, taking in the whole Torres
del Paine mountain range, with the Serrano River and a wind-stunted
forest in the foreground (these spectacular vistas are worth the significant added expense, especially if you can snag a room with a balcony).
Pros: impressive public areas; a stunning location with all-encompass-
ing views. **Cons:** it's enormous, so guided tours can be a bit chaotic
when the hotel's near capacity; rooms are tight on space. $ *Rooms
from: 205750 pesos* ✉ *Lago Toro, Torres del Paine* ☎ *61/222–4181 for
reservations (Puerto Natales)* ⊕ *www.hotelrioserrano.cl* 📞 *95 rooms*
⦿| *Multiple meal plans.*

\$\$\$\$ ⬛ **Las Torres Patagonia.** Owned by one of the earliest families to settle in
HOTEL what became the park, Las Torres has a long history, and is the closest
hotel to the main trails into the heart of the Torres del Paine massif;
originally an estancia, then a popular hostería, the facility upgraded to
a two-night-minimum, all-food-and-excursion-inclusive resort, in the
style of Hotel Explora. **Pros:** friendly and efficient; homey atmosphere;
couldn't be closer to the mountains. **Cons:** not cheap and prices keep
rising; may be closer to the mountains, but the views are more sweeping
at hotels Explora or Río Serrano. $ *Rooms from: 335000 pesos* ✉ *Lago
Amarga* ☎ *61/360–364* ⊕ *www.lastorres.com* 📞 *84 rooms* ⊙ *Closed
mid-Apr.–mid-Sept.* ⦿| *Multiple meal plans.*

USHUAIA AND TIERRA DEL FUEGO

8

Tierra del Fuego, a more or less triangular island separated from the
southernmost tip of the South American mainland by the twists and
bends of the Estrecho de Magallanes, is indeed a world unto itself. The
vast plains on its northern reaches are dotted with trees bent low by
the savage winds that frequently lash the coast. The mountains that rise
in the south are equally forbidding, traversed by huge glaciers slowly
making their way to the sea.

The first European to set foot on this island was Spanish explorer Her-
nando de Magallanes, who sailed here in 1520. The smoke that he
saw coming from the fires lighted by the native peoples prompted him
to call it Tierra del Humo (Land of Smoke). King Charles V of Spain,
disliking that name, rechristened it Tierra del Fuego, or Land of Fire.

Tierra del Fuego is split in half. The island's northernmost tip, well
within Chilean territory, is its closest point to the continent. The
only town of any size here is Porvenir. Its southern extremity, part of
Argentina, points out into the Atlantic toward the Falkland Islands.
Here you'll find Ushuaia, the main destination, on the shores of the
Canal Beagle. Farther south is Cape Horn, the southernmost point of
land before Antarctica (still a good 500 miles across the brutal Drake
Passage).

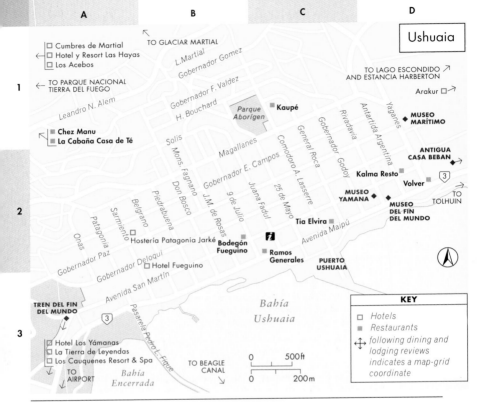

Map labels:

A **B** **C** **D**

Cumbres de Martial
Hotel y Resort Las Hayas
Los Acebos

TO GLACIAR MARTIAL

L.Martial

Gobernador Gomez

TO LAGO ESCONDIDO
AND ESTANCIA HARBERTON

TO PARQUE NACIONAL
TIERRA DEL FUEGO

Gobernador F. Valdez

Arakur

1

Leandro N. Alem

Gobernador F. Valdez

H. Bouchard

Parque
Aborigen

Kaupé

MUSEO
MARÍTIMO

Chez Manu
La Cabaña Casa de Té

Solis

Mons. Fagnano

Magallanes

Gobernador E. Campos

Comodoro A. Lasserre

General Roca

Gobernador Godoy

Rivadavia

Antártida Argentina

Yaganes

ANTIGUA
CASA BEBAN

Kalma Resto

Volver

2

Onas

Patagonia

Sarmiento

Belgrano

Piedrabuena

Don Bosco

J.M. de Rosas

9 de Julio

Juana Fadul

25 de Mayo

Tia Elvira

Avenida Maipú

MUSEO
YAMANA

MUSEO
DEL FIN
DEL MUNDO

TO
TOLHUIN

Gobernador Paz

Gobernador Deloqui

Hostería Patagonia Jarké

Bodegón
Fueguino

Ramos
Generales

PUERTO
USHUAIA

Hotel Fueguino

Avenida San Martín

Bahía
Ushuaia

TREN DEL FIN
DEL MUNDO

Pasarela Pedro L. Fique

3

Hotel Los Yámanas
La Tierra de Leyendas
Los Cauquenes Resort & Spa

TO
AIRPORT

Bahía
Encerrada

TO BEAGLE
CANAL

0   500 ft
0   200 m

KEY
Hotels
Restaurants
following dining and
lodging reviews
indicates a map-grid
coordinate

USHUAIA

230 km (143 miles) south of Río Grande; 596 km (370 miles) south of Río Gallegos; 914 km (567 miles) south of El Calafate; 3,580 km (2,212 miles) south of Buenos Aires.

At 55 degrees latitude south, Ushuaia (pronounced oo-swy-ah) is closer to the South Pole than to Argentina's northern border with Bolivia. It is the capital and tourism base for Tierra del Fuego, the island at the southernmost tip of Argentina.

The city rightly (if perhaps too loudly) promotes itself as the southernmost city in the world (Puerto Williams, a few miles south on the Chilean side of the Beagle Channel, is a small town). You can make your way to the tourism office to get your clichéd, but oh-so-necessary, "Southernmost City in the World" passport stamp. Ushuaia feels like a frontier boomtown, at heart still a rugged, weather-beaten fishing village, but exhibiting the frayed edges of a city that quadrupled in size in the '70s and '80s and just keeps growing. Unpaved portions of Ruta 3, the last stretch of the Pan-American Highway, which connects Alaska to Tierra del Fuego, are finally being paved. The summer months (December through March) draw more than 120,000 visitors, and dozens of cruise ships. The city is trying to extend those visits with events like March's Marathon at the End of the World and by increasing the gamut of winter activities buoyed by the excellent snow conditions.

A terrific trail winds through the town up to the Martial Glacier, where a ski lift can help cut down a steep kilometer of your journey. The chaotic and contradictory urban landscape includes a handful of luxury hotels amid the concrete of public housing projects. Scores of "sled houses" (wooden shacks) sit precariously on upright piers, ready for speedy displacement to a different site. But there are also many small, picturesque homes with tiny, carefully tended gardens. Many of the newer homes are built in a Swiss-chalet style, reinforcing the idea that this is a town into which tourism has breathed new life. At the same time, the weather-worn pastel colors that dominate the town's landscape remind you that Ushuaia was once just a tiny fishing village, snuggled at the end of the Earth.

As you stand on the banks of the Canal Beagle (Beagle Channel) near Ushuaia, the spirit of the farthest corner of the world takes hold. What stands out is the light: at sundown the landscape is cast in a subdued, sensual tone; everything feels closer, softer, and more human in dimension despite the vastness of the setting. The snowcapped mountains reflect the setting sun back onto a stream rolling into the channel, as nearby peaks echo their image—on a windless day—in the still waters.

Above the city rise the last mountains of the Andean Cordillera, and just south and west of Ushuaia they finally vanish into the often-stormy sea. Snow whitens the peaks well into summer. Nature is the principal attraction here, with trekking, fishing, horseback riding, wildlife spotting, and sailing among the most rewarding activities, especially in the Parque Nacional Tierra del Fuego (Tierra del Fuego National Park).

GETTING HERE AND AROUND

Arriving by air is the preferred option. Ushuaia's Aeropuerto Internacional Malvinas Argentinas (✉ *Peninsula de Ushuaia* ☎ *2901/431–232*) is 5 km (3 miles) from town and is served daily by flights to and from Buenos Aires, Río Gallegos, El Calafate, Trelew, and Comodoro Rivadavia. There are also flights to Santiago via Punta Arenas in Chile. A taxi into town costs about US$8.

Arriving by road on the Ruta Nacional 3 involves Argentine and Chilean immigrations/customs, a ferry crossing, and a lot of time. Buses to and from Punta Arenas make the trip five days a week in summer, four in winter. Daily buses to Río Gallegos leave in the pre-dawn hours, and multiple border crossings mean an all-day journey. Check prices on the 55-minute flight, which can be a much better value. There is no central bus terminal, just individual company locations.

There is no regular passenger transport (besides cruises) by sea.

CRUISE TRAVEL TO USHUAIA

As you sail into Ushuaia, the captain almost always takes you around the picturesque lighthouse at the "end of the world": a beacon for the southernmost city perched on the edge of the Canal Beagle. The port is just two blocks from the main street, leaving you in a central location once you disembark.

Crab really is king in Tierra del Fuego; king crab, or *centolla*, is delicious and readily available.

Before undertaking the five-minute walk into town, stop at the Tourism Office (right in front of the port), where you can gather information and take advantage of the free Wi-Fi. Most city attractions can be reached on foot, although if you're spending the night here, you may need to take a taxi to your hotel. If you're in Ushuaia only for the day, lace on some good shoes, as the city is built on a hill and requires calves of steel.

ESSENTIALS

Bus Services Tecni-Austral ⊠ *Roca 157* ☏ *2901/431-408.*

Visitor Information Ushuaia Tourist Office ⊠ *Av. San Martín 674* ☏ *2901/432-001, 2901/424-550* ⊕ *www.turismoushuaia.com* ⊙ *Weekdays 9 am–10 pm, weekends 9–8 (reduced hrs in winter)* ⊠ *Av. Prefectura Naval Argentina 470* ☏ *2901/437-666.*

EXPLORING

TOP ATTRACTIONS

Canal Beagle. Several tour operators run trips along the Canal Beagle, on which you can get a startling close-up view of sea mammals and birds on **Isla de los Lobos, Isla de los Pájaros,** and near **Les Eclaireurs Lighthouse.** Catamarans, motorboats, and sailboats usually leave from the tourist pier at 9:30, 10, 3, and 3:30 (trips depend on weather; few trips go in winter). Trips start at US$50 and some include hikes on the islands. Check with the tourist office for the latest details; you can also book through any of the local travel agencies or scope out the offers yourself by walking around the kiosks on the tourist pier.

Estancia Harberton (*Harberton Ranch*). This property—50,000 acres of coastal marshland and wooded hillsides—was a late-19th-century gift from the Argentine government to Reverend Thomas Bridges, who authored a Yamana–English dictionary and is considered the patriarch of Tierra del Fuego. His son Lucas wrote *The Uttermost Part of the Earth*, a memoir about his frontier childhood. Today the ranch is managed by Bridges's great-grandson, Thomas Goodall, and his American wife, Natalie, a scientist and author who has cooperated with the National Geographic Society on conservation projects and operates the impressive marine mammal museum, **Museo Acatushun** (⊕ *www. acatushun.com*). Most people visit as part of organized tours, but you'll be welcome if you arrive alone. They serve up a tasty tea in their home, the oldest building on the island. For safety reasons, exploration of the ranch can only be done on guided tours (45–90 minutes). Lodging is available, either in the Old Shepherd's House or the Old Cook's House (US$400 for a double, with breakfast). Additionally, you can arrange a three-course lunch at the ranch by calling two days ahead for a reservation. Most tours reach the estancia by boat, offering a rare opportunity to explore the **Isla Martillo** penguin colony and a sea-lion refuge on **Isla de los Lobos** (Seal Island) along the way. ⊠ *85 km (53 miles) east of Ushuaia* ☎ *2901/422–742* ⊕ *www.estanciaharberton.com* ☒ *Approx. US$10* ⊘ *By tour only: Oct.–Apr., daily 10–7 (last tour at 5:30).*

Fodor's Choice
★

Glaciar Martial. If you've never butted heads with a glacier, and especially if you won't be covering El Calafate on your trip, then you should check out Glaciar Martial, in the mountain range just above Ushuaia. Named after Frenchman Luís F. Martial, a 19th-century scientist who wandered this way aboard the warship *Romanche* to observe the passing of the planet Venus, the glacier is reached via a panoramic *aerosilla* (ski lift). Take the Camino al Glaciar (Glacier Road) 7 km (4 miles) out of town until it ends (this route is also served by the local tour companies). Even if you don't plan to hike to see the glacier, it's a great pleasure to ride the 15-minute lift, which runs daily 10–4:30, weather permitting (it's often closed in winter), and costs about US$3. If you're afraid of heights, you can instead enjoy a small nature trail here, and the pretty teahouse. You can return on the lift, or continue on to the beginning of a 1-km (½-mile) trail that winds its way over lichen and shale straight up the mountain. After a steep, strenuous 90-minute hike, you can cool your heels in one of the many gurgling, icy rivulets that cascade down water-worn shale shoots or enjoy a picnic while you wait for sunset (you can walk all the way down if you want to linger until after the aerosilla closes). When the sun drops behind the glacier's jagged crown of peaks, brilliant rays beam over the mountain's crest, spilling a halo of gold-flecked light on the glacier, valley, and channel below. Moments like these are why this land is so magical. Note that temperatures drop dramatically after sunset, so come prepared with warm clothing.

Fodor's Choice
★

Museo Marítimo (*Maritime Museum*). Part of the original penal colony, the Presidio building was built to hold political prisoners, murderous estancia owners, street orphans, and a variety of Buenos Aires' most violent criminals. Some even claim that singer Carlos Gardel landed in one of the cells for the petty crimes of his misspent youth. In its day it held 600 inmates in 380 cells. Today it's on the grounds of Ushuaia's naval base and holds the Museo Marítimo, which starts with exhibits

8

on the canoe-making skills of the region's indigenous peoples, tracks the navigational history of Tierra del Fuego and Cape Horn and the Antarctic, and even has a display on other great jails of the world. You can enter cell blocks and read about the grisly crimes of the prisoners who lived in them and measure yourself against their eerie life-size plaster effigies. Of the five wings spreading out from the main guard house, one has been transformed into an art gallery and another has been kept untouched—and unheated. Bone chattering cold and bleak, bare walls powerfully evoke the desolation of a long sentence at the tip of the continent. Well-presented tours (in Spanish only) are conducted at 11:30, 4:30, and 6:30 daily. ⊠ *Gobernador Paz at Yaganes* ☎ *2901/437–481, 2901/436–321* ✑ *Approx. US$13 (valid for 2 days)* ☉ *Nov.–April, daily 9–8; May–Oct., daily 10–8.*

Tren del Fin del Mundo (*End of the World Train*). Heavily promoted but a bit of a letdown, the Tren del Fin del Mundo purports to take you inside the Parque Nacional Tierra del Fuego, 12 km (7½ miles) away from town, so you have to drive to get there, and it leaves visitors a long way short of the most spectacular scenery in the national park. The touristy 40-minute train ride's gimmick is a simulation of the trip El Presidio prisoners were forced to take into the forest to chop wood; but unlike them, you'll also get a good presentation of Ushuaia's history (in Spanish and English). The train departs daily at 9:30, noon, and 3 (only 10 and noon in low season). One common way to do the trip is to hire a remis that will drop you at the station for a one-way train ride and pick you up at the other end, then drive you around the Parque Nacional for two or three hours of sightseeing (which is far more scenic than the train ride itself). ⊠ *R3, Km 3042* ☎ *2901/431–600* ⊕ *www. trendelfindelmundo.com.ar* ✑ *US$36.*

WORTH NOTING

Antigua Casa Beban (*Old Beban House*). One of Ushuaia's original houses, the Antigua Casa Beban long served as the city's social center. Built between 1911 and 1913 by Fortunato Beban, it's said he ordered the house through a Swiss catalog. In the 1980s the Beban family donated the house to the city to avoid demolition. It was moved to its current location along the coast and restored, and is now a cultural center with art exhibits. ⊠ *Maipú at Pluschow* ☎ *2901/431–386* ✑ *Free* ☉ *Weekdays 10–8.*

Canal Fun. This unconventional tour goes to **Monte Olivia**, the tallest mountain along the Canal Beagle, rising 4,455 feet above sea level. You also pass the **Five Brothers Mountains** and go through the **Garibaldi Pass,** which begins at the Rancho Hambre, climbs into the mountain range, and ends with a spectacular view of Lago Escondido. From here you continue on to Lago Fagnano through the countryside past sawmills and lumber yards. To do this tour in a four-wheel-drive truck with an excellent bilingual guide, contact Canal Fun; you'll drive *through* Lago Fagnano (about 3 feet of water at this point) to a secluded cabin on the shore and have a delicious asado, complete with wine and dessert. In winter they can also organize tailor-made dogsledding and cross-country skiing trips. ⊠ *Roca 136* ☎ *2901/437–395, 2901/1551–1827* ⊕ *www.canalfun.com.*

Lago Escondido (*Hidden Lake*). One good excursion in the area is to Lago Escondido and **Lago Fagnano** (Fagnano Lake). The Pan-American Highway out of Ushuaia goes through deciduous beech forests and past beaver dams, peat bogs, and glaciers. The lakes have campsites and fishing and are good spots for a picnic or a hike. This can be done on your own or as a seven-hour trip, including lunch, booked through the local travel agencies (around US$60 standard tour, US$100 with lunch and 4X4 tour).

Museo del Fin del Mundo (*End of the World Museum*). See a large taxidermied condor and other native birds, indigenous artifacts, maritime instruments, a reconstruction of an old Patagonian general store, and such seafaring-related objects as an impressive mermaid figurehead taken from the bowsprit of a galleon at this museum. There are also photographs and histories of El Presidio's original inmates, such as Simon Radowitzky, a Russian immigrant anarchist who received a life sentence for killing an Argentinean police colonel. The museum is split across two buildings—the first, and original, is in the 1905 residence of a Fuegonian governor at Maipú 173. The newest museum building, opened in 2008, is farther down the road at Maipú 465, where you can see extended exhibitions of the same style. ⌧ *Maipú 173, at Rivadavía* ☎ *2901/421–863* ⌦ *Approx. US$9 (covers both museums)* ◷ *Oct.–April, weekdays 10–7, weekends 2–8; May–Sept., Tues.–Fri. 10–5, weekends 2–7.*

Museo Yamana. Tierra del Fuego was the last land mass in the world to be inhabited—it was not until 9,000 BC that the ancestors of those native coastal inhabitants, the Yamana, arrived. The Museo Yamana chronicles their lifestyle and history. The group was decimated in the late 19th century, mostly by European diseases. The bicentenary of Charles Darwin's birth passed with great fanfare in 2009, but his attitudes towards the indigenous people, dismissing them as "miserable, degraded savages" in *The Voyage of the Beagle,* are belied here by descriptions of the Yamana's incredible resourcefulness in surviving a bitter climate. Photographs and good English placards depict the Yamana's powerful, stocky build and bold body-paint; their use of seal fat to stay warm; their methods of carrying fire wherever they went, even in small canoes; and their way of hunting cormorants, which were killed with a bite through the neck. ⌧ *Rivadavía 56* ☎ *2901/422–874* ⊕ *www.tierradelfuego.org.ar/mundoyamana* ⌦ *Approx. US$8* ◷ *Oct.–April, daily 10–8; May–Sept., daily noon–7.*

8

OFF THE
BEATEN
PATH

Tres Marias Excursions. Although there are a number of boat tours through the Canal Beagle or around the bays to Tierra del Fuego National Park, one offers an experience that will put you in the shoes of the earliest explorers to visit the far south. The operators of Tres Marias Excursions offer a half-day sailing trip to Island H, an outcrop in the middle of the channel, with cormorant colonies, families of snow geese, seaweed stands, and a weather station that records the howling winds blowing in from the misnamed Pacific Ocean. The guides are skillful sailors and storytellers. On a gusty day you'll marvel at the hardiness of the Yamana people, who survived frigid winters wearing little or no clothing by setting fires behind natural and manmade windbreaks. You'll find the same plant and moss species that grow in the high Andes; they thrive here at sea level because the conditions kill off less hardy, temperate species. On the way back you visit a sea lion colony, but won't soon forget arriving in Ushuaia under full sail as the late sun hits the mountains. At US$60 it's only a little more expensive, and a lot more adventurous, than the motorized alternatives trawling for business at the dock. ⊠ *Port* ☎ *2901/436–416* ⊕ *www.tresmariasweb.com* ⊙ *Tours only Oct.–Mar.* .

WHERE TO EAT

$$$
ARGENTINE

✕ **Bodegón Fueguino.** A mustard-yellow pioneer house that lights up the main street, this traditional eatery is driven by its ebullient owner Sergio Otero, a constant presence bustling around the bench seating, making suggestions, and revving up his staff. Sample the *picada* plate (king crab rolls, Roma-style calamari, marinated rabbit) over an artisanal Beagle Beer—the dark version is the perfect balm on a cold windy day. Lamb dominates the mains, and the emphasis is on hearty rather than fashionable. Tables filled with locals and visitors make for a boisterous atmosphere. Don't worry about the no-reservations policy as you won't have to wait long. ⑂ *Average main: US$18* ⊠ *San Martin 859* ☎ *2901/431–972* ⊕ *www.tierradehumos.com* ⌂ *Reservations not accepted* ⊙ *Closed Mon.* ⊹ *B2.*

$$$$
SEAFOOD
Fodor's Choice
★

✕ **Chez Manu.** *Herbes de Provence* in the greeting room, a tank of lively king crabs in the dining room: French chef Manu Herbin gives local seafood a French touch and creates some of Ushuaia's most memorable meals with views to match. Perched a couple of miles above town across the street from the Hotel Glaciar, the restaurant has stunning views of the Beagle Channel. The first-rate wine list includes Patagonian selections, while all dishes are created entirely with ingredients from Tierra del Fuego. Don't miss the baby scallops or the centolla au gratin. ⑂ *Average main: US$33* ⊠ *Camino Luís Martial 2135* ☎ *2901/432–253* ⊕ *www.chezmanu.com* ⊙ *Closed Mon., and 2 wks May–June. No lunch Tues.* ⊹ *A1.*

$$$$
MODERN
ARGENTINE

✕ **Kalma Resto.** Beautiful dishes and a contemporary twist on traditional Patagonian flavors meet at this funky little restaurant at the end of the world. Owner and chef Jorge says that recipes are inspired by his grandma's classics, but there is also a hint of Peruvian and Mediterranean with signature dishes like octopus ceviche, centolla and Canal Beagle mussels, and paella. The wine list has plenty of Patagonian wines to help you while away a couple hours at this slow-paced and charming restaurant. ⑂ *Average main: US$26* ⊠ *Antártida Argentina 57* ☎ *2901/425–786* ⊕ *www.kalmaresto.com.ar* ⊙ *Closed May and June. No lunch July–Oct.* ⊹ *D2.*

$$$$
ARGENTINE

✕ **Kaupé.** The white picket fence, manicured lawns, and planter boxes play up the fact that this out-of-the-way restaurant used to be a family home. Inside, polished wooden floors, picture windows, and tables covered in wine glasses offer a sophisticated dining experience with an intimate touch. The star ingredient is centolla, best presented as chowder with a hint of mustard. This restaurant is on a steep ridge above town and offers good views, only a little bit spoiled by the radio antennae sticking up from plots next door. Still, it's seafood served with panache

Can't beat the view in Ushuaia, the world's southernmost city.

and warmth in a dining room that belies the status quo of the kitschy restaurants near the waterfront. But it can be hard to find; even taxi drivers get lost in the warren of streets above town. ⓢ *Average main: US$22* ✉ *Roca 470* ☎ *2901/422–704* ⊕ *www.kaupe.com.ar* ☙ *Reservations essential* ⊙ *Closed Sun.* ✛ *C1.*

$$$$ ✕ **La Cabaña Casa de Té.** This impeccably maintained riverside cottage
ARGENTINE is nestled in a verdant stand of lenga trees, overlooks the Canal Beagle, and provides a warm, cozy spot for delicious looseleaf tea or comforting snacks before or after a hike to the Glaciar Martial. (It's conveniently located at the end of the Martial road that leads up from Ushuaia, tucked in behind the ski lift.) An afternoon tea with all the trimmings will satiate any peckish trekker, fondues are served at lunchtime, and at 8 pm in summer the menu shifts to pricier dinner fare with dishes like salmon in wine sauce (mainly for the guests at the adjoining cabin accommodation). ⓢ *Average main: US$20* ✉ *Camino Luís Martial 3560* ☎ *2901/434–699* ⊕ *www.lacabania.com.ar* ⊙ *Closed Apr. and May* ✛ *A1.*

$$$ ✕ **Ramos Generales.** Entering this café on the waterfront puts you in
ARGENTINE mind of a general store from the earliest frontier years of Ushuaia, which is why locals call it the *viejo almacen* (old grocery store). As you walk from room to room admiring the relics (like the hand-cranked Victrola phonograph), the hubbub around the bar reminds you that a warehouse like this was not just a store to pick up supplies; it was also a place for isolated pioneers to socialize and gather all the latest news from the port. Burgers and picada platters are uninspiring; choose fresh-baked bread or scrumptious lemon croissants instead, and try the *submarino*—a mug of hot milk in which you plunge a bar of dark

chocolate (goes well with a panini). $ *Average main: US$18* ⊠ *Maipú 749* ☎ *2901/424–317* ⊕ *www.rgramosgenerales.com.ar* ☯ *Closed 3 wks in May* ✛ *C2.*

$$$$
ARGENTINE

✕ **Tia Elvira.** On the street that runs right along the Beagle Channel, Tia Elvira is a good place to sample the local catch. Garlicky shellfish appetizers and centolla are delicious; even more memorable is the tender *merluza negra* (black sea bass). The room is decked out with nautical knickknacks that may seem on the tacky side for such a pricey place. The service is friendly and familial. $ *Average main: US$28* ⊠ *Maipú 349* ☎ *2901/424–725* ☯ *Closed Sun.* ✛ *C2.*

$$$$
ARGENTINE

✕ **Volver.** A giant king crab sign beckons you into this red-tin-wall restaurant, where the maritime bric-a-brac hanging from the ceiling can be a little distracting. The name means "return" and it succeeds in getting repeat visits on the strength of its seafood. Newspapers from the 1930s line the walls in this century-old home; the service is friendly and relaxed. The culinary highlight is the centolla, which comes served with a choice of five different sauces. ■ **TIP**→ **This is among the best places to try Tierra del Fuego's signature dish.** $ *Average main: US$25* ⊠ *Maipú 37* ☎ *2901/423–977* ☯ *Closed Mon. No lunch Sun.* ✛ *D2.*

WHERE TO STAY

Choosing a place to stay depends in part on whether you want to spend the night in town, several miles west toward the national park, or uphill in the hotels above town. The hotels with the best views all require a taxi ride or the various complimentary shuttle services to reach Ushuaia.

$$$$
RESORT

▦ **Arakur.** You can see this brand-new luxury hotel towering in the distance in front of Monte Olivia; it's one of the most extensive spa-and-resort complexes in Ushuaia and overlooks the entire bay and town from its own nature reserve out of town on the road to Cerro Castor. **Pros:** brand-new; modern design with luxury fittings; sweeping views; nature reserve at doorstep. **Cons:** expensive; sterile atmosphere; far from town. $ *Rooms from: US$639* ⊠ *Cerro Alarken, via Av. Héroes de Malvinas 2617* ☎ *2901/442–900* ⊕ *www.arakur.com* ⤳ *125 rooms, 6 suites* ⭢⭥ *Breakfast* ✛ *D1.*

$$$$
B&B/INN

▦ **Cumbres de Martial.** This charming complex of cabins and bungalows, painted a deep berry purple, is high above Ushuaia in the woods at the base of the ski lift to the Glaciar Martial; each spacious room has an extremely comfortable bed and a small wooden deck with terrific views down to the Canal Beagle. **Pros:** easy access to the glacier and nature trails; stunning views of the channel; romantic cabins; spa. **Cons:** you need to cab it to and from town; few restaurant options or services within walking distance. $ *Rooms from: US$332* ⊠ *Camino Luís Martial 3560* ☎ *2901/424–779, 2901/434–699* ⊕ *www.cumbresdelmartial. com.ar* ⤳ *6 rooms, 4 cabins* ☯ *Closed Apr. and May* ⭢⭥ *Breakfast* ✛ *A1.*

$$
B&B/INN

▦ **Hostería Patagonia Jarké.** Jarké means "spark" in a local native language, and this B&B is a bright, electric addition to Ushuaia; the three-story lodge cantilevers down a hillside on a dead-end street in the heart of town. **Pros:** warm, welcoming rooms with decent views; good price for Patagonia. **Cons:** steep walk home; can't compete with the views from the larger hotels farther uphill; noise travels through walls.

$ *Rooms from: US$135* ✉ *Sarmiento 310, at G. Paz* ☎ *2901/437–245* ⊕ *www.patagoniajarke.com.ar* ⤴ *15 rooms* ⏣ *Breakfast* ✢ *A2.*

$$$ ⟐ **Hotel Fueguino.** In downtown Ushuaia, the Fueguino boasts all the
HOTEL modern amenities: a conference center; a gym; a spa; shuttle service;
outgoing, professional, multilingual staff; and one of the better Wi-Fi
signals in town. **Pros:** modern; central. **Cons:** barking dogs can keep you
up all night in downtown location. $ *Rooms from: US$280* ✉ *Gober-*
nador Deloqui 1282 ☎ *2901/424–894* ⊕ *www.fueguinohotel.com* ⤴ *53*
rooms ⏣ *Breakfast* ✢ *B2.*

$$$ ⟐ **Hotel Los Yámanas.** This cozy hotel 4 km (2½ miles) from the center
HOTEL of town is named after the local tribe and offers a rustic mountain
aesthetic. **Pros:** some stunning views from rooms; peaceful location;
sauna is lovely. **Cons:** far from town; questionable taste in decora-
tion. $ *Rooms from: US$230* ✉ *Costa de los Yámanas 2850, Km 4*
☎ *2901/446–809* ⊕ *www.hotelyamanas.com.ar* ⤴ *41 rooms* ☾ *Closed*
May ⏣ *Breakfast* ✢ *A3.*

$$$$ ⟐ **Hotel y Resort Las Hayas.** In the wooded foothills of the Andes, Las
HOTEL Hayas overlooks the town and channel below; ask for a canal view
and, since the rooms are all decorated differently and idiosyncrati-
cally, sample a variety before settling in. **Pros:** good restaurant; charming staff and managers speak English; good spa. **Cons:** décor doesn't
suit everyone; wall prints can be distracting; needs a refurb. $ *Rooms*
from: US$305 ✉ *Camino Luís Martial 1650, Km 3* ☎ *2901/430–710,*
11/4393–4750 in Buenos Aires ⊕ *www.lashayashotel.com* ⤴ *88 rooms*
⏣ *Breakfast* ✢ *A1.*

$$$ ⟐ **La Tierra de Leyendas.** "The Land of Legends" is a honeymooners'
B&B/INN delight; it sweeps up awards often, meaning the secret's out, but this
adorable B&B run by Sebastian and Maria still bears their personal
touch down to the family photos on the walls. **Pros:** an extraordinarily
quaint find for western Ushuaia; enthusiastic, personal, and atten-
tive service; all seven rooms have views. **Cons:** the street name is no
joke—it's insanely windy; the immediate surroundings are a bit bar-
ren; need to book a month or more in advance; closed during winter.
$ *Rooms from: US$208* ✉ *Tierra de Vientos 2448* ☎ *2901/446–565*
⊕ *www.tierradeleyendas.com.ar* ⤴ *7 rooms* ☾ *Closed mid-Apr.–mid-*
July ⏣ *Breakfast* ✢ *A3.*

$$$ ⟐ **Los Acebos.** From the owners of Las Hayas (just around the corner
HOTEL on the winding mountain road), Los Acebos is a modern hotel on
FAMILY a forested ridge with a commanding view over the Beagle Channel;
spacious and super-clean rooms feature the same iconoclastic décor
as Las Hayas, including the trademark fabric-padded walls, only this
time with a '60s-style color scheme. **Pros:** good price for spacious and
superclean rooms; expansive views of the channel from the restaurant. **Cons:** a tad out of the way for a spa-less facility. $ *Rooms from:*
US$269 ✉ *Luis F. Martial 1911* ☎ *2901/424–234, 11/4393–4750 for*
reservations (Buenos Aires office) ⊕ *www.losacebos.com.ar* ⤴ *60*
rooms ⏣ *Breakfast* ✢ *A1.*

8

$$$$
HOTEL
Fodor's Choice
★

⌂ **Los Cauquenes Resort and Spa.** Right on the shore of the Beagle Channel about 8 km (5 miles) west of town, this resort is in a private community with privileged beach access and a nature hike that starts right outside your room. **Pros:** luxurious spa offers comprehensive range of treatments and massages; free transfer into city; private boat excursions offered. **Cons:** rooms can get uncomfortably hot; thin walls can make for noisy nights. Ⓢ *Rooms from: US$343* ⊠ *De la Ermita 3462, Barrio Bahía Cauquén* ☎ *2901/441–300* ⊕ *www.loscauquenesushuaia.com.ar* ⌂ *54 rooms* ⎀*Breakfast* ✚ *A3.*

NIGHTLIFE

Ushuaia has lively nightlife in summer, with its casino, discos, and intimate cafés all close to each other.

Bar Ideal. This cozy and historic bar and café opens from 9 am onwards. ⊠ *San Martín 393, at Roca* ☎ *2901/437–860* ⊕ *www.elbarideal.com.*

El Náutico. The biggest and most popular pub in town, El Náutico attracts a young crowd with disco and techno music. ⊠ *Maipú 1210* ⊕ *www.nauticodiscopub.com* ☾ *Closed Sun.–Thurs.*

Tante Sara. This popular café-bar in the heart of town has a casual, old-world feel. Locals kick back with a book or a beer; they pour the local artisanal brews too. During the day it's one of the few eateries to defy the 3–6 pm siesta, and stays open late. Their other branch, at San Martín 175, closes at 8:30 pm. ⊠ *San Martín 701* ☎ *2901/423–912* ⊕ *www.tantesara.com.*

SHOPPING

Boutique del Libro–Antartida y Patagonia. Part of a bookstore chain, this branch specializes in Patagonian and polar exploration. Along with dozens of maps and picture books, postcards, and posters, it offers adventure classics detailing every Southern expedition from Darwin's Voyage of the Beagle to Ernest Shackleton's incredible journeys of Antarctic survival. While books in English are hard to come by in the rest of Argentina, here you're spoiled for choice, and the Antarctica trip logbooks on sale at the counter might inspire you to extend your travel farther south. ⊠ *San Martín 1120* ☎ *2901/432–117* ☾ *Closed Sun.*

Laguna Negra. If you can't get to South America's chocolate capital Bariloche, you'll find some of the best sweets in Argentina at this boutique/café in the center of town. Planks of homemade chocolate include coconut crunches, fudges, and brittles, along with Tierra del Fuego's best selection of artisanal beers, chutneys, and spices. In the small coffee shop at the back, drop a glorious slab of dark chocolate into a mug of piping hot milk—one of the best submarinos in town. Locals pop in for a quick cup of hot chocolate at all hours, even as other cafés close for the lull between 3 and 8 in the evening. If you get hooked, there's another branch on the main street of El Calafate. ⊠ *San Martín 513* ☎ *02901/431–144* ⊕ *www.lagunanegra.com.ar* ☾ *Daily 9–9.*

The banner tree, or *Tuta complementaria*, is whipped by Patagonian winds from the time it's a mere shoot; the result has a bannerlike effect, hence the name.

PARQUE NACIONAL TIERRA DEL FUEGO

21 km (13 miles) west of Ushuaia.

This park is one of the main reasons that travelers make a trip to the tip of Argentina. Its deep forests, glistening lakes, and wind-whipped trees will not disappoint. An easy day trip from Ushuaia, this 60,000-hectare park offers varied outdoor experiences and many wildlife-spotting opportunities.

EXPLORING

Fodor's Choice ★ **Parque Nacional Tierra del Fuego.** The pristine park offers a chance to wander through peat bogs, stumble upon hidden lakes, trek through native *canelo, lenga,* and wild cherry forests, and experience the wonders of wind-whipped Tierra del Fuego's rich flora and fauna. Everywhere, lichens line the trunks of the ubiquitous lenga trees, and "chinese lantern" parasites hang from the branches.

Everywhere, too, you'll see the results of government folly, *castoreros* (beaver dams) and lodges. Fifty beaver couples were first brought in from Canada in 1948 so that they would breed and create a fur industry. In the years since, without any predators, the beaver population has exploded to plague proportions (more than 100,000) and now represents a major threat to the forests, as the dams flood the roots of the trees; you can see their effects on parched dead trees on the lake's edge. Believe it or not, the government used to pay hunters a bounty for each beaver they killed (they had to show a tail and head as proof). To make matters worse, the government, after creating the beaver problem, introduced weasels to kill the beavers, but the weasels killed birds instead; they then introduced foxes to kill the beavers and weasels, but they also killed the birds. With eradication efforts failing, some tour operators have accepted them as a permanent presence and now offer beaver-viewing trips.

Visits to the park, which is tucked up against the Chilean border, are commonly arranged through tour companies. Trips range from bus tours to horseback riding to more adventurous excursions, such as canoe trips across Lapataia Bay.

Several private bus companies travel through the park making several stops; you can get off the bus, explore the park, and then wait for the next bus to come by or trek to the next stop (the service only operates in summer; check providers with the tourism office). Another option is to drive to the park on Ruta 3 (take it until it ends and you see the famous sign indicating the end of the Pan-American Highway, which starts 17,848 km [11,065 miles] away in Alaska, and ends here). If you don't have a car, you can also hire a remis to spend a few hours driving through the park, including the Pan-American terminus, and perhaps combining the excursion with the Tren del Fin del Mundo. Trail and camping information is available at the park-entrance ranger station or at the Ushuaia tourist office. At the park entrance is a gleaming restaurant and teahouse set amid the hills, **Patagonia Mia** (✉ *R3, Entrada Parque Nacional* ⊕ *www.patagoniamia.com*); it's a great place to stop for tea or coffee, or a full meal of roast lamb or Fuegian seafood. A nice excursion in the park is by boat from lovely **Bahía Ensenada** to **Isla Redonda,** a wildlife refuge where you can follow a footpath to the western side and see a wonderful view of the Canal Beagle. This is included on some of the day tours; it's harder to arrange on your own, but you can contact the tourist office to try. While on Isla Redonda you can send a postcard and get your passport stamped at the world's southernmost post office. You can also see the Ensenada bay and island (from afar) from a point on the shore that is reachable by car.

Other highlights of the park include the spectacular mountain-ringed lake, **Lago Roca,** as well as **Laguna Verde,** a lagoon whose green color comes from algae at its bottom. Much of the park is closed from roughly June through September, when the descent to Bahía Ensenada is blocked by up to 6 feet of snow. Even in May and October, chains for your car are a good idea. No hotels are within the park—the only one burned down in the 1980s, and you can see its carcass as you drive by—but there are three simple camping areas around Lago Roca. Tours to the park are run by **All Patagonia** (✉ *Juana Fadul 58* ☎ *2901/433–622* ⊕ *www.allpatagonia.com*). ⊕ *www.parquesnacionalesargentina.com* 🖃 *Approx. US$17.*

EN ROUTE If you're in Ushuaia in the days leading up to New Year's Eve, drop in on **La Pista del Andino** campsite, on the edge of town. You'll be dwarfed by a mad mix of four-wheel-drive vehicles, enormous customized German trucks, and worn-out bicycles with beaten panniers. It's a tradition among overland explorers to spend Christmas and New Year's in the southernmost city in the world, and this turns out to be one of the most unusual "motorhog" celebrations around. Their routes zigzag across

South America and are often painted on the sides of their vehicles—which have been known to be equipped with everything from rooftop tents to satellite dishes. Travelers share stories of crossing places like Siberia or northern Africa, and if you're lucky you'll encounter some who've ridden, driven, or pedaled the Pan-American Highway all the way from Alaska down to Ushuaia, a 17,000-mile journey that takes years to complete.

SPORTS AND THE OUTDOORS

FISHING

The rivers of Tierra del Fuego are home to trophy-size freshwater trout—including browns, rainbows, and brooks. Both fly- and spin-casting are available. The fishing season runs November through April; license fees range from US$50 per week to US$65 per season for nonresidents. Fishing expeditions are organized by the various local companies.

Asociación de Caza y Pesca. Founded in 1959, the Asociación de Caza y Pesca is the principal hunting and fishing organization in the city. ⊠ *Av. Maipú 822* ☎ *2901/423–168* ⊕ *www.cazaypescaushuaia.org.*

Rumbo Sur. The city's oldest travel agency can assist in setting up fishing trips. ⊠ *Av. San Martín 350* ☎ *2901/421–139* ⊕ *www.rumbosur.com.ar.*

Wind Fly. In summer this outfitter is dedicated exclusively to fishing, and offers classes and arranges trips. ⊠ *Av. 25 de Mayo 155, Ushuaia* ☎ *2901/431–713, 2901/1551–6809* ⊕ *www.windflyushuaia.com.ar.*

MOUNTAIN BIKING

A mountain bike is an excellent mode of transport in Ushuaia, giving you the freedom to roam without the rental-car price tag. Good mountain bikes normally cost about US$10 for a half day or US$15 for a full day. Guided tours are about the same price.

All Patagonia. Guided bicycle tours (including rides through the national park) are organized by All Patagonia. ⊠ *Juana Fadul 40, Ushuaia* ☎ *2901/433–622* ⊕ *www.allpatagonia.com.*

Ushuaia Extreme. You can rent bikes or do a tour with Ushuaia Extreme. ⊠ *San Martín 1306, Ushuaia* ☎ *2901/423–582* ⊕ *www.patagoniabiketour.com.*

Rumbo Sur. One of the city's biggest travel agencies, Rumbo Sur can arrange cycling trips. ⊠ *San Martín 350, Ushuaia* ☎ *2901/421–139* ⊕ *www.rumbosur.com.ar.*

SCENIC FLIGHTS

The gorgeous scenery and island topography of the area is readily appreciated on a Cessna tour.

Aeroclub Ushuaia. Half-hour- and hour-long trips are available through Aeroclub Ushuaia. The half-hour flight (US$105 per passenger, US$140 per solo passenger) with a local pilot takes you over Ushuaia, Parque Nacional Tierra del Fuego, and the Canal Beagle with views of area glaciers, waterfalls, and snowcapped islands south to Cape Horn. A 60-minute flight (US$175 per passenger, US$235 per solo passenger) crosses the Andes to Escondida and Fagnano lakes. ⊠ *Antiguo*

Aeropuerto, Luis Pedro Fique 151, Ushuaia ☎ *2901/421–717* ⊕ *www. aeroclubushuaia.org.ar.*

Heli-Ushuaia. All sorts of helicopter trips are available from Heli-Ushuaia, beginning with a seven-minute spin at US$99 per person. There are plenty of longer trips and excursions if you have money to burn. ✉ *Laserre 108, Ushuaia* ☎ *2901/444–444* ⊕ *www.heliushuaia.com.ar.*

SKIING

Canopy Ushuaia. Located at the Glaciar Martial, Canopy Ushuaia offers skiing in winter and canopy lines in summer. ✉ *Cerro Martial, Luis Fernando Martial 3551, Ushuaia* ☎ *2901/1550–3767* ⊕ *www. canopyushuaia.com.ar.*

Cerro Castor. With off-piste and alpine skiing and almost guaranteed snow, this has become a popular ski haunt for European Olympic teams looking for summer snow. Pistes range from beginners to black-diamond runs with more than 31 trails and four high-speed lifts. You can rent skis and snowboards and take ski lessons at this resort 26 km (17 miles) northeast of Ushuaia on Ruta 3. Day passes are around US$70 in high season, and there are restaurants, bars, and a ski lodge on site. The resort is open June through October. ✉ *R3, Km 26, Ushuaia* ☎ *2901/422–244* ⊕ *www.cerrocastor.com.*

Club Andino. Ushuaia is the cross-country skiing (*esquí de fondo* in Spanish) center of South America, thanks to enthusiastic Club Andino members who took to the sport in the 1980s and made the forested hills of a high valley about 20 minutes from town a favorite destination for skiers. It's a magnet for international ski teams who come from Europe to train in the northern summer. ✉ *Fadul 50, Ushuaia* ☎ *2901/422–335* ⊕ *www.clubandinoushuaia.com.ar.*

Haruwen. You can ride in dog-pulled sleds, rent skis, go cross-country skiing, get lessons, and eat at Haruwen, Hostería Los Cotorras, and Hostería Tierra Mayor; contact the Ushuaia tourist office for more information.

UNDERSTANDING ARGENTINA

SPANISH VOCABULARY

MENU GUIDE

SPANISH VOCABULARY

	ENGLISH	SPANISH	PRONUNCIATION
BASICS			
	Yes/no	Sí/no	see/noh
	Please	Por favor	por fah-vor
	Thank you (very much)	(Muchas) gracias	(**moo**-chas) **grah**-see-ass
	You're welcome	De nada	deh **nah**-da
	Excuse me	Con permiso	con pehr-**mee**-so
	Pardon me	¿Perdón?	pehr-**don**
	Could you tell me.?	¿Podría decirme.?	po-**dree**-ah deh-**seer**-me
	I'm sorry	Lo siento/Perdón	lo see-**en**-to/pehr-**don**
	Hello!/Hi!	¡Hola!	**o**-la
	Good morning!	¡Buen día!	bwen **dee**-a
	Good afternoon!	¡Buenas tardes!	**bwen**-as **tar**-des
	Good evening/Good night!	¡Buenas noches!	**bwen**-as **no**-ches
	Goodbye!	¡Chau!/¡Adiós!	chow/a-dee-**os**
NUMBERS			
	0	Cero	seh-ro
	1	Un, uno	oon, **oo**-no
	2	Dos	doss
	3	Tres	tress
	4	Cuatro	**kwah**-troh
	5	Cinco	**sin**-koh
	6	Seis	**say**-iss
	7	Siete	see-**yet**-eh
	8	Ocho	och-oh
	9	Nueve	nweh-veh
	10	Diez	dee-**ess**
DAYS OF THE WEEK			
	Sunday	domingo	doh-**ming**-oh
	Monday	lunes	**loo**-ness

ENGLISH	SPANISH	PRONUNCIATION
Tuesday	martes	**mar**-tess
Wednesday	miércoles	mee-**er**-koh-less
Thursday	jueves	**hweh**-vess
Friday	viernes	vee-**er**-ness
Saturday	sábado	**sah**-bad-oh

USEFUL PHRASES

Do you speak English?	¿Habla usted inglés? / ¿Hablás inglés?	**ab**-la oo-**sted** ing-**less** / **ab**-las ing-**less**
I don't speak Spanish	No hablo castellano	No **ab**-loh cas-**teh**-sha-no
I don't understand	No entiendo	No en-tee-**en**-doh
I understand	Entiendo	en-tee-**en**-doh
I don't know	No sé	No seh
What's your name?	¿Cómo se llama usted? / ¿Cómo te llamás?	ko-mo seh **shah**-mah oo-**sted** / ko-mo teh **shah**-mass
My name is.	Me llamo.	meh **shah**-moh.
What time is it?	¿Qué hora es?	keh **o**-rah ess
It's one o'clock	Es la una	ess la **oo**-na
It's two/three/four. o'clock	Son las dos/tres/ cuatro	son lass doss/tress/ **kwah**-troh
Yes, please/	Si, gracias.	see, **grah**-see-ass
No, thank you	No, gracias.	noh, **grah**-see-ass
How?	¿Cómo?	**ko**-mo
When?	¿Cuándo?	kwan-doh
Tonight	Esta noche	**ess**-tah **noch**-eh
What?	¿Qué?	Keh
What is this?	¿Qué es esto?	keh ess **ess**-toh
Why?	¿Por qué?	por keh
Who?	¿Quién?	kee-**yen**
Telephone	teléfono	tel-**eff**-on-oh
I am ill	Estoy enfermo(a)	ess-**toy** en-**fer**-moh(mah)

ENGLISH	SPANISH	PRONUNCIATION
Please call a doctor	Por favor, llame a un médico	Por fah-**vor**, **shah**-meh a oon **meh**-dik-oh
Help!	¡Auxilio!	owk-**see**-lee-oh
Fire!	¡Incendio!	in-**sen**-dee-oh
Look out!	¡Cuidado!	kwee-**dah**-doh

OUT AND ABOUT

Where is.?	¿Dónde está.?	**don**-deh ess-**tah**.
the train station	la estación de tren	la ess-tah-see-**on** deh tren
the subway station	la estación de subte	la ess-tah-see-**on** deh **soob**-teh
the bus stop	la parada del colectivo	la pah-**rah**-dah del col-ek-**tee**-voh
the post office	el correo	el cor-**reh**-yoh
the bank	el banco	el **ban**-koh
the hotel	el hotel	el oh-**tel**
the museum	el museo	el moo-**seh**-yoh
the hospital	el hospital	el oss-pee-**tal**
the elevator	el ascensor	el ass-**en**-sor
the bathroom	el baño	el **ban**-yoh
Left/right	izquierda/derecha	iss-kee-**er**-dah/ deh-**rech**-ah
Straight ahead	derecho	deh-**rech**-oh
Avenue	avenida	av-en-**ee**-dah
City street	calle	**cah**-sheh
Highway	carretera/ruta	cah-ret-**eh**-rah
Restaurant	restaurante/restorán	rest-ow-**ran**-teh/ rest-oh-**ran**
Main square	plaza principal	**plass**-ah prin-see-**pal**
Market	mercado	mer-**kah**-do
Neighborhood	barrio	**bah**-ree-oh

MENU GUIDE

With so much meat on the menu, you'll need to know how to order it: *jugoso* (juicy) means medium rare, *vuelta y vuelta* (flipped back and forth) means rare, and *vivo por adentro* (alive inside) is barely warm in the middle. Argentineans like their meat *bien cocido* (well cooked).

aceite de olivo: olive oil

alfajores: Argentine cookies, usually made with dulce de leche and often covered with chocolate, though there are hundreds of varieties

arroz: rice

bife de lomo: filet mignon

bife de chorizo: like a New York strip steak, but double the size (not to be confused with *chorizo*, which is a type of sausage)

budín de pan: Argentine version of bread pudding

cabrito: roasted kid

cafecito: espresso

café con leche: coffee with milk

centolla: King crab, a Patagonian specialty

chimichurri: a sauce of oil, garlic, and salt, served with meat

chinchulines: small intestines

chorizo: thick, spicy pork-and-beef sausages, usually served with bread (*choripan*)

churros: baton-shaped donuts for dipping in hot chocolate

ciervo: venison

chivito: kid

cordero: lamb

cortado: coffee "cut" with a drop of milk

dulce de leche: a sweet caramel concoction made from milk and served on pancakes, in pastries, on cookies, and on ice cream

empanadas: pockets stuffed with meat—usually beef—chicken, or cheese

ensalada de fruta: fruit salad (sometimes fresh, sometimes canned)

estofado: beef stew

facturas: small pastries

huevos: eggs

humitas: steamed cornhusks wrapped around cornmeal and cheese

jamón: ham

lechón: roast suckling pig

lengua: tongue

licuado: milk shake

locro: local stew, usually made with hominy and beans, that's cooked slowly with meat and vegetables; common in northern Argentina

medialuna: croissant

mejillones: mussels

merluza: hake

milanesa: breaded meat cutlet, usually veal, pounded thin and fried; served as a main course or in a sandwich with lettuce, tomato, ham, cheese, and egg

milanesa a la napolitana: a breaded veal cutlet with melted mozzarella cheese and tomato sauce

mollejas: sweetbreads; the thymus glands, usually of the cow but also can be of the lamb or the goat

morcilla: blood sausage

pejerrey: a kind of mackerel

pollo: chicken

provoleta: grilled provolone cheese sprinkled with olive oil and oregano

puchero: boiled meat and vegetables; like pot-au-feu

queso: cheese

salchichas: long, thin sausages

sambayon: an alcohol-infused custard

tamales: ground corn stuffed with meat, cheese, or other fillings and tied up in a corn husk

tenedor libre: all-you-can-eat meat and salad bar

tinto: red wine

trucha: trout

TRAVEL SMART
ARGENTINA

GETTING HERE AND AROUND

Argentina extends approximately 3,650 km (2,268 miles) from tip to tail, and many of its attractions are hundreds of miles apart. So you can save a lot in terms of both time and money by carefully plotting your course. Buenos Aires lies about two-thirds of the way up Argentina's eastern side, on the banks of the Río de la Plata. It's the country's capital and its main transportation hub.

TRAVEL TIMES FROM BUENOS AIRES		
TO	BY AIR	BY BUS
Montevideo, Uruguay	45 minutes	8 hours
Atlantic Coast	1 hour	5–6 hours
Córdoba	1¼ hours	9–11 hours
Mendoza	1¾ hours	12–14 hours
Puerto Iguazú	1¾ hours	16–19 hours
Salta	2¼ hours	18–21 hours
Bariloche	2¼ hours	21–23 hours
El Calafate	3¼ hours	40 hours

Three of the country's main draws are about 1,000 km (621 miles) from Buenos Aires as the crow flies: Puerto Iguazú, the base for exploring Iguazú Falls, in northeastern Misiones Province; Salta, the gateway to the Andean Northwest; and Mendoza, in the wine region, near the Chilean border. Slightly farther, this time southwest of Buenos Aires, is Bariloche, the hub for the Lake District of northern Patagonia. El Calafate, the hub for southern Patagonia and the launch pad for the Glaciar Perito Moreno, is a whopping 2,068 km (1,285 miles) southwest of Buenos Aires.

Flying within the country makes sense given these huge distances. That said, domestic flights are expensive, and flight delays are fairly regular occurrences.

Many visitors opt to take the more reliable overnight sleeper buses for trips of up to 1,000 km (621 miles). A well-developed network of long-distance buses connects Buenos Aires with cities all over Argentina; buses also operate between many urban centers without passing through the capital.

▋ AIR TRAVEL

TO ARGENTINA

There are direct daily flights between Buenos Aires and several North American cities, with New York and Miami being primary departure points. Many airlines also serve Buenos Aires via Santiago de Chile or São Paulo in Brazil, which adds only a little to your trip time.

Aerolíneas Argentinas, the flagship airline, operates direct flights between Buenos Aires and JFK once a day and Miami twice a day. Since its renationalization in 2008, Aerolíneas' reputation for chronic delays has greatly improved, although strikes do still ground planes.

Chilean airline LAN is Aerolíneas' biggest local competition. LAN flies direct from Buenos Aires to Miami, and via Santiago de Chile or Lima to JFK, Dallas, San Francisco, and Los Angeles, often in partnership with Brazilian airline TAM. LAN also allows you to bypass Buenos Aires by flying into Mendoza and Córdoba from JFK and Miami, both via Santiago de Chile.

U.S. carriers serve Buenos Aires, too. There are direct flights from Atlanta on Delta and from Houston on United; American flies nonstop from JFK, Miami, and Dallas.

Flying times to Buenos Aires are 11–12 hours from New York, 10½ hours from Atlanta, Dallas or Houston, and 9 hours from Miami.

WITHIN ARGENTINA

Most domestic flights operate from Buenos Aires, so to fly from the extreme south of the country to the extreme north, you often have to change planes here.

Aerolíneas Argentinas and its partner Austral link Buenos Aires to more Argentine cities than any other airline, with flights running to Puerto Iguazú, Salta, Mendoza, Córdoba, Bariloche, Ushuaia, and El Calafate at least once a day. LAN also flies to these cities. Andes Líneas Aéreas operates flights between Buenos Aires, Salta, and Puerto Madryn; and sometimes provides direct service between Puerto Iguazú and Salta and Córdoba, bypassing Buenos Aires.

AIR PASSES

Aerolíneas Argentinas has two coupon-based air passes, the South American Pass and the Visit Argentina Pass, both of which must be purchased before you arrive. Although you do not need to fly in and out of the continent with Aerolíneas to take advantage of either, prices are cheaper if you do. Each allows you to travel to between three and 12 destinations, using one coupon per flight; coupons from the two passes may also be combined.

The South American Pass includes all countries the carrier serves within the region (Brazil, Chile, Colombia, Paraguay, Peru, Uruguay, and Venezuela). All routes operate from Buenos Aires, except Rio de Janeiro to Puerto Iguazú and Santiago de Chile to Mendoza. Coupons cost between $90 and $250. The Visit Argentina Pass is valid for domestic flights. Coupons cost $180 each except for ones covering Patagonia, which cost $220 (prices drop to $150 and $200, respectively, if you fly into Argentina with Aerolíneas). The downside with these passes is that each connection you make through Buenos Aires counts as a flight and, therefore, requires a coupon. If you want to visit Buenos Aires, El Calafate, and Iguazú with the Visit Argentina Pass, for example, you would need to buy four coupons.

If you plan to take at least three flights within Argentina or South America in general, you might save money with Visit South America pass offered by the One-World Alliance (of which LAN is a member). Flights are categorized by mileage; segments (both domestic and international) start at $160.

Airline Contacts Aerolíneas Argentinas ⊕ *www.aerolineas.com.ar.* **Andes Líneas Aéreas** ⊕ *www.andesonline.com.* **American Airlines** ⊕ *www.aa.com.* **Delta Airlines** ⊕ *www.delta.com.* **LAN** ⊕ *www.lan.com.* **United Airlines** ⊕ *www.united.com.*

Airline Security Issues Transportation Security Administration ⊕ *www.tsa.gov.*

Air Passes South American Pass ☎ 800/333–0276 for Aerolíneas Argentinas ⊕ *www.aerolineas.com.ar/en-us/cheap_flights/south_american_pass.* **Visit Argentina Pass** ☎ 800/333–0276 for Aerolíneas Argentinas ⊕ *www.aerolineas.com.ar/en-us/cheap_flights/visit_argentina.* **Visit South America Pass** ☎ 866/435–9526 for LAN ⊕ *www.lan.com/en_us/sitio_personas/southamericanairpass/index.html or www.oneworld.com/flights/single-continent-fares/visit-south-america.*

AIRPORTS

Airports in Argentina are mostly small, well maintained, and easy to get around. Security at most isn't as stringent as it is in the States—computers stay in cases, shoes stay on your feet, and there are no random searches.

BUENOS AIRES

Buenos Aires' Aeropuerto Internacional de Ezeiza Ministro Pistarini (EZE)—known as Ezeiza—is 35 km (22 miles) southwest of the city center. Ezeiza is the base for international flights operated by Aerolíneas Argentinas and its partner Austral; both airlines run a limited number of domestic flights to Puerto Iguazú, El Calafate, Bariloche, Trelew, Córdoba, Ushuaia, and Rosario from here as well. These all depart from the newest terminal, C; inbound international flights on Aerolíneas, however, arrive at Terminal

A, a pleasant, glass-sided building. Other major international carriers also use Ezeiza's Terminal A. SkyTeam-member airlines (including Delta) are the notable exception: they operate entirely out of Terminal C. At this writing, Terminal B is being renovated.

A covered walkway connects all three terminals. Both A and C have a few small snack bars, a small range of shops—including a pharmacy—a public phone center with Internet services, and a tourist information booth. The ATM, 24-hour luggage storage, and car-rental agencies are in Terminal A.

⚠ Avoid changing money in the baggage claim area. The best exchange rates are at the small Banco de la Nación in the Terminal A arrivals area; it's open round the clock.

Most domestic flights operate out of Aeroparque Jorge Newbery (AEP). It's next to the Río de la Plata in northeast Palermo, about 8 km (5 miles) north of the city center. Both it and Ezeiza are run by the private company Aeropuertos Argentinos 2000.

ELSEWHERE IN ARGENTINA
Several other airports in Argentina are technically international, but only because they have a few flights to neighboring countries; most flights are domestic.

Aeropuerto Internacional de Puerto Iguazú (IGR) is close to Iguazú Falls; it's 20 km (12 miles) from Puerto Iguazú and 10 km (6 miles) from the park entrance. The northwest is served by Salta's Aeropuerto Internacional Martín Miguel de Güemes (SLA), 7 km (4½ miles) west of the city of Salta.

The airport for the wine region and western Argentina is Aeropuerto Internacional de Mendoza Francisco Gabrieli (MDZ), usually known as El Plumerillo. It's 10 km (6 miles) north of Mendoza. Northern Patagonia's hub is Bariloche, 13 km (8 miles) west of which is the Aeropuerto Internacional San Carlos de Bariloche Teniente Luis Candelaria (BRC), known

as the Aeropuerto de Bariloche. The gateway to southern Patagonia is Aeropuerto Internacional de El Calafate Comandante Armando Tola (ECA), 18 km (11 miles) east of El Calafate itself.

Airport Information Aeroparque Jorge Newbery ☎ 11/5480–6111 ⊕ www.aa2000. com.ar. **Aeropuerto Internacional de Ezeiza Ministro Pistarini** ☎ 11/5480–2500 ⊕ www. aa2000.com.ar.

▌ BOAT TRAVEL

Ferries run frequently across the Río de la Plata between Buenos Aires and the Uruguayan cities of Colonia and Montevideo. Seacat or Colonia Express catamarans, which take an hour or less to Colonia and three hours to Montevideo, offer the best value. Full-price round-trip tickets cost around 1,000 and 1,250 pesos, respectively, but they often drop as low as 650 and 770 pesos if you book online (same-day return tickets are sometimes even less). Buquebus offers similar services on high-speed ferries. Round-trip tickets cost 1,350 pesos to Colonia and 1,550 pesos to Montevideo, but there are substantial off-peak and midweek discounts.

All three companies also sell packages that include bus tickets to La Paloma, Montevideo, and Punta del Este direct from Colonia's ferry terminal. You can order tickets by phone or online. Buquebus and Seacat leave from a terminal at the northern end of Puerto Madero. The Colonia Express terminal is on Avenida Pedro de Mendoza (the extension of Avenida Huergo) at 20 de Septiembre, south of Puerto Madero. It's best reached by taxi.

Contacts Buquebus ☎ 11/4316–6500 ⊕ www.buquebus.com. **Colonia Express** ☎ 11/4317–4100 for English-speaking operator ⊕ www.coloniaexpress.com. **Seacat** ☎ 11/4314–5100 ⊕ www.seacatcolonia.com.

▌ BUS TRAVEL

Frequent, comfortable, and dependable long-distance buses connect Buenos Aires with cities all over Argentina and with neighboring countries. Bus travel can be substantially cheaper than air travel and far less prone to delays. As a result, locals and visitors alike often choose overnight sleeper services for trips up to 14 hours long.

The Plataforma 10 website lets you assess routes, compare prices, and buy tickets for long-distance bus rides throughout Argentina, as well as ones to top international destinations like Montevideo. Most major bus companies have their own online timetables; some allow you to purchase tickets online or by phone. Websites also list alternative *puntos de venta* (sales offices)—in many cases you can buy tickets from booths in shopping malls or subway stations, though outside of peak season you can usually buy them at the terminal right up until departure time. Many now accept credit cards; even so, you should be prepared to pay in cash. In January, February, and July, get your ticket as far in advance as possible (a week or more, at least) and arrive at the terminal extra early.

Most long-distance buses depart Buenos Aires from the Terminal de Omnibus de Retiro, which is often referred to as the Terminal de Retiro or simply Retiro. Ramps and stairs from the street lead you to a huge concourse where buses leave from more than 60 numbered platforms. There are restrooms, restaurants, public phones, lockers, news kiosks, and a tourist office on this floor.

If you didn't buy tickets in advance, you can get them from the *boleterías* (ticket offices) on the upper level; there are also two ATMs here. Each company has its own ticket booth; they're arranged in zones according to the destinations served, which makes price comparisons easy. The terminal's comprehensive Spanish-language website lists bus companies by destination, including their phone number and ticket booth location. *(See individual chapters for information about local bus stations.)* Keep your wits about you in the terminal: pickpockets and bag-snatchers often prey on distracted travelers.

Long-distance buses have toilets, air-conditioning, videos, and snacks. The most basic service is *semi-cama*, which has minimally reclining seats and often takes a little longer than more luxurious services. It's worth paying the bit extra for *coche cama* (also called *ejecutivo*), which has large, business-class-style seats and, sometimes, pillows and blankets. The best rides of all are on *cama suite* services, where fully reclinable seats are often contained in their own little booth.

On routes between nearby towns you can usually choose between regular buses (*común*) and air-conditioned or heated ones with reclining seats (*diferencial*). The companies that run local services rarely have websites—you buy tickets directly from the bus station.

Contacts Plataforma 10 ⊕ *www. plataforma10.com.* **Terminal de Ómnibus Retiro** ✉ *Av. Antártida Argentina at Av. Ramos Mejía, Retiro, Buenos Aires* ☎ *11/4310–0700* ⊕ *www.tebasa.com.ar.*

▌ CAR TAVEL

Argentina's long highways and fabulous scenery make it a great place for road trips. However, if you're only going to be staying in Buenos Aires and other big cities, parking limitations and downright crazy traffic make renting a car more trouble than it's worth. Stick with public transportation, including taxis, or hire a *remis* (car and driver), which can take you around the countryside, too.

GASOLINE

Gas stations (*estaciones de servicio*) are in and near most towns and along major highways. Most are open 24 hours and include full service, convenience stores, and sometimes ATMs. In rural areas, stations have small shops and toilets; however, they are few and far between and have reduced hours.

On long trips, fill your tank whenever you can, even if you've still got gas left, as the next station could be a long way away (signs at stations often tell you how far). Attendants always pump the gas and don't expect a tip, though most locals add a few pesos for a full tank. Credit cards often aren't accepted—look for signs reading "*Tarjetas de crédito suspendidas*" ("No credit cards") or "*Solo efectivo*" ("Cash only").

The major service stations are YPF, Shell, Petrobras, and Esso. Locals say that YPF gas is the highest quality; it is also the cheapest. Prices are often higher in the north of Argentina. South of an imaginary line between Bariloche and Puerto Madryn, gas is heavily subsidized and costs roughly half what it does elsewhere. There are three grades of unleaded fuels, as well as diesel and biodiesel. GNC is compressed natural gas, an alternative fuel. Stations with GNC signs may sell only this, or both this and regular gas.

PARKING

On-street parking is limited in big cities. Some have meter systems or tickets that you buy from kiosks and display on the dashboard. In meter-free spots there's often an informal "caretaker" who guides you into your spot and charges 2–5 pesos to watch your car, which you pay when you leave.

Car theft is common, so many agencies insist that you park rental cars in a guarded lot. Many hotels have their own lots, and there are plenty in major cities: look for a circular blue sign with a white "E" for *estacionamiento* (parking). In downtown Buenos Aires, expect to pay 25–30 pesos per hour, or 70–120 pesos for 12 hours. Rates are much lower elsewhere. Illegally parked cars are towed only from restricted parking areas in city centers. Getting your car back is a bureaucratic nightmare and costs around 450 pesos.

ROAD CONDITIONS

The streets of many Argentine cities are notorious for potholes, uneven surfaces, and poorly marked intersections. Most major cities have a one-way system whereby parallel streets run in opposite directions: never going the wrong way along a street is one of the few rules that Argentineans abide by. Where there are no traffic lights at an intersection, you give way to drivers coming from the right, but have priority over those coming from the left.

Two kinds of roads connect major cities: *autopistas* (two- or three-lane freeways) and *rutas* (single or dual carriageways) or *rutas nacionales* (main "national routes," usually indicated with an "RN" before the route number). Both types of roads are subject to regular tolls. Autopistas are well maintained, but the state of rutas varies hugely. In more remote locations even rutas that look like major highways on maps may be narrow roads with no central division. Always travel with a map, as signposts for turnoffs are scarce.

Night driving can be hazardous: some highways and routes are poorly lighted, routes sometimes cut through the center of towns, cattle often get onto the roads, and in rural areas farm trucks and old cars seldom have all their lights working. Outside of the city of Buenos Aires, be especially watchful at traffic lights, as crossing on red lights at night is common practice. A useful road-trip website is ⊕*www.ruta0.com,* which calculates distances and tolls between places and offers several route options.

ROADSIDE EMERGENCIES

All rental-car agencies have an emergency help line in case of breakdowns or accidents—some services take longer than others to arrive. The best roadside assistance is usually that of the Automóvil Club Argentina (ACA), which sends mechanics and tow trucks to members traveling anywhere in the country. The ACA also offers free roadside assistance to members of North American clubs and automobile associations. However, bear in mind when you call for assistance that most operators speak only Spanish.

If you have an accident on the highway, stay by your vehicle until the police arrive, which could take a while, depending on where you are. If your car is stolen, you should report it to the closest police station.

Contacts American Automobile Association (AAA). ☎ 800/564–6222 ⊕ www.aaa.com. **Automóvil Club Argentino (ACA).** ☎ 11/4808–4000, 800/777–2894 for emergencies ⊕ www.aca.org.ar. **Police** ☎ 101.

RULES OF THE ROAD

You drive on the right in Argentina, as in the United States. Seatbelts are required by law for front-seat passengers. You must use your headlights on highways at all times. The use of cellular phones while driving is forbidden, and turning left on two-way avenues is prohibited unless there's a left-turn signal; there are no right turns on red. Traffic lights turn yellow before they turn red, but also before turning green, which is interpreted by drivers as an extra margin to get through the intersection, so take precautions.

The legal blood-alcohol limit is 500 mg of alcohol per liter of blood, but in practice breathalyzing is common only in Buenos Aires and along the highways of the Atlantic coast during January and February. In towns and cities a 40-kph (25-mph) speed limit applies on streets and a 60-kph (37-mph) limit is in effect on avenues. On autopistas the limit is 130 kph (80 mph), and on rutas it ranges between 100 kph (62 mph) and 120 kph (75 mph). On smaller roads and highways out of town it's 80 kph (50 mph). Locals take speed-limit signs, the ban on driving with cell phones, and drunk driving lightly, so drive very defensively.

Police tend to be forgiving of foreigners' driving faults and often waive tickets and fines when they see your passport. If you do get a traffic ticket, don't argue. Most tickets aren't payable on the spot, but some police officers offer "reduced" on-the-spot fines in lieu of a ticket: it's bribery, and you'd do best to insist on receiving the proper ticket.

In Buenos Aires, buses and taxis have exclusive lanes on major avenues. On other streets they often drive as though they have priority, and it's good to defer to them for your own safety.

If you experience a small accident, jot down the other driver's information (full name, license number, insurance provider, and policy number) and supply your own. In cities, the standard procedure is to call the police and wait for them at the site of the accident. Otherwise, go to the nearest police station in the area to file a report. Contact your rental agency immediately.

Paved highways run from Argentina to the Chilean, Bolivian, Paraguayan, and Brazilian borders. If you do cross the border by land, you'll be required to present your passport, documentation of car ownership, and insurance paperwork at immigration and customs checkpoints. It's also common for cars and bags to be searched for contraband, such as food, livestock, and drugs.

RENTAL CARS

Daily rates range from 430 pesos to 1,550 pesos, depending on the type of car and the distance you plan to travel. This generally includes tax and 200 free km (125 free miles) daily. Note that most cars have manual transmissions; if you need an automatic, request one in advance and be prepared to pay extra—usually only the more expensive vehicle categories have them.

Reputable firms don't rent to drivers under 21, and drivers under 23 often have to pay a daily surcharge. Children's car seats are not compulsory, but are available for about 35 to 50 pesos per day. Some agencies charge a 10% surcharge for picking up a car from the airport.

A collision damage waiver (CDW) is mandatory and is usually included in standard rental prices. However, you may still be responsible for a deductible fee (known locally as a *franquicia* or *deducible*)—a maximum amount that you'll have to pay if damage occurs. It ranges from 3,000 to 6,000 pesos for a car and can be much higher for a four-wheel-drive vehicle. You can reduce the figure substantially or altogether by paying an insurance premium (anywhere from 40 to 1,000 pesos per day); some companies have lower deductibles than others.

In general, you cannot cross the border in a rental car. Many rental companies don't insure you on unpaved roads and have special insurance clauses that make you responsible for most of the value of the car if it flips over in an accident, which is commonplace on unpaved roads in Patagonia. Discuss your itinerary with the agent to be certain you're always covered.

Rental Agencies Alamo ☎ *810/999–25266, 11/4811–5903 in Buenos Aires* ⊕ *www.alamo. com.* **Avis** ☎ *810/9991–2847, 11/4326–5542 in Buenos Aires* ⊕ *www.avis.com.ar.* **Budget** ☎ *810/999–2834, 11/4326–3825 in Buenos Aires* ⊕ *www.budget.com.ar.* **Dollar** ☎ *800/555–3655, 11/4315–1670 in Buenos Aires* ⊕ *www.dollar.com.ar.* **Hertz** ☎ *810/222–43789, 11/4816–8001 in Buenos Aires* ⊕ *www. hertzargentina.com.ar.*

ESSENTIALS

■ ACCOMMODATIONS

Argentina has a broad variety of hotels, and the healthy competition between them generally translates into high quality and reasonable rates. Nearly all hotels—even hostels—include breakfast in the room price, but not all include the 21% tax in their quoted rates. Prices are also linked to municipality-run rating systems, which are based on a checklist of amenities (often outdated) rather than detailed evaluation. You can get wildly different things for your money, so do your homework. In destinations popular with locals, room prices soar in high season (usually January, February, and July), and some establishments won't take bookings for less than seven days. In the off-season the same places can be a steal.

APARTMENT AND HOUSE RENTALS

There are hundreds of furnished rentals available by the day, week, or month in Buenos Aires and other cities. International outfits such as HomeAway and AirBnB (which also lets individual rooms) list an enviable selection of properties. Reputable local reservations services like ApartmentsBA.com, ByT Argentina, and Buenos Aires Habitat have large online databases, too.

When choosing your rental, remember that air-conditioning is a must in central and northern Argentina between December and March. Always check exact street locations on a map, as listings sometimes exaggerate a property's proximity to particular neighborhoods, landmarks, or subway stations. Likewise, apartments are often more worn than they appear in gleaming website photos.

Most online apartment agencies act as intermediaries between you and the owner: an English-speaking representative meets you at the apartment, you sign a contract, pay the owner, and are given the keys. You pay for your entire stay up front, and usually have to pay a deposit equivalent to a week's rent, which is returned when you leave. Note that though you give a credit card number to secure your reservation, actual payment is nearly always in cash only. Read cancellation policies carefully: many agencies don't refund if you're not happy with your apartment choice.

Rental Contacts Air BnB ⊕ *www.airbnb.com.* **ApartmentsBA.com** ☎ *646/827–8796 in the U.S., 11/5254–0100 in Buenos Aires* ⊕ *www.apartmentsba.com.* **Buenos Aires Habitat** ☎ *305/735–2223 in the U.S., 11/4815–8662 in Buenos Aires* ⊕ *www.buenosaireshabitat.com.* **ByT Argentina** ☎ *11/4876–5000* ⊕ *www.bytargentina.com.* **HomeAway** ⊕ *www.homeaway.com.*

ESTANCIAS

You get a taste of Argentine country life—including home-cooked meals and horseback riding—when you stay at a ranch. Estancias Travel and Estancias Argentinas are two good booking services, but you usually get better rates if you call the estancia directly.

When booking, ask specifically about what activities and drinks are included in rates, and bear in mind that many establishments accept only cash payments. Be sure to factor in travel times and costs when planning your stay: remoter locations may be reachable only by private transport, often at a hefty cost.

Estancia Reservations Estancias Argentinas ☎ *11/4343–2366* ⊕ *www.estanciasargentinas.com.* **Estancias Travel** ☎ *11/5236–1054* ⊕ *www.estanciastravel.com.*

■ COMMUNICATIONS

INTERNET

Free or inexpensive Internet access is widely available in major urban centers. Both budget establishments and high-end hotels tend to have free Wi-Fi, though connection quality varies greatly. Many bars and restaurants in big cities also have free Wi-Fi—look for stickers on their windows; these are typically open networks and you don't need to ask for a password to use them.

In the capital, wider coverage comes courtesy of BA WiFi, a free service provided by the city government in many subte stations, Metrobus shelters, public libraries, museums, cultural centers, and even major streets and squares. The BA WiFi website lists an ever-growing number of hot spots. Civic and provincial governments elsewhere in the country offer similar services on major public thoroughfares or in libraries. You can also find Wi-Fi in many business and event centers, some airports, and in other public spaces—piggybacking is common practice.

If you're traveling without a laptop or smartphone, some hotels provide Internet access through room televisions; many also have a PC in the lobby for guests to use. Using a *locutorio* (telephone and Internet center) is another option, although these are becoming less common. Expect to pay between 6 and 15 pesos per hour to surf the Web.

Contact BA WiFi ⊕ *www.buenosaires.gob.ar/ modernizacion/wi-fi-gratis.*

PHONES

The country code for Argentina is 54. To call landlines in Argentina from the United States, dial the international access code (011) followed by the country code (54), the two- to four-digit area code without the initial 0, then the six- to eight-digit phone number. For example, to call the Buenos Aires number 011/4123–4567, you would dial 011–54–11–4123–4567.

Any number that is prefixed by a 15 is a cell-phone number. To call cell phones from the United States, dial the international access code (011) followed by the country code (54), Argentina's cell-phone code (9), the area code without the initial 0, then the seven- or eight-digit cell-phone number *without* the initial 15. For example, to call the Buenos Aires cell phone (011) 15/5123–4567, you would dial 011–54–9–11–5123–4567.

CALLING WITHIN ARGENTINA

Argentina's phone service is run by the duopoly of Telecom and Telefónica. Telecom covers the northern half of Argentina (including the northern half of the city of Buenos Aires) and Telefónica covers the south. However, both companies operate public phones and phone centers throughout Argentina, called *locutorios* or *telecentros.*

Service is efficient, and direct dialing—both long-distance and international—is universal. You can make local and long-distance calls from your hotel (usually with a surcharge) and from any public phone or locutorio. Public phones are increasingly rare and usually broken; those that aren't accept coins. Phone cards can be used from both public and private phones by calling a free access number and entering the card code number.

At locutorios, ask the receptionist for *una cabina* (a booth), make as many local, long-distance, or international calls as you like (a small LCD display tracks how much you've spent), then pay as you leave. There's no charge if you don't get through. Note that many locutorios don't allow you to call free numbers, so you can't use prepaid calling cards from them.

All of Argentina's area codes are prefixed with a 0, which you need to include when dialing another area within Argentina. You don't need to dial the area code to call a local number. Confusingly, area codes and phone numbers don't all have the same number of digits. The area code for Buenos Aires is 011, and phone numbers have 8 digits. Area codes for the rest of the country have three or four digits, and start with 02 (the southern provinces) or 03 (the northern provinces); phone numbers have six or seven digits.

For local directory assistance (in Spanish), dial 110. Local calls cost 23 centavos for two minutes at peak periods (weekdays 8–8 and Saturday 8–1) or four minutes the rest of the time. Long-distance calls cost 57 centavos per *ficha* (unit)—the farther the distance, the less time each unit lasts. For example, 57 centavos lasts about two minutes to places less than 55 km (35 miles) away, but only half a minute to somewhere more than 250 km (155 miles) away.

To make international calls from Argentina, dial 00, then the country code, area code, and number. The country code for the United States is 1.

CALLING CARDS
You can use prepaid calling cards (*tarjetas prepagas*) to make local and international calls from public phones, but not locutorios. All cards come with a scratch-off panel, which reveals a PIN. You dial a free access number, the PIN, and the number you wish to call.

Many *kioscos* (convenience stores) and small supermarkets sell a variety of prepaid calling cards: specify it's for *llamadas internacionales* (international calls), and compare each card's per-minute rates to the country you want to call. Many cost as little as 9 centavos per minute for calls to the United States. Telecom and Telefónica also sell prepaid 5-, 10-, and 20-peso calling cards from kioscos and locutorios. They're called Tarjeta Ciudades and Geo Destinos, respectively. Calls to the United States cost 19 centavos per minute using both.

Calling Card Information Telecom
☎ *800/888-0110* ⊕ *www.telecom.com. ar.* **Telefónica** ☎ *800/333-4004* ⊕ *www. telefonica.com.ar.*

MOBILE PHONES
All cell phones in Argentina are GSM 850/1900 Mhz. Cell numbers use a local area code, then the cell-phone prefix (15), then a seven- or eight-digit number. To call a cell in the same area as you, dial 15 and the number. To call a cell in a different area, dial the area code, including the initial 0, then 15, then the number.

There are three main phone companies here: Movistar (owned by Telefónica), Claro, and Personal. Although they're similar, Claro has the most users and is said to have the best rates, while Movistar has the best coverage, and Personal the best customer service. All three offer 3G, but service is patchy even in the big cities, and most local users complain that they spend more time on 2G than 3G.

The best way to use your own smartphone in Argentina is to get it unlocked before you travel, then purchase a prepaid local SIM card (*tarjeta SIM*) once you land. You can buy one for 15 to 20 pesos from any of the companies' offices and sales stands, which are easy to find country-wide. Top up credit by purchasing pay-as-you-go cards (*tarjetas de celular*), available from kioscos, locutorios, supermarkets, and gas stations, or by *carga virtual* (virtual top-ups) at kioscos and locutorios, where sales clerks add credit to your line directly while you wait.

⚠ **Pickpockets often target tourists for their cell phones, so consider leaving your latest-generation model at home and packing an older one instead. Alternately, you can buy a basic pay-as-you-go handset and SIM card on arrival for about 400 pesos.**

Using data packages for anything other than, say, email eats your pay-as-you-go credit quickly. The wisest strategy is to save your credit for local calls and restrict internet use to times when you have Wi-Fi access. While connected to Wi-Fi take advantage of services like Skype or Google Hangouts that let you touch base with folks back home for free (or a fraction of what roaming would cost).

Local charges for calling a cell phone from a landline depend on factors like the company and time of day, but most cost between 50 centavos and 1.50 pesos per minute. In general, you pay only for outgoing calls from cell phones, which cost around 3 pesos a minute. Calls from pay-as-you-go phones are the most expensive and calls to phones from the same company as yours are usually cheaper.

Contacts Claro ☎ *800/1232–5276* ⊕ *www. claro.com.ar.* **Movistar** ☎ *11/5321–1111* ⊕ *www.movistar.com.ar.* **Personal** ☎ *800/444–0800* ⊕ *www.personal.com.ar.*

∎ CUSTOMS AND DUTIES

Customs uses a random inspection system that requires you to push a button at the inspection bay—if a green light appears, you walk through; if a red light appears, your bags are X-rayed (and very occasionally opened). Officially, foreign tourists are allowed to bring up to 2 liters of alcoholic beverages, 400 cigarettes, and 50 cigars into the country duty-free. You are also allowed another $300 worth of purchases from the duty-free shops, which most of Argentina's international airports have, after you land. In practice, however, most officials wave foreigners through customs controls and are rarely interested in alcohol or tobacco. Personal clothing and effects are admitted duty-free, provided they have been used, as are personal jewelry and professional equipment. Fishing gear and skis present no problems.

If you enter the country by bus from Bolivia, Brazil, or Paraguay, you, your bags, and the vehicle may be subject to lengthy searches by officials looking for drugs and smuggled goods.

Argentina has strict regulations designed to prevent the illicit trafficking of antiques, fossils, and other items of cultural and historical importance. For more information, contact the Dirección Nacional de Patrimonio y Museos (National Heritage and Museums Board).

Information in Argentina Dirección Nacional de Patrimonio y Museos ☎ *11/4381– 6656* ⊕ *www.cultura.gov.ar.*

U.S. Information U.S. Customs and Border Protection ⊕ *www.cbp.gov.*

∎ ELECTRICITY

The electrical current is 220 volts, 50 cycles alternating current (AC), so most North American appliances can't be used without a converter. Older wall outlets take continental-type plugs, with two round prongs, whereas newer buildings take plugs with three flat, angled prongs or two flat prongs set at a "v" angle.

Brief power outages (and surges when the power comes back) are fairly regular occurrences, especially outside of Buenos Aires, so it's a good idea to use a surge protector with your laptop.

∎ EMERGENCIES

In a medical emergency, taking a taxi to the nearest hospital—drivers usually know where to go—can be quicker than waiting for an ambulance. If you do call an ambulance, it will transport you to the nearest hospital—possibly a public one that may well look run-down; don't worry, though, as the medical care will be excellent. Alternatively, you can call a private hospital directly.

For theft, wallet loss, small road accidents, and minor emergencies, contact the nearest police station. Expect all dealings with the police to be a lengthy, bureaucratic business—it's probably only worth bothering if you need the report for insurance claims.

American Embassy American Embassy ✉ *Av. Colombia 4300, Palermo, Buenos Aires* ☎ *11/5777–4354 for emergency assistance, 11/5777–4873 for emergencies after hrs* ⊕ *argentina.usembassy.gov.*

General Contacts Ambulance and Medical ☎ *107.* **Fire** ☎ *100.* **Police** ☎ *101.*

∎ HEALTH

MEDICAL CONCERNS
No vaccinations are required for travel to Argentina. However, the National Centers for Disease Control & Prevention (CDC) recommend vaccinations against hepatitis

A and B and typhoid for all travelers. A yellow fever vaccine is also advisable if you're traveling to Iguazú. Each year there are cases of cholera in northern Argentina, mostly in the indigenous communities near the Bolivian border; your best protection is to avoid eating raw seafood. Malaria is a threat only in low-lying rural areas near the borders of Bolivia and Paraguay. In 2009 outbreaks of dengue fever (another mosquito-borne disease) were widespread in northern Argentina, especially in Misiones Province (where Iguazú Falls is), but following comprehensive public health campaigns, there have been no more serious outbreaks. All the same, cases are regularly reported as far south as Buenos Aires. The best preventive measure against both dengue and malaria is to cover your arms and legs, use a good mosquito repellent containing DEET, and stay inside at dusk.

American trypanosomiasis, or Chagas' disease, is present in remote rural areas. The CDC recommends chloroquine as a preventive antimalarial for adults and infants in Argentina. To be effective, the weekly doses must start a week before you travel and continue four weeks after your return. There is no preventive medication for dengue or Chagas'. Children traveling to Argentina should have current inoculations against measles, mumps, rubella, and polio.

In most urban areas in Argentina, including Buenos Aires, people drink tap water and eat uncooked fruits and vegetables. However, if you're prone to tummy trouble, stick to bottled water. Take standard flu-avoidance precautions such as hand-washing and cough-covering, and consider contacting your doctor for a flu shot if you're traveling during the austral winter.

OTHER ISSUES

Apunamiento, or altitude sickness, which results in shortness of breath and headaches, may be a problem when you visit high altitudes in the Andes. To remedy any discomfort, walk slowly, eat lightly, and drink plenty of fluids (avoid alcohol). In northwestern Argentina, coca leaves are widely available (don't worry, it's totally legal). Follow the locals' example and chew a wad mixed with a dab of bicarbonate of soda on hiking trips: it does wonders for altitude problems. You can also order tea made from coca leaves (*maté de coca*), which has the same effect. If you experience an extended period of nausea, dehydration, dizziness, or severe headache or weakness while in a high-altitude area, seek medical attention. Dehydration, sunstroke, frostbite, and heatstroke are all dangers of outdoor recreation at high altitudes. Awareness and caution are the best preventive measures.

The sun is a significant health hazard, especially in southern Patagonia, where the ozone layer is said to be thinning. Stay out of the sun at midday and wear plenty of good-quality sunblock. A limited selection is available in most supermarkets and pharmacies, but if you use high SPF factors or have sensitive skin, bring your favorite brands with you. A hat and decent sunglasses are also essential.

Health Warnings National Centers for Disease Control & Prevention (*CDC*). ☎ *800/232-4636* ⊕ *www.cdc.gov/travel*. **World Health Organization** (*WHO*). ⊕ *www. who.int*.

HEALTH CARE

Argentina has free national health care that also provides foreigners with free outpatient care. Although the medical practitioners working at *hospitales públicos* (public hospitals) are first-rate, the institutions themselves are often underfunded: bed space and basic supplies are at a minimum. Except in emergencies you should consider leaving these resources for the people who really need them. World-class private clinics and hospitals are plentiful, and consultation and treatment fees are low compared with those in North America. Still, it's good to have some kind of medical insurance.

LOCAL DO'S AND TABOOS

CUSTOMS OF THE COUNTRY

Welcoming and helpful, Argentineans are a pleasure to travel among. City dwellers here have more in common with, say, the Spanish or Italians, than other Latin Americans. However, although cultural differences between here and North America are small, they're still palpable.

Outside Buenos Aires, siestas are still sacrosanct: most shops and museums close between 1 and 4 or 5 pm. Locals are usually fashionably late for all social events—don't be offended if someone keeps you waiting over half an hour for a lunch or dinner date. However, tardiness is frowned upon in the business world.

Fiercely animated discussions are a national pastime, and locals relish probing controversial issues like politics and religion, as well as soccer and their friends' personal lives. Political correctness isn't a valued trait, and just about everything and everyone—except mothers—is a potential target for playful mockery. Locals are often disparaging about their country's shortcomings, but Argentina-bashing is a privilege reserved for Argentineans. That said, some anti-American feeling—both serious and jokey—permeates most of society. You'll earn more friends by taking it in stride.

Sadly, the attitudes of many Argentines toward foreigners vary greatly according to origin and race. White Europeans and North Americans are held in far greater esteem than, say, Peruvians or Bolivians. Racist reactions—anything from insults or name calling to giving short shrift—to Asian, black, or Native American people are, unfortunately, not unusual. Although there's little you can do about this in day-to-day dealings, Argentina does have an antidiscrimination body, Institución Nacional contra la Discriminación, la Xenofobia y el Racismo (INADI ⊕ *www.inadi.gov.ar*), that you can contact if you're the victim of serious discrimination.

GREETINGS

Argentineans have no qualms about getting physical, and the way they greet each other reflects this. One kiss on the right cheek is the customary greeting between both male and female friends. Women also greet strangers in this way, although men—especially older men—often shake hands the first time they meet someone. Other than that, handshaking is seen as very cold and formal.

When you leave a party it's normal to say good-bye to everyone in the room (or, if you're in a restaurant, to everyone at your table), which means kissing everyone once again. Unlike other Latin Americans, Argentineans use the formal "you" form, *usted,* only with people much older than they or in very formal situations, and the casual greeting ¡Hola! often replaces *buen día, buenas tardes,* and *buenas noches.* In small towns, formal greetings and the use of *usted* are more widespread.

LANGUAGE

Argentina's official language is Spanish, known locally as *castellano* (rather than *español*). It differs from other varieties of Spanish in its use of *vos* (instead of *tú*) for the informal "you" form, and there are lots of small vocabulary differences, especially for everyday things like food. Intonation varies greatly around Argentina, but it is markedly singsong in Buenos Aires. Another *porteño* peculiarity is pronouncing the letters "y" and "ll" as a "sh" sound. Elsewhere these same letters are pronounced "y" or "j" and "ly". In the northern half of Argentina, the typical Spanish "r" is trilled much more softly.

In hotels, restaurants, and shops that cater to visitors, many people speak at least some English. All the same, attempts to speak Spanish are usually appreciated. Basic courtesies like *por favor* (please) and *gracias* (thank you) are a good place to start. Even if your language skills are basic and phrase-book-bound, locals generally make an effort to understand you. If people don't know the answer to a question, such as a request for directions, they'll tell you so.

OUT ON THE TOWN

A firm nod of the head or raised eyebrow usually gets waiters' attention; "*disculpa*" (excuse me) also does the trick. You can ask your waiter for *la cuenta* (the check) or make a signing gesture in the air from afar.

Alcohol—especially wine and beer—is a big part of life in Argentina. Local women generally drink less than their foreign counterparts, but there are no taboos about this. Social events usually end in general tipsiness rather than all-out drunkenness, which is seen as a rather tasteless foreign habit.

Smoking is very common in Argentina. Anti-smoking legislation in several cities—including Buenos Aires, Mendoza, and Córdoba—has banned it in all but the largest cafés and restaurants (these are required to have extractor fans and designated smoking areas). Elsewhere you are likely to get smoke with your steak, although larger eateries may offer no-smoking sections (*no fumadores*); make sure to ask before you are seated. Smoking is prohibited on public transport and in government offices, banks, and cinemas.

Public displays of affection between hetero-sexual couples attract little attention in most parts of the country. Although same-sex marriage is now legal throughout Argentina, beyond downtown Buenos Aires same-sex couples may attract hostile reactions.

All locals make an effort to look nice—though not necessarily formal—for dinner out. Older couples get very dressed up for the theater; younger women usually put on high heels and makeup for clubbing.

If you're invited to someone's home for dinner, a bottle of good Argentine wine, a shop-bought cake or dessert, or chocolates are all good gifts to take the hosts.

SIGHTSEEING

You can dress pretty much as you like in Buenos Aires: skimpy clothing causes no offense.

Argentinean men almost always allow women to go through doors and to board buses and elevators first, often with exaggerated ceremony. Far from finding this sexist, local women take it as a God-given right. Frustratingly, there's no local rule about standing on one side of escalators to allow people to pass you.

Despite bus drivers' best efforts, locals are often reluctant to move to the back of buses. Pregnant women, the elderly, and those with disabilities have priority on the front seats of city buses, and you should offer them your seat if these are already taken.

Children and adults selling pens, notepads, or sheets of stickers are regular fixtures on urban public transport. Some children also hand out tiny greeting cards in exchange for coins. The standard procedure is to accept the merchandise or cards as the vendor moves up the carriage, then either return the item (saying *no, gracias*) or give them money when they return.

Most Argentineans are hardened jaywalkers, but given how reckless local driving can be, you'd do well to cross at corners and wait for pedestrian lights.

In nonemergency situations you'll be seen much quicker at a private clinic or hospital, and overnight stays are more comfortable. Many doctors at private hospitals speak at least some English. Note that only cities have hospitals; smaller towns may have a *sala de primeros auxilios* (first-aid post).

MEDICAL INSURANCE AND ASSISTANCE

Consider buying trip insurance with medical-only coverage. Neither Medicare nor some private insurers cover medical expenses anywhere outside of the United States. Medical-only policies typically reimburse you for medical care (excluding that related to preexisting conditions) and hospitalization abroad, and provide for evacuation. You still have to pay the bills and await reimbursement from the insurer, though.

Another option is to sign up with a medical-evacuation assistance company. Membership gets you doctor referrals, emergency evacuation or repatriation, 24-hour hotlines for medical consultation, and other assistance. International SOS and AirMed International provide evacuation services and medical referrals. MedjetAssist offers medical evacuation.

Medical Assistance Companies AirMed International ⊕ *www.airmed.com.* **MedjetAssist** ⊕ *www.medjetassist.com.*

Medical-Only Insurers International Medical Group ☎ *800/628–4664* ⊕ *www. imglobal.com.* **International SOS** ⊕ *www. internationalsos.com.* **Wallach & Company** ☎ *800/237–6615, 540/687–3166* ⊕ *www. wallach.com.*

OVER-THE-COUNTER REMEDIES

Towns and cities have a 24-hour pharmacy system: each night there's one *farmacia de turno* (on-duty pharmacy) for prescriptions and emergency supplies.

In Argentina, *farmacias* (pharmacies) carry painkillers, first-aid supplies, contraceptives, diarrhea treatments, and a range of other over-the-counter treatments, including some drugs that would require a prescription in the United States (many antibiotics, for example). Note that acetaminophen—or Tylenol—is known as *paracetamol* in Spanish. If you think you'll need to have prescriptions filled while you're in Argentina, be sure to have your doctor write down the generic name of the drug, not just the brand name.

Farmacity is a supermarket-style drugstore chain with branches all over Buenos Aires and other major cities, including Córdoba, Mendoza, and Salta; many of them are open 24 hours and offer a delivery service.

Pharmacies Farmacity ☎ *11/4322–7777* ⊕ *www.farmacity.com.ar.*

▌ HOLIDAYS

January through March is summer holiday season for Argentines. Winter holidays fall toward the end of July and beginning of August. Most public holidays are celebrated on their actual date, except August 17, October 12, and November 20, which move to the following Monday. When public holidays fall on a Thursday or Tuesday, the following Friday or preceding Monday, respectively, is also declared a holiday, creating a four-day weekend known as a *feriado puente.*

Año Nuevo (New Year's Day), January 1. **Carnaval** (Carnival), Monday and Tuesday six weeks before Easter. **Día Nacional de la Memoria por la Verdad y la Justicia** (National Memorial Day for Truth and Justice; commemoration of the start of the 1976–83 dictatorship), March 24. **Día del Veterano y de los Caídos en la Guerra de Malvinas** (Malvinas Veterans' Day), April 2. **Viernes Santo** (Good Friday), March or April. **Día del Trabajador** (Labor Day), May 1. **Día de la Revolución de Mayo** (Anniversary of the 1810 Revolution), May 25. **Día de la Bandera** (Flag Day), June 20. **Día de la Independencia** (Independence Day), July 9. **Paso a la Inmortalidad del General José de San Martín** (Anniversary of General

José de San Martín's Death), August 17.
Día del Respeto a la Diversidad Cultural
(Day of Respect for Cultural Diversity),
October 12. **Día de la Soberanía Nacio-nal** (National Sovereignty Day; Anniver-sary of the Battle of Vuelta de Obligado),
November 20. **Inmaculada Concepción de María** (Immaculate Conception), Decem-ber 8. **Christmas**, December 25.

▌MAIL

Correo Argentino, the mail service, has
an office in most towns or city neigh-borhoods; some locutorios also serve as
collection points and sell stamps. Older
postboxes are dark blue and yellow,
newer ones dark and light blue: most are
found either inside or directly outside post
offices. Mail delivery isn't dependable: it
can take 6 to 21 days for standard letters
and postcards to get to the United States.
Regular airmail letters cost 19 pesos for
up to 20 grams.

If you want to be sure something will
arrive, send it by *correo certificado* (reg-istered mail), which costs 52 pesos for
international letters up to 20 grams. Valu-able items are best sent with express ser-vices like DHL, UPS, or FedEx—delivery
within one to two days for a 5-kilogram
(11-pound) package starts at about 2,000
pesos. A similar size package would cost
670 pesos to send with Correo Argentino
and would take up to a week to arrive.

Argentina's post-code system is based on a
four-digit code. Each province is assigned
a letter (the city of Buenos Aires is "C,"
for instance) that goes before the number
code, and each city block is identified by
three letters afterward (such as ABD). In
practice, however, only big cities use these
complete postal codes (which look like
C1234ABD; the rest of Argentina uses the
basic number code (1234, for example).

Contacts Correo Argentino ⊕ *www.correoargentino.com.ar.*

▌MONEY

Although prices here have been steadily
rising, the number of pesos you get for
your dollar has been increasing as well.
So Argentina is still a good value if you're
coming from a country with a strong cur-rency. Eating out is very affordable, as are
mid-range hotels. Prices are usually sig-nificantly lower outside Buenos Aires and
other large cities. Room rates at first-class
hotels all over the country approach those
in the United States, however.

ITEM	AVERAGE COST
Cup of coffee and three *medialunas* (croissants)	25–35 pesos
Glass of wine	25–30 pesos
Liter bottle of local beer at a bar	40–50 pesos
Steak and fries in a cheap restaurant	60–90 pesos
One-mile taxi ride in Buenos Aires	11 pesos
Museum admission	Free–50 pesos

You can plan your trip around ATMs—cash is king for day-to-day dealings.
Always withdraw more well before your
current supply is spent, particularly in
small towns with few ATMs, as these
often run out of money, especially over
weekends or during holiday season. U.S.
dollars can be changed at any bank and
are often accepted as payment in clothing
stores, souvenir shops, and supermarkets.

Note that there's a perennial shortage
of change in Argentina. Hundred-peso
bills can be hard to get rid of, so ask for
50s when you change money. Traveler's
checks are useful only as an emergency
reserve.

You can usually pay by credit card in
high-end hotels countrywide and in nicer
restaurants and stores in big cities. But be
advised that even establishments display-ing stickers from different card companies
may suddenly stop accepting them: look

out for signs reading *tarjetas de crédito suspendidas* (credit card purchases temporarily unavailable). Outside of urban areas, plastic is less widely accepted. Visa is the most widely accepted credit card, followed closely by MasterCard. American Express is also accepted in hotels and restaurants, but Diners Club and Discover might not even be recognized. If possible, bring more than one credit card, as some establishments accept a single type. You usually have to produce photo ID—preferably a passport, but otherwise a driver's license—when making credit card purchases.

Nonchain stores often display two prices for goods: *precio de lista* (the standard price, valid if you pay by credit card) and a discounted price if you pay in *efectivo* (cash). Many travel services and even some hotels also offer cash discounts—it's always worth asking about.

Prices throughout this guide are given for adults. Substantially reduced fees are almost always available for children and senior citizens.

ATMS AND BANKS

ATMs, called *cajeros automáticos,* are found all over Buenos Aires and other big cities. Most smaller towns have at least one ATM; gas stations on major highways also sometimes have them. If you plan to be away from urban areas or major tourist destinations for long, take ample cash with you. There are two main systems. Banelco, indicated by a burgundy-color sign with white lettering, is used by Banco Comafi, Citibank, BBVA Banco Francés, HSBC, Banco Galicia, ICBC, Banco Itaú, Banco Macro, Banco Santander Río, and Banco Patagonia. Link, recognizable by a green-and-yellow sign, is the system used by Banco Provincia, Credicoop, Banco Hipotecario, and Banco de la Nación, as well as nearly all banks belonging to other provinces. Cards on the Cirrus and Plus networks can be used on both systems.

Many banks have daily withdrawal limits of 2,000 pesos or less. Sometimes ATMs

will impose unexpectedly low withdrawal limits (say, 600 pesos) on international cards—this is more common on Banelco than Link machines. You can get around it by requesting a further transaction before the machine returns your card, but first check whether your bank back home charges high per-withdrawal fees. It's safer to make withdrawals from ATMs in daylight hours.

ATM Locations Banelco ⊕ *www.banelco.com. ar.* **Link** ⊕ *www.redlink.com.ar.*

CURRENCY AND EXCHANGE

Argentina's currency is the peso, which equals 100 centavos. Bills come in denominations of 100 (violet), 50 (navy blue), 20 (red), 10 (ocher), 5 (green), and 2 (light blue) pesos. Coins are in denominations of 2 pesos and 1 peso (both heavy and bimetallic), as well as 50, 25, and 10 centavos. U.S. dollars are widely accepted in big-city stores, supermarkets, and at hotels and top-end restaurants (usually at a slightly worse exchange rate than you'd get at a bank). You always receive change in pesos, even when you pay with U.S. dollars.

Following a series of devaluations, the official exchange rate at this writing is around 8 pesos to the U.S. dollar. You can change dollars at this rate at most banks (between 10 am and 3 pm), at a *casa de cambio* (money changer), or at your hotel. All currency exchange involves fees, but as a rule banks charge the least and hotels the most. You need to show your passport to complete the transaction.

Heavy restrictions on locals buying U.S. dollars has led to a parallel—i.e., black market—exchange rate, known locally as the "*dólar blue,*" usually about 20% above the official rate. Although technically illegal, the dólar blue is so well established that major newspapers publish it alongside the official exchange rate. Many establishments are keen to bypass the lengthy bureaucracy involved in buying dollars officially and may offer to accept payment in them at the blue rate. On busy streets (like Calle Florida in Buenos Aires), you'll likely be propositioned by touts from small shops that are referred to locally as *"cuevas,"* or caves. Most are safe, but try to change relatively small amounts regularly to minimize any possible trouble.

■ **TIP→ You may not be able to change currency in rural areas at all, so don't leave major cities without adequate amounts of pesos in small denominations.**

Exchange-Rate Information Oanda.com ⊕ *www.oanda.com.* **XE.com** ⊕ *www.xe.com.*

▌ PACKING

Argentinean city dwellers are an appearance-conscious bunch who choose fashion over comfort any day. Though locals are stylish, they're usually fairly casual. Your nicer jeans or khakis, capris, skirts, and dress shorts are perfect for urban sightseeing. Combine them with stylish walking shoes or leather flats; sneakers are fine if they're out-about-town and hip. In summer, many local women seem to live in nice flip-flops or sandals. With the exception of truly posh establishments, a dirty look is usually the only punishment restaurants give the underdressed; refusing entry is almost unheard-of. A jacket and tie or stylish dress is necessary only if you plan on some seriously fine dining.

In most smaller towns and villages dress is more practical and sometimes more conservative. Wherever you go in the country, take good-quality sunglasses, sunblock, and a cap or hat: the sun can be strong. A good insect repellent is useful in Buenos Aires in the summer and invaluable in Iguazú year-round.

If you're visiting the northern half of Argentina, temperatures in lower-lying areas (including Buenos Aires) rarely fall below freezing, but a heavier coat or jacket is still a must in winter; in the high-altitude towns of the northwest, temperatures drop dramatically at night, so bring a jacket even in summer. In southern Patagonia, proper cold-weather gear is essential regardless of the season.

Pharmacies in major cities stock a good range of toiletries and hygiene products (note that only no-applicator tampons are available, however). Pharmacies, supermarkets, and kiosks sell condoms (*preservativos*), and oral contraceptive pills are available over the counter.

Toilet paper is rare in public restrooms, but you can buy pocket packs of tissues (known as *pañuelos descartables* or by their brand name, Carilinas) in kiosks. Antibacterial wipes and alcohol gel, available in pharmacies, can make bathroom trips more pleasant in remote areas.

▌ PASSPORTS

As a U.S. citizen, you need a passport valid for at least six months to enter Argentina for visits of up to 90 days. Argentina operates a reciprocal entry fee scheme for citizens of countries that charge Argentineans for visas, which includes U.S. citizens. At this writing, the fee (valid for multiple entries over a 10-year period) is $160. You pay in cash or by credit card at booths near immigration, after which you receive a tourist visa stamp on your passport. You can also pay the fee online before you travel, through the Dirección Nacional de Migraciones (National Directorate for Migrations) website.

If you need to stay longer, you can apply for a 90-day extension (*prórroga*) to your tourist visa at the Dirección Nacional de Migraciones. The process takes a morning and costs about 300 pesos. Alternatively, you can exit the country (by taking a boat trip to Uruguay from Buenos Aires, or crossing into Brazil near Iguazú, for example); upon reentering Argentina, your passport will be stamped allowing an additional 90 days. Overstaying your tourist visa is illegal and incurs a fine of 300 pesos, which you must pay at the Dirección Nacional de Migraciones. Once you have done so, you must leave the country within 10 days. You should carry your passport or other photo ID with you at all times: you need it to make credit-card purchases, change money, and send parcels, as well as in the unlikely event that the police stop you.

Officially, children visiting Argentina with only one parent do not need a signed and notarized permission-to-travel letter from the other parent. However, as Argentinean citizens *are* required to have such documentation, it's worth carrying a letter just in case laws change or border officials get confused. Single Parent Travel is a useful online resource that provides advice and downloadable sample permission letters.

For information on passport and visa requirements to visit the Brazilian side of Iguazú Falls, see the Planner pages at the start of Chapter 3, Side Trips from Buenos Aires.

Contacts Dirección Nacional de Migraciones ✉ *Av. Antártida Argentina 1355, Retiro, Buenos Aires* ☎ *11/4317-0234* ⊕ *www. migraciones.gov.ar.* **Embassy of Argentina** ⊕ *www.embassyofargentina.us.* **Single Parent Travel** ⊕ *www.singleparenttravel.net.*

U.S. Passport Information U.S. Department of State ☎ *877/487-2778* ⊕ *www.travel.state. gov.*

▌ SAFETY

Argentina is safer than many Latin American countries. However, street crime is still a concern—mainly pickpocketing, bag snatching, and occasionally mugging—especially in Buenos Aires. Taking a few precautions when traveling in the region is usually enough to keep you out of harm's way.

CRIME

Walk with purpose; if you don't look like a target, you'll likely be left alone. Avoid wearing flashy jewelry. Keep a grip on your purse or bag, and keep it in your lap if you're sitting (never leave it hanging on the back of a chair or on the floor). Try to keep your cash and credit cards in different places about your person (and always leave one card in your hotel safe, if possible), so that if one gets stolen you can fall back on the other.

Tickets and other valuables are best left in hotel safes, too. Avoid carrying large sums of money around, but always keep enough to have something to hand over in the unlikely event of a mugging. Another time-honored tactic is to keep a dummy wallet (an old one containing an expired credit card and a small amount of cash) in your pocket, with your real cash in an inside or vest pocket: if your "wallet" gets stolen you have little to lose.

Women can expect pointed looks, the occasional *piropo* (a flirtatious remark, usually alluding to some physical aspect), and some advances. These catcalls rarely escalate into actual physical harassment. The best reaction is to make like local women and ignore them; reply only if you're really confident with Spanish curse words. If you're heading out for the night, it's wise to take a taxi.

There's usually a notable police presence in areas popular with tourists, such as San Telmo and Palermo in Buenos Aires. This deters potential pickpockets and hustlers somewhat. However, Argentineans have little faith in their police forces: officers are often corrupt, and at best, the police are well-meaning but underequipped.

The most important advice we can give you is to not put up a struggle in the unlikely event that you are mugged. Nearly all physical attacks on tourists are the direct result of their resisting would-be pickpockets or muggers. Comply with demands, hand over your stuff, and try to get the situation over with as quickly as possible—then let your travel insurance take care of it.

PROTESTS

Argentineans like to speak their minds, and protesters frequently cause major traffic jams by blocking streets or clogging squares in downtown Buenos Aires. Some denounce government policies; others may show support for them.

Demonstrations are usually peaceful, but exercise caution if you happen across one.

SCAMS

Beware of scams such as a kindly passer-by offering to help you clean a stain that has somehow appeared on your clothes: while your attention is occupied, an accomplice picks your pocket or snatches your bag.

Taxi drivers in big cities are usually honest, but occasionally they decide to take people for a ride, literally. All official cabs have meters, so make sure this is turned on. It helps to have an idea where you're going and how long it will take. Local lore says that if you're hailing taxis on the street, those with lights on top (usually labeled "Radio Taxi") are more trustworthy. Late at night, try to call for a cab—all hotels and restaurants, no matter how cheap, have a number and will usually call for you.

When asking for price quotes while shopping in touristy areas, always confirm whether the amount is given in dollars or pesos. Some salespeople, especially street vendors, have found that they can take advantage of confused tourists by charging dollars for goods that are actually priced in pesos.

Advisories and Other Information Transportation Security Administration (*TSA*). ⊕ *www.tsa.gov*. **U.S. Department of State** ⊕ *www.travel.state.gov*.

▌ TAXES

Argentina has a $29 departure tax for international flights and an $8 departure tax for domestic flights. These are included in your ticket price when you fly from some airports, including Buenos Aires'. Otherwise you can pay by credit card or in cash at booths in airports (pesos, dollars, and euros are accepted). Hotel rooms carry a 21% tax. Cheaper hotels and hostels tend to include this in their quoted rates; more expensive hotels add it to your bill.

Argentina has 21% V.A.T. (known as IVA) on most consumer goods and services. The tax is usually included in the price of goods and noted on your receipt. You can get nearly all the IVA back on locally manufactured goods if you spend more than 70 pesos at stores displaying a Global Blue duty-free sign. You'll be given a Global Blue refund check for the amount you're entitled to; then, after getting it stamped by a customs official at the airport, you can cash it at the clearly signed tax refund booths. Allow an extra hour to complete the process.

Tax refunds Global Blue ☏ *11/5238-1970* ⊕ *www.globalblue.com*.

▌ TIME

Argentina is three hours behind G.M.T., or three hours ahead of U.S. Central Standard Time. Although Argentina does not currently observe Daylight Saving, it has in the past, so double-check time differences when you travel.

Time-Zone Information Timeanddate.com ⊕ *www.timeanddate.com/worldclock*.

▌ TIPPING

Propinas (tips) are a question of rewarding good service rather than an obligation. Restaurant bills—even those that have a *cubierto* (bread and service charge)—don't include gratuities; locals usually add 10% to 15%. Bellhops and maids expect tips only in the very expensive hotels, where a tip in dollars is appreciated. You can also give a small tip (10% or less) to tour guides. Porteños round off taxi fares, though some cabbies who frequent hotels popular with tourists seem to expect more. Tipping is a nice gesture with beauty and barbershop personnel—5% to 10% is fine.

TIPPING GUIDELINES FOR ARGENTINA	
Bellhop at high-end hotels	$1–$5 per bag, depending on the level of the hotel
Hotel maid at high-end hotels	1$–$3 a day (either daily or at the end of your stay, in cash)
Hotel room-service waiter	$1 to $2 per delivery, even if a service charge has been added
Taxi driver	Round up the fare to the next full peso amount
Tour guide	10% of the cost of the tour if service was good
Waiter	10%–15%, depending on service
Restroom attendants	Small change, such 1 or 2 pesos.

▌ TRIP INSURANCE

Comprehensive trip insurance is valuable if you're booking a very expensive or complicated vacation (particularly to an isolated region) or if you're booking far in advance. Comprehensive policies typically cover cancellation and interruption, letting you cancel or cut your trip short because of a personal emergency, illness, or, in some cases, acts of terrorism in your destination. Such policies also cover evacuation and medical care. (For trips abroad you should at least have medical-only coverage; *for more information,* ⇨ *see Medical Insurance & Assistance under Health, above.*) Some also cover you for travel delays because of bad weather or mechanical problems, as well as for lost or delayed baggage.

Another type of coverage to look for is financial default—that is, when your trip is disrupted because a tour operator, airline, or cruise line goes out of business. Generally you must buy this when you book your trip or shortly thereafter, and it's available to you only if your operator isn't on a list of excluded companies.

Always read the fine print of your policy to make sure that you are covered for the risks that are of most concern to you. Compare several policies to make sure you're getting the best price and range of coverage available.

Insurance Comparison Sites Insure My Trip. com ☎ 800/487–4722 ⊕ www.insuremytrip. com. **Square Mouth.com** ☎ 800/240–0369, 727/564–9203 ⊕ www.squaremouth.com.

▌ VISITOR INFORMATION

All major cities and most smaller tourist destinations have tourist offices that can provide maps as well as information on accommodation and sightseeing. The quality of these offices varies according to local funding, but employees are usually friendly and helpful. The city of Buenos Aires has tourist information booths around the city. Its extensive website includes downloadable maps, free MP3 walking tours, and insightful articles on porteño culture, though at this writing, all information was available in Spanish only.

Each Argentine province also operates a tourist office in Buenos Aires, usually called the "Casa de [Province Name] en Buenos Aires." The government umbrella organization for all regional and city-based tourist offices is the Secretaría de Turismo (Secretariat of Tourism). Their no-frills website has links and addresses to these offices, and other practical information.

Limited tourist information is also available at Argentina's embassy and consulates in the United States.

Contacts Argentine Secretariat of Tourism ☎ 800/555–0016 in Argentina ⊕ www.turismo. gov.ar. **Embassy of Argentina** ⊕ www. embassyofargentina.us. **Turismo Buenos Aires** (*Dirección de Turismo del Gobierno de la Ciudad de Buenos Aires*). ☎ 0800/999–2838 in Argentina ⊕ www.turismo.buenosaires.gob.ar.

ONLINE RESOURCES

The like-minded travelers on the Travel Talk Forums at Fodors.com are eager to answer questions and swap travel tales. The regional information and downloadable maps on the government-run Argentina Travel website are a great pre-trip planning resource. Welcome Argentina has good overviews of Argentina's different regions.

The website of the *Buenos Aires Herald*, the city's English-language daily, gives a conservative take on major local news stories. The website of English-language monthly newspaper *The Argentina Independent* has traveler-oriented news and cultural information. Run by American expats, *What's Up Buenos Aires* is a slick bilingual guide to contemporary culture and partying in the city.

The Museo Nacional de Bellas Artes contains the world's biggest digital collection of Argentine art and has lots of background on Argentine artists. Todo Tango is a comprehensive bilingual tango site with lyrics, history, and free downloads.

Wines of Argentina is overflowing with information about Argentina's best beverage. For insight into local cooking, restaurants, and ingredients, head to Saltshaker, the blog of American food writer Dan Perlman. Another food-obsessed American, Allie Lazar, is the sassy voice behind the unflinchingly detailed—and usually hilarious—restaurant and bar reviews at Pick Up the Fork.

All About Argentina Argentina Travel ⊕ *www.argentina.travel.* **Argentine Secretariat of Tourism** ⊕ *www.turismo. gob.ar.* **Embassy of Argentina** ⊕ *www. embassyofargentina.us.* **Fodors.com** ⊕ *www. fodors.com/community.* **Welcome Argentina** ⊕ *www.welcomeargentina.com.*

Culture and Entertainment Museo Nacional de Bellas Artes ⊕ *www.mnba. gob.ar.* **Todo Tango** ⊕ *www.todotango. com.ar.* **What's Up Buenos Aires** ⊕ *www. whatsupbuenosaires.com.*

Food and Drink Pick Up the Fork ⊕ *www. pickupthefork.com.* **Saltshaker** ⊕ *www. saltshaker.net.* **Wines of Argentina** ⊕ *www. winesofargentina.org.*

Media The Argentina Independent ⊕ *www. argentinaindependent.com.* **Buenos Aires Herald** ⊕ *www.buenosairesherald.com.*

Great Reads Sample the work of Argentina's greatest writers with Jorge Luis Borges's *Labyrinths: Selected Stories and Other Writings* and Julio Cortázar's *Blow-Up and Other Stories.* Bruce Chatwin's *In Patagonia* is the classic piece of travel writing on Argentina. Delve deeper into the lives of two (in)famous Argentineans with Tomás Eloy Martínez's *Santa Evita,* a fictional look at Eva Perón's life and death, and Jon Lee Anderson's excellent biography *Che Guevara: A Revolutionary Life.*

On-screen Juan José Campanella's Oscar-winning thriller *The Secret in Their Eyes* is set in the politically troubled Buenos Aires of the early 1970s. A remorse-struck gaucho is the stormy star of Fernando Spiner's *Aballay,* an arty Argentine Western filmed in Tucumán Province. A hapless traveling salesman is the unlikely hero of Carlos Sorín's Patagonian road movie *Intimate Stories.* Lucrecia Martel's *The Holy Girl* is an oppressive but brilliantly made film about a Catholic schoolgirl in Salta. Bariloche is the backdrop to Fabián Bielinsky's eerie psychological drama *The Aura.*

INDEX

Cover: Danita Delimont/AWL Images Ltd [Description: Gauchos herd sheep near Lake Argentina on the Patagonian grasslands near El Cala Fate, Argentina]. 1, Ignacio Alvarez/age fotostock. 2-3, Julian Rovagnati / Shutterstock. 5, ARCO/P. Wegner/age fotostock. Chapter 1: Experience Argentina: 8-9, Andrew Mirhej, fodors.com member. 10 (top), jd_miller, fodors.com member. 10 (center), M. Scanel, fodors.com member. 10 (bottom), Andrew Mirhej, fodors.com member. 14, Tony Morrison/South American Pictures. 15 (left), Jacynth Roode/iStockphoto. 15 (right), berhbs, fodors.com member. 16 (left), pdqu2, fodors.com member. 16 (top center), Tokyo Tanenhaus/Flickr. 16 (bottom center), feserc/ Flickr. 16 (right), fortes/Flickr. 17 (left), iStockphoto. 17 (top center), Clive Ellston, fodors.com member. 17 (bottom center), rm/Shutterstock. 17 (right), iladm/Shutterstock. 18, Andy Christodolo/Cephas Picture Library/Alamy. 19, Jefferson Bernardes / Shutterstock. 20, Brand X Pictures. 21 (left), AFP PHOTO/ALI BURAFI/ Newscom. 21 (right), Juanderlust, fodors.com member. 22, Diego_3336/Flickr. 23, MIMOHE/Shutterstock. 26, Galina Barskaya/Shutterstock. 28, Pablo Caridad/iStockphoto. 29 (left), Image Asset Management/age fotostock. 29 (right), José Francisco Ruiz/age fotostock. 30 (left), Eduardo M. Rivero/age fotostock. 30 (top right), Wikimedia Commons. 30 (bottom right), Jordi Camí/ age fotostock. 31 (right), Apeiron-Photo/Alamy. 31 (left) Wikimedia Commons. 32 (bottom right), Pictorial Press Ltd/Alamy. 32 (top right, left), A.H.C./age fotostock. 33 (bottom right), Griffiths911/wikipedia.org. 33 (left), Archivo Gráfico deClarín (Argentina)/Wikimedia Commons. 33 (top right), Tramonto/age fotostock. 34 (bottom right), DYN/Getty Images/Newscom. 34 (top), Nikada/iStock photo. 34 (left), Christopher Pillitz/alamy. 35 (top), Roberto Fiadone/wikipedia.org. 35 (bottom left), wikipedia.org. Chapter 2: Buenos Aires: 37, Dan Leffel/age fotostock. 38, Christine Yuan, fodors.com member. 39 (top), EL UNIVERSAL/Newscom. 39 (bottom), Seamus, fodors.com member. 40, caron malecki, fodors.com member. 44, blmurch/Flickr. 47, lilap/Flickr. 48-49, iStockphoto. 59, James Wong, fodors.com member. 62, Alfredo Maiquez/age fotostock. 65, christine592/Flickr. 67, Dan DeLuca/wikipedia.org. 68, caron malecki, fodors.com member. 71, giulio andreini/age fotostock. 77, wabauer, fodors.com member. 78, Jose Fuste Raga/age fotostock. 79, Beth/Queen/ZUMA Press/Newscom. 80, Wim Wiskerke/Alamy. 91, Martin Byrne, fodors.com member. 96, GUY Christian/age fotostock. 105, Christopher Pillitz/ Alamy. 106, 2litros > raimundo illanes/Flickr. 111, Ernesto Ríos Lanz/age fotostock. 112, wikipedia.org. 113, eyalos.com/Shutterstock. 114 (top), Picture Contact/Alamy. 114 (2nd from top), Christina Wilson/ Alamy. 114 (3rd from top), Michel Friang/Alamy. 114 (bottom), Jason Howe/ South American Pictures. 115 (top), Archivo General de la Nación/wikipedia.org. 115 (bottom), Danita Delimont/Alamy. 121, Jon Hicks/Alamy. Chapter 3: Side Trips: 129, David Lyons/Alamy. 130, Dario Diament/Shutterstock. 131 (bottom), Carla Antonini/Wikimedia Commons. 132, Pablodda/Flickr. 142-143, Jeremy Hoare/Alamy. 144, Chris Sharp/South American Pictures. 145, Pablo D. Flores. 146, Jeremy Hoare/Alamy. 147, SuperStock. 148 (top), Hughes/age fotostock. 148 (bottom), Johannes Odland/ Shutterstock. 155, Ken Welsh/age fotostock. 156, Gerad Coles/iStockphoto. 157, Sue Cunningham Photographic/Alamy. 158-59, Fritz Poelking/age fotostock. 158 (inset), Albasmalko/wikipedia.org. 159 (inset), flavia bottazzini/iStockphoto. 160, travelstock44/Alamy. 161, vittorio sciosia/age fotostock. Chapter 4: Side Trips to Uruguay: 165, Ricardokuhl | Dreamstime.com. 166, kasinaz / Shutterstock. 167, Ksenia Ragozina / Shutterstock. 168, Afagundes | Dreamstime.com. 176, Toniflap / Shutterstock. 187, Alberto/Flickr. 195, Demetrio Carrasco / age fotostock. Chapter 5: The Northwest: 201, Fabian von Poser/age fotostock. 202, JOSE ALBERTO TEJO/Shutterstock. 203 (top), Colman Lerner Gerardo/ Shutterstock. 203 (bottom), Alicia Nijdam/Flickr. 204, Ignacio Alvarez/age fotostock. 205 (top), B. Hennings, Nürnberg, Germany/wikipedia.org. 205 (bottom), Alicia Nijdam/wikipedia.org. 206, Guerretto/Flickr. 214, Ignacio Alvarez/age fotostock. 216-17, Wolfgang Herzog/age fotostock. 218, WYSOCKI Pawel/age fotostock. 219 (top), Walter Bibikow/age fotostock. 219 (bottom), borderlys/ Flickr. 220-21, ARCO/Therin-Weise/age fotostock. 222 (top), Clive Ellston, fodors.com member. 222 (bottom), Joris Van Ostaeyen/iStockphoto. 223 (top), Lee Torrens/Shutterstock. 223 (bottom), Humawaka/wikipedia.org. 224, Ignacio Alvarez/age fotostock. 227, Clive Ellston, fodors.com member. 230, Angel Manzano/age fotostock. 233, Nacho Calonge/age fotostock. 241, ARCO/Stengert, N/age fotostock. 250, Heeb Christian/age fotostock. Chapter 6: Mendoza and the Wine Regions: 253, David Noton Photography/Alamy. 254, CASA DEL VISITANTE Familia Zuccardi, Mendoza. 255 (top), iStockphoto. 255 (bottom), dubonnet, fodors.com member. 256, Jason Maehl/Shutterstock. 257 (top), José Carlos Pires Pereira/iStockphoto. 257 (bottom), fainmen/Flickr. 258, CASA DEL VISITANTE Familia Zuccardi, Mendoza. 268, Yadid Levy/age fotostock. 275, Heeb Christian/age fotostock. 278-79, Cephas Picture Library/Alamy. 282, Luc./Flickr. 286-87, Bon Appetit/Alamy. 286 (bottom), Dizzy/ Alamy. 288 (top), Douglas Peebles/Stock Connection/Aurora Photos. 288 (2nd from top), Clay McLachlan/Aurora Photos. 288 (3rd from top), WinePix/Alamy. 288 (bottom), Karen Ward/South American Pictures. 289 (top), Pablo Abuliak. 289 (2nd from top), John and Brenda Davenport, fodors.

com member. 289 (3rd from top), Pablo Abuliak. 289 (bottom), matetic.com. 291 (top), Pablo Abuliak. 291 (center), CASA DEL VISITANTE Familia Zuccardi, Mendoza. 291 (bottom), Mark Surman/Flickr. 292, Tony Morrison/South American Pictures. 299, Pablo Abuliak. 306, Andre Charland from Canada/ wikipedia.org. 311, Jason Maehl/Shutterstock. Chapter 7: The Lake District: 315, Hitmans | Dreamstime.com. 316 (top), rm/Shutterstock. 316 (center), Sam Chadwick/Shutterstock. 316 (bottom), Rafael Franceschini/Shutterstock. 317 (top), ricardo.martins/Flickr. 317 (bottom), JOSE ALBERTO TEJO/ Shutterstock. 318, FLPA/Krystyna Szuleck/age fotostock. 319 (top), Greg Cooper/iStockphoto. 319 (bottom), wikipedia.org. 320, HappyTrvlr, fodors.com member. 321 (top), Josh Roe, fodors.com member. 321 (bottom), ArielMartin/Shutterstock. 322, Alfonsitomaria/wikipedia.org, 332, Walter Bibikow/ age fotostock. 334, Walter Bibikow/age fotostock. 340-341, hdcaplan, Fodors.com member. 346-47, Diana Proemm/age fotostock. 348, Karl Weatherly/age fotostock. 351, Jason Friend/Alamy. 357, ImageState/Alamy. 362, ImageState/Alamy. **Chapter 8: Patagonia:** 365, R. Matina/age fotostock. 366, David Thyberg/Shutterstock. 367 (top), Gerad Coles/iStockphoto. 367 (bottom), Pablo H Caridad/ Shutterstock. 368, A Maywald/age fotostock. 369 (top), Eduardo Rivero/Shutterstock. 369 (bottom), Pablo H Caridad/Shutterstock. 370, Karen Coleman, fodors.com member. 379, Gareth McCormack/ Alamy. 380, WYSOCKI Pawel/age fotostock. 381, Gareth McCormack/Alamy. 382, Colin Monteath/ age fotostock. 383, Galen Rowell/Mountain Light/Alamy. 384 (top), Jan Baks/Alamy. 384 (bottom), Heeb Christian/age fotostock. 385, Peter Essick/Aurora Photos. 386 (left), Laura Hart/Shutterstock. 386 (top center), Michael S. Nolan/age fotostock. 386 (top right), jan.kneschke/Flickr. 386 (bottom right), ARCO/P. Wegner/age fotostock. 387 (top left), Danita Delimont/Alamy. 387 (bottom left), Derek Dammann/iStockphoto. 387 (bottom center), iStockphoto. 387 (top right), David R. Frazier Photolibrary, Inc./Alamy. 387 (bottom right), David Ryan/Alamy. 393, Michael S. Nolan/age fotostock. 399, Juan Carlos Muñoz/age fotostock. 407, Heeb Christian lage fotostock. 409, Raymond Forbes/age fotostock. 413, Anna Hainze, fodors.com member. 419, Lois Zebelman, fodors.com member. 420, Tony West/Alamy. 426, Michele Molinari/Alamy. 434, Marco Simoni/age fotostock. 440, Colin Monteath/age fotostock. 445, Dave Houser/age fotostock. 449, Danny Aeberhard/South American Pictures. Back cover (from left to right): longhorndave/Flickr; Claudio Elias/wikipedia.org; Julian Rovagnati / Shutterstock. Spine: Linda Hilberdink Photography / Shutterstock

About Our Writers: All photos are courtesy of the writers except for the following: Alan Kellin, courtesy of Jocelyn Mandryk; Karina Martinez-Carter, courtesy of Lucas Lara; Sorrel Moseley-Williams, courtesy of Time Out Buenos Aires.

NOTES

NOTES

NOTES